FOURTH EDITION

TERRORISM TODAY

THE PAST, THE PLAYERS, THE FUTURE

Jeremy R. Spindlove

Clifford E. Simonsen

Prentice Hall
Upper Saddle River, New Jersey
Columbus, Ohio

Library of Congress Cataloging-in-Publication Data

Spindlove, Jeremy R.
 Terrorism today : the past, the players, the future/Jeremy R. Spindlove, Clifford E. Simonsen.
  p. cm.
 Simonsen's name appears first on earlier editions.
 Includes index.
 ISBN-13: 978-0-13-500637-5 (alk. paper)
 ISBN-10: 0-13-500637-6 (alk. paper)
 1. Terrorism. 2. Terrorism—History. 3. Terrorism—Prevention. I. Simonsen,
Clifford E. II. Title.
 HV6431.S53 2010
 363.325—dc22

                                                                      2008046438

Editor in Chief: Vernon R. Anthony
Editor: Tim Peyton
Marketing Manager: Adam Kloza
Senior Marketing Coordinator: Alicia Wozniak
Production Manager: Renata Butera
Production Coordination: Shiny Rajesh
Manager, Rights and Permissions: Zina Arabia
Manager, Visual Research: Beth Brenzel
Manager, Cover Visual Research & Permissions: Karen Sanatar
Image Permission Coordinator: Jan Marc Quisumbing
Composition: Integra Software Services Pvt. Ltd.
Cover Design: Bruce Kenselaar
Printer/Binder: Hamilton Printing Company
Cover Printer: Lehigh/Phoenix Color
Cover Photo: Hemera Technologies/Jupiter Images, Inc.

Pearson Prentice Hall™ is a trademark of Pearson Education, Inc.
Pearson® is a registered trademark of Pearson plc
Prentice Hall® is a registered trademark of Pearson Education, Inc.

Pearson Education Ltd., London
Pearson Education Singapore, Pte. Ltd.
Pearson Education Canada, Inc.
Pearson Education—Japan
Pearson Education Australia PTY, Limited

Pearson Education North Asia Ltd., Hong Kong
Pearson Educación de Mexico, S.A. de C.V.
Pearson Education Malaysia, Pte. Ltd.
Pearson Educacion Upper Saddle River,
  New Jersey

Prentice Hall
is an imprint of

www.pearsonhighered.com

10 9 8 7 6 5 4 3 2 1
ISBN-13: 978-0-13-500637-5
ISBN-10: 0-13-500637-6

This edition is dedicated to my good friend Cliff

CONTENTS

LIST OF MAPS

PREFACE

When the authors decided to write the first edition of an introductory text about a subject as complex and rapidly changing as terrorism, it became a daunting yet intriguing task. The very concept of terrorism includes such a wide range of activities that the most difficult task became how to make a text short enough to be effective for instructors, casual readers, and students, but long enough to convince colleagues, professionals, and practitioners that it adequately covers an acceptable depth into this fascinating discipline. We must admit that, at times, it seemed like we were trying to paint a moving bus—the players, organizations, and operations often changed faster than the speed at which we could write the words, and this continues to be the case!

This fourth edition, which picks up where the third left off, is also written in an admittedly broad-brush manner. We re-examine where terrorism came from, where it is today, and where it seems to be going as we reel from the effects of global terrorist attacks and threat, the War on Terror, and the arrangement of new pieces on the world chessboard of terror. This new world arrangement has need of new and specific countermeasures.

There is no easy answer to the question "What is terrorism?" As you read this book, it will become apparent to you that most terrorism actions are committed by groups of fanatics or dissidents, often with conflicting goals and little interface. Of course, there are exceptions to every rule. Many of these groups are continuing their plans to upset security and safety in the United States and around the globe. We hope that the knowledge we have assembled in this book will stimulate students and others to seek out ways to offer better safety and security to all persons worldwide.

Your authors have attempted to provide a clear overview of many of the sectors and operations that comprise the broad terms *terrorism* and *counterterrorism*. We explore some specific subjects and locations in greater depth than others, reduce redundancy, and cover as many differences and similarities as possible. We present this fourth edition with the firm belief that any learning experience should be enjoyable as well as educational. We offer instructors a text that we have organized and written with the goal of making teaching and the learning experience as interesting and effective as possible. We cover the essentials of the subject and include a large array of pedagogical tools in each chapter.

Security is an ancient need for humans—a basic rung on the ladder of Maslow's hierarchy of needs. Never has America's and mankind's sense of security been so badly shaken as by the events of 9-11 and by escalating terrorist acts abroad and in the American homeland. As with most fields of human endeavor that are just now entering into an academic discipline, the available material presenting scientific theory, literature, and research is not extensive in the field of terrorism.

THE TRADITION CONTINUES

The methodology for textbook development, which we have used successfully in the past for several other introductory texts, has continued to be the foundation and cornerstone for this fourth edition of *Terrorism Today*. We have built on the comments of readers, instructors, and students to the book's previous editions:

- An engaging writing style, resulting in a book that is highly readable and effective as an informational, teaching, and learning tool.
- A balanced treatment of practical examples, technology, history, and data from available documents and academic research.
- An eye-pleasing design for easy reading, with features such as clearly presented examples of current and historical photographs, illustrations, and other supplemental materials to augment the basic text.

- A systems approach to exploring the varied elements of terrorism, terrorists, and the various motives for terrorist groups as a potentially integrated and interrelated series of subsystems.
- An unbiased presentation of a wide range of topics, making for a text suitable for instructors and students from many disciplines and points of view.
- In-chapter and end-of-chapter materials that augment the textual materials with examples of events, persons, stories, terms to remember, maps and Web sites for further research.
- An *Instructor's Manual* that features test banks and other aids for busy instructors, a set of PowerPoint materials by chapter, and other aids. Many are ideal for adjunct instructors who are tilling the fields of law enforcement and security, or others in academia or the military.

ORGANIZATION OF THE TEXT

This fourth edition has again been divided into three major parts and fifteen chapters that build from historical backgrounds to predictions about terrorism in the twenty-first century. Each chapter begins with a set of Learning Objectives which should be accomplished after completion of the text. Information on specific terror events of note is included in the body of the text to illustrate and frame each chapter. Extensive endnotes, placed at the end of each chapter, provide helpful content and applicability to the subject matter. These should be considered as important as the textual materials themselves for presentation and study. The materials we have selected come from the best and most currently available sources in the field. We presented them in their original form, or blended them into our own writing to minimize confusion.

Part One: The Definitions and History of Terrorism

Part One offers an in-depth, historical look at terrorism and its origins. Learning about the types of terror and their history will provide the student/reader with the background necessary to understand the rapid evolution of terrorism in the present and into the future.

CHAPTER 1: IN SEARCH OF A DEFINITION FOR TERRORISM   Chapter 1 presents some basic definitions for terminology used throughout the following chapters. The information will allow the readers to understand and differentiate between terrorist acts and ordinary criminal acts. The chapter presents defining issues, operational terms, useful typologies, as well as forms and tactics of terrorism in today's troubled world. Terrorism as criminal behavior and its use as a method for change are detailed. Such acts as ambush, assassination, arson, bombing, hijacking, hostage-taking, kidnapping, blackmail, and protection are included. The initiation and development of the Department of Homeland Security are covered in detail.

CHAPTER 2: A BRIEF HISTORY OF TERRORISM   Chapter 2 describes an act of violence as a logical progression but one that can take place in microseconds within a single individual. Violence perpetrated for ideological reasons and for a systematically organized cause or complaint is shown to be much different. Pogroms by religions, the Inquisition, the Holocaust, the PLO, the Phoenix Program, Tiananmen Square, and guerrilla warfare are among examples that illustrate how individual terrorism can grow into a national or religious crusade. Chapter 2 also explores the motives and methods employed by individual terrorists or groups with some perceived agenda as compared to the motives of a state for suppressing dissent and revolution. Readers are introduced to the concept of state-sponsored terrorism, a concept that supports terrorist groups and individual terrorists with weapons, money, and supplies to achieve a government's goals. Discussions range from the Crusades to the continuing frictions between major religions around the world today.

Part Two: Terrorism around the World

Part Two brings the readers to the terrorist events—both left and right wing—of the twentieth and early twenty-first centuries. We examine the right-wing factions in various countries and regions, their similarities and differences, and their goals and objectives. We also look at the left-wing factions in various countries and regions, using a similar methodology, and we contrast the two. Part Two covers regions and nations in the investigation of terrorism, its many different forms and factions, and their interrelationships.

CHAPTER 3: THE UNITED STATES OF AMERICA   Chapter 3 examines the events leading up to 9-11 and the "dots" that were never connected to prevent that cataclysmic event. We also examine what has happened since 9-11 in the War on Terror. We examine and analyze the general types of "home-grown" terrorism in the United States to see how they compare with terrorism in other parts of the world. The United States is no longer free from the violent terrorist actions that have been plaguing the rest of the world. How America has now had to defend its Homeland with a lessening of civil liberties and the introduction of "watch lists" and renditions is discussed.

CHAPTER 4: CANADA AND THE CARIBBEAN   Chapter 4 examines the problems of immigration, illegal aliens and refugees, and the threat that poses not just to Canada but also to the United States. Canada has for several decades expounded on its program of "multi-culturism," and this chapter reviews how the Canadian homeland has thus become a haven for fundraising activities for such terror groups as the Tamil Tigers and Sikh extremists. Canada has also been singled out for attack by Osama bin Laden and al-Qaeda affiliates. Canada has suffered one of the worst terrorist attacks, prior to 9-11, namely the downing of Air India flight 182 in the Irish Sea, and this chapter examines that case and its failing in detail.

CHAPTER 5: GREAT BRITAIN AND NORTHERN IRELAND   Chapter 5 examines the background for the "Irish Problem" and brings readers up to date with examples of friction and terrorism on both sides of the issues. The Troubles as they have been termed, lasted for more than forty years and have only now reached the final peaceful chapter. This long chapter provides a model for examining other terror spots of the world. It shows similarities and differences in the use of terrorism in meeting political or religious goals. Ireland and mainland Britain have been embroiled in the violence of terrorism for more than four decades. Here, we examine the current political processes and the methods employed to reach a solution to the violence. We also discuss the concerns of security forces and the export of terror knowledge to other international terror groups. The rise of Islamic extremism and suicide attacks by young British-born men on the London transport system are also discussed.

CHAPTER 6: WESTERN EUROPE   Chapter 6 examines terrorism, past and present, in Western Europe. We discuss how the French have used or supported terrorist acts in the past and how Germans were led into blind obedience and violence many times. The chapter examines how the Italian Mafia and Mussolini's fascist thugs in Italy used terrorism and discusses the changing political patterns of the Italians over the centuries. We look at the turbulent history of Spain—from the Inquisition to the fascist reign of terror under Franco, to the many terrorist activities in Spain, especially those involving the Basque separatists and Islamic extremists. In the twenty-first century, Europe is now seen as the target for international terror cells plotting and planning mayhem in other regions as well as their adopted homelands.

CHAPTER 7: EASTERN EUROPE AND THE BALKANS   Chapter 7 recounts the sad history of the multiracial, multireligious region formerly known as Yugoslavia, from the partisan terrorism and German terrorism in World War II to the divided state that has seen constant interracial and interreligious fighting since Yugoslavia's breakup. Terrorism and even genocide will be the main weapons in these battles for ethnic purity. We examine the Russians and their long history of national terrorism to keep the populace under control, from the Czars, to the Soviet Union, and Stalin's murder of fifty million of his countrymen. We discuss Chechnya and other Islamic states in the Russia of today, after the fall of the former Soviet Union, and their continuing use of tactics of terror.

CHAPTER 8: NORTH AFRICA AND THE MIDDLE EAST   Chapter 8 examines this critical area of the world, where terror is the primary weapon in local and international conflicts. Slowly, we realize that all of the conflicts are similar in that troubled region and terror is the primary weapon used by all sides. We discuss the battle that Jews, Christians, and Arabs have been waging for 3,000 years in this hotbed of terrorism. The chapter details the problems faced in this ancient fight for land and minds. Algeria, Libya, Egypt, and other hot spots of state-sponsored and religious terrorism are covered as well.

CHAPTER 9: THE PERSIAN GULF   Chapter 9 explores the Persian Gulf states, which have been involved in active warfare or constant terrorism (religious or political) for a very long time. This area—the most valuable source of the world's petroleum—remains a hotbed of violence and terrorism today. We discuss the persecution of the Kurds in Iraq, the use of oil revenue to sponsor worldwide terrorism, and the constant threat of the use of nuclear, biological, and chemical weapons stirring the pot of terrorism in this area. The second Gulf War and the fall of Saddam Hussein from power have had a destabilizing effect on the entire region. We also examine the struggles for prominence among the states that ring the Persian Gulf.

CHAPTER 10: NORTHEAST, CENTRAL, AND SOUTHERN AFRICA   Chapter 10 examines the Dark Continent, from the long struggle for freedom from apartheid in South Africa to a quite different struggle in Robert Mugabe's dictatorship in Zimbabwe. We explore the genocide in the Congo, Uganda, and Rwanda, as well as the tribalism that divides most of these regions. We discuss the threat of right-wing-directed warfare against the new Black governments—a new and seriously escalating problem. Africa is a continent of both significant potential and almost insurmountable problems.

CHAPTER 11: SOUTHERN AND SOUTHEAST ASIA   Chapter 11 looks at past and present terrorism in southern and southeast Asia. India has a long history of terrorism; as well, it possesses nuclear weapons. The war against the United Kingdom showed India that terrorism can work. Following independence, India has had to combat attacks from religious factions and from rebel causes. Pakistan and India have a long-standing state of war, which could easily go nuclear, and the Punjab has used terrorism to try to gain independence from India. We re-examine Afghanistan, the first battlefield of the post-9-11 War on Terror. We also discuss Sri Lanka, formerly Ceylon, which has suffered a long, ongoing war with the Tamil Tigers and other splinter groups. The devastation from the 2005 tsunami compound the problems in this region. The terrorism conducted in other theaters of the world is found in many parts of Southeast Asia, and the local conflicts, religious and ideological, seem to echo the themes seen elsewhere on the globe. From the Khmer Rouge in Cambodia to the guerrilla fighters in the jungles of Malaysia and Indonesia, terrorism has seemed to find a long-term home in Southeast Asia.

CHAPTER 12: THE PACIFIC RIM   Chapter 12 explores the countries of the Pacific Rim. We examine China, which has moved past its terror-filled period following the ascension of Communism. Terror as a philosophy can be traced back through Chinese history as a viable means to control that vast nation. From the fighters against the government at the turn of the twentieth century, to World War II and the Japanese occupation, to the terrorist tactics of the Marcos regime, the history of the Philippines has also shown that terror can be a useful tool in controlling a large, scattered, and very poor country. Japan has been stricken with fanatical terrorism that extends back into history through the occupation of China and the Pacific Islands in World War II up to the use of chemical weapons attacks on subways in the present. Indonesia and Malaysia have many terrorist organizations residing within their borders.

CHAPTER 13: LATIN AMERICA AND SOUTH AMERICA   Chapter 13 discusses Latin America's struggles with terrorism. The so-called "banana republics" have long suffered from repressive dictators who used terrorism against the people, as well as rebels who used terrorism against the governments. We examine major conflicts in terms of past history and present status and the roles of Mexico and Cuba in these struggles. Mexico has a long history of terrorism and revolution. The "other America" has been rife with terrorist activities for a long time, from The Shining Path of Peru to the "disappeared" in Brazil and Argentina. We discuss the drug cartels in Colombia and other states, as well as various political upheavals. The violence and danger of this region, as well as suppressive Latin American governments, invite terrorist organizations to emerge.

Part Three: The War on Terror

Part Three discusses the varying efforts of nations around the world to detect or defeat terrorism, to find other ways to deal with it, and to manage the threats of terrorism in the post-9-11 era. We examine what the future of terrorism might be.

CHAPTER 14: COUNTERING TERRORISM Chapter 14 examines the efforts of the world to counter terrorism—both politically and operationally. We determine which methods are effective and which have failed. These range from national paramilitary groups to local activities by regular citizens. We study in detail the importance of intelligence gathering, the cycle of intelligence, and the proper uses of intelligence against terrorism. The threats to aviation from acts of terror, along with maritime piracy, are discussed. The chapter examines worldwide counter-terrorist groups and strategies, from the Delta Force in the United States, to the Mossad in Israel, and to the Special Air Service in the United Kingdom, and many other highly organized and effective groups both police and military. We discuss the strategies of the United Nations and regional governments and their successes and failures. The threats posed by chemical and biological agents have to be considered as the world prepares for the unexpected and the possibility of attack with weapons of mass destruction (WMD).

CHAPTER 15: THE FUTURE AND THE "WAR AGAINST TERRORISM" *"Predicting stuff is difficult, especially if it's in the future,"* according to cartoon character Pogo Possum. In that vein, the authors try in Chapter 15 to predict the most likely spots where the pressure from terrorism will be found at the start of the twenty-first century, and what possible effects the War on Terror will have in the future. We also look at the possible and probable threat from weapons of mass destruction (WMD) and the use of the internet as a means of self-radicalization.

ACKNOWLEDGMENTS

How do authors begin to acknowledge those persons whose support, encouragement, assistance, and belief in our dream have allowed us to develop, refine, and produce a fourth edition of a book that attempts to cover an almost encyclopedic, worldwide view of terrorism? To try to acknowledge each of them individually would take several pages, and we shudder to think we might miss some of them.

The list begins with our families and close personal friends, then our colleagues and international friends in academia, as well as professionals and practitioners in terrorism at the international, federal, state, and local levels. Perhaps most important were the efforts of reviewers who were kind enough to examine our work. Fourth edition reviewers include: Les Boggess, Fairmont State University; Timothy Capron, California State University, Sacramento; Louise Cooper, Mitchell Community College; David Copp, Chaminade University; Lew Hall, Evangel University; Stacey Hervey, Community College of Denver; Collin Lau, Chaminade University of Honolulu; Dennis McLean, Tallahasse Community College; Filiz Otucu, Plymouth State University; and James Simmerman, Missouri Valley College.

To each of them we extend our deepest appreciation and gratitude for encouraging and assisting us in putting together a text about this important topic that seems to work. We would, however, like to single out a few of the special people at Pearson Education who helped the authors turn their prose, ideas, and concepts for a book about terrorism into a textbook that will greatly assist students, readers, and instructors alike. First, our executive editor, Tim Peyton, gets applause for allowing us to write and for leading us through the land mines of this fourth edition with minimal problems and a lot of positive support. Tim fought for our ideas and listened to our suggestions to use new concepts and techniques, rather than just staying with the status quo. Alicia Kelly, editorial assistant gets a big hug and "thank you." She was a calm place in the often-wild storm of writing and got us through the rapids of production in fine style. Our production editor, Renata Butera, was also calm and professional in the midst of what could have become a frantic effort to stay on schedule.

We also must offer our continuing thanks to our families, friends, and relatives and, in particular, two persons who provided us with continuous support and solace—our dear wives, Fran and Esther, who put up with our disappearances to basement offices! While they will enjoy with us whatever modest success we may garner from this new edition, they have also had to put up with the periodic absences and the frequent bouts of frenzied revisions and changes, often from long distances by phone or e-mail. Jeremy's work colleagues and, in particular, Glenn Ross and Glenn Welsh for their input and knowledge on South Africa, and Cliff's clients have been extremely supportive and understanding, and we thank you, too. Our appreciation also goes to Gary Wilson, a good friend and colleague and former Royal Ulster Constabulary Police officer; to Dave Roberts in Edmonton for his technical and moral support; to Mike McGuire and Diane Cooper for their photographic input and advice on security operation, and Arik Garber, who arrived in Lebanon with the IDF as Jeremy evacuated to Syria! Last, but not least, thanks to our good friend Dave Loban for his assistance and photographic support and extensive knowledge of Northern Ireland. We have found out over the past few years that writing can be a lonely task, especially when it involves such a specific and rapidly changing field. It is often not easy to discuss the book with anyone else, while we are in the frantic throes of creation and revision. We deeply appreciate the understanding and support we have received over the past periods of hard work and love you all for understanding and caring.

ABOUT THE AUTHORS

Jeremy R. Spindlove Presently, Jeremy R. Spindlove holds the position of Director of Safety and Risk Management for Exel Inc., a global leader in supply chain management. Based in Vancouver, Canada, his responsibilities extend throughout Canada and the United States. He has had firsthand experience in terrorism—first, through his service in the Surrey Constabulary (UK) as a first responder on the scene in 1974 when a Provisional Irish Republican Army cell detonated two bombs, one in the Horse and Groom and the second in the 7 Stars pub in Guildford, which killed six and wounded more than sixty. Jeremy went on to be recruited by British Airways as an overseas security officer to supervise air terminal security operations for the airline in Baghdad, Iraq, for two years; in Amman, Jordan, for three months; and in Beirut, Lebanon, for six months. He traveled globally throughout the network conducting airport risk assessments for BA. On his return to the UK, Jeremy set up a fraud investigation unit, tracking and intercepting illegal immigrants transiting the UK en route to North America on forged passports and travel documents. He has been assigned to security duties escorting H.M. Queen Elizabeth to the Far East in 1987 and to Rome in 1988. Jeremy immigrated to Canada in 1988 and holds dual Canadian/British citizenship. He has held critical security leadership positions as Manager of Security and then Director of Airport Security at Vancouver International Airport. He is a qualified Passenger Screening Instructor and, during his airport tenure in 1994, served on a Canadian Advisory Board reviewing airport and aviation security regulations. In 1996, he moved to the Tibbett and Britten Group North America as Manager and, later, Director of Loss Prevention, Health and Safety for Western Canada and the United States, advancing to his present position with broader responsibilities. Jeremy Spindlove was presented the Royal Humane Society Award by Britain's Queen Elizabeth in 1976 for his courage in saving a woman's life. He is a longtime member of the International Society for Industrial Security and the Academy of Criminal Justice Sciences, and the co-author of the three successful previous editions of *Terrorism Today: The Past, the Players, the Future.* He is a frequent guest commentator on airport security and terrorism for Canada's Global News Network. He has also authored a contributory text on victims of terrorism entitled *Victimology—A Study of Crime Victims and Their Roles*, edited by Judith M. Scarzi and Jack McDevitt.

Clifford E. Simonsen, Ph.D. Presently the President of Criminology Consultants Inc., Clifford E. Simonsen has an extensive background and education as related to the topics of terrorism, crime, and criminal behavior. His extensive education includes B.S., University of Nebraska at Omaha, Law Enforcement and Corrections; M.S., Florida State University, Criminology and Corrections; MPA, The Ohio State University, Correctional Administration; and Ph.D., The Ohio State University, Administration of Criminal Justice and Deviant Behavior. Cliff retired after $32\frac{1}{2}$ years as a Military Police Colonel. His extensive education in the military includes the Military Police Officer Basic Course, the Military Police Officer Advanced Course, the Advanced Police Administration Course, the U.S. Army Command and General Staff College, the OR/SA Executive Course, the Industrial College of the Armed Forces, and the U.S. Army War College.

Cliff has been an active member and supporter of many prestigious professional associations, including American Correctional Association (ACA) International Committee, Washington State Correctional Association (WCA), American Society for Industrial Security (ASIS) (lifetime award), Certified Protection Professional CPP (lifetime award), The International Association of Professional Security Consultants (IAPSC), International Academy of Criminology (IAC), Academy of Criminal Justice Sciences (ACJS), and The Retired Officers Association (TROA).

His honors and awards include Two Meritorious Service Awards U.S. Army; Legion of Merit, U.S. Army; Korean National Police Medal of Merit, Korean Government, Outstanding Service International Association of Halfway Houses, Outstanding Achievement as a Scholar, Washington State Council on Crime and Delinquency, Fellow of the International Institute for Security and Safety Management, IISSM, New Delhi, India.

His books in print include *Corrections in American: An Introduction,* 11th Edition; *Juvenile Justice Today*, 5th Edition; and *Terrorism Today: The Past, the Players, and the Future,* 3rd Edition, all published by Pearson.

PART ONE

The Definitions and History of Terrorism

CHAPTER 1

In Search of a Definition for Terrorism

Above the gates of hell is the warning that all who enter should abandon hope. Less dire but to the same effect is the warning given to those who try to define terrorism.[1]

Learning Objectives

The study and review of this chapter will enable you to

1. Understand the many different definitions of terrorism;
2. Look back over the last two decades to discover how those definitions were developed;
3. Recognize that the definition of terrorism is complex and no one finite definition is acceptable for all forms of such violence and menace by either the United Nations or individual governments;
4. Prepare your own definition for terrorism.

Terms to Remember

Army of God
Assassination
Freedom fighters
Laws
Mores
National Liberation
    Army

Office of Intelligence and
    Analysis
Oklahoma City Federal
    Building
Prescribed
Proscribed
Reign of Terror

Roe v. Wade
Simple continuum
Sympathizers
Terrorist incident
USA Patriot Act 2001
War on Terror

OVERVIEW

Terrorism constitutes one of the most serious threats to global peace and security. Although it is not a new phenomenon, finding a universally accepted definition that fits every terrorist event has not been achieved with any measure of success. Terrorism, in its many difference shades, has been around for centuries. Since the terror attacks of 9-11, the bombings of the London subway system, and the Madrid train station attacks, the fear of terrorism has spawned a massive governmental and private security industry aimed at protecting individuals, tourists, travelers, long-established institutions, and industries. The specter of a feared but unknown doom has required the expenditure of huge sums of money to protect us from the threat of dangerous, threatening, and mysterious archcriminals we call, for lack of a better title, "terrorists." A constant fear of more such attacks has become an everyday reality to citizens of the United States and their allies. This threat has forced airlines to make drastic changes in their methods for securing thousands of flights each day. It has also caused major delays, and has forced travelers to make drastic changes in planning, scheduling, and taking personal security measures for trips, especially abroad. The television, internet, print, and radio news media happily respond and immediately inform and frighten the public about terrorist acts from around the globe. We need to understand at the outset that there is no globally accepted definition of terrorism. To a vast majority of American citizens, it may seem that terrorism is all about the events that took place in New York, Washington, and a field in Pennsylvania on September 11, 2001. But that would certainly detract from the established terrorist events that have been played out by such groups as the Provisional IRA, ETA in Spain, and of course the Middle East terrorist organizations, many with roots going back over several decades.

This chapter examines and asks several key questions: "Just who is this larger-than-life monster that we call a 'terrorist?' What are terrorist acts?" Can we protect ourselves against them? How do we define this deadly and frightening activity we so casually refer to as "terrorism?" Combs, discussing this problem, says "Terrorism is a political as well as a legal and military issue; its precise definition in modern terms has been slow to evolve. Not that there are not numerous definitions available—there are hundreds! But few of them are of sufficient legal scholarship to be useful in international law, and most of those which are legally useful lack the necessary ambiguity for any political acceptance."[2] The attacks of 9-11 provided a wake-up call to everyone in the Government, which quickly passed the **USA Patriot Act of 2001**. This legislation provides funding and oversight on a massive scale.

We shall now commence the daunting task of trying to define "terrorism" and/or "terrorist behavior." The terms must be carefully constructed so that they project the precise meanings intended. A **terrorist incident**, generally speaking, is any violent act that can become a broader

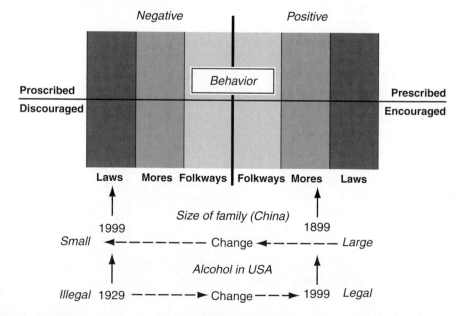

FIGURE 1-1   Continuum of Behavior (Clifford E. Simonsen).

threat as the purpose and intention for such action becomes clearly known, and the act is clearly of a criminal nature. What it is (and is not) called hinges on finding a commonly understood meaning for the all too simple term, terrorism. This chapter will lay a foundation for the reader/student to use throughout the rest of this text.

This is a journey into the fascinating phenomena of terrorism and terrorists. To better understand these concepts, we must explore some historical context and the specific rules that society has developed over time to define the use of criminal and antisocial acts to meet political or social goals. Behavior in social groups, whether they are for primitive tribes or complex modern nation-states, can be regarded as points on a **simple continuum**, as shown in Figure 1-1.

TERRORISM: SEARCHING FOR A DEFINITION

It is perhaps too easy to use terms such as "terror," "terrorism," and "terrorist" for acts and persons that shock the senses of most reasonable people. The **Reign of Terror**, which took place in France from 1792 to 1794, has been accepted by most scholars as the first event to be commonly called "terrorism." During that very bloody Revolution, those who resisted the dictums of the revolutionaries faced arrest, imprisonment, and death by the guillotine. Most of these decisions were made without the benefit of trials or any other legal procedure. Brutal members of the revolutionary groups went to extreme lengths to eliminate every possible threat to their revolution, eventually seeking out those with even moderate to mild opposition to their cause. Those who considered themselves to be possible targets of the revolutionaries finally decided to adopt countermeasures for their self-preservation. On July 27, 1794, members of the Jacobin dissenters murdered *Robespierre* and his council of supporters. The Reign of Terror, in which over 400,000 "suspects" (including children and women) had been imprisoned, hanged, or beheaded by guillotine, finally came to an end. But the seminal concepts of terror tactics as a part of a political strategy grew directly out of this bloody episode. From a devastating beginning . . . terrorism, and terrorist acts, became defined as, "the systematic application of violence to establish and maintain a new political or religious system." Such a definition may be difficult to use today, primarily, because it fails to separate terrorism from other acts of aggression that use terror as only a small component, not the primary objective, of such behavior. For example, terror in conventional warfare between nation-states is a natural by-product of the violence and confusion of combat. Military objectives and tactics are usually chosen in order to effect the quickest elimination of an enemy's force, its morale, and will to fight through the destruction or disruption of its command, control, communication, and support and supply networks. Victory is decided by force of numbers, skill at arms, weapon superiority, or strategy and tactics, or a combination thereof. Terror, however, is not intended to be a primary factor or function in such military actions.

Trained soldiers (in wartime), or citizens frightened into surrender or compliance but not physically injured are the most logical and realistic targets of terrorism; other casualties are easily classified according to the way they were injured or killed. Rosie offers a tentative definition of terrorism for our consideration: "The use and/or threat of repeated violence in support of, or in opposition to, some authority, where violence is employed to induce the fear of similar attack in as many non-immediate victims as possible so that those so threatened accept and comply with the demands of the terrorists."[3]

Within this wordy, but somewhat awkward, definition, we can perhaps work out a methodology for describing the variety of behaviors springing from terrorists acting from a wide range of motives. At the same time, this definition remains neutral with regard to the great variety of individual traits that characterize particular groups. It can be applied to political terrorism, revolutionary terrorism, state terrorism, religious terrorism, insurgencies, and all the many other variations. It eliminates the need for suggesting a particular type of motivation as part of the definition of terrorism and creates a temptation to infer that terrorism has to be politically motivated.

The modern-day assassin is the Middle East suicide bomber or the "Right-to-Life" shooter of doctors and staff at abortion clinics. Both calculate their acts to induce fear and anxiety in a wider number and variety of people, hoping to have a major impact on a far-larger population than those likely to be injured by the acts themselves. The perpetrators of such acts would, most likely, believe that these drastic means could, and would, coerce a wider group into abandoning certain commercial practices or medical procedures, that lie at the root of the shooter's angry actions. Certainly, these groups definitely do carry out acts of terrorism, but they are not necessarily considered to be politically motivated in the larger sense.

This definition of terrorism also excludes acts of violence in which the terror component is incidental, or secondary to some other primary objective. The death of the owner operator of a major logging company, for example, may be the primary goal of some environmental extremists who wish to eliminate his voice or his particular kind of leadership. Or, more likely, the owner could be about to influence some item of legislation that is clearly in opposition to the environmental extremist group's goals. In this situation, the fear generated by the killing is of secondary importance to the actual silencing of that individual. This act should probably be more accurately labeled as "murder" or "assassination," rather than as terrorism. If the extremist group that killed this leader were also to issue a statement of demands, however, and threaten that more such industrialists and even private citizens would be attacked if the group's demands were not met, then it would be more accurate to refer to the group's actions as "terrorism."

It is clear that labeling persons or groups as terrorists does not preclude also categorizing those same persons or groups as "madmen," "guerrillas," "ideologues," or "revolutionaries." An example could go as follows: "A grocery store owner, who plays baseball on weekends, might be sometimes referred to as a, 'baseball player.' But he has not, however, stopped being a grocer." Members of the IRA (Irish Republican Army), PLO (Palestine Liberation Organization), or ETA (Euzkadi Ta Azkatasuna) may be revered as **freedom fighters** by their subgroups of the local political system. But, to others in the same system, they clearly continue to be seen as "terrorists." Without some recourse to established definitional parameters, these kinds of labels are just a matter of value judgment. If the person making the judgment does not agree with the objectives of the group using such methods to gain some goal, they will be called (with very few exceptions) terrorists. The group thus categorized immediately denies this, of course, and calls itself a **National Liberation Army**, or a "Workers Army" or some similar identifying term. The overwhelming conclusion is that a terrorist group invariably has no legitimacy and therefore its goals have no validity. The label of terrorist then becomes a catchall term of derision and, thus, obscures whatever legitimate complaints the group may have had. In order to understand the phenomenon of terrorism, one must always assess the divergent views of what precisely constitutes terrorism and then ask, "What is the current definition in use?" Reaching a general consensus on a universal definition of terrorism has generated many hot debates in the Social Sciences. It is clear that no single definition seems to satisfy every terrorist or act of terrorism. It is clear, also, that there is no "one-size-fits-all" for terrorist/terrorism situations.

Terrorism is clearly a very special type of violence. It is a tactic used in many situations—peace, conflict, and even war. The threat of terrorism can be ever present, and anywhere, and an attack, such as the one on the World Trade Center on 9-11, can occur when least expected. A terrorist attack as horrible as 9-11 has already happened however; it was the kind of event that almost always forces a transition from peaceful coexistence to conflict—or war. Combating terrorism is a factor that must be considered in all military plans and operations. Combating terrorism requires a continuous state of intelligence gathering and awareness, and should be a constant practice, rather than a particular type of military operation. Terrorism is also a criminal offense under nearly every national and international legal code. With few exceptions, acts of terrorism are forbidden in war—just as they are in times of peace.[4]

SOME APPROACHES TO DEFINING TERRORISM

In addition to the definitions just discussed, the following diverse definitions are also used to describe terrorism:

Simple: Violence or threatened violence intended to produce fear or cause change.

Legal: Criminal violence violating legal codes and punishable by the state.

Analytical: A specific political and/or social factor behind individual violent acts.

State-sponsored: National or other groups used to attack Western or other vested interests.

State: Power of the Government used to repress its people to the point of submission.[5]

In his book *Political Terrorism* (1983), Alex Schmid surveyed 100 scholars and experts in the field and asked for their definition of terrorism. This analysis found two constant characteristics:

1. An individual being threatened,
2. The terrorist act's meaning is derived from the choice of target and victims. Schmid's analysis concluded that the following elements are common throughout the 100 definitions surveyed:
   - Terrorism is an abstract concept with no real essence.
   - A single definition cannot account for all the possible uses of the term.
   - Many different definitions often share common elements.
   - The meaning of terrorism derives from the victims or targets.[6]

Schmid also provided the following from his research of those 100 definitions:

Terrorism is an anxiety inspiring method of repeated violent action, employed by (semi-)clandestine individual, group or state actors, for idiosyncratic, criminal or political reason, whereby—in contrast to assassination—the direct targets of violence are not the main target.

The perpetrators of terrorism may truly believe their cause to be altruistic and that it serves for the betterment of society. In Bruce Hoffman's (1998) excellent work, *Inside Terrorism*, he states that the terrorist is fundamentally a violent intellectual who is prepared to use and, indeed, is committed to using, force in the attainment of perceived goals.

Hoffman also adds that by distinguishing terrorists from other types, such as thugs or common criminals, we come to appreciate that terrorism is

- Primarily political in aims and motives;
- Violent or—equally important—threatens violence;
- Designed to have far-reaching psychological repercussions, beyond the immediate victim or target;
- Conducted by an organization with an identifiable chain of command or conspiratorial cell structures (whose members wear no uniform or identifying insignia); and
- Perpetrated by a sub-national group or nonstate entity.[7]

Once we accept that terrorism is simply a means to an end—nothing more and nothing less—we can apply the term to an event without the inclusion of moral beliefs and sociological-political mumbo-jumbo. The operatives of the PLO are clearly terrorists. But that fact, standing alone, does not mean that their aims and objectives are not without some real reason and validity. Members of the Provisional IRA might be described as "freedom fighters," but even if they do not personally accept the label of terrorist, they would almost always be deemed to be terrorists by those whom their actions affect, be they the general public, government or specific individuals. Militant groups, particularly those like the Irish terror groups and Spain's ETA, whose *modus operandi* includes bombings in public places and targeted assignations, are universally condemned and labeled as terrorists.

It is often easier for one to perceive a long-established, freely elected (even dictatorial, religious, or royalist) regime as "legitimate" than it is to accept that a handful of individuals with views significantly different from those of the majority might deserve the same classification. This is especially true if the individuals use methods that provoke moral indignation against a sanctioned, "legitimate" target, such as the government. When an indiscriminate "enemy" label is applied to those not actually supportive of a dissenting aggressor's objective, the situation becomes far more disturbing, even more so because the aggressors frequently use violence as a means to their ends. Wearing no uniforms to indicate their presence, they employ weapons that may not need to be personally fired or activated (e.g., mail bombs, car bombs, time bombs, etc.). Likewise, unknown aggressors kill unknown victims for reasons that are seldom made clear until after the event has occurred.

There will always be some "bottom-line" considerations, of course, even when the targets are "acceptable enemies" in the eyes of many. Violence against the former Soviet-backed regimes, for example, finds more favor among Western observers, even when such strikes could be clearly defined as terrorist actions. But if the nature of the assault transgresses certain unwritten, but widely accepted, boundaries of decency or fair play, then condemnation is more likely to be applied. The downing of a Russian helicopter gunship by elements of dissenting Chechen rebels, for example, is more likely to be interpreted (except by supporters of the Russians) as acceptable than would be the downing of a civilian airliner by the PLO. The deliberate slaughter of armed soldiers in an ambush is more easily accepted than is the slaughter of small children. In descending order, "fair game" for terrorists or dissenters might be depicted as follows:

1. Military personnel;
2. Government officials;
3. Civilians unconnected in any way with the continuance of the policy against which the terrorist is fighting.

This same attenuated sample list might constitute the basis of a target selection for almost any military offensive. On the other hand, an actual terrorist group would consider the following order to be more appropriate for maximum impact:

1. Civilians unconnected in any way with the continuance of the policy against which the group is fighting;
2. Government officials;
3. Military personnel.

This second, seemingly illogical, order is the one that is very logical for terrorists because maximum fear and anxiety can be generated by attacks against noncombatants. This kind of prioritizing demonstrates to the populace as a whole that the targeted regime is clearly unable to protect them. Such actions are generally a far safer technique—for the terrorist group—than trying to prove that the regime cannot protect itself. Terror groups will choose to cause outrage and revulsion in their target audience in order to maintain the required level of terror, fear, and anger against government agencies. The reader/student should now have a clearer basis for understanding that, while strategies incorporating acts of terrorism in the past centuries have changed somewhat in delivery and methods, the primary purposes of terrorist acts have always remained generally constant:

- To bring attention to perceived grievances or causes by some act or acts that are shocking and draw attention;
- To use the media by attracting coverage of such acts in order to get the widest possible dissemination of the message;
- To contain reaction by the public at large through fear and intimidation;
- To coerce change and destabilize opponents through the threat of further and continued use of such acts until the grievances or causes are recognized and acted upon.

Over a quarter of a century ago, Jenkins argued that "terrorism is theatre; therefore terrorists do not want a lot of people dead . . . they want a lot of people watching and listening."[8] In recent years, that rationale has significantly diminished with the advent of Islamist terror attacks. This watching and listening has been used over the centuries—from a few villagers who stood by, while terrorists acted out or gave their speeches, up to today's instant and live worldwide television coverage by all of the major networks of the most vile acts, piped directly into millions of homes. It is seldom that one hears much about the barbarous acts committed in Third-World countries such as Rwanda, Congo, Zimbabwe, Burma, or Sudan on the evening news in other than a quick sound bite. But let a few armed attackers take over a commercial airliner from a developed country, with 150 to 300 or so paying passengers, and the media flocks to stand by and listen to the demands of the terrorists, and broadcast them around the globe.

Following the London subway suicide attacks, the British government sought to define terrorism as it might apply to the current threat and attack scenarios. At the time, the existing legislation, the Prevention of Terrorism Act of 1989, which had been formulated to deal with Irish nationalist terrorism, defined terrorism as "the use of violence for political ends, and includes any use of violence for the purpose of putting the public or any section of the public in fear." As it is written this is obviously a very broad definition of terrorism and excludes violence for religious ends or for a nonpolitical ideological end. Subsequently the Terrorism Act, 2000, was developed to remedy the defects of the 1989 definition. In the United States, the Homeland Security Act of 2002 defines terrorism as "any activity that involves an act that is dangerous to human life or potentially destructive of critical infrastructure or key resources; and is a violation of the criminal laws of the United States or of any State or other subdivision of the United States and appears to be intended to intimidate or coerce a civilian population; to influence the policy of a government by intimidation or coercion or to affect the conduct of a government by mass destruction, assassination, or kidnapping."

Another current UK definition for terrorism can be found in The Reinsurance (Acts of Terrorism) Act, 1993, section 2(2), which states: "In this section 'acts of terrorism' means acts of persons acting on behalf of, or in conjunction with any organization which carries out activities directed towards the overthrowing or influencing, by force or violence, of Her Majesty's government in the United Kingdom or any other government de jure or de facto."

This chapter just begins our study of this topic we call terrorism and examines the difficulty in deciding just what that term really means. George Rosie further highlights this difficulty as follows: "Terrorism is a complex, multifaceted, and often baffling subject. The organizations involved have a way of emerging, splintering, disappearing and then reappearing, which makes it very difficult for the average person to follow. Individuals come and go, are jailed, die, go underground, or apparently vanish. Counter terror bureaucracies are formed then reformed, names are changed, and leaders are shuffled around, like deck chairs on the Titanic, as they are promoted, demoted, forced to resign, or put out to pasture. Incidents proliferate across the world, some of which can trigger a chain of events that will destabilize a whole region and bring nations and governments to the edge of ruin. At the same time, major terrorist actions can shock for a short while, and then be quickly forgotten (except by those who were directly affected by the inevitable tragedy). Treaties are written, theories propounded, grievances aired, tactics discussed, occasionally to some effect, but usually not. Causes are picked up by the world's media, examined, probed, and then all too soon often overlooked, until the next explosion occurs, or the next airliner is hijacked."[9]

We now continue our examination of what terrorism is (and what it is not) with a few more commonly used definitions. Acts of terrorism conjure emotional responses in the victims (those hurt by the violence and affected by the fear) as well as in the practitioners. Even the U.S. government cannot agree on one, single definition. Following are a few more common definitions of terrorism:

- Terrorism is the use or threatened use of force designed to bring about political change—Brian Jenkins.
- Terrorism constitutes the illegitimate use of force to achieve a political objective when innocent people are targeted—Walter Laqueur.

- Terrorism is the premeditated, deliberate, systematic murder, mayhem, and threatening of the innocent to create fear and intimidation in order to gain a political or tactical advantage, usually to influence an audience—James M. Poland.
- Terrorism is the unlawful use or threat of violence against persons or property to further political or social objectives. It is usually intended to intimidate or coerce a government, individuals, or groups, or to modify their behavior or politics—U.S. Vice President's Task Force, 1986.
- Terrorism is the unlawful use of force or violence against persons or property to intimidate or coerce a government, the civilian population, or any segment thereof, in furtherance of political or social objectives—FBI definition.
- The calculated use of violence or the threat of violence to inculcate fear; intended to coerce or to intimidate governments or societies in the pursuit of goals that are generally political, religious, or ideological—Department of Defense definition.[10]

THE FBI CONSTRUCT

The FBI seems to have developed a very useful construct of what is to be considered terrorism in the United States. This issue concerns foreign power-sponsored or foreign power-coordinated activities that:

a. Involve violent acts, dangerous to human life, that are a violation of the criminal laws of the United States or any state, or that would be a criminal violation if committed within the jurisdiction of the United States, or any state;

b. Appear to be intended to:
- Intimidate or coerce a civilian population;
- Influence the policy of a government by intimidation or coercion;
- Affect the conduct of a government by assassination or kidnapping.

c. Occur totally outside of the United States, or transcend national boundaries in terms of the means by which they are accomplished, the persons they appear intended to coerce or intimidate, or the locale in which their perpetrators operate or seek to find asylum.

Investigating acts of terrorism overseas includes interviewing victims, collecting forensic evidence, and apprehending terrorist fugitives. The FBI coordinates all overseas investigations with the U.S. Department of State and the host foreign government.[11]

THE U.S. DEPARTMENT OF DEFENSE (DOD) CONSTRUCTS

Christopher G. Essig stated at the United Nations, quoting from his paper, *Terrorism: Is It a Criminal Act or an Act of War?* "This is discussed in depth at the Army War College at Carlisle Barracks, Pennsylvania, and its implications for National Security in the 21st century, but there is no single determination for classifying all acts of terrorism, neither as acts of war, nor criminal acts. In light of a predicted terrorist threat significant enough to threaten the survival of the nation (catastrophic terror), this determination is less a legal or academic exercise and more practically one based on how such a determination governs this situation (law enforcement or national security?) to respond to the threat. More important is how that response protects our nation's interests and our status in the world community. Catastrophic terror makes relying solely on a law enforcement response a dangerous option. Yet, reflecting on the changing strategic environment, an act of war determination, in a classical legal sense, is equally impractical. A new determination, carrying the same weight as an act of war must be developed and accepted, domestically and internationally, to provide legal response options offering greater latitude to law enforcement and national security forces. This latitude will provide the means to better meet threats to national security in the 21st century."

Terrorism, as further defined by the DOD, is usually considered to be calculated, and the selection of a target preplanned and rational. The perpetrators know the effect they seek. Terrorist violence is considered to be neither spontaneous nor random. Terrorism is intended to produce fear in someone other than the victim. In a layperson's terms, "terrorism is a psychological act conducted primarily for its impact on a specific audience." It is abundantly clear that the attack on 9-11 was calculated and that the terrorists knew what they were doing, but the impact caused exactly the opposite to what they had expected . . . and awakened, a sleeping giant! Or in awakening this sleeping giant, maybe, the expectations of the Islamist terrorists were in fact realized. In the decade since 9-11, the Islamist threat has hardened against western democracies as well as secular Middle East regimes. Many believe that the attacks of 9-11 and the subsequent invasions of both Iraq and Afghanistan were exactly what the Islamists hoped to achieve. For the Islamists, the presence of foreign troops in the Middle East gives them the excuse they so dearly need to extend, prolong, and widen their jihad to global proportions.

The DOD definition also addresses goals. Terrorism may be motivated by political, religious, or ideological objectives. In one sense, terrorist goals are invariably political—extremists are driven by religious or ideological beliefs and usually seek political power to compel general society to conform to their views. The objectives of terrorism distinguish it from other violent acts aimed at personal gain, such as criminal violence. However, the definition permits including violence by organized crime when it also seeks to influence government policy. Some drug cartels and other international criminal organizations engage in political action when their activities influence governmental functioning. As noted previously, the essence of terrorism is the intent to inculcate fear into persons other than its direct victims in order to make a government or other audience finally change its political behavior.

Terrorism is common practice in insurgencies, but insurgents are not necessarily terrorists, especially if they comply with the rules of war and do not engage in forms of violence that could be clearly identified as terrorist acts. While the legal distinction is clear, it rarely inhibits terrorists, who convince themselves that their actions are justified by an even higher law or principle. Their single-minded dedication to a goal, however poorly it may be articulated, and renders legal sanctions relatively ineffective. In contrast, however, war is subject to rules of international law. Terrorists recognize no rules. No person, place, or object of value is immune from terrorist attack. To them, there are no innocents.

THE UNITED NATIONS

The United Nations General Assembly has been struggling with defining terrorism since the 1960s, and between 1963 and 1999 the UN came up with 13 international conventions aimed at terrorist actions and, in particular, outlawing airline hijackings and diplomatic hostage taking. The UN came up with a draft, which still remains contentious to many member states – however, the General Assembly has resolved to fight terrorism, even if it has failed to adequately define the term.

The United Nation's Global Counterterrorism Strategy was adopted by Member States on September 8, 2006. The strategy—in the form of a Resolution and an annexed Plan of Action—is a unique global instrument that will enhance national, regional, and international efforts to counter terrorism. This is the first time that all Member States have agreed to a common strategic approach to fight terrorism, not only sending a clear message that terrorism is unacceptable in all its forms and manifestation, but also resolving to take practical steps individually and collectively to prevent and combat it. Those practical steps include a wide array of measures ranging from strengthening state capacity to counter terrorist threats to better coordinating United Nation's counterterrorism activities. The adoption of the strategy fulfils the commitment made by world leaders at the 2005 September Summit and builds on many of the elements proposed by the Secretary-General in his May 2, 2006, report entitled *Uniting against Terrorism: Recommendations for a Global Counterterrorism Strategy.*[12]

STRUCTURES OF TERRORIST GROUPS

Terrorists tend to organize themselves all over the world in ways that enable them to function well in the specific environment in which they are located, and then be able to carry out the acts of terrorism. We shall now discuss some general organizational principles for terrorists that shed insight into how a terrorist thinks. Above all else, the most important thing to a terrorist is tight security. Why? Because they are always operating in a hostile environment!

It does not matter if the terrorists are in Europe, Japan, or the United States, as wherever they are is a hostile environment. Their safety and security is best protected by what is called a "cellular structure." This is primarily most important, because the structure ensures that not one of them can identify any more terrorists than those in their specific cell of operation. It is like a safety net for them.

Terrorist groups—those that are not supported by a specific government—always create what is called a tight support structure of **sympathizers** or many other people who may have been coerced into supporting or helping them for various reasons.

Such a support system can be either active or passive. By that we mean intelligence collection, recruiting, monetary support, logistics, dissemination of propaganda, or worse, a young person strapped up with explosives and sent to a specific target for self-destruction. This is clearly horrid, but it is a reality in terrorism just as is the use of women and children as human shields for covert operations. It is a fact in the lifestyle of terrorism and terrorists, wherever they are to be found.

COMMON TERRORIST QUALITIES

What qualities does a terrorist leader look for when selecting his followers for an operation? It is difficult to give a categorical or simple answer to this question. However, certain qualities separate terrorists who form the "hard core" of terrorist organizations from those who comprise the peripheral elements, whose activities are mostly seen in a supportive role.

First, they must believe passionately in the justness of their cause! This is a most important quality, because this is also the motivating factor for all their subsequent actions.

Second, they must possess a killer instinct, in other words, a predilection to kill, not in anger, not in the heat of the moment, not during a fight or a battle, but kill at any time, anywhere, in absolute cold blood, and without any pangs of conscience or feelings of pity and remorse for the targeted victims.

Third, they must possess an ability to act effectively as loners, if circumstances so warrant, even though in their private lives they may not be loners. Members of conventional armies, and insurgent and guerrilla organizations, train, live, and move together. They normally operate in groups, although there may be circumstances when individual members may have to operate totally alone. On the contrary, in the case of terrorist organizations, they may train and occasionally live together, but more often their members operate as loners unless they are tasked for specific operations, such as the hijacking of an aircraft or a kidnapping.

About 60 percent of the terrorist incidents reported every year are operations in which the terrorists acted as loners for assassinations, sniper missions, throwing of hand grenades, planting of explosives, suicide bombings, and so on. Thus, operating as a loner requires greater physical and mental courage and individual determination, and even greater dedication and loyalty than operating in groups. Independent groups that have been inspired by al Qaeda and the Islamist extremist preachings of Osama bin Laden have seen a level of "religious" violence and considerable bravery on behalf of the autonomous cell members, unmatched by the likes of European groups such as ETA and the Irish terrorist groups.

Fourth, they must have a very high degree of physical courage, because a terrorist risks not only death, but even worse than death—capture, physical torture, and long imprisonment, if caught.

The development of bureaucratic states led to a profound change in terrorism. Modern democratic governments have continuity that older, charismatic, royal, religious-based, or inherited governments do not. Terrorists soon found that the death of a single individual, even a Monarch, did not necessarily make a great enough impact to produce the policy changes they had sought. Terrorists reacted by turning to an indirect method of attack. By the early twentieth century, terrorists began to attack people who were previously considered "innocents" to generate political pressure from and by the public. These indirect attacks managed to create a public atmosphere of anxiety, fear, and an undermining of confidence in government. Their very unpredictability, and apparent randomness, makes it virtually impossible for governments to protect all potential victims. The public then cries out for safety and protection that the state cannot give. Frustrated and fearful, the people then demand that the government make concessions to the terrorists in order to stop the attacks.

Modern terrorism behavior and philosophy offers its practitioners many advantages. First, by not recognizing innocents, terrorists can acquire and attack an infinite number of targets. They can select their target and then determine when, where, and how to attack. This range of choices gives terrorists a high probability of success with minimum risk. If the attack goes wrong, or fails to produce the intended results, they can simply deny responsibility.

Ironically, as democratic governments become more common, it may be getting even easier for terrorists to operate. The first terrorist bombing of the World Trade Center in New York City, the **Oklahoma City Federal Building** disaster, the bombing of the two U.S. embassies in Kenya and Tanzania, and the suicide attack on the U.S.S. *Cole* in Yemen—all were *dots* that were not connected, culminating in the horrendous attacks on the World Trade Center on 9-11! Such "follow-the-dots roadmaps" proved how easy it could be for terrorists to operate in a free or democratic society. Authoritarian governments, whose populace may have even better reasons to revolt, may also be less constrained by requirements for due process and impartial justice when combating terrorists. As national leaders and politicians address terrorism, they must consider several relevant characteristics:

1. Anyone can be a victim. (Some terrorists may still operate under certain cultural restraints, such as a desire to avoid harming women; but essentially, there are no more innocents these days.)
2. Attacks that may appear to be senseless and random may not be senseless or random to the perpetrators/terrorist; their attacks have made perfect sense. Acts such as suicide bombings in public places of assembly or shooting into crowded restaurants are guaranteed to heighten public anxiety. This is always the terrorists' immediate objective.
3. The terrorist or terrorist group needs to publicize the attack. If no one knows about it, it will not generate the desired fear and pressure on government. The need for publicity often drives target selection—the greater the symbolic value of the target, the more publicity the attack brings to the terrorists and the more fear it generates. The media often provide the notoriety, intentionally or inadvertently, that the terrorists desire, simply by just covering the terrorist event.
4. Any leader planning for effective ways to combat terrorism must understand that nothing can protect every possible target all the time. It must be seen clearly that terrorists would most likely just change their attack tactics from more-protected targets to less-protected ones. This is the key to defensive measures.[13]

Motivations for Terrorists

Terrorists are inspired by many and diverse motives. One can even classify them into three distinct categories: *rational*, *psychological*, and *cultural*. Many combinations and variations of these factors may shape a terrorist. Rational terrorists will think through their goals and options, often conducting a sort of "cost/benefit analysis" of expected results. They seek information to determine whether there are less costly or more effective ways with which to achieve their individual or group objectives. To assess the risk, they weigh the target's defensive capabilities against their own offensive abilities to accomplish an attack. They analyze the terrorist group's capabilities to sustain the effort. The essential question is whether terrorism will probably work and accomplish the desired goals, given societal conditions at the time. The terrorist's rational analysis is similar to that of a military commander or a business entrepreneur considering available resources and courses of action. Groups considering terrorism as an option always ask a crucial question: "Can terrorism induce enough anxiety to attain their goals without causing a backlash that will destroy the cause and perhaps even the terrorists themselves?" To misjudge the answer to that question is to court disaster. In the case of the attacks of 9-11, they generated a backlash now known, perhaps a little too simply but aptly, as the **War on Terror**. Psychological motivations for resorting to terrorism usually derive from the terrorist organizations' or individuals' personal depth of dissatisfaction with their life and accomplishments. Individuals find a reason to be involved in a dedicated terrorist action. Although no clear psychopathy can always be found among terrorists, there is a nearly universal element in them that can be described as the "true believer." Terrorists seldom even attempt to consider that they may be wrong or that other views might have some merit. Terrorists tend to project their own antisocial attitudes and motivations onto others, creating a polarized "us-versus-them" outlook. They attribute evil motives to anyone outside their own group. This enables the terrorists to dehumanize their victims and removes any sense of ambiguity from their minds. The resulting clarity of purpose appeals to those who crave and need a use of violence to relieve their constant anger.

Another common characteristic of the psychologically motivated terrorist is the desperate need to belong to a like-minded group. With some terrorists, group acceptance is a stronger motivator than the stated political objectives of the organization. Such individuals define their social status by group acceptance.

Terrorist groups with strong internal motivations find it necessary to justify the group's existence continuously. A terrorist group must, as a minimum, commit some violent acts to maintain group self-esteem and legitimacy. Another result of psychological motivation is the intensity of the group dynamics among terrorists. They tend to demand unanimity and are intolerant of any dissent or different opinions. With the enemy clearly identified and determined to be unequivocally evil, pressure to escalate the frequency and intensity of operations is ever-present. The need to belong to the group discourages any possible resignations, and the fear of compromise disallows their acceptance; compromise is also usually rejected. Terrorist groups lean toward inflexible positions. Having placed themselves "beyond the pale" (forever unacceptable to ordinary society), they cannot consider any compromise. They can then expect any negotiation to be dishonorable, even treasonous. Such dynamics also make any announced group goal nearly impossible to achieve. By definition, a group that has achieved its stated purpose is no longer necessary. As a result, success threatens the psychological well-being of its members. Therefore, when a terrorist group approaches its stated goal, it is inclined to pause and redefine it. The group may reject the achievement as false or inadequate, or the result of the duplicity of the unknown, unnamed "them." Terrorist groups also often suffer from a nagging fear of success. One effective psychological defense against success is to define goals so broadly that they are impossible to achieve. Even if the world proclaims the success of a political movement, the terrorists can deny it and fight on. Cultural concepts also shape values and motivate people to actions that seem unreasonable to outside observers. For example, Americans are often generally reluctant to appreciate the intense impact that cultural factors have on behavior. They too often easily accept the myth that rational behavior guides all human actions. It is easy to reject as unbelievable such things as vendettas, martyrdom, suicide bombers, and self-destructive group behavior when Americans observe them in others. There is disbelief that such things as the destruction of a viable state can be done just for the sake of ethnic purity, especially when the resulting state becomes economically or politically unstable.

The treatment of life, in general, and individual life, in particular, is a cultural characteristic that has a tremendous impact on terrorism. In societies in which people identify themselves in terms of group memberships (family, clan, or tribe), there may be a willingness to accept levels of self-sacrifice seldom seen elsewhere. At times, terrorists seem to be eager to give their lives for their organization or cause. The lives of "others," even strangers, whom they perceive as being totally evil by their terrorist value system, can therefore be snuffed out without any sense of remorse. Other factors include the manner in which aggression is channeled and the concepts of social organization. In many political systems, there are effective, nonviolent means for succession to power. A culture may have a high tolerance for nonpolitical violence, such as banditry or ethnic turf battles, and remain relatively free of political violence. The United States, for example, is one of the most violent societies in the world; yet political violence remains a rare aberration. By contrast, both France and Germany, with low tolerance for violent crime, have had long histories of political violence.

A major cultural determinant of terrorism is the perception of "outsiders" and anticipation of their threat to long-held ethnic values or to a terrorist group's survival. Fear of cultural dilution or extermination leads to violence that, to someone who has not experienced it, seems irrational. All human beings are sensitive to threats to their personal values and beliefs, those with which they identify themselves. These include language; religion; tribal, racial, or group membership; and a sense of homeland territory. The possibility of losing any of these can trigger defensive, even xenophobic, reactions.

Religion may be the most volatile of cultural identifiers because it encompasses values and beliefs deeply rooted in a long-standing and ancient cultural paradigm. A threat to one's religion puts not only the present at risk but also one's entire cultural past, present, and future. Many religions, including Christianity and Islam, are so confident they are right that they have often used force to make converts or to eliminate nonbelievers. Terrorism in the name of religion can be especially violent, and will be discussed in detail in Chapter 2. Like all terrorists, those who are religiously motivated view their acts with moral certainty and even divine sanctions. What would otherwise be extraordinary acts of desperation becomes a religious duty in the mind of the religiously motivated terrorist. This helps explain the high level of commitment among religious extremist groups and suicide bombers, and their willingness to risk their own deaths.

TERRORISM AS CRIMINAL BEHAVIOR

The broad range of violent activities that are often labeled as "terrorism" can now be seen as difficult, even as impossible, to define in a simplistic and universal way. There are some specific acts that seem to straddle the behavioral continuum in such a way so as to cloud the effort to somehow distinguish between criminal acts and terrorist acts. Some so-called terrorist acts are so specific and localized as to be outside the scope of the broader definitions. We shall now examine a few of them that seem especially relevant as we examine crime and terror in the twenty-first century.

HOSTAGE TAKING

Taking hostages, whether for political reasons or for extortion of funds to support terrorist groups, is an often-used tactic. The policy of the United States is to make no concessions to terrorists who hold official or private U.S. citizens as hostages. The United States will not pay ransom, release prisoners, change its policies, or agree to other acts that might encourage terrorism. At the same time, the United States will use every available and appropriate resource to gain the safe return of American citizens who are being held hostage by terrorists. Hostage-taking is defined under international law (the International Convention Against the Taking of Hostages, adopted December 17, 1979) as "the seizing or detaining, threatening to kill, injure, or continue to detain a person in order to compel a third party to do, or abstain from doing, any act as an explicit or implicit condition for the release of the seized or detained person. Such activity is also considered a criminal act in most countries around the world, as a part of extortion or kidnapping for profit." It is generally accepted in the international community that local governments are responsible for the safety and welfare of persons within the borders of their nations. Terrorist threats and public safety shortcomings in many parts of the world have caused the United States to develop enhanced physical and personal security programs for U.S.

citizens, and to establish cooperative arrangements with the U.S. private sector to help warn and protect business travelers. The United States has established bilateral counterterrorism assistance programs, and close intelligence and law enforcement relationships with many nations to help prevent terrorist incidents, or to resolve them in a manner that will deny the terrorists political or financial benefits from their actions. The United States also seeks to employ adequate and effective judicial prosecution and punishment for terrorists and criminals who seek to victimize the U.S. government, or its citizens, and will use all appropriate legal methods toward these ends, including extradition alone and/or, hopefully, with appropriate cooperation from the other governments. After many serious incidents, the United States has finally concluded that paying ransom or making other concessions to terrorists in exchange for the release of hostages only increases the probability and danger that others will then be taken hostage—*ad infinitum*. In some very poor nations, kidnapping and ransom are considered growth industries. The official U.S. policy is to reject any demands for ransom, prisoner exchanges, and deals with terrorists in exchange for hostage release. At the same time, every effort will be made, including contact with representatives of the captors, to obtain the release of the hostages, without responding to the stated demands of the terrorists. U.S. policy also strongly encourages U.S. companies and private citizens not to respond to terrorist ransom demands. It believes that good security practice, relatively modest security training and expenditures, and continual close cooperation with embassy and local authorities will lower the risk to Americans abroad who are living and working in such high-threat environments.

Although the United States is concerned for the welfare of its citizens, it cannot support requests from private companies that host governments should violate their own laws or abdicate their normal law enforcement responsibilities. On the other hand, if the employing organization or company of a hostage works closely with local authorities and follows U.S. policy, U.S. Foreign Service posts can be involved actively in efforts to bring such stressful incidents to a safe conclusion. This includes providing reasonable administrative services and, if desired by the local authorities and the American organization, full participation in strategy sessions. Requests for U.S. technical assistance or expertise are considered on a case-by-case basis. The full extent of U.S. government participation must await an analysis of each specific set of circumstances. This again demonstrates the problems involved with making precise definitions of who can do what in a situation that may or may not be terrorism.

LEGAL ISSUES IN HOSTAGE-TAKING

Under current U.S. law (18 USC 1203, Act for the Prevention and Punishment of the Crime of Hostage-Taking, enacted in October, 1984, on implementation of the UN convention on hostage-taking), seizure of a U.S. national as a hostage anywhere in the world is a crime, as is any hostage-taking action in which the U.S. government is a target or the hostage-taker is a U.S. national. Such acts are, therefore, subject to investigation by the FBI and to prosecution by U.S. authorities.

ASSASSINATION

On September 11, 2001, terrorist leader Osama bin Laden and his al Qaeda cohorts struck a blow not only against Americans, but also against western social values, and have, by these acts, created a lingering and justifiable fear that they will attempt to strike at the United States again. This fear tended to increase pressure on U.S. officials and, around the talk-show circuit, to perhaps reconsider "**assassination**" as a method of solving problems with world leaders whom we consider to be dangerous. The old argument still remains, "How many lives would we have saved if Hitler had been assassinated in 1938?" This argument is strong and, for a long time, many countries have ordered and approved using "extreme sanction" against leaders of unfriendly countries or against leaders of criminal or terrorist organizations. "Cut the head off the snake," was considered a good response to perceived danger. But, ordering an assassination today would mean moving away from long-established policy and practice.

Time will tell whether or not the United States can ever accumulate the needed backing of the international community to head into "a sure-to-spiral upward" path of assassinations adopted to meet perceived solutions to growing problems. The problem is similar to that of euthanasia—"Who decides when a person is so evil, or in such bad health, that their elimination is the only alternative?" This issue will have a long discussion period, in times when cooler emotions may eventually prevail. The situation in Iraq showed what methods had to be used to oust Saddam Hussein—and his trial and execution will help to clarify whether such actions were justifiable or considered too extreme.

Examples of Past Hostage Crises

FRONT DE LIBERATION DU QUEBEC (FLQ)—OCTOBER 3RD 1970   Members of the Front kidnap the British Trade Commissioner, James Cross, as he is leaving his home, and five days later FLQ members kidnap Pierre Laporte, the Vice Premier of Quebec. The Canadian Prime Minister invokes the War Measures Act similar in effect to a declaration of Marshall Law. The FLQ issues a long list of demands, including the release of "political prisoners," a demand for $500,000 in gold, as well as publication of the FLQ Manifesto and safe passage out of Canada to either Algeria or Cuba. Laporte is murdered by his kidnappers and his body dumped in the trunk of a car. Police successfully negotiate the release of James Cross and allow five of the terrorists passage to Cuba. The kidnappers and murderers of Laporte are arrested in December of the same year.

FIGURE 1-2   James Cross, British Trade Commissioner, kidnapped by members of the FLQ, is photographed playing cards during his captivity in November 1970 (Canadian Press).

FIGURE 1-3   Kidnapping of German industrialist Hanns-Martin Schleyer on the streets of Cologne, Germany, on September 5, 1977. Herr Schleyer's driver and bodyguards were killed during the abduction and are seen lying covered beside the cars (Canadian Press).

BLACK SEPTEMBER—MARCH 1973   Eight members of the Palestinian group Black September raid a diplomatic event at the Saudi Arabian Embassy in Khartoum and seize the American Charge d'Affaires, George Curtis Moore, the American Ambassador to Sudan, Cleo Noel Jr., and Guy Eid from the Belgian Embassy. The terrorist demands included the release of Sirhan Sirhan, Robert Kennedy's assassin, the release of a Black September leader from a Jordanian prison and several members of the Baader Meinhof terror gang being held in Germany. President Nixon and the two other governments refuse to negotiate, and the Black September terrorists execute all three men in the basement of the Embassy.

HANNS-MARTIN SCHLEYER—RED ARMY FACTION SEPTEMBER (RAF) 1977   Members of the RAF attack a convoy of vehicles carrying Schleyer, and kill his driver and three police escorts. They demand the release of members of the RAF from German prisons in exchange for Herr Schleyer. The German government refuses to negotiate, and the RAF, with help from PLO terrorists, hijacks a Lufthansa jet and land it at Mogadishu Airport in Somalia. The German Special force GSG-9 storms the aircraft killing all but one of the hijackers. In retaliation, the RAF kills Hans Schleyer and dumps his body in the trunk of a car in Mulhouse, France.

TALIBAN KIDNAPPINGS—AFGHANISTAN JULY 2007   The Taliban kidnapped 23 South Koreans, working as Christian aid volunteers, on a highway in central Afghanistan in July 2007. The pastor leading the team and another man were shot dead soon after the abduction. All the remaining hostages were released on August 11, 2007, after protracted negotiations with South Korea. Under the agreement, South Korea reaffirmed a pledge to withdraw its 200 troops from Afghanistan by the end of the year, as previously planned, and agreed to prevent any evangelical activities by South Korean churches in Afghanistan. The Taliban, for its part, dropped a demand that eight senior Taliban prisoners be released in exchange for the South Koreans.[14]

There are some obvious concerns with the Korean incident as it seems highly probable that the Korean government capitulated to Taliban demands and surrendered millions of dollars for the return of their citizens. At the same time, a German hostage, also held by the Taliban, has not been released. In light of the exposure and arrest of Islamist networks uncovered in Germany during the summer of 2007, that government has stood firm in its resolve not to negotiate with the Taliban. Paying a ransom is not unusual; however, the agreement to end all missionary work in the country will likely send the wrong message to other Islamist groups who have now witnessed that South Korea has not only the ability and willingness to pay a ransom but to also restrict or prohibit missionary work in a foreign country. This may mean that in countries where there has been violent opposition to Christians and missionaries but where incidents of kidnapping have rarely occurred, such as India, Pakistan, and Indonesia, this incident may be seen as an opportunity to embrace the same style of attack to force out foreign Christians.

PRO-LIFE TERRORISM

When, and how, does legitimate protest in a free democracy become terrorism? On January 3, 1997, the peace of the New Year was shattered by bomb blasts and injuries at the Northside Family Services Clinic in Atlanta, Georgia, rekindling fears and memories of the bombing at the Summer Olympics in that stately southern city. The first blast occurred at the start of the business day, whereas the second blast was set and deliberately delayed to catch federal agents, firefighters, ambulance attendants, and clinic workers as they responded to the scene forty-five minutes later. The second blast resulted in major and minor injuries, and serious damage to the five-story building. The blasts occurred less than a week before the twenty-eighth anniversary of the Supreme Court's decision in *Roe v. Wade*,[15] which had legalized abortion. Was this explosion simply individual rage and violence, or was it a terrorist act?

The Task Force on Terrorism concluded that terrorism is a technique—a way of engaging in certain types of criminal activity—to attain particular ends. This would be a process by which a group would create "an overwhelming fear for coercive purposes," such fear to be raised not only in the immediate victims, but also within the audience of community or society. It seems that this definition fits within the parameters of the violence against abortion clinics by extremist members of the Pro-Life movements across the nation. The technique used in the Atlanta bombings is one well known from the efforts of terrorist groups like the Irish Republican Army (IRA). Experts on terrorism refer to this method as the "congregate effect." The goal is to get people to gather around or near the first bombing and then explode a second or third device with devastating impact. Such planning is not typical of a random act of violence by a single dissident.

As we discussed earlier, the FBI defines terrorism as, "the unlawful use of force or violence against persons or property to intimidate or coerce a government, the civilian population, or any segment thereof, in furtherance of political or social objectives." Again, the acts of violence against abortion clinics by those who wish to get the Supreme Court to reverse *Roe v. Wade* seem to fit neatly within this definition.

"Limited political" and "sub-revolutionary" terrorism are the terms usually applied to those acts in which the goal is to influence through coercive fear certain public policies or practices. While violence, harassment, disruptions, arson and bombings, demonstrations, and action plan documents in total squarely fit the FBI's definition, the Department of Justice has concluded that abortion clinic violence is not terrorism and that there is no national conspiracy to engage in terrorism. It is not clear whether the FBI addressed the question of regional or local conspiracies in this decision, although the Justice Department continues to investigate the alleged conspiracy among antiabortion activists, and to indict activists on federal conspiracy and arson charges.

A Social Construction of Abortion Clinic Violence/Terrorism

The United States has experienced a religious revival, off and on, since at least 1977. This was in part due to the New Millennium and in part due to a reactionary movement fueled by rising crime, anti-Semitism, racism, political demagoguery, and a desire to make the past become the future. The New Right has emerged with a goal of political and cultural hegemony in the United States.

Antiabortionists, in particular, define abortion as a "violation of their moral precepts." The movement gained some momentum with the elections of such pro-life Presidents as Ronald Reagan and George W. Bush. Such movements can be characterized as:

- Adopting a "pro-family" stance;
- Stressing parental rights;
- Emphasizing strong families;
- Expressing moral indignation of abortion, which is perceived as murder;
- Stressing the patriarchal family as the ideal model;
- Emphasizing a fear of changes occurring in family systems;
- Opposition to same-sex marriage or "civil rights."

Thus, this is a backlash movement, and the heart of the effort is to fight the shifts and changes under way in American culture by focusing concerns on reproductive control, including abortion, women's rights, and male domination over women's bodies. For pro-life extremists, those not holding the same moral and religious beliefs are viewed, in dualistic terms, as good-bad, saved-damned, chosen-evil, and God's children-the spawn of Satan. Such moral absolutes permit causal attribution, assigning to one's opponents both malicious intent as well as evil character. Such a mind-set encourages and validates the use of force against opponents, or "sinners". Indeed, it is a moral requirement to punish offenders using whatever force necessary to restrain the wicked and make them virtuous. This could include violence against persons and property, as well as threats of violence (e.g., verbal statements, confrontations at abortion clinics, telephoning the mother of an abortion clinic patient and stating that her yet-unborn grandchild is going to be killed) or other threats. This kind of behavior could fit any number of the previously listed definitions of terrorism.

The antiabortion movement and the New Right interact and network in many ways, including the use of television evangelists who support and condone, workshops, books, training sessions, Bible colleges, and demonstrations. Some in this movement state that their followers ought not to engage in violence, but they then also argue that violence is to be expected because "truly moral" people have no other recourse—they have been "pushed" to these extremes. Thus, one could argue that frustration and anomie are underlying causes of abortion clinic violence and demonstrations.

Abortion and Religious/Political Organizations

Although abortion clinic demonstrators come from a wide section of society, it could be argued that most demonstrators are middle class, religiously influenced, and motivated by postmillennium eschatology—the "parousia" (second-coming)—and a long-range hope for the revitalization of the Church and re-Christianization of American society. The four major religious strategy groups are the Lambs of Christ, Operation Rescue, Pro-Life Action League, and Missionaries to the Pre-Born. Other groups exist (Rescue America, for example), but little is known about their relative composition or influence. Since academic study of the more radical factions of the Pro-Life Movement is at best scant, research lags behind changing events, although diverse written materials appear to be abundant.

The major groups, seminal leaders, and examples of their strategic literature are:

- Lambs of Christ, founded by "Father Doe" (Father Norman Weslin).
- Operation Rescue, founded in 1986 by Randall Terry. In 1991, in Wichita, Kansas, Terry organized the "Summer of Mercy" event, where coordinated acts of civil disobedience were staged. The group is best described as a Christian antiabortion organization founded in the United States. The group advocates civil disobedience as a strategy to oppose abortion. It holds prayer vigils outside abortion clinics and uses graphic symbols to protest abortion.
- Pro-Life Action League, headed by Joseph Scheidler.
- Missionaries to the Pre-Born, headed by Joseph Foreman, with Matt Trewhella as chief strategist.

This group's basic concern is with abortion clinic bombings, killings, and disturbances.

A fairly coherent body of literature and existing personal narratives have not been carefully examined by scholarly inquiries or students of terrorism. Writer and researcher Jeffrey Kaplan is one exception to this criticism.

Abortion Clinic Violence and Disruption

The National Abortion Federation compiles national statistics forwarded by family planning programs and abortion service providers. Relying on voluntary reporting creates many of the same problems associated with the Uniform Crime Reports, and data should be utilized as only estimates of the extent of abortion clinic violence and disruptions. For example, data are gathered on "stalking," defined as the "persistent following, threatening, and harassing of an abortion provider, staff member, or patient away, from the clinic." Stalking may be so frequent that some clinic staffers may relegate it to "routine behavior" and not bother to report the incidents. Harassing calls at any hour of the day or night may also be underreported. There is no equivalent of the National Crime Victimization Survey to permit estimates of the extent of underreporting.

Violence at abortion clinics in western democracies has been a common enough event over the last quarter of a century. There have been attacks on specific clinics in North America that have been directed at medical practitioners, in particular, with the intent to intimidate and cause serious injury. A clinic in Fort Lauderdale was firebombed in 2000, and in June 2003 another clinic was firebombed. In 2003, Paul Hill was executed for killing an abortion clinic doctor and his bodyguard. There have been a series of nationwide campaigns that involved not only abortion clinics but also "gay" bars and churches.[16]

Tracking events and attacks on abortion clinics and associated staff is the responsibility of the National Abortion Federation, and examples of antiabortion activities likely to be underreported in the data gathered by the Federation include the following:

- Beheading of a cat of a clinic worker;
- Spray painting the van of a county councilwoman with the word "baby killer" to coerce her to vote for the termination of lease of a Planned Parenthood Agency;
- Poisoning dogs of a physician who performs abortions in his office;
- Threatening a clinic worker by holding a sledge hammer over her head;
- Holding red meat up before a physician's children, while asking them why their father "kills babies";
- Shooting a judge;
- Picketing physicians' and council members' homes;
- Slashing tires of clinic workers;
- Telephoning patients in the middle of the night and yelling, "baby killer";
- Calling parents of clinic patients to accuse their daughters of sexual and moral misconduct, and calling them "whore," "tramp," "slut," "pin cushion," "Ms. Community Chest."

It is estimated that many more similar acts go unreported.

Such harassment techniques are aimed at inducing fear, similar to the goals of acts of terrorism. Private practices and public policies are influenced by such coordinated efforts. It would not exceed the limits of logic to argue that religious political terrorists are attempting to impose their moral beliefs and practices on a nation by the use of and the threat of the use of violence to gain sufficient power to affect political institutions, especially local and state law making bodies.

There is ample evidence of persistent action against abortion providers, and at least some suggestion of a decline in overall incidents in the past few years.

Army of God

As we have seen in the media, those who are against abortion feel that it is their inalienable right to attack those on the other side of the issue. Networks of like-minded individuals have sprung up in North America, and most believe that violence is the only means to ending abortions. The Army of God is one such group that could be deemed a terrorist organization. An excerpt from the Army of God manual says that the Army of God " . . . ; is a real Army, and God is the General and Commander-in-Chief. The soldiers, however, do not usually communicate with one another. Very few have ever met each other. And when they do, each is usually unaware of the other's soldier status. That is why the Feds will never stop this Army. Never. And we have not yet even begun to fight." Army of God member James Kopp, alias Atomic Dog, was convicted for the fatal shooting of Dr. Barnett Slepian in 1998. Also thought to be linked to Kopp are the shootings that injured Dr. Garson Romalis in Vancouver, British Columbia, in November 1994; Dr. Hugh Short in Ancaster, Ontario, on November 1995; an unnamed physician in Rochester, New York, in October 1997; and Dr. Jack Fainman in Winnipeg, Manitoba, in November 1997.

Clayton Waagner, who was convicted of sending over 550 anthrax threat letters to clinics in 2001, signed many of his letters with "Army of God." He also posted threats to kill forty-two individuals working at abortion clinics on the Army of God Web site.[17]

Future Scenarios

It is clear that after a somewhat calm period after 1996, the level of violence at abortion clinics and against providers has been rising again. There was a significant drop in incidents of violence against abortion providers since the peaks seen in the early 1990s, but a sharp increase in the number of incidents of disruption. When you combine these two categories, it becomes clear that the total increase in incidents is threefold.

Protesters in general have undertaken new strategies for removing abortion providers and reducing opportunities for abortion. After having failed to secure a reversal of *Roe v. Wade,* and facing U.S. Supreme Court affirmation of buffer zones, antiabortion strategists may have concluded that they might gain more by focusing their activities on local and state governments. Instead of militant antiabortion activism, these groups are challenging the tax-exempt status of Planned Parenthood organizations by searching for legal flaws in the wording of charters and bylaws; seeking revocation of property-tax exemptions of nonprofit organizations; pushing local statutes and ordinances; and encouraging passage of antiabortion laws. The National Abortion Federation points out that there is little evidence that the Pro-Life movement has stopped women from having abortions. Nonetheless, it has caused untold trauma, unnecessary and unconscionable health risks, and the loss of personal dignity and privacy for hundreds of thousands of women. It also points out several factors at work in the 21 percent decline in antiabortion violence in 1996:

- The deterrent effect of the passage and enforcement of the Freedom of Access to Clinic Entrances Act.
- Utilization of legal tools such as injunctions, buffer zones, and restraining orders.

The FBI, however, has decided that antiabortion violence is not terrorism, possibly for political or other reasons. However, this may be for such diverse administrative reasons as wanting to focus attention on international homegrown terrorism, or to downplay the real or imagined existence of domestic terrorists to the public. By not defining abortion clinic violence as terrorism, the responsibility for bombing and arson investigation shifts to the Department of the Treasury and the Bureau of Alcohol, Tobacco and Firearms (ATF), a smaller agency with considerably fewer resources than the FBI. Perhaps the federal government can now begin to refocus attention on this violent behavior as a true form of domestic terrorism.

CONSTITUTIONAL RIGHTS

Finally, we raise the question of subversion of constitutionally guaranteed federal rights. The Fourteenth Amendment of the U.S. Constitution defines "residents" as being citizens of both the federal government and of the state in which they reside. It expressly forbids states from making any ordinance, law, or regulation that abridges the federal rights of citizens. If there is a constitutional right to abortion, and the effects (whether by "color" or "usage") of local, county, or state government clearly abridge that right, is that right an issue that might be considered by federal courts? If one defines antiabortion terrorism as an effort to impose a set of religious beliefs on others, is there a colorable question of separation of church and state? Students of constitutional history may later consider these early-millennium years as an odious period of challenge to and denial of their liberties.

Clearly, terrorism is a complex, multifaceted, and often baffling subject to define. The players involved have a way of rising to prominence, splintering, disappearing for years, and then suddenly reappearing. Counterterrorisms bureaucracies are formed and then reformed, names are changed, and leaders are shuffled around as they are promoted, demoted, killed, or forced to resign. Incidents proliferate across the world, some of which can trigger off a chain of events that will destabilize a whole region and bring nations to the edge of ruin. At the same time, major terrorist actions can shock for a short while and then be eventually forgotten by all except those seriously impacted by the tragedy. Treatises are written, theories propounded, grievances aired, and tactics discussed, occasionally, to some effect, but more often, not. Causes are picked up by the world media, examined, probed, and then all too often overlooked in the rush to cover some new breaking story—until the next bomb explodes, or the next airliner is hijacked or downed, like those in Russia in 2004; or another cataclysmic event, like the attacks on 9-11, happens in some major city, as London experienced in July 2005, and the bungled attacks in Glasgow, Scotland, in July 2007.

With the various definitions of terrorism and their application to specific events, you should have a good foundation for the study of terrorism and terrorist acts. Terrorism drastically shocks the senses and promotes fear and concern around the world. In the next chapter, we shall review state-sponsored and religious terrorism from several viewpoints. Terrorist causes are often looked upon as bizarre or weird in the context of the present. But most issues (political, religious, racial, or ethnic) have a long, historic pattern that always needs to be discovered and examined in a particular context. We believe that those who understand the historic foundations of these issues that have shaped the free world, since the attacks of 9-11, will never again be able to view the evening news in the same way ever again.

You can now appreciate that there is neither a universally accepted nor a simple definition of terrorism. According to acknowledged terrorism expert Walter Laqueur, "the only characteristic generally agreed upon, is that terrorism involves violence and the threat of violence." This criterion alone does not produce a useful definition as it includes many acts not usually considered terrorism, such as war, organized crime, revolution, or even a simple riot. *Asymmetric warfare* and *low-intensity operations* are military terms for tactics that sometimes include terrorism. At its core, the definition of terrorism is not so much a description of a particular kind of violence, like bombing or assassination, but a way to characterize an act of violence relative to terrorists and their point of view.

Terrorism, then, is a term that attempts to define, as a separate phenomenon, a philosophy of coordinated violence that tends to have a high degree of social impact on a targeted society. Rebels in opposition to an established social order may perpetrate terrorist violence, or a state may inflict it upon its own citizens or those of another state. One study by the U.S. Army discovered over 100 definitions that have been used. A few more of such examples will highlight and emphasize the problem of settling upon any precise definition:

U.S. CODE OF FEDERAL REGULATIONS   "The unlawful use of force and violence against persons or property to intimidate or coerce a government, the civilian population, or any segment thereof, in furtherance of political or social objectives" (28 C.F.R. Section 0.85).

CURRENT U.S. NATIONAL SECURITY STRATEGY   "Premeditated, politically motivated violence against innocents."

U.S. DEPARTMENT OF DEFENSE   The "calculated use of unlawful violence to inculcate fear; intended to coerce or intimidate governments or societies in pursuit of goals that are generally political, religious, or ideological."

A 1984 U.S. ARMY TRAINING MANUAL   "Terrorism is the calculated use of violence, or the threat of violence, to produce goals that are political or ideological in nature."

BRIAN JENKINS   "Terrorism is the use or threatened use of force designed to bring about political change."

VICE PRESIDENT'S TASK FORCE   "Terrorism is the unlawful use or threat of violence against persons or property to further political or social objectives. It is usually intended to intimidate or coerce a government, individuals, or groups, or to modify their behavior or politics."

JAMES M. POLAND   "Terrorism is the premeditated, deliberate, systematic murder, mayhem, and threatening of the innocent to create fear and intimidation in order to gain a political or tactical advantage, usually to influence an audience."

As is so often the case, a planned series of attacks by any disparate group will cause governments to establish emergency and often far-reaching legislation aimed at protecting the nation. After the suicide attack on 9-11, the U.S. government moved quickly to pass the Patriot Act, which addressed and formalized into law a U.S. response to how terrorism would be combated from within.

THE USA PATRIOT ACT 2001

An Act H. R. 3162 In the Senate of the United States

The USA Patriot Act came into law on October 26, 2001, and aimed at expanding police powers to investigate terrorism in the Homeland. The Act is broken into ten titles as listed below.

The short table of contents for this Act is as follows:

Title I—Enhancing Domestic Security Against Terrorism

- Sec. 101. Counterterrorism fund.
- Sec. 102. Sense of Congress condemning discrimination against Arab and Muslim Americans.
- Sec. 103. Increased funding for the technical support center at the Federal Bureau of Investigation.
- Sec. 104. Requests for military assistance to enforce prohibition in certain emergencies.
- Sec. 105. Expansion of National Electronic Crime Task Force Initiative.
- Sec. 106. Presidential authority.

Title II—Enhanced Surveillance Procedures

- Sec. 201. Authority to intercept wire, oral, and electronic communications relating to terrorism.
- Sec. 202. Authority to intercept wire, oral, and electronic communications relating to computer fraud and abuse offenses.
- Sec. 203. Authority to share criminal investigative information.
- Sec. 204. Clarification of intelligence exceptions from limitations on interception and disclosure of wire, oral, and electronic communications.

- Sec. 205. Employment of translators by the Federal Bureau of Investigation.
- Sec. 206. Roving surveillance authority under the Foreign Intelligence Surveillance Act of 1978.
- Sec. 207. Duration of FISA surveillance of non-United States persons who are agents of a foreign power.
- Sec. 208. Designation of judges.
- Sec. 209. Seizure of voice-mail messages pursuant to warrants.
- Sec. 210. Scope of subpoenas for records of electronic communications.
- Sec. 215. Access to records and other items under the Foreign Intelligence Surveillance Act.
- Sec. 216. Modification of authorities relating to use of pen registers, and trap and trace devices.
- Sec. 219. Single-jurisdiction search warrants for terrorism.
- Sec. 220. Nationwide service of search warrants for electronic evidence.

Title III. International Money Laundering Abatement and Antiterrorist Financing Act 2001

- Sec. 314. Cooperative efforts to deter money laundering.
- Sec. 330. International cooperation in investigations of money laundering, financial crimes, and finances of terrorist groups.
- Sec. 351. Amendments relating to reporting of suspicious activities.
- Sec. 352. Anti-money laundering programs.
- Sec. 372. Forfeiture in currency reporting cases.

Title IV. Protecting the Border

- Sec. 401. Ensuring adequate personnel on the northern border.
- Sec. 403. Access by the Department of State and the INS to certain identifying information in the criminal history records of visa applicants and applicants for admission to the United States.
- Sec. 412. Mandatory detention of suspected terrorists; habeas corpus and judicial review.
- Sec. 416. Foreign student monitoring program.
- Sec. 417. Machine readable passports.

Title V. Removing Obstacles to Investigating Terrorism

- Sec. 501. Attorney General's authority to pay rewards to combat terrorism.
- Sec. 502. Secretary of State's authority to pay rewards.
- Sec. 503. DNA identification of terrorists and other violent offenders.

Title VI. Providing for Victims of Terrorism, Public Safety Officers, and Their Families

- Sec. 611. Expedited payment for public safety officers involved in the prevention, investigation, rescue, or recovery efforts related to a terrorist attack.
- Sec. 622. Crime victim compensation.
- Sec. 624. Victims of terrorism.

Title VII. Increased Information Sharing for Critical Infratrsucture Protection

- Sec. 711. Expansion of regional information sharing system to facilitate federal, state, and local law enforcement response to terrorist attack.

Title VIII. Strengthening Criminal Laws Against Terrorism

- Sec. 801. Terrorist attacks and other acts of violence against mass transportation systems.
- Sec. 803. Prohibition against harboring terrorists.

- Sec. 812. Postrelease supervision of terrorists.
- Sec. 813. Inclusion of acts of terrorism as racketeering activity.
- Sec. 814. Deterrence and prevention of cyber terrorism.

Title IX. Improved Intelligence

- Sec. 901. Responsibilities of Director of Central Intelligence regarding foreign intelligence collected under Foreign Intelligence Surveillance Act 1978.
- Sec. 908. Training of government officials regarding identification and use of foreign intelligence.

Title X. Miscellaneous

- Sec. 1001. Review of the Department of Justice.
- Sec. 1005. First responder assistance act.
- Sec. 1006. Inadmissibility of aliens engaged in money laundering.
- Sec. 1014. Grant program for state and local domestic preparedness support.
- Sec. 1016. Critical infrastructure protection.[18]

Civil libertarians were less than happy about the sweeping powers of the Patriot Act, particularly sections that authorized roving wiretaps, which effectively allowed police to obtain a wiretap warrant on *any* phone used by a *suspected* terrorist. Prior to the Patriot Act, police would have to seek judicial approval/authorization for each individual phone. Lawmakers sought to minimize the effect on civil liberties by including a sunset clause, which would cause the act to expire at the end of four years. In even the most primitive societies, certain acts or groups of acts have been universally forbidden or discouraged, or **proscribed**. Such acts include murder, rape, incest, kidnapping, and treason (or some form of rebellion affecting the entire social group's safety and the leadership's authority). In contrast, most societies have encouraged or sponsored, or **prescribed**, behaviors such as marrying, having children, hunting, growing food, and other actions that clearly benefit the group's, or tribe's, common social welfare and survival. Terrorism often falls into the range of behaviors that are not only a violation of laws, but also a violation of the politics and practices (**mores**) of a social group or tribal organization. Often the violation of codified **law** requires that a person must call a public safety officer to make an investigation or an arrest. All of these behaviors are related to the ways that social groups or subcultures choose to respond to transgressions that violate their mutually agreed-to standards of conduct. In 2001, shortly after 9-11, the U.S. Department of Homeland Security was born out of public outrage and the aftereffects of the attacks. Terrorism from abroad had struck at the United States and awakened a "sleeping giant," one that realized that the world had changed. Something had to be done quickly to assure Americans that the government was going to respond strongly and would not allow something terrible like this to happen again at the hands of foreign terrorists. As we approach the end of the first decade of the twenty-first century, and the events of 9-11 recede into time, only the lasting effects of security are clear to us all. The world has not necessarily become a safer place, particularly for U.S. citizens traveling abroad; the United States is engaged in a conventional war against insurgents in both Iraq and Afghanistan, and is still a target for the hatred and ire of Islamist terror cells, be they foreign or home grown. However, since 2001, the U.S. government has:

- Created the Department of Homeland Security (DHS) by merging twenty-two separate agencies into a cohesive department with a primary mission of protecting the U.S. homeland;
- Provided billions of U.S. dollars to DHS to support federal, state, and local preparedness through 2008;
- Leveraged detection technology and deployed additional personnel to enhance border and transportation security, increasing spending by nearly $9 billion;

- Protected the nation's aviation system by deploying a well-trained screener workforce and state-of-the-art screening equipment; and
- Secured $5.6 billion as part of President Bush's Project BioShield to buy cutting-edge drugs, vaccines, and other medical supplies for biodefense.

THE DEPARTMENT OF HOMELAND SECURITY (DHS)

The President proposes to create a new Department of Homeland Security, the most significant transformation of the U.S. government in over half century, by largely transforming and realigning the current confusing patchwork of government activities into a single department, whose primary mission is to protect our homeland. The creation of a Department of Homeland Security is one more key step in the President's national strategy for homeland security.

—From the Department of Homeland Security, June 2002—George W. Bush

Department Subcomponents and Agencies

- Department Components
- Office of the Secretary
- Advisory Panels and Committees

Homeland Security leverages resources within federal, state, and local governments, coordinating the transition of multiple agencies and programs into a single, integrated agency, focused on protecting the American people and their homeland. More than 87,000 different governmental jurisdictions at

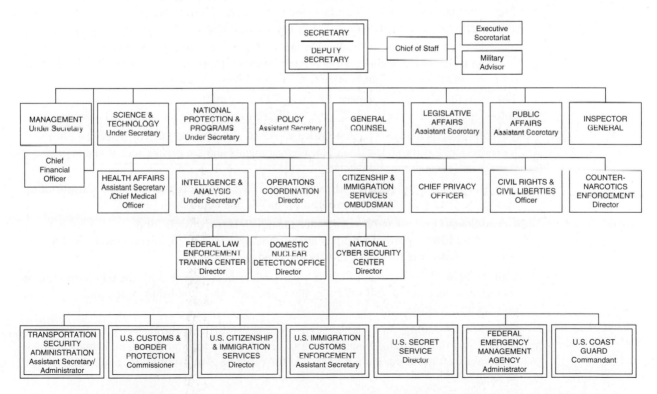

FIGURE 1-4 Structure of The U.S. Department of Homeland Security (U.S. Department of Homeland Security).

the federal, state, and local level have homeland security responsibilities. The comprehensive national strategy seeks to develop a complementary system connecting all levels of government, without duplicating effort. Homeland security is truly a "national mission."

The following list contains the major components that currently make up the Department of Homeland Security.

Department Components

The Directorate for National Protection and Programs works to advance the Department's risk-reduction mission. Reducing risk requires an integrated approach that encompasses both physical and virtual threats, and their associated human elements.

The Directorate for Science and Technology is the primary research and development arm of the Department. It provides federal, state, and local officials with the technology and capabilities to protect the homeland.

The Directorate for Management is responsible for Department budgets and appropriations, expenditure of funds, accounting and finance, procurement; human resources, information technology systems, facilities and equipment, and the identification and tracking of performance measurements.

The Office of Policy is the primary policy formulation and coordination component for the Department of Homeland Security. It provides a centralized, coordinated focus to the development of Department-wide, long-range planning to protect the United States.

The Office of Health Affairs coordinates all medical activities of the Department of Homeland Security to ensure appropriate preparation for and response to incidents having medical significance.

The **Office of Intelligence and Analysis** is responsible for using information and intelligence from multiple sources to identify and assess current and future threats to the United States.

The Office of Operations Coordination is responsible for monitoring the security of the United States on a daily basis and coordinating activities within the Department and with governors, Homeland Security Advisors, law enforcement partners, and critical infrastructure operators in all 50 states and in more than 50 major urban areas nationwide.

The Federal Law Enforcement Training Center provides career-long training to law enforcement professionals to help them fulfill their responsibilities safely and proficiently.

The Domestic Nuclear Detection Office works to enhance the nuclear detection efforts of federal, state, territorial, tribal, and local governments and the private sector, and to ensure a coordinated response to such threats.

The Transportation Security Administration (TSA) protects the nation's transportation systems to ensure freedom of movement for people and commerce.

United States Customs and Border Protection (CBP) is responsible for protecting our nation's borders in order to prevent terrorists and terrorist weapons from entering the United States, while facilitating the flow of legitimate trade and travel.

United States Citizenship and Immigration Services is responsible for the administration of immigration and naturalization adjudication functions, and establishing immigration services policies and priorities.

United States Immigration and Customs Enforcement (ICE), the largest investigative arm of the Department of Homeland Security, is responsible for identifying and shutting down vulnerabilities in the nation's border, and for economic, transportation, and infrastructure security.

The United States Coast Guard protects the public, the environment, and U.S. economic interests in the nation's ports and waterways, along the coast, on international waters, or in any maritime region, as required to support national security.

The Federal Emergency Management (FEMA) prepares the nation for hazards, manages federal response and recovery efforts following any national incident, and administers the National Flood Insurance Program.

The United States Secret Service protects the President and other high-level officials, and investigates counterfeiting and other financial crimes, including financial institution fraud, identity theft, computer fraud, and computer-based attacks on our nation's financial, banking, and telecommunications infrastructure.

Office of the Secretary

The Office of the Secretary oversees activities with other federal, state, local, and private entities as part of a collaborative effort to strengthen borders, provide for intelligence analysis and infrastructure protection, improve the use of science and technology to counter weapons of mass destruction, and to create a comprehensive response and recovery system. The Office of the Secretary includes multiple offices that contribute to the overall Homeland Security mission.

The Privacy Office works to minimize the impact on the individual's privacy, particularly the individual's personal information and dignity, while achieving the mission of the Department of Homeland Security.

The office for Civil Rights and Civil Liberties provides legal and policy advice to Department leadership on civil rights and civil liberties issues, investigates and resolves complaints, and provides leadership to Equal Employment Opportunity programs.

The Office of Inspector General is responsible for conducting and supervising audits, investigations, and inspections relating to the programs and operations of the Department, and recommending ways for the Department to carry out its responsibilities in the most effective, efficient, and economical manner possible.

The Citizenship and Immigration Services Ombudsman provides recommendations for resolving individual and employer problems with the United States Citizenship and Immigration Services in order to ensure national security and the integrity of the legal immigration system, increase efficiencies in administering citizenship and immigration services, and improve customer service.

The Office of Legislative Affairs serves as primary liaison to members of Congress and their staffs, the White House, and Executive Branch, and to other federal agencies and governmental entities that have roles in assuring national security.

The Office of the General Counsel integrates approximately 1700 lawyers from throughout the Department into an effective, client-oriented, full-service legal team, and comprises a headquarters office with subsidiary divisions and the legal programs for eight Department components.

Office of Counternarcotics Enforcement

Office of Public Affairs

Executive Secretariat

Military Advisor's Office

Advisory Panels and Committees

The Homeland Security Advisory Council provides advice and recommendations to the Secretary on matters related to homeland security. The Council is composed of leaders from state and local government, first responder communities, the private sector, and academia.

The National Infrastructure Advisory Council provides advice to the Secretary of Homeland Security and the President on the security of information systems for the public and private institutions that constitute the critical infrastructure of the U.S. economy.

The Homeland Security Science and Technology Advisory Committee serves as a source of independent, scientific, and technical planning advice for the Undersecretary for Science and Technology.

The Critical Infrastructure Partnership Advisory Council was established to facilitate effective coordination of federal infrastructure protection programs with the infrastructure protection activities of the private sector and state, local, territorial, and tribal governments.

The Interagency Coordinating Council on Emergency Preparedness and Individuals with Disabilities was established to ensure that the federal government appropriately supports the safety and security of individuals with disabilities in disaster situations.

The Task Force on New Americans is an interagency effort to help immigrants learn English, embrace the common core of American civic culture, and become fully American.

The necessity to create a government department that would address protection for the homeland came as a direct result of the attacks on the United States on September 11, 2001. DHS established five key components with five Directorates: Border and Transportation Security, Emergency Preparedness and Response, **Information Analysis and Infrastructure Protection**, Science and Technology, and Management. There are also three Mission Agencies: Coast Guard, U.S. Citizenship and Immigration Services, and U.S. Secret Service.[19]

Over the years since those attacks, a warning system has been developed to immediately advise the public of the threat status in the United States. Many observers do not find, given the passage of time and the frequency of output of these "advisories," that they actually have any real effect on the public at large. The details of these advisories are as follows.

HOMELAND SECURITY PRESIDENTIAL DIRECTIVE-3

Purpose

The Nation requires a Homeland Security Advisory System to provide a comprehensive and effective means to disseminate information regarding the risk of terrorist acts to federal, state, and local authorities, and to the American people. Such a system would provide warnings in the form of a set of graduated "Threat Conditions" that would increase as the risk of the threat increases. At each Threat Condition, federal departments and agencies would implement a corresponding set of "protective measures" to further reduce vulnerability or increase response capability during a period of heightened alert.

This system is intended to create a common vocabulary, context, and structure for an ongoing national discussion about the nature of the threats that confront the homeland and the appropriate measures that should be taken in response. It seeks to inform and facilitate decisions appropriate to different levels of government, and to private citizens at home and at work.

Homeland Security Advisory System

The Homeland Security Advisory System shall be binding on the executive branch, and recommendatory, although voluntary, to other levels of government and the private sector. There are five Threat Conditions, each identified by a description and corresponding color. From lowest to highest, the levels and colors are:

Low = Green;

Guarded = Blue;

Elevated = Yellow;

High = Orange;

Severe = Red.

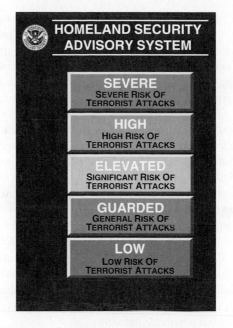

FIGURE 1-5   Homeland Security Advisory System (U.S. Department of Homeland Security).

The higher the Threat Condition, the greater the risk of a terrorist attack. Risk includes both the probability of an attack occurring and its potential gravity. Threat Conditions shall be assigned by the Attorney General in consultation with the Assistant to the President for Homeland Security. Except in exigent circumstances, the Attorney General shall seek the views of the appropriate Homeland Security Principals or their subordinates and other parties, as appropriate, on the Threat Condition to be assigned. Threat Conditions may be assigned for the entire nation, or they may be set for a particular geographic area or industrial sector. The assigned Threat Conditions shall be reviewed at regular intervals to determine whether adjustments are warranted.

For facilities, personnel, and operations inside the territorial United States, all federal departments, agencies, and offices other than military facilities shall conform their existing threat advisory systems to this system and, henceforth, administer their systems consistent with the determination of the Attorney General with regard to the Threat Condition in effect.

The assignment of a Threat Condition shall prompt the implementation of an appropriate set of protective measures. Protective measures are the specific steps an organization shall take to reduce its vulnerability or increase its ability to respond during a period of heightened alert. The authority to craft and implement protective measures rests with the federal departments and agencies. It is recognized that departments and agencies may have several preplanned sets of responses to a particular Threat Condition to facilitate a rapid, appropriate, and tailored response. Department and agency heads are responsible for developing their own protective measures, and other antiterrorism or self-protection and continuity plans, and resourcing, rehearsing, documenting, and maintaining these plans. Likewise, they retain the authority to respond, as necessary, to risks, threats, incidents, or events at facilities within the specific jurisdiction of their department or agency and, as authorized by law, to direct agencies and industries to implement their own protective measures. They shall continue to be responsible for taking all appropriate proactive steps to reduce the vulnerability of their personnel and facilities to terrorist attack. Federal department and agency heads shall submit an annual written report to the President, through the Assistant to the President for Homeland Security, describing the steps they have taken to develop and implement appropriate protective measures for each Threat Condition. Governors, mayors, and the leaders of other organizations are encouraged to conduct a similar review of their organization's protective measures.

The decision whether to publicly announce Threat Conditions shall be made on a case-by-case basis by the Attorney General in consultation with the Assistant to the President for Homeland Security. Every effort shall be made to share as much information regarding the threat as possible, consistent with the safety of the nation. The Attorney General shall ensure, consistent with the safety of the nation, that state and local government officials and law enforcement authorities are provided the most relevant and timely information. The Attorney General shall be responsible for identifying any other information developed in the threat assessment process that would be useful to state and local officials, and others, and conveying it to them as permitted, consistent with the constraints of classification. The Attorney General shall establish a process and a system for conveying relevant information to federal, state, and local government officials, law enforcement authorities, and the private sector expeditiously.

The Director of Central Intelligence and the Attorney General shall ensure that a continuous and timely flow of integrated threat assessments and reports is provided to the President, the Vice President, Assistant to the President and Chief of Staff, the Assistant to the President for Homeland Security, and the Assistant to the President for National Security Affairs. Whenever possible and practicable, these integrated threat assessments and reports shall be reviewed and commented upon by the wider interagency community.

A decision on which Threat Condition to assign shall integrate a variety of considerations. This integration will rely on qualitative assessment, not quantitative calculation. Higher Threat Conditions indicate greater risk of a terrorist act, with risk including both probability and gravity. Despite best efforts, there can be no guarantee that, at any given Threat Condition, a terrorist attack will not occur. An initial and important factor is the quality of the threat information itself. The evaluation of this threat information shall include, but not be limited to, the following factors:

1. To what degree is the threat information credible?
2. To what degree is the threat information corroborated?
3. To what degree is the threat specific and/or imminent?
4. How grave are the potential consequences of the threat?

Threat Conditions and Associated Protective Measures

1. **Low condition (green).** This condition is declared when there is a low risk of terrorist attacks. Federal departments and agencies should consider the following general measures in addition to the agency-specific protective measures they develop and implement:
   1. Refining and exercising, as appropriate, preplanned protective measures;
   2. Ensuring personnel receive proper training on the Homeland Security Advisory System and the specific preplanned department or agency rotective easures; and
   3. Institutionalizing a process to assure that all facilities and regulated sectors are regularly assessed for vulnerabilities to terrorist attacks, and all reasonable measures are taken to mitigate these vulnerabilities.

2. **Guarded condition (blue).** This condition is declared when there is a general risk of terrorist attacks. In addition to the protective measures taken in the previous Threat Condition, federal departments and agencies should consider the following general measures in addition to the agency-specific protective measures that they will develop and implement:
   1. Checking communications with designated emergency response or command locations;
   2. Reviewing and updating emergency response procedures; and
   3. Providing the public with any information that would strengthen its ability to act appropriately.

3. **Elevated condition (yellow).** An elevated condition is declared when there is a significant risk of terrorist attacks. In addition to the protective measures taken in the previous Threat Conditions, federal departments and agencies should consider the following general measures in addition to the protective measures that they will develop and implement:
   1. Increasing surveillance of critical locations;
   2. Coordinating emergency plans as appropriate with nearby jurisdictions;
   3. Assessing whether the precise characteristics of the threat require the further refinement of preplanned protective measures; and
   4. Implementing, as appropriate, contingency and emergency response plans.

4. **High condition (orange).** A high condition is declared when there is a high risk of terrorist attacks. In addition to the protective measures taken in the previous Threat Conditions, federal departments and agencies should consider the following general measures in addition to the agency-specific protective measures that they will develop and implement:
   1. Coordinating necessary security efforts with federal, state, and local law enforcement agencies or any National Guard, or other appropriate armed forces organizations;
   2. Taking additional precautions at public events, and possibly considering alternative venues or even cancellation;
   3. Preparing to execute contingency procedures, such as moving to an alternate site or dispersing their workforce; and
   4. Restricting threatened facility access to essential personnel only.

5. **Severe condition (red).** A severe condition reflects a severe risk of terrorist attacks. Under most circumstances, the protective measures for a severe condition are not intended to be sustained for substantial periods of time. In addition to the protective measures in the previous Threat Conditions, federal departments and agencies also should consider the following general measures in addition to the agency-specific protective measures that they will develop and implement:
   1. Increasing or redirecting personnel to address critical emergency needs;
   2. Assigning emergency response personnel, and prepositioning and mobilizing specially trained teams or resources;
   3. Monitoring, redirecting, or constraining transportation systems; and
   4. Closing public and government facilities.[20]

Summary

Finding a definition for terrorism continues to elude us all; many exist and more will be forthcoming over the years. The word is used daily to describe all manner of atrocities, many related to global events and others totally unconnected to conventional terrorism. This chapter has taken a broad approach to looking at the many and various definitions that are currently favored by government, academia, and the judiciary, and though each of the definitions listed has some descriptive bearing on the word "terror" as we observe it today, it will change with the types of terror events we become exposed to. The world is changing, and the definition for terror will also change. After 9-11, what has taken place in the United States is the stark realization that terrorists have successfully targeted the United States and that they continue to threaten, quite possibly, from within the United States itself. In these intervening years since 9-11, many attempts have been made, which were thwarted by vigilance and intelligence gathering. Homeland Security was developed to protect the homeland; so far it has been successful, whether by luck or not, but as they always say, terrorists have to get lucky only once, but law enforcement has to be lucky all the time. The use of the term "War on Terror" only has context for the United States in general, and the Bush administration in particular. We will see in the next chapter that although the al Qaeda led by Osama bin Laden has designs on a global jihad, global terrorism has been fought by a large number of nations on a global scale for decades, and in this we will consider the European, Middle East, as well as Central American terrorist organizations. Although this chapter will give the student pause for thought on how best to create a definition for terrorism, it will, we believe, continue to be elusive as the nature of terrorism constantly changes.

Web Sites

1. **Perspectives on Terrorism**—*http://www.csmonitor.com/specials/terrorism/start.htm*
2. **Constitutional Rights Foundation**—*http://www.crf-usa.org/terror/What_Is_Terrorism_rev.htm*
3. **George Mason University' History News Network**—*http://hnn.us/articles/299.html*
4. **The Peace Encyclopedia**—*http://www.yahoodi.com/peace/terrorism.html*
5. **International Assessment and Strategy Center**—*http://www.strategycenter.net*

Endnotes

1. David Tucker. *Skirmishes at the Edge of Empire* (Praeger, Westport, 1997, p. 51).
2. Cindy C. Combs. *Terrorism in the Twenty-First Century* (Upper Saddle River, NJ: Prentice Hall, 1997).
3. George Rosie. *International Terrorism: A New Mode of Conflict* (Los Angeles: Crescent, 1975, p. 4).
4. The Hague Regulation of 1907 and the Geneva Conventions of 1949.
5. George Rosie. *The Directory of International Terrorism* (New York: Paragon House, 1987).
6. *U.S. Army Field Manual 100–20*, "Combating Terrorism." Stability and Support Operations (Washington, DC: Department of Defense, U.S. Government Printing Office, 1993), Chapter 8.
7. Editors: "FBI Counterterrorism Responsibilities." FBI Web site, see Internet index (Washington, DC: Department U.S. Government Printing Office, Department of Justice, 1996.)
8. *U.S. Army Field Manual*, "Combating Terrorism."
9. Ibid.
10. Jonathan R. White. *Terrorism: An Introduction* (Pacific Grove: Brooks/Cole Publishing, 1991, p. 13).
11. Alex P. Schmidt. *Political Terrorism* (Cincinnati, OH: Transaction Books, Anderson Press, 1983, p. 107).
12. UN General Assembly Adopts Global Counterterrorism Strategy—www.UN.org.
13. Bruce Hoffman. "Defining Terrorism," *Inside Terrorism* (New York: Columbia University Press, 1998, p. 19).
14. New York Times on line. www.nytimes.com/2007/08/31/world/asia/31afghan.html.
15. Bruce Hoffman. *RAND Newsletter* (Winter 1994).
16. http://www.religioustolerance.org/abo_viol.htm.
17. http://prochoice.org/about_abortion/violence/army_god.html.
18. An Act: H. R. 3162 in the Senate of the United States of America.
19. Department of Homeland Security. http://www.dhs.gov/index.shtm.
20. Homeland Security Presidential Directive #3. http://www.whitehouse.gov/news/releases/2002/03/20020312–5.html.

A Brief History of Terrorism

*Fight in the cause of Allah those who fight you, but do not
transgress limits; for Allah loves not transgressors.*

QUR'AN, CHAPTER 2, VERSE 190

Learning Objective

The study and review of this chapter will enable you to

1. Discuss how the use of terrorism has evolved;
2. Discuss multiple view points on the topic of historical terrorism;
3. Understand how rogue states play a key role in global terrorism;
4. Discuss jihad and why this term is so important in the fight against terrorism;
5. Discuss how suicide terror is not a new phenomenon but one that has been used by terrorists through the centuries.

Terms to Remember

Air-India flight 182	Improvised Explosive	Muslim Council of Britain
Ayatollah Khomeini	Device (IED)	Rogue states
Ethnic cleansing	Islamism	State-sponsored terrorism
Formation of intent	Jamaat al-Fuqra	Union of Russian Men
Hashish-eater	Jihad	

OVERVIEW

When did terrorism begin? As noted in Chapter 1, the word "terrorism" was coined during the French Revolution and the Jacobean reign of terror. However, that does not mean that individual and group acts—what we might classify as today's terrorism—cannot be traced back to the earliest activities of humankind. This chapter will briefly examine human violence and how it evolved into the label of "terrorism," as used to describe today's world events. We shall examine the evolution of human behavior into what we have attempted to define (with considerable difficulty) in Chapter 1. This viewpoint will provide the reader with a different perspective on the behavioral aspects of violence as just another point on the "Continuum of Behavior" discussed in Chapter 1.

VIOLENCE AND TERRORISM

What are the conditions that can generate violence? What are the possible justifications for using violence as a stepping-stone to terrorism? What is it that allows a person or a group to apply violence to a specific situation, complaint, or event and believe it to be a logical, or natural, response? Violence is the application of destructive and harmful power that results in measurable damage caused by a conscious decision by an individual, or individuals, to apply it. Violence in this sense has had broad usage throughout the history of the world, demonstrated by the application of great force to achieve specific short-term goals by persons acting alone, or in mobs, or even as part of an organized group of like-minded individuals.

If we think about the paradigm of violence as seen in the fury of a wounded or humiliated animal, we can readily see that violence, or something very much like it, is not even a uniquely *human* behavior. Animals also release their energies in violent and destructive ways. In fact, it is the very similarity of such behavior by brutes that makes violence so distasteful to a rational human mind.[1]

In the earliest social groups, or tribes, violence could be identified, controlled, or quickly dealt with by either individual or group retaliation. Violent people were considered to be behaving like animals and were banished to the wilds, forced to live as "outlaws," those who chose to operate outside the rules/laws of the group. Probably the earliest examples of what might be called terrorist behaviors were those actions intended to frighten another group into running away, or surrendering by the threat of violence. Individuals took actions such as painting themselves in bright patterns and colors, brandishing weapons and shouting threats, killing enemies and placing their heads on poles, or perhaps wearing the skins, teeth, and claws of violent animals, and so on. The goal was to shock or frighten the "enemy" so badly that it would either run away in fear or finally submit and surrender to the will of its adversaries.

Modern societies are composed of diverse religious, ethnic, and racial groupings that often seem out of context or not in sync with the ruling structures. Use of one-on-one violence as a way to draw attention to an individual (or group) and grievance becomes more difficult. When public officials seem to be inaccessible, a natural temptation for a frustrated constituent is to burst into their office, pound on the desk, or perhaps even wave a weapon; or stalk the officials and then attack them verbally or physically at an open-air market or other public place. At the extreme, some may even attempt to seriously injure or even kill. When an unwilling or uncaring bureaucracy refuses to respond to a perceived grievance, it can result in some spectacular and destructive behavior. Shooting a politician or destroying public property is not always a rational choice for the aggrieved person's situation. However, the motivation is often to not just stand there, but "do something" out of anger, frustration, and a deep sense of hopelessness. The self-perceived hapless "victim(s)" begins to see all of society as a monstrous machine, out to get him or them! It is against this background that the distraught and frustrated person begins to believe that some kind of a serious "payback" blow must be struck. In today's global societies, there is a definite tendency to consider violence as an attractive, attention-getting solution, as most actions are social in nature. There are very few constructive, autonomous, and well-thought-out actions open to those who are not writers, doctors, or self-employed professionals. The doing of virtually anything worthwhile usually requires cooperation with, and actions of, others. Violence and destruction, however, are among a small number of things that are easily available to a single individual. The aggrieved needs no assistance or permission to shoot at drivers from a freeway overpass or to drive a car into a group of pedestrians. But this "natural" desire to "do something" can often easily be channeled into a "violent" something. The fast-moving pace of modern society may make one feel that it is critical to do something—anything—whether it is bad or good! The catchy phrase is relevant here: "Don't just stand there . . . do something!" Violence, precisely because it is usually structured as an individual decision, leaves an individual with a feeling of actually having active involvement.

An act of violence can be described as a logical three-step progression:

1. **Formation of intent**
2. Execution
3. Immediate consequences.

All can take place in microseconds. The feeling that whatever we do is not caused by something of our own design has been verified and replaced by thoughts that are all unique and individually formed in regard to one's own action(s).

Violence perpetrated for ideological reasons, and for a systematically promoted cause or complaint, is significantly different. Organizations in the business of doing such things frequently suffer from too much thinking and discussion, and very little action. In the mind of an individual person, being told to do something does not nearly match the satisfaction of an act both conceived and performed by that specific person. Individuals who take violent action on their own, on the other hand, can take satisfaction in the self-empowered nature of their individually conceived act. They then can both claim and accept responsibility for their acts: "I did that, and I'm proud of it." Acts of violence planned and executed by a group, on the other hand, always have to share diluted credit. As a result, the blame or credit is spread so broadly it fails to satisfy anyone.

For example, Lachs presents a thoughtfully surprising positive side of the horrors of war: "Many people report that great danger leads to an exhilaration that renders an experience vibrant. Some say they can never recapture the keen sense of being totally alive that they felt in battle, or even when they merely supported the war effort."[2] The often dull and predictable regularity of most individuals' daily lives seems to validate such claims as just believable and natural. Living in a boring routine, in a cocoon-like, safe society, eventually makes life dull. War makes one begin to contemplate one's death, and life—up close and personal—feeling and living the moment with crystal clarity. Something akin to this effect happens in connection with violence. In these outbursts, the adrenaline flows in great quantities, the eyes focus tightly into "tunnel vision," and blood rushes to the brain and other vital organs. Any soldier in combat, or police officer who has been involved in a street shootout, can describe that effect absolutely clearly. This is a drug that is not available on the street or in a pharmacy, but, once experienced, can be just as addictive.

WHEN DID VIOLENCE BECOME TERRORISM?

By definition, the assassination of Julius Caesar, in 44 B.C., was an act of terrorism. This holds true as well when a modern political assassination is defined as terrorism.[3] Most modern political scientists generally treat assassination as a terrorist act, whether by an individual acting alone (as John Hinckley did when he shot President Ronald Reagan) or in concert with a group (as with Charles Manson's "groupies," in the attempted shooting of President Ford).

Group terrorism became common as early as the Middle Ages. In fact, the word "assassin" comes from the Arabic term hashashin, which literally means **hashish-eater**. It was used to describe a sectarian group of Muslims who were employed by their spiritual and political leader (the local Caliph) to spread terror in the form of murder and destruction among their religious enemies, with the promise of instant acceptance, of being directly transported to paradise, if they were killed, themselves.[4] This promise is similar to the incentives claimed for suicide bombers in the Israel-Palestinian ongoing "cycle of violence," and the highjackers of the four civilian aircraft used in the attacks of 9-11, or the current crop of radical suicide bombers in Iraq and Afghanistan. Marco Polo's travel journals included lurid tales of murder committed by these assassins. These early terrorists were motivated not only by promises of eternal reward in the "afterlife," but also by unlimited access to sex, hashish, and other drugs. Even the Crusaders made mention of this group of fanatics and the terror they inspired.[5]

The region from which the original assassins emerged was then known as Persia (the present-day Iran). In recent times, the **Ayatollah Khomeini** became the religious leader of the Shi'ites in Iran during its religious revolution in the late 1970s. It is widely believed and accepted that the young men in the Iran-Iraq War had been told that they would go directly to paradise if they fought bravely and died fighting for Allah. Reports from that war claimed that fifteen- and sixteen-year-olds were walked into the guns of their enemies, the Iraqis, in waves, unarmed and unafraid. The potent combination of religious and political fanaticism is the legacy of the Brotherhood of Assassins.

Islam, Christianity, Judaism, and Hinduism are not, by doctrine, violent religions. Generally speaking, neither are most of the other major religions. However, the mixture of religion and politics has quite often resulted in violence, frequently against innocent victims, which makes it, according to the definition we suggested in Chapter 1, clearly "terrorism." The Middle East, as the home of three major world religions, has been plagued by a variety of violent sects and religions. The creation of violent sects, however, and the blending of religion and politics, are similar to the Brotherhood of Assassins, and continue to fan the flames of violence. Religion is a special kind of "narcotic" that can both motivate terrorist actions in its name and deaden consciences to the slaughter inflicted on innocent people.

If terrorist acts were perceived as the proper way to "right the wrongs" committed by government, then the use of political assassins would not always be looked upon with disfavor. Vidal, a leading French legal scholar, has noted that, whereas formerly the political offender was treated as a public enemy, he or she is today considered a friend of the public good—a person of progress, desirous of bettering the political institutions of his country, having laudable intentions, hastening the onward march of humanity. His only fault is that he wishes to go much too fast, and then he employs, attempting to realize the progress that he desires, using means irregular, illegal, and violent.[6]

Not until the middle of the twentieth century was the murder of a head of state, or any member of his family, formally designated as terrorism. Even today, those who commit the "political" crime of murdering a head of state can often enjoy a type of special protection in the form of political asylum.[7]

More than 2,000 years ago, the first known acts of what we now call terrorism were perpetrated by a radical offshoot of the Zealots, a Jewish sect active in Judea during the first century A.D. The Zealots resisted the Roman Empire's rule of what is today Israel through a determined campaign primarily involving assassinations. Most of the violence perpetrated occurred in broad daylight with the intent to inculcate fear into the local as well as the wider community. They acted like our twentieth and twenty-first century terrorists, sending their open message to the Romans and any of the local population that may have considered siding with the Roman occupation.

We have seen many instances of suicide attacks used by Islamic extremists in the twenty-first century, and this was also evident in early history when an Islamic movement called the Assassins used the same type of tactic. Between the tenth and twelfth centuries, the Assassins waged numerous suicide attacks against the Christian Crusaders who had invaded parts of the area we now refer to as the Middle East. The Assassins embraced the same notions of self-sacrifice and suicidal martyrdom evident in Islamic extremist ideology today. The Assassins, 800 years ago, believed that violence was a divine act that assured their ascendancy to heaven, should they perish during the task.

STATE-SPONSORED AND RELIGIOUS TERRORISM

State terrorism, whether it is internal (against its own people or dissenters) or external (using or funding outside terrorist groups or individuals), offers a real threat to international stability and security. Internal terrorism can often inspire the formation of resistance movements, which then may resort to revolutionary or terror tactics. This cycle of terror and violence can result in a whirlwind that can suck in all sanity within its reach—innocent or guilty. Exportation of the support for external terror, sponsored by rogue states, has resulted in a proliferation of terrorist attacks worldwide. Even nations whose official policy specifically rejects the use of terror have been guilty of providing financial and operational aid, often clandestinely, to those who would promote and perform their terrorism. Early attacks on Jews in what is now Israel were sponsored and supported by religious leaders such as Haj Muhammed Amin Al-Husseini (1893–1974), the Grand Mufti of Jerusalem who dedicated his entire life to forcibly removing Jews from Arab land. After his death in 1974, his dedication to the Arab cause was carried on by his nephew Yasser Arafat.

State-Sponsored Terrorism as Warfare in the Twenty-First Century

There is no global consensus as to a definition of **state sponsored terrorism**. During the second half of the twentieth century, various countries began to use terrorist organizations to promote state interests in the international domain. In some cases, states have established "puppet" terrorist organizations, whose purpose is to act on behalf of the sponsoring state, to further the interests of the state, and to represent its positions in domestic or regional fronts. The patron state provides its beneficiary terrorist organization with political support, financial assistance, and the sponsorship necessary to maintain and expand its struggle. The patron uses the beneficiary to perpetrate acts of terrorism as a means of spreading its ideology throughout the world or, in some cases, the patron ultimately expects the beneficiary to gain control of a state or impart its ideology to the general public. The following list details countries designated by the United States as sponsors of terrorism. (See Figure 2-1.) Iran, besides sponsoring insurgent acts in Iraq, has ongoing association with and provides support to Hezbollah, Hamas, Palestinian Islamic Jihad, and al Qaeda. Hezbollah is a Lebanese-based terrorist organization formed in 1982 by Iranian Revolutionary Guards Corps and is closely allied to the Syrian Ba'ath Party regime. With Iran and Syrian support, this organization is accountable for the 1983 bombing of the U.S. Marine Corps barracks in Beirut, the 1982 Israeli embassy bombing in Argentina, the bombing of the Jewish Cultural Center in Buenos Aires, and the 1996 Khober Towers bombing in Saudi Arabia. Hamas, based in the Palestinian territories, is also sponsored by Iran, and its terror wing the Izz al Din al Qassam Brigades are involved in suicide attacks against Israeli targets. Hamas was formed in 1987 and since 2000 has conducted over 425 attacks, with 377 killed and 2,070 injured. Hamas is also responsible for the 2002 suicide bomb attack at Natanya, which killed 23 people. PIJ is a fanatical terrorist organization, hard core and committed to the destruction of Israel, and is controlled and funded by Iran.

Countries determined by the Secretary of State to have repeatedly provided support for acts of international terrorism are designated pursuant to three laws: section 6(j) of the Export Administration Act, section 40 of the Arms Export Control Act, and section 620A of the Foreign Assistance Act. Taken together, the four main categories of sanctions resulting from designation under these authorities include restrictions on U.S. foreign assistance; a ban on defense exports and sales; certain controls over exports of dual use items; and miscellaneous financial and other restrictions.

Designation under the above-referenced authorities also implicates other sanctions laws that penalize persons and countries engaging in certain trade with state sponsors. Currently there are five countries designated under these authorities: Cuba, Iran, North Korea, Sudan, and Syria.

Country	Designation Date
Cuba	March 1, 1982
Iran	January 19, 1984
North Korea	January 20, 1988
Sudan	August 12, 1993
Syria	December 29, 1979

FIGURE 2-1   List of State Sponsors of Terrorism (U.S. Department of State).
Source: U.S. Department of State.

State Sponsor: Implications

Designating countries that repeatedly provide support for acts of international terrorism (i.e., placing a country on the terrorism list) imposes four main sets of U.S. Government sanctions:

1. A ban on arms-related exports and sales.
2. Controls over exports of dual-use items, requiring a thirty-day Congressional notification for goods or services that could significantly enhance the terrorist-list country's military capability or ability to support terrorism.
3. Prohibitions on economic assistance.
4. Imposition of miscellaneous financial and other restrictions, including
   • Requiring the United States to oppose loans by the World Bank and other international financial institutions;
   • Lifting diplomatic immunity to allow families of terrorist victims to file civil lawsuits in U.S. courts;
   • Denying companies and individuals tax credits for income earned in terrorist-listed countries;
   • Denial of duty-free treatment for goods exported to the United States;
   • Authority to prohibit any U.S. citizen from engaging in a financial transaction with a terrorist-list government without a Treasury Department license; and
   • Prohibition of Defense Department contracts above $100,000 with companies controlled by terrorist-list states.[8]

State-sponsored terrorism can achieve strategic ends where the use of conventional armed forces is neither practical nor effective. The high costs of modern warfare and concern about nonconventional escalation have turned terrorism into an efficient, convenient, and generally discrete weapon for attaining sponsor-state interests in the international realm. Some specific advantages are

• **Low cost—financially:** Terrorism offers a relatively inexpensive method of making a point for insurgent groups who lack the finances, personnel, or armaments to win against a nation's army on a conventional battlefield. Terrorist tactics also can provide small non-"superpower" nations a low-cost way to wage war, whether overtly or clandestinely, on a hostile state whose resources provide a serious obstacle to waging a full-scale war.

• **Low cost—politically:** For states, particularly those that can successfully provide and hide clandestine support for terrorist groups, the political cost can be quite low as long as such support remains secret. On the other hand, profit in arms sales might become temptingly high. When such support is not too obvious, as with Libya, other nations have often tended to look the other way.

• **High yields—financially:** States that are arms dealers to terrorists can usually profit quite handsomely, with little or no political, military, or economic impact. Sometimes being caught results in the recall of a couple of ambassadors, but seldom is there any impact on diplomatic or trade relations.

• **High yields—politically:** For dissenters who decide to use terrorism as a political weapon, the political currency can be very large in value. This is especially true when the targeted government's reactions are not supported by citizens in the middle and could lead to a regime being ousted from power. Major concessions can then be "bought" when a successful terrorist incident shocks the populace too much.

• **Low risk—politically and financially:** The costs of financing terrorist operations can be much less than those of maintaining a fully equipped and trained army. And the individuals carrying out these operations are not subjected to as much risk as there would be in conventional warfare. In a successful terrorist operation, the rewards are often very big. For a failed operation, the losses are generally small, unless the failure can be traced back to a state sponsor. The finding of these linkages has become very costly in financial and, more importantly, political terms.[9]

Such state sponsors, as Iran led by President Mahmoud Ahmadinejad since 2005, show us all types of megalomanics in charge of a country that has designs on nuclear weapons. Ahmadinejad joined the Revolutionary Guards in 1986, and there have been reports, denied by Iran, that he was one of the student leaders that held Americans hostage in the U.S. Embassy in Tehran. He is virulently anti-Semitic, denies that the Holocaust took place, and wants to see Isreal wiped off the face of the earth. His involvement in supporting the insurgency in Iraq is well documented, and much of the weaponry being used and the fighters involved have been both trained and funded by his regime.

In May 2002, Colin Powell, former U.S. Secretary of State, clearly designated the governments that are supporting terrorism. Those named were Cuba, Iran, Iraq, Libya, North Korea, Sudan, and Syria. Since the U.S. led invasion, Iraq is no longer on the list, and Libya is making moves to be fully accepted back into the "international community." By and large these governments have continued to provide support to international terrorism, either by engaging in terrorist activity themselves, or by providing arms, training, safe havens, diplomatic facilities, financial backing, logistics, and/or other support to terrorists. The U.S. policy of bringing maximum pressure to bear on state sponsors of terrorism and encouraging other countries to do likewise has paid significant dividends. There has been a clear decline in state-sponsored terrorism in recent years. A broad range of bilateral and multilateral sanctions serves to discourage state sponsors of terrorism from continuing their support for international acts of terrorism, but continued pressure is essential. In January 1991, President George Herbert Bush informed the U.S. Congress that he was continuing sanctions against Libya as the "Libyan government continues to employ international terrorism and to support it, in violation of international law and international rules of conduct." Currently Libya has become cooperative with both the United Kingdom and United States in extraditing terrorist suspects, and in 2006 signed a treaty to that effect with the UK government. The United States continues to designate Cuba, Iran, Syria, Sudan, and North Korea as states sponsoring terrorism.

THE TURKS AND THE FIRST CRUSADE

The Turks were not originally from Turkey as most people think—they were a nomadic people from Central Asia, known today as Turkmenistan ("Land of the Turks"). One Turkish tribe, the Seljuks, began moving into the Anatolian peninsula, or the area we now call Turkey. These Turks were Muslims, but a Christian Emperor, Michael VIII, controlled the peninsula. The Emperor appealed to Pope Urban II to help him rid Anatolia of "unbelievers." The Pope received Michael's call for assistance, but decided to use the situation to advance a more ambitious plan. Jerusalem was considered Holy Land to Christians, Jews, and Muslims, but in 1095, Muslims controlled the city. The message from Emperor Michael VIII presented Pope Urban II with an opportunity to justify and wage a "War of the Cross," or Crusade, retake the Holy Lands, and eradicate the unbelievers.

Pope Urban II persuaded the Knights of Europe to join in the Crusade, by appealing to their religious convictions. They were told that Muslim Turks were robbing, raping, and killing Christian pilgrims journeying to Jerusalem. The Pope suggested that the knights fight Muslims instead of continuing to fight one another. Crusaders left their homes and families for a long journey into the unknown. While they did not succeed in ridding the Holy Lands of nonbelievers, the Crusaders found other, more worldly benefits:

- An increase in trade with Europe;
- Travels to new lands and learning about new and interesting cultures;
- Spices that allowed food to last longer and taste better;
- The fine cloths manufactured in the Middle East.

The Christians had recaptured the Holy Lands by the end of the Second Crusade, but a Muslim general named Saladin launched a **jihad** (an Islamic holy war) and recaptured Jerusalem. Saladin was neither an Arab nor a Turk—he was Kurdish. The Kurds lived between the Turks and

Arabs in the mountainous lands of northern Iraq and eastern Turkey, even as they do to this day. When Saladin recaptured Jerusalem in 1187, the Christians launched a Third Crusade, perhaps the most famous, led by "King Richard the Lion-Hearted" of England. The Christians fought hard in the Third Crusade, but Saladin was able to hold Jerusalem for the Muslims. The two warriors agreed to a truce that left the Muslims controlling the Holy Lands, but with Christians free to visit their shrines. Although many other so-called Holy Wars have taken place over countless centuries, the Crusades are considered to be the eight campaigns into the Holy Lands that occurred from 1095 A.D. until 1291 A.D. The following is a listing of those eight major campaigns:

- The First Crusade, 1095–1099
- The Second Crusade, 1147–1149
- The Third Crusade, 1189–1192
- The Fourth Crusade, 1202–1204
- The Fifth Crusade, 1218–1221
- The Sixth Crusade, 1228–1229
- The Seventh Crusade, 1248–1254
- The Last Crusade, 1270–1291

Hundreds of wars and attempts at extermination of certain groups of people have stemmed from religious, ethnic, racial, and tribal differences since the Crusades, and even before— Catholics against Protestants, Jews against Arabs, Sikhs against Hindus, Hindus against Muslims, Tutsis against Hutus, Communists against Democracies, Kosovo against Serbia, Khmer Rouge against Republicans, Shiites against Sunnis. The endless list goes on and on, all with the same religious fervor. The main weapon in these latter-day attempts at **ethnic cleansing** has been terrorism, using the greatest terror of all—genocide. From the inquisition to ethnic cleansing, the resulting terror has created deep splits among religions, tribes, and ideologies throughout the world.

RELIGIOUS TERRORISM   Were the Crusades simply a form of terrorism in the name of religion? One definition of "genocide" is as follows: "A conspiracy aimed at the total destruction of a group and thus requires a concerted plan of action. The instigators and initiators of a genocide are cool-minded theorists first, and barbarians only second. The specificity of genocide does not arise from the extent of the killings, nor their savagery or resulting infamy, but solely from the intention: the destruction of a group."[10]

The founder of Islam, the Prophet Mohammed, died in 632 A.D. Abu Bekr became Caliph, or "the one who comes after." Abu Bekr wanted everyone around the world to follow Islam and, "to submit to Allah." He then set about to organize, convert, and subjugate the entire world to Allah, whom he believed was the one true God. A century after Mohammed's death, the lands of Islam under Arab leadership stretched from Spain in the West across North Africa, and most of the modern Middle East into Central Asia and northern India. The Arabs were great traders whose influence reached as far as Southwest Asia. The Arabs were interested in learning and in other cultures. Western Europe was mired deep in the "Dark Ages," so-called because the great civilizations of Greece and Rome had fallen. The Arabs, however, had made great advances in mathematics, medicine, and physical science. They provided us with Arabic numerals, which made possible great advances in mathematics (algebra, in fact, is an Arabic word).

ISLAM

The modern day terrorism and the events unfolding globally have a considerable amount to do with not just religion but extreme and fanatical elements preaching a firebrand and extreme version of that religion. We are of course referring to Islam and the far-reaching effects of that fanaticism. Islam, considered one of the oldest of religions, refers to the doctrines of the Prophet Mohammed dating back to the sixth century. Mohammed was born in Mecca and is revered as God's representative, and in Islam, God is referred to as Allah. Muslim adherents can be found in vast numbers throughout the globe and number around one-fifth of the global population. At the dawn of the tenth century, Islam and the Caliphs held control over a vast section of the globe, stretching from India in the east to Spain in the west. Jerusalem was considered the Holiest of places not just by Christians but also by Muslims and Jews, and this brings us to the Crusades. During the Middle Ages, religion was at the forefront when it came to territorial conquest, and the Kings of European countries, including France and England, mounted a series of campaigns, in fact, a total of eight between 1096 and 1270—the aim being not only the conquest of rich lands but also to establish their religious claim to Jerusalem. Control of Jerusalem was to change numerous times during the Crusades. Islam itself has been consumed with internal battles over the centuries on the rightful succession of Caliphs (rulers). A split within the religion created two separate groups of adherents within the Muslim faith, Shia and Sunni; the Sunni Muslims have the larger following and dominate the countries of the Middle East. Osama bin Laden's al Qaeda adherents are followers of the Sunni version of Islam who believe in and follow the teachings of the Prophet Mohammed. The Shia sect, on the other hand, believes that the rightful Prophet of Islam is Ali, a cousin of Mohammed. The Middle East conflict is currently drawn along religious lines in Iraq and Iran; both countries have Shia Muslims as the dominant sect within their respective nations. The former President of Iraq, Saddam Hussein, prior to being ousted by U.S. troops, held power with a Sunni minority government and inflicted his awesome power not just against the Kurds but also against any and all Shia opponents of his totalitarian regime for over a quarter of a century. Since the terrible attacks against the United States on 9-11, the Madrid trains bombings in Spain, the London tube train and bus bombings of 2005, and the global wave of Muslim violence some months after a Danish newspaper Jyllands-Posten produced cartoons linking the Prophet Mohammed to violent acts, many in both the media and in general discussion have linked Islam with extreme violence and fanaticism. Politicians have even referred to Islamist fascism as having declared war on the West.

Islamism

Islamism is an ideology that demands man's complete adherence to the sacred law of Islam and rejects as much as possible outside influence. It is imbued with a deep antagonism toward non-Muslims and has a particular hostility toward the West. It amounts to an effort to turn Islam, a religion and civilization, into an ideology.

Islamism is, in other words, yet another twentieth-century radical utopian scheme. Like Marxism-Leninism or fascism, it offers a way to control the state, run society, and remake the human being. It is an Islamic-flavored version of totalitarianism. Islamism is also a total transformation of traditional Islam. Islamism is not a medieval program but one that responds to the stress and strains of the twentieth century.

Islamism is a huge change from traditional Islam. One illustration: Whereas traditional Islam's sacred law is a personal law, a law a Muslim must follow wherever he is, Islamism tries to apply a Western-style geographic law that depends on where one lives. Take the case of Sudan, where traditionally a Christian was perfectly entitled to drink alcohol, for he is a Christian, and Islamic law applies only to Muslims. But the current regime has banned alcohol for every Sudanese. It assumes Islamic law is territorial, because that is the way a Western society is run.

Islamism has few connections to wealth or poverty; it is not a response to deprivation. There is no discernible connection between income and Islamism. The ideology appeals primarily to modern people; I am always fascinated to note how many Islamist leaders (e.g., in Turkey and Jordan) are engineers.

Islamism is a powerful force. It runs governments in Iran, Sudan, and under the Taliban, Afghanistan. It is an important force of opposition in Algeria, Egypt, Turkey, Lebanon, and the Palestinian Authority. Islamists are also present in the United States and, to a stunning extent, dominate the discourse of American Islam.

The Islamists' success in Iran, Sudan, and Afghanistan show that were they to come to power elsewhere, they would create enormous problems for the people they rule, for the neighborhood, and for the United States. Their reaching power would lead to economic contraction, to the oppression of women, to terrible human rights abuses, to the proliferation of arms, to terrorism, and to the spread of a viciously anti-American ideology. These are, in short, rogue states, dangerous first to their own people and then to the outside world.[11]

JIHAD

Jihad is a term that the West has come to know and fear. This term dates back to the Middle Ages. In the linguistic sense, the Arabic word *jihad* means struggling or striving and applies to any effort exerted by anyone. In this sense, a student struggles and strives to get an education and pass course work; an employee strives to fulfill his/her job and maintain good relations with his/her employer; a politician strives to maintain or increase his popularity with his constituents and so on. The terms strive or struggle may be used for/by Muslims as well as non-Muslims; for example, Allah, the One and Only True God says in the Qur'an:

> We have enjoined on people kindness to parents; but if they strive (Jahadaka) to make you ascribe partners with Me that of which you have no knowledge, then obey them not . . .
>
> (The Holy Quran, 29:8; also see 31:15)

In the above verse of the Qur'an, it is non-Muslim parents who strive (*jahadaka*) to convert their Muslim child back to their religion. In the West, *jihad* is generally translated as "holy war," a usage the media has popularized. According to Islamic teachings, it is unholy to instigate or start war; however, some wars are inevitable and justifiable.

If we translate the words "holy war" back into Arabic, we find *harbun muqaddasatu*, or for "the holy war," *al-harbu al-muqaddasatu*. We challenge any researcher or scholar to find the meaning of *jihad* as holy war in the Qur'an or authentic Hadith collections or in early Islamic literature. Unfortunately, some Muslim writers and translators of the Qur'an, the Hadith, and other Islamic literature translate the term *jihad* as "holy war" because of the influence of centuries-old Western propaganda.

This could be a reflection of the Christian use of the term "Holy War" to refer to the Crusades of a thousand years ago. However, the Arabic words for "war" are "harb" or "qital," which are found in the Qur'an and Hadith.

For Muslims, the term *Jihad* is applied to all forms of striving and has developed some special meanings over time. In its defence of Islam, Allah declares in the Qur'an:

> To those against whom war is made, permission is given (to defend themselves), because they are wronged—and verily, Allah is Most Powerful to give them victory—(they are) those who have been expelled from their homes in defiance of right—(for no cause) except that they say, 'Our Lord is Allah'. . .
>
> (The Holy Quran, 22:39–40)

> Fight in the cause of Allah against those who fight against you, but do not transgress limits. Lo! Allah loves not aggressors. . . . And fight them until persecution is no more, and religion is for Allah. But if they desist, then let there be no hostility except against transgressors.
>
> (The Holy Quran, 2:190, 193)[12]

In trying to understand the modern-day applications of jihad, the following from the Ontario Consultants on Religious Tolerance is perhaps easier to comprehend:

A small percentage of Muslims who are from the extreme, radical, and violent wing of Islamic Fundamentalism, and who are . . . *passionate, [deeply] religious, and anti-Western . . .*[13] might dwell on passages or verses dealing with conflict, war, and resistance to oppression. Many conclude that the Qur'an expects them to engage in acts of terrorism, assassinations, suicide bombings, armed aggression against persons of other religions, oppression of women, executing innocent persons, etc.

Those Muslim Fundamentalists who are not extreme, violent, and radical, and those Muslims from mainline or liberal wings of the religion, might concentrate on passages and themes of spirituality, justice, personal struggle, peace, freedom, etc.

They are consulting the same book with a different emphasis and achieve very different results. We see the same split among Christians as they study Islam and the Qur'an.

Some emphasize the earlier passages in the Qur'an, which emphasize cooperation with the Jews and Christians—the *People of the Book*. They tend to interpret *Jihad* in terms of personal struggle toward purity.

Others emphasize later passages of the Qur'an, which were received during a time of conflict. They tend to interpret *Jihad* as holy war.

They come to opposite conclusions about whether Islam is a religion of peace or war.[14]

Since September 11, 2001, the global jihad and, probably in more particular terms, the war against the United States, can be easily witnessed in the hatred we see in the media. The media is a strong communicator, particularly in the Middle East, with a diet of hate being spewed forth by religious leaders calling for death to Americans. Not only is the insidious nature of their broadcasts abhorrent, but they are also educating their children on a diet of jihad to become suicide bombers and murderers.

Following the attacks in London in July 2005, there was considerable revulsion at the fact that young British Muslims were responsible for the attacks. The original thought was that these were marginalized youth who had some axe to grind, but the truth here is that all came from good backgrounds, and were well educated and part of mainstream society. However, the Muslim Councils in Great Britain, far from denouncing the perpetrators, claimed that it was the Muslim community that was under attack and that the young men were not Muslims. This was a claim voiced by Mohammed Naseem, chairman of the Birmingham Center Mosque. Blaming the attacks squarely on Tony Blair (former Labor Party Prime Minster) for his government's support of the U.S. led war in Iraq, Dr. Azzam Tammimmi from the Muslim Association of Britain stated in the London Evening Standard: "and God knows what will happen afterwards, our lives are in real danger and it would seem, so long as we are in Iraq and so long as we are contributing to injustices around the world, we will continue to be in real danger. Tony Blair has to come out of his state of denial and listen to what the experts have been saying, that our involvement in Iraq is stupid." Among those experts would have to be included the leader of the **Muslim Council of Britain**, Sir Iqbal Sacranie, who has labeled Israel a "Nazi state" responsible for the "ethnic cleansing" of Palestine.[15]

The defensive nature of Islam's religious leaders became more evident when Sir Iqbal's comments during a televised BBC Panorama program in August 2005 colorfully compares suicide bombers from Hamas with Mahatma Gandhi and Nelson Mandela. He went on to state that those fighting oppression and occupation were in fact freedom fighters and not terrorists. He referred to Sheikh Yassin, the former leader of Hamas, as a "renowned Islamic scholar."

THE MEDIA AND TERRORISM

Prior to 9-11, the media in North America would not be concentrating that much on terrorism as a daily topic, but since that date, terrorism has become the Number One topic for every news media outlet. Although we could consider the 9-11 attack as a single and one-off event, the speculation about what will come next consumes the media. Although the number of terrorist attacks is at their lowest for twenty years, media reporting on terrorism is at its most sustained. Everything that has the possibility of being terrorist related now gets ample and even excessive media coverage. The media is sometimes at fault for glamorizing a terrorist event, and one such event is the hijacking of an Israeli airliner over Europe in 1970 by a Palestinian group led by a vivaciously portrayed Leila Khaled. The media created an impression the she was an adventurer to be admired, while at the same time ignoring her criminal acts. Scant coverage was provided to the Israeli security officer who shot and killed her colleague. Terrorists need publicity if they are to inspire fear and respect, and secure favorable understanding of their cause, if not their act of itself. The first airliner attack on the World Trade Center was not caught on news media film, but the second airliner hitting the Twin Towers most certainly was—whether the terrorists intended this or not, the coverage they received and the fear, panic, and attention they got has created a frenzy of news coverage ever since. Margaret Thatcher's metaphor that publicity is the oxygen of terrorism underlines the point that public perception is a major terrorist target, and the media are central in shaping and moving it. For terrorism, the role of the media is critical.[16]

Terrorists' Needs and the Media

- Terrorists are not in the market to go out and buy media space; so publicity, free publicity that a group can generate is a definite asset. From the terrorist perspective, an unedited interview with Osama bin Laden as took place in May 1997 by CNN was an enormous coup for al Qaeda. For news networks, access to a terrorist will always be a coup and a hot story, and is treated as such.

- The sympathetic ear of the media and whatever spin they may decide to place on the media report is to the terrorists' advantage. One may not agree with terrorist acts, but this does not preclude being sympathetic to their plight and cause. Terrorists believe that the public needs to be educated and that their cause is a just one, and terrorist violence is the only course of action available to them.

- Terrorist organizations may also seek to court or place sympathetic personnel in press positions—particularly in wire services. The Al-Jazeera news network in the Middle East continues to be a particular favorite news wire service of terrorists as its avenue to disseminate information.

- Legitimacy. Terrorist causes want the press to give legitimacy to what is often portrayed as ideological or personality feuds, or divisions between armed groups and political wings. For the military tactician, war is the continuation of politics by other means; for the sophisticated terrorist, politics is the continuation of terror by other means. IRA and Hamas are examples of groups having "political" and "military" components. Musa Abu Marzuq, for example, who was in charge of the political wing of Hamas, is believed to have approved specific bombings and assassinations.[17] Likewise, the "dual hat" relationship of Gerry Adams of Sinn Féin—the purported political wing of the IRA—to other IRA activities is subject to speculation. Distinctions are often designed to help people join the ranks or financially contribute to the terrorist organization.

They also need the press to provide a level of legitimacy to the findings and viewpoints of specially created nongovernmental organizations (NGOs) and study centers that may serve as covers for terrorist fund raising, recruitment, and travel by terrorists into the target country. The Palestinian Islamic Jihad-funded and controlled World and Islam Studies Enterprise is but one known example.[18] In hostage situations, terrorists need to have details on identity, number, and value of hostages, as well as details about pending rescue attempts and details on the public exposure of their operation. Particularly where state sponsors are involved, they want details about any plans for military retaliation.

- Terrorist organizations seek media coverage that causes damage to their enemy. This is particularly noticeable when the perpetrators of the act and the rationale for their act remain unclear. Terrorists need the media to spread and magnify the panic and fear on their behalf, to facilitate economic loss (like scaring away investment and tourism); one example of this comprised the threats proclaiming that a summer bombing campaign of tourist locations along the Spanish coast by ETA would take place. The local populous and the visiting populations would then loose faith in their governments' ability to protect them, and to trigger government and popular overreaction to specific incidents and the overall threat of terrorism.

What Government Leaders Want from the Media

Governments seek understanding, cooperation, restraint, and loyalty from the media in efforts to limit terrorist harm to society. In the West, where there is freedom of the press to a great extent, governments' need cooperation from the press to push their agenda in efforts to punish or apprehend those responsible for terrorist acts, specifically:[19]

- Both governments and terrorists want to advance their agendas but, of course, from completely different perspectives. From their perspective, the media should support government courses of action when operations are under way and disseminate government-provided information when requested. This includes understanding of policy objectives, or at least a balanced presentation (e.g., why governments may seek to mediate, yet not give in to terrorist demands).
- An important goal is to separate the terrorist from the media to deny the terrorist a platform, unless doing so is likely to contribute to his imminent defeat.[20]
- Another goal is to have the media present terrorists as criminals and avoid glamorizing them; to foster the viewpoint that kidnapping a prominent person, blowing up a building, or hijacking an airplane is a criminal act regardless of the terrorists' cause.
- In hostage situations, governments often prefer to exclude the media and others from the immediate area, but they want the news organizations to provide information to authorities when reporters have access to the hostage site.
- They seek publicity to help diffuse the tension of a situation, not contribute to it. Keeping the public reasonably calm is an important policy objective.
- It is generally advantageous if the media, especially television, avoids "weeping mother" emotional stories on relatives of victims, as such coverage builds public pressure on governments to make concessions.
- During incidents, they wish to control terrorist access to outside data to restrict information on hostages that may result in their selection for harm; government strongly desires the media not to reveal planned or current antiterrorist actions or provide the terrorists with data that helps them.
- After incidents, they want the media not to reveal government secrets or detail techniques on how successful operations were performed, and not to publicize successful or thwarted terrorist technological achievements and operational methods so that copycat terrorists do not emulate or adapt them.[21]
- They want the media to be careful about disinformation from terrorist allies, sympathizers, or others who gain from its broadcast and publication. Many groups have many motives for disseminating inaccurate or false data, including, for example, speculation as to how a plane may have been blown up or who may be responsible.
- They want the media to boost the image of government agencies. Agencies may carefully control leaks to the press, giving scoops to newsmen who depict the agency favorably and avoid criticism of its actions.
- They would like journalists to inform them when presented with well-grounded reasons to believe a terrorist act may be in the making or that particular individuals may be involved in terrorist activity.
- In extreme cases, where circumstances permit, vital national security interests may be at stake, and chances of success high, they may seek cooperation of the media in disseminating a ruse that would contribute to neutralizing the immediate threat posed by terrorists. In common criminal investigations involving heinous crimes, such media cooperation is not uncommon,

when media members may hold back on publication of evidence found at a crime scene, or assist law enforcement officials by publishing misleading information or a non-promising lead to assist authorities in apprehending a suspect by, for example, lulling him or her into a false sense of security.

Evolving technology has played an immense role in allowing terrorists to publicize and expand their reach into any home that has access to the Internet; with programs such as You Tube and live video streaming, terrorists have successfully been able to disseminate whatever acts they want shown. From Iraq we have had examples of beheadings of kidnapped westerners, road side detonations of **Improvised Explosive Devices (IEDs)**, items of news that mainstream media would not normally show in television news reports. This ability on the part of the terrorist groups has allowed media, more particularly in the Middle East, to inspire attacks against the West. Although the media has a duty to report responsibly and track down the next biggest news scoop, the reporters themselves have become targets for terrorists in the modern era; the case of Daniel Pearl from the Wall Street Journal in 2002 is a case in point. Many, if not all, journalists view getting to the story a primary objective over their own personal safety. Pearl, aged 38, the Wall Street Journal's South Asia bureau chief, was taken hostage in Pakistan in January 2002. At the time, he was attempting to track down and interview the leader of **Jamaat al-Fuqra**; after meeting a go-between at a Karachi restaurant, he was taken to a house, where two weeks later his execution was videotaped and broadcast for the world to see. Al Qaeda's #3 man, Khaled Sheikh Mohammed, claims responsibility for Pearl's death. With their ability to manipulate their audience through the medium of the Internet, is there necessity to set any specific code of conduct on mainstream news coverage while attempting to preserve the independence of the media's role? This is a hotly debated topic, and although there may be voluntary guidelines, there are four other policy decisions that may help preserve that independence and overcome some objections to their treatment of terrorism:

1. To consider matters relating to the timing of news. Temporary withholding of news may be legitimate in some instances such as a kidnapping.
2. Making deliberate attempts to balance coverage (an extremely difficult goal to attain) may counteract some of the negative effects of terrorism.
3. To acknowledge that news tailoring is a fact of everyday news production and focus on reporting that might be expected to lessen tensions and aid the negotiating process.
4. To accept that the media have an important role to play in public education and, at times other than during terrorist incidents, to feature items regarding the ethics of using violence for political ends, the legitimate needs of law enforcement in a democratic society, the nonromantic side of terrorism, and the existence of avenues of dissent. Part of this role must also encompass a vigorous determination to investigate and report on the injustices and inequalities in society that, if left to fester, may be the cause of acts of terrorism.[22]

Of course the case of Daniel Pearl, we all hope, is the most extreme of attacks, but journalists have suffered threats and intimidation from groups with links to terrorism. Journalists do not need to travel to Karachi to be threatened, intimidated, kidnapped, or murdered, as it can happen in North America. Canada, a country known for its liberal approach to minority groups and immigration, is a nation that has embraced the political agenda of multi-centralism. Canada has at least forty terrorist groups active within its boundaries as a report from the Canadian Security Intelligence Service informs us. Investigative journalists have long studied and dug deeply into the involvement of Sikh extremists in the Air India bombing in 1985. **Air-India Flight 182** exploded in midair on June 23, 1985, while at an altitude of 31,000 feet above the Atlantic Ocean, not far from the coast of Ireland; all 329 on board were killed, of whom 136 were children and 280 were Canadian citizens. Until September 11, 2001, the Air India bombing was the single deadliest terrorist attack involving aircraft. The downing of Air India is directly linked back to Sikh extremism, which had largely either been ignored or gone unchecked in the early 1980s in western Canada. Protesters on the streets of Vancouver, calling for the death of Indira Ghandi for her involvement in the storming of the Golden Temple in Amritsar, were largely ignored by police. Sikh extremists were therefore emboldened to carry on with their activities. Many moderate Sikhs were fearful of speaking out inside their own communities, let alone talking to the police. In this community of fear, the extreme members of the Sikh Babba Khalsa movement openly plotted revenge, culminating in the Air India bombing. It has taken over twenty years for Canada to even hold a trial of the suspects, and during this time frame, Sikhs were pressured and coerced into silence. As for the media, such local and respected journalists as Kim Bolan, an investigative journalist for the Vancouver Sun newspaper, sought to dig deeper into this movement and suffered numerous death threats. Tara Singh Hayer, a moderate Sikh, and founder of the Indo-Canadian Times newspaper, had been an advocate for a Sikh homeland, Khalistan. His moderate views were very much in contrast with the Sikh extremists of the Babbar Khalsa movement, who focused on violence to gain a Sikh homeland. Tara Hayer was attacked by a youth in his office in 1988 and was paralysed from the waist down. This, however, did not deter him from continuing his moderate campaign. He had also provided a written statement to the Royal Canadian Mounted Police concerning the investigation of the Air India bombing, in which Ajaib Singh Bagri was implicated. Bagri is a staunch Khalsa member. On November 18, 1998, while getting out of his car and into his wheelchair in the garage of his home, Tara Singh Hayer was assassinated by a single gunshot.

Even in such a free and inclusive society as exists in Canada, the threats from terrorists and their organizers has continued against journalist. In the instance related above, the police and security services have done little to curb the activities of Babbar Khalsa and their affiliated organizations. In October 2007, fifteen years after the death of Talwinder Singh Parmar who most investigators believe was the mastermind of the Air India bombing in 1985, Sikhs in western Canada held a three day memorial to honor his life.

STATE TERROR AND GENOCIDE

State-approved use of power and resources to terrorize and attempt to liquidate a specific group of citizens, immigrants, and religious or ethnic groups has created some ambivalence about what to label as a proper designator. Raphael Lemkin, in his 1944 book, *Axis Rule in Occupied Europe*, coined the word "genocide." He constructed this term from the Greek word *genos* (race or tribe) and the Latin suffix *cide* (to kill). At the end of World War II, the War Crimes Tribunal in Nuremberg was at a loss as to what this crime should be called. History was of little use in finding a proper word to fit the nature of the crimes that Nazi Germany had engaged in at its extermination and concentration camps. "Ethnic cleansing" has been used in recent years to soften the term for eradication of specific groups of people. But hard or soft, the word "genocide" better describes "the destruction of a nation or an ethnic group." It implies the existence of a coordinated plan, aimed at total extermination, to be put into effect against individuals selected as victims purely, simply, and exclusively because they are members of some target group.[23]

"Mass murder," the term that was often used at the time, is an inadequate description of the atrocities committed in Nazi-occupied territories. It could not account for the motives, which arose solely from "racial, national, homosexual, gypsy, or religious" considerations, not the conduct of the war. Genocide required a separate definition, as it was clearly not just against the rules of war, but also a crime against humanity. Raphael Lemkin was the first person to put forward the theory that genocide is not a war crime and that the immorality of genocide should not be confused with the amorality of war.[24]

Terrorist acts have too often created a vicious "cycle of violence," with those against whom the terror-violence is first carried out becoming so angered that they themselves resort to terrorism in response. This is clear in the present situation in the Israel/Palestine disputes in the

Middle East and the Northern Ireland "troubles," which have resulted in the deaths of thousands of innocent people by countering "their" violence with "our" violence in an endless cycle of "tit-for-tat." Each violent action calls for an equal or greater violent reaction—ad infinitum. When the violence is nonselective, and innocent people are killed by car bombs and purely random acts of violence, the reaction of the victims is likely to "break all the rules" in their selection of targets and become terrorist violence itself. "Round and round it goes and where it stops nobody knows" becomes the theme song of terrorism. In the same way as in a case of homicide, the natural right of the individual to exist is implied, so in the case of genocide as a crime, the principle that any national, racial, or religious group has an equal right to exist is then clearly evident. Attempts to eliminate such groups violate this right to exist and to develop within the international human community. Lemkin's efforts and his single-minded persever-ance brought about the Convention for the Prevention and the Punishment of the Crime of Genocide, which was voted into existence by the Convention of the General Assembly of the United Nations in 1948. After stating in Article I that genocide is a crime under International Law, the Convention laid down the following definition:

> Any of the following acts committed with intent to destroy, in whole or in part, a national, ethnical, racial, or religious group, as such:

> - Killing members of the group;
> - Causing serious bodily or mental harm to members of the group;
> - Deliberately inflicting on the group conditions of life calculated to bring about its physical destruction in whole or in part;
> - Imposing measures intended to prevent births within the group;
> - Forcibly transferring children of the group to another group;
> - A criminal act . . . with the intention of destroying . . . an ethnic, national, or religious group . . . targeted as such.[25]

The controversial thousand-plane carpet-bombings that took place over Germany; incendiary and nuclear bombs over Japan during World War II; and, in more recent times, Napalm and Agent Orange over Vietnam; the poison gas attacks on the Kurds in Iraq; and the killing of over 500,000 Tutsis by the Hutus in Rwanda, all claimed their victims in a totally haphazard manner. Intrinsic meaning is lost when words like "genocide" or "holocaust" are used loosely to describe any human disaster with a large number of victims, regardless of the cause. It would be hard to deny that some form of evil has always existed in the world. But if such evil is seen in general, impersonal terms such as barbarism, man's inhumanity to man, chance circumstance, or plain hatred, then there are no individual culprits toward whom an accusing finger can be pointed. So-called "collective blame" is just another way of denying the facts.

CYCLICAL NATURE OF TERRORISM

Perhaps the most prominent proponents of individual and collective violence as a means of destroying governments and social institutions were the Russian anarchists. These were revolutionaries within Russia who sought an end to the Czarist state of the late nineteenth century. "Force only yields to force," and terror would provide the mechanism of change, according to the Russian radical theorist Alexander Serno-Solovevich.[26]

In the writings of two of the most prominent spokesmen for revolutionary anarchism, Mikhail Bakunin and Sergei Nechaev, one finds philosophies often echoed by modern terrorists. Bakunin, for example, advocated in his *National Catechism* (1866) the use of "selective, discriminate terror." Nechaev, in his work, Revolutionary Catechism, went further in advocating both the theory and practice of pervasive terror-violence. He asserted of the revolutionary: "Day and night he must have one single thought, one single purpose: merciless destruction. With this aim in view, tirelessly and in cold blood, he must always be prepared to kill with his own hands anyone who stands in the way of achieving his goals."[27]

This is surely a very large step in the evolution of a terrorist from the use of a lone political assassin in earlier centuries. Even the religious fanatics of the Assassins were arguably less willing to kill "anyone" to achieve a political objective. But this difference may well have existed more on paper than it did in practice. In spite of this written willingness to "kill anyone" who stood in the way, even the Socialist Revolutionary Party resorted primarily to selective terror-violence, and took special pains to avoid endangering innocent bystanders. The **Union of Russian Men**, which formed to combat the growing revolutionary movement "by all means," was not only sanctioned by the Tsar, but granted special protection by him. This reactionary group engaged in a variety of terrorist activities, including, but not limited to, political murders, torture, and bombing. The Okrana (the Czarist secret police) also used vicious counterterror against the militant revolutionaries in an unabated attack until World War I began. John Thompson, commenting on the rising tide of "terrorism" in Russia during the last half of the nineteenth century, explained the relationship of state and revolutionary terrorism in this way: "Wrong a man . . . deny him all redress, exile him if he complains, gag him if he cries out, strike him in the face if he struggles, and at the last he will stab and throw bombs."[28]

During the struggle to gain a homeland free of Nazi terror, the Jewish Irgun had also committed terrorist acts against the indigenous population. Israel finally declared itself to be an independent state in 1948. Then, some of the dispossessed people within its borders and those who fled to surrounding states began a terrorism campaign against the new nation of Israel, whose terror/violence against the Palestinian people sparked a conflict, which today continues to rend the fragile fabric of peace in the Middle East. Born in bloodshed, violence, and desperation, Israel continues to struggle against the terrorist violence that its very creation evoked.[29]

CONTEMPORARY EVENTS: HISTORICAL ROOTS

If contemporary terrorism is somehow different from historical terrorism, how is it different? One reason for briefly reviewing the historical pattern and roots of terrorism is to be able to discover whether that pattern still remains accurate in the contemporary world. If terrorism today is just like the terrorism of previous centuries, but with better weapons, then we can use historical patterns to more accurately predict behavior. Then we can construct responses based on successful attempts that were used to combat this phenomenon in the past. If terrorism today is actually different, however, historical patterns are less useful in designing responses, although such patterns may still be of use in understanding the dynamics of such a phenomenon. Terrorism has clearly existed for centuries. What we need to know, as we move ahead in the twenty-first century, is whether these new forms of terrorism are actually that much different from their historical counterparts.

Related to the differences between historical and modern terrorism are important developments in the contemporary world. Modern methods of travel, for example, make it possible to carry out an assassination in the morning in country "X" and be halfway around the world from that nation within a matter of hours. Modern communications, too, have created a "smaller world." Events in places like Nigeria, Cape Town, or Sri Lanka, for instance, are immediately transmitted in a dozen ways to London, New York City, Tokyo, Seattle, and Omaha. Such rapid communications, too, have served to expand the theater and enlarge the audience to which the terrorist plays out the drama of death and violence. To catch the attention of America, the Third World terrorists need not hijack airliners, and fly to New York City and Washington DC, and crash them into the World Trade Center Towers and the Pentagon.

The dramatic increase in the arsenal of weapons available to modern terrorists is also now worth serious consideration. The would-be assassin does not need to rely on a rifle or a handgun to eliminate his victim. A letter bomb, an envelope containing anthrax, or explosives can do the job without endangering the perpetrator, as the Unabomber in the United States has demonstrated. The potential for destruction through chemical and biological weapons has not yet been fully field-tested either, as will be discussed in Chapter 14, although the Sarin toxin attacks in subways in Japan in 1995 gave ample evidence of the potential for such biochemical weapons when used in the vulnerable mass transit system of a modern city. Perhaps, until recently, the consequences of using such weapons were too dramatic for most groups to contemplate. But modern technology has certainly put at the terrorist's disposal a vast array of lethal and largely indiscriminate weapons, of which the Sarin toxin apparently used in Japan represents only a very simple example. With this arsenal, the selection of victims has become devastatingly indiscriminate.

We hope the student can now see that, as historical precedents for terrorism grow, it becomes very hard to distinguish between legitimate and illegitimate violence. As nations born out of a climate of violence, such as Ireland and Israel, become themselves illegitimate, it is increasingly difficult to condemn the terrorist for using such methods, also employed in the struggles for independence and survival. The longer the history of terrorism the harder it is to make the label of "terrorism" stick to the actions of any group or nation.

Summary

If violence begets terrorism, then terrorism must be as old as society, and must have begun with the first peoples of the earth. This chapter was not especially long. It was deliberately written that way to tweak the curiosity of the reader/student and, hopefully, make them want to learn more. Understanding terrorism without learning something about the history of a terrorist group, individual terrorists, and the conditions that spawned them is much like eating soup without salt. It feeds the body but is pretty bland and tasteless. Following chapters will involve places, cultures, and issues that have strange names and exotic locations, as well as many well-known names and places that have been touched by terrorism. Some will be covered in more depth than others. All of them will reveal something about the social, religious, or economic conditions that allowed the cancer of violence to grow into terrorism, whether by the state or by groups of people—those that have gone beyond the pale. Part Two will take the reader on an exciting and interesting trip around the world, examining the most significant terrorist locations, starting with the problems before and after the attacks of 9-11 in North America, and a tour of the major regions of the world. Throughout history, from the time of the ancient Egyptians, who always took time to kill every member of a defeated army, to the "Killing Fields" of Cambodia, Rwanda, and the Sudan, ethnic cleansing and genocide continue as either a state form of terror or conducted by individual terror groups for whatever social, religious or political gain or goal. State-sponsored terrorism in the twentieth century alone resulted in untold millions of deaths. Human rights movements, such as Amnesty International and others, have begun to shine bright light on the depredations committed by nations against their own people. Power and religious fanaticism have driven the kinds of terrorism that resulted in Hitler's Holocaust and the conflicts between the Irish Catholics and Protestants, the Jews and Arabs, Shia and Sunni Muslims, and dozens of other conflicts around the globe. Instantaneous television coverage of these atrocities has finally begun to make the world aware that the most pernicious forms of terrorism are not those used by a single fanatic throwing bombs. In Part Two we will explore in detail the causes of terrorism in many nations and cultures.

Web Sites

1. **Center for the Study of Terrorism and Political Violence**—*www.st-andrews.ac.uk*
2. **Human Rights Watch**—*www.hrw.org*
3. **Center for Defense Information**—*www.cdi.org*
4. **White Aryan Resistance**—*www.resist.com*
5. **The Constitutional Rights Foundation**—*http://www.crf-usa.org/terror/terrorism_links.htm*
6. **Southern Poverty Law Center**—*http://www.splcenter.org*

Endnotes

1. John Lachs. "Violence as Response to Alienation," *Alienation and Violence* (Middlesex, UK: Science Reviews Ltd., 1988, pp. 147–160).
2. Ibid., p. 15.
3. Cindy C. Combs. *Terrorism in the Twenty-First Century* (Upper Saddle River NJ: Prentice Hall, 1997).
4. Ibid., p. 21.
5. See M. Hodgson. *The Order of the Assassins* (London, UK: The Institute of Ismaili Studies, 1960); B. Lewis. *The Assassins: A Radical Sect in Islam* (London, UK: The Institute of Ismaili Studies, 1968).
6. B. Harwood. *Society of the Assassin: A Background Book on Political Murder* (London: International Institute for Strategic Studies, 1996).
7. Carl Sandburg. *Abraham Lincoln: The War Years*. Vol. 4 (Cambridge, MA: MIT Press, 1939, p. 482).
8. Country Reports on Terrorism—Released by the Office of the Coordinator for Counter Terrorism April 28, 2006, http:///wwwstate.gov.
9. Political asylum is sanctuary or refuge for a person who has committed a crime such as assassination of a political figure. It is granted by one government against requests by another government for the extradition of that person to be prosecuted for this "political" crime. *Funk and Wagnall's Standard Dictionary*, Comprehensive International Ed., vol. 1, p. 86, col. 3.
10. U.S. State Department of State. 2002–2003, *Patterns of Global Terror Report.*
11. Distinguishing between Islam and Islamism—Center for Strategic Studies June 30, 1998.
12. Jihad Explained—The Institute of Islamic Information and Education Brochure #18 Chicago.
13. Craig Branch, *Act of War—Jihad*, Apologetics Resource Center, http://www.apologeticsresctr.org/act_of_war.htm.
14. B.A. Robinson, Ontario Consultants on Religious Tolerance Originally written: March 28, 2003, http://www.religioustolerance.org/isl_jihad.htm.
15. Jewish Chronicle May 27, 2005.
16. CRS Issue Brief **Raphael F. Perl**, Specialist in International Affairs Foreign Affairs and National Defense Division, Congressional Research Service October 22, 1997.
17. *Islamic Terrorism from Midwest to Mideast* by Steven Emerson, Christzan Science Monitor, August 28, 1996.
18. *Terrorism and the Middle East Peace Process: The Origins and Activities of Hamas in the United States*, testimony by international terrorism consultant, Steven Emerson, before the Senate Subcommittee on the Near East and South Asia, March 19, 1996, p. 11.
19. *Impact of Television on U.S. Foreign Policy*, April 26, 1994, U.S. Congress, House Committee on Foreign Affairs, 103rd Congress, 2nd Session, GPO, Washington, 1994, p. 53.
20. In the case of the anonymous "Unabomber," it was publication of a manifesto in the New York Times and Washington Post that triggered the leads and actions by the suspect's family, which resulted in an arrest.
21. "Spiriting Off of Fugitive by U.S. Irks Pakistanis" by John F. Burns, *New York Times*, June 23, 1997, p. A9.
22. Grant Wardlaw. *Political Terrorism, Theory, Tactics and Counter Measures* (Melbourne, Australia: Cambridge University Press, 1989, p. 85).
23. The U.S. Central Intelligence Agency, *World Fact Book*.
24. Ibid.
25. Ibid.
26. Ibid.
27. U.S. Department of State, *Country Reports on Human Rights Practices*, 1998.
28. Ralph Lemkin. *Axis Rule in Occupied Europe* (Warsaw, Poland. University of Stockholm, 1944),
29. Convention for the Prevention and Punishment for the Crime of Genocide; General Assembly of the United Nations, 1948.

PART TWO

Terrorism around the World

CHAPTER 3

The United States of America

*We shall continue to target you at home and abroad, just as you
target us at home and abroad . . .*

FROM AN AL QAEDA AUGUST 2007
VIDEO—ADAM GADAHAN, AKA AZZAM, THE AMERICAN

Learning Objectives

The study and review of this chapter will enable you to

1. Examine the threat that exists from Islamic extremism in the United States;
2. Debate the values in a democracy for the need for draconian measures—extraordinary rendition;
3. Explain how right wing and left wing groups have impacted the terror scene in the United States;
4. Explain why the war on terror will likely continue for decades to come.

Terms to Remember

Autonomous jihad	Hamas	New World Order
Domestic terrorist acts	Jamaat al-Fuqra	Patriot
Extraordinary rendition	Jihadi-Salafi	Task Force on Violence
Fatwa	Khalid Sheikh	against Abortion Providers
Freedom of Access to Clinic	Mohammed (KSM)	(TFVAAP)
Entrances (FACE)	Militias	World Trade Center

OVERVIEW

As the events of September 11, 2001, remain indelibly marked on Americans as a whole, the ensuing declaration of a "War on Terror" might best be described as a war against the al Qaeda terrorist organization and its globally inspired movement. This global movement, although unlikely receiving direct orders from Osama bin Laden, has been able to inflict enormous damage on the West. In broader terms, during the last thirty years of the twentieth century, most terror groups and

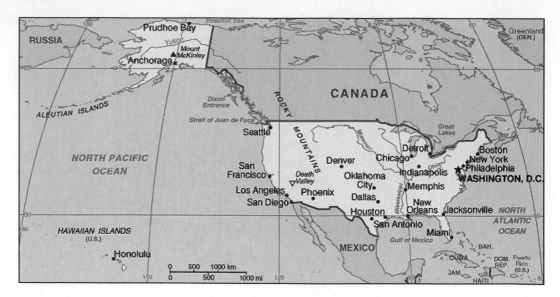

FIGURE 3-1   Map of USA (Central Intelligence Agency, *The World Factbook*, 2008).

subgroups operating throughout the world had their specific stated agenda; al Qaeda and its inspired followers have no political agenda in mind. In attacking the West in particular, their prime agenda is to set up Islamic Caliphates and overthrow Western democracies and secular states. The United States, like Europe, has been attacked, and the challenge now is to determine how to undermine as well as understand what it is that is driving impressionable and somewhat unremarkable young men and women to turn on their adopted homelands? In Britain, the attacks in 2005 were the work of "homegrown terrorists," so make no mistake, the same threat exists in the United States. In this chapter, we will review the events of the last two decades with obvious emphasis on jihad in America. The following "Failure to connect the Dots" indicates that although the indications were all there, connecting the so-called dots was either beyond the intelligence community's ability, or that the unspeakable events coming were too unfathomable to be credible.

FAILURE TO CONNECT THE DOTS

Dot #1—1993: World Trade Center Bombing in New York City

A car bomb exploded underneath the **World Trade Center** in New York, killing six people and injuring more than a thousand others. The bombing shocked the United States, which had not suffered from the terrorist acts that have plagued other parts of the world. Mario Cuomo, then New York State Governor, said: "No foreign people or force has ever done this to us. Until now, we felt invulnerable." At approximately 12:18 P.M. on February 26, 1993, an improvised explosive device in the back of a rental vehicle exploded on the second level of the parking basement. The resulting blast produced a crater approximately 150 feet in diameter and five floors deep in the parking basement. That structure consisted mainly of steel-reinforced concrete, twelve to fourteen inches thick. The epicenter of the blast was approximately eight feet from the south wall of World Trade Center Tower One, near a support column. The device had been placed in the rear-cargo portion of a 1-ton Ford F350 Econoline van, which had been rented from a Ryder Rental agency in Jersey City. Approximately 6,800 tons of concrete and steel were displaced by the massive blast. The main explosive charge consisted primarily of approximately 1,200 to 1,500 pounds of homemade (nitrogen fertilizer-based) explosive and urea nitrate. The fusing system was made from twenty 220-minute lengths of nonelectric, burning-type fuses. The fuse material ended up in lead azide acting as the terminator/initiator. Also incorporated into this thrown-together homemade device, and placed under the main explosive charge, were three large metal cylinders of highly compressed hydrogen gas. The resulting massive explosion killed six people and injured more than a thousand. Over 50,000 people were evacuated from the huge World Trade Center complex during the hours immediately following the blast. The initial inspection, on February 27, was described as a scene of "massive devastation, almost surreal in appearance." There were small pockets of fire, electrical sparks arcing from damaged wiring, and dozens of parked automobile alarms whistling, howling, and honking. The explosion ruptured two of the main sewage-removal lines from both of the World Trade Center towers and the Vista Hotel, plus several water mains from the air-conditioning system. In all, more than 2 million gallons of water and sewage drained into the tower and was then pumped out of the crime scene.

Dot #2—1995: The Oklahoma City Bombing

According to a classified Pentagon study, the Oklahoma City bombing was caused by more than one bomb. Two independent Pentagon experts concluded that five separate bombs caused the destruction of the Oklahoma City Federal Building in April 1995. A huge truck bomb destroyed most of that building, leaving 168 people dead and more than 500 others injured. Preliminary reports indicated that the bomber might have been from the Middle East. After many more unconfirmed rumors, prejudice and public anger rose to a fever pitch. The arrest of Timothy McVeigh and his subsequent trial, conviction, and execution, as well as the arrest and conviction of his friend and accomplice, Terry Nichols, grated on the already raw nerves of an entire nation. When it was revealed that both were members of local right-wing **militias**, it became clear that American, not foreign, domestic terrorists had planned and committed this terrible act. Those two events and many others since have caused officials and security and law enforcement agencies in the United States to rethink and reorganize their perceptions of where serious terrorist threats might really lie. But the dots still had not yet been connected, and the general public soon slipped back into their everyday lives.

Dot #3—1998: U.S. Embassies Targeted in Africa

On August 7, 1998, very powerful, almost simultaneous, explosions rocked two U.S. embassies in East Africa. The blasts took place at almost the exact same time, 10:30 A.M. local time, in Kenya and Tanzania. Embassy officials confirmed that the explosions were the result of car bombs detonated near the two embassies, one in the Kenyan capital of Nairobi, and the other in Dar es Salaam, the capital of Tanzania. In Kenya, the explosion toppled the tall Ufundi Cooperative Bank building over onto the U.S. Embassy. The blast occurred shortly after the U.S. Ambassador, Prudence Bushnell, had met with the Kenyan Trade Minister at the nearby bank. She was taken from the site on a stretcher, feared to be badly injured, but later found to have sustained only minor wounds from flying glass and debris. The bank building, located between the trade center and the embassy, was leveled almost to the ground. Apparently the bomb had been placed there, rather than at the embassy itself, because of the embassy's bombproof construction. In Tanzania, another massive explosion left a large crater outside of the U.S. Embassy. An eyewitness stated: "The people at the front of the building didn't stand a chance." The blast occurred near the spot where a gasoline tanker-truck had been observed parked in the embassy parking lot. More than sixty people were killed in that explosion, with at least another 500 wounded, ranging from serious to moderate injuries. No one claimed immediate responsibility for the attacks, and officials stated that they felt certain that the blasts were unrelated to U.S. relations with either of the countries where the blasts occurred. There was, however, a good deal of suspicion pointing toward Osama bin Laden's work. The Saudi millionaire and terrorist financial-backer had made repeated threats against America. There is no doubt that his extensive terror network could have been capable of carrying out the attacks, but still the dots had not yet been connected; nor was an imminent threat to the mainland of the United States anticipated.

Dot #4—2000: The Suicide Bombing of the U.S.S. *Cole*

A gaping hole in the hull of the U.S.S. *Cole* testified to the force of the suicide terrorist bombing that killed seventeen sailors as the U.S. Navy vessel was docked in Yemen in October 2000. Counterterrorism officials later concluded that the bombing was carried out by al Qaeda.

Americans generally believed that acts of extreme terror and aggression would continue to be perpetrated against not only military, but also civilian targets, in far-off places around the globe. Many still felt that the U.S. mainland was well protected from foreigners attacking them in the safety of the homeland. The results of those actions by foreign terrorists has not made the world a safer place, but did launch three wars—one against the Taliban government in Afghanistan, another against the oppressive regime of Saddam Hussein in Iraq, and the third, the global war on terror.

It was in 1995 that full-blooded terrorism of a homegrown nature surfaced in the United States with Timothy Mcveigh's bombing of the Alfred P Murrah Federal Building in Oklahoma City, which killed 150 people. This was notably the most vicious attack by an American citizen on fellow Americans. McVeigh was a member of the **Patriot** movement that developed in the early 1990s, a group that believed in the true American ideals of individualism, armed citizens, and minimum interference from governments. McVeigh used a rented Ryder truck as his method of bomb delivery and packed it with ammonium nitrate, fuel oil, and Tovex high explosive. Following the attack, most counterterrorism experts were candid in stating that they had not predicted the sort of attack that was carried out in Oklahoma. In 1995, there were a considerable number of right-wing "militia" groups, rabidly antiestablishment and antigovernment, stemming not from social injustices but more likely from proposed gun control legislation. After the ATF raid on the Waco compound of the Branch Davideons, there was notable unrest and disillusionment from "patriot," "militia," and "constitutionalist" groups who believed that the attack at Waco was a massacre by the authorities. The early 1990s were not a time when U.S. terrorism experts were paying much, if any, attention to Islamic extremists in their midst, or believed that any may exist. Any homegrown terrorist would likely fall into the following groups: Skinheads, Ku Klux Klan, Neo Nazi groups, Militias and, of course, single-issue terrorists such as the Unabomber. Islamist issues were not center stage in the United States at the commencement of the 1990s.

In the mid-1990s, international terrorism within the United States was generally not considered to be a major issue or threat—*yet*. Nevertheless, there were indications that if some foreign terrorist group became angry enough at the United States, and was determined enough to act out that anger, it could create major problems to U.S. commerce, infrastructure, and population, given leadership and financing.

The levels of far-away terrorism experienced in places like Beirut, Belfast, Paris, London, Madrid, Kabul, Islamabad, and Palestine did not carry much impact all the way to the American shores; nor did terrorism create major nervousness or any impact on the American lifestyle. Public credibility about threats from foreign terrorism in the United States is not enhanced when a violent act occurs. Even then, media "talking heads" merely issue a brief sound bite and then quickly move on to another story. Later, the media reveal that the act was not foreign terrorism after all! Such reporting creates confusion and mistakes. Three especially relevant examples of this syndrome are

1. The bombing of a van belonging to Naval Captain Will Rogers III, the former Captain of the U.S.S. *Vincennes*;
2. The Aegis missile-equipped U.S. Navy warship that mistakenly shot down an Iranian civilian airliner during the Iran-Iraq War;
3. The mysterious "Middle Eastern man" who was brought back to the United States for questioning in regard to the bombing of Alfred P. Murrah Federal Building in Oklahoma City.

In all three cases, the media jumped the gun and came to the conclusion that these had been foreign terrorist bombings, planned and executed by someone other than U.S. domestic terrorists.

When contrary facts surfaced about these stories, the public reached a different conclusion. The public subsequently put less credence in media reports and ignored any comments presented by the media in regard to reports of terrorism for a long time.

Mainland United States, after all, had never been subjected to as much political violence or international terrorism as other areas like Europe, the Balkans, the Middle East, Northern Ireland, the Persian Gulf, Africa, or South and Southeast Asia. A few exceptions come to mind—the Symbionese Liberation Army (SLA), the Black Panthers, the Weathermen, and the Unabomber— but such **domestic terrorist acts** have been few and far between. On the other hand, the IRA's ongoing slaughter of innocent women and children with car bombs (as the reader will learn about in Chapter 5) continued to be frequent and unremitting. But, after August 7, 1998, the United States was slowly awakening to the fact that it was no longer immune to larger-scale attacks, clearly identifiable as foreign terrorist acts. The first World Trade Center explosion became (perhaps) a significant marker of the first salvo by foreign terrorists using politically motivated actions that attack random victims. The bombing was intended to incite fear as well as add a determined and well-planned external terrorist signature to an act of violence.

But terrorism in the United States was not to be limited to those with external agendas from foreign sources, as demonstrated by the attack on the Federal Building in Oklahoma City, Oklahoma. The terrorists in this case were Americans, members of a paramilitary survivalist militia from Michigan. They had responded to a long-festering anger over the U.S. government's bungling of the **"Waco Massacre"** of the Branch Davideons, a fringe religious group headed by David Koresh.

DOMESTIC TERRORISM

The face of domestic terrorism in the United States continues to change. The FBI has of course defined *domestic terrorism* "as groups of individuals who are based and operate entirely in the United States and Puerto Rico without foreign direction and whose acts are directed at elements of the U.S. government or population". This definition is suitably wide enough to class terror events from both the ideological left and right. If we study traditional attacks in the United States, we can see that domestic issue terror can then be categorized accordingly as

- Revolutionary nationalist groups
- Extreme right-wing ideological groups (Ku Klux Klan)
- Extreme left-wing ideological groups (Weather Underground)
- Foreign groups operating in the United States
- Religious extremist groups.

The FBI identified a further decline in traditional left-wing domestic extremism, and an increase in activities among extremists associated with right-wing groups and special-interest, radical organizations.

Left-Wing Terrorism

Over several decades, left-wing oriented extremist groups posed the predominant domestic terrorist threat in the United States. In the 1980s, however, the FBI neutralized many of these groups by arresting key members who were conducting criminal activity. The failure of Communism and the fall of the former Soviet Union in 1989 deprived many leftist groups of a coherent ideology or tangible support. As a result, membership and belief in the "cause" in these groups have waned.

The United States still faces a threat from some left-wing extremists, including a few Puerto Rican terrorist groups and a Cuban group. Although Puerto Rico voted to remain within the U.S. Commonwealth in 1993, some extremists still plan and conduct minor terrorist acts to draw attention to their support for independence.

Right-Wing Terrorism

Right-wing extremist groups, located at the opposite end of the political spectrum, generally adhere to an antigovernment or racist ideology. These groups still continue to attract some followers. Many of these recruits feel disenfranchised by rapid changes in the U.S. culture and economy, or are seeking some form of personal affirmation. As American social structures continue to change, the potential for escalating hate crimes by extremist right-wing groups is an increasingly valid concern. Of particular note, many state and local law enforcement organizations consider a broader range of activities and acts as terrorist, or potentially terrorist, than does the FBI. The official FBI statistics do not count many threatening acts by organizations such as the skinheads, street gangs, and drug dealers as terrorist acts. States and municipalities are equally adamant in identifying right-wing (neo-Nazi, the Ku Klux Klan, anti-Semitic, anti-federalist, and militias), and issue-specific (antiabortion, animal rights, environmentalist) organizations as major potential sources for supporters of terrorism in the United States.

The burgeoning militia movement in the United States was placed under a blinding spotlight that shined on the admissions by Timothy McVeigh and Terry Nichols. Such paramilitary, rabid, antigovernment groups also continue to attract supporters. Several factors have contributed to the increase of this generally antigovernment mood. In a changing political environment, issues such as gun control legislation, the United Nations' involvement in international affairs, seemingly unsupported U.S. efforts around the world by our former allies, and clashes between dissidents and law enforcement are cornerstones of militia ideology. When you tie in the neo-Nazi zeal and radical philosophies, you have an explosive situation. Some militia members firmly believe that the U.S. government is deeply involved in a conspiracy to create a "**New World Order**." According to their adherents and radical believers, international boundaries will be dissolved and the United Nations will be allowed to become the ruling power in the world. Other militia advocates believe that the federal government has gotten either too powerful or simply illegal and out of control. Many of these militants continue to conduct paramilitary training and stockpile illegal weapons in preparation for an armed Armageddon-type of confrontation with the government. A few of these extreme militia members could pose a serious terrorist threat. Counterterrorism efforts by the United States and others will be covered in depth in Chapter 14.

Special-Interest Extremists

Special-interest extremists continue to conduct acts of politically oriented crime and terrorism. Violent antiabortion advocates are responsible for many of these activities. The Department of Justice's **Task Force on Violence against Abortion Providers (TFVAAP)** decreased the number of abortion-related crimes from the high 1994 levels. Although the number of incidents has declined, the TFVAAP has still investigated more than 100 violations of the **Freedom of Access to Clinic Entrances (FACE)** Act. Two of the most prominent abortion-related events in the 1990s included the following:

- On February 22, 1995, Dr. Elizabeth Karlin, a physician in Madison, Wisconsin, received two letters with death threats. Vincent Whitaker, an inmate at a local county jail, who was serving a sixty-seven-year sentence for reckless injury with a motor vehicle, later admitted writing the letters. On September 12, 1995, Whitaker was tried and convicted of two counts of the FACE Act and sending threats through the U.S. mail. On November 21, 1995, Whitaker was sentenced to an additional sixty-three months of imprisonment.
- In August 1995, John Salvi, the suspected murderer of two receptionists during a December 30, 1994, shooting spree at an abortion clinic in Brookline, Massachusetts, was declared competent to stand trial. Salvi was charged under Massachusetts law with the murders of Shannon Lowney and Lee Ann Nichols, and five other counts of aggravated assault. He received a life sentence in March 1996 and died, of possible suicide, in November the

same year. The Civil Rights Division of the Department of Justice, through the TFVAAP, investigates any instance in which customers or providers of reproductive health services are criminally threatened, obstructed, or injured while seeking or providing services.

Revolutionary Nationalist Groups

The U.S. government's experience with the Puerto Rican nationalist group, Los Macheteros, dates back to an armed robbery on September 12, 1983, at an armoured car depot in West Hartford, Connecticut. After the day's pickups were done, a guard named Victor M. Gerena suddenly turned on his two comrades. He then restrained them at gunpoint, injected both with an unknown substance, and began packing blocks of currency into his rented car.

Authorities eventually determined that Gerena's robbery had been planned by Los Macheteros, a group founded in the 1970s by Ojeda Rios, a musician who had turned communist and Puerto Rican revolutionary. Using bombings and attacks on police officers and U.S. government personnel, the group pushed for an end to U.S. control of the island.

The FBI caught up with the leader of this group in Puerto Rico in September 2005; Filiberto Ojeda Rios was tracked to a farmhouse, where it was surrounded by agents and during the ensuing shootout Rios died of a single gunshot wound.[1]

Left-Wing Aggression

The radical student movements, civil rights marches, and anti-Vietnam war demonstrations of the 1960s galvanized a large number of student organizations to frame their struggles around an antiestablishment theme. As the Vietnam War intensified, so too did the attitudes and activities of the growing student movements. One such group that supported the use of terrorism and violence was the Weather Underground Organization (Weathermen), which had its roots within the Students for Democratic Society, and aimed at a revolutionary overthrow of the United States government. The group engaged mainly in sporadic bomb attacks at police stations and at the Pentagon. However, when the Vietnam War ended in 1973, the Weather Underground began to dissolve.

THE BLACK PANTHERS AND NATION OF ISLAM

The New Black Panther Party for Self-Defense takes its name from the original Black Panther Party, formed by Huey Newton and Bobby Seale in Oakland, California, in 1966. The original Panthers combined militant Black Nationalism with Marxism and advocated black empowerment and self-defence, often through violent confrontation. By 1969, the group had an estimated 5,000 members spread through twenty chapters around the country. In the early 1970s, however, the group lost momentum and most of its support due to internal disputes, violent clashes with police, and infiltration by law enforcement agencies. Despite the collapse, the group's mystique continued to influence radicals, and by the early 1990s a new generation of militant activists began to model themselves after the original Panthers. Essentially a black supremacist movement but with anti-Semitic undertones, the Nation of Islam has been around since the 1930s, and became more prominent with notorious speeches from NOI national spokesman Malcolm X until his assassination in 1965.

THE KU KLUX KLAN

Ku Klux Klan (KKK) has its beginnings in small town America and was essentially born out of boredom and small town life by six Confederate veterans, in December 1885. The Klan began life as a social club in Pulaski, Tennessee, not far from the Alabama border. As a means of distraction, the members began to ride around town at night wearing white sheets, and then extended this to pointed hats; they adopted this bizarre costume as their official regalia. They formed up like a college fraternity and began to hold elaborate initiation ceremonies for new members, with a form of hazing rituals. The KKK would likely have faded away as quietly as they had been formed, but in 1886 the membership expanded to other towns, and activities became more sinister and violent toward the black communities. As the KKK expanded and developed, it engaged in some of the most brutal terror attacks over the early decades of the twentieth century. It was well-known for decades as the major advocate for white supremacy and power, and segregation of the races is foremost among its agenda. KKK members allege there was a conspiracy between Jewish people, white liberals, blacks, and other minorities to take over the United States.

Since 1865, KKK has provided a vehicle for racial hatred in America, and its members have been responsible for atrocities that are difficult for most people to even imagine. Although the membership and actions of the traditional and historical KKK declined in the last half of the twentieth century, there are too many other groups that go by a variety of names and symbols that have been at least as dangerous as the KKK ever was.

Some of these comprise teenagers who shave their heads and wear storm-trooper jackboots, display swastika tattoos, and call themselves "skinheads" or "neo-Nazis." Some of them are young men who wear camouflage fatigues and practice guerrilla-warfare tactics at secret locations for training in weaponry and violence. Some of them are conservatively dressed professionals who publish materials filled with their bizarre beliefs—ideas that range from denying that the Nazi Holocaust against the Jews in World War II had ever happened, to those with the conviction that the federal government is an illegal body and that all governing power should rest with county sheriffs or militias. Despite their peculiarities, they all share the deep-seated hatred and resentment that had given life to the Klan and terrorized racial minorities, the weak, and Jews in this country for almost a century and a half.

The Klan itself has had three periods of significant strength in American history: first, in the latter half of the nineteenth century, then again in the 1920s and, more recently, during the 1950s and early 1960s, when the Civil Rights Movement was at its height. The Klan finally experienced a small resurgence in the 1970s, but it never again approached its past level of influence. Since then, with open and universal access to the Internet, the Klan has become just one element in a much broader spectrum of white supremacist and hatred activity. It is important for the student/reader to understand, however, that violent prejudice is not limited to the KKK or any other white supremacist organization. People who have no ties to any organized group, but who share their virulent hatred, commit bombings, assaults, murders, and arsons every year.

Learning about the past gives critical information for making sense out of the present, and then planning for the future. Historical research explains the roots of racism and prejudice, which sustains the Ku Klux Klan beliefs even into the twenty-first century. As for current events, that is an even easier lesson for most minorities who grew up in the racially torn years of the 1950s. Young civil rights activists, working alongside John Lewis, Andrew Young, the late Dr. Martin Luther King, Jr., Julian Bond, and many others, saw the KKK as an all-too-visible power in many of the places they went to organize voter registration and protest segregation. They knew what the Klan was, and often had a pretty good idea of who its members were. They also knew what Klan members would happily do to them if they thought they could get away with it.

Now, of course, you can turn on your television set and see people in Klan robes or military uniforms again handing out hate literature on street corners. You can read in almost any newspaper stories about crosses being burned in the yards of minorities or mixed-race couples, and it seems as if we are suddenly thrust back into the 1960s. Some claim the Klan today should just be ignored and it will fade away. Past history, however, will not let us ignore current events. Those who would use violence to deny others their rights must not be ignored. The law must be exercised to stay strong, and even racists must learn to respect the law. The background of the KKK and its battles with the law illustrate why hate groups cannot be ignored. It is not a pretty part of American history—some of the things you read here will make you angry or ashamed; some will turn your stomach and make you sick at heart. But it is important that we try to understand the villains as well as the heroes in our past if we are to continue building a nation where equality, freedom, and democracy are preserved.

Victims of the Klan

The image of a Black man, hanging lifeless by a rope from a tree limb, has become a symbol for the worst of Klan violence. Between 1889 and 1941, 3,811 Black people were lynched for "crimes" such as threatening to sue a White man, attempting to register to vote, joining labor unions, being "disrespectful" to a White man, even looking at a White woman, or just for no reason at all. During the American Revolution, the term *Lynch Law* described an informal court run by Colonel Charles Lynch of Bedford County, Virginia, who tried Tories and criminals in an effort to restore law and order to the frontier. Lynch's punishments consisted generally of fines or an occasional whipping. In the 1850s, the KKK used "Lynch Law." Later, the term was used to commonly describe a quick finding of guilty and the hanging of one of a group's objects of hate.

Today, there is a trend to spread hate and racism by forming so-called militias that freely use the worldwide Internet to spread their twisted messages of hatred and intolerance. In the late 1920s, during the years of prohibition, gangs and mobsters preyed on society and each other with deadly violence. Mobsters gunned down those who opposed or interfered with their bootlegging and traumatized all those who witnessed, or heard of, such carnage. These acts, it is now clear, were not just criminal, but serious terrorist acts. Terror strikes at the public's basic need for safety. Serial killers are unwitting terrorists when their deeds are publicized, and street gangs in American cities today use drive-by shootings as a tactic for creating fear and terror in their "hoods." These demonstrations keep their rivals in check and neighborhood citizens afraid to report these and other crimes against their own communities to the police. The same kinds of fear-inducing methods have long been the favorite tactics of the Mafia, or "Cosa Nostra" ("Our Thing"). From killings in schools and fast food places, to motorcycle gangs terrorizing an entire town, all forms of violence can be utilized as a means to incite terror.

With a population rapidly approaching over 300 million, the United States remains a "nation of immigrants," people who came to a great and prosperous land, legally and illegally, from the four corners of the earth. They come here in hope of finding opportunities for a better life. As far as terrorism was concerned, many of these immigrants escaped from various forms of it, leaving their

FIGURE 3-2 Members of the Knights of the Ku Klux Klan hold a rally on the steps of the Lebanon County Courthouse on April 24, 1999 in Lebanon, PA (Canadian Press).

home countries to come to a place where such actions were unthinkable. As we have now seen, the history of the United States does not support that premise, and many forms of terror have scarred its brief but bloody past—and even now sometimes mar its present.

The United States has the most powerful, diverse, and technologically advanced economy in the world. It boasts a per-capita annual income that is the highest among all major industrial nations. In this market-oriented economy, private individuals and business firms make most of the decisions, and the government buys needed goods and services predominantly in the private marketplace. American business firms enjoy considerably greater flexibility than their counterparts in Western Europe and Asia in their decisions to expand capital plant, lay off surplus workers, and develop new products.

A growing terrorism threat in the United States is not only from foreign sources, but also from dissatisfied, domestic purveyors of violence, hate, and terror.

OSAMA BIN LADEN AND AL QAEDA THREAT TO AMERICA

Osama bin Laden, the master planner behind the 9-11 attacks and prior terror events such as the bombing of the U.S.S. *Cole* in Yemen and the two embassy bombings in Nairobi and Dar es Salaam, announced a "**fatwa**," an interpretation of an Islamic law, in a London Arabic newspaper in 1998. In this proclamation, he stated that the United States had declared war against God and His messenger. Bin Laden called for the killing of Americans anywhere on earth as being a sacred duty of all Muslims. In a television interview with ABC, taped in Afghanistan, bin Laden expounded even further on this theme by stating the importance for Muslims to kill Americans more so than other infidels.

Bin Laden is one of a large number of sons of a Saudi construction magnate—a wealthy son who went to Afghanistan to fight against the Soviet invasion in 1980. Arabs from across the Middle East, Africa, and Asia headed to Afghanistan to wage jihad against the Soviets. Bin Laden's actual involvement in the fighting has never been established. However, his role became that of a key financier for the movement in Afghanistan. When bin Laden was in Afghanistan, the United States and Saudi Arabia supplied him with hundreds of millions of U.S. dollars in secret aid and support to the jihad. The ultimate defeat and the full pullout of the Soviet forces from Afghanistan in 1988 left bin Laden and his cohorts with an interesting dilemma— what to do next? Bin Laden and his Islamic fighters from across the globe had managed to defeat the mighty Soviet Army and, in doing so, had set up a base for their operations in Afghanistan. Strangely, a literal translation of "al Qaeda" is "the base," or "the foundation." The al Qaeda of the 1980s was a far cry from what it is today. In those post-Soviet months, the group developed and organized along corporate structures, complete with departments that dealt with arms procurement, media relations, and propaganda and intelligence. In Afghanistan, bin Laden worked closely with a Palestinian cleric, Abdullah Yusuf Azzam, who was nicknamed the "Godfather of Jihad." During the 1980s, Azzam was the central figure in the global development of the militant Islamist movement. He built a scholarly, ideological, and practical paramilitary infrastructure for the globalization of Islamist movements, which, until then, had been focused on separate national, revolutionary, and liberation struggles. Azzam envisioned a pan-Islamic transnational movement that would transcend the political map of the Middle East drawn by non-Islamic colonial powers.[2] Azzam traveled throughout Europe, the Middle East, and North America, where he visited more than fifty cities to raise money and preach jihad. His belief was that Afghanistan was a model for future struggles with the objective of establishing an Islamic Caliphate across all Muslim lands under foreign occupation. Azzam's radical ideology, combined with his skill at organizing paramilitary training for more than 20,000 Muslim recruits from about twenty countries around the world, created an international cadre of highly motivated and experienced militants, intent on perpetuating his vision of global Islamic revolution. In his book, *Join the Caravan*, Sheik Azzam implored Muslims to rally in defense of Muslim victims of aggression, to restore Muslim lands from foreign domination, and to uphold the Muslim faith.[3]

Azzam's success, and that of his fighters in Afghanistan, was solidified with the support of the CIA and Saudi Arabia. When the CIA began supplying Azzam's fighters with FIM-92 Stinger man-portable, surface-to-air missiles, the conventional military superiority of the Soviet MI-24 helicopters was neutralized, deeply demoralizing the Soviet troops and hastening victory for the Mujahideen fighters.

Azzam and his two sons were killed in a car bomb attack in Peshawar, Pakistan, in November 1989. His radical thoughts and ideology live on, however, through his related paramilitary manuals and a London-based media organization, Azzam Publications.

Azzam combined hatred for the West, Christians, and Jews, whom he routinely accused of carrying out diabolical conspiracies against Islam, with nostalgia for the days of the Islamic Caliphate, when non-Muslims were still treated formally as second-class citizens. It was the United States that seemed to epitomize for Azzam the ongoing Jewish-Christian conspiracy. Ironically, it was in the United States that Azzam was able to raise huge amounts of money, enlist new fighters and, most important, provide the political freedom to freely coordinate with other top radical Islamic movements. Azzam helped bring about the mobilization of the Muslim Brotherhood Movement more than did any other leader. Today, the military wing of **Hamas** in the West Bank is called the Abdellah Azzam Brigades.[4]

FLIGHT TRAINING

Germany was the major launching pad for the four primary members of the 9-11 suicide plot developed by Osama bin Laden in Afghanistan. The recruits were all well versed in the ways of Western society and were fervently anti-West in their ideologies. They would adequately suit bin Laden's needs for the attack on America. Mohamed Atta, Hani Hanjour, Marwan al Shehhi, and Ziad Jarrah completed their foundational training in Kandahar in 1999, and came to the United States in early 2000 to begin flight training. By now, al Qaeda possessed leaders who were able to evaluate, approve, and supervise the planning and direction of a major operation; a personnel system that could recruit candidates, indoctrinate them, vet them, and give them the necessary training; communications sufficient to enable planning and direction of operatives and those who would be helping them; an intelligence effort to gather required information and form assessments of enemy strengths and weaknesses; the ability to move people great distances; and the ability to raise and move money necessary to finance an attack.[5]

The planning stage inside the United States involved financing and training operatives for the 9-11 attack. The team members began training at flight schools in Florida and Oklahoma. All of the students were in the United States on "visitor" visas. According to the 9-11 Commission Report the flight training was paid for by funds wired from Dubai between June and September 2001. Al Qaeda had assembled pilots but determined they would also require other teams to assault the cockpits and subdue the crews of the targeted flights. Twelve of the thirteen who were selected for this task came from Saudi Arabia; the thirteenth came from the United Arab Emirates. In assessing these teams, a Saudi investigation noted that members came from a variety of backgrounds:

- All were between twenty and twenty-eight years old;
- Most were unemployed;
- Most had little more than high school education;
- Most were probably unmarried; and
- Four came from a cluster of towns in an isolated and underdeveloped region of Saudi Arabia.

All of the hijackers who made the trip to the United States were not hindered by immigration or customs. None had arrived through Canada, as originally thought. Al Qaeda trained all of these terrorists in Afghanistan for this specific operation.

Throughout the summer months of 2001, the hijackers, including the trained pilots, undertook surveillance flights across the United States in the types of aircraft that they planned to hijack.

At the same time, they tested the security system by carrying box cutters either on their person or in carry-on baggage.

Following the devastating 9-11 assault on the United States, there was an immediate outcry for a response in kind and to determine where to direct such a response. Osama bin Laden and his support network in Taliban-controlled Afghanistan came quickly to the forefront of targets. A meeting was held on September 13, 2001, between Deputy Secretary of State, Richard Armitage; Maleeha Lodhi, Pakistan's Ambassador to the United States; and Mahmud Ahmed, the head of Pakistan's Intelligence Service. The Deputy Secretary stated that the United States wanted Pakistan to take the following steps:

- Stop al Qaeda operatives at its border and end all logistical support for bin Laden;
- Give the U.S. blanket overflight and landing rights for all necessary military and intelligence operations;
- Provide territorial access to the United States and allied military intelligence and other personnel to conduct operations against al Qaeda;
- Provide the United States with intelligence information;
- Publicly condemn the terrorist acts; and
- Cut off all shipments of fuel to the Taliban and stop recruits from going to Afghanistan.

The United States also wanted Pakistan to break relations with the Taliban government if the evidence implicated bin Laden, and al Qaeda, and the Taliban continued to harbor them.

Combined and improved dissemination of intelligence has been credited for many successes in the aftermath of 9-11, and Britain and Europe have been in the forefront of information sharing and cooperation. The British experience with homegrown terror and the openness of the threat posed by Islamic clerics, such as the hook-handed Abu Hamza al-Masri, a credible cleric yet, alone, was not immediately recognized, as a security threat to either Britain or its allies. However Masri currently is wanted in the United States for his formation of a terrorist training camp in Oregon in 1999 and for his involvement in a kidnapping in Yemen. While he languishes in a British prison, the justice system in the United Kingdom has authorized his extradition to the United States once he completes his sentence for soliciting murder and inciting racial hatred. Al-Masri openly praised the success of the 9-11 attacks, and one of his young and impressionable students at his London mosque was Richard Reid, the shoe bomber.

The threat from within the United States will continue to focus on the minds of the security and intelligence community. Attempts by citizens to assemble and procure items to make bombs, both conventional and nonconventional, such as that by U.S. citizen Jose Padilla, will remain a high priority. He was arrested at Chicago O'Hare Airport on suspicion of plotting a dirty bomb attack. With the U.S. ability to hold such persons as "enemy combatants" continuing to be challenged, he was eventually indicted in 2005 and, although not charged with plotting to detonate a dirty bomb, was convicted along with three others in 2007. The fact remains that he is in prison and also cooperating with the FBI about any involvement he may have had with al Qaeda while outside of the United States.

9-11 AND ITS AFTERMATH

The terrorist attacks could have, and many commentators say should have, been prevented, had the security guards at major U.S. airports stopped the hijackers from boarding their flights. The training for the crews operating on those flights worked against them, and in the hijackers' favor, in that the crews did what they were trained to do—keep the passengers calm and do as the hijackers instructed. Unfortunately, they were never to know the true intentions of the hijackers, until it was too late.

The intelligence community knew that Osama bin Laden had threatened to "cut off the head of the serpent" (the United States) and cause mass casualties; it also knew that bin Laden was

FIGURE 3-3   View of the area in New York City where the World Trade Center once stood (Clifford E. Simonsen).

planning to do something with aircrafts. An FBI Field Office knew that several pilots were in training, but even with all of this information, the "dots were never connected." Could we have then expected anything else? Hindsight is always 20/20 when we reflect back on what might or could have been done, or should have been done differently. Intelligence gathering is not a finite art, and it is invariably the case that after an event takes place, previously gathered information adds up to a large arsenal of circumstantial evidence on the trail of the terrorist masterminds. In 2001, aviation security (passenger screening) was one of the lowest-paid and most menial tasks at airports, particularly in the United States. Aviation security suffered a major blow to its performance and credibility—and rightly so. For more than two decades, the industry has lacked any desire to beef up security—a fact clearly laid bare on 9-11. Airline crew training programs had never covered how to tackle determined terrorists, and the cockpits had an almost "open-door" policy for visitors. No one suspected that dedicated terrorists would commit mass suicide in such a ghastly manner as occurred on 9-11. Historical terror events and "dots" pointed clearly to a buildup by internationalized terror fanatics from the Islamic world, with serious planning for inflicting attacks against U.S. targets. So, it was purely a matter of *when* and not *if* an attack would come to the U.S. shores. However, the United States and the rest of the world were not prepared for the outcome or the reaction to it. The failure of the United States and other intelligence organizations to correctly intercept the 9-11 operatives could be blamed on historical events. Since the end of the Cold War, the need for covert operatives had been in decline. Many CIA specialists were moved to different areas of activity, such as the Balkans or Africa. Further, the levels of new recruits to the CIA continued to decline. By the end of the last decade of the twentieth century, the CIA was virtually stripped of any incoming new recruits. Recruits to the CIA typically took a period of seven years of training to become fully effective.

Chronology of Events of 9/11/2001

08:46:40	Hijacked American Airlines Flight 11 flew into the upper portion of the North Tower of New York's World Trade Center. The aircraft cut through floors 93 to 99.
09:03:11	Hijacked United Airlines Flight 175 flew into the South Tower of the World Trade Center. The aircraft cut through floors 77 to 85.
09:37	Hijacked American Airlines Flight 77 crashed into the west wall of the Pentagon in Washington DC.
09:40	The FAA suspends all U.S. air traffic. This is the first time that this drastic action has been undertaken.
09:58:59	In a period of ten seconds, the South Tower of the World Trade Center collapses.
10:10	A portion of the west side of the Pentagon collapses.
10:10	United Airlines Flight 93, also hijacked, crashes in Shanksville, Somerset County, Pennsylvania.
10:28	The North Tower of the World Trade Center collapses.

More than 2,600 people died at the World Trade Center; 125 died at the Pentagon; and 256 died on the four aircraft. The death toll on 9-11 surpassed that of the surprise Japanese attack on Pearl Harbor in December 1941.[6]

The "War on Terror" materialized through a pre-9-11 directive concerning al Qaeda and evolved into National Security Presidential Directive 9 entitled, "Defeating the Terrorist Threat to the United States." This directive would extend to a global war against terrorism—not just aimed at al Qaeda, but also at nations that harbored terrorists, and terror groups and organizations.

FIGURE 3-4   World Trade Center, New York, following the attacks on September 11, 2001 (U.S. Department of Homeland Security).

In October 2001, U.S. forces began their attack on Afghanistan, along with a coalition of forces, aimed at dislodging the Taliban and capturing Osama bin Laden. In August 2006, the U.S. government issued its National Strategy for Combating Terrorism document. With a continuingly evolving threat, the central theme was about winning the "War on Terror" which, to many observers, is maybe more than ten years away! The document makes its central platform that to win the war, the United States must

- Advance effective democracies as the long term antidote to the ideology of terrorism;
- Prevent attacks by terrorist networks;
- Deny weapons of mass destruction to rogue states and terrorist allies who seek to use them;
- Deny terrorists the support and sanctuary of rogue states;
- Deny terrorists control of any nation they would use as a base and launching pad for terror; and
- Lay the foundations, and build the institutions and structures needed to carry the fight forward against terror, and help ensure ultimate success.

Setting this document aside, the next step is to understand how the radicalization of Muslims has taken place, and how that threat may exist in the United States. The 2005 attacks in the United Kingdom were from radicalized young men who were either born in the UK or immigrated at a young age. The fact that all were unremarkable and had drawn little or no attention is something that the United States will have to consider when attempting to define how the next attack will materialize from inspiration and ideology—inspiration gathered from the spectacular events of 9-11, and ideology from the al Qaeda leader Osama bin Laden preaching a global jihad, turning young men into inspired "Holy Warriors". One of the main perpetrators captured by the United States as one of the masterminds of the 9-11 attacks was **Khalid Sheikh Mohammed** (KSM), who currently resides in Guantanamo Bay. Under interrogation, this man has provided a possible treasure trove of information; however, no doubt some of the intelligence gathered will be viewed with skepticism for its content and accuracy. In March 2007, the Pentagon released written and oral statements by KSM.

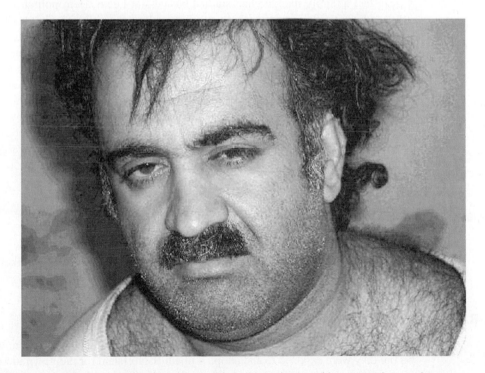

FIGURE 3-5 Al Qaeda operational leader Khalid Sheikh Mohammed in a 2003 photo, who confessed before a U.S. military tribunal to having planned and supported more than 30 terrorist attacks including 9/11 (Canadian Press).

The released statements shed new light on the extent of KSM's al Qaeda activities and his claims to be involved in the media organization, and the group's intent to produce biological weapons. He declared that he was responsible for the 9-11 operation from A to Z, and he also claimed to have been "directly in charge, after the death of Sheikh Abu Hafs al-Masri Subbj Abu Sittah, of managing and following up on the call for the production of biological weapons such as anthrax and others, and following up on dirty bomb operations on American soil."[7]

RADICAL ISLAM AND THE UNITED STATES

As we look to the future, we have to determine what threats are posed to the U.S. Homeland from radicalized Muslims. Jihadism is a flourishing ideology, and while it thrives, those wishing to embrace such an ideology continue to pose a threat. The experiences in Britain and Europe from radicalized Muslims could well be the example for the next attack on the United States. Governments cannot protect every building and every citizen, and therefore cannot protect every target. The threat from the homegrown jihadist comes from a reality that those trying to enter the United States will use whatever legal and illegal means they can employ, whether they originate from countries in the U.S. Visa Waiver Program, or have entered illegally through either Canada or Mexico; they may also be current U.S. citizens currently conspiring to attack the country from within. It is a tactical reality that these individuals exist and are already on U.S. soil.

In review of the terrorist attacks by homegrown terrorists in the United Kingdom in 2005, we can begin to get a picture of a radicalized jihadist. He is invariably the child of moderate Muslim immigrants, and aged under thirty-five. The jihadist comes from a varied ethnic background and, contrary to popular belief, is not economically destitute, but rather has a full-time job and is well educated. There is little evidence to suggest that they have any criminal background, therefore making them more unremarkable! Mohammad Siddique Khan, one of the 2005 London bombers, was in fact a family man; he had studied business at Leeds Metropolitan University from 1998 to 2001 and was working as a teaching assistant with young children. So what transformation did this young man undergo that would lead him to become a suicide bomber in his country of birth?

The **jihadi-Salafi** ideology is the driver that motivates young men and women, either born or living in the West, to carry out "**autonomous jihad**" via acts of terrorism against their host countries. This ideology has served as the inspiration for groups such as those that carried out the Madrid train attacks in 2004, The Dutch Hoftsad Group, the 2005 London bombers, as well as the eighteen Canadians arrested in Toronto in 2006. The New York Police Department (NYPD) Intelligence Division undertook a review of radical Islam to better understand the phases that went into the process of radicalization, and their review paper identified four specific phases in the process:

1. Pre-radicalization
2. Self-identification
3. Indoctrination
4. Jihadization

Although the NYPD model is sequential, individuals do not always follow a perfectly linear progression; however, those that do pass through the entire process are quire likely to become involved in the setup and organization of terror attacks.

PRE-RADICALIZATION

This is the point of origin for individuals before they began this progression. It is their life situation before they were exposed to and adopted jihadi-Salafi Islam for their own ideology. The majority of the individuals involved in plots came from unremarkable backgrounds and jobs, and lived seemingly normal crime-free lives. The Toronto 18 terror suspects reportedly were well integrated into Canadian society.

SELF-IDENTIFICATION

This is the phase where individuals, influenced by both internal and external factors, begin their exploration of Salafist Islam, gradually gravitate away from their old identity, and begin to associate themselves with like-minded individuals and adopt this ideology as their own. In the Toronto case, the suspects had struggled with their identity, and some had formed a religious club and chat groups; they had also adopted the tradition Muslim style of dress, and some grew beards. The catalyst for this religious seeking is a cognitive opening or crisis, which shakes ones certitude in previously held beliefs and opens an individual to be receptive to new worldviews. What those worldviews are and what specific event sparks the religious changes could be many varied events, be it social, economic, or world events involving Muslims, or even a family member's death.

INDOCTRINATION

This is the period when the individual progressively intensifies his beliefs and wholly adopts Salafist teachings and ideology, and concludes that the conditions and circumstances exist for action to further and support the jihadi cause. In most events, this phase is driven by a "spiritual sanctioner." While the initial self-indoctrination process may be an individual act, association with like-minded individuals is an important factor as the process deepens. By the indoctrination phase, this self-selecting group becomes increasingly important as radical views are encouraged as well as reinforced by the religious sanctioner.

JIHADIZATION

This is the phase in which the group members accept their individual duty to participate in jihad and self-designate themselves as holy warriors, or mujahideen. Ultimately, the group will begin operational planning for a terrorist attack. These activities include planning, reconnaissance, preparation, and execution. While the previous phases can take months or even years to reach Jihadization' this final phase can be a very rapid process taking only a few months or weeks to run its course.[8]

The far-reaching inspiration of Osama bin Laden and his al Qaeda terrorist organization has resulted in attempts by self-styled jihadists to attack U.S. targets. One such attack that was disrupted by the FBI in early 2007 was that of a group of Islamists who planned to attack the Fort Dix Army camp. Six men began practicing with semiautomatic weapons in rural Pennsylvania, and in January 2006, a video tape of their activities that they had taken to a local store to have it transferred into a DVD format raised the clerk's suspicion, who contacted the FBI. During the ensuing investigation of the group, the FBI successfully infiltrated the group. All the members of the group held down normal jobs throughout the planning phases. The six conspirators, four ethnic Albanians from the former Yugoslavia, a Turkish immigrant, and a U.S. citizen from Jordan, planned to buy M16's AK-47's as well as rocket propelled grenades, and mount an attack on the New Jersey Army Base at Fort Dix and kill as many service personnel as they could. The far-reaching tenets of Osama bin Laden's jihadist ideology come after from the belief that

- This is a clash of civilizations. Militant jihad is a religious duty before God. The clash is necessary for the salvation of one's soul and to defend the Muslim nation.
- Only two camps exist, and there can be no middle ground in an apocalyptic showdown with both the West and the Muslims that do not agree with al Qaeda's vision of "true Islam."
- Violence is the only solution, peace is an illusion.
- Many of the theological and legal restrictions on the use of violence by Muslims do not apply to this war.

- The United States' power is based on its economy and, thus, large-scale mass-casualty attacks, especially focussed on U.S. and Western economic targets, are a major goal.
- Muslim governments that are religiously unacceptable and cooperate with the West must be violently overthrown.[9] The U.S. government has been steadfast on its position relative to enemy combatants that now reside at Guantanomo Bay. The United States has also adopted tactics that have been broadly criticised by such groups as Amnesty International for its actions.

Another example of homegrown threats against the United States, successfully investigated by FBI, is the "Lackawanna Group," a reference to the working class town of Lackawanna, south of Buffalo, where the Islamist conspirators came from, and is home to 3,000 Muslim Americans, whose families come from the Republic of Yemen, on the Arabian Peninsula. The inspirational leader of the Lackawanna Group was Kamal Derwish who, although born in Buffalo and raised in Saudi Arabia, is steeped in that country's fundamentalist breed of Islam, known as Wahhabism. Derwish had trained in al Qaeda camps in Afghanistan and fought with Muslims in Bosnia. After returning to Saudi Arabia in 1997, he had been jailed for extremist activities. He returned to the United States in 2001 and began to inspire a group of like-minded young Muslims at his local mosque. This can be likened to the events that happened at London's Finsbury Park mosque, where Abu Hamza al Masri preached his hatred of the West. In the Spring of 2001, the following group members flew to Afghanistan for training: Mukhtar al-Bakri, Sahim Alwan, Jaber Elbaneh, Faysal Galab, Yahya Goba, Shafal Mosed, and Yasein Taher. Juma Al Dosari, who it is believed had fought with other Muslim fighters alongside Kamal Derwish in Bosnia, arrived in the United States in early 2001 and joined the Lackawanna Group. The Buffalo FBI Field Office is alerted to the Yemeni group via an anonymous letter, and, although the group is investigated, no charges can be substantiated. Following the 9-11 attacks, Al Dosari leaves to fight with the Taliban in Afghanistan, and is captured sometime in the fall of 2001 while fighting with the Taliban.

He is declared an enemy combatant and is sent to the U.S. Naval Base on Guantanamo Bay, Cuba, where he is questioned. Al Dosari's interrogation confirms that the Lackawanna suspects were the targets of an al Qaeda recruitment operation. Mukhtar al-Bakri is arrested by Bahraini Police in September 2002, and subsequently is interviewed by the CIA. He reveals the names of the other members of the Lackawanna Group; Sahim Alwan, Faysal Galab, Yahya Goba, Shafal Mosed, and Yasein Taher are arrested. In early November 2002, Kamal Derwish is killed in Yemen by a CIA Predator Drone while tracking the al Qaeda plotters of the U.S.S. *Cole* attack. Although Derwish was an American citizen, the government will not discuss his death or any connections he may have or have had with al Qaeda. This very brief example indicates the very real problems that exist within the Muslim communities within the United States. The Lackawanna Group is sentenced to between seven and ten years in prison in 2003, and has been cooperating with the government.

The Lackawanna case is just possibly the tip of an as-yet-undiscovered iceberg of terrorist cells that, although unlikely being directed by al Qaeda, are inspired by the terrorist movement to act independently.

How Muslims integrate and how they view themselves not only in the United States but also in other Western countries is an ongoing concern not just to religious groups but to governments as well. The overwhelming view from research companies such as Pew Research point out that many Muslims feel better off in Western society although their standard of living is often not comparable to that of the general population in the host country. Certainly, rioting in France in 2007 was the result of young Muslim men angry at the lack of opportunity and no doubt upset at the secular stance the French government takes toward them and their beliefs.

WATCH LISTS

The value of watch lists is still uncertain as, presumably, terrorists do not plan to fly using their official name or with a genuine passport!

Testimony before the Committee on Homeland Security and Governmental Affairs, U.S. Senate, October 2007

Pursuant to Homeland Security Presidential Directive 6, the Attorney General established Terrorist Screening Centers (TSCs) in September 2003 to consolidate the government's approach to terrorism screening and provide for the appropriate and lawful use of terrorist information in screening processes. TSC's consolidated watch list is the U.S. government's master repository for all records of known or appropriately suspected international and domestic terrorists used for watch list-related screening.

- When an individual makes an airline reservation, arrives at a U.S. port of entry, or applies for a U.S. visa, or is stopped by state or local police within the United States, the frontline screening agency or airline conducts a name-based search of the individual against applicable terrorist watch list records. In general, when the computerized name-matching system of an airline or screening agency generates a "hit" (a potential name match) against a watch list record, the airline or agency is to review each potential match. Any obvious mismatches (negative matches) are to be resolved by the airline or agency. Page 3 GAO-08-194T.

   The National Counterterrorism Center and the FBI rely upon standards of reasonableness in determining which individuals are appropriate for inclusion on TSC's consolidated terrorist watch list. In general, individuals who are reasonably suspected of having possible links to terrorism—in addition to individuals with known links—are to be nominated. As such, inclusion on the list does not automatically prohibit an individual from, for example, obtaining a visa or entering the United States. As of May 2007, TSC's watch list contained approximately 755,000 records.

- From December 2003 (when TSC began operations) through May 2007, agencies encountered individuals who were on the watch list about 53,000 times. Many individuals were encountered multiple times. Actions taken in response included arresting individuals and denying others entry into the United States. Most often, however, agencies questioned and then released the individuals because there was not sufficient evidence of criminal or terrorist activity to warrant further legal action. Nevertheless, such questioning allowed agencies to collect information on the individuals, which was shared with law enforcement agencies and the intelligence community.

- Screening agencies do not check against all records in the consolidated watch list, partly because screening against certain records (1) may not be needed to support the respective agency's mission or (2) may not be possible owing to the requirements of computer programs used to check individuals against watch list records. Not checking against all records may pose a security risk. Also, some subjects of watch list records have passed undetected through agency screening processes and were not identified, for example, until after they had boarded and flew on an aircraft. Federal agencies have ongoing initiatives to help reduce these potential vulnerabilities.

- The federal government has made progress in using the consolidated watch list for screening purposes, but it has not (1) finalized guidelines for using watch list records within critical infrastructure components of the private sector or (2) identified all appropriate opportunities for which terrorist-related screening should be applied. Further, the government lacks an up-to-date strategy and implementation plan—supported by a clearly defined leadership or governance structure—which are important for enhancing the effectiveness of terrorist-related screening.

Several actions have been recommended to promote a more comprehensive and coordinated approach to terrorist-related screening. Among them are actions to monitor and respond to vulnerabilities and to establish up-to-date guidelines, strategies, and plans to facilitate expanded and enhanced use of the list. The Department of Homeland Security and the FBI generally agreed with GAO findings and recommendations.[10]

EXTRAORDINARY RENDITION

Nearly a decade after the attacks on 9-11, the United States and its principal ally, Great Britain, are still vigorously prosecuting the War on Terror. Afghanistan has been largely forgotten as the United States moved on to the removal of Saddam Hussein, his subsequent capture, and execution in Iraq, and has become bogged down in the ensuing aftermath of insurgent Islamic forces from both within and outside that battered country. At home in the United States, the question of dealing with terrorists and the need to gather much more and reliable intelligence has become a major priority for the Bush Administration. The U.S. government does not recognize those captured in both Afghanistan and Iraq as being prisoners of war, but rather as "enemy combatants." This has led to speculation surrounding treatment of the detainees in Guantanomo Bay, as well as the significant fallout from the abuses at Abu Ghraib prison near Baghdad. While these events may be of little interest to the wider American public, the stories are front-page and never-ending news for the Muslim media in the Middle East. Some argue that U.S. plans for democratizing areas of the Gulf and other regions of the Middle East have an effect on the levels of insurgent attacks on U.S. troops in Iraq. There are over a quarter of a million U.S. troops now based in the Middle East.

Back home, the need for solid intelligence continues. Complaints have been made by Amnesty International and others that the United States, in its race and determination to go to extraordinary lengths to gather information, is violating both U.S. and international laws. By categorizing detainees as enemy combatants, the United States does not apply the rigorous standards required under the Geneva Conventions. What is taking place and being driven in secret, presumably by the CIA, is an activity referred to as "**extraordinary rendition**," which has been defined as "the transfer of an individual, with the involvement of the United States or its agents, to a foreign state in circumstances that make it more likely than not, that the individual will be subjected to torture, or cruel, inhuman, or degrading treatment."[11] This practice has not had much press in the United States, likely because of the secret manner in which it is being conducted. However, there are cases of "rendition" that took place prior to 9-11, and certainly the practice has been even more widespread since that tragic event. Specifically, critics claim the United States is violating International Conventions that ban the use of torture. Since 9-11, dozens of "enemy combatants" have been sent to third-party countries such as Morocco, Saudi Arabia, Yemen, Egypt, and Jordan. All of these countries—in particular, Egypt and Jordan—have close ties to the CIA and all have been cited by the U.S. State Department as using torture in interrogations. Detainees have been taken often under cover of darkness and transported by private jet to these countries for interrogation. The interrogation tactics used would be illegal if conducted inside the United States. The Convention against Torture prohibits torture carried out at the "instigation of or with the consent or acquiescence" of officials. Handing someone over to a foreign intelligence service with the knowledge that the person will be tortured fits within the prohibitions of the Convention. It also appears that U.S. officials engage in the treatment of detainees that may include torture. Witnesses have reported that captives are "softened up" by the U.S. military. The detainees are said to have been blindfolded and thrown into wells, bound in painful positions, subjected to loud noises, and deprived of sleep. There is growing resistance to the use of torture even from law enforcement officials.[12] Article 3 of the United Nations Convention Against Torture, to which the United States is a signatory, states that "no party shall expel, return ('refouler') or extradite a person to another State where there are substantial grounds for believing that person would be in danger of being subjected to torture. For the purpose of determining whether there are such grounds, the competent authorities shall take into account all relevant considerations including, where applicable, the existence in the State concerned of a consistent pattern of gross, flagrant, or mass violations of human rights."

Maher Arar—Canadian Citizen

While the number of cases and the extent to which the government is involved in rendition is uncertain, there is a significant case that has embarrassed both the U.S. and Canadian governments for the manner in which a Canadian citizen, transiting through JFK en route back into Canada, was detained and sent on to Syria. Arar came to Canada with his family and had no intention, according to him, of returning to Syria. In the wake and paranoia of 9-11, it is entirely probable that mistakes were made in targeting individuals for this form of treatment. Failings by the Canadian intelligence service and the RCMP led to an individual being forcibly removed from an in-transit location to Syria, where he remained incarcerated and, according to Amnesty International, was severely tortured. He was released on October 5, 2003, 374 days after first being deported to Syria. No charges have been brought against him by Syria, the United States, or Canada even though it was alleged that he had contact with al Qaeda sympathizers.

USA Patriot Improvement Act

On March 9, 2006, President Bush signed The USA PATRIOT Improvement and Reauthorization Act of 2005. Since its enactment in October 2001, the Patriot Act has been vital to winning the War on Terror and protecting the American people. The legislation signed today allows intelligence and law enforcement officials to continue sharing information and using the same tools against terrorists already employed against drug dealers and other criminals. While safeguarding Americans' civil liberties, this legislation also strengthens the U.S. Department of Justice (DOJ) so that it can better detect and disrupt terrorist threats, and it also gives law enforcement new tools to combat threats. America still faces dangerous enemies, and no priority is more important to the President than protecting the American people without delay.

THE PATRIOT ACT CLOSES DANGEROUS LAW ENFORCEMENT AND INTELLIGENCE GAPS

The Patriot Act Has Accomplished Exactly What It Was Designed to Do

- It has helped us detect terrorist cells, disrupt terrorist plots, and save American lives.
- The Patriot Act has helped law enforcement break up terror cells in Ohio, New York, Oregon, and Virginia.
- The Patriot Act has helped in the prosecution of terrorist operatives and supporters in California, Texas, New Jersey, Illinois Washington, and North Carolina.

The Patriot Act Authorizes Vital Information Sharing to Help Law Enforcement and Intelligence Officials Connect the Dots Before Terrorists Strike. The Patriot Act enables necessary cooperation and information sharing by helping to break down legal and bureaucratic walls separating criminal investigators from intelligence officers.

The Patriot Act Eliminates Double Standards by Allowing Agents to Pursue Terrorists with the Same Tools They Use Against Other Criminals. Before the Patriot Act, it was easier to track a drug dealer's phone contacts than a terrorist's phone contacts, and it was easier to obtain a tax cheat's credit card receipts than to trace the financial support of an al Qaeda fund-raiser. The Patriot Act corrected these double standards—and America is safer as a result.

The Patriot Act Adapts the Law to Modern Technology. The Patriot Act allows Internet service providers to disclose customer records voluntarily to the government in emergencies involving an immediate risk of death or serious physical injury, and permits victims of hacking crimes to request law enforcement assistance in monitoring trespassers on their computers.

The Patriot Act Preserves Our Freedoms and Upholds the Rule of Law. The legislation signed today adds over thirty new significant civil liberties provisions.

THE PATRIOT ACT REAUTHORIZATION SAFEGUARDS OUR NATION

The Patriot Act Reauthorization Creates a New Assistant Attorney General for National Security. By creating a new Assistant Attorney General for National Security, this legislation fulfills a critical recommendation of the Commission on the Intelligence Capabilities of the United States regarding Weapons of Mass Destruction. This will allow the Justice Department to bring its national security, counterterrorism, counterintelligence, and foreign intelligence surveillance operations under a single authority.

The Patriot Act Reauthorization Tackles Terrorism Financing. This bill enhances penalties for terrorism financing and closes a loophole concerning terrorist financing through "hawalas" (informal money transfer networks) rather than traditional financial institutions.

The Patriot Act Reauthorization Protects Mass Transportation. This bill provides clear standards and tough penalties for attacks on our land- and water-based mass transportation systems, as well as commercial aviation.

THE PATRIOT ACT REAUTHORIZATION COMBATS METHAMPHETAMINE ABUSE

The Patriot Act Reauthorization Includes the Combat Methamphetamine Epidemic Act of 2005. This bill introduces commonsense safeguards that will make many ingredients used in methamphetamine manufacturing more difficult to obtain in bulk and easier for law enforcement to track. For example, the bill places limits on large-scale purchases of over-the-counter drugs that are used to manufacture methamphetamines, and requires stores to keep these ingredients behind the counter or in locked display cases. It increases penalties for smuggling and selling methamphetamines.[13]

INTERNATIONAL TERRORISM

Following the attacks of 9-11, foreign terrorists of every stripe could not but now think of the United States as being vulnerable—an easy priority target. Despite the rapid mobilization efforts by Homeland Security on land, rail, in the air, and elsewhere, terrorists and their supporters continue to live in and travel with relative ease throughout the United States. Ironically, the U.S. drug-using population still continues to help finance terrorism around the world by being a major consumer of the entire spectrum of illegal drugs. These narco-dollars continue to fill the war chests of terrorist groups around the world. Narco-terrorists purchase cut-down cocaine shipped from Colombia through Mexico and the Caribbean, brown tar heroin, marijuana, and, increasingly, methamphetamine from Mexico. The American user continues as a consumer of high-quality Southeast Asian heroin from the Golden Triangle regions. America is a major illicit producer of its own cannabis, depressants, stimulants, hallucinogens, methamphetamine, and designer drugs such as Ecstasy. This creates a multibillion-dollar need for drug-money-laundering centers. And then the cycle repeats itself, on and on.

RELIGIOUS EXTREMISM

Jamaat Al-Fuqra

There resides, somewhat eerily, a network of possible terrorists-in-waiting within a little-known organization called **Jamaat al-Fuqra**, which has the literal translation, "community of the impoverished." This group's Islamic roots in the United States date back as far as 1980, when it was founded by Sheik Mubarak Ali Gilani, a Pakistani cleric, who incorporated the group under the name of "Muslims of America." The organization has tax-exempt status in the United States, and has an educational section that supports student training in Pakistan. The group has done little to draw attention to itself in mainstream United States, and all but denies its very existence. One of al-Fuqra's first members was Stephen Paul Paster, who had converted to Islam and was convicted of bombing a hotel that was owned by an Indian cult in Portland, Oregon, in 1983. On his release from prison, Paster went to Pakistan, where he joined Gilani and other instructors teaching advanced courses in Islamic military warfare. On a broader scale, al-Fuqra members are believed to have been involved in fighting in Chechnya, Bosnia, Afghanistan, Kashmir, and Lebanon. U.S. sources believe some of its members are affiliated with the al-Kifah Refugee Center in Brooklyn, New York. Following the first attack on the World Trade Center in 1993, the FBI determined that Muslim men, including participants in the attack, had been recruited at the al-Kifah refugee office in Brooklyn and sent to training camps in Afghanistan—first to fight the Soviet army, and later to engage in a jihad against the United States. In 1993, the FBI also learned of a plot to blow up bridges, tunnels, and landmarks in New York. That investigation led to the conviction of Omar Abdul al-Rahman, the "Blind Sheikh," for soliciting others to commit all of those acts of terrorism in 1993. A further connection links the infamous "shoe bomber," Richard Reid, to the Brooklyn office. More recently, *The Wall Street Journal* reporter Daniel Pearl was investigating Gilani in Pakistan when he was kidnapped and murdered.

U.S. Visa Waiver Program

Countries that are allowed to participate in the Visa Waiver Program must meet certain legislatively established criteria as set forth in the Immigration and Nationality Act (U.S.C. 1187), the Border Security Act, and the Enhanced Border Security and Visa Entry Reform Act (EBSVERA).

> Among these criteria are requirements that
>
> Governments provide reciprocal, visa-free travel for U.S. citizens (ninety days for tourism or business purposes);
>
> Governments issue secure, machine-readable passports that satisfy internationally accepted standards;
>
> Governments certify that they have a program to incorporate biometric identifiers into their passports in accordance with International Civil Aviation Organization standards;
>
> Governments certify that they report the theft of blank passports on a timely basis to the U.S. government, and do so in practice;
>
> The refusal rate for nonimmigrant visitor visa applications for nationals of the country is less than 3 percent for the previous two fiscal years; and
>
> The incidence of nationals of the country traveling as nonimmigrant visitors who are denied admission, withdraw their application, and violate the terms of a VWP admission is less than 2 percent of the total number of nonimmigrant nationals traveling to the United States during the previous fiscal year.
>
> Currently, twenty-seven countries participate in the Visa Waiver Program, as shown in Table 3-1.

While an incredible array of measures is being put in place to control foreigners entering the United States, we must not lose sight of the so-called holy warriors who are in our midst—those probable converts to Islam, and second- and third-generation Americans who have already learned their trade in the theaters of conflict in the Balkans, the Middle East, and Afghanistan. It is entirely possible that the next attack on U.S. soil may be committed by U.S. passport holders.

Table 3-1 List of designated State sponsors of Terrorism	
Country	**Designation Date**
Cuba	March 1, 1982
Iran	January 19, 1984
North Korea	January 20, 1988
Sudan	August 12, 1993
Syria	December 29, 1979

Summary

You may want to recall the early events of Bill Clinton's regime when the United States suffered a "Fire fight from Hell," as it was described in Newsweek Magazine. We of course refer to the debacle in Somalia when the United States had the objective of seizing Somali warlord Mohammed Aidid. What had started out as a peacekeeping mission in Mogadishu turned into a race to capture Aidid who had been undermining UN humanitarian aid in the region. The resulting loss of life to American Marines was starkly played out on TV screens around the world. The Mogadishu failure brought back haunting memories from the failed attempt to rescue U.S. hostages in Tehran two decades earlier and had subsequently cost President Carter the 1980 election. Bin Laden and his cohorts believe the cost in military deaths will be too unpalatable

for the U.S. public, and he continues to taunt a receptive global media with that fact. In reality, the United States has not suffered from an al Qaeda-inspired attack since 9-11, but history has shown us that Islamist supporters of al Qaeda are prepared to plan over a considerable period of time in order to mastermind their plans—no doubt the increase in Homeland Security and good old fashioned police work has gone a long way to delay, deter, and disrupt Islamist elements readying themselves for attacks on U.S. targets. That another attack is on the way is a certainty, but predetermining when and where the attack will come from is the major challenge for authorities. The next chapter discusses terrorism in Canada and the Caribbean. The threat from Islamist and other groups from those countries, in particular Canada, will be reviewed.

Web Sites

1. **Center for Defense Information**—*www.cdi.org*
2. **White Aryan Resistance**—*www.resist.com*
3. **Terror Attack Database**—*www.ic.org.il*
4. **National Counter Intelligence Center**—*www.nacic.org*
5. **U.S. Department of Homeland Security**—*www.dhs.gov*
6. **Stormfront**—*http://www.stormfront.org*
7. **Army of God**—*http:///www.armyofgod.com*

Endnotes

1. Washington Post. www.washingtonpost.com/wpdyn/content/article/2005/09/28/AR.htm.
2. www.religioscope.com/info/doc/jihad/azzam_defence_1_table.htm.
3. Clark Staten—Domestic Terrorism—The enemy from Within. www.emergency.com/domsterr.htm.
4. Steve Emerson—*Abdullah Assam: The Man before Osama bin Laden.* www.iacsp.com/itobli3.htm.
5. Executive Summary 9-11 Commission Report.
6. 9-11 Commission Report and Executive Summary of the 9-11 Commission Report.
7. Global Intelligence Brief—Stratfor—*The Masterminds many roles in al Qaeda.* www.stratfor.com (March 15, 2007).
8. New York Police Department—*NYPD Radicalization in the West: The Homegrown Threat,* Michael D Silber, Arvin Bhatt—Senior Intelligence Analysts, NYPD Intelligence Division.

9. Philip P Purpura. *Terrorism and Homeland Security: An Introduction with Applications* (Butterworth: Heinmann, 2006, p. 30).

10. U.S. Government Accountability Office.

11. Association of the Bar of the City of New York and Center for Human Rights and Global Justice. Torture by Proxy: International and Domestic Laws applicable to "Extraordinary Renditions" (New York: ABCNY and NYU School of Law, 2004).

12. Michael Ratner: War on Terror: The Guantanamo Prisoners, Military Commissions and Torture. www.ccr-ny.org/v2/viewpoints/viewpoint.asp.

13. The White House. www.whitehouse.gov/news/releases/2006/03/20060309–7html.

CHAPTER 4

Canada and the Caribbean

Victory is reserved for those who are willing to pay its price.

SUN TZU

Learning Objectives

The study and review of this chapter will enable you to

1. Discuss how support for terrorism and fund-raising in Canada poses a threat to the United States;

2. Understand that Canada's liberal attitude to immigration has helped the spread of the threat of terrorism;

3. Discuss how Sikh terrorism has been on the rise in Western Canada;

4. Explain how effective the Tamil Tigers have been at raising funds from within Canada.

Terms to Remember

Akali Dal	Che Guevara	Macheteros
Babbar Khalsa	Dal Khalsa	Multiculturalism
Bill C-36	FLQ	Operation Blue Star
Canada Security and Intelligence Service (CSIS)	Jarnail Singh Bhindranwale	

OVERVIEW

Canada is associated with terrorist activity and has been a home base for terrorist organizations dating as far back as the 1980s. The country's first experience with terror was strictly a homegrown affair with the French seperatist movement in Quebec in the 1970s, but a much more violent form of terrorism during the 1980s was a direct result of events taking place on the Indian subcontinent. This chapter looks at the Sikh terrorist movement that downed an Air India Boeing 747 aircraft off the coast of Ireland, and Canada's inability at the time to recognize the threats being posed by external forces. After 9-11, there was considerable criticism from politicians in the United States concerning the porous border between the two countries. The Canadian government has always fostered a very liberal approach to immigration policy in stark contrast to its near neighbor to the south. In a Security Report released in 2002 by Canada's Security and Intelligence agency, it was stated that there were more terrorist organizations active in Canada, with the possible exception of the United States, than anywhere else in the world. There are believed to be more than forty such organizations that, although not directly involved with violence within Canada, are involved in terror-related activities, including fund-raising; lobbying through front organizations; providing support for terrorist operations abroad; procuring weapons and material; intimidating and manipulating immigrant communities in Canada, such as Tamil/Sri Lankan migrants in Toronto; and, the obvious concern to the United States, the facilitating of access to the United States.

In this chapter, we will discuss the multicultural nature of Canada, and how weak immigration and refugee controls have allowed terrorist groups to plan, coordinate, and attack targets on a global scale. Canada is considered to be the easiest country in the developed world in which to obtain refugee status.

PUERTO RICO

The Commonwealth of Puerto Rico is closely intertwined and associated with the United States. The island's inhabitants possess all the rights and obligations of U.S. citizens, except for the right to vote in U.S. presidential elections and the obligation to pay federal taxes. The United States also governs over the Virgin Islands, Guam, and American Samoa. Puerto Rico is slightly less than three times the size of Rhode Island. The Taino Indians, who inhabited the territory originally, called the island Boriken, or Borinquen (a word that, with various modifications, is still popularly used to designate the people and the island of Puerto Rico). The Taino Indians, who came from South America, inhabited a portion of the island when the Spaniards arrived. While the post-Colombian native language is Spanish, the status of official languages has been a central issue in Puerto Rican education and culture since 1898. Until 1930, U.S. authorities insisted on making English the primary language of instruction in the schools, the intent being to produce English-speaking persons of American culture. But strong resistance to the policy finally brought about a

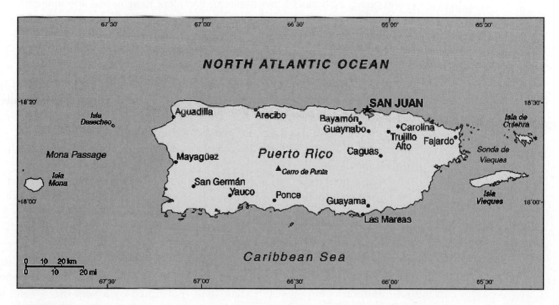

FIGURE 4-1 Map of Puerto Rico (Central Intelligence Agency, *The World Factbook*, 2008).

change to the use of Spanish as the basic school language, with English becoming a second language studied by all students. In 1991, the Puerto Rican legislature, following the lead of the pro-Commonwealth Popular Democratic Party and Governor Hernandez Colon, endorsed a bill that made Spanish the island's official language, thus reversing a 1902 law that gave Spanish and English official recognition. In 1993, pro-statehood Governor Pedro J. Rosello, signed legislation restoring equal status to English and Spanish again for a population of close to 3.9 million. Puerto Rico's population density is 1,100 persons per square mile—among the worlds highest. Only Bangladesh, the Maldives, Barbados, Taiwan, South Korea, and the city-states of Hong Kong and Singapore are more crowded.

It is estimated that some 2 million Puerto Ricans have migrated to the United States over the years. Had these people remained in Puerto Rico, the island would be so densely populated that there would be virtually no room for people to live. Because of the massive migration to mainland United States, more Puerto Ricans are now said to live in New York City than in San Juan.

Besides the slaves imported from Africa (Sudan, Congo, Senegal, Guinea, Sierra Leone, and the Gold, Ivory, and Grain coasts), other ethnic groups brought to work on the plantations joined the island's rich racial mix. Fleeing Simón Bolívar's independence movements in South America, Spanish loyalists fled to Puerto Rico, a fiercely conservative Spanish colony, during the early 1800s. French families also flocked to Puerto Rico from both Louisiana and Haiti. As changing governments or violent revolutions depressed the economies of Scotland and Ireland, many farmers from those countries also journeyed to Puerto Rico in search of a better life.

While Puerto Ricans have had a fairly peaceful existence, they have seen some incidents that were considered terrorism in nature, or close to it. The most notable occurred when a quasi-terrorist group, the **Macheteros,** blew up eleven jet fighters of Puerto Rico's National Guard near San Juan. Ronald Fernandez, professor of sociology and author of ***Los Macheteros: The Violent Struggle for Puerto Rican Independence***, has spent many years researching Puerto Rico. He writes of the Macheteros's frustrations and susceptibility to lashing out:

> On August 25, 1989, Filiberto Ojeda Rios, acting as his own attorney, gave his closing argument to the jury in a U.S. court in San Juan. The indictment, drawn in the name of the United States of America, charged that Ojeda Rios had shot at and assaulted agents of the Federal Bureau of Investigation. President Reagan had appointed the prosecutor, and President Carter, the American flag standing in the courtroom, had appointed the judge, but the jury was all Puerto Rican.
>
> Far from denying his actions, Ojeda Rios embraced them, and asked the jury to uphold the right of the Puerto Rican people to use force in self-defense against the unwanted, foreign presence of the United States. There are no American heroes (in this story), nor is there a happy ending. Yet, it is imperative for Americans to know our own contribution to the perpetuation of colonialism. When the sun rose on October 12, 1992, marking 500 years of colonialism, Americans would have done well to take a look at Puerto Rico and the destruction wrought there in the name of "democracy."
>
> The island today has a per-capita income less than one-half that of Mississippi, the poorest state in the United States. Its rates of suicide, mental illness, drug addiction, crime, alcoholism, and sterilization of women are among the highest in the world.[1]

The hotly contested issue of the eventual status of Puerto Rico continues. In 1991, in an island-wide vote, Puerto Ricans rejected an amendment that would have "reviewed" their commonwealth status. In the referendum, commonwealth status was reaffirmed by a very close vote, with statehood,

788,296 (46.3 percent); commonwealth, 826,326 (48.6 percent); independence, 75,620 (04.4 percent); and nulls, 10,748 (00.7 percent). This issue has caused a lot of tempers to flare up again, but those in opposition fall short of forming newer terrorist groups.

We have seen that the United States still seems to be "the land of the free and the home of the brave." But its very freedom, in a world of terrorism, can be an "Achilles' heel." As the world economic situation continues to destabilize and the American economy stays strong, the gap between those who can get ahead (haves) and those who cannot (have-nots) continues to widen. And, as that gap grows, the disenchanted and disenfranchised of both left and right movements in the United States, and around the globe, will become a more active threat to its peace and tranquility. Chapter 15 will go into great depth on U.S. efforts to provide coordinated and effective homeland security protection for a nation that has felt too secure and, for too long, protected by two oceans, from the fears of international terrorism.

CANADA

In November 2002, Osama bin Laden listed Canada as a state to be attacked by his followers. **Bill C-36** of Canada's Anti-terrorism Act provides the government of Canada with the ability to create a list of "entities." Through Canada's criminal code, the term *entity* is defined as a person or group, trust, partnership, or fund, or an unincorporated association or organization. The government can therefore list an entity as a terrorist organization if it satisfies the following legal test that there are reasonable grounds to believe the entity has

- Knowingly carried out;
- Attempted to carry out;
- Participated in, or facilitated, a terrorist activity.
- Or is knowingly acting on behalf of, at the direction of, or in:
- Association with, an entity that has knowingly carried out, attempted to carry out, participated in or facilitated a terrorist activity.[2]

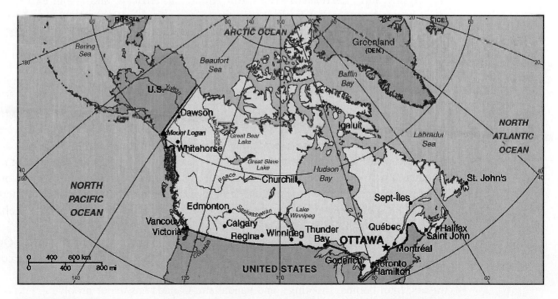

FIGURE 4-2   Map of Canada (Central Intelligence Agency, *The World Factbook*, 2008).

Canada has one of the longest "undefended borders" in the world, but that may not be the case any longer. After the United States declared war on terror, it realized that its northernmost neighbor could pose a threat to U.S. national security—from terrorist groups within Canada's leaky borders. The United Nations Human Development Agency heralds Canada as the best country in which to live. Unfortunately, terrorist elements read UN material as well, and the country has become a haven for terror groups actively campaigning and fund-raising for terrorism around the globe. The undefined border between Canada and the United States no longer exists and, since the horrific terrorist strikes on New York and Washington DC on 9-11, the United States no longer believes the border with Canada can continue to remain undefended. After the attacks, U.S. National Guardsmen were rushed to the border, and the number of border control officers along the 4,000-mile border has more than tripled.[3]

Juliet O'Neill, of the *Ottawa Citizen*, said in 1996, "You're more likely to be struck down by lightning or die in a car crash than find yourself victim of a terrorist attack in Canada."[4] Although that remark might have seemed appropriate at the time, that certainly is not now the case. Canada must assume that it is a prime target for terrorist attacks even if that premise is based solely on an edict from Osama bin Laden. The **FLQ** (Front du Liberation de Quebec) crisis in 1970 was the first time that Canada came face-to-face with terrorist violence. Then, the mid-1980s Armenian attacks on Turkish diplomats in Ottawa occurred. And lastly, Sikh extremists were involved in the crash of an Air India jet that blew up over the coast of Ireland, killing 329 passengers, who were mostly Canadians. This incident occurred in June 1985 on the same day as an explosion in the baggage collection hall at Tokyo Airport from a bag arriving on a Canadian Pacific airliner from Vancouver.

Canada is a nation founded on immigration and, many would say, tolerance as well and, as such, admits more than 300,000 immigrants plus 25,000 asylum seekers a year. Thanks to its very liberal attitudes and policies, Canada does not incarcerate those who claim refugee status. In actual fact, it seldom fails to allow them out into the ethnic communities of Toronto, Montreal, and Vancouver, where they become invisible.

The major concern is that Canada is being used as a base for organizing, fund-raising, consciousness-raising, transport, and logistics for international terrorists from among the many refugees as well as honest immigrants who have come there. These groups range from the Tamil Tigers and Islamic extremists; to Protestant and Irish Catholic paramilitaries, although that threat has significantly decreased; even Latin American, African, and Asian extremists are present. Canada stays on the alert for homegrown terrorism from a list that is referred to as "issue group extremists." Examples of these are animal rights extremists, armed Indians, antiabortion radicals, neo-Fascists, bikers, and skinheads.

Immigration and Canada

The opportunity for terrorists to sneak into the country under the guise of refugees has distinct concerns for Canada's Security and Intelligence Service (CSIS). A report issued by CSIS in 2002 stated, ". . . there were more international terrorist organizations active in Canada than anywhere in the world. This can be attributed to Canada's proximity to the United States . . . and to the fact that Canada is a country built upon immigration, represents a microcosm of the world . . . terrorist groups are present here whose origins lie in regional, ethnic, and nationalist conflicts, including the Israeli-Palestinian one as well as those in Egypt, Algeria, Sudan, Afghanistan, Lebanon, Northern Ireland, the Punjab, Sri Lanka, Turkey, and the former Yugoslavia."

Of course, potential violence and disputes over land and politics—should Quebec someday choose separation in a referendum—are always on the agenda of Canadian counterterrorism agencies. Among tactics used by low-level terrorist groups in recent years are consumer scare threats, mail bombs, shootings, and vandalism. Canada has major problems with illicit production of cannabis for the domestic and U.S. drug market. Use of hydroponics technology permits growers to plant large quantities of high-quality marijuana indoors. With its links to the Far East and a long coastline, Canada has a continuing and growing role as a transit point for heroin and cocaine entering the U.S. market. There are many connections between organized crime and terrorism—while high-quality Canadian hash travels south to the vibrant California markets, the return route brings weapons and cocaine, and thus links to terrorism. The trade in illegal drugs between Canada and the United States is viewed as significant and the terrorist group that may be involved in this trade would likely be the Tamil Tigers with bases of operation in Toronto and Montreal; however, the trafficking of people, which gets little news coverage, is an area of considerable concern to Homeland Security in the United States. As stated earlier, Canada's liberal attitudes to immigration sets the stage for a two-tier system of legality and illegality. Few of the people who traveled here through the conventional system should be regarded with suspicion (although this system is in desperate need of sweeping reforms), while the refugee system is subjected to considerable and unending abuse. Canada's immigration and refugee system needs a very radical overhauling, and the Canadian government appears to recognize that, but few changes have been made to make it happen. Evidence of frontline corruption has been evidenced in Hong Kong and Eastern Bloc countries where Canadian authorities have "failed" to properly verify the backgrounds of immigrant applicants. It would be easy for potential terrorists or their supporters to beat this style of such casual scrutiny. As the past is always so often an indicator of what may happen in the future, we need only look at the threats posed from the failure to check student visas and the abuse that they are subject to. Many of the al Qaeda terrorists who operated so successfully in Europe, and then in the United States, did so on student visas. Canada is certainly no better at screening these applicants than its Western allies, or at tracking down those that have overstayed their visas or welcome. The abuse of the refugee system is one that Canada is currently living with, and yet seems ill prepared to combat with any degree of diligence. During the 1980s, a surge in illegal immigrant activity from India, Sri Lanka, Vietnam, and Cambodia, to mention just a few, saw the Canadian immigration and refugee system under serious assault. False and counterfeit documentation is a central process in people-smuggling operations. Groups of up to twenty will travel through major international airports, possibly being escorted. After they have managed to successfully get by the airline's cursory passport check, the passports or immigration documents are returned to the escort during flight for reuse on the next mission, or are flushed down the aircraft toilets—on arrival in Canada, the undocumented traveller then presents himself or herself to be a refugee claimant. Your authors spent a number of years in the United Kingdom intercepting a large number of these illegal immigrants/refugees during the 1980s, at which time the majority were originating from across the globe and, in many cases, from Sri Lanka, Afghanistan, Saudi Arabia, Somalia, Algeria, and the Sudan. A number of terrorists have been caught entering Canada with false passports—Mokhtar Haouari and Ahmed Ressam both did that in February 1994 (Ressam had arrived in France with a fake Moroccan passport in the name of Nasser Resam in 1993, arrived in Montreal with an altered French passport in the name of Tahar Mejadi, and subsequently traveled to Afghanistan for terrorist training under a Canadian passport to the name of Benni Noris). Mohamed Zeki Mahjoub, a Toronto area convenience store clerk, who is also suspected of being a major "fixer" for Islamic Jihad, came to Canada with a doctored passport. Aynur Saygili, a PKK member, who came to Canada to take over a Kurdish cultural organization, also had a doctored passport when entering Canada.

Babba Khalsa International (BKI) member Iqbal Singh arrived in Canada in 1991 as an undocumented refugee (after hopping through several countries with false documentation).[5]

Front de Liberation du Quebec (FLQ)

Liberal and extreme-thinking young residents of Quebec were eager for change and the right to establish a separate, French-speaking sovereign state within Canada. Terrorism in such a liberal country as Canada has been rare, but the turbulent days of the radical 1960s saw terrorism come to Central Canada in the shape of a separatist movement, the Front de Liberation du Quebec (FLQ).

From its beginnings in 1963, its goal was the separation of the Province of Quebec from what is termed English-speaking Canada. Canada is part of the British Commonwealth and therefore pays allegiance to the Crown. In the 1960s, French-speaking Quebec wanted separation to create its own sovereign country within Canada. The debate on separation and sovereignty still continues to this day. In the 1960s, the left-wing FLQ espoused a workers' revolution as a means of achieving its goal. The FLQ, along with many French-speaking Canadians, strongly resented the control that English Canadians exerted on both politics and the economy in the Province of Quebec. The Parti Quebecois, still a political party today, has actively pursued an agenda of separation.

The political boost that the FLQ needed came from an unexpected direction. On a visit to Montreal in 1967, the President of France, General Charles De Gaulle, in what has become a famous speech, ended with the phrase, "Vive le Quebec Libre" (Long live free Quebec). Throughout the 1960s, the FLQ targeted Anglophile areas of Montreal for bomb attacks.[6]

More than 200 explosions took place between 1963 and 1970, with the Quebec government, and even the Canadian federal government, seemingly powerless to intervene. The FLQ used robberies in the traditional fashion of financing their operations and also as a reason to hit any Anglophile businesses. The major terrorist event that spelled the end for the FLQ was the kidnapping of the British Trade Commissioner, James Cross, and the Province of Quebec's Labor Minister, Pierre Laporte. The kidnapping produced little value to the FLQ but gave the Prime Minister at the time, Pierre Trudeau, the reason he needed to use a firmer hand against all subversive elements, not only in Quebec, but throughout the rest of Canada. The two VIPs were kidnapped in October 1970. The dead body of Laporte was found days later in the trunk of a car. All Canadians were appalled that the FLQ would go to such drastic lengths. The brutal murder turned public and political opinion sharply against the group. James Cross was located in a suburb of Montreal by the Royal Canadian Mounted Police (RCMP). After protracted negotiations, the kidnappers were allowed to fly to Cuba in exchange for the release of James Cross. They had also demanded the release of colleagues serving prison sentences for FLQ offenses, but these demands were never met. One of the founder members of the FLQ, Raymond Villeneuve, was convicted of planting a number of bombs and was sentenced to twelve years in prison. A national referendum held in Canada in October 1995 saw a narrow defeat for the separation movement; however, by then Villenueve had been released from prison and was again assisting with a new, younger breed of Quebec separatists, also hell-bent on tearing up the Canadian Constitution. The Movement de Liberation Nationale du Quebec is deemed extremely small with only a couple of dozen die-hard activists, and consists of some former militant members of the now-defunct FLQ.[7] This terrorist movement, the only one of note in normally reserved and peaceful Canada, has shown that this country is not immune to such social violence.

INTERNATIONAL TERRORISM—SIKH TERRORISM

Canada has had an official multicultural policy since 1971, which in so many regions has had the negative effect of ghettoizing non-English speaking communities in the major Canadian cities of Montreal, Toronto, and Vancouver. Canada has been home to numerous generations of hardworking Sikh immigrants for most of the twentieth century, but it was political events and actions of Indian Prime Minster Indira Gandhi that was to have a profound effect on Sikhs and Canadian security services. Gandhi had been convicted of corruption in 1975, but had steadfastly refused to resign. Following more than a year of emergency rule, Gandhi was defeated in the country's next General Election. Dirty politics were then to be the name of the political game and, in order to return to political dominance, Gandhi needed to target the alliance between the party that represented Sikh interests and the Hindu party in the Punjab region. **Akali Dal** (AD), which represented those Sikh interests, had to be seriously undermined by the Gandhi political machine. Financing of all Sikh temples in India was controlled by the Shiromani Gurdawara Pradbandhk Committee (SGPC), an organization that was also backing the Akali Dal party. The temples were fabulously wealthy, not to mention influential, and having control and influence with the temples meant power. Gandhi and her political party determined to undermine the AD by supporting and promoting a more radical Sikh movement. The intent of Gandhi's Congress Party was to show AD simply as soft supporters of Sikh ideals. The man targeted to lead the political embarrassment of AD was the now infamous **Jarnail Singh Bhindranwale**; at the time he was relatively unknown but, nonetheless, a popular religious leader. The Congress Party helped promote a new Punjab-based Sikh party, the **Dal Khalsa** (party of the pure), for Bhindranwale. The Congress Party was also aware that Bhindranwale was a powerful advocate for an independent Sikh homeland and was not immune from using violence to achieve his goals. Bhindranwale quickly established his religious standing and manipulated the various Sikh teachings to his own ends, and through this evolved a dedicated armed following of his ideals. By the start of the 1980s, the Dal Khalsa movement was implicated in several murders of religious opponents, and it was now clear to most political observers that Indira Gandhi and the Congress Party had lost what little control they thought they may have exercised over Bhindranwale and his Dal Khalsa movement. Dal Khalsa had begun to establish training camps at some of the Sikh temples, and formed an alliance with the All India Sikh Students Federation, which had a violent history in its own struggle to determine a separate Sikh state.

Numerous failed attempts by the Indian Government's intelligence service to infiltrate Dal Khalsa accounted for the deaths of more than 100 operatives from the security services. Subsequently, the central government took control of the state of Punjab and, in retaliation, the Dal Khalsa movement took control of the Golden Temple, with several hundred of its armed militants. The Sikh religion holds the Temple as its Holiest of Temples and central to the religion. Indian security police surrounded the temple in an Operation named **Operation Blue Star** in June 1984 and demanded that Bhindranwale surrender. He refused and was killed during the fierce assault that followed. The number of those killed in the assault included many innocent pilgrims, and, although the death toll has never been confirmed, it is believed to have run to several thousand. Bhindranwale's Dal Khalsa movement had attracted global support in Sikh communities that were in favor of an independent Sikh homeland, and none more so than Dal Khalsa members in British Columbia. The assault on the Golden Temple in Amritsar gave the Sikh radical element all the legitimacy they required. The temple storming gave rise to Sikh extremism in Canada and many street protests in Vancouver; Canada's Pacific coast turned violent. Moderate Sikhs within the Sikh community were attacked and beaten, and although demonstrations were observed by the police, they failed to take any actions or sanctions, and the beatings went unprosecuted. On October 31, 1984, two of Indira Gandhi's Sikh bodyguards attacked and killed her, blaming her for the desecration of the Golden Temple. Rioting ensued throughout India, and many Sikhs fled to the safer Punjab area. In Western Canada, among the Babbar Khalsa International movement, there was elation. However, the Sikh extremists were planning another attack against the Indian Government.

Babbar Khalsa (BK)

The Babbar Khalsa was founded in India in 1978. Originally, its founder, Sukhdev Singh Dasuwal, was a follower of Bhindranwale, but he broke away to form his own group and later tried to kill Bhindranwale. Within several years, branches of the BK were established in a number of Western countries, being most active in Canada and Britain. Outside India, they operate as the Babbar Khalsa International (BKI). The BK was present at the Golden Temple in June of 1984 with Bhindranwale and his armed followers. A number of Babbars left only days before the assault on the holy complex, putting inter-group rivalries above the defence of the temple.

Philosophically, the Babbars concentrated on changing or, more accurately, controlling the lifestyles of individual Sikhs, and were never hesitant about using violence and murder as a way of enforcing a strict fundamentalist code of discipline. So strict are they in the interpretation of Sikh doctrine and practices, that observers have often noted their similarity to a religious cult. By the early 1990s, the Canadian-based Talwinder Singh Parmar had broken away from the BKI and formed the Azad Babbar Khalsa ("Independent Babbar Khalsa").[8]

Sikh extremists were to become a major concern to **Canada's Security and Intelligence Services (CSIS)**. The Air India disaster, which claimed more than 300 lives, was the single-largest loss of life to aircraft terrorism prior to the attacks on September 11, 2001. Of those who plunged so needlessly into the Irish Sea, 154 were Canadians.

Sikh extremism was not new to Canada, and CSIS was actively watching the various Sikh extremists, particularly in Toronto and Vancouver. Sukhdev Singh Babbar and Talwinder Singh Parmar founded Babbar Khalsa International (BKI). The first cell or unit of BKI, led by Talwinder Parmar, was discovered in Canada in 1981. BKI has branches not only in Canada, but also the United States, France, Germany, Switzerland, and Pakistan. The group's objective is for an independent Sikh state that would be named Khalistan. Parmar was a prime suspect in the Air India bombing, and his associate, Inderjit Singh Reyat, the bomb maker, indicated under interrogation that he had been making a bomb for Parmar for an attack in India. Parmar's rise to significance came after he returned from a trip to India in May 1982. The Indian government requested his extradition for the murder of two police officers in Punjab in November 1981. Parmar remained out of Indian custody, but was detained in Europe in May 1984 just as Operation Blue Star was being mounted by government troops against the Golden Temple in Amritsar, considered to be the holiest of Sikh temples. Followers of Sikh separatist Jarnail Singh Bhindranwale had occupied the temple, and when negotiations between police and the separatists failed, Prime Minister Indira Gandhi ordered troops to clear the temple. The resulting loss of life accounted for 83 soldiers and

FIGURE 4-3 Inderjit Singh Reyat (left) and Talwinder Singh Parmar enter the courthouse in Duncan, BC, on November 8, 1985 (Canadian Press).

490 Bhindranwale followers. Indira Gandhi was to die soon after at the hands of her Sikh body-guards. Almost as if it were a war cry, the attack on the Golden Temple generated significant support across Canada for the Sikh separatist movement, and demonstrations were coordinated from Montreal to Vancouver.

Speaking Out Against Sikh Terrorism

Apart from some very diligent members of the local press, some influential Sikhs have stood up to the extremist Sikh movements in Western Canada—unfortunately the fight has been taken straight to them with devastating consequences. Tara Singh Hayer, Order of British Columbia (OBC), was one such Vancouver businessman who was outspoken against the extremist movement. As a symbol of the struggle for human rights, peace, and freedom of expression, Mr. Hayer paid an enormous personal price for his beliefs. Aware that discrimination thrives on ignorance, Mr. Hayer worked tirelessly to promote understanding between ethnic and cultural groups.

After immigrating to Canada in 1970, he worked as a miner, teacher, truck driver, and a manager of a trucking firm before becoming a full-time journalist. In 1978, he established the community newspaper, The Indo-Canadian Times, and has built it into the leading Punjabi language newspaper in North America.

In August 1988, he survived an attempt on his life, which left him in a wheelchair. Despite this attack, Mr. Hayer has never wavered in his commitment to tolerance, peace, and understanding between cultural communities.

In 1992, he was honored with the Commemorative Medal for the 125th anniversary of Canada and a Certificate of Appreciation from the R.C.M.P. Among his other awards, Mr. Hayer received the Journalist Award from the Municipality of Surrey, a city just south of Vancouver, for courageous and outstanding contribution to Punjabi Journalism in Canada. He also received the International Award of Distinction for Journalism from the International Association of Punjabi Authors and Artists.

Tara Singh Hayer continued, even when faced with violence, to be a voice of moderation and reason.

In the early and mid-1980s, Hayer was affected by the "nationalist fervor" of Sikhs. The aftermath of Operation Blue Star at the Golden Temple in Amritsar made an indignant Hayer a Khalistan supporter. But his mental makeup and liberal mindset did not allow him to remain a Khalistan supporter for long. He was revolted by the violence and mayhem associated with the movement. He returned to the path of moderation. The 1985 explosion on an Air-India plane drew fearless criticism from Hayer. Thereafter, Hayer remained estranged from the Sikh extremists and their supporters in Canada. Tara Hayer was shot to death as he got out of his vehicle and into his wheelchair at his home in Surrey, British Columbia, on November 18, 1998.[9]

News reports showed Parmar inciting crowds in Vancouver with his rhetoric and threats of death to Rajiv Gandhi. By 1985, reports and intelligence from CSIS indicated that a Sikh backlash for the Amritsar attacks was probable but could not specifically identify a target. What was to become the target was the Boeing 747, Air India flight 182 from Montreal to London, which had originated in Vancouver. Parmar returned to India in 1988 and was subsequently shot by Indian police in 1992. After the Air India bombing, Parmar was the prime suspect in the downing of Air India flight 182 as revenge for the Golden Temple attack by the Indian government.[10]

In November 2007, a prominent Liberal politician, Ujjal Dosanjh, called for tougher laws to combat the rise of extremism in Canada. Dosanjh, a former Attorney General and Premier of British Columbia, had himself been the victim of Sikh extremism before and after the Air India bombing. Moderate Sikhs residing in British Columbia endured death threats, physical attacks, and fire bombings from the extreme Sikh movement throughout the 1980s and 1990s. The resulting climate of fear and intimidation was not taken seriously enough by the police or politicians, which paved the way for the Air India bombing. Dosanjh believes that if the authorities had taken action, more witnesses would likely have come forward with more information.[11]

Talwinder Singh Parmar

In March 1984, the Indian government appealed for the extradition of Talwinder Singh Parmar from Canada. The request was refused on the technicality that Canada could not extradite fugitives to a country which did not recognize the Queen as its head of state. In November 1985, the RCMP conducted a raid on the homes of suspected Sikh radicals, Talwinder Singh Parmar, Inderjit Singh Reyat, Surjan Singh Gill, Hardial Singh Johal, and Manmohan Singh. Following the sweep, Parmar and Reyat were arrested on weapons, explosives, and conspiracy offences. The charges against Parmar were dropped owing to lack of evidence. Reyat paid a fine for the weapons' offences, but investigators initially failed to link him to the Air India bombing. Reyat then moved to Coventry, England.[12]

THE BOMBING OF AIR INDIA FLT 182

Two Canadian Sikhs—Ripudaman Singh Malik, a fifty-seven-year-old millionaire businessman, and Ajab Singh Bagri, a Sikh preacher and sawmill worker from the British Columbia interior—were charged with eight counts, including conspiracy to murder, for the downing of Air India. The third conspirator and confident to Talwinder Parmar was Inderjit Singh Reyat, who pleaded guilty in 2003 to manslaughter for supplying the bomb-making materials that destroyed the Air India flight. The court sentenced Reyat to a term of five years in prison following his plea bargain. The Air India investigation and trial has lasted over twenty years. On March 16, 2005, both men were found not guilty on all eight counts in British Columbia Supreme Court and, as a result, were set free. The verdict stunned the British Columbia Sikh community and, likely, divided it as well. It was deemed the worst act of terrorism in Canadian history: 331 people were killed in two decisive and deliberate explosions—one in a Japanese airport, another aboard Air India flight 182. When Air India was downed, Canada relied on the newly created CSIS for its intellignece gathering, and in the twenty plus years since then, the Canadian Security Intelligence Service has been at the forefront of this investigation along with the RCMP. There have been claims of interference and total mismanagement of the entire case, and for over twenty years Canadians have grappled with this unsolved crime for which no one has yet been brought to justice.

Only one person has so far been sentenced for involvement in this bombing attack. What went wrong? Why and how did these two men manage to be found not guilty? In presiding Judge, Justice Ian Josephson's 600 pages of judgment, he pointed to evidence that was "markedly short" of reasonable doubt. Much of the evidence presented against Malik and Bagri came down to evidence provided by unreliable and often unbelievable witnesses supplying hearsay evidence. There was also condemnation for the actions of CSIS, who had the main suspects under surveillance when they were testing the explosives. CSIS subsequently destroyed surveillance tape evidence. Judge Josephson singled this out as "unacceptable negligence." In addition to the problems of lack of physical evidence, the prosecution called Reyat as one of its star witnesses. The judge found him to have "patently and pathetically fabricated" his testimony. At the end of twenty years, Canada, unfortunately, has little to show for this investigation. The immediate effect of the 1985 disaster was the introduction of the requirement to match passengers with their bags. Of course, where a human element is involved, there is always room for error. The terror scenario played out again in the 1980s with the bombing of a Pan Am 747 aircraft over Lockerbie, Scotland, by agents of Colonel Qaddafi's Libyan regime.

LIBERALISM TOWARD REFUGEES

How Canada accommodates its refugee problems is well documented, and many take extreme advantage of the liberal program that allows convicted terrorists to remain within the safe haven, Canada. One example of abuse of the refugee system is the case of Mahmoud Mohammad, who immigrated to Canada in 1987 with his family from Lebanon. Mohammad is a former member of the Popular Front for the Liberation of Palestine (PFLP) who, in 1968, attacked an El Al aircraft on the tarmac at Athens International Airport. Mohammad and an accomplice fired more than eighty rounds and threw six hand grenades at the aircraft, killing one passenger in the attack. He was sentenced to eighteen years in jail, but was released after only two years when Palestinian terrorists hijacked a Greek airliner and demanded his release. Since then, Mohammad has resided in southern Ontario, having lied on his immigration application. The Canadian Immigration Service has been trying to deport him since 1988. His lawyers argue that he should not be deported owing to his poor health. This is surely democracy working at its very best.

The story of Mahmoud Mohammad is a classic example of why Canada is often seen as such a liberal haven for organizations looking to raise funds without interruption from the government. Canada is one of the few Western governments that did not recognize and list the Tamil Tigers (LTTE) from Sri Lanka as a terrorist organization until a change in government in 2006 saw as one of its first acts a Conservative government listing the Tigers as a "terrorist organization." Thousands of Sri Lankan refugees have come to Canada over the last few decades, and a large number came via Europe on forged passports. As noted earlier, Canada tends not to incarcerate refugees but rather allows them into society until their status hearings take place. In many instances, this can take several years and often results in an amnesty and the granting of landed immigrant status. With Canada's vast numbers of illegal/refugee entrants/claimants, it is virtually impossible to check backgrounds to find out how bona fide the claims really are.

The Liberation Tigers of Tamil Eelam (LTTE) is a violent separatist organization fighting in Sri Lanka. This group has the dubious reputation of being the originators of suicide bombings, as we know them today. The government of Sri Lanka believes that of all funds raised by the LTTE annually (Canadian $120 million), 25 percent originates through funding from front organizations, proceeds of crime, and drug activity, as well as from Tamil residents located in Canada. The LTTE has been associated with trafficking people into Canada on forged travel documents for more than two decades. The resulting influx into Canada has meant that a huge Tamil community has built up, allowing LTTE to levy war taxes on Tamils. When they arrive in Canada, many Tamils find that much of their community life is controlled by LTTE front organizations. In Canada, the term *multiculturalism* is used to define almost anything that is not White and Anglo Saxon to such an extent that the government has funded many of the Tamil Tiger front organizations involved in immigrant settlement services, as well as Tamil media and housing. From a fund-raising point of view, Canada must be seen as a dream location because any opposition voiced publicly is invariably met with claims of racism and intolerance. In 2000, two liberal Cabinet members, including the Finance Minister and former Liberal Prime Minister Paul Martin, attended a fund-raising event for a group identified as a front for the Tamil Tigers. When opposition members questioned the pair about the event in Parliament, the Liberal response was to smear the questioners as racists.[13]

The Case of Omar Khadr

Terrorist organizations require the support of networks able to fund activities in other theaters of conflict—Canada is seen by a host of organizations as a rich breadbasket in which to gather funds, and al Qaeda's support network has been operating effectively through the Khadr family in Ontario, close to the U.S. border. It is believed that millions of dollars have been accrued for the al Qaeda network from within Canada. When the Soviet Union invaded Afghanistan in 1980, Khadr (senior) went to Afghanistan, where he met Osama bin Laden. Khadr became involved with Human Concern International (HCI), which purported to raise funds for refugees from the Afghan war. As a Canadian, Khadr sought out funding to support HCI, and funds were channeled to it from the Canadian government through the International Development Agency (CIDA). Much of the money has gone toward an al Qaeda training camp through offices in Peshawar. Injured in a land mine incident, he returned to Canada in 1992 for medical aid. When he recovered, he returned to Pakistan. There, Pakistani police arrested him in 1995 for his involvement in the car bombing attack of the Egyptian Embassy in Islamabad. Fortune was on Khadr's side—Canada's prime minister at the time, Jean Chretien, interceded personally with the Pakistanis on his behalf. Khadr was released and returned to his now native Canada. After the attacks on 9-11, Khadr disappeared, and nothing was known of him until his fourteen-year-old son Omar was captured after a gun battle in Afghanistan in 2002. It is believed Khadr was killed during the same action. In the attack, Omar hurled a grenade at a U.S. Army medic; the medic subsequently succumbed to his wounds.[14]

The trial for Omar Khadr is currently underway in the United States; however, there is little or no mention at all of the related activities of his immediate family:

- Wife Maha Elsamnah took her then fourteen-year-old son Omar from Canada to Pakistan in 2001 and enrolled him in al Qaeda training.
- Daughter Zaynab, twenty-three, was engaged to one terrorist, and married another al Qaeda member in 1999. Osama bin Laden himself was present at the nuptials. Zaynab endorses the 9-11 atrocities and hopes her infant daughter will die fighting Americans.
- Son Abdullah, is an al Qaeda fugitive who is constantly on the move to elude capture. Canadian Intelligence states he ran an al Qaeda training camp in Afghanistan during the Taliban period, something Abdullah denies.
- Son Abdul Karim, half-paralyzed by wounds sustained in the October 2002 shoot-out that left his father dead, is presently a prisoner in a Pakistani hospital.[15]

The Canadian refugee claimant system is under considerable strain, not to mention abuse from those countries' citizens seeking to implant sleepers for terrorist activities within the country. Some excellent examples of this abuse are readily available. Mohamed Harkat arrived in Canada on a forged Saudi Arabian passport after flying in from Malaysia. He was initially unassuming and found casual work in the Ottawa region of Ontario once his refugee application was granted in 1997. He went on to marry a Canadian woman. Since 1997, he has come under scrutiny from CSIS and is accused of being involved with the al Qaeda in Pakistan and also other Islamist terror groups prior to coming to Canada. In 1994, Abdul Jabarah arrived as a refugee claimant with his family from Kuwait. He is believed to have been recruited by al Qaeda in 1990 and was killed in a police raid in Saudi Arabia in 2003 after his terror cell was involved in a series of truck bombings. Nizar Ben Muhammed Nawar was one of 1300 Tunisian students who entered Montreal in 1999 and immediately dropped out of sight along with more than 100 other students after the 9-11 attacks. He appears to be an al Qaeda recruit who has returned to Tunisia and is actively involved in terror attacks back in his home country. A member of Hizbollah, Omar el Sayed was arrested in Edmonton, Alberta; he had entered Canada on a forged Dutch passport in 1998. He was arrested for possession of fake identification papers, and was wanted on drugs and weapons charges in Germany. A judge allowed him out on bail in 2002 and he very quickly disappeared. Canada's relaxed approach, if that is the correct phrase to use, dates back to the 1951 United Nations Convention of Refugees which, in simple terms, defined a refugee as someone escaping a country and having a well-founded fear that they would be prosecuted for their beliefs if they were to be returned to their home state. No defined policy on refugees existed in Canada until the late 1960s as, until then, it was supposed that it would be dealing with European refugees from the World War II; however, Canada accepted around 3,000 refugees per year between 1960 and 1979, and from 1979 to 1998 that figure changed to almost 25,000 accepted refugee claims per year. Canada sees itself as a predominantly liberal state founded on immigration, to a certain degree; and of course Canada's relaxed approach and its almost open-door policy on refugees opened the flood gates—while the vast majority settled well in Canada, there were those that came for different reasons and used Canada's liberalism to help fund their stay in the country. In a 1985 legal challenge in Regina *v.* Singh, a soon-to-be-deported Singh, who was being deported for his ties to Sikh terrorism, successfully argued that Canada's Charter of Rights and Freedoms extended to applicants such as him, and he was in fact entitled to the same rights and freedoms as any Canadian citizen. This meant that however weak or ridiculous the case, every case had to be heard, and since mostly all refugees could claim indigence, they were entitled to have their case or cases publicly funded by the Canadian taxpayer. Overnight, a legal system sprang up to support the needs of refugee claimants with the bill being paid for by Canadians.

CUBA

The Republic of Cuba is situated on an island and is the largest country in the Caribbean. It is located between the Caribbean Sea and the North Atlantic Ocean, just ninety miles south of Florida, and is slightly smaller than Pennsylvania. The United States leases the U.S. Naval Base at Guantanamo Bay. The base remains a geographical part of Cuba, and only mutual agreement of the two nations or U.S. abandonment of the area can terminate the lease. This has been a serious bone of contention in U.S./Cuban relations for decades. The population of this communist state is almost 11 million. Its ethnic makeup is unique and diverse, with 51 percent being Mulatto, 37 percent White, 11 percent Black, and 1 percent Chinese. The state government is the primary player in the Cuban economy and controls practically all foreign trade. The government has undertaken several reforms in recent years to stem excess liquidity, increase labor incentives, and alleviate serious shortages of food, consumer goods, and services. The liberalized agricultural markets introduced in October 1994, where state and private farmers sell above-quota production at unrestricted prices, have broadened legal consumption alternatives and reduced black market prices. Government efforts to lower subsidies to unprofitable enterprises and to shrink the money supply caused the peso's black market value to move from a peak of 120 to the dollar in the summer of 1994 to a low of 20 to 21 to the dollar at the end of 1996. New taxes helped drive down the number of legally registered, self-employed workers from 208,000 in January 1996 to 180,000 by December. Havana announced that GDP declined by 35 percent from 1989 to 1993, the result of lost Soviet aid and domestic inefficiencies. The drop in GDP was turned around in 1994, when Cuba reported a 0.7 percent growth rate. Government officials claimed that GDP increased by 2.5 percent in 1995 and 7.8 percent in 1996. Export earnings rose an estimated 40 percent in 1996 to $2.1 billion. This trend is a good sign that Cuba may be making a move back into the economy of the region. Some say this is largely owing to the strength of increased sugar shipments to Russia and higher nickel production through a joint venture with a Canadian firm. With the economic recovery, imports rose for the second straight year, growing by an estimated 26 percent to $3.5 billion. Despite these moves, however, the economy has dropped again, and living standards for the average Cuban have not improved significantly.

Fidel Castro

Kim Il-Sung, Deng Xiaoping, Peron, Khrushchev, Kadar, Franco, and Tito are all famous dictators who are long departed. But Fidel Castro remained as the longest-serving leader of any country in the modern world. Castro had all but destroyed his country with iron-fisted leadership, yet managed to stay in power until his resignation due to ill health in February 2008. Born on August 13, 1926, Fidel Castro led a revolt against the Batista dictatorship and became the President of Cuba in 1959. He remained ensconced in his palace in Havana, seemingly as solidly as he was forty years ago. Recent data suggest that nearly half the Cuban workforce is unemployed and that most Cubans live on a bare subsistence of only 1,400 calories a day. Foreign investment, which peaked at $563 million in 1994, was probably as low as $30 million in 1998. Part of this decline was owing to the fall of the Soviet Union. Worst of all, Cuba has lost its long-held position as the world's largest producer of sugar. Barely 3 million tons are being produced a year—an all-time low.

Castro was a "classic" dictator in that he emerged not from the historical center of his society but from its physical and moral peripheries. His father was a rough and deceitful "Gallego" from the impoverished north of Spain. Like Napoleon the Corsican, Hitler the Austrian, and Stalin the Georgian, who came from similar difficult backgrounds, Castro has a perversely captivating combination of seductiveness and violence. As a boy, he tried to burn down his parents' house and burn up his father's car. Legend says that young Fidel would regularly hang over a canyon while the trains thundered by. Above all, he was always the perfect Machiavellian, naturally mastering every technique of political, physical, and psychological manipulation over the Cuban people, his troops, and leaders around the world.

When he was at the Jesuit high school, Castro was fascinated with reading about the European Fascists. From Mussolini, he took the Italian's hysterical rhetorical gestures. From Hitler, he borrowed the Austrian's lessons in the sociology of revolution. Hitler had created a power base from the alienated and devastated German lower classes. Castro created his own base from poor workers and farmers. And so, once he marched into Havana in January of 1959, Castro immediately began using his unique system of revolutionary control. He brought down the upper classes, and then the middle classes, by seizing their lands and removing their privileges, or by simply terrorizing them. He managed to remove any competitors to power, either by sending them to places where they would surely die (**Che Guevara** in Bolivia, 1967; Frank Pais on the streets of revolutionary Santiago de Cuba, 1957) or, when that did not work, by executing them (General Ochoa in Havana, 1989). Meanwhile, his military and intelligence organizations assured, and still assure, his physical control over the island. Castro has been extraordinarily adept at using the traditional Cuban fear of the "Miami Cubans" and the hated "Americanos" to hold his own people ignorant and in check.[16]

"Hatred is an element of struggle; relentless hatred of the enemy that impels us over and beyond the natural limitations of man and transforms us into effective, violent, selective, and cold killing machines. Our soldiers must be thus; a people without hatred cannot vanquish a brutal enemy."

Thus spoke Che Guevara in 1967. Guevara was one of the most radical of Castro's entourage who was, as mentioned earlier, sent by Fidel to die in Bolivia. Guevara used hatred or, as he put it, "relentless hatred" to "impel us over and beyond the natural limitations of man." This use of hatred to encourage the dehumanization of one's enemy is but another manifestation of the doctrine found throughout the centuries to justify mass murder and torture. It has been used to apparently great success in Cuba, keeping Castro in power for more than forty years.

THE DOMINICAN REPUBLIC AND HAITI

These two small countries share an island and have been involved in strife, war, rebellion, and terrorism in the Caribbean to some extent, although minor. We shall examine them briefly as a possible source of future problems in that region. First we look at the Dominican Republic.

The Dominican Republic

Noted more for its major league baseball players in the United States, the Dominican Republic is located on the eastern two-thirds of the island of Hispaniola, between the Caribbean Sea and the North Atlantic Ocean. Haiti borders it. It is slightly more than twice the size of New Hampshire, with a population of about 7.9 million. The ethnic mix is a reflection of past developments, with Whites, 16 percent; Blacks, 11 percent; and mixed races, 73 percent. The population is 95 percent Roman Catholic.

Economic reforms launched in late 1994 contributed to exchange rate stabilization, reduced inflation, and strong GDP growth in 1995–1996. In 1996, there was increased mineral and petroleum exploration; a new investment law that allows for repatriation of capital dividends, has drawn more investment to the island. President Leonel Fernandez Reyna, who came to power in August 1996, inherited a trouble-ridden economy hampered by a pressured peso; a large external debt; nearly bankrupt, state-owned enterprises; and a manufacturing sector hindered by daily power outages. In December, Fernandez presented a bold economic reform package—including such reforms as the devaluation of the peso, income tax cuts, a 50 percent increase in sales taxes, reduced import tariffs, and increased gasoline prices—in an attempt to create a market-oriented economy that can compete internationally. The legislature, however, has been slow to act on several of the economic measures. The Dominican per-capita purchasing power is $3,670—three times that of its neighbor, Haiti. The Dominican Republic has been very quiet in the wake of the events of 9-11 and seems to be satisfied with staying out of the kinds of conflicts it has engaged in the past.

The Republic of Haiti

The Republic of Haiti occupies the western one-third of the island of Hispaniola, bordering on the west of the Dominican Republic. It is slightly smaller than Maryland and has a population that is predominately Black (95 percent), with Mulattos and Whites making up 5 percent. These more than 6.5 million people are crowded into one-half the land space of their neighbor, the Dominican Republic. Haitians are predominately Roman Catholic (80 percent), and an overwhelming majority also practices voodoo.

Haiti is clearly one of the poorest countries in the world. About 75 percent of the Haitian population lives in abject poverty. Nearly 70 percent of all Haitians depend on the agriculture sector, which consists mainly of small-scale, subsistence farming, and employs about two-thirds of the economically active workforce. The country has experienced little or no job creation since President Rene Preval took office in February 1996. Failures to reach agreements with international sponsors have denied Haiti badly needed budget and development assistance. Meeting aid conditions in 1997 was especially challenging in the face of mounting popular criticism of reforms.

François **Papa Doc** Duvalier was the Absolute Dictator of Haiti from 1957 to 1971. His nickname came from his career as a physician. He became Director General of the Haitian National Public Health Service in 1946, and subsequently served as Minister of Health and of Labor. After opposing Paul Magloire's coup in 1950, he hid in the interior, practicing medicine, until he was granted a general political amnesty in 1956. In 1957, with army backing, "Papa Doc" was overwhelmingly elected president. Reelected in a sham election in 1961, he declared himself "President for Life" in 1964. His regime, the longest in Haiti's history, was a brutal reign of terror; political opponents were summarily executed, and the notorious Tonton Macoutes (secret police) kept the populace in a state of abject terror and fear. Under Duvalier, the economy of Haiti continued to deteriorate, and the illiteracy rate remained at about 90 percent. Duvalier nevertheless maintained his hold over Haiti. His practice of voodooism encouraged rumors among the people that he possessed supernatural powers. He died in 1971, after arranging for his son, Jean-Claude ("Baby Doc"), to succeed him.

Jean-Bertrand Aristide became president of Haiti in December 1990, elected in a landslide, only to be ousted seven months after taking office. He went into exile in Venezuela and later the United States. Three years later, a 20,000-member U.S.-led multinational force intervened to forcibly disband the army and restore Aristide to power.

President Aristide was a radical Catholic priest who defended liberation theology. He worked among Haiti's poor and was part of a group of progressive priests who opposed the Duvalier dictatorship. Expelled from his religious order in 1988 because of his revolutionary teachings, he became the candidate of a coalition of leftist parties in the 1990 presidential elections and was elected with an overwhelming majority. Party infighting plagued Aristide toward the end of his five-year term; however, and continued for the new administration of Rene Preval, who took over in February 1998.[17] In the relative safety of the new UN-protected Haiti, Aristide recently launched a new umbrella movement to invigorate and unify the governing Lavalas coalition. Many Haitians still had hopes of seeing Aristide back in the National Palace in the year 2000. Aristide has insisted that his latest efforts are not a challenge to Preval, a friend and activist whom he belatedly endorsed for president in 2002. By law, Aristide could not seek a consecutive term as president of Haiti.

To emphasize that the appearance of safety in this battered nation is not necessarily reality, in 1998 unknown gunmen opened fire on the National Palace and police headquarters in the latest apparent effort to try to destabilize Haiti's new government. At least one person was killed, a civilian working at the police station, and a policeman was slightly injured. UN soldiers and Haitian police officers returned fire, but no casualties were reported. UN helicopters also took to the air and patrolled the city. There have been death threats against Preval, former President Aristide, and several liberal Haitian legislators. The distinctive sounds of gunfire ring out almost nightly in Port-au-Prince, the Haitian capital.

Preval has blamed the attacks on soldiers from the army that ousted Aristide in 1991. The army was reformed after an American-led military intervention restored the exiled Aristide in October 1994. Preval also has speculated that the subversion could be connected to his controversial plan to privatize some state-owned enterprises. The fate of this beleaguered, poor, and downtrodden country is far from settled. The state terrorism created by the two despotic Duvaliers, and a combination of violence and voodoo has left a legacy of former state terrorists ready to leap into the vacuum created by the departure of the UN operation. Time will tell if this dire prediction will come to pass.[18]

Summary

Canada, thanks to its liberal policies on immigration and refugees, continues to experience a flood of thousands of "refugees" from Third-World countries. No doubt, many of the refugees are genuine, but some have only escaped from the view of their "oppressive regimes," and continue to foster and promote terrorism from within Canada. The downing of an Air India B747 off the southern coast of the Republic of Ireland on June 22, 1985, which killed 329 people, 82 of them children, was the worst ever single terrorist attack prior to 9-11. Most of the people on board Air India Flight 182 were Canadian citizens. Canada's only previous brush with an organized attack using terror tactics has been Quebec's experience with the FLQ. Whether the cause of separation will see any resurgence of an FLQ-styled organization is not yet apparent. Sporadic problems in the Caribbean and in Cuba continue to flare. Most of the terrorist and insurgent problems in the islands have been as a result of economic downturns, and inefficient and corrupt governments. Cuba remains firmly under the control and dictates of an aging Fidel Castro, and his power continues to dominate in the region as well as covertly influence Latin American states. As the events of 9-11 recede to form part of history, we must expect the new generation of terrorists to come from the ranks of extreme Islam— those terrorists with designs on launching jihad against both Canada and the United States will very likely come from within our own borders. Canada, as a center for terrorism support and financing, is a continuing problem as it relates to the expatriate Tamil community. Britain, as we shall see in Chapter 5, has experienced and suffered from attacks by homegrown terrorists, those that immigrated to a new homeland only to repay their adopted country with terror and death.

Web Sites

1. **The Mackenzie Institute**—*www.mackenzieinstitute.com*
2. **MITP Terrorism Knowledge Base**—*www.tkb.org*
3. **Canadian Security and Intelligence Service**— *www.csis-scrs.gc.ca*
4. **Department of Justice—Canada** *www.doj.ca*
5. **Anti-Defamation League**—*http://www.adl.org/ terror/tu/tu_0401_canada.asp*
6. **Ministry of Defense**—*http://www.defence.lk/ new.asp?fname=20080416_03*

Endnotes

1. U.S. Department of State, *Background Notes: Geographic Entities and International Organizations.* http//www. state.com.
2. *Canada Gazette*, Part II (June 19, 2003). Published by the Queen's Printer for Canada.
3. John Bissett. Troubled Borders, Canada, The United States and Mexico, John Bissett, former Executive Director Canadian Immigration Services speaking at the 2nd North American Meeting on the Trilateral Commissions New York, November 14–16, 2003.

4. Juliet O'Neill. *The Ottawa Citizen* (August 3, 1996).

5. The Mackenzie Institute.

6. George Rosie. *The Directory of International Terrorism* (New York: Paragon House, 1987, p. 123).

7. Canadian Press. "Neo-FLQ Group to Fight for Breakup." (December 3, 1995).

8. John Thompson is President of the Mackenzie "Overseas Terrorism in Canada" Chapter Two—Terrorism in Canada's History. www.mackenzieinstitute.com.

9. Government of British Columbia. www.protocol.gov.bc.ca.

10. Stewart Bell. *Cold Terror, How Canada Nurtures and Exports Terrorism Around the World.* (Etobicoke: John Wiley and Sons, 2004, p. 19).

11. Kim Bolen, "MP calls for tougher laws to deal with extremists" The National Post November 22, 2007.

12. CBC archives www.cbc.ca.

13. John Thompson. "How the Tigers Came to Canada," *The National Post* (February 28, 2005).

14. Daniel Pipes. "The Khadrs: Canada's First family of Terrorism," *New York Sun* (March 11, 2004).

15. Ibid.

16. Offices of the General Customs Receivership, Santo Domingo (1907). Courtesy National Archives.

17. *The Columbia Encyclopedia*, 5th ed. (New York: Columbia University Press, 1993). Licensed from Inso Corporation. Aristide, Jean-Bertrand. http://bartleby.com.

18. Michael Norton. Associated Press Writer (Port-au-Prince, Haiti, August 19, 1996).

CHAPTER 5

Great Britain and Northern Ireland

I say rejoice, by Allah, London shall be hit.
Posting on Al-Hesbah Jihadist Web site shortly before the
July 2007 attacks

Learning Objectives

The study and review of this chapter will enable you to

1. Describe the organizational structure of Irish terrorist groups;
2. Discuss the sectarian issues that have divided Ireland for over a century;
3. Identify the methods used by the British government to destabilize and confront the Irish terrorists;
4. Discuss the threat that homegrown terrorism poses to the United Kingdom.

Terms to Remember

Abu Hamza al Masri
Antiterrorism Crime and
   Security Act of 2001
Black and Tans
Decommission
Diplock Commission
Good Friday Agreement
H-Blocks
Home Rule Bill

Internment
Irish Free State
Irish National Liberation
   Army (INLA)
Irish Republican Army (IRA)
Operation Crevice
Police Service of Northern
   Ireland

Provisional Irish Republican
   Army (PIRA)
Royal Ulster Constabulary
   (RUC)
Sectarian
Sinn Féin
Troubles

1974—November 2: PIRA places two bombs inside the Mulberry Bush and the Tavern in the Town, two pubs in the center of Birmingham, killing 21, and injuring 160.

2005—July 7: Central London. British suicide bombers with links to Islamist terror groups detonate bombs on three subway trains and one London double-decker bus, killing more than 57 and injuring over 700.

2007—June 29: In the early hours, two cars packed with gas cylinders and nails were found before they could detonate in the nightclub district of central London—the following afternoon, two men in a four-wheel drive jeep ram the passenger terminal at Glasgow airport containing similar materials as the London bombs.

OVERVIEW

Britain has been no stranger to acts of domestic terrorism from Irish terror groups during the last thirty years of the twentieth century. During this same period, successive British governments have allowed an influx of Islamic extremists to enter the country, who have inspired, trained, and funded radical elements to fight jihad abroad and, of course more recently, against their adopted homeland. We will be examining the rise of Islamic extremism in Britain and its effect on British society. This chapter examines what is still considered to be one of the most successful and logistically well-organized and ruthless terror groups of its time—the **Provisional Irish Republican Army (PIRA)**—as well as other terror factions operating in both Northern Ireland and mainland Britain. Attempts to disarm Irish terror groups continued to be a major political challenge for the Labor government of former Prime Minister Tony Blair. The Good Friday Agreement, or Belfast Agreement, signed on Friday April 10, 1998, came as a major sticking point in achieving a measure of independence for Northern Ireland. We will examine how Irish terrorists have turned away from the gun and toward political strategies to attain their goals. We shall also consider whether the events of 9-11 may have exerted influence on the pursuit of peace in Northern Ireland.

FIGURE 5-1 Map of Great Britain and Northern Ireland (Central Intelligence Agency, *The World Factbook*, 2008).

On July 28, 2005, the **Irish Republican Army (IRA)** formally renounced violence and instructed its active units and volunteers to cease all activities and "assist the development of purely political and democratic programmes through exclusively peaceful means." The long-term effects of this on Northern Ireland will be apparent only with the passage of time. Other disaffected splinter groups, both Protestant and Catholic, are also involved in "The Troubles." Of concern to European countries, and to Britain in particular, has been the discovery of foreign terror cells linked with Osama bin Laden. Nearly a decade has elapsed since the suicide attacks in New York and Washington on September 11, 2001, and Great Britain, the United States' staunchest ally in the "War on Terror," has gone to draconian lengths to deter and defeat the rise of Islamic extremism within its shores. This chapter examines the rise of Islamic extremism in Britain, reviewing the measures being taken to limit and track down those that have become involved with suspected al Qaeda terrorist operations. Britain has become a recruiting haven for young Islamic radicals. These connections, in the wider context of the 9-11 attacks and the workings of the al Qaeda network, will also be discussed. Great Britain's "special relationship" with the United States, as well as being its staunchest ally, has made it a specific target for Osama bin Laden's al Qaeda network. The bomb attack outside the British Embassy in Turkey in 2004 was al Qaeda's first specific, targeted attack against British interests. The introduction of new laws aimed at curbing terrorism has meant a tenuous return to an internment process used unsuccessfully in Northern Ireland in the 1970s and early 1980s. As Britons struggled with the realization that a form of Islamic terror had come to its shores, Britons were ill prepared for the reality that the attacks were the work of young British men who were educated and raised in England. The type of terror they were now witnessing was more commonly associated with terror attacks in the Middle East rather than London!

IRELAND: A HISTORY OF PAIN AND TERROR

In the early sixteenth century, James I, the King of England, provided land in areas of Ireland to Scottish settlers in hopes of establishing the Protestant church in Ireland. He hoped to convert the Irish to Protestantism and persuade them to forfeit their lands, thus assuring Protestant ascendancy to the throne of England. James II's inability to work with Parliament and his appointments of Catholics into prominent positions led to both William and Mary, who were staunch Protestants, being "invited" by Parliament to invade England and seize the throne. In November 1688, in what was termed the "Glorious Revolution," William (a Dutchman from the House of Orange), with a predominantly Dutch army, invaded England and was victorious in a bloodless coup. James II was captured while fleeing from London, but William ensured his safe passage to France where he would live in exile. However, by 1689, William III and Mary II coruled England, while James amassed an army in France with which to oppose them.

In 1690, James II,[1] supported by French and Irish armies, fought William III in the famous "Battle of the Boyne." James II was defeated, and Protestant rule then prevailed throughout Ireland. The Protestants were the landowners of Ireland, while the Catholics held on to a tenuous existence, and suffered great deprivations and poverty. To this day, Protestants celebrate the victory of William III over King James II's Catholic army. Orange Lodges (so-called for William of Orange) still hold annual marches and celebrations in the Protestant regions of Ireland on July 12. The first Orange Lodge was founded in Loughhall, County Armagh, in 1795. (See "Protestant Marching Season" for more on this fraternal organization.)

In 1801, the Act of Union resulted in Ireland becoming part of Great Britain, and in 1886, British Prime Minister Gladstone tabled the first **Home Rule Bill** for Ireland. Irish Protestants opposed it. The second Home Rule Bill was then introduced, which resulted in street fighting throughout Ulster.

In 1905, an Irish journalist, Arthur Griffith, founded the political organization called **Sinn Féin** (pronounced Shin Fain), a Gaelic term meaning "we ourselves." The aims of the newly formed Sinn Féin were to aggressively seek Irish self-government. The Irish Republican Brotherhood (IRB), known as the Fenian Movement in the 1850s, was a secret revolutionary group committed to the use of force that wanted total independence from Great Britain, and the formation of an Irish Republic. This group was active in Ireland in the early 1900s. Led by the distinguished Dublin lawyer, Sir Edward Carson, and Captain James Craig, MP (Member of Parliament) for East Down, 471,414 Protestants signed the "Ulster's Solemn League and Covenant" on September 28, 1912, to oppose and resist Home Rule.[2]

In 1914, in spite of strong Protestant opposition, the British Parliament finally passed a Home Rule Bill. However, the outbreak of the World War I of 1914–1918 prevented it from being put into effect. It would be fair to say that the large majority of the Irish people supported the British in the conflict with Germany, but the Republican Movement in Ireland, led by Patrick Pearse, viewed the war as an opportunity to gain total independence from Britain. In Dublin on Easter Monday, 1916, fighting broke out, but was rapidly suppressed by British troops. Fifteen Republicans were executed following the uprising. Michael Collins, who took part in the rising, and would later play such a significant part in coordinating the IRA's military, was imprisoned for a short period for his part in what became known as the "Easter Rebellion." There was little support for the abortive Easter Rebellion, but the prompt execution of the protagonists earned widespread Irish sympathy. Collins was released from prison in 1916; he began to organize the "volunteers," and was successful in infiltrating the Royal Irish Constabulary and gathering valuable intelligence. To counter Collin's activities, the British created a secretive group of operators, tagged as the "Cairo Gang," who were tasked with stopping the infiltrations and "eliminating" the volunteers.

In the general election of 1918, the Republicans, who had already gained control of Sinn Féin, won 73 of the 105 Irish seats in Britain's Parliament. The Republicans never used their "seats" in London, however, and chose to meet, instead, in Dublin. They named themselves the House of Deputies (or Dial Eireann) and, on January 21, 1919, this body declared publicly that all of Ireland was now independent from Britain. The British government passed "The Government of Ireland Act—1920" and officially created two separate countries. The result was wide-scale fighting and terrorism throughout Northern Ireland in 1920 and 1921. As a means of combating "The Troubles" in Ireland, the British government hastily assembled a fighting force, known infamously to this day as the "**Black and Tans**." They are best described as an auxilliary force established to support the Royal Irish Constabulary (RIC), and first recruited in 1920 with members coming from the ranks of returning soldiers from the World War I of 1914–1918. Employed to contain the Irish insurgents, they became synonymous with brutality in efforts to contain the Republican insurgency. They get their nickname from the mixed style of uniform they wore: khaki trousers, and dark vests or shirts. They quickly came to represent the symbol of a harsh British rule and were viewed by Irish Republicans as an army of occupation. Etched into Irish history, the Black and Tans, and the RIC were often involved in reprisal attacks against Republicans. On what became the first "Bloody Sunday," on November 21, 1920, after the IRA killed fourteen British undercover officers, the Black and Tans surrounded a Gaelic football match in Croke Park, Dublin. Shooting broke out, and twelve spectators and players were killed, and sixty wounded.[3] The Black and Tans burned and rampaged through several Irish villages north of Dublin. This not only shocked the British public, but also brought about their recall from Ireland and their subsequent disbanding in July 1921.

The Government of Ireland Act of 1920 divided Ireland into two separate countries (made up of four provinces, Ulster, Munster, Connaught, and Leinster, and comprising thirty-two counties). The six (predominantly Protestant) counties of Ulster in the north would make up Northern Ireland, while the other three counties of Ulster would join with the remaining twenty-three (predominantly Catholic) counties of the other provinces to form Southern Ireland. The counties in the north accepted the Act, and the state of Northern Ireland was formed. However, the Republicans in the South rejected the Act, and fighting broke out between the Irish Republican Army (IRA) and British troops.

In 1921, Britain and the Irish Republicans signed a treaty creating the South as a dominion of Great Britain to be called the **Irish Free State**. There was disagreement between the various and sundry Republican factions. One group led by Eamon de Valera, one of the icons for the IRA, wanted total separation from Britain and a reunification with Northern Ireland. An opposition group led by Michael Collins,[4] and later William Cosgrave, was in favor of the treaty. The Republic of Ireland came into being in 1949 with the passing of the Ireland Act.

In 1922, civil war broke out in Ireland, and the fighting continued until 1923. The warring factions then formed opposing political parties within the Irish Free State. Eamon de Valera became leader of Sinn Féin, and William Cosgrave led the Cumann na nGaedheal Party. Michael Collins was killed in an ambush in West Cork, and the Irish Republican Army (IRA) was outlawed, but it continued to exist, and to harass and attack British interests.

"THE TROUBLES," 1968–1998

There is little doubt that in the early days of "The Troubles" (the term for fighting between Catholics and Protestants), the PIRA was considered to be more of a nuisance than a terrorist threat to the security of a sovereign nation. "The Troubles" began with civil rights marches in Northern Ireland. In October 1968, the newly formed Northern Ireland Civil Rights Association organized a march in Londonderry to show its strength and its frustration at the discrimination by the Protestant majority. The Catholic minority in the North, probably in copycat fashion of the civil rights marches in the United States led by Dr. Martin Luther King, Jr., started marching for better access to jobs, housing, and a fairer share of the economy; sadly, the marches and marchers quickly turned violent and, in an attempt to quell the situation, the British government urged the Northern Ireland Prime Minister Terrence O'Neill to make far-reaching reforms to prevent further outbreaks. The then British Home Secretary, James Callaghan, on seeing the images of violence being broadcast, later wrote, "Ulster had arrived in the headlines."[5] Without the ability to sway the Unionist politicians, however, reforms were doomed to failure. Rioting broke out in the summer of 1969, and the British government sent troops in to restore order and protect the Catholic enclaves. The end of 1970 could count the triggering of 153 bombs and incendiary devices against Protestant businesses in Northern Ireland.

In the thirty-plus years of "The Troubles," more than 3,000 people on both sides of the religious divide have been killed. To place some meaning and dimension to that figure—if one were to do a comparison based population size with a comparable terrorist campaign in the United States, the resulting death toll would have reached over 600,000! The enormity of "The Troubles" should not be minimized, for its effect on several generations has been long lasting and devastating. The first Catholic to die in the "Troubles" was a teenager who was struck on the head by a baton wielded by a member of the RUC during street demonstrations and violence on July 14, 1968.

Religion and discrimination have been the battleground, stemming from centuries of social injustice—a region divided by a clearly dominant Protestant presence over a Catholic minority. This led to discrimination against Irish Catholics in almost every facet of their everyday life, from finding employment to finding housing. For instance, almost exclusively, Protestant members staffed the police service of the day, the **Royal Ulster Constabulary (RUC)**. (Although, it is important to note, the service was always open to the Roman Catholic minority, but those who chose to join were, along with their families, victims of intimidation from within their own community.)

As a result of the The Independent Commission on Policing for Northern Ireland set up in 1998 (more commonly known as the Patten Report), an Act of Parliament—the Police (Northern Ireland) Bill of May 2000, ultimately led to the rebirth of the RUC as the Police Service of Northern

Ireland (PSNI) on November 4, 2001. Now, somewhat divested of its antiterrorism role, it was to be brought back into a more all-encompassing community role.

In addition to the changes made to the police force, other changes finally came into effect at the end of the twentieth century, including the removal of the word "Royal" from the police department's title, as well as other recommendations unpopular with the Unionists, who viewed the change as pandering to the Republican movement.

It is worth noting that while much criticism was leveled at the RUC, the sacrifice made by the men and women who served in the force cannot be overlooked. During the Troubles, 302 officers lost their lives, and many thousands were injured; the force received a vast number of awards and commendations:

- 16 George Medals
- 103 Queens Gallantry Medals
- 111 Queens Commendations.

On April 12, 2000, Her Majesty, the Queen, in presenting the force with the George Cross (awarded for acts of great heroism or for the most conspicuous courage in circumstances of extreme danger) said in part of her speech

> *Due, in no small measure, to the bravery and dedication over the years of the men and women of the Royal Ulster Constabulary, Northern Ireland is now a much more peaceful and stable place in which to live.*

The 1960s were a decade of tumultuous change, with the British Empire giving up its colonies without a fight. Britain had just withdrawn from one of its last colonies—Aden, which is situated in the Persian Gulf—after a total breakdown of law and order achieved through terrorist violence. The IRA concluded that it could topple the British government, which it thought would back down if confronted by the kind of violence that had occurred in Aden. As a result of a split in the ranks of the IRA, the Provisional IRA (PIRA) was formed in 1969 as the clandestine armed wing of Sinn Féin, a legal democratic socialist political movement dedicated to the removal of British forces from Northern Ireland. The Official IRA, which had been in existence at that time for more than forty years, declared a ceasefire in 1972. A further split in the Provisional Movement resulted from the policies of the Sinn Féin leader Gerry Adams between 1994 and 1998. In the fall of 1997, one faction accepted the **Good Friday Agreement**, and the other, a newly formed splinter of PIRA, the Real IRA (or New IRA, as it is sometimes called), continued armed resistance to the British occupation of Northern Ireland. Together with the civil rights issues, and the American debacle in Vietnam, the PIRA aimed to make good use of what it considered positive factors. To the PIRA, Northern Ireland was seen as just another British colony, waiting its turn for independence from the mother country. With this and recent history in mind, the terrorists believed that the killing of British soldiers would very quickly influence the decision-making processes of the British government and public opinion on the mainland.

POLITICAL OBJECTIVES

Before the student/reader can appreciate and understand the kinds of terror campaigns that have been waged by the IRA, PIRA, and Loyalist paramilitaries in the province, it is important to acquire a basic understanding of the political goals of these groups. The IRA of the 1920s was demanding, and continues to demand, one united Ireland, and total separation from the United Kingdom. In support of this, the Nationalists turned to using campaigns of terror. The Easter Uprising was among the first in a long chain of terrorist incidents and acts conducted throughout the twentieth century. To emphasize that point, in the early 1920s, bands of IRA men were relentlessly pursued by the Black and Tans. In the 1960s, Cathal Goulding, the Army Council's Chief of Staff for the IRA, considered and then established a viewpoint toward shifting the IRA away from violence as the only means to achieve its ends. His idea was the formation of both a Catholic and a Protestant workers group, aimed at the overthrow of capitalism and achieving his goal of a united Ireland. As a result, the end of 1969 found a situation rampant with internal disarray and a split in the IRA ranks. Goulding's ideas offended many Catholics who saw themselves as the defenders of the Catholic enclaves of the North, as well as IRA members. When renewed fighting broke out in 1969, following the civil rights marches, the IRA's lack of weaponry rendered it incapable of protecting the northern Catholics. At a special IRA convention held in Dublin in August 1969, it was voted, predominantly by the southerners, to adopt a policy of political activism. Further, it allowed election of Sinn Féin members to both the Dublin and British parliaments. To the men of the North, this was viewed as recognition of partition, or "sleeping with the enemy." Led by Sean McStiofain, the Provisional Irish Republican Army (PIRA) was formed the following month. Rory O'Brady, Leo Martin, Billy McKee, Francis Card, and Seamus Twomey led the PIRA in 1969. They believed that physical violence could solve their political problems. Subsequently, splinter groups were formed from the ranks of the IRA. The PIRA was formed as a splinter group from the IRA as well as a smaller group, the **Irish National Liberation Army (INLA)**.

Sinn Féin,[6] the name of the political party representing the original IRA, was adopted by the splinter Provisionals as their "political wing." Gerry Adams, a prominent civil rights advocate when the Troubles began, had long been suspected as being involved directly with the PIRA Army Council; however, he is responsible for Sinn Féin's rise to prominence and power over the past three-plus decades as the political party that will achieve the goal of separation. A sense of fear surrounds the Sinn Féin party, in truth, because so many of its members have gravitated from the ranks of the PIRA and its active service units. The PIRA has used terror campaigns to great effect in Northern Ireland against its Protestant neighbors, members of British Army units, and the predominantly Protestant RUC. Sectarian reprisals by Loyalist paramilitaries targeted Catholic families, mainly in Belfast and Londonderry, with Protestant groups targeting innocent civilians purely on the grounds that they were Catholics. PIRA carried out indiscriminate attacks on the British mainland against a broad array of targets. Many were military and government establishments, but the brutal sophistication and indiscriminate nature of the attacks caused death and destruction to the population. Attack targets ranged from pubs frequented by soldiers, to shopping centers, business districts, airports, and the official London residence of the British Prime Minister—10 Downing Street. The objective was to successfully attack British military, political, and economic targets with the aim of undermining the political will of the government, frightening the citizens, and sapping the British economy. The PIRA has also attacked prominent British subjects and, in 1975, assassinated Ross McWhirter, the coauthor of the Guinness Book of Records, who had offered a reward for the capture of IRA terrorists.

The political aims of Sinn Féin/Irish Republican groups continue to be the complete removal of British rule and the establishment of a united Ireland. How could that objective be achieved? In the minds and viewpoints of IRA members of the 1960s, the only way to reach their goal was to wage war. After more than thirty years of "The Troubles," there still is hope for long-lasting peace, but the Irish people ask, "Must it be peace at any price?" The bombs and guns have had the effect of motivating the political leaders on all sides toward a peace agreement. This appears to be achievable—but, again, at what cost? As noted, more than 3,600 people, both military and civilian, have died during the long course of "The Troubles." Groups that have split away from the IRA over the last thirty years to form the Provisional IRA, the Continuity IRA, and the Real IRA, cannot be seen as having lost total contact with the political organization, Sinn Féin.

Protestants believe that both Gerry Adams and Martin McGuiness have had a long association with the IRA and PIRA, and view them as terrorists-turned-politicians. The political "end game" has seen the prominent and eventual rise to political power of both Adams and McGuiness. Both men hold positions of considerable influence in the ongoing negotiations with Britain's Labor government. Both men have been elected to sit in the British House of Commons. However, neither has taken his seat to date, as that would require the men to swear an allegiance to Her Majesty, the Queen of England, an act they view as repugnant. A landmark date for these two men came on January 21, 2002, when they were greeted in London by British Prime Minister Tony Blair and then occupied their new offices in the Palace of Westminster. Although the peace process has achieved a lot, the PIRA has never really "gone away." The tenuous ceasefire has been breached time and again by both the Loyalists and the Republicans, with punishment beatings and attacks. Sinn Féin continues to be seen as the party that can make significant inroads with the mandarins in Westminster. However, during the period since the signing of the peace accord, the Loyalist paramilitaries have not moved their political base and have no real representation in the political arena.

Other paramilitary players have stood for government election in Northern Ireland; during the infamous hunger strikes in 1981, Bobby Sands, a Republican prisoner in the Maze Prison, began his hunger strike "until death". The publicity and press coverage that the prisoners garnered allowed his name to become so prominent that he was nominated to run in a local by–election' however, he died in prison in May the same year, three weeks after being elected as MP for Fermanagh and South Tyrone. A further nine hunger strikers would die in the Maze Prison.

Internment

Modern-day **internment** relates to the attempts to contain the fervent Irish Republican Movement. However, this style had previously been tested from 1939 to 1945 and again from 1956 to 1962. For terrorist organizations to have success, they must first achieve political recognition, or at least gain some kind of special status. When internment was reintroduced on August 9, 1971, it resulted in the rounding up by the British Army of 342 mainly Republican sympathizers drawn from a list supplied

FIGURE 5-2 Sinn Féin Leader Gerry Adams (center) stands at the head of the coffin bearing hunger striker Bobby Sands during the funeral procession to Milltown cemetery, Belfast (Canadian Press).

by the RUC Special Branch. They were placed in detention indefinitely without trial (an ability afforded to the Unionist government of the time under the Special Powers Act, 1922) in an old and disused former Royal Air Force base at Long Kesh outside Belfast. The introduction of internment by Northern Ireland's Prime Minister, Brian Faulkner, did nothing to decrease the levels of violence in Northern Ireland. To the contrary, the violence soon escalated. The rounding up of civilians from Republican areas of Belfast and Londonderry placed more than 400 persons in detention in August 1971, and those numbers swelled to over 900 by 1972. What was remarkable was that no Loyalist suspects were rounded up for internment, but neither were many members of the Provisional IRA, the majority of whom had fled south. The effectiveness of this process soon came into question when it was clear that no significant Republicans were among those interned; however, this may, in part, have been due to poor and outdated intelligence. The deteriorating events in the North led the British government to suspend the Northern government in Stormont Castle and use Direct rule from London. Housed in Long Kesh (renamed the Maze Prison), detainees were incarcerated with convicted paramilitary prisoners. The paramilitary prisoners soon began to demand special status, which, at the time, was applied only to internees. The Republican paramilitary prisoners viewed themselves as political prisoners and demanded to be recognized as such. In 1974, the British government, under the direction of the Secretary of State for Northern Ireland, William Whitelaw, granted "Special Category Status" to paramilitary prisoners as well as the internees. Special Category Status gave prisoners the following privileges:

- Freedom of association with others in the prison (previously available only to internees);
- One prison visit per week;
- The option of wearing prison uniforms;
- Weekly food parcels; and
- No requirement to perform prison work.

The Maze Prison became a fertile training ground for Republicans, and with more than 1,000 Special Category prisoners, the ability of prison staff to control their activities soon became questionable, at the very least. Special Category Status was finally ended in 1976 by Merlyn Rees, the Secretary of State. The Maze Prison had constructed new blocks to house Republican prisoners. Their design in the shape of an "H" had them aptly named as the *H-Blocks*. Those prisoners moved to the H-Blocks held that they were political prisoners and not criminals, and therefore had a right to Special Category Status. Their demands were not met, and they escalated their action by refusing to wear prison clothes or to wash. If one looks at the hypocrisies of terrorism (which is mostly oppression committed in the name of freedom), we will see there are several:

- Terrorists unilaterally suspend democracy for their own acts.
- Terrorists expect democratic principles to be fully applied to them if they are captured.
- Terrorists seek special recognition from governments they do not recognize.
- Terrorists avoid mentioning violation of their victims' human rights.[7]

Special Category Status was ended on March 1, 1976, and Republican prisoners were moved into the H-Blocks within the Maze Prison. With their status now revoked, the Republican prisoners took internal action by refusing to wear prison clothing, and wearing only a prison blanket. The prisoners' actions fell on deaf ears of the British government, and, in 1979, that government was being led by "the Iron Lady," Margaret Thatcher. The culminating events of the protests were undoubtedly the hunger strikes and the associated deaths, which made headline news around the world. The hunger strikes ended in October 1981, after which the British government allowed the prisoners to wear their own clothes. Ironically, the Maze Prison was not to be closed down for another nineteen years. After the 1998 Good Friday Agreement, when more than 400 paramilitary prisoners—both Republican and Loyalist—were released, the remaining half-dozen were scattered to different prisons. The Maze Prison was finally closed down in 2000. During the period of internment—August 9, 1971, until December 5, 1975—1,981 people had been detained: 1,874 were Catholic/Republican, and the remaining 107 were Protestant/Loyalist.

The PIRA campaign was operating at full capacity at the beginning of the 1970s; one of the most violent days was in July 1972, when the IRA detonated a total of twenty-seven bombs in Belfast, killing seven and wounding 130 others. The bombs were indiscriminate, and injured both Catholics as well as Protestants.

LOGISTICS AND FINANCING OF TERROR

For the PIRA of the 1970s and beyond to have any success against the British Army, it had to establish and possess a large arsenal of weaponry with which to fight its campaign. The most obvious method of raising funds for terrorist activities had often been bank robberies. (In December 2004, a £26.5 million robbery, the largest in the history of Northern Ireland, from the Northern Bank was attributed by police on both sides of the border to the PIRA.) While this method was used in the early days of the campaign, it was not necessarily the PIRA's only avenue for funds. Terrorism is clearly not just a cost-effective means of political representation at a broad level, but terrorist tactics can be inexpensively implemented in terms of finance. Fertilizers and other commercially available chemical compounds found in household products will, for the foreseeable future, remain part of the basic arsenal of even the most powerful terrorist groups.[8]

The PIRA has been successful in raising funds by committing armed robberies, kidnappings, extortion, money laundering, smuggling, and drug dealing. It also raises funds through foreign aid and legitimate business ventures. Armed robberies and terrorists go hand in hand, and the audaciousness of planning for most of the major robberies in Northern Ireland has been laid at the feet of PIRA. The most spectacular robbery, and possibly the largest in Northern Ireland's history, involved the Northern Bank of Ireland and the theft of more than 20 million pounds-sterling in December 2004. Intelligence pointed toward this being a PIRA operation owing to its sophistication and the amount of planning required to carrying it out. Indications are that armed backup units were in place, should any police units unexpectedly stumble onto the raid. Why would PIRA risk this kind of activity while delicate talks were ongoing with respect to the Peace Accord? From a historic point of view, the PIRA had previously carried out spectacular operations when events such as peace talks involving the British government had to be disrupted or otherwise stalled. For example, shortly after a breakout from the Maze Prison, one of the escapees was part of a PIRA cell that detonated a bomb in the Grand Hotel in Brighton on October 12, 1984. The nighttime bombing (when the explosive was planted at least a month before the event and placed on a long-term timer) was aimed directly at the Conservative government of Margaret Thatcher. Patrick McGee was convicted of planting the bomb in the Grand Hotel three weeks prior. (McGee was released in 1999 as part of the Good Friday Peace Agreement.) The resulting explosion killed five people and injured more than thirty. The PIRA later issued a statement claiming that it had placed the 100-pound bomb in the Grand Hotel:

> *Today we were unlucky, but remember, we only have to be lucky once; you will have to be lucky always. Give Ireland peace and there will be no war.*

Financing also comes from the Northern Aid Committee (NORAID), and from the Friends of Sinn Féin—both fund-raising operations that have operated successfully in the United States.

Kidnapping for ransom, as another method of generating funds, has been used less by the Republican terrorists than we would probably expect. This may well be in part due to the terrorists not wanting to alienate the society within which they live and operate. Most of the notable kidnappings for ransom occurred in the 1970s and involved wealthy industrialists or members of their

FIGURE 5-3 The Grand Hotel, Brighton, with its façade and frontage rebuilt after a massive bomb attack on the Conservative Party Conference held there on October 12, 1984. The Provisional IRA directly targeted the government and ministers of Prime Minister Margaret Thatcher in this attack (Jeremy R. Spindlove).

immediate family. Kidnappings have also involved racehorse stock. In February 1981, Shergar, the British Derby winner, was taken from the Ballymoney Stud Farm. The horse was owned by a syndicate led by the Aga Khan, and although it is believed that no ransom was ever paid by the syndicate, the horse has never been recovered.[9]

Revenues generated and obtained from illegitimate sources have been used to fund the purchase of legitimate business interests in the North, from nightclubs to taxi companies and security companies, to name but a few. Broadening the scale of legitimate business interests allows the terrorists the opportunity to permeate all levels of Northern Ireland society.

Extortion for fund-raising was an early method employed by PIRA in the 1970s. The group demanded money "with clear menace" from local clubs, pubs, and businesses. This evolved into more sophisticated applications when PIRA established legal security companies that businesses would need to hire to protect themselves from threats by Loyalist terror groups. As the years have rolled by, PIRA has managed to skillfully continue less-overt forms of extortion in such a way as to distance itself from the thuggery image, often seen as the hallmark of Loyalist groups. The Ulster Defence Association (UDA) and its methods are often reviled for their thuggery. The public image of this group is that of thugs out for easy money to fund a lavish lifestyle rather than support a political campaign.

It remains unclear just how involved the terrorist groups, both Republicans and Loyalists in the North, have been in the drug trade. Certainly, the PIRA has acted as escorts to certain international drug shipments, but its involvement in the supply chain remains unclear. Anyone wishing to buy drugs in PIRA-controlled neighborhoods would likely need approval from the PIRA leadership. Figures are not currently available in regard to the scale of the drug trade and its specific connection to terrorist activities. There have certainly been punishment beatings, and even killings of citizens, both for drug use and for selling drugs. How far the Loyalists and Republicans have moved into this murky underworld is not clear. But it is safe to assume that, if there is an abundant supply of drugs, this kind of marketing will at some point supply finances for weapons and terrorist activity.

Weapons procurement has been a major project for the PIRA. Its accumulations of weaponry are largely owing to the support it has received from rogue states, none more so than Libya, which has enabled the PIRA to stockpile considerable quantities of weapons, ammunition, and explosives over the last thirty years. Libya and its leader, Colonel Qaddafi, were drawn toward the PIRA most likely as a result of the hunger strike deaths of the ten PIRA members. Libya saw itself as a country that emerged from the yoke of colonialism and had considerable sympathy for the Revolutionary Movement in Northern Ireland. Libya's support of PIRA in the early 1970s is believed to have been to the tune of more than $3 million in hard currency, as well as arms and explosives. One notable incident involved a shipment containing at least five tons of Russian made weapons that was intercepted by Irish authorities in 1974. The shipment was destined for the PIRA and was hidden in the hold of the freighter *Claudia*. Irish authorities intercepted her off the coast of Ireland. The number of prior shipments has never been fully confirmed, but sources believe at least three others successfully reached the terrorists.[10]

Although the IRA had a representative in Tripoli, the relationship began to sour, the amount of the funds dwindled with the seizure of the *Claudia*, and arms shipments from Libya ceased. Libya's interference was seen by both the U.S. government of Ronald Reagan and the British government of Margaret Thatcher as acts of a state that clearly sponsored terrorism. The eventual destabilizing of the Qaddafi regime by whatever means was a likely goal of the CIA under the leadership of William Casey. Libya had been linked to terror attacks in Europe, and increasing numbers of public protests by dissident Libyan exiles were causing embarrassment to the Libyan regime. Bombings of the Libyan Consulate in Germany and the assassination of the Libyan ambassador in Rome in 1984 created a tense atmosphere within Libyan diplomatic missions in Europe. A significant event in April 1984 occurred in central London when a group of vocal anti-Qaddafi supporters demonstrated outside the Libyan Embassy (Libyan Peoples Bureau). While police were in attendance to ensure an orderly atmosphere, automatic gunfire erupted from the Libyan Embassy.

A police officer, WPC Yvonne Fletcher, lay dying in the street. Relations between Britain and Libya, and the United States and Libya, continued to deteriorate when the United States asserted its right to have ships in the Gulf of Sirte, an area claimed as sovereign by the Libyans. In 1986, U.S. warplanes, with cooperation from Britain, bombed Tripoli with the intent of "removing" Qaddafi. Although forbidden by the United States, assassination was clearly on the minds of the politicians at this time. The bombing raid killed more than eighty, including Qaddafi's adopted baby daughter. Qaddafi and PIRA now had a common enemy and enmity—both sides had cause to despise the Thatcher government. The PIRA held Margaret Thatcher responsible for the hunger strikers' deaths in 1981, and Qaddafi held her complicit in the Tripoli bombings. Arms shipments were once again resumed, and PIRA acquired huge shipments of weapons and Czech-made Semtex explosives. In the fall of 1986, 105 tons of weapons arrived from Libya, including 40 general-purpose machine guns; 1,200 AK 47s; 26 Russian-built DHSK heavy-duty machine guns; RPG-7 grenade launchers; and a large quantity of Semtex high exposives.[11]

In one of their more cowardly attacks, the PIRA targeted the British Royal family, and in August 1979, detonated a bomb in a small fishing vessel being operated by Lord Louis Mountbatten, cousin to the Duke of Edinburgh, husband of Queen Elizabeth II. The bomb attack also killed eighty-two-year old Lady Brabourne, mother-in-law to Mountbatten's daughter, and three teenage boys. Lord Mountbatten was seventy-nine years old. On the same day, the PIRA also killed a patrol of eighteen British soldiers in a roadside bombing at Warrenpoint, County Down.

THE IRISH REPUBLICAN ARMY (IRA), OR PROVISIONAL IRISH REPUBLICAN ARMY (PIRA)

Official records do not indicate the exact membership numbers of the many Northern Ireland paramilitary groups, but it is widely believed that the number of IRA members reached a peak of around 1,500 to 2,000 active members in the war-torn years of the 1970s. Membership declined over the next fifteen years until the announced ceasefire in 1994, at which point membership was probably only 300 to 500. Still considered to be one of the most powerful and effective terror organizations of the last century, the IRA traces its roots to the Easter Rebellion of 1916 in what is now the Republic of Ireland, and gets its name from the first "volunteers" who fought for a free Irish State. The birth of the Provisional IRA came when the IRA split in December 1969, between the "Officials" and the "Provisionals." Confusion was rampant, as both organizations had a military wing, the "Official" and "Provisional" IRA, and both had a political wing, the "Official" and "Provisional" Sinn Féin. It was the "Official" IRA that declared a ceasefire in the summer of 1972 and, from then on, the term *IRA* was used for the organization that had developed from the "Provisional" IRA. From a splinter group of a small and badly equipped paramilitary grouping, the "Provisional" IRA developed into a comparatively large, well-financed, well-equipped guerrilla/terrorist organization that has been involved in what it calls "an armed campaign" for almost three decades. The IRA's development of wider connections in countries like Libya, Spain, North America, and South America for logistical and weaponry support expanded it into a truly international terrorist organization.

The IRA has been known to conduct activities outside of Northern Ireland and mainland Britain. It is active in Europe, and has set up safe houses during the early 1990s for operations aimed at military and government targets in the Netherlands, France, and West Germany. Ease of movement and lack of border controls in the Benelux countries made opportunities for movement just that much simpler. Weapons seizures in Europe in the early 1990s and two active service unit (ASU) arrests likely slowed down any advances that PIRA may have contemplated for extensive operations in Europe. The PIRA has more or less observed the ceasefire put in place since the end of the last decade. No doubt, the strong influence of McGuiness and Adams has been brought to bear as Sinn Féin has used its political power base to edge closer to a peaceful solution after thirty long years of violence. In August 2001, the credibility of the PIRA and Sinn Féin was brought into question when Colombian security forces arrested PIRA's head of engineering while he was developing mortars for the Revolutionary Armed Forces of Colombia (FARC) guerillas. Three suspected members of PIRA were arrested on August 11, 2001, at Bogotá's El Dorado International Airport, charged with training FARC in explosives handling and urban terrorist tactics. Of the three Irishmen arrested, one was identified as Niall Connolly, who had been in Latin America for at least a decade, according to Colombian and British officials.

Since 1996, however, Connolly had lived in Havana under the pseudonym David Bracken and acted as the Sinn Féin ambassador to the Fidel Castro government. He reportedly traveled frequently to Venezuela, Panama, Nicaragua, and El Salvador, where he is believed to have established contacts with individuals and groups interested in arms smuggling, drug trafficking, and supporting the FARC's expanding insurgency in Colombia. Sinn Féin denied having any relationship with Connolly or knowledge of his activities in Latin America, but Cuba's Foreign Ministry released a statement on August 17, 2001, stating that Connolly had lived in Cuba for five years as Sinn Féin's Latin America representative.[12] Ulster Unionists feared that the IRA was, on one hand, talking peace and decommissioning, while on the other, conducting training and seeking high-powered weapons. The other two suspects were identified as James "Mortar" Monaghan and Martin McCauley. Monaghan was formerly a member of Sinn Féin's ruling executive body. According to Garda Commissioner, Pat Byrne, both men are experts in the design and manufacture of increasingly effective homemade mortars for use against military and political targets in Northern Ireland and mainland Britain. The two are also skilled in the use of mercury-tilt switches designed to blow up people in cars, and radio-controlled "command" bombs for use against armored vehicles. These are technologies that would have significantly enhanced FARC's explosive-handling capabilities. Remote-controlled explosive devices have been a strong feature of terrorist operations over the last two decades in Northern Ireland, particularly in the border regions.

The U.S. Central Intelligence Agency reportedly supplied the Colombian government with satellite footage of the three suspects training FARC rebels inside a demilitarized zone. Colombian officials have described the FARC–PIRA link as a "business relationship," in which the PIRA trades advanced explosives-handling techniques for illegal drugs, cash, or weapons. The three PIRA men spent three years in jail and were released on condition that they remain in Colombia pending an appeal from the Colombian government of their convictions. They were convicted of training Marxist rebels, in December 2004. The three men have since disappeared, and the Colombians have requested the support of Interpol to track them down. The men could face up to seventeen years in prison.

PIRA members most likely schooled FARC rebels in how to mix high-powered synthetic explosives to extend the range of homemade gas-cylinder mortars. The FARC needed to extend the roughly 400-meter range of its homemade mortars because of better defenses at military compounds built with American assistance. This implies that the guerrillas are considering attacks on compounds, which typically house U.S. military and civilian defense personnel assigned to "Plan Colombia," an antidrug initiative.

Soon after the 9-11 attacks in New York City, David Trimble, the former First Minister of the Northern Ireland Assembly, made the following statement about PIRA's head of engineering in the British Parliament on Thursday, October 4, 2001:

> *Terrorism is terrorism, and requires no further qualification, so could I ask you (the Prime Minister) to reject the spurious distinction some people seek to draw between international and domestic terrorism. . .recent events all show that the Irish Republican Movement is part of an international terrorist network, and that there is still no sign that it is making the changes required by the Belfast Agreement.*[13]

It is not surprising that the PIRA has established itself as one of the most ruthless and well-organized terror groups in history. It has achieved success against significant odds, and the modern day **Troubles** have their origins in the working-class areas of West Belfast and Londonderry, back in 1969.

By the late 1960s and early 1970s, PIRA had changed dramatically in its makeup. By the end of the 1960s, the Catholic minority was under increasing pressure and assault from Protestant gangs. Catholic enclaves had to be protected from Protestant gangs who were burning, shooting, and bombing Catholic housing districts. Born out of necessity and pressure from the authorities, the PIRA evolved from a loosely knit organization to one with a military structure, employing geographically based brigades, battalions, and companies. The PIRA reorganized to form cells based on the continental cellular structure and better adapted to modern-day terrorist activities. Autonomous Active Service Units (ASU) were formed within these cells, and were difficult to penetrate or identify, as each cell had only three to four members. They were given code names and were directed by controllers. It was difficult to operate in the Catholic housing districts of Belfast and Londonderry, as everyone knew everyone else. However, away from Northern Ireland, these cells have proven to be successful paramilitary units in operations against mainland Britain. The PIRA owed much of its success to the effectiveness of the cell system.

As part of its mainland campaign after the collapse of the 1974–1975 ceasefire, it centered a majority of its attacks on London. Londoners were basically unfazed by the bombing campaign and stoically went about their business as usual. The PIRA was always concerned about the activity of the British SAS, and in one now-famous incident, the Balcombe Street siege, the PIRA cell gave up without a fight when news was leaked that the London Metropolitan Police were handing over to the SAS. What had started out as a botched raid on a London restaurant, saw the four-man PIRA team chased down by uniformed police officers. The gang holed up in a residential area, Balcombe Street, and took an elderly couple hostage for six days before surrendering peacefully. The gang was also responsible for the death of Ross McWhirter, and a number of bomb attacks.

CONTINUITY IRISH REPUBLICAN ARMY

The Continuity IRA (CIRA) was a breakaway, or splinter group of Republicans from the mainstream Provisionals. CIRA may have been in existence in the South for several years. In 1986, some of those Republicans attending the Sinn Féin Ard Fheis (party conference) walked out in protest, but they never presented the threat to the organization posed by the dissidents in 1969. The group was led by Ruairí Ó Brádaigh, who went on to form the Republican Sinn Féin, and other veteran activists. Despite the purity of their beliefs, the Ó Brádaigh wing failed to persuade enough Provisionals to join them. The split was small and contained. The fear of reprisals from PIRA was ever-present, and it was years before the Continuity IRA revealed its existence. That, in itself, was a comment on the group's frailty.[14]

DIRECT ACTION AGAINST DRUGS

Sometimes PIRA uses the name Direct Action Against Drugs (DAAD) when it wishes to claim responsibility for certain operational activities in Northern Ireland. It is basically a cover name for the Provisionals, and is not a separate or distinct terror group in the North.

REPUBLICAN SINN FÉIN

The Republican Sinn Féin (RSF) is a breakaway group from Sinn Féin. It formed in 1986. The party decided to end its traditional abstention policy, and those who opposed the move walked out to form the RSF. The group was led by Ruairí Ó Brádaigh, former President of Sinn Féin, and Dáithí Ó Conaill, former Chief of Staff of the Irish Republican Army (IRA). At the 1988 RSF Ard Fheis, or annual conference, the party reaffirmed its support for the "armed struggle." RSF rejected the 1993 Downing Street declaration, and is also squarely against the current peace process. There have been claims that CIRA is, in effect, the military wing of RSF, but RSF leaders have denied this.[15]

REAL IRISH REPUBLICAN ARMY

The Real Irish Republican Army (RIRA) is somewhat smaller in numbers than the PIRA, and estimated at around thirty members. RIRA formed in the fall of 1997 at the time the PIRA was announcing its ceasefire. This breakaway group of Republicans was adamantly against the "peace agreement" and the direction from the Sinn Féin leadership of Gerry Adams. Viewed as one of the most dangerous groups in existence after the Good Friday Agreement, one of its most devastating accomplishments was the bomb attack of the town center of Omagh on August 15, 1998. Twenty-nine civilians were killed in this bombing, and more than 200 were wounded. It was, singly, the worst terrorist attack in Northern Ireland history. Following this atrocity, the group was forced to call a ceasefire. In spite of this, the group remains in existence and gets its support from those not aligned with the peace process. As long as there is a modicum of deadlock and lack of progress, this group is likely to continue to try to sway support away from the PIRA. The Real IRA 2008

New Years Statement published in the Sovereign Nation newspaper is very clear about their intent moving forward:

> The Irish Republican Army will continue to carry out armed attacks against the British military and political apparatus in Ireland, and those who assist in anyway their illegal occupation. Once again the constitutional nationalist and establishment parties are attempting to sell the lie that the RUC/PSNI are a civic police force, and this has been borne out by recent events, that the RUC/PSNI are primarily a political police force whose primary function is to protect British interests in Ireland. It is for this reason that the IRA have carried out a number of attacks against the British police in Ireland, these attacks will continue.

It operates in much the same way as does the PIRA, with bomb attacks on security forces and commercial locations, and targeting mainland Britain. Its leadership includes Bernadette Sands Mckevitt, the sister of Bobby Sands, an PIRA member who died from a hunger strike, and Francie Mackey, a one-time Sinn Féin counselor for Omagh. Its weapons and explosives likely come from PIRA sources, and there is concern that the group is purchasing weapons through Balkan states.

OTHER IRISH TERRORIST GROUPS

Irish National Liberation Army (INLA)

Also known as People's Liberation Army (PLA), People's Republican Army (PRA), and Catholic Reaction Force (CRF), this small terror group is an offshoot of the breakup of the IRA in the late 1960s. The group rejects the ideology of both the official IRA and the Provisional IRA. The INLA is considered more Marxist in orientation than the PIRA. Formed in the early 1970s with a relatively small membership of about thirty, it is headquartered in Dublin. Its goals and activities on the terrorist front were centered in and around Belfast and Londonderry. The group's political objectives were the formation of a thirty-two-county Socialist Republic in Ireland, the forced removal by any means, including violence, of British troops from Northern Ireland, and the overthrow of the elected government of the Republic of Ireland. The INLA expresses its solidarity with other national liberation and terrorist organizations around the world. Its leadership consisted of Harry Flynn, Gerard Steenson, Thomas Power, and Dominic McGlinchey. McGlinchey, Steenson, and Power were all killed in bitter feuding between INLA and the PIRA in the late 1980s. The INLA's most audacious act of terror remains the 1979 assassination of Airey Neeve, the British Conservative Party spokesman on Northern Ireland. Neeve was killed when a powerful bomb destroyed his car as he was leaving the Houses of Parliament in London. He was a highly decorated veteran of World War II and wrote a study of the Nuremberg trials. In his study's final chapter, he was to reflect on the impact the Nuremberg trials had had on his life, and the fight between good and evil; his words are extremely telling: "Before our eyes the problems of race and terrorism are a frightening reminder of Hitler's example. Those who use terror to gain their political ends are the heirs of his Revolution of Destruction however much they may claim to represent opposing doctrines."

This incident marked INLA's first operation outside Ireland. The group was decimated in the 1980s as a result of the "Supergrass" trials. The word supergrass is an outgrowth of an eighteenth-century slang term, copper (meaning *informer*), which rhymed into grasshopper, later shortened to just "grass." "Super" was added to precede "grass" in the late twentieth century to imply informing on a truly grand scale. In the context of Northern Ireland, the Supergrass strategy involved "reforming" terrorists by allowing them to divulge information in court about fellow terrorists and current prisoners in exchange for a new identity in a new country. Police in Northern Ireland used this strategy in the fight against terrorism, and the evidence at that time was admissible in court. Supergrasses were initially responsible for a number of arrests and convictions of Irish terror suspects; the evidence provided was not required to be corroborated. The strategy of this kind of evidence gathering was used throughout the 1980s, but very rarely since then. Uncorroborated testimony is among the more dubious practices in a court of law. These Supergrassers were designated as such by INLA and PIRA militants for those who informed on their former comrades. By the end of the decade, the problems with admission of Supergrass evidence as part of the court process led to the release of many imprisoned INLA and PIRA members. The result—a bloody feud between the INLA and PIRA—killed many militants. INLA still remains brutal and unpredictable. The organization was responsible for the murder of Billy Wright, a Loyalist Protestant and Maze Prison militant, on December 27, 1997. The result of this assassination was a spate of **Sectarian** attacks, in which eight Catholics were murdered. The INLA has been observing a ceasefire since August 1998.

Ulster Volunteer Force

The Ulster Volunteer Force (UVF), a Loyalist paramilitary group, also operates under the names Protestant Action Group and Protestant Action Force. Its current force and numbers are difficult to determine, but as its high point in the 1970s, it is assumed to have had around 1,800 active members. By 2006, that number had dwindled to a significant hard core, but the group still had several hundred supporters. UVF was considered to be the largest of the Loyalist paramilitary organizations. It was formed at the outset of "The Troubles" in 1966. The group took its name from its Irish forefathers—the original UVF was formed in 1912 to oppose, by force, the Home Rule Bill for Ireland. Members of the UVF joined the 36th (Ulster) Division of the British army, and suffered many dead and injured at the Battle of the Somme. As they went over the top that day and charged the enemy lines, the Ulster soldiers shouted, "No surrender," echoing the same cry used by the apprentice boys in the siege of Londonderry of 1688. Over the years, it is believed that more than 40,000 people became members of this organization. Its limited goals are aimed at securing the North's constitutional position within the United Kingdom and to aggressively defend its Protestant heritage.

The endless cycle of violence—tit-for-tat killings and bombings—that has typified Northern Ireland life for more than a quarter of century, can be laid squarely at the doorsteps of both Protestant and Catholic paramilitaries. On many occasions, these groups use different names of ally groups to claim responsibility for attacks. The Loyalist paramilitary groups invariably did not claim specific responsibility for their murders—they moved and operated under various subgroups in their terrorist structure.

The UVF has been responsible for scores of assassinations in Northern Ireland, mostly of innocent Catholics. The UVF leader in the 1960s was Augustus (Gusty) Spence, who killed a Catholic man in a pub on the Shankill Road, Belfast, in June 1966, and was subsequently sentenced to life in prison. The UVF is also credited with the simultaneous bombings of Dublin and Monaghan on May 17, 1974, which killed thirty-three civilians.

Throughout the 1970s, the UVF's main battleground became the Shankill Road area of Belfast and parts of County Antrim. The group was proscribed in 1974, thus making it an illegal organization. The UVF continued its bloody sectarian attacks, killing twelve people in October 1975. Raids by security forces in 1977 saw twenty-six suspects arrested for the killings. Their subsequent convictions resulted in a total of 700 years imprisonment. The decline in the UVF's fortunes came about mostly from informers, whom the British security services were able to skillfully manipulate for information on past attacks, resulting in further arrests and convictions throughout the 1990s. In spite of these setbacks, the UVF continued to attack innocent

Catholics throughout the 1990s. In 1996, a number of disaffected members of the UVF's mid-Ulster brigade formed the Loyalist Volunteer Force (LVF). For its political influence, the Progressive Unionist Party (PUP) is considered as its front in much the same way as Sinn Féin and PIRA.

Along with many other paramilitary groups, the UVF did declare a ceasefire in 1994. Declaring and keeping a ceasefire are two different matters; later in the decade, the UVF was frequently accused of violating the ceasefire agreement. As late as August 2005, the UVF continued its sectarian attacks. Estimates of the level of membership and the size of the arsenal of weapons available to the UVF are difficult to make. The original Ulster Volunteers were founded by Lord Carson in 1912 to act as a militia movement to resist Home Rule. In 1914, the Volunteers smuggled 35,000 rifles into Larne, County Antrim. Later, men of the UVF joined the British Army en masse as the 36th Ulster Division, which suffered huge losses at the Battle of the Somme. Gusty Spence announced that the UVF and the Red Hand Commando would "assume a nonmilitary, civilianized role." The UVF continued to feud with other loyalist group, which caused the British government to announce in 2005 that it no longer recognized the UV's 1994 ceasefire. Since 2005, the group's leadership has attempted to distance the UVF from criminal activities, although with very questionable results. The Independent Monitoring Commission, formed in 2004 to monitor paramilitary organizations in Northern Ireland, in its April 2006 report stated that the UVF remained an active and violent paramilitary organization. By May 2007, with most other groups either out of commission or having declared a permanent ceasefire, the UVF declared that it was renouncing violence and ending its terror campaign. It also stated that it was not disarming but, like the PIRA in the past, was simply putting their weapons and explosives beyond reach. The announcement was made by Gusty Spence, the leader of the UVF.

Ulster Democratic Party (UDP)

The UDP also uses the name Ulster Loyalist Democratic Party (ULDP). The group was formed in 1989 as a political front for the Ulster Defence Association (UDA). The ULDP was the original political mouthpiece of UDA in 1981. This organization had little or no political gains and successes. PIRA assassinated its leader John McMichael with a car bomb at his Lisburn home in December 1987. The UDP strategy was to outwardly portray itself as a distinct political movement, and was not aligned with the UDA; we have seen this with PIRA and Sinn Féin. The government banned membership of UDP in 1992. Under the terms of Section 30(3) of the Northern Ireland Emergency Provisions Act of 1996, the following Loyalist groups were proscribed:

> The Red Hand Commandos
> The Ulster Freedom Fighters
> The Ulster Volunteer Force
> The Ulster Defence Association.

The following are the proscribed Republican groups:

> The Irish Republican Army
> The Irish National Liberation Army
> The Irish Peoples Liberation Organization
> Women's wing of the Irish Republican Army (Cumann na mBan)
> Youth Wing of the Irish Republican Army (Fianna na hEireann)
> Saor Eire (Free Ireland).

The UDP was finally dissolved in November 2001. It seems logical that infighting and disagreement over the Good Friday Agreement was the cause of the disbandment of the organization.

Ulster Defense Association (UDA)/Ulster Freedom Fighters (UFF)

The Ulster Defense Association (UDA) is also considered to be one of the largest Loyalist paramilitary groups in Northern Ireland. The group also uses the name Ulster Freedom Fighters as a cover for its terrorist actions. An abundance of Loyalist defense associations sprang up in the first years of "The Troubles," which saw numerous attacks in the 1970s on Catholics. Members of the UFF claimed responsibility for these attacks, but they were effectively being conducted by UDA members. The two groups can be termed as one. It is hard to understand why the UDA was not proscribed until August 1992. Along with the UVF, the UDA had significant numbers located in Belfast and was a commanding force to either attack Catholics or challenge the British army presence.

The UDA's aim was to create an independent Northern Ireland, both within the European Union and the Commonwealth. To create the correct political mindset, it needed to create a viable political forum, so it formed the New Ulster Political Research Group (NUPRG) in 1978. In June 1981, the Ulster Loyalist Democratic Party (ULDP) was established, replacing the NUPRG. The ULDP also proposed independence for Northern Ireland within the British Commonwealth. The UDA was politically savvy and was able to create a document by 1987 that set out its vision for a new political settlement and structure for the North. In spite of UDA's obvious links with terrorism, the proposal document did receive some favorable reviews from politicians and the British government's Northern Ireland Office. When politics and terrorism are mixed, it is often the case that a terrorist/political leader becomes a target for opposition terrorist groups. The UDA leader in 1987 was John McMichael, who was killed that year by a PIRA bomb. The UDA/UFF continued its attacks on Catholics into the 1990s, and against Republican supporters. Along with other Loyalist paramilitaries, the UDA/UFF joined in the 1994 ceasefire, and members of the Ulster Democratic Party were involved in the multiparty talks in 1996. The Good Friday Agreement remained a political football throughout the remainder of the century. Many groups on both sides were opposed to various sections of the agreement.

UDA/UFF continued a campaign of violence into 2001 not only against Catholics but it also had an internal feud with another Loyalist group—the UVF. This feuding and the sporadic attacks on Catholics culminated in the government declaring that the UDA/UFF, the UVF, and the Loyalist Volunteer Force (LVF) had ended their ceasefires. Sporadic feuding continued within the UDA, and on February 22, 2003, the UDA declared a ceasefire. The LVF was formed in 1996 as a breakaway group from the Loyalist UFF. LVF is a violent, anti-Catholic movement that is strongly opposed to the ceasefire agreement of 1994. Its membership is likely small, and probably accounts for maybe three dozen active members. It was held responsible for a series of sectarian attacks aimed at Catholic civilians. The British government proscribed the LVF in 1997. The LVF was led by Billy "King Rat" Wright. Wright was serving a prison sentence inside Northern Ireland's Maze prison when, allegedly, Republican prisoners from the Irish National Liberation Army (INLA) murdered him on December 27, 1997. As has been the case throughout "The Troubles," no terror act by one side goes without retaliation from the other. In the two weeks following Billy Wright's death, sectarian violence accounted for the murders of eight Catholics by members of the LVF and UFF.

The LVF agreed to a ceasefire in May 1998, but continues to oppose the peace process. Because of its relatively small numbers, this group may have been continuing its sectarian attacks under the cover of other Loyalist groups. In 1998, under the auspices of the Independent International Commission on Decommissioning (IICD), it began to decommission some of its arsenal of weapons. Any weapons and explosives it may have limited access to are likely under the control of other Loyalist groups. It is believed that no other Loyalist terror groups have decommissioned any weapons or explosives; however, the UVF has claimed to put their weapons "beyond reach."

The LVF, at its peak, had around 300 members, and the group has not been credited with carrying out any attacks since February 2003. Billy Wright was "succeeded" by Mark Fulton, a close acquaintance who reportedly idolized the founder of the LVF; Fulton has been described as Wright's hit man and is thought to be personally responsible for over a dozen sectarian murders. While in jail, awaiting trial on charges of conspiracy to murder a rival loyalist, Fulton died of strangulation on June 9, 2002, one month after being replaced as the group's leader, in an apparent suicide. Mark Fulton was found in his jail cell in the isolation wing of the prison with a belt wrapped around his neck.[16]

Red Hand Defenders

The Red Hand Defenders (RHD) formed in late 1998, probably from a group of Loyalist paramilitaries disaffected by the Good Friday Agreement. There has been ongoing speculation that RHD is simply a cover name for UDA and LVF members to carry on their sectarian campaigns. This would be to their benefit, as only those paramilitaries on formal ceasefire were able to benefit from the early prison-release program within the accord. If this is the case, then clearly the RHD is established as a cover and has no real existing members as they would all be considered members of either the UDA or the LVF.

Under the RHD cover name, Catholic attacks continued. During the 1998 marching season, RHD conducted what seems to be a revenge bomb attack, killing an RUC officer. This attack followed the RUC decision to restrict the Orange Order from marching along the Garvaghy Road in Portadown, County Armagh. The RDH has also claimed responsibility for the killing of Rosemary Nelson, a prominent Catholic human rights lawyer, in Lurgan in March 1999. RHD and the Orange Volunteers seemed to surface around the same period, and it is thought that the OV may be another cover for Loyalists.

Orange Volunteers

The Orange Volunteers (OV) is a Protestant Loyalist paramilitary with ties to the Orange Order. The group originated at the outset of "The Troubles." It was at that time second only to the UDA and the UVF in size and support. The group was believed to be inactive by the end of 1980, but its name came up once again in 1998 at the same time as the Red Hand Defenders. Like other paramilitaries of the time, OV was made up of those disaffected by the Good Friday Agreement and is likely closely linked with, if not drawing on, the same membership as the RHD. The operational effectiveness of this "new" group is unsophisticated and has utilized homemade blast bombs (pipe bombs) and hand grenades. It may be that this small group of dissidents is also involved in crime . . . most particularly drug dealing.

TURF WARS

The early 1970s could be described as turf wars among the warring factions of the IRA, the Irish National Liberation Army (INLA), the Ulster Freedom Fighters (UFF), and the Ulster Volunteer Force (UVF). Tit-for-tat murders and revenge killings of both Catholics and Protestants were common, driven mostly by pure hatred.

This was epitomized by the infamous "Shankhill Butchers," a gang of UVF members led by "The Master Butcher" Lenny Murphy, operating in West Belfast with the purpose of intimidating the Catholic community and carrying out merciless, cutthroat killings. In those early days, there was a real struggle for supremacy in the housing districts and ghettos of West Belfast. The feuding was partly ideological and partly material in that they were fighting for control of the criminal rackets in Belfast and Londonderry. Violence within the various terror groups has been carried on as a measure of discipline within the membership. Since the Good Friday Agreement came into force, much of the continued violence has related to criminal activities within the paramilitaries, both Protestants and Catholics.

One Protestant fighter stands out among all others mainly for his audacious attacks against Republicans. In March 1988, the crack British counterrevolutionary warfare unit from the Special Air Service Regiment (SAS) killed three PIRA members on the island of Gibraltar. At the funeral of the three dead PIRA operatives at Milltown Cemetery, with the world's press watching, a man approached the gathering from the road and began to hurl grenades at the assembled Republicans, including Gerry Adams. In the ensuing mayhem, the Protestant Michael Stone was arrested; he was charged and sentenced, and was subsequently released in 2000 under the terms of the Good Friday Agreement. His actions did not end there; in 2006, he single-handedly stormed into the foyer of the Northern Ireland Assembly, waving a handgun and knife, before being tackled by security staff.

Civil Liberty Issues

Civil rights and civil liberty issues in Northern Ireland have aided, confused, and complicated the processes of both peace and terror. In many instances, the British government has used human rights violations as a tool, both legislatively and as a method of controlling the violence in Ulster.

FIGURE 5-4 A mural painted on a street in Belfast, Northern Ireland (Clifford E. Simonsen).

The Catholic marches of the late 1960s sparked the rioting and bloodshed that led to larger and larger troop deployments in Ulster. By the start of the 1970s, the British government had made significant moves to curtail the actions of the paramilitary groups with the introduction of internment. This policy had little strategic effect, but provided PIRA members with tremendous sympathy—they were seen as "martyrs for the cause."

During this period, there was a serious issue of how the courts could, and should, deal with terror organizations in Northern Ireland. By nature, the terror campaign also harassed, coerced, and intimidated court witnesses, juries, and magistrates. The **Diplock Commission**[17] was set up to look at ways of dealing with the legal aspects of controlling a terrorist in a free and democratic society. With the aim of ensuring the safety and integrity of the security forces, and giving them the unfettered ability to bring the terrorists before the courts, the Northern Ireland Emergency Provisions Act was passed in 1973. The measures, seen as draconian, served the security services well. The Act provided for terrorist offenses to be listed as "scheduled" offenses:

- Scheduled offenses were to be tried by a senior judge sitting alone, with more than the rights of appeal;
- Bail was prohibited for scheduled offenses unless granted by the High Court, with stringent conditions attached;
- Persons could be held on police arrests without warrant for seventy-two hours;
- Suspects arrested by the military could be held for four hours;
- Security forces had extensive powers for search and seizure;
- Those arrested for weapons and explosives offenses had the onus of proof reversed for them to prove their innocence; and
- The Secretary of State could issue detention orders from information gathered if the security forces believed the information and evidence to be valid.[18]

The Diplock Courts still remain in force in Northern Ireland, some thirty years after they were established as an "emergency power" to defeat the terrorists. The ongoing consensus of both the government and the judiciary was that the jury system, and the ability to try those charged with scheduled (terrorist) offenses, would be severely hindered through witness or jury intimidation. Sitting judges could also draw inference from the refusal of an accused to speak or give evidence; his silence could therefore be used as an admission of guilt. There is a lower standard of admissibility for confession evidence than that set in other criminal courts. This has given rise to claims that the security forces and police have used highly unethical and degrading methods for "breaking" suspects.

With many convictions for terrorist offenses gathered through this sweeping legislation, the PIRA still managed to make both political and publicity points for its predicament. Once in prison, the terrorist took virtual control of his or her destiny and intimidated prison officers both inside and outside the confines of jail. These laws were adopted in the early 1970s, and since then have undergone frequent reviews and amendments. In 1988, fifteen years after it was enacted, the Prevention of Terrorism Act, designed to give sweeping powers to security forces in Britain, was challenged in the International Court. The provision within the Act to detain terrorist suspects for up to seven days violated the European Convention on Human Rights. In 1999, the Home Secretary announced the establishment of a review group comprising representatives of the Northern Ireland Office, the Northern Ireland Court Service, the Attorney General's Office, the Director of Public Prosecutions (Northern Ireland), and the then Royal Ulster Constabulary. Underlying the work of the review group was the general consensus that normalization should occur as soon as possible, and that the restoration of jury trial would be seen as a normalizing event. In a report to the Secretary of State for Northern Ireland in May 2000, the review concluded that the time was not yet right for an immediate return of jury trial. The principal reason for this was the conclusion that the risk of jury intimidation remained significant.[19]

The Terrorism Act of 2000 came to force in February 2001, and reformed much of the mechanisms and powers dealing specifically with terrorism in Northern Ireland. However, the provisions of this Act extended to all forms of domestic and foreign terrorism within the United Kingdom. Certain provisions of previous terrorism legislation, applicable only to Northern Ireland, could be extended for a maximum of five years. The Act broadened the definition of terrorism to include actions or threats of action that are designed to:

- Influence the government;
- Intimidate the public;
- Advance a political, religious, or idealogical cause;
- Involve serious violence against a person or serious damage to property;
- Endanger a person's life;
- Create a serious risk to the health or safety of the public; or
- Interfere with an electronic system.

Special powers within the Act include special entry, arrest, and search and seizure authority without a warrant under certain circumstances.

Periodic reviews of the emergency powers specifically relating to Northern Ireland have been undertaken. While the perception may well be that life has returned to a level of normalcy, this is not necessarily expressed by the judiciary in its reviews. Examples of the powers available to both police and military forces came from Sections 81 to 88 of the Terrorism Act of 2000, Schedule 5. Lord Berriew, in reviewing the Act, concluded that Section 81 allows a police officer to enter and search any premises if he or she has reasonable suspicion that a person is or has been concerned in the commission, preparation, or instigation of acts of terrorism. Section 82 provides that any police officer may arrest, without warrant, any person he or she has reasonable grounds to suspect is committing, has committed, or is about to commit a scheduled offense, or an offense under the Act that is not a scheduled offense, and may enter and search any premises or other place for that purpose. Section 82(3) empowers a police officer to seize and retain anything that he or she suspects is being, has been, or is intended to be used in the commission of a scheduled offense. Section 83 provides a power of arrest and detention for a period not exceeding four hours to a member of Her Majesty's Forces on duty who reasonably suspects that a person is committing, has committed, or is about to commit any offense, together with corresponding powers of entry and seizure.

This Act was further supported with the enactment of the **Antiterrorism Crime and Security Act of 2001**, which addressed terrorism and foreign nationals. Civil rights movements have objected to provisions in both of these Acts, specifically in sections where the burden of proof is reversed in suspected terrorism cases. In reflecting on 9-11, the legislation was also aimed at those Britons involved with attacks overseas. For instance, the British press reported that in December 2000, a British Muslim from Birmingham, England, was alleged to have conducted a suicide attack on an Indian army barrack in Srinagar; in another, a Briton was reportedly plotting a terrorist attack, earlier the same year, against Israel.

PROTESTANT MARCHING SEASON

The Reverend Ian Paisley

Ian Paisley has been the charismatic face of Protestant reaction to Republicanism (Catholics). In Northern Ireland, he is the leader of the Democratic Unionist Party of Northern Ireland and Moderator of the Free Presbyterian Church. As the vocal and popular face of the Unionist movement, he was often sentenced for unlawful assembly as he conducted marches and protests around the province in the years leading up to the "Troubles". He even coined a battle cry first heard at the siege of Londonderry in 1688, "No surrender", when thirteen apprentice boys closed the gates of the city on the Jacobite army. In his hard-line Protestantism, he loudly proclaimed opposition to any and every concession offered to the Catholic community in Northern Ireland. He was an outspoken opponent of the Good Friday Agreement. However, in 2007, Ian Paisley was sworn in at Stormont Castle as Northern Ireland's First Minister, and was photographed alongside the other senior member of the power-sharing executive and his old arch enemy, Martin McGuiness from Sinn Féin. With the guns silent and politics the order of the day, Paisley announced he would retire from politics in March 2008.

The Loyalists, including the entire Orange Order, were determined not to be part of any Republic. It seems almost incredible to people outside the Province of Northern Ireland that the act of marching, seemingly so irrelevant to most, should cause such widespread anger and revulsion. Marching in almost military style has been a part of Protestant history in the North for over 200 years. The lore and beliefs have been passed from generation to generation. To understand what motivates such sectarian hatred between the Catholics and Protestant communities requires a review of the historical roots of marching.

Marching season is the time between Easter Monday and the end of September, when more than 2,000 parades and marches are held throughout the North. There are, however, specific march dates in history that create more flashpoints on the calendar than do other marches. The Protestants celebrate the victory of Protestant King William over Catholic King James I at the Battle of the Boyne, on July 12, 1690. But, there is more than just the celebration of a victory. To the Protestant Orangemen, it is the need to display their undying allegiance to the Crown and Protestantism. Sometimes referred to as "Orangeism," it could also be described as Ulster Unionism on the march. The Orange Order and the Ulster Unionist Council constitute an integrated political movement that is determined that Northern Ireland will remain within the United Kingdom along with England, Scotland, and Wales, and will never be absorbed by a Catholic-dominated, all-Ireland republic.[20] Both the Orange Order and the Apprentice Boys say that marching is an essential part of their Protestant culture. The Apprentice Boys is a Loyalist organization similar to the Orange Order. This group holds an annual commemoration of the ending of the 105-day siege of Londonderry in 1688. The Apprentice Boys march with a crimson flag first carried by Protestant supporters of William of Orange who were besieged in Londonderry by an Irish Jacobite army.

The challenges to peace during marching season are many, as the marchers wind their way through long-established routes in Catholic strongholds such as the Garvaghy Road in Portadown and the Lower Ormeau Road in Belfast. Both areas have been rife with outbursts of violence in recent years. The Independent Commission on Policing in Northern Ireland made a recommendation in 1998 that it should be a condition for the approval of a parade that the organizers provide their own marshals. Further, the organizers and the police should work together to plan the policing of such events. This should include, as appropriate, representatives of the neighborhoods involved along the parade route. Whether this can happen in reality, time alone will tell. The Catholic communities, through which Protestants demand the right to march, have so much hostility to marching because it would take but one small incident to provoke an outbreak of serious sectarian violence.

The Loyal Orange Institution, or Orange Order, was founded in 1795 after a Protestant victory at Loughgall, County Armagh. This is referred to as the "Battle of the Diamond." In September 1795, several hundred Defenders (Catholics) assembled at a crossroads called the Diamond, near Loughgall in County Armagh. They had come to attack the house of one Dan Winter, where they were convinced the "peep-o-day boys" (Protestants) stored their guns and met to conspire against Catholics. The Battle of the Diamond, on Monday, September 21, lasted a brief fifteen minutes. The "peep-o-day boys" suffered no losses, but as many as forty-eight Defenders were said to have been killed. The first Orange Lodge was established that evening. One James Sloan, an innkeeper, became the first Grand Secretary, with power to issue warrants to whichever group of Protestants that wanted to follow his rule and set up Orange Lodges. They were required to swear an oath of allegiance to "His Majesty, King George III, and his successors so long as he and they support the Protestant ascendancy."[21]

Sectarian Violence

The terror groups on both sides of this complex situation have focused on the police and the military as their legitimate targets. The long-established hatred and revulsion of some Catholics for Protestants, and vice versa, has caused the senseless deaths of many innocent civilians. People have been killed purely for their religious affiliations, whether they are from PIRA or a Loyalist paramilitary. Tit-for-tat killings have been a hallmark of Northern Ireland's history through most of the twentieth century and into the twenty-first. (An obvious parallel is the conflict between the Israelis and Palestinians.) The start can be dated as far back as June 17, 1922, when the IRA issued an order for the destruction of property owned by Orangemen. According to police reports, at 2:30 that morning, IRA men executed six unarmed Protestants and a policeman. The attack was motivated purely along religious lines and had no significance in the struggle for the IRA. In 1976, a similar, but far more gruesome, attack took place in the Kingsmills area in South Armagh and claimed the lives of ten Protestant workers, who were stopped on their bus ride home from work, taken from the vehicle, and executed in a hail of bullets by members of the PIRA. Marching season, as discussed earlier, is the time of year when sectarianism comes into play. Protestants have viewed the treatment of Sinn Féin and the Republican movement as an erosion of their own political and economic power base. As they lose ground, this violence, sectarian in nature, has begun to spread. In 2001, in the weeks leading up to the 9-11 attacks in the United States, Protestants pelted Catholic primary school-children with rocks and verbal abuse as they made their way to school through the Protestant Ardoyne district of Belfast. These scenes were more reminiscent of an earlier age in the southern United States involving bussing of black students to school. The Holy Cross School in Ardoyne district has existed for more than thirty years, but the demographics of the area around it have changed. Mainly a Protestant area when "The Troubles" began, many of the middle-class Protestants moved away throughout the 1990s, and more Catholic families have moved into the area, to the chagrin of Protestants.

FIGURE 5-5 Homemade improvised explosive device used by the Provisional IRA (Gary Wilson).

FIGURE 5-6 October 24, 1990—Buncrana Road Checkpoint, Coshquin, near Londonderry. The PIRA kidnapped the family of Patrick Gillespie, who was a civilian cook at a British Army base and thus considered a collaborator by the PIRA. While his family was held hostage, he was forced to drive the Buncrana Checkpoint in a vehicle packed with explosives. As he reached the checkpoint the PIRA remotely detonated the explosives in the vehicle, killing Mr. Gillespie and five soldiers from the King's Regiment (Gary Wilson).

FIGURE 5-7 Devastation from the Buncrana Road checkpoint bombing (Gary Wilson).

THE PIRA AND INTERNATIONAL TERROR

The Sinn Féin and Irish Republican terror groups had a problem, and that problem was credibility. The requirement to **decommission** weapons was all-important to the Peace Accord. Although some decommissioning had taken place, there was a double standard—the PIRA turned in the old weapons, but then actively pursued acquiring new ones. In May 2002, the PIRA purchased a quantity of Russian-made AN-94 assault rifles. In April 2002, the Israelis identified pipe bomb devices made by PIRA terrorists in the hands of Palestinian terrorists. Paul Collinson, a former officer with the Royal Engineers Bomb Disposal, who worked for the Red Cross at the Jenin refugee camp in Palestine, commented, "The pipe bombs I found in Jenin are exact replicas of those in Northern Ireland. The size of bomb, the way they put the nail in, the way of igniting it with a light bulb filament, where they drilled the holes through, the use of a command wire and the means of initiating the bomb; these are all the same."[22] As we can tell from this report, the PIRA continues to ply its terrorism trade on an international scale not only in the Middle East, but also, as mentioned earlier, in South America. This broader involvement of the PIRA on the international stage was also a focus of the U.S. House of Representatives International Relations Committee. This committee concluded that Irish, Iranian, Cuban, and Spanish terror groups had probably been sharing techniques and honing their terror skills, while using illicit drug proceeds for payment. Gerry Adams, as the President of Sinn Féin, not surprisingly turned down an invitation to testify before the Congressional committee on the topic.

How closely linked are Sinn Féin and the Irish terror groups? There is little doubt that Adams and McGuiness have the ability to exert significant pressure, whether direct or implied, on the workings of the PIRA and the Army Council. In early 2002, a daring raid was made on the Northern Ireland Police Special Branch offices at Castlereagh. The PIRA managed to seize highly confidential documents that named police informants and undercover operations. To most observers in the security services, it is highly probable that the PIRA Army Council ordered and conducted this seizure. In its quest for a peace deal with the men of terror, is it possible that the Labor government of former Prime Minister Tony Blair was appeasing them to a far greater extent than was really acceptable? Most, if not all, terror groups come to the table to talk peace only when they are in such a desperate situation that signing a deal or calling a ceasefire is all that is left to them. In 1994, the PIRA called a ceasefire—not when they were winning the battle, but when they were, in fact, losing it. Both Adams and McGuiness are notable survivors. So, as the political process moves along, with no real sense of urgency, there is a lot of double-talk as well as double standards. To control the dissidents within the Republican movement, it would seem wholly logical for the PIRA to continue as before, but allowing Sinn Féin the freedom to express concern, sometimes outrage and, more frequently, denial of knowledge of PIRA activities when it comes to the thorny topics of bomb making and weapons acquisition.

There are many differences between the struggle for peace in Northern Ireland and the struggle for peace in the Middle East. In Northern Ireland, there are still many political problems to be resolved, as well as centuries of fear and distrust standing between Catholics and Protestants. However, for Northern Ireland there is a tunnel, and there even appears to be some light at the end of it. For the Middle East also the light has at last been turned on with the death of Arafat, and a new zeal from the United States to broker a lasting peace plan between the Palestinians and the Israelis.

THE NORTHERN IRELAND PEACE PROCESS

It seems almost inconceivable, but entirely probable, that the devastation from the 9-11 attacks on New York's World Trade Center prompted many terror groups, particularly the PIRA, to begin some decommissioning and moves toward peace. It is generally agreed that the peace process was developed from a combination of factors: A realization, by both the PIRA and the British Army, that the war could not be won militarily, and the decision by the PIRA to develop political strategies through its political party Sinn Féin, as an alternative way to fight for its political goals:

- The willingness of the Social Democratic Labour Party (SDLP) to engage with Sinn Féin in pursuing common nationalist political goals by peaceful means;
- A changing social and economic context in which many of the discriminations against Catholics were addressed, and in which a legal and social infrastructure to address issues of inequality, equality, and respect for diversity began to be developed;
- An increased willingness by many within civic society, for example, among businesses, trade unions, and community groups, to actively engage in the process of contact and political leverage for peace;

- The development of some new (albeit small) political parties by the Loyalists, and by the Women's Coalition, which enabled some new thinking on the political landscape; and
- A changing international context, including proactive involvement from the U.S. government, and many U.S. businessmen and politicians, as well as assistance with developing peace processes from South Africa.[23]

In August 2001, just a few weeks before 9-11, the Good Friday Agreement was on the verge of collapse. The PIRA had failed to follow through on its decommissioning of weapons. Strangely, the events of 9-11 appear to have had a sobering effect on the men of violence in the troubled region of Northern Ireland. After more than thirty years, and with endless bombings and more than 3,600 killed in sectarian violence, both main players—the British government, which has endured with an occupying army in the North for over three decades, and the Irish terror organizations—eventually came to the conclusion that the perpetual fighting must end. From the terrorist standpoint, the use of the gun, albeit used to good effect, has not had its desired effect of removing British occupying forces from Northern Ireland. Early attempts at peace settlements in the two decades preceding the Good Friday Agreement were doomed to failure, and Direct Rule from Britain had returned. As history moves forward, the events that would hinder any lasting peace have principally been the decommissioning of weapons in the possession of the paramilitary groups and the PIRA's foreign involvement in Colombian and Middle East terrorism. For many decades, the romantic image of Irish freedom fighters taking on the Britons was lore in the Irish-American communities of New York and Boston. Media coverage of terrorism—live and on U.S. television screens—has required a fundamental shift in the IRA's attitude toward decommissioning of weapons. The IRA has received significant amounts of financial aid from U.S. organizations and groups in support of its cause; however, in the aftermath of 9-11, the romantic view of the cause for most Americans faded quickly.

Decommissioning

The decommissioning of weapons was a central issue in making any peace process a reality.

In September 1997, the Independent International Commission on Decommissioning (IICD) was established to oversee the decommissioning of paramilitary weapons from both sides.

The 1998 Belfast Agreement committed all participants to the total disarmament of all paramilitary organisations. The plan and agreement called on both sides to work constructively with the decommissioning teams to use any influence they may have to achieve the decommissioning of all paramilitary arms within two years of the referendum, in May 1998. Although this target was never met by the men of violence, progress was nonetheless made. The first act of decommissioning under the scheme was witnessed by the IICD in December 1998, when the Loyalist Volunteer Force (LVF) decommissioned a quantity of weapons.

Caches of weapons and explosives have been stockpiled through the last two decades of the twentieth century. These arms shipments came from state sponsors of terrorism, specifically Colonel Qaddafi of Libya. This would surely be repugnant to the American public still recovering from the aftermath of 9-11.

At the end of October 2001, the PIRA, under the scrutiny of IICD, "put beyond use" (a term used by the PIRA to signify destruction) a large quantity of weapons and explosives. The first round of PIRA decommissioning was orchestrated shortly after the arrest in Colombia of two senior members of the Republican movement and FARC guerrilas. This can only have been an embarrassment to the Sinn Féin leadership, and something that would likely damage relations between the Republicans and their U.S. support networks. On the other side of the equation, the Ulster Democratic Unionist Party, under the leadership of the Reverend Ian Paisley, was not satisfied with the manner in which the destruction of the weapons and explosives had taken place, and was demanding a full listing of weapons destroyed. However, this may be viewed as a landmark event that gave the British government a further opportunity to announce the removal and closure of the network of army watchtowers along the border with the Republic. Further decommissioning took place in 2003 and 2004, but the PIRA still retains the ability to use force. While they may have decommissioned all of their arms, they have not actually disbanded, and no one except the PIRA has any definitive knowledge as to the number and types of weapons that remain cached. This being said, in 2005 PIRA issued the following statement:

> *The leadership of Oglaigh nahEireann (IRA) announced on 28 July that we had authorised our representative to engage with the IICD to complete the process of verifiably putting arms beyond use. The IRA leadership can now confirm that the process of putting arms beyond use has been completed.*

> Signed: P. O'Neill.

General John de Chastelain has indicated that the following estimates are an accurate representation of the PIRA arsenal that was decommissioned:

- 1,000 rifles
- 2 tonnes of Semtex
- 20–30 heavy machine guns
- 7 surface-to-air missiles (unused)
- 7 flame throwers
- 1,200 detonators
- 11 rocket-propelled grenade launchers
- 90 handguns
- 100+ grenades.[24]

The peace process, starting with the Good Friday Agreement, has stumbled along for more than half a decade. The aim of a coalition of parties was to lead what might be termed a "joint assembly" made up of all "interested parties," including the political wing of the Irish Republican Army, Sinn Féin. The inclusion of Sinn Féin, and the perception that its leaders still have links and influence over PIRA activities, has had a definite impact on the power-sharing process. Unionist parties were adamant that they could not work out a government with Sinn Féin so long as the Provisionals retained possession of their weapons and munitions. But, with the final decommissioning of the IRA arms, a power-sharing government for Northern Ireland has become a reality. In May 2007, Ian Paisley and Martin McGuiness were sworn in at Stormont Castle as Northern Ireland's First Minister and Deputy First Minister, respectively, and both Republican groups (Catholics) and the Unionists (Protestants) now make up the power-sharing executive in Northern Ireland.

On October 23, 2001, the IRA issued the following statement on the BBC regarding the subject of disarmament:

> The IRA is committed to our republican objectives and to the establishment of a united Ireland based on justice, equality, and freedom. In August 1994, against a background of lengthy and intensive discussions involving the two governments and others, the leadership of the IRA called a complete cessation of military operations in order to create the dynamic for a peace process. "Decommissioning" was no part of that. There was no ambiguity about this. Unfortunately, there are those within the British establishment and the leadership of Unionism who are fundamentally opposed to change. At every opportunity, they have used the issue of arms as an excuse to undermine and frustrate the process. It was for this reason this decommissioning was introduced to the process by the British government. It has been used since to prevent the changes that a lasting peace requires. In order to overcome this and to encourage the changes necessary for a lasting peace, the leadership of Oglaigh na hEireann (IRA) has taken a number of substantial initiatives. These include our engagement with the Independent International Commission on Decommissioning (IICD) and the

inspection of a number of arms dumps by the international inspectors, Cyril Ramaphosa and Martti Ahtisaari. No one should doubt the difficulties these initiatives cause for our volunteers, our supporters, and us. The political process is now on the point of collapse. Such a collapse would certainly, and eventually, put the overall peace process in jeopardy. There is a responsibility upon everyone seriously committed to a just peace to do our best to avoid this. Therefore, in order to save the peace process, we have implemented the scheme agreed with the IICD in August. Our motivation is clear. This unprecedented move is to save the peace process and to persuade others of our genuine intention.

Signed P. O'Neill.[25]

The PIRA's reluctance for verification of arms decommissioning continued to be a stumbling block for the Republicans and the Loyalists.

The "Agreement" is a document that goes a long way in addressing political, social, economic, and judicial inequalities that, to many, would seem to have been root causes of the thirty years of "The Troubles." Three of the most common points, decommissioning, security and policing, and justice have been cause for not just debate, but at times the near breakdown of the whole Agreement. The following sections taken from the Agreement form some of the most contentious points:

PRISONERS

1. Both governments will put in place mechanisms to provide for an accelerated programme for the release of prisoners, including transferred prisoners, convicted of scheduled offences in Northern Ireland or, in the case of those sentenced outside Northern Ireland, similar offences (referred to hereafter as qualifying prisoners). Any such arrangements will protect the rights of individual prisoners under national and international law.

2. Prisoners affiliated to organizations that have not established or are not maintaining a complete and unequivocal ceasefire will not benefit from the arrangements. The situation in this regard will be kept under review.

3. Both governments will complete a review process within a fixed time frame and set prospective release dates for all qualifying prisoners. The review process would provide for the advance of the release dates of qualifying prisoners, while allowing account to be taken of the seriousness of the offences for which the person was convicted and the need to protect the community. In addition, the intention would be that, should the circumstances allow it, any qualifying prisoners who remained in custody two years after the commencement of the scheme would be released at that point.

4. The governments will seek to enact the appropriate legislation to give effect to these arrangements by the end of June 1998.

5. The governments will continue to recognize the importance of measures to facilitate the reintegration of prisoners into the community by providing support both prior to and after release, including assistance directed toward availing of employment opportunities, retraining and/or re-skilling, and further education.

As mentioned earlier, the decommissioning of weapons by paramilitaries has been a major stumbling block for politicians, particularly from the Unionists.

DECOMMISSIONING

1. Participants recall their agreement in the Procedural Motion adopted on September 24, 1997, "that the resolution of the decommissioning issue is an indispensable part of the process of negotiation," and also recall the provisions of paragraph 25 of Strand 1 above.

2. They note the progress made by the Independent International Commission on Decommissioning and the governments in developing schemes that can represent

a workable basis for achieving the decommissioning of illegally held arms in the possession of paramilitary groups.

3. All participants accordingly reaffirm their commitment to the total disarmament of all paramilitary organizations. They also confirm their intention to continue to work constructively and in good faith with the Independent Commission, and to use any influence they may have to achieve the decommissioning of all paramilitary arms within two years following endorsement in referendums North and South of the agreement, and in the context of the implementation of the overall settlement.

4. The Independent Commission will monitor, review, and verify progress on decommissioning of illegal arms, and will report to both governments at regular intervals.

5. Both governments will take all necessary steps to facilitate the decommissioning process to include bringing the relevant schemes into force by the end of June.

SECURITY

1. The participants note that the development of a peaceful environment on the basis of this agreement can and should mean a normalization of security arrangements and practices.

2. The British government will make progress toward the objective of a return as early as possible to normal security arrangements in Northern Ireland, consistent with the level of threat and with a published overall strategy, dealing with
   i. The reduction of the numbers and role of the Armed Forces deployed in Northern Ireland to levels compatible with a normal peaceful society;
   ii. The removal of security installations;
   iii. The removal of emergency powers in Northern Ireland;
   iv. Other measures appropriate to and compatible with a normal peaceful society.

3. The Secretary of State will consult regularly on progress and the response to any continuing paramilitary activity with the Irish government and the political parties, as appropriate.

4. The British government will continue its consultation on firearms regulation and control on the basis of the document published on April 2, 1998.

5. The Irish government will initiate a wide-ranging review of the Offences Against the State Acts 1939–85 with a view to both reform and dispensing with those elements no longer required as circumstances permit.[26]

Decommissioning continued as the central issue for both sides; the demand that photographic evidence be produced by the IRA for confirmation purposes had been handled with considerable reluctance on the part of the IRA. The power base for the IRA and Sinn Féin had rested as much on the gun and the bomb as it did on the vote. The governments of both Dublin and London have believed that terrorism cannot be defeated but must be appeased, and this has caused them to waver in negotiations—firstly, demanding concessions from the IRA, next backing down or withdrawing the demand, and then pressuring the democratic parties not to make the same demands. Success in the elections has gone to those parties that have openly opposed serving in government assemblies with armed terrorists. Appeasement will surely win in the end!

POWER-SHARING EXECUTIVE

The Northern Ireland peace process has been a long and protracted process, and has at times almost crashed and burned! The appetite for a power-sharing government has come after nearly forty years of sectarian violence, and political posturing and squabbling. May 8, 2007, became a landmark day in the history of Northern Ireland's "Troubles"—a power-sharing local authority had been brokered and recognized by the governments of both the Republic of Ireland and the United Kingdom. The Rev. Ian Paisley, leader of the dominant party among Northern Ireland's protestant community, and Martin

McGuiness, the deputy head of Sinn Féin Republican Party, were both sworn in as leader and deputy leader, respectively, to lead the new Northern Ireland government. The events were in effect an end to political and direct rule from London, which had been in effect since the Northern Ireland Assembly was suspended in 2002. If we look back over the last thirty-five years, it seems almost inconceivable that these two men, Paisley and McGuiness, would ever speak to each other let alone form the leadership nuclei of a new power-sharing government—in the past, Paisley has long accused McGuiness of being an IRA terrorist and he had acquired the nickname of "Dr. No" for his continued rejection of the Good Friday Agreement. The May 8th oath that both men swore also included a commitment to the Northern Ireland Police, something the Republicans had long resisted as the police were viewed as part of the Union enemy. As the first decade of the twenty-first century draws to a close, the Troubles are officially over in Northern Ireland, and what remains of the men of violence? They have certainly not disappeared but have continued to act as organized crime units, controlling drugs and other illegal activities. It is hoped that with cooperation, with the police now enshrined in the new government approach to business, the police service will be able to curb the actions of former terrorists now engaged in criminal activity.

The Police Service of Northern Ireland

The Police Service of Northern Ireland—historically, the Royal Ulster Constabulary (RUC)—has long been composed disproportionately of Protestant and Unionist members. The total percentage of Catholics within the force is only about 7 percent. Over the last three decades, the RUC has been identified with political control, formerly from the Unionist government in Stormont and latterly during the period of Direct Rule from Westminster, not as upholders of the law, but as defenders of the state, and the nature of the state itself has remained the central issue of the political argument.

In 1998, the British government appointed the former Governor of Hong Kong, Chris Patten, to head the Independent Commission on Policing in Northern Ireland. The Commission's report made 175 recommendations for change. When the recommendations were presented, the Sinn Féin party was adamant that the only way forward for the Peace Accord was a full implementation of all the recommendations, including the striking of the word "Royal" from the police title. The former RUC has survived a torrid thirty years of strife and assault from the Republican terror groups. The police force has always had a predominantly Protestant flavor and has lost some 300 officers, who were murdered in terrorist acts; more than 9,000 have been injured during this time frame. Policing in the North cannot be likened to the work of any other police force operating in a Western democracy. It has had to handle terrorist incidents like no other force as part of everyday policing, which can hardly be considered the norm in Western civilization. In 1985, INTERPOL stated that the RUC was the most dangerous force anywhere in the world in which to serve, even surpassing that of Colombia. The Patten Report, entitled "A New Beginning: Policing In Northern Ireland," covered every region of the force from recruitment, IT, size of force, composition by religious affiliation, culture and ethos, public order policing, and human rights. The aim of the recommendations was to attract and sustain support for the new organization from the entire community. The problems faced by the police service in Northern Ireland are, in a sense, unique in a divided society, each side with its own particular history and culture. But many problems are similar to those confronting police services in democratic societies elsewhere. The Independent Commission studied policing in other countries, and while it could discover no model that could simply be applied to Northern Ireland, it was able to find plenty of examples of police services wrestling with the same sort of challenges. The challenge for the police service in the North was how it could be accountable to the community it serves if its composition—in terms of ethnicity, religion, and gender—is vastly different to that of its society. In the words of the founder of the British police service, Sir Robert Peel, the police service's main objective is the prevention of crime rather than the detection and punishment of offenders. The end of the 1990s saw the debate in Britain on policing as it affected ethnic minorities and communities, and the police service's relationship with those communities. There is obviously no perfect model for Northern Ireland, and there is no example of a country that, to quote one European police officer, "has yet finalized the total transformation from force to service." The commitment to a fresh start gives Northern Ireland the opportunity to take best practices from elsewhere and to possibly lead the way in overcoming some of the toughest challenges of modern policing.[27]

The Provisional IRA made an announcement on Thursday, July 28, 2005, that it had "formally ordered an end to the armed campaign" that goes well beyond its 1997 ceasefire. The statement went on to confirm that it would allow Protestant and Catholic clergy to witness future disarmament. Although the British government and also the White House welcomed PIRA's statement, there was no rejoicing on the streets in Northern Ireland, most likely owing to the fact that in the past the PIRA has issued hollow and deceptive statements. Whether there is any substance to this proclamation will also depend on whether any breakaway faction takes up arms in place of PIRA. It is notable that PIRA talks only of disarming and not disbanding, which indicates it will reserve the right to rearm should the political picture change.

COUNTERING IRISH TERRORISM

With the advent of terrorism, the British government developed wide-scale antiterrorist and counterterrorist measures against the terror groups in Northern Ireland. Never before in its modern history had a British peacetime government to deal with internal terrorist activities on the scale that emerged from Northern Ireland. On many occasions, Britain has met violence with violence and has had some innovative ideas to counter the terrorists. Among those innovations are its shoot-to-kill policy, internment, removal of a defendant's right of silence during judicial proceedings, and the prohibiting of news media broadcasting statements of PIRA and Sinn Féin. With the "Irish question" appearing now to be answered after more than three decades of political and sectarian violence, one has to question how effective the countermeasures really were. The hostility shown by and to Margaret Thatcher helped to feed the terror campaign against British economic, military, and political targets. She constantly reiterated that she would "never give in" to the IRA. Each side's inability to achieve a military victory should be obvious to the other. The lessons for the rest of the world from Northern Ireland's conflict would seem to be the following:

- Authorities must pursue every effort to make political compromises with dissidents before violence becomes institutionalized.
- Authorities cannot achieve a military victory over terrorists and still maintain civil liberties and democratic institutions.
- Counterterror techniques by authorities that kill, injure, or frighten noncombatants provide support for terrorist groups. Indeed, revolutionary terrorist groups depend on the authorities to perpetrate provocation and outrages against noncombatants.
- Terrorist groups can be devastatingly effective with very few members, given the worldwide availability of sophisticated weapons and explosives.
- Terrorist groups can sustain community support by using both the latent sympathy of citizens, as well as intimidation.
- Even the most technologically sophisticated, well-organized, well-financed, and highly motivated counterterrorist methods can be frustrated by a small group of terrorists that have some community support.[28]

Britain's counterterrorism organizations have had some notable successes. The Special Air Service Regiment (SAS), which continued to thwart and strike at Republican terrorists through the 1980s and 1990s, was instrumental in preventing terrorist attacks and setting up offensive traps, resulting in the capture and often the death of terrorists. The SAS has had significant success against the IRA, and has been responsible for a number of successful ambushes against the terrorists. Many have been spectacular in nature, resulting in heavy loss of life to the terrorists. Notable among its successes was an ambush on the island of Gibraltar of an unarmed ASU that British and Spanish intelligence had determined was about to carry out an attack on the British colony. Britain was

FIGURE 5-8   Helicopters were used widely by the British military to patrol the dangerous region of South Armagh (Dave Loban).

widely criticized at the time for this action. In the environment of post 9-11, one has to wonder whether the same criticism would be applied now.

Judicial processes were already the primary weapon used against the terror groups in Northern Ireland, and Britain's early response in sending in troops to protect Catholics from Protestants did not have the desired effect. The PIRA was up against the entire intelligence resources of a major

FIGURE 5-9   Fortified towers with powerful CCTV systems were constructed to monitor the region of South Armagh (Dave Loban).

Western government, and those resources were significant. The brigade and battalion structures of the PIRA, established at the latter end of the 1960s, became targets for penetration by the RUC. Informants were placed within the organization, and several senior IRA members were arrested. As noted previously, the PIRA remodeled its battalions into smaller cells where only a minority of people knew who was who. The British government was prepared to meet violence head-on with its special counterrevolutionary warfare force, the British Special Air Service Regiment (SAS).[29]

DOMESTIC TERRORISM IN MAINLAND BRITAIN

The Angry Brigade

British politicians and the public have suffered under both the threat and the reality of indiscriminate terror acts by the IRA since the early 1970s. Almost totally forgotten by many, however, is a small terror group that came to life in the 1960s—the decade that saw the Beatles, widespread drug use, and fundamental changes in societal views and values. The Angry Brigade is Britain's only noteworthy, homegrown terror group.

One of the earliest workers' movements was the Chartist Movement, which started in the 1830s. Prior to this time, there were other forms of autonomous revolt by workers in the textile mills of the midlands and the North of England. As a result of threatened job losses caused by industrialization, workers formed into armed groups of both the employed and unemployed. They rioted and caused property damage.

Few may recall the Angry Brigade; however, the group was real and did exist. The members of this group were dissimilar in almost every way to the Irish terrorists and had no clearly defined enemy to focus on, other than wealthy, middle-class Conservatives running business corporations. Unlike the terrorist groups waging war in both Northern Ireland and the mainland, the Angry Brigade was a loosely formed group of Communist-style workers' party members. The philosophy of the brigade was that of a militant, pro-labor, left-wing revolutionary movement.

The Angry Brigade came to some prominence in the late 1960s. Little has been heard of the group since the main protagonists were jailed in 1971. The group could be termed a copycat, and it likened itself to the Weathermen in the United States, and, in a later period, to the German terrorist group led by Baader and Meinhoff. With no military knowledge or background, the Angry Brigade espoused Marxist theories in the hope that workers would find them acceptable. In the 1960s, Britain was a changing society in a great many respects, with a strong Conservative government under Alec Douglas Hume. Modernization and growth in the factories, particularly in the auto industry and the dockyards, was the order of the day. The leaders of the Angry Brigade sought to change government policy and usher in a new era of socialism by murdering politicians and bombing public buildings.

Activist or Terrorist

As pure activists in a workers' party struggle against the perceived enemy, the state, and big business, the Angry Brigade issued communiqués and proclamations stating their cause. The Brigade hoped to gain recognition by professing support for the Irish Nationalist Movement and such mirror-image revolutionaries as the Symbionese Liberation Army (SLA) in the United States. Closer to home, the group espoused support for the activities of the Red Brigade in Italy and the German Red Army faction. There is no recorded information that the group received any support, either of a financial or a military nature, from either of these terrorist organizations. What is certain is that the Brigade caused explosions aimed primarily at political and business figures. The group was hunted down by London's Metropolitan Police and prosecuted for its terrorist and criminal acts. The Angry Brigade's members believed that they were engaged in a workers' struggle that could only come to fruition if the working masses rebelled against their masters. This altruistic goal was never realized, however, possibly owing to the atrocious nature of the Brigade's attacks.

Angry Brigade Terrorist Acts

The Angry Brigade is believed to have been involved in a number of bombings in London aimed at banks, corporations, and foreign-interest businesses, such as the Bank of Bilbao. The Brigade supported the Basque Separatists in Spain. It is unclear what this group hoped to achieve by attacking the homes of the Commissioner of the Metropolitan Police and a Member of Parliament. Certainly, these actions demonstrated an ability to coerce and intimidate, but their overall effectiveness can be dismissed as having minimal effect in making any changes in the political arena. Unlike the PIRA, the Brigade had no political machinery similar to that of Sinn Féin, or any media support. The Angry Brigade was broken up through a series of arrests in 1971, and the ringleaders, who became known as the Stoke Newington Eight, were sent to prison for long terms in 1972. The group still remains one of the only examples of homegrown, internal terrorism in Great Britain.

Wales and Terror for the Tourist

To a casual observer, the region of the United Kingdom known as Wales seldom conjures up visions of terrorist activity. In fact, Wales is better known for its tourist attractions at Caernavon Castle, the Mountains of Snowdonia, Welsh choirs, famous actors, mining, and the sport of rugby. So, is Wales a nest of terror groups or a convenient hiding place for the indigenous terrorist? Over the past three decades, there has been the odd discussion of an independent Welsh homeland, which occasionally has been brought to the attention of Britons by acts of arson. These acts were usually aimed at unoccupied holiday homes and cottages in the Wales countryside. Claiming responsibility for these acts of arson is a group calling itself the Miebion Glyndwr, or Sons of Glendower. This group takes its name from Owen Glendower, a Welsh leader from the fifteenth century, who vowed to fight the English and their rule over Wales. The arson attacks on remote cottages resulted in more than 100 having been destroyed since the first attack in 1979. The group appears disorganized and factional, with no political platform for its support. About twenty Welsh activists have been convicted and jailed for some fifteen of the attacks. There appears to be little significance to the arsons and no clear links between them. A group calling itself Cadwyr Cymru (the Defenders of Wales) has claimed responsibility for some of the arsons, but many might well have been committed for insurance purposes.

Animal Rights Militia

Animal rights activists have been prevalent in Great Britain for several decades, but the Animal Rights Militia is the only one of their many groups to have moved toward terror tactics, and bombings aimed at companies and research institutes. In 1986, bombs were planted under cars, and at the homes of prominent research scientists and animal importers. Although adequate warnings were given, this marked the group's trend toward violent action. This group, while perhaps using what could be terrorist tactics, is still considered more like criminals than true terrorists. The Antiterrorism Act of 2000, although logically aimed at curbing the IRA and other Northern Ireland terror groups, could also be focused on the Animal Liberation Front, an activist organization that is believed responsible for a number of bomb attacks against animal research establishments and the agricultural industry. Attacks on fast-food establishments in Belgium appear to have been the work of the same group.

ISLAMIC EXTREMIST THREATS TO THE UNITED KINGDOM

Over the last three decades, Islamic groups have managed to relocate to the United Kingdom as a sanctuary or base for various activities, for fund-raising, and primarily to escape their own repressive regimes. Britain's liberal policies have made it easy for Islamic groups to set up official charities to raise funds for their own causes. Terrorists wanted in other countries were given safe haven in the United Kingdom and left free to foment hatred against the West. Extremist groups such as Hizb ut-Tahrir remained legal despite being banned in many European and Muslim countries.

Radicals such as Abu Qatada, Omar Bakri Mohammed, Abu Hamza, and Mohammed al-Massari were allowed to preach incitement to violence and jihad![30] After the 9-11 attacks and in the years since, the British government is convinced that it is on the hit list of Islamic extremists, and this not only because it has taken on a major support role to U.S. involvement in Iraq. Indeed, as early as 1998, Osama bin Laden was quoted in *TIME* magazine: "Our work targets world infidels. Our enemy is the crusader alliance led by America, Britain, and Israel. It is a crusader-Jewish alliance." Britain's military presence in Afghanistan also makes the country a prime target. The Muslim population in Britain runs to just over 2 million, and a constant inflow of refugees—both legal and illegal—crosses into the country from Europe on an almost daily basis. So, how deeply entrenched were Muslim fanatics within the Muslim faith in Britain? The answer is quite startling; according to British officials, up to 16,000 British Muslims are either actively engaged in or support terrorist activities, while up to 3,000 are estimated to have passed through al Qaeda training camps, with several hundred thought to be primed to attack the United Kingdom.[31]

Islamic groups operating within mainland Britain are often from terrorist organizations that appear on the U.S. State Department list of overseas terrorist organizations. These groups include Gama'a al-Islamiyya, Hamas, Shining Path, the Liberation Tigers of Tamil Eelam, Hezbollah, and the Kurdistan Workers' Party. All of these groups had been actively recruiting and raising funds freely in the United Kingdom until September 11, 2001.

Al Qaeda is a relatively modern-day phenomenon that had been in existence a little over a decade, and only became seriously connected with terrorism in the days after the attacks on the U.S. embassies in Nairobi and Dar es Salam, and the waterborne suicide attack on the U.S.S. *Cole*

FIGURE 5-10 This undercover photo shows the July 21, 2005, London terror plot defendants training and praying at a Lake District camp in Cumbria, northern England. The picture shows Ramzi Mohammed (left) and Yassin Omar (hooded top) on the training camp trip. Ramzi Mohammed was accused of trying to bomb the Oval tube station, and Yassin of trying to bomb the Warren Street tube station just two weeks after the July 7 blasts in the center of London (Canadian Press).

in Yemen. It is clear and becoming clearer that the reach and spread of al Qaeda throughout the world, and particularly on the European continent, is posing one of the most significant risks to Western democracies.

Britain continues to be viewed as one of Europe's most liberal societies; however, that view may be changing following the introduction of tough, new antiterrorism legislation by the Home Secretary. There were 5,890 applications for asylum in the United Kingdom in the third quarter of 2007 (July to September). This was 19 percent higher than the previous quarter and less than 1 percent higher than the third quarter of 2006. The top five applicant nationalities were Chinese, Eritrean, Iraqi, Iranian, and Afghan. In 2006, there were 23,610 asylum applications received, 8 percent less than in 2005 (25,710). In 2007, British Intelligence announced that there were more than 2,000 residents in Britain who were considered a threat to national security, and that number has been steadily rising.

U.K. Asylum Statistics–Initial Decisions

There were 5,230 initial decisions in the third quarter of 2007, 12 percent lower than the previous quarter. Of these, 17 percent were granted asylum, 12 percent were granted either Humanitarian Protection or Discretionary Leave, and 71 percent were refused. The number of initial decisions made fell by 24 percent between 2005 and 2006, from 27,395 to 20,930. Of the 20,930, 10 percent were granted asylum, 11 percent were granted Humanitarian Protection or Discretionary Leave, and 79 percent were refused.[32]

London has become a haven for young Muslim immigrants as well as asylum seekers; however, with diminishing prospects for work, they have managed to adapt to the generosity of a welfare state that provides for their physical well-being. Many have resorted to attending institutions such as the Finsbury Park Mosque, where many observers would say that they were brainwashed into global movements such as al Qaeda, and then sent throughout the world to carry out jihad. Evidence has been uncovered linking Richard Reid, who attempted to detonate an explosive device in his shoes on board a U.S. trans-Atlantic flight in December 2001, Zacarias Moussaoui, the so-called twentieth hijacker (9-11), as well as the millennium bomber, Ahmed Ressam. A mosque is a holy place of worship, and the Finsbury Park Mosque was one of the largest in London. Before its forced closure in 2002, the mosque was open to worshipers as well as casual visitors. The one-eyed, hook-handed Imam Sheik **Abu Hamza al Masri** continued to be outspoken in his support for Osama bin Laden. In a television interview, he made no apologies and showed no remorse for the 9-11 attack on the World Trade Center. So, was Finsbury Park Mosque a fertile and covert breeding ground for al Qaeda? The mosque itself attracted many Muslims from the diverse ethnic communities in the London area, namely, Pakistanis, Bengalis, Egyptians, and Algerians. Abu Hamza is himself an Egyptian, and has been in the United Kingdom for more than twenty-five years. His presence was imposing—a missing eye and a hook in place of his right hand—to young and impressionable Muslims who would see little future for themselves in the Western democracies and be easily indoctrinated by the Imam and his cohorts. A Canadian Broadcast Corporation (CBC) documentary on recruiting al Qaeda in Britain focused squarely on the mosque in Finsbury. The detailed exposé included hidden videotaping of recruiting activities inside the mosque, as well as videos of terrorist training tactics, such as how to slit a person's throat. The problem for British police lay in its inability to pinpoint any crime that the Imam may have committed. UK authorities shut down the Finsbury Park Mosque in 2002, but that did not stop the one-eyed Abu Hamza from preaching on the street outside the mosque, with dialogue such as, "Seek the way of death . . . if you die to defend your religion, you are a martyr . . . die honorably, don't die humiliated."[33] The United States has been trying to build a case against the cleric, based on evidence of his involvement in setting up a training camp in Bly, Oregon, in 1999–2000, with the intention to stockpile weapons there for jihad training. He has also been charged in the United States with conspiracy for his involvement with an Islamic group in Yemen that took sixteen tourists hostage in 1998. The allegations are that Abu Hamza al-Masri provided a satellite phone to the Islamic Army of Aden and spoke to the conspirators before the attack. On May 27, 2004, British police arrested Abu Hamza. He remained in custody, while the United States attempted to have him extradited. However, in October 2004, the British charged Abu Hamza on ten counts ranging from inciting racial hatred to soliciting or encouraging the murder of others—"namely, a person or persons who did not believe in the Islamic faith, in particular the Jewish people." He is currently serving a seven-year prison sentence for soliciting murder and inciting racial hatred.

Al-Masri faces eleven charges in the United States, including charges related to a 1998 kidnapping in Yemen and the formation of a terrorist training camp in Oregon in 1999. In 2006, a Britsh court ruled that he could be extradited once he has completed his sentence in the United Kingdom.

The Prevention of Terrorism Act 2005

A system of control orders under the Prevention of Terrorism Act 2005 has replaced the Part 4 powers under the Antiterrorism, Crime, and Security Act 2001. The Prevention of Terrorism Act allows for control orders to be made against any suspected terrorist, whether a UK national or a non-UK national, or whether the terrorist activity is international or domestic. The Home Secretary is required to report to Parliament as soon as reasonably possible after the end of the relevant three-month period on how control order powers have been exercised during that time.

FIGURE 5-11   A banner hung from the window of the Finsbury Park Mosque, London, on September 11, 2002. A conference was being held by some of the most radical Muslim clerics in Britain, organized by al-Muhajiroun, who wanted to turn Britain into a Muslim state (Canadian Press).

The facts about Control Orders

- Control orders enable the authorities to impose conditions upon individuals ranging from prohibitions on access to specific items or services (such as the Internet), and restrictions on association with named individuals, to the imposition of restrictions on movement or curfews. A control order does not mean "house arrest."
- Specific conditions imposed under a control order are tailored to each case to ensure effective disruption and prevention of terrorist activity.
- The Home Secretary must normally apply to the courts to impose a control order based on an assessment of the intelligence information. If the court allows the order to be made, the case will be automatically referred to the court for a judicial review of the decision.
- In emergency cases, the Home Secretary may impose a provisional order, which must then be reviewed by the court within seven days.
- A court may consider the case in open or closed session—depending on the nature and sensitivity of the information under consideration. Special advocates will be used to represent the interests of the controlled individuals in closed sessions.
- Control orders will be time limited and may be imposed for a period of up to twelve months at a time. A fresh application for renewal has to be made thereafter.
- A control order and its conditions can be challenged.
- Breach of any of the obligations of the control order without reasonable excuse is a criminal offence punishable with a prison sentence of up to five years, or an unlimited fine, or both.
- Individuals who are subject to control order provisions have the option of applying for an anonymity order.
- To date, the government has not sought to make a control order requiring derogation from Article 5 of the European Convention on Human Rights.

Terrorism Act 2006

The Terrorism Act contains a comprehensive package of measures designed to ensure that the police, intelligence agencies, and courts have all the tools they require to tackle terrorism and bring perpetrators to justice.

The Act received Royal Assent on March 30, 2006. This Act was not a direct response to the July attacks on London, as new terrorism legislation had already been planned.

After the attacks, however, consultations with law enforcement and intelligence agencies were held to make sure that their views were considered when developing the legislation.

Content of the Terrorism Act

The Terrorism Act specifically aims to make it more difficult for extremists to abuse the freedoms we cherish and encourage others to commit terrorist acts.

The Act creates a number of new offences. Once it is brought into force, it will be a criminal offence to commit the following:

- **Acts preparatory to terrorism**–This aims to capture those planning serious acts of terrorism.
- **Encouragement to terrorism**–This makes it a criminal offence to directly or indirectly incite or encourage others to commit acts of terrorism. This will include the glorification of terrorism, where it may be understood as encouraging the emulation of terrorism.
- **Dissemination of terrorist publications**–This will cover the sale, loan, or other dissemination of terrorist publications. This will include those publications that encourage terrorism, and those that provide assistance to terrorists.
- **Terrorist training offences**–This makes sure that anyone who gives or receives training in terrorist techniques can be prosecuted. The Act also criminalizes attendance at a place of terrorist training.

The Act also makes amendments to existing legislation, including

- Introducing warrants to enable the police to search any property owned or controlled by a terrorist suspect;
- Extending terrorism stop and search powers to cover bays and estuaries;
- Extending police powers to detain suspects after arrest for up to twenty-eight days (though periods of more than two days must be approved by a judicial authority);
- Improved search powers at ports;
- Increased flexibility of the proscription regime, including the power to proscribe groups that glorify terrorism.

Facts and Figures

The UK police terrorism arrest statistics (excluding Northern Ireland) from September 11, 2001 to March 31, 2007 show 1,228 arrests were made:

- 1,165 arrests under the Terrorism Act 2000;
- 63 arrests under legislation other than the Terrorism Act where the investigation was conducted as a terrorist investigation.

Of the total 1,228 arrested

- 132 charged with terrorism legislation offences only;
- 109 charged with terrorism legislation offences and other criminal offences;
- 195 charged under other legislation offences including murder, grievous bodily harm, firearms, explosives offences, fraud, and false documents;
- 76 handed over to immigration authorities;
- 15 on police bail, awaiting charging decisions;
- 1 warrant issued for arrest;
- 12 cautioned;
- 1 dealt with under youth offending procedures;
- 11 dealt with under mental health legislation;
- 4 transferred to Police Service of Northern Ireland custody;
- 2 remanded in custody, awaiting extradition proceedings;
- 669 released without charge;
- 1 awaiting further investigation.

Of those charged

- 41 Terrorism Act convictions to date;
- 183 convicted under other legislation: murder and explosives offences (including conspiracies), grievous bodily harm, firearms offences, fraud, false documents offences, etc. (this includes the twelve cautions detailed above);
- 114 at or awaiting trial.[34]

As has been the case in many other regions of the world, laws in Britain have had to be created and amended to accommodate the terrorist acts. However, the laws being enacted have been subject to Human Rights challenges, and in Britain, the Law Lords as recently as April 2006 issued a declaration that Section 3 of the Terrorism Act 2005 was actually incompatible with the right to a fair trial under Article 6 of the European Convention on Human Rights. In 1989, the European Court of Human Rights extended the scope of the provision in the European Convention on Human Rights that prohibits torture and degrading treatment. For Western countries attempting to deport illegal immigrants, including suspected terrorists, they were now prohibited from doing so if the judge thought that abuses might be practiced at the country to which the suspect was being deported. The very liberal interpretation by British judges has made removal from Britain a very onerous prospect, and ultimately this plays into the hands of the terrorists wishing to seek out a safe haven.

The British government believes it is under attack from Islamic extremists, and has gone to extraordinary lengths to inform the public that it is not a case of *if* an attack will happen, but *when.* Fear mongering aside, the resilience of the British government has relied on draconian measures to hold at bay those it feels have been or may likely be involved or connected to terrorism. To get a greater understanding of how widespread the threat of radical Islam is to the social fabric of Britain, one needs to also appreciate that immigration has played a major part in all this. Travel the streets of London, and you will witness a melting pot of languages and people from around the world that have made not only London, but also provincial towns and cities their home. But let us be candid; immigration does not always translate into integration. When you see the numbers of Muslim enclaves, as that is what they are, in the northern mill towns such as Bradford or Oldham, and the strict adherence to Muslim religious dress, you have to question whether this is rural Britain or a village on the Indian subcontinent. In the 1970s and 1980s, the possibility of seeing Muslim women swathed from head to toe in black, with only a slit for the eyes, was extremely rare, but today in Muslim Britain, it is a common sight, and one has to wonder whether this is more a political than religious statement to taunt the British people and its government. The areas noted above are not referred to or recognized by a religious divide, as the politically correct term might better be Asian; any references to religion or religious sensitivities seem to weigh heavily on politicians of all stripes. To many observers, the theory is that Britain became a target for Islamic militants only after its support for U.S. President Bush's campaign in Iraq. However, that is not your authors' view of the current state of affairs. As we noted earlier, Muslims from around the globe have relocated to the United Kingdom, and have been doing so for more than twenty-five years. In Britain, hundreds of thousands of Muslims lead law-abiding lives, and live and work in peace and harmony. Nevertheless, moderation among the majority appears to be a highly relative concept considering their widespread hostility toward Israel and the Jews, for example, or the way the very concept of Islamic terrorism or other wrongdoing is automatically denied.[35] Long before the events of 9-11 unfolded, and the coalition invasion of Taliban-controlled Afghanistan, and then Iraq, London and the United Kingdom were home to radical Muslims. One prime example is the case of Dhiren Barot who, as far back as 1999, was plotting an attack on London's Heathrow airport. Barot was an airline ticket agent, and his plans included detonating a bomb on a bus in the tunnel connecting the arterial roads to the center of the airport, and exploding a bomb in a tube train under the River Thames with the intent to flood the underground chamber and cause an untold number of deaths as a result. Barot was grammar school educated, and converted from Hinduism to Islam, and in 1995, long before George Bush became President, he attended a training camp in Kashmir. He is a staunch believer that terror works, and that it is a religious duty of all Muslims. So, if we believe that foreign policy can dictate a sea change in Muslim terrorist actions, we need to think again. It is purely a convenient excuse for the Muslim extremists to use and cite both Iraq and Afghanistan. Change can only come from within the Muslim community itself, and removing troops from Iraq or Afghanistan will only convince the impressionable young extremists that terror does work.

Hizb Ut-Tahrir

Such organizations as this have been flourishing for several decades in the United Kingdom, but are banned in many other countries, in particular the Middle East and Asia. One of the difficulties we see with Islamist groups such as Hizb ut-Tahrir (HT) is how to interpret the groups' intentions—while the various government ministries have determined that HT does not advocate terrorism and is therefore not a threat within the United Kingdom, Hizb ut-Tahrir in Britain emphasizes the importance of Muslims choosing loyalty to their religion above loyalty to Britain or any other country, whether majority Muslim or non-Muslim. HT has thousands of followers in over forty countries but its members have not won elections in any government. This makes it very difficult to establish its position on any international issues. HT media releases show an anti-Western sentiment that has been characteristic of most Islamist movements. It rejects democracy as Western and un-Islamic.

TABLIGHI JAMAAT

This organization, considered a radical and extreme Islamist movement, actually has its European headquarters in the northern English town of Dewsbury and has been in situ since 1978. The organization has its own extreme views on Islam's place in the world and is considered by British security experts to be the leading force in Islamic extremism and a fertile recruiting ground for young men—Mohammed Siddequ Khan, the leader of the London bomb plot in July 2005, has links to Jamaat. The number of adherents that come to the Dewsbury mosque is quite startling—they come from all over England and Western Europe to meet and be preached to in Dewsbury. To the many law abiding Muslims in Britain, it is entirely true to say that their religion is being hijacked by those with an extremist agenda, and it is unfortunate that the voices of moderate Muslims are no longer heard, let alone listened to. With the influx of Muslims in the 1970s came their highly traditional faith influenced by Suffism that was therefore passive and quiescent. Over a few years, theirs became an increasingly activist faith centering on the mosques that were now generating a highly radicalized ideology, and according to the Pakistani Bishop of Rochester (Christian), a whole generation of Muslim children was indoctrinated with a set of inflammatory ideas about the need for Islam to achieve primacy over the non-Islamic world.[36] The fuel for the radicalization process came about from two important events in the 1980s and 1990s, the first being the Soviet invasion of Afghanistan, which saw British forces training and equipping Afghan fighters (mujahideen) against the Soviets who they eventually drove out of their homeland; these Muslim fighters had now found a cause and a vocation—holy war. The second event was the Bosnian war in which a steady stream of media depicted the massacres of Muslims by Christian neighbors. The thousands of Islamic fighters from both Afghanistan and Bosnia found their way west.

SPECIAL IMMIGRATION APPEALS COMMISSION (SIAC)

Non-United Kingdom nationals detained under the draconian measures of the Antiterrorism Crime and Security Act had only one avenue for appeal open to them. Set up by the British Government Home Office Department, the SIAC, was a legal in-camera forum presided over by three High Court Judges. The presumption of innocence now is at issue and, under international human rights law, the presumption of innocence applies to all persons charged with a criminal offense, even during times of emergency, and requires the state to prove such charge "beyond a reasonable doubt." In these cases, there is no charge being laid; however, the detainee has no rights under this legislation to know firsthand why he or she is being detained. The requirement for the Crown in these cases—to prove beyond a reasonable doubt the probable guilt of any detainee—is not required. Groups such as Amnesty International claim that this legislation is a perversion of justice.

Under international human rights law, the right to the presumption of innocence, which applies to all persons charged with a criminal offense, including during times of emergency, requires the state to prove the charge "beyond reasonable doubt."

The SIAC has ruled that under the Antiterrorism, Crime and security Act 2001 (UK) ATCSA, the burden of proof that the Home Secretary has to meet in order that the SIAC may confirm the certification of individuals as "suspected international terrorists" falls well short of "beyond reasonable doubt." According to the SIAC, under the ATCSA, the onus upon the Home Secretary is lower than that needed in a civil case, such as cases involving contractual disputes.

The SIAC stated: "The standard of proof is below a balance of probabilities (i.e., the standard in civil cases) because of the nature of the risk facing the United Kingdom, and the nature of the evidence which inevitably would be used to detain these appellants."[37]

Like the U.S. detention in Guantanamo Bay, British suspects are held indefinitely at London's Belmarsh Prison, a top-security facility. Fighting terrorism in a democracy is no easy task, and the application of the rule of law makes the problems dangerous and far-reaching. The effects that this type of legislation may be having on foreigners from the Middle East and North Africa, and their attitude to their host countries are easy to imagine. If these minorities felt any sense of marginalization prior to the events of 9-11, is it any wonder that some would find sympathy with extreme Islamic ideals? The Antiterrorism Act gives the Home Secretary powers to detain foreign nationals who are thought to be a potential danger to the United Kingdom; however, the catch here is that they cannot be deported to their country of origin because they face persecution there and no other country will accept them. Under normal circumstances, detainees would be charged with a criminal offense and brought to court. In the situation since 9-11, Britain has detained suspects based on intelligence provided by MI5 and MI6, giving rise to the suspicion that they are linked to international terrorism. It would therefore seem that British authorities do not have any hard evidence with which to lay criminal charge against its detainees, and that the government is unwilling to divulge such information and the sources of such information.

Police have correctly targeted young Muslims since the 9-11 attacks. This has had the effect of pushing some young Muslims, who are resentful of the treatment, toward such figures as Abu Hamza. It is entirely probable that the draconian measures are creating wider alienation and actually nourishing hatred. An example of this is Omar Bakri, the head of al-Mohjeroum, an Islamic extremist group, and the self-proclaimed representative of Osama bin Laden in the United Kingdom. In May 2004, Bakri was linked with suicide attacks in Israel. The psychology of suicide and bombings is one of his more extreme teachings. Young Muslims are also taking their extreme views and actions to other locations — Richard Reid (the "shoe bomber") currently resides in a U.S. jail after his attempt to destroy an aircraft in flight in December 2001. Omar Sharif and Asif Hanif, two young British Muslims, ended up on a suicide mission for Hamas. They detonated a bomb in an Israeli restaurant in April 2003, killing three and injuring fifty-five. Hamas subsequently issued a video of the two young men in which they are seen urging others to follow their example. Omar Sharif's bomb failed to detonate at the scene, and he was discovered dead a week later off the coast of Israel. Many British radicals were mobilized by the invasion of Afghanistan and the ousting of the Taliban. Hassan Butt, a spokesman for al-Mohjeroum, had traveled to Pakistan and had established himself there as a facilitator for those westerners traveling to Pakistan wanting to fight with the Taliban. Butt told the British Broadcasting Corporation (BBC) in a 2002 interview that he had recruited 200 Britons for combat with the Taliban, and went on to warn that "if they do return, I do believe they will take military action within Britain."

LONDON—JULY 7, 2005

For decades, London has been home to a network of extreme Islamist groups that have consistently used the liberal society in Britain to preach hatred abroad. The mass immigration of Muslims to Europe was an unintended consequence of the post-World War II guest-worker programs. Backed by friendly politicians and sympathetic judges, foreign workers, who were supposed to stay temporarily, benefited from family reunification and became permanent residents. Muslims now constitute the majority of immigrants in most Western European countries. Jihadist networks span Europe, thanks to the spread of radical Islam among the descendants of guest workers. A Nixon Center study of 373 mujahideen in Western Europe and America between 1993 and 2004 found more than twice as many Frenchmen as Saudis, and more Britons than Sudanese, Yemenites, Emiratis, Lebanese, or Libyans. Fully a quarter of the jihadists on the list were Western European nationals and eligible to travel visa-free to the United States.[38] The threat of an attack on the British capital has been an increasing security concern since the invasions of Afghanistan and Iraq. Britain is one of the core group of countries that bin Laden and his

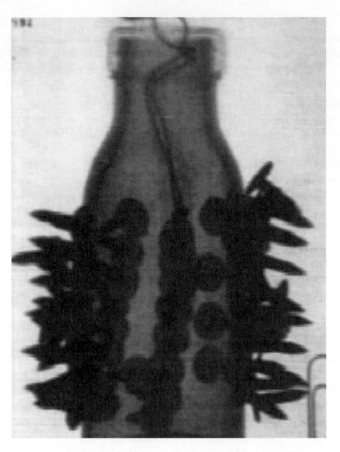

FIGURE 5-12 In the wake of the July 2005 London bombings, this X-ray photo was taken of a bottle bomb (one of 16) found in one of the suicide bombers' cars at Luton station (Canadian Press).

fanatics have listed for an attack, so it was no surprise to authorities when it eventually came. However, the method of delivery in the London subway attacks was what most disturbed the authorities.

July 7, 2005, dawned clear and sunny; it heralded the start of the G8 Economic Summit in Edinburgh, Scotland, attended by world leaders and the world's press. Thursday, July 7, happened to be the day after London had been awarded the 2012 Summer Olympic Games, and most Londoners were in a jubilant and celebratory mood. That would all change at around 8:50 A.M. at the height of the "rush hour."

Terror Attack Timeline—July 7, 2005

08:50—A bomb with approximately 10 pounds of high explosives is detonated by a suicide bomber aboard a westbound Circle Line Underground train about 100 yards into a tunnel after departing Edgware Road station.

08:50—A second explosive device detonates on a Piccadilly Line Underground train just after it left Kings Cross Station. This bomb also was estimated to contain approximately 10 pounds of high explosives.

08:50—A third explosion occurs on a Circle Line Underground train as it approaches Liverpool Street Station. This device is also believed to have contained about 10 pounds of high explosive.

09:47—A fourth explosion takes place on the upper deck of a Number 30 London Transport bus traveling from Hackney Wick to Marble Arch. The bus had been diverted from its normal route, and the explosion occurred outside the offices of the General Medical Council in Russell Square. The blast destroyed most of the upper deck, killing thirteen people.

The bombings from all four attacks left 57 dead and more than 700 injured. The timing of the attacks shows that this was well planned and scripted, and intended to cause maximum damage to human life, and to make the statement that the terrorist cell and probably future bombers/terrorists have the capability to strike at the heart of the British capital. This may have been a symbolic gesture on the part of the bombers, as it has become clear that all four attacks were the acts of suicide bombers. The motivations for the attacks will be the subject of months of analysis and investigation; however, it is clear that the bombers were all male, and three of the four were born in the United Kingdom, of Pakistani descent. The fourth, who came to Britain from Jamaica with his parents when he was a baby, had been a recent convert to Islam. All four fit into the age and education level characteristic of Hamas bombers in Israel. In London, unlike the United States and Canada, the motorway system, the streets of most major cities, and the transportation systems are lined with closed-circuit television (CCTV) cameras. Shortly after these attacks, CCTV footage showed the bombers gathering as a group at a regional train station before embarking on their journey to London. The vehicle they traveled in was recovered and valuable evidence gathered. It now seems that the intelligence community had identified at least one of the bombers as a potential Islamic extremist; however, a risk assessment did not determine that this target was a sufficient risk to warrant in-depth surveillance. This might seem strange, but we believe this is all part of connecting the dots. Does this possible miss indicate a tactical error on the part of Britain's security services? The sheer numbers of British-born Muslims now makes the task of identifying those who may pose a risk far more complex than simply keeping close tabs on foreign nationals visiting the country. As we mentioned in Chapter 3, the fairly lax U.S. Visa Waiver program allows virtual unrestricted access by British and other European nationals to the United States. This specific attack would likely have been organized by external forces that supported the cell or team by providing the ingredients for the bomb, timing devices and detonators, as well as the expertise to construct such a device. Tracking down the support network will be the main role for the police investigators. The British police have a wealth of experience in dealing with terrorism through their activities with Irish terror groups on the mainland, but this is the first instance of a terror attack carried out by suicide bombers and marks a dramatic turn in events. If suicide missions have the aim of disrupting transportation and sending fear through the traveling public, then the events that took place exactly two weeks after these attacks are worthy of discussion. On July 21, 2005, reports began coming in at around 12:30 in the afternoon of more bomb attacks on the London Underground system and bus transportation. In eerily similar circumstances, three backpack bombs were left on trains at the Oval Kennington, Shephards Bush, and Warren Street Underground stations. A small detonation appears to have taken place in each case, but no injuries were reported. The fourth bomb went off on the top deck of a Number 26 bus in Hackney, again without causing injury. This second round of attacks, although fitting in nicely to our preconceived views of al Qaeda and its affiliated groups, is likely to have been the work of al Qaeda-inspired Islamist sympathizers willing to make the statement that the threat remains, and that the security and police service are powerless to prevent future attacks. This incident could have been the warning of more to come.

The July 21 Failed Bomb Attack Timeline

- **12.25 P.M.**—Mukhtar Said Ibrhaim, Yassin Hassan Omar, and Ramzi Mohammed are believed to have entered Stockwell tube station.
- Yassin Hassan Omar traveled north on the Victoria Line.
- Mukhtar Said Ibrhaim traveled to Bank station on the Northern Line.
- **12.34 P.M.**—Ramzi Mohammed went north on the Northern Line attempting to detonate his improvised explosive device before reaching the Oval Kennington station; he ran out of the station.

- Yassin Hassan Omar attempted to detonate his improvised explosive device (IED) on the Victoria Line train as it approached Warren Street Station; he too ran out of the station.
- **1.06 P.M.**—Mukhtar Said Ibrhaim left Bank Station and boarded number 26 bus to Hackney Wick and attempted to detonate his device as he disembarked at Harrow Road.
- Hussein Osman is believed to have embarked at Westbourne Park onto a Hammersmith and City Line train heading west. He attempted to detonate his device near Sheppards Bush Station; he ran from the station.
- July 23—Unexploded device is found in Little Wormwood Scrubs Park.
- July 25—Yassin Hassan Omar is arrested in Birmingham.
- July 29—Said Ibrhaim and Ramzi Mohammed are arrested in West London.
- Hussein Osman is arrested in Rome by Italian police.

The bombs all failed to detonate and, this, as it turned out, was more owing to luck than ineptitude on the part of the terrorists. The bombs consisted of hydrogen peroxide mixed with chapatti flour, and detonators created out of high-strength hydrogen peroxide, acid, and acetone, which were placed in tubes of cardboard with light bulbs wired to batteries. United Kingdom forensic experts believe that they failed to detonate because the initiator was not sufficiently powerful to set off the main charge.

Name	Age	Residence	National/ethnic identity	Conviction	Sentence
Mukhtar Said Ibrahim	29	London	Eritrean/British national	Conspiracy to murder	40 years
Yassin Omar	26	London	Somali	Conspiracy to murder	40 years
Ramzi Mohammed	25	London	Somali	Conspiracy to murder	40 years
Hussein Osman	28	London	Ethiopian	Conspiracy to murder	40 years
Younis Tsouli	23	London	Moroccan/British national	Incitement to terrorist murder	10 years
Wassem Mughal	23	Chatham	United Arab Emirates	Incitement to terrorist murder	6.5 years
Tariq al-Daour	20	London	British	Incitement to terrorist murder	7.5 years
Yassin Nassari	28	London	British	Possessing terrorist related info	3.5 years
Omar Altimimi	37	Bolton	Unk	Possessing terrorist related info	9 years
Mohammed Naved Bhatti	27	Harrow	British	Conspiracy to cause explosions	20 years
Junade Feroze	31	Blackburn	British	Conspiracy to cause explosions	22 years
Zia ul Haq	28	London	British	Conspiracy to cause explosions	18 years
Abdul Aziz Jahil	34	Luton	British	Conspiracy to cause explosions	26 years
Omar Abdul Rehman	23	Bushey	British	Conspiracy to cause explosions	15 years
Qaisar Shaffi	28	London	British	Conspiracy to murder	15 years
Nadeem Tarmohamed	29	London	British	Conspiracy to cause explosions	20 years

FIGURE 5.13 List of convicted jihadists planning to emulate the July 2005 bombing campaign in London (Reproduced with permission from *Jane's Information Group—Jane's Terrorism and Security Monitor*).

In July 2007, four men were jailed for forty years each for attempting to carry out suicide bomb attacks on London's transport system. Muktah Said Ibrahim, the group's leader, had traveled to Pakistan in December 2004 to hone and learn his bomb-making skills at the same time as two of the July 7 bombers, Mohammed Sidique Khan and Shehzad Tanweer, were there. There was no evidence that the two attacks in London were linked, but the judge believed that both attacks were masterminded in Pakistan.

OPERATION CREVICE

In April 2007, five men were convicted of conspiracy to cause explosions using homemade devices, and although the group had discussed many targets and had acquired the fertilizer base for their bomb they appear not to have formulated a target or a defined target plan for their operation. **Operation Crevice** was a combined operation between the British, U.S., Canadian, and Pakistani security services, which ultimately led to the arrest of the five men. All five were born and raised in Britain, and had become radicalized in local mosques and had then traveled to Pakistan for training. The convicted men, Salahuddin Amin, 32; Omar Khyam, 25; Anthony Garcia, 25; Jawad Akbar, 23; and Waheed Mahmood, all received life sentences. The group came together in 2002, and several of them traveled back and forth between the United Kingdom and Pakistan to facilitate training. Following training, they began to focus on assembling an explosive device, but appear to have abandoned the idea of smuggling components for their bomb in favor of a homemade version. In September 2003, Anthony Garcia purchased 600 kilograms of ammonium nitrate, which they kept in a self-storage lockup in West London. In February 2004, staff at the depot notified police of the suspicious amount of fertilizer being stored. It appears that at this time several of the conspirators were already under surveillance. Members of the group were bugged, and conversations about target selection were recorded. Waheed Mahmood had previously worked for the National Grid and had stolen discs detailing the location of high-pressure gas pipelines. Having decided to use fertilizer, the group was having difficulty acquiring detonators, and it is alleged that they contacted a Canadian citizen, Mohammad Momin Khawaja, to supply them. Khawaja flew to the United Kingdom and met with Khyam; he did not bring detonators with him, but they discussed using remote long-range detonators for their attack. The group then bought airline tickets to Pakistan, and it was at that juncture that the group was arrested as the police and security services feared that the plot to detonate a bomb was now complete. The authorities had in fact exchanged the fertilizer for another inert substance. This conspiracy was being hatched at the same time as the July 7, 2005, attack on the London Underground system was taking place. It seems quite remarkable that this group that had traveled to Pakistan, and had actively trained and were highly motivated to carry out a mission, had only received rudimentary training and little or no direction from al Qaeda about how and where to target their attack. It became clear at their trial that Omar Khyam was training in Pakistan at the same time as the July 7 bomber, Mohammed Siddique Khan who, together with Shaheed Tanweer (July 7), were picked up on surveillance in the UK meeting with Khyam and Garcia.[39]

Shoot to Kill Policy

This policy was mentioned earlier in relation to an SAS assault on a PIRA active service unit in Gibraltar in the 1980s. Now, some two decades later, we are witnessing police on the streets of London carrying automatic weapons. They have the authority to shoot first if a suspect fits a profile of a suicide bomber, and to ask questions afterward. The danger in this is that innocents can and do get killed—in the SAS case, the ASU in question was known to the security services; however, they were not armed. In London, on Friday, July 22, 2005 (as Scotland Yard detectives were still investigating the failed suicide bombs of July 21 in London), a young, olive-skinned man ran from police in Stockwell after being repeatedly ordered to stop. He was wearing a heavy overcoat in 70-degree temperatures, and ran down into the Underground station and onto a waiting train. At this point, officers shot him in the head a total of seven times, and once in the shoulder (according to autopsy reports). Later, it was determined that the man was not a suicide bomber, but a Brazilian electrician Jean Charles de Menezes, who had no connection to any ongoing terrorist investigation or activity. Life on the streets of London has changed. Our archtypical view of the friendly British Bobby is now gone, and we can expect to see more such tragedies. In November 2007, the London Metropolitan Police were found guilty of endangering the public over the shooting death of Menezes and fined £175,000 with £385,000 in costs. The London Metropolitan Police Commissioner, Sir Ian Blair, was forced to resign in September 2008 by the new Lord Mayor of London who informed Sir Ian that he had lost confidence in him to continue in his position as Commissioner.

Points for Consideration

While the scheduling of the G-8 Summit, with world media attention, may be significant in the timing of the London attacks, the announcement of London's selection to host the Olympics would be far too recent an event for the terrorists to have planned for. It did, however, give added opportunity to the planners and the attackers. The complete lack of a specific, credible threat for another attack, either in the United Kingdom or Europe, does little to alleviate the threat. The London Underground and bus attacks are shown to be consistent with al Qaeda's approach to taking traditional terror tactics and using them on a scale not seen before. Consistent with current insurgent attacks in Iraq, the bus bombing may have been a required element in order to video the actual attack sequence. This attack has all the hallmarks of an al Qaeda or al Qaeda-inspired attack, as it is the only group currently executing this type of atrocity on a global scale.

Although prior attacks have not taken place in London, al Qaeda-affiliated groups have targeted British interests in both Europe and the Middle East:

November 20, 2003—Simultaneous car/truck bomb attacks occur on Hong Kong Shanghai Bank Corporation (HSBC) Headquarters and the British Consulate in Istanbul, Turkey.

June 6, 2004—A British Broadcasting Corporation (BBC) film crew is attacked in Riyadh, Saudi Arabia.

September 15, 2004—A British national is gunned down in Riyadh, Saudi Arabia.

March 19, 2005—A car bomb is detonated outside a British-operated cinema in Doha, Qatar.

The Threat Continues

We have detailed some of the major events that have involved radical homegrown Islamists; however, the threat has not diminished. At the end of June 2007, a car bomb was detected by authorities in the heart of London; before it could explode, a second vehicle was found a few hours later—the treasure trove of evidence that these unexploded vehicle bombs was able to provide put the police hot on the trail of resident Islamists. Within twenty–four hours, another attack took place at the International Airport in Glasgow, Scotland. At around 3.00 P.M., two men in a Jeep SUV rammed the entrance doors to the terminal; they had soaked themselves in gasoline, and the rear of the Jeep contained propane tanks. The driver and passenger were Bilal Abdullah and Kafeel Ahmed, respectively, both twenty-seven-year old doctors. Kafeel Ahmed died from the 90 percent burns to his body in August 2007. The terrorists in this instance turned out to be highly qualified and respectable doctors; a third doctor was arrested the following day. Although the attack and the improvised bombs were crudely made, there was the possibility that had all three vehicles detonated as planned, then there would have been a significant injury count. There is speculation that due to the failure of the two bomb laden vehicles in London that the Jeep (used in the Glasgow attack) may have been at a third as yet unknown location, somewhere in London. However, when the two primary vehilces failed to detonate, is is probable that the cell decided to relocate away from the London area and try for a softer but nonetheless spectacular target. On the other hand, the Labor Party had a new Prime Minister in Gordon Brown, a Scotsman; so this may have been an attempt to send the new Prime Minister a harsh message. As for the perpetrators, it seems that the reach of extreme Islam knows no bounds in its ability to radicalize even these professional young men. It could also be that they were inspired and not directed by al Qaeda, and had no organizational links to transnational jihadist networks. If it is determined that they did have jihadist links, it seems clear that the organization is incapable of supplying skilled terrorists, which in part will likely be because of conterterror activities of the security services. The threat to the United Kingdom is most definitely not from external forces but from internal, and the comment by Prime Minister Gordon Brown that Briton faces a threat that is "long-term and sustained" in nature would seem appropriate.

Cold War Returns to Britain—The Death of Aleaxander Litvinenko

In November 2006, a former Russian spy died an agonizing death in a central London hospital from radiation poisoning. It was determined that Litvinenko had been exposed in some manner to Polonium-210. The dose that he was administered could only have been prepared or manufactured in a nuclear facility and was administered to him through his food in a lethal dose. The radiation killed his cells causing his organs to shut down. According to a 2000 database produced by Stanford University's Institute for International Studies, approximately 88 pounds of radioactive material including weapon-usable uranium and plutonium were removed without authorization from nuclear facilities in the former Soviet Union. Litvinenko was an outspoken critic of Russian leader Vladimir Putin, who, while on his death bed, he accused of being complicit in his poisoning. Polonuim poisoning is a very unusual method of assassination unless it was intended to send a message to the wider ex-patriot Russian community in London. While the Russsian leader and his government have strongly rebuffed any suggestion of government involvement, the British authorities believe Litvinenko was killed by a former KGB agent, Andrei Lugovoi, and have unsuccessfully sought his extradition from Russia to stand trial in the United

EXTREME RIGHT-WING GROUPS

The issues of immigration and violence by right-wing groups against immigrants are not new phenomena for Britain. Hate crimes have been prevalent throughout the last thirty years of the twentieth century. The British National Party has a political agenda that demands Britain become independent from Europe and stop the influx of immigrants. The party also calls for the deportation of criminal and illegal immigrants. While this party maintains this stance, it has attracted a hooligan element that attacks indiscriminately persons of foreign origin. The loosely knit group at the center of these attacks—the Skinheads—is associated with football violence. Skinheads first appeared in Britain around the early 1970s, and could be found in almost every city in the country. This group is definitely a cult rather than an organization with any political aspirations. Skinhead youths have changed little since those early days of the 1970s: shaved heads, Nazi insignias, tattoos, checked shirts, blue jeans, and steel-toed "bovver" boots in the Doc Martens style. They were easily spotted angry young men who symbolized a tough, working-class background. The Skinheads were known for their violent rampages and became synonymous with extreme nationalism. Their favored targets for violent attacks were Jews, homosexuals, and Asians. Their style of dress soon went out of fashion; however, a hard-core—albeit small—movement much along the lines of neo-Nazi exists today. Their hate attacks target Jewish cemeteries and Asian shopping areas. Many of the attacks appear random in nature, but there is a belief that some attacks involving English soccer clubs are planned in advance. They are often seen at marches and parades with the British National Party, although there is no evidence to suggest that any Skinheads are members. The ebb and flow of this cult-like movement has endured for almost thirty years, and has spread its aggressive attitudes toward Jews and immigrants across Europe and North America.[40]

Summary

For almost forty years, the British and Irish security forces have had to combat the threat of Irish terror attacks both in Northern Ireland and the mainland. The experiences gained in tackling, combating, and prosecuting the men and women of Irish terror will have put them, hopefully, in a strong position to take on the homegrown jihadists who are even now plotting further suicide attacks on their adopted homeland. Intelligence assets and protocols designed to thwart the PIRA are now redirected to an entirely different and more troubling threat. The suicide attacks in 2005 on the London Underground and subsequent attempts in 2007 to suicide bomb Glasgow airport are an indication of the lengths to which these committed individuals will go to prosecute their cause. While the attack in Glasgow was far less sophisticated and well planned out, it leads observers to the belief that good intelligence is disruptive to their cause. The threat remains, and further attacks will undoubtedly soon come to fruition. Britain views itself in the forefront of threats from al Qaeda and jihadist groups, as it continues to be the staunchest ally of the United States in the War on Terror. Britain may be the breeding ground for fertile, young Muslim minds, but it is also clear that the spread and influence of al Qaeda continues unabated throughout the countries of Europe.

Web Sites

1. **Federation of American Scientists**—*www.fas.org/ irp/world/para/ira/htm*
2. **Conflict and Politics in Northern Ireland**—*http://cain. ulst.ac.uk*
3. **Jane's Information Group**—*www.janes.com*
4. **The Security Service MI5**—*http://www.mi5.gov.uk*
5. **Muslim Public Affairs Committee**—*http://mpacuk.org/*
6. **The Jamestown Foundation**—*http://www. jamestown.org/terrorism/news/article.php? articleid=2373989*

Endnotes

1. *The World Book Encyclopaedia*, vol. 11, S.V. "James II."
2. *The World Book Encyclopaedia*, vol. 10, S.V. "home rule."
3. http://en.wikipedia.org/wiki/Black_and_Tans.
4. Ibid.
5. (Quote taken from The Troubles—The Background to the Violence in Northern Ireland, Edited by Taylor Downing, a Channel Four Book.)
6. Strategic Forecasting: http://www.stratfor.com/standard/ analysis_view.php.
7. Paul Medhurst. *Global Terrorism* (New York: United Nations Institute for Training & Research Program of Correspondence and Instruction, 2002, p. 70).
8. John Horgan and Max Taylor. "Playing the Green Card—Financing the IRA." *Terrorism and Political Violence*, vol. 11, no. 2 (Summer 1999), 1–38.
9. *Press Association News.* "New hope of solving Shergar mystery." (April 4, 1996).
10. U.S. Department of State. Libya/PIRA background paper (July 1998).
11. Brendan O'Brien. *A Pocket History of the IRA* (Dublin: O'Brien Press, 2000, p. 108).
12. Strategic Forecasting: http://www.stratfor.com/standard/ analysis_view.php.
13. BBC News Service (October 4, 2001, 13.09 GMT).
14. Ed Moloney. *A Secret History of the IRA* (Penguin Books, 2002, Toronto Canada, p. 289).
15. Gayle Olsen-Raymer. *Terrorism: A Historical and Contemporary Perspective* (New York: American Heritage Custom Publishing, 1986, p. 197).
16. MIPT Terrorism Knowledge Base. http://www.mipt.org/
17. *The Diplock Report: Report of the Commission to Consider the Legal Procedure to Deal with Terrorist Attacks in Northern Ireland.* Cmnd.5185 (London: HMSO, 1972, p. 13).
18. Jim Smyth. "Stretching the Boundaries: The Control of Dissent in Northern Ireland." *Terrorism: An International Journal*, vol. 11 no. 4 (1988) (Queens University, Belfast; Taylor and Francis, 1988, pp. 289–295).
19. *Report on the Operation in 2003 of Part VII of the Terrorism Act 2000*, sec. 5, Nonjury Trial Section, 74, 75.
20. Andrew Boyd. *The Orange Order, 1795–1995* (1995), www.history.com.
21. Ibid.
22. *The Weekly Telegraph*, London (May 7, 2002, p. 13).
23. CAIN: http://cain.ulst.ac.uk.
24. Force Estimates—Janes Intelligence Review.
25. IRA Statement on Decommissioning: www.cnn.com/ world.
26. Extract Northern Ireland Peace Agreement: http:// www.nio.gov.uk/agreement.htm.
27. *A New Beginning in Northern Ireland*, Extract 1.3 and 1.4 London: 2, 3.

28. J.W. Soule. "Problems in Applying Counterterrorism to Prevent Terrorism: Two Decades of Violence in Northern Ireland Considered." *Terrorism: An International Journal*, vol. 12, no. 1 (1989).

29. Jonathan R. White. *Terrorism: An Introduction* (Pacific Grove, CA: Brooks/Cole Publishing, 1991, pp. 220–221).

30. Melanie Phillips. *Londonistan* (London: Encounter Books, 2007, p. xi).

31. *Draft Report on Young Muslims and Extremism*, UK Foreign and Commonwealth Office, 2004; Robert Winnett and David Leppard. *Sunday Times*, 10 July 2005.

32. Immigration, Research and Statistics, Home Office. http://www.statistics.gov.uk/cci/nugget.asp?id=261.

33. Mathew Mcallester. "Islamic radicals draw attention in Great Britain." (May 23, 2004), www.startribune.com.

34. "These statistics are compiled from police records by the offices of the National Coordinator for Terrorist Investigations. (They are subject to change as cases go through the system.)" Crown Copyright 2007. http://www.homeoffice.gov.uk/security/terrorism-and-the-law/.

35. Melanie Phillips. *Londonistan* (London: Encounter Books, 2007, p. 6).

36. Ibid, p. 9.

37. The SIAC judgment, 29 October 2003, p. 14, para. 48. In making this ruling, the SIAC relied on the precedent set in the case of *Secretary of State for the Home Department v Rehman* (2001) UKHL 47, in which the House of Lords concluded that no particular standard of proof was required of the Secretary of State in reaching his judgment or assessment that an individual's deportation was conducive to the public good.

38. Robert S. Leiken. Nonresident Fellow, Foreign Policy Studies. *Europe's Angry Muslims*. The Brookings Institute (July 7, 2005).

39. Janes Terrorism and Security Monitor—June 2007.

40. Anti-Defamation League. *The Skinhead International, A Worldwide Survey of Neo-Nazi Skinheads* (New York: ADL, 1995). ADL, 823 UN Plaza New York. http://www.nizkor. org/hweb/orgs/american/adl/skinhead-international.

CHAPTER 6

Western Europe

*The ones that truly believe are the ones who
become suicide pilots.*

FRENCH TERRORISM EXPERT ROLAND JACQUARD

Learning Objective

The study and review of this chapter will enable you to

1. Discuss reaction to left-wing terrorism in Germany;

2. Explain the threats posed by Palestinian supported terror groups in Europe in the 1960s and 1970s;

3. Explain the connection between the attacks of 9-11 and foreign terror cells;

4. List the terrorist groups that changed the way in which governments would in future handle terrorist threats and actions.

Terms to Remember

Army for the Liberation of Armenia (ASALA)
Carlos the Jackal
Communist Combatant Cells (CCC)
Dev Sol
Euzkadi Ta Azkatasuna (ETA)
Frente Revolucionario Anti-Fascista Y Patriotico (FRAP)

Grupo Especial De Operaciones (GEO)
Herri Batasuna Party
Kurdistan Workers Party (PKK)
Milli Görüs
National Organization of Cypriot Combatants (EOKA)
North Atlantic Treaty Organization (NATO)

November 17
Partisan Action Group (GAP)
Red Army Faction
Union of Islamic Communities and Organizations in Italy (UCOII)

August 2, 1980—84 people die in what was at the time Europe's worst terrorist attack when a massive bomb detonated at Bologna Railway Station in northern Italy.

June 29, 2002—A bomb detonates in the hands of Savvas Xeros and starts a chain reaction of arrests of November 17's members.

March 11, 2004—201 people are killed when bombs are detonated at Madrid railway stations.

OVERVIEW

Domestic terrorism in Spain had been the exclusive domain of the Euzkadi Ta Azkatasuna (ETA) terror organization in the Basque region . . . that is until May 2004. ETA has continued its bloody bombing campaigns, in spite of an earlier ceasefire agreement and concessions in areas such as local government and education. In this chapter, we examine the effects of Islamic extremism and the attacks of March 2004 in Madrid and the wider implications for other European countries fighting the menace of extremism. France, in contrast, still contends with sporadic attacks from dissident Algerian factions as well as the homegrown Corsican terrorists. Like other countries in Europe, France has also seen immigrant jihadists joining the war in Iraq and fighting against the United States. Germany, unused to being viewed as a terror haven, is firmly on the map in that regard as the launching pad for the planning of some of the suicide hijackers of 9-11. Germany has also been contending with terror of a subtly different kind—from that of secretive al Qaeda cells some with plans to attack U.S. interests in Germany. This chapter also discusses terror by hate groups that target ethnic minorities such as the neo-Nazi Skinhead factions. In the broad battle for the suppression of terrorist acts, we shall also examine the role played by the European countries in freezing monetary assets of terrorist support networks. Italy has also seen the effects a free society has on the abilities of terror cells to propagate and pursue their ugly mission of terror. In Greece, terrorism has been the province of the shadowy **November 17** group. Until the spring of 2002, authorities had made no headway in managing, or even attempting, to arrest any of its members.

SPAIN

Spanish Nationalism and the Basques

The Basque region of Spain spills north across the Pyrenees and into southern France, and it is estimated that half a million Basques live on French soil, with approximately 2.5 million living within the borders of Spain. Historical facts about the initial origin of the Basque people are uncertain; however, it is known that they have been living in this region since long before the Gauls and Iberians settled in Spain and France. The Basques have their own language called Euskera that is not derived from any other European language or dialect. With the size of the region's population, it would be logical to expect that Basque territory might be a self-governing principality, similar to Monaco. However, the Basque people do not have their own homeland and, in similar fashion to the Irish Republican movement, have been fighting for self-government and their own homeland since the first quarter of the twentieth century. General Francisco Franco came to power during the Spanish Civil War of 1936–1939 and ruled Spain as an iron-fisted dictator until his death in 1975. In the intervening years since then, Spain has achieved rapid economic growth and prosperity.

Basque Separatism

As the twentieth century drew to a close, there were only two European regions of nationalist conflict. Of course, the most notable and most documented has been the long terrorist campaign for separation from England waged in Northern Ireland. The Basques of the Pyrenean region of Spain have long waged their own internal struggle for a national identity and have not enjoyed a separate homeland or autonomy since the twelfth century. Amazingly, they have managed to maintain and protect their own language and culture over the centuries. General Franco's approach to dealing with the Basque Nationals was to suppress them at all costs by incorporating the Basque region into Spain at the end of the Spanish Civil War and outlawing both their culture and their unique language. Franco's actions led to a rebirth of Basque Nationalistic fervor in the late 1950s. Spain continues to suffer from the scourge of terror attacks perpetrated by the frustrated ETA. In 1999, ETA broke its "unilateral and indefinite" ceasefire and recommenced a bombing and assassination campaign. Since the turn of the century, attacks have increased and, like the attacks by Irish Republicans, the Basque

FIGURE 6-1   **Map of Spain** (Central Intelligence Agency, *The World Factbook*, 2008).

separatists favor the indiscriminate use of remotely detonated bombs in public places to make their point, as well as assassination of local and state officials. Following the 9-11 attacks in the United States on New York and Washington DC, the U.S. government, which re-designated ETA every two years as a Foreign Terrorist Organization, went one step further in October 2001. At this time, ETA was designated, under the President Bush's September 23, 2001 Executive Order 13224, a "Specially Designated Global Terrorist Organization." Executive Order 13224 was specifically aimed at those persons and groups that provide financial support and assistance to terrorist organizations. More specifically, the order further blocked property and prohibited transactions with persons who commit, threaten to commit, or support terrorism. In February 2002, under Executive Order 13224, the U.S. Department of the Treasury designated twenty-one Spanish nationals as members of, assisting in, sponsoring, or providing financial, material, or technological support for, or financial and other services to, or in support of ETA's acts of terrorism, and are otherwise believed to be acting for, or on behalf of them. These twenty-one individuals were identified by the European Union on December 21, 2001, for their involvement in terrorist acts.[1]

Euzkadi Ta Azkatasuna (ETA)

In 1959, the Basques formed the Euzkadi Ta Azkatasuna (Basque Fatherland and Freedom). This group was then dedicated to promoting Basque independence. ETA was not originally formed as a terrorist group . . . but, following General Franco's vicious oppression of the Basques, the group was more or less compelled to retaliate with more violence. ETA, much like the Irish IRA, gathered its membership support from the working classes. The members come from regions that identify with the strong and unique ethnic identity of the Basque people. The members are invariably young, frustrated, and nationalists with deep anger against their lack of autonomy. The majority of Basques favor nationalism, but do not support the terrorists' violent "any means to an end" approach to resolve a political goal of self-government and determination. ETA has, over the past twenty-five years or more, been a fragmented organization that has seen many offshoots of the original groups formed, disbanded, and re-formed again.

A political report, commissioned in 1986 by the Basque regional government, described the Basque region as being amenable to political solutions. It also described ETA as "an unfortunate child of the Franco Dictatorship." Much of the report suggested political solutions such as how to accommodate Basque Nationalism within the framework of Spain and the European Economic Community (EEC). One of the recommendations was that Basque terrorists, who under Spanish law were tried in Madrid's "special courts," should instead be tried in their Basque courts. And further, they recommended that policing of terrorists should come under the control of Basque police and not those of Spain's National Police.[2]

Since its inception in the 1950s, ETA has been riddled with ongoing internal squabbling, bitter dissension, and discontent. The group split apart in 1966, into what was known as ETA-Zarra (or old ETA) and ETA-Berri (or young ETA). ETA-Zarra was further divided into two subgroups: ETA-5 and ETA-6. The subgroup ETA-5 was then divided further into **ETA-Military** and ETA-Politico Military, and the most hardened and seasoned campaigners for armed action come from the subgroup ETA-Military.[3] These splits have caused confusion and consternation among the Basque people as to which of these proliferating schisms . . . to support or oppose. "Actions Unite–Words Divide" is the slogan adopted by ETA-Military, and their terrorist members adopted the same cell-like structure as that used by the Provisional IRA terrorists on active service unit duties. ETA-military commandos, or irurkos, were made up of three-man cells called "Sleeping Commandos" and were organized in the late 1970s by the ETA-Military Commander, Miguel Apalategui.[4] The "sleepers" were to be called up from the Basque community to perform a single terrorist act and then return to their jobs under relative anonymity. To finance its terror campaign, ETA used robbery and extortion as its main means of sustenance.

Development of the ETA Organization

ETA's growth, and its Youth Movement, can be traced back to the Basque Nationalist Party (PNV). The party had been an exiled force since Franco's defeat of Spain's Republicans in the 1939 Civil War. The PNV then operated as a government in exile, as another group based in France. The Basque Youth Movement was determined to ensure that the Basque's unique language and culture would not die. ETA's political position was purely democratic. In 1957, a group of young Basques traveled to France to try to convince the government in exile to organize and lead an armed struggle against the hated General Franco. The PNV leader, Jose Maria Leizaola, and his government, flatly rejected the idea. ETA's First Assembly came about in May 1962 when a small group of university students and activists gathered to discuss how to go forward and gain support for their ideals. Much of what they discussed at that First Assembly was the example set by other groups struggling for a national identity against such regimes as Fidel Castro in Cuba, and others struggling against their colonial masters throughout Africa and the Middle East. This became the first few steps along ETA's path toward terrorism. Determined not to be easily captured by the police, they set up their own three-man cell structure and defined ETA as a "Revolutionary Movement for National Liberation."

The works and writings of Mao Tse-tung played a significant role in the development of ETA's organization. Impressed by Mao, a young Basque named Jose Ortiz, studying in Paris, attempted to rouse others in ETA to the same level of understanding that he had found in his readings of Mao. Then, the Second ETA Assembly, in 1963, set about attempting to rid itself of Maoist influences. No split occurred as a result of the Second Assembly but shortly thereafter, the Maoist militants within the organization produced their own mini-manual, *Insurrection in Euskadi*. The tract brought forth the Basque determination to embark on a war of revolution. A Third Assembly in 1964 broke away from the old, established Nationalist PNV, and, influenced by the Maoists within ETA, redefined the group as being anti-capitalist and anti-imperialist. An ETA leader defined the new direction as: "The primacy of the human person and of his rights is the basis for any political action." As ETA ideology veered toward the left, the worried French government took action against ETA founder members on French territory and removed them from the frontier region with Spain.

Eustakio Mendizabel Benito headed up ETA at the start of 1970. Benito's group was known as the "Military Front of ETA." He believed passionately in securing a homeland for the Basque people and preserving their language, and had a deep concern about the future. Benito financed his terrorist operations, like so many other such groups, by resorting to criminal activities such as armed robbery, extortion, and kidnappings. The group had no training in the art of weaponry or the use of explosives. Members actively purchased arms through the underground arms networks and bought, as their first consignment, 500 new, 9-mm Firebird Parabellum pistols. They also stole explosives from local factories and rock quarry operations.

ETA members are known to have received training from the Popular Front for the Liberation of Palestine (PFLP) at its training base in South Yemen. One of the ETA's most audacious acts was the assassination of Luis Carrero Blanco, who served as the vice president of Spain under General Franco from 1967 until his death on December 20, 1973. When General Franco stepped down from office in June 1973, Carrero Blanco succeeded him as the Prime Minister of Spain. ETA has become more advanced and well equipped, and has formed alliances with the Revolutionary Armed Forces of Colombia (FARC) terrorists and members of the PIRA (Northern Ireland). While the "public face" of the PIRA would desire that the public appreciate and believe its moves to decommission all weapons and explosives had been honest, its terror arsenal has been replaced with explosives provided by ETA. One can only make the obvious assumption that the explosives have been traded for the bomb making and training expertise that has been a well-known hallmark of the PIRA.

New Century—New Campaign

The previously mentioned ceasefire, which ended in 1999, had probably been misread and likely misunderstood by both the Spanish government and the popular press. It was widely reported that ETA was on its knees and ready to capitulate. At a secret meeting between ETA and the Spanish government in 1999, the government presumed that ETA was ready to deal. However, what actually took place at that meeting has never been revealed. In fact, ETA quickly resumed hostilities against the Spanish government. Similar ceasefires had taken place in Northern Ireland, and many observers have felt that these ceasefires, far from being the death knell for the terrorists, were a time for covert rebuilding and recruiting of new blood into this type of terror organization. The **Basque Socialist Coalition**, known as the **Herri Batasuna** (Peoples Unity) Party led by Arnoldo Ortiz, officially denies any links or involvement with the ETA terrorist organization. Throughout the spring and early summer of 2002, ETA terrorists engaged in a very prolonged campaign targeting Spain's lucrative tourist industry. The ebb and flow of terrorist success is most often measured by the terror group or its organization's ability to remain at large and to function in a cohesive manner. Spanish authorities, in a cooperative effort with France, have seen some spectacular successes in capturing ETA's leadership. In October 2004, French police had arrested seventeen Basque separatists in the Pyrenees region of France. Not only were the arrests a blow to the ETA organization, but at the same time, they uncovered caches of arms and more than 700 kilograms of explosives, including potassium chlorate, an ingredient used in the manufacture of bombs. Subsequently, the Spanish government passed legislation that made political parties that supported terrorism illegal. To follow this through, the government officially declared the Herri Batasuna Party illegal in 2003. The Spanish law also ensured that there could be no resurgence under a new name, so that when former members of the banned group reappeared with the intention of running in local elections in 2003 under the name Autodeterminaziorako Bilgunea (AuB), these lists were determined to be nothing more than Batasuna in a new guise and were similarly banned by the Spanish Constitutional Court. ETA has continued to seek out new targets to attack and one such target has been the lucrative Spanish holiday market and in its effort to attack the tourists visiting Spain during summer months planned a bombing attack on a cross channel ferry, fortunately the authorities disrupted these plans and no attack has taken place yet. The group also attacked Madrid airport over the Christmas season in 2006.

On November 4, 2004, Ortiz attended a mass in San Sebastian and called out for an end to the violence. The War on Terror had caught up with Batasuna, and by June 2003, the organization's name appeared on both the European and U.S. Department of State lists of terrorist organizations.[5] Although Batasuna does have considerable Basque support, the new upsurge in Islamic extremism in Europe no doubt had a big effect on the Spanish population and even more particularly so since the bombings of the Madrid train stations in March 2004. The president of the mainstream Nationalist Party and also one of the fathers of Basque Nationalism, Xavier Arzalluz, commented publicly, "The time has come to fight for the independence of the Basque region in the streets!" Ostensibly, the appeal that set the Herri Batasuna Party apart from others was that it conjured up memories of the repressive regime of General Franco. The legislation may have had the markings of a bygone era, but Herri Batasuna's political influence would continue to exist in some format and, along with it, some 200,000 voters, many of whom could become willing supporters of a separatist movement. Many observers compare the ETA movement to the Irish Republican Army and their "Troubles" in Northern Ireland. ETA's campaign, however, was actually markedly different from the IRA's, as it specializes in kidnappings and extortion. This has rarely been a trademark of the Irish terrorist. The future for ETA does not look very good.

The outlawing of Herri Batasuna and associated parties won't stop ETA from exploding more bombs and assassinating more Spanish officials. In spite of the fact that large numbers of the Herri Batasuna Party have been arrested for their involvement and support of ETA attacks, the party continued to maintain its position by publicly stating that it had no ties, neither institutional nor political, to ETA. The Spanish Judge Baltazar Garzon has stated that Herri Batasuna was inextricably linked to legal groups and organizations that continued to provide economic and political support to ETA. From these groups it finds new recruits for the possibly ailing ETA ranks. Although there are no valid estimates of ETA strength, it still continues to use indiscriminate bombings.[6]

Similar to its Irish republican counterparts in Northern Europe, ETA has not been able to maintain a long and lasting peace accord. The nearly five-decades-old battle for a truly Basque homeland has cost more than 850 lives, and the current ceasefire that was proclaimed in the summer of 2006 came to a halt within six months . . . with an ETA bombing attack on Madrid Airport on December 30th of that year and although they did not declare the ceasefire over, the Spanish government most certainly considered it over. Formal notification by ETA came on June 5, 2007, with an announcement that their "permanent ceasefire" was over, stating "minimum conditions for continuing a process of negotiations that do not exist."[7] The Spanish, who may have had some lingering sympathy toward the ETA struggle have been turned away with the diet of violence that was unleashed in the Madrid railway attacks of 2004 and although the ETA organization has not been as active as in pre-Madrid or 9-11 years they do still pose a threat. For a peace process to evolve the same conditions as in Northern Ireland would likely be required to include a cessation of violence and a verified decommissioning of weapons and explosives. The parallels to Irish terror are quite often drawn but in essence there are fundamental differences between the two conflicts. There is no equivalent sectarian divide of Catholics and Protestants and neither is there dual involvement of the two governments, the British in London and the Republic of Ireland in Dublin.

While the ETA has returned to violence, the Irish issue is almost settled with a power sharing administration between the two major protagonists. The Basque region of Spain has had more power devolved to it than Northern Ireland did, and current attitudes to any separation of any region of Spain is pathologically opposed by politicians in Madrid, while at the same time the democratic processes in the UK, which frequently debates the separation of Scotland and Wales, is based on the wishes of the general public. For any resounding political success with ETA there must first be consensus on what the common ground is for a peace process among the ruling parties in Madrid . . . something that is non-existent at the moment.

FIGURE 6-2   The Basque separatist group ETA detonated a bomb at Madrid's new airport terminal on December 30, 2006. The bombing marked the fiery end to a nine-month ceasefire that had spurred the greatest hopes in a decade of a peaceful end to the conflict (Canadian Press).

Opposition to ETA

Accion Nacional Espanila (ANE), Spanish National Action, was a right-wing terror movement that specifically targeted Basque separatists. The group was formed in the 1970s and operated against the Basques in the regions of northern Spain. The group is known to be responsible for reprisal killings of many ETA terrorists and sympathizers, and has also been active in bombings on both sides of the Spanish border. Spanish and French cooperation in 2001 combined to produce results, leading to the arrests of thirty-seven ETA members residing in France. Going along with the United States in its war against terror, the French agreed to extradite immediately to Spain any ETA members who had warrants issued against them. In the past, the stumbling block for the French had been the political issue surrounding nationalism, which invariably led to interminably long delays in the extradition process.

Spain has been effective in combating terrorism with its paramilitary Special Operations Group, **Grupo Especial De Operaciones (GEO)**. GEO is part of the Spanish National Police and is stationed in Guadalajara, near the capital, Madrid. The GEO has special response capabilities and is responsible for VIP protection duties, as well as countering and responding to terrorism. It was designed, set up, and organized along the lines of many other special counterterrorism units throughout Europe, and is specifically focused on dealing with terrorist attacks, including aircraft hijackings, maritime threats, and hostage-taking. The GEO can also be utilized in a support role for Spanish police operations outside the realm of terrorism, and is trained and active in protecting visiting heads of state and providing security for high-profile events such as the Olympic Games held in Barcelona in 1992.

GEO has had some noteworthy successes over the last decade and was responsible for foiling the assassination attempt on King Juan Carlos in 1995, as well as an attempt by the ETA to attack the Barcelona Olympics in 1992. GEO remains the foremost threat to terror cells and activity on the Spanish mainland.

ETA History Timeline

1959—Euskadi Ta Askatasuna (ETA), or Basque Homeland and Freedom, founded during dictatorship of General Franco to fight for self-determination.

1968—Police chief murdered in ETA's first planned killing.

1973—Franco's Prime Minister, Luis Carrero Blanco, killed when his car passes over ETA explosives in Madrid.

1980—ETA's bloodiest year. Almost 100 killed, despite Spain's return to democracy.

1985—First ETA car bombing in Madrid. American tourist killed while jogging and sixteen Civil Guards wounded.

1987—ETA supermarket bombing attack in Barcelona—twenty-one shoppers killed. ETA apologizes for "mistake."

1995—The Popular Party opposition leader, Jose Maria Aznar, later prime minister, escapes ETA bomb. Saved by vehicle's armour plating.

1998—ETA announces truce. It lasts fifteen months.

2000—A former Socialist health minister, Ernest Lluch, shot dead in Barcelona.

FIGURE 6-3 ETA car bomb explosion outside a police station in Calahorra in northern Spain on March 21, 2008 (Canadian Press).

2004—Al Qaeda train bombings in Madrid kill 191 people and reinforce Spanish revulsion against violence. ETA's suspected leader and twenty-one suspects arrested.

2005—Spain's parliament gives government permission to open peace talks with ETA if the group lays down its arms.

2006—Permanent ceasefire announced, lasts approximately six months.

2007—ETA ceasefire at an end.[8]

Frente Revolucionario Anti-Fascista Y Patriotico (FRAP)

Although little remembered today, Spain suffered from other terror groups, one of which was the left-wing Maoist group **FRAP**.[9] In an ironic twist, FRAP received worldwide recognition when members were sentenced to death in 1975 for killing a Spanish policeman in Madrid. The worldwide outcry led to demands for Spain to be thrown out of the United Nations. Unmoved by these outbursts for clemency, the Spanish government followed through with the executions as planned on September 27, 1975.

Grupa De Resistencia Antifascista Primo Octobre (GRAPO)

The **Anti-Fascist Resistance Group of October First (GRAPO)**[10] was another left-wing terror group active in the 1970s at about the same time as FRAP. Four Spanish police officers were killed in a retaliatory action over the execution of five left-wing terrorists. The group takes its name from this action on October 1, 1975. GRAPO was also responsible for at least one attempt on the life of King Juan Carlos of Spain. Juan Carlos Delgado de Codex led the group until he died in 1979, while attempting to evade arrest.

After 9-11 . . . Spain embraced the global assault on international terrorism and now it strongly supports mutual assistance as a strategy to deny safe haven to terrorists. Mutual agreements and cooperation with the French have enabled both countries to root out ETA suspects on the French side of the border. Spain has also been responsible for the break-up and arrest of two suspected al Qaeda-affiliated cells in late September and November of 2001. In July 2002, Spanish police continued to chase down suspected al Qaeda members operating on the Spanish mainland. In July 2002, the Spanish police arrested three men who were alleged to be of Syrian origin . . . two were naturalized and the third held Spanish residency. The police found videotapes from a 1997 visit to the United States in the suspects' possession. The footage shows various angles of the New York World Trade Center towers. The Spanish Interior Minister, Angel Acebes, has stated that the footage "was obviously not what a tourist would make." In addition, other high-profile locations had been taped, including the Golden Gate Bridge in San Francisco, the Sears Tower in Chicago, the Empire State Building, and the Disneyland theme park in California. While this footage was filmed some four years prior to the 9-11 attacks, it gives considerable weight to the theory that al Qaeda is very well organized and plans its attacks in meticulous detail and far in advance. Photos of the bridges focused on the construction of the bridge supports, while another two videos showed violent mujahideen "terrorist training," fighting, and suicide bombers.[11]

The suspected cell leader was Syrian-born Imad Barakat Yarkas, also known as Abu Dahdah. Yarkas is believed to be an organizer and financier for Islamic extremists operating in Spain. Along with two other suspects charged in connection with the 9-11 attacks are Moroccan-born Driss Chebli and another Syrian, Ghasoubun. Spanish prosecutors are seeking 74,000 years of jail time for each of the accused and fines of 893 million euros.[12] The wider prospects for international terrorism in Spain have focused mainly on Algerian nationals residing in or visiting the country. Since 9-11, Spanish authorities have made significant headway in this respect when Mohammed Atta, one of the 9-11 suicide pilots, met with an Islamic cell operating in Madrid in the summer of 2001. Atta's motives and his activities in Spain have not been established, but one may draw the inference that he was meeting and planning strategies for terrorist attacks. Spanish authorities have established that Atta tried to visit an Algerian who was serving a prison term for forgery. In trying to determine how widely spread the Osama bin Laden network is, Atta would seem able to give the most direct evidence of links among activities in France, Spain, and the United States. Atta was present in Spain at the same time as Tunisian immigrant and former pro soccer player, Nizar Trabelsi, who was later arrested in a plot to bomb the U.S. Embassy in Paris. If Atta met with Trabelsi, the next rational conclusion would be that the attacks in New York and Washington were to be coordinated with bombing attacks in Europe.[13] As the investigation and links continue to be investigated, the widespread nature of the cell structure in Europe appears to infect France, Spain, Italy, Germany, the Netherlands, as well as the Eastern European countries. Spain's significance on the terror map also indicates that Ahmed Ressam visited Spain prior to his arrest in the plot to blow up the Los Angeles International Airport on New Year's Eve in 1999.

ISLAMIC EXTREMISTS' ATTACK ON SPAIN

The characteristics of the attack on Madrid's rail system on March 11, 2004, bear some wide discussion. First, this was the worst act of terrorism on Spanish soil since the end of its civil war more than sixty years ago. Second, the Conservative government was quick to blame ETA for this attack. A similarly quick response by U.S. authorities initially blamed Islamic extremists for the attack on the Alfred P. Murrah building in Oklahoma City, and it was later determined to be a homegrown version of terrorism. ETA's modus operandi was not necessarily characteristic of this attack for the following reasons:

1. ETA has usually claimed responsibility for its attacks, but did not do so on this occasion.
2. ETA has invariably given advance warnings of its attacks, often to minimize civilian casualties.
3. The leader of the banned Batasuna Party publicly denied any ETA involvement and indicated an Arabic involvement (this was considered an unusual comment on Batasuna's part).

FIGURE 6-4 Rescue workers work around the destroyed intercity train at Atocha station in Madrid after a number of blasts rocked railway stations in Madrid on March 11, 2004. The bombs were detonated by Islamist militants (Canadian Press).

The ten, almost simultaneous, attacks in Madrid were immediately blamed on ETA, which would have meant that ETA had changed its targets away from the police, judiciary, and politicians, and was now going after the public in general. It was not long before authorities found a videotaped message outside a mosque and, thus, the wider political implications for both Spain and the rest of Europe were about to be realized.

Up until the Madrid bombings, Spain's ruling Conservative government led by Jose Maria Aznar was a committed ally and supporter, not just of the U.S. and British War on Terror but also of deploying Spanish troops to the war in Iraq. To the Spanish voter, the realization was clear—three days before a general election an Islamic extremist cell had detonated bombs in Madrid, killing more than 200. An already disillusioned public that did not support the War in Iraq was now going to turn what was likely to have been a Conservative victory into a stunning defeat. The Spanish returned the Socialist Party under the control of Jose Luis Rodriguez Zapatero to power. The power to openly change the direction of a nation was about to be shown to the men of terror. The first act by the Socialist government was to pull Spanish troops out of Iraq. To many, this was seen as a cowardly reaction to terrorism. What is also becoming apparent is that the Islamic extremists who attacked the Spanish public with such devastation were supporters of the al Qaeda movement. With Osama bin Laden residing in the mountains of Afghanistan, would he or his direct group be capable of coordinating such an attack in Spain? Al Qaeda might be evolving into more of a "movement" and a cause for which young, disaffected Muslims have come to identify. This one attack changed the political will of a nation, and its effects caused Spain to turn its back on a previously stated commitment in Iraq. Does Spain's about-turn mean that the country is bending to the will of the terrorists? Some would say yes: however, since the Madrid attacks, the Spanish have managed to unearth a considerable treasure trove of Islamic extremists operating within its borders. Iraq aside, the threat is clear and the cause is also clear: Islamic extremism is not on the decline, but is increasing, and the longer the War on Terror is centered in Iraq, the more it will continue to grow.

The fanaticism of the terrorists and their will to destroy not only innocents but also themselves was played out in the Madrid suburb of Leganes in April 2004. The group that had claimed responsibility for the Madrid train station bombing had stated that it would turn Spain into an inferno if it did not pull its troops out of Iraq and Afghanistan and cease its support for the United States. The letter containing this threat was supposedly from a group calling itself "Abu Dujana Al Afgani" (Ansar Group, al Qaeda in Europe). Significant concern for Europe, and not just Spain, is the link believed between this group and Abu Musab al-Zarqawi, the Jordanian terrorist conducting his insurgency campaign in Iraq. While this may be speculation, what is known is that Ansar al-Islam is an extreme Islamic terrorist organization that has been held responsible for numerous attacks in Iraq, Turkey, and Jordan. The Spanish police cornered the main suspects in the Madrid train station bombings in an apartment in Legenes. Before the raid could begin, the terror cell in that apartment building detonated a bomb that destroyed part of the building. In the following confusion, several of the suspects may have fled the area. The explosion killed three people. To Spaniards the term 11M is as significant as 9-11 is profoundly disturbing for Americans. 11M symbolizes the March 11, 2004, Madrid station bombings that killed 191 and injured nearly 2,000 other commuters. The culmination of the investigation saw a number of young radical Islamists in a Madrid court in October 2007. The three lead suspects convicted of murder and attempted murder each received sentences of 34,000 to 40,000 years in prison; however, Spain does not have the death penalty and the longest a prisoner can serve is forty years so the 34,000 term was largely symbolic. A total of twenty-one out of twenty-eight defendants were convicted of the lesser charge of belonging to a terrorist organization.

FRANCE

A Long Acquaintance with Terrorism

On the face of it, France has not seen the same level of terrorist activity as have, perhaps, other major European countries. This does not imply that France has been left out of the problems facing other governments in dealing with terrorists. However, European terrorists and Middle Eastern terror groups have always needed bases, not only safe houses, but also safe countries from which to mount their terror campaigns without too much political or police interference. Until the Madrid bombings, Europe was perceived to be a logistics base for terror groups and cells. However, the reality is that Europe (France included) has become a fertile recruiting ground for the likes of Abu Musab al-Zarqawi, the Jordanian leading the insurgent attacks in Iraq. The country of choice for many terrorist groups and terrorists has often been France. From a strategic point of view, terror groups have considered France an ideal location from which to strike and then return to hide. It has borders with Spain, Italy, Germany, Switzerland, Belgium, and Luxembourg, plus an efficient transportation network of roads, air, sea, and rail systems.

France has not been immune to terror. History books are full of atrocities perpetrated during the French Revolution. (As noted earlier, the word "terrorism" was born from that time.) What needs more consideration and discussion is the type of terror groups that utilize France for their base of operations and their reasons for doing so. The next section discusses some specific groups that have successfully used France as a base to mount terror operations and even to carry on turf wars outside their own countries.

FIGURE 6-5   Map of France (Central Intelligence Agency, *The World Factbook*, 2008).

Terrorism means different things to different people. The German Federal Republic uses the legal process to combat terrorism, considering terrorism as the use of criminal acts for political purposes. Without belaboring the topic of definition, the student may want to consider that terrorism could easily be termed an import–export industry.

The Popular Front for the Liberation of Palestine (PFLP) in France

In the late 1960s and 1970s, France became a European safe haven for the beleaguered terrorist organization, the Popular Front for the Liberation of Palestine (PFLP). The PFLP was one of the most militant and aggressive Palestinian groups linked to the Palestine Liberation Organization (PLO). Wadi Haddad controlled and led the "external" operations from a secure base, in either South Yemen or Aden, and directed PFLP operations in Europe. The PLO had set up safe houses in Paris for its planned attacks in Europe. The audacious attacks carried out by this group include some of the most spectacular attacks in recent history: the attacks at Zurich Airport in 1969, the Dawson Field hijackings in 1970, and the attack on OPEC (**The Organization of Petroleum Exporting Countries**) headquarters in Vienna in 1975, led by Ilich Ramirez Sanchez, better known as Carlos the Jackal,[14] who now resides in a French prison cell. The Jackal was finally linked to the following attacks:

- 1972—Massacre of eleven Israeli athletes by Palestinian gunmen at the Munich Olympic Games.
- 1973—Edward Sieff, whose family owned Marks and Spencer's department stores, was attacked and wounded.
- 1974—Armed assault and take over of the French Embassy in the Hague by members of the Japanese Red Army.
- 1975—Two French intelligence agents were killed while investigating the Orly Airport attack on an Israeli airliner.
- 1975—Attack on the OPEC headquarters in Vienna in which three people died and eleven were taken hostage.
- 1976—Air France, airliner to Entebbe, Uganda, hijacked
- 1982—Bombing attack on the Paris—Toulouse Express.
- 1983—Bombing attack on Marseille's main railway terminal killing five people.

The justification for terrorism has been argued vigorously. However, since the end of the World War II, the use of terror as a means to an end has had several primary benefits: (1) to receive local and, in most cases, worldwide attention for a specific cause or causes; (2) as an outlet for political impotence and frustration; and (3) to carry out combative measures for countries or states not in the financial position to take direct action themselves. In the political arena, the latter would occur where a state did not wish to take direct confrontational action but rather use the cloak of terror, for which it could always deny any involvement in the aftermath of the event. The Palestinian cause will be dealt with under a separate chapter; however, many organizations like the PLO, and various other offshoots, used France in the 1960s and 1970s as a friendly base for their operations.

Japanese Red Army

The Japanese Red Army terror group was also prominent in France in the 1970s. This group was pledged to a worldwide Marxist revolution. It actively supported and was very much involved in the Palestinian struggle in the Middle East.[15] The group was formed in the early 1970s and is based on feudal Japanese Samurai warrior traditions, as well as Marxism. The Japanese Red Army operated throughout the world and has been involved in major international terror attacks in support of the Palestinian cause. The group participated in the ferocious attack on Lod Airport in Israel,[16] killing Puerto Rican pilgrims in the departure lounge. The group also murdered two U.S. sailors in Italy in 1988. In continuous worldwide support of its Palestinian brethren, the group also hijacked an airliner and held the passengers hostage, demanding the sum of $6 million (U.S.) in ransom.

Action Direct (AD)

France is a center of operations for international terrorism, but it also has had its own brand of internal terrorists. AD was a Marxist terrorist group unlike many of its other European and Middle Eastern counterparts. It evolved, not out of the 1960s, but the late 1970s and early 1980s. Considered a left-wing revolutionary group, it began as a Communist revolutionary organization and limited its focus to virulent anti-American sentiment. One of its more audacious attacks was a raid on the Goldenberg Restaurant in Paris in August 1982 when gunman opened fire, killing six patrons and injuring a further twenty-two other diners.

With its strong views on American interference in European affairs, it adopted the anti-American rhetoric of the Palestinian cause and began to attack Israeli and Zionist targets as well as those associated with capitalism and imperialism, such as the **North Atlantic Treaty Organization (NATO)**. France had withdrawn from NATO in July 1967. As AD evolved, it began to build a network of other left-wing terror groups operating in Europe, particularly in Germany, France, and Belgium. The Communist Combatant Cells (CCC) in Belgium,[17] the Red Brigade in Italy, and the German-based Red Army Faction, supported AD's campaign against NATO. Thus, with its original base in Paris, AD also became an international terror organization.

There is some skepticism in official quarters that this group had to feed off and be supported by the other left-wing groups. It must be noted that since the unification of East and West Germany, the level of left-wing violence and terror has decreased. This, however, does not indicate that the group has split up or disintegrated, and AD will most likely continue, in some form, to espouse and support its philosophical goals.

Alien Invaders

To say that French soil had been invaded from a far-away planet would not be a correct assessment in any shape or form. However, in recent times it has been the breeding ground for unwelcome guests from the European and Middle East theaters of terrorist conflict. On the home front, there has been the **Front de la Liberation Nationale de la Corse (FLNC)**, a group of Corsican separatists, as well as the extreme left-wing AD group. Another is the Armee Republicaine Bretonne (ARB). The ARB and the FLNC are distinct in their aims as compared to the AD. They are purely regional French factions with the goal of local autonomy. AD, on the other hand, has somewhat fuzzy international ideological goals. Confusingly, to the casual or the uninformed observer, AD has gone after anti-Jewish interests, which, one would normally associate with the extreme right-wing as opposed to the extreme left. France's tolerance for the number of groups active within its borders is probably born out of its own realization of how the French Republic was created. This tolerance has led many other groups to use Paris as a primary base for internal and external operations. The Corsican Army (Armata Corsa), a vicious terrorist organization, on the other hand, has its roots in the criminal classes of Corsica and seems to function partly on the nationalist scene and partly on the criminal side of life. It does, however, denounce the Mafia-style activities that have plagued the island of Corsica. Armata Corsa seeks to create an island state that is independent from France, and also the return of Corsican terrorists imprisoned in mainland France. The group has been mainly involved in attacks against public figures and buildings as well as tourist locations, and has concentrated nearly all the attacks on the island itself.

With the disintegration of the Empire of the Shah of Iran, students in Paris took control of the Iranian Embassy to show their support for Ayatollah Khomeini. The city was a tolerant host to both sides, with both pro- and anti-Khomeini supporters making their protests public. Both groups clashed during a street protest.

The **Army for the Liberation of Armenia (ASALA)** represents another region of Europe. This French group of exiled Armenians was intent on promoting its cause and airing its grievances against the government of Turkey. ASALA's grievances go back in history to 1915–1922, when the Turks massacred more than 1 million Armenians Headquartered in the Middle East its actions are attention seeking and aimed at securing a homeland of its own. Most Armenians lived within former Soviet Bloc countries.

By far the most aggressive groups operating out of Paris have been the Palestine Liberation Organization (PLO) and the Algerian Islamic terrorist group known as the Armed Islamic Group (GIA). The PLO's headline-catching events included the rocket attack at Orly Airport, when in broad daylight two Lebanese Palestinians calmly parked their car near the runway and, armed with a RPG-7 rocket launcher, fired at an El Al flight taxiing for take-off. Fortunately, the rocket missed the El Al aircraft and hit an empty Yugoslav jetliner.[18] The two terrorists escaped capture at the airport. Not to be outdone by the failure, another attack was scheduled for Orly Airport six days later. By this time, the airport was strongly protected by military security. The group entered the airport with an assembled bazooka, much to the astonishment of the armed police, and a furious gun battle between police and terrorists ensued amid hundreds of passengers and spectators in the airport building. As for the GIA, their actions in France in the mid-1990s included attacks on the Paris Metro subway system. Approximately 5 million Muslims live in France out of a total population of 58 million. GIA's actions in France resulted in bombings throughout 1995 and, in July of that year, a gas canister bomb exploded in the subway, killing seven and injuring eighty-six. Algeria, a former French colony, had been fighting a rising tide of Islamic radicalism. Rather than accede to it, the Algerian government, at that time under Liamine Zeroual, used military force to repress GIA. Because of its support for the Algerians, the French thus became a very legitimate target for the GIA, who hoped to force France to withdraw its support for Algeria. Aircraft hijackings, by GIA terrorists, seem to be almost a prediction of the tragic events of 9-11. In December 1994, armed terrorists disguised as police officers boarded an Air France jet in Algiers and hijacked it to France. The aircraft was reportedly packed with explosives to be detonated over the capital city of Paris. The aircraft landed in Marseilles and was stormed by members of the crack anti-terror group Groupe d' Intervention de la Gendarmerie Nationale (GIGN), which ended the fifty-four-hour siege that culminated in the death of three of the hostages and all of the terrorists. Following the events of 9-11, the French government has been unstinting in its support of the War on Terror. French officials expressed their determination to eradicate the "perverse illness" of terrorism, and have offered military and logistics support. France played a leading role and supported the invoking of Article 5 of the UN Treaty, which covers a mutual-defense clause. As part of Operation "Enduring Freedom," the French provided logistical support with its army, navy, and air force.

In April 2001, Fateh Kemal was sentenced in Paris for operating a support network believed to be linked to al Qaeda. He was sentenced to eight years in jail. The French were able to establish links between Kemal's operatives and Ahmed Ressam, the millennium bomber arrested by U.S. Customs agents when he was crossing from Canada into Washington State with a bomb intended for a terrorist attack at the Los Angeles International Airport. On the day before the 9-11 attacks, French authorities began to investigate a group linked to al Qaeda that planned to attack U.S. targets in France. The group's leader, Djamel Beghal, was extradited from the United Arab Emirates (UAE) to France in October 2001 as part of that investigation. It was a very patient intelligence work which revealed that Kemal was both an expert document forger, head of the network of which the Roubaix gang was a part and had also spent time in Afghanistan, where he'd been in contact with Bin Laden. The French authorities believe it is clear that in the decentralized, compartmentalized, and intersecting root system of Islamic networks, Kemal had been given the responsibility for creating and transporting false ID documents to be used by militants being assembled in Turkey, Bulgaria, Belgium, France, Bosnia, and North America.

Kemal and twenty-three associates were convicted for activities related to association with terrorist enterprises. There was no demonstrative proof of their service or allegiance to Bin Laden, although such links would be impossible to verify given the dispersed, cellular nature of these operations (thus organized precisely to prevent police from following a linear trail back to the top) and their vague hierarchy and direction.[19]

Under Executive Order 13224, French authorities froze 54 million dollars, the assets of the former Taliban government of Afghanistan. Although France has been a strong UN ally, the U.S. desire to seek death penalty for Zacarias Moussaoui, the only man arrested in connection with the

9-11 attacks, has meant a lack of cooperation between the French intelligence services and those of the United States. Both the French and German governments have been supplying evidence to the United States concerning Moussaoui, but not material that could lead to his execution. In spite of this, the French have been party to counter-terrorism discussions at the G-8 summit meetings.[20]

AL QAEDA IN FRANCE

With France's close ties to the North African continent during its colonial era, it is not surprising that many immigrants from Morocco and Algeria ended up in France. The planning and recruiting for the 9-11 attack did not take place in Muslim countries, but mainly on the continent of Europe—in Germany, France, and England in particular. The security and intelligence failures can be linked back to Europe and a failure to follow up on specific intelligence reports from the French security services. As for al Qaeda, most of its French cells were made up of second-generation immigrants, and as investigations have shown (particularly in Germany after 9-11), most of the combatants showed little or no interest in Islam in their own countries. It seems the seeds of Islamic radicalism may have been planted in the mosques of Europe. Radical Islamic beliefs are not the sole domain of Muslims. Richard Reid, the infamous "shoe bomber," and two French-native brothers, David and Jerome Courtailler, are converts to Islam. Lionel Dumont, a French citizen from the northern French town of Roubaix, and also a convert to Islam, saw military service with the French in Somalia. In the early 1990s, he went to the former Yugoslavia and joined a mujahideen group, the Takfir wal Hirja, in Bosnia. He returned to France and formed an organization with others from the North African communities, called the Gang of Roubaix, which was involved in several terrorist attacks. His links to al Qaeda have never been confirmed, and so far he has evaded arrest from French authorities.[21]

During President Bush's reelection campaign in 2004, he commented publicly, "More than three quarters of al Qaeda have been brought to justice." This comment may well have sounded great for the electorate but as we have seen, al Qaeda has become or is becoming a rallying cry movement for young and impressionable Muslims around the globe, more particularly those in Western countries such as France. The first prominent example is British citizen Richard Reid who boarded an American Airlines flight in Paris bound for Miami on December 22, 2001, and attempted to detonate a bomb hidden in his shoes. Richard Reid may seem an unlikely candidate for an Islamic convert—nevertheless his troubled youth brought him into contact with those that would ultimately set him on a path to terrorism:

1992–1994—The British Home Office says Richard Reid was twice incarcerated at Feltham (Middlesex) Young Offenders Institution in West London—for ten days in 1992 and a month in 1994. It was not known what charges led to Reid's incarceration there.

Late 1998 and early 1999—Brixton Mosque chairman Abdul Haqq Baker says Reid and Zacarias Moussaoui—the only person so far charged with conspiracy in the 9-11 terrorist attacks on the United States—attended the same South London mosque during this period, though it is not known if they were there at the same time.

July 2001—Israeli government officials say Reid travelled to Israel for "around ten days" before traveling by land to Egypt.

August to December 2001—Reid reportedly lives in Amsterdam, working in restaurants.

Early December 2001—Reid allegedly spends ten days in Brussels, Belgium, staying at the Dar Salam hostel in an Arab and North African neighborhood.

December 5/6, 2001—Reid tells Belgian authorities he'd lost his British passport. The British Embassy issues him a new one.

December 15, 2001—Reid reportedly checks out of the Brussels hostel and arrives in Paris, France, the next day.

December 17, 2001—Reid buys round-trip ticket from Paris to Miami, Florida, to Antigua. Police say he appears to have spent his entire time in the area around the Gare du Nord, one of the city's major train stations.

December 21, 2001—French authorities question Reid after a security agent becomes suspicious because Reid is traveling without checked luggage. Authorities eventually say Reid can board his flight, American Airlines Flight 63, but by then it has already left Paris.

December 22, 2001—Reid boards American Airlines Flight 63, which is following the same route as the flight he'd missed a day earlier. Ninety minutes later he allegedly tries to use a match to light explosives hidden in his shoes, and is subdued when passengers and crew jump on him and strap Reid to his seat. Doctors aboard the aircraft sedate him. Plane diverts to Boston, Massachusetts, and Reid is arrested and charged with interfering with a flight crew.

December 28, 2001—A federal judge denies Reid bail and remands him to jail in Plymouth, Massachusetts, which is about 30 miles south of Boston.[22]

Reid was sentenced to life in prison in Federal Court in Boston on January 30, 2003. To many Reid has been cast as a bungling amateur when in fact the opposite is the case as there is ample evidence that this man had been in contact with other jihadis, and had received terror training. With respect to Moussaoui, the intelligence sources on both sides of the Atlantic should have picked up on the activities and involvement of Zacarias Moussaoui. French intelligence tracks nearly all North Africans traveling from France to Pakistan and/or Afghanistan. British newspapers reported that the French Directorate of Territorial Security repeatedly informed its counterparts in Britain that Zacarias Moussaoui, who was residing in London in the early 1990s, had made trips to both Afghanistan and Pakistan. Further, he was considered to be involved in terrorism. As part of the investigation into the murder of three French Consular staff in Algeria, Moussaoui's name was found in an address book that was seized. Unfortunately, information provided to the British appears to never have been acted upon.[23]

The FBI had been warned in advance of the 9-11 attacks, and that Moussaoui was associated with Osama bin Laden. Moussaoui was arrested on an immigration violation; the French intelligence report was never acted upon.[24] Zacarias Moussaoui was born in France and, like other suspects arrested in Germany, was not known as an Islamic extremist. In 1992, he went to England and shared an apartment with the French Courtailler brothers while he studied for a degree. Sometime during this period he came under the spell of the fanatical Muslim cleric, Abu Qatada.

It is also becoming clear that Europe is currently the recruiting haven for Islamic militants. In January 2005, the French government confirmed that three of its citizens were killed in fighting with Iraqi insurgents against the United States and coalition troops. Iraq has all the attractions for Islamic youth, as did the war in Afghanistan more than two decades ago. The Iraqi invasion has therefore increased the recruiting level in European countries from the multitudes of disillusioned Muslims.

Italy has more than 1 million Muslims and 10,000 native Italians who have converted to Islam. Muslim associations are common in most European countries. The **Union of Islamic Communities and Organizations in Italy (UCOII)** is heavily influenced by Islam and has a Syrian-born head, Mohamed Nour Dachan. Italians and Europeans are increasingly concerned about the rise of extreme Islamic fundamentalism. In 2002, Randa Ghazy, a fifteen-year-old Italian girl who lived and studied in Milan, aroused considerable controversy. The girl wrote a book, *Seguundo Palestina* (*Dreaming Palestine*), which was published and has sold tens of thousands of copies. The book glorifies Arab teenagers who have embraced the jihad against the "Zionists." The book, which is characterized by an anti-Semitic and Islamist approach to the Arab-Israeli conflict, praises suicide attacks against the Jews. The youngster also appeared on TV and radio talk shows and has reached a level of notoriety and even respectability. Although UCOII has, in the past, condemned fundamentalist terrorism, its influential secretary, Hamza Roberto Piccardo, has repeatedly expressed his approval of suicide attacks within Israel.[25] The growth of such extreme organizations and the recruiting of European Muslims for the global jihad have only been exacerbated by the war in Iraq. European countries have reported mainly second-generation immigrants from Middle Eastern and North African countries where the young and often disillusioned are seen as excellent candidates for radical recruiters for the jihad in Iraq and elsewhere. Having seen events unfold in London, it is no surprise to note how global the jihad network of Muslim extremists is becoming. The French connection to jihad is also relevant. Jihad is being spread by young Algerian immigrants to France, many of whom are second-generation Algerians. Several European countries were targeted by a French-Algerian named Jamal Beghal, who was arrested in July 2001 in the United Arab Emirates as he was about to transfer from a flight from Pakistan to a flight to Europe. The truly transnational nature of jihad is evident here: This man, with links to al Qaeda, had lived in London and attended the Finsbury Park Mosque along with Richard Reid (the shoe bomber), the Courtailler brothers, Zacarias Moussaoui, and Nizar Trabelsi. Beghal had attended training camps in Afghanistan and recruited mostly young Algerians living in France for the cause of jihad. Beghal's network conducted surveillance and plotted to attack the U.S. Embassy in France and a U.S. Air Force Base in Belgium. It is highly probable that all had links through the Algerian Salafist Group for Preaching and Combat (GSPC) to al Qaeda. Members of Beghal's group considered themselves to be takfiris (i.e., extreme religious literalists who view anyone who does not subscribe to their extreme and literal interpretation of the Koran as unbelievers and worthy of attack).

The threat from within Western Europe comes from the Middle East and North African immigrant population and the threat in the United Kingdom has come from second generation immigrants and from converts to Islam. The same trend is evident in France. In Paris during November 2005, two Muslim youths died while being chased by French police, which sparked a week of rioting. France is home to over 5 million Muslims, many live in slum areas of the major cities and finding work is difficult at best. The presence of so many disgruntled youth, both immigrant and second generation, provides ample fodder for radical Muslim extremists to recruit for jihad either in Europe, the Middle East, or North America.

GERMANY

A Mixed History of Fascism, Terrorism, and Democracy

Historically, Germany survived two world wars, was divided into two nations, paid the price of Nazism as well as Communism, and, at the end of the twentieth century, rose again as a major industrial power in Europe. The history books clearly describe the years between the two world wars as being economically harsh for Germany. This section will deal with the rise of terrorist groups in Germany. However, it is important to look back at some significant periods of the twentieth century that affected the German people as well as their neighboring countries. Between the two world wars, Germany saw the rise of the Nazi Party and the ultimate power of its leader, former Austrian Corporal, Adolph Hitler. Germany was humbled by its reparation payments and crippled by the devastation of the dismal, worldwide Great Depression of 1929. The German populace faced massive unemployment and starvation. The reparation repayment was renegotiated under the terms of the Young Plan, against which Adolf Hitler campaigned long and hard throughout Germany. By July 1932, the Nazi Party held 38 percent of the seats in the German Parliament (Reichstag).[26] Hitler's passionate, self-appointed mission was to lead the badly depressed Germany back to greatness, rid it of Communist and other influences, and purge the society of its ills. To achieve this, he had to gain absolute power and control. In 1933, Paul Von Hindenburg, then president of Germany, proclaimed Hitler as chancellor (prime minister). With total control, Hitler then proclaimed his government as the "Third Reich." With that, Germany's dictator began his own reign of terror on the German people. By the end of July 1933, through legal processes, Hitler had destroyed the German constitution and outlawed freedom of the press, unions, and all political parties with the exception of the National Socialist Party (the "Nazi" Party). His own breed of police, the dreaded Gestapo, hunted down all opponents of the government. Many were arrested on suspicion alone, and more often than not, were jailed or shot.

FIGURE 6-6   Map of Germany (Central Intelligence Agency, *The World Factbook*, 2008).

The Nazis used terror-like tactics to gain control over the populace, and to keep it. All German children, both boys and girls, were required to join the Hitler Youth or the Society of German Maidens. These children of Germany were indoctrinated into the Nazi philosophy and military discipline and were used as spies to inform on family members who did not embrace Nazi doctrines. A sophisticated network of spies monitored and reported on the German people and fostered an atmosphere of physical and psychological terror.

Germany's New Order

There have been hundreds of accounts, books, and films about Hitler's "Final Solution" for the Jewish problem. His belief was that the German people were a genetically superior race and that his country had to be purged of the impure, non-Aryan peoples. Those groups singled out for special treatment were Jews, Gypsies, Poles, homosexuals, and Slavs. The term *Holocaust* is widely used to define the mass murder of over 6 million Jewish people. Hitler and his Nazi Party members began their reign of terror on the Jews as early as 1933, almost immediately after Hitler came to power. Sometime in early July 1933 (the date has never been precisely confirmed), beginning around the ninth of the month and lasting for about forty-eight hours, Nazi Party members destroyed thousands of Jewish businesses and synagogues throughout Germany, killed dozens of Jews, and sent almost 40,000 to concentration camps. The night is referred to as *Kristallnacht* (night of the broken glass).

When the German armies rolled across Europe, a similar fate awaited Jews in those countries that Germany had conquered. The names of the camps still strike fear and loathing: Belsen, Auschwitz, Buchenwald, Dachau, and many others. Hitler's unique brand of terror, which accounted for the mass murder of many millions of Jews and other persons considered non-Aryan or those who did not fit his Aryan picture of perfection, was a simple means to an end. The Nazi leadership saw it as the cleansing of a nation and those it had conquered. Such use of political terrorism was considered a weapon of psychological warfare.

Post-World War II Germany and Terrorism

After the end of World War II, a long period of rebuilding and healing took place. By the 1960s, the Federal German Republic was experiencing three different types of terrorism. (1) Left-wing terrorism came about from the imported views of radical students and their opposition to the U.S. war in Vietnam. (2) Right-wing terrorists opposed the left-wing radicals in a continuation of the anti-Communist past. (3) Criminals also adopted the terror group's actions and copied and mimicked their attacks for personal criminal gain.

The 1960s were a period of widespread student revolt and protest, although in Germany there was no real catalyst to take the protests to the next stage. Student protests were the order of the day on many university campuses in Europe and the United States as a platform for anti-Vietnam War protests. Modern terrorism, particularly in Germany's case, has been typified by indiscriminate violence, sensationalized by the murder of innocents.

The student body of left-wing radicals at the Berlin Free University, in a somewhat copycat style, protested against American involvement in Vietnam. The protests were restricted mainly to marches and the distribution of leaflets, but there was no catalyst in place to take any serious action at a higher level that would involve violence directed at the authoritarian government. Two main protagonists came to the forefront of the student protests—Andreas Baader and Gudrun Enselin.[27] As on many university campuses of the 1960s, both Communism and Marxism were prevalent. This was also the case at the Berlin Free University. Baader, Enselin, and, later Meinhof, were all committed Marxists. Out of the Berlin University was developed the Red Army Faction. The RAF was led by Gudrun Enselin and by the freewheeling Andreas Baader, who presented more of a playboy image than that of a terrorist.

Kidnapping and holding for ransom was a hallmark of many of the terrorist groups operating in Europe and the Middle East during the turbulent years of the 1960s and 1970s. The kidnapping of a prominent German industrialist Herr Hanns-Martin Schlayer by members of the Red Arm Faction is an example of how desperate the various groups were for media and government attention. Schlayer and his entourage were attacked in a Cologne suburb and his bodyguards were killed. The intent was to trade their captive for captured RAF members and for Andreas Baader. Schlayer was executed by his abductors when the German authorities failed to acquiesce to the demands.

Red Army Faction (RAF)

This group of committed Marxists sought to engage the United States in a combative role by extending the Vietnam War to German soil. They achieved this by attacking U.S. interests in West Germany, and particularly U.S. servicemen and military bases. Many books describe Andreas Baader as more of a delinquent and a follower than a committed terrorist. He seemed, in many accounts, to draw pleasure from being at the center of an infamous criminal network. To finance its program of violence, the group resorted to a series of bank robberies and other crimes.

The igniting factor that sparked this group into action on a grand scale was, in fact, an eloquent German lawyer, Horst Mahler, who joined the student movement to give it impetus toward a violent action. In 1968, Enselin and her boyfriend Baader attempted to destroy two Frankfurt department stores with firebombs. They were both captured and sentenced and, a year later, temporarily released during an amnesty for political prisoners. When the amnesty was over, they fled to France as fugitives. They returned to West Germany to join with Horst Mahler, but Baader was again arrested. At this point in the group's development, Ulrike Meinhof came into the picture.

Meinhof was the editor of an underground newspaper called *Konkert*.[28] The paper had been launched in the 1950s, sponsored and supported by Communist groups in East Germany. Meinhof is reputed to be a close friend of Gudrun Enselin, and it was Enselin who persuaded Meinhof to assist in Andreas Baader's prison breakout. The jailbreak on May 14, 1970, resulted in changing the name of the group to the Baader-Meinhof Gang. Over the following two years, Meinhof spent time in Jordan not far from the capital, Amman, and received training in weaponry from the Palestinians. Meinhof and colleagues became skilled in the use of what was to be their favorite weapon, the famed Russian Kalashnikov (better known as the AK-47 assault rifle). Having received training from the PLO, the group went into action and was involved in the attack on the Organization of Petroleum Exporting Countries (OPEC) headquarters in Vienna, Austria, on December 21, 1975. At this point, the RAF joined forces with a group that called itself the "Arab Revolution," a cover name for the Popular Front for the Liberation of Palestine (PFLP).[29]

Ilich Ramirez Sanchez, better known as "**Carlos the Jackal**," led the assault on the OPEC building in Vienna in 1975 that targeted the oil-producing countries, was more a case of raising money than having a significant political impact. The Saudi Arabian and Iranian governments are believed to have paid a ransom of $50 million for the safe return of their nationals. Among the five strong groups that attacked the building were two German terrorists—Gabrielle Tiedermann and Hans-Joachim Klein. During a gun battle with Austrian security officers, Klein was captured and seriously injured. No political demands were made except the demand that the Austrians broadcast a political statement for the Baader–Meinhof group. The Austrians allowed the terrorist and a number of the hostages to fly to Algiers and then to Tripoli. The large amount of ransom money was transferred to a bank in Aden to bankroll further terrorism.

German authorities arrested the principals of the Baader–Meinhof Gang, which numbered about 100 active supporters. In 1972, Baader, Meinhof, and Enselin were sentenced to long prison terms. The group was housed in the maximum security Stammheim Prison. Ulrike Meinhof, suffering from acute depression, hanged herself in her prison cell on May 9, 1976. As for the remainder of the group's members, it is something of a controversy as to how they met their ends. On the night of November 18, 1977, several members of the Baader–Meinhof group died from self-inflicted gunshot wounds in their prison cells.[30] Many have asked how guns could have been smuggled into a top-security prison. The most likely answer to that is lawyers for the group brought in the weapons to attempt a breakout.

The deaths coincided with news of a dramatic rescue by the anti-terrorist group GSG-9 in October 1977. The GSG-9 stormed a Lufthansa aircraft at Mogadishu, Somalia, killing three hijackers and rescuing the ninety passengers. It would seem to be entirely logical that the Red Army Faction, or as it was usually called, the "Baader–Meinhof Gang," would cease to exist. However, it exists to this day and its growth has not been stemmed by arrests of prominent members over the past two decades. With arrests of successive leaders and gang members, the RAF has continued to rise like a Phoenix from its own ashes. It is believed that its growth in the 1970s and 1980s was due, in part, to an elaborate communications system and network set up among the imprisoned terrorists, their lawyers, and the activists still working for the cause. Public opinion soured toward the RAF in 1977, an opinion that had generally held them up as romantics fighting for a misunderstood cause. This was naturally embellished by the popular press, which continued to sensationalize the group's criminal activities and misdeeds. However, the previously mentioned hijacking of a Lufthansa airline to Mogadishu, Somalia, by terrorists supported by the RAF resulted in the murder of the aircraft's pilot, Jurgen Schumann. This single act helped turn public opinion against the group.

TERRORISM AND THE OLYMPIC GAMES MOVEMENT

High profile targets will always be on a terrorist groups' agenda and one of the most significant and historic attacks against innocent civilians is encapsulated in the massacre of Israeli athletes at the Munich Olympic Games Village between September 5 and 6, 1972. At a time when European countries relied on their police as front line troops to handle criminal attacks of all nature—the attack by members of the Palestinian terrorist group Black September were to cause a complete rethink and evolution of police response to terrorist threats and for West Germany it caused the Federal Police to create a crack counter terror unit, the Grenzschutzgruppe-9 (GSG-9). The Black September attack was intended to force the Israeli government to release more than 200 Palestinians being held in Israeli jails, as well as RAF members being held by West German authorities. The initial attack resulted in the immediate death of several athletes and coaches and over the next twenty-four hours the police negotiated with the terrorists to get them and their hostages to a local airfield. It was at this point that the German police attacked in an attempt to rescue the hostages. The resulting firefight saw all nine hostages and their captors killed.

The RAF probably reached the pinnacle of its terrorist existence toward the end of the 1970s. The group was responsible for the assassination of the West German Attorney General, Seigfred Buback, and Hans-Martin Schleyer. The group went so far as to attempt to murder the head of NATO in Europe—U.S. Army Four-Star General Alexander Haig. The RAF was still active in the 1980s and by then had joined forces with a little-known German terror unit called the June Second Movement and another called the Red Cells. Little is known of their members or their numbers; however, it seems likely that the groups continue to operate independently of each other. The significance of the date, June 2, is in remembrance of Benno Ohnesorg, who was killed on that date in 1967 during a student protest that turned into a riot. The most notorious act carried out in the name of the RAF was the abduction of Peter Lorenz, a candidate for the post of mayor of West Berlin. The ransom paid was for the release of four of the group's compatriots who were then flown to South Yemen.

A Reawaking of Germany's Past

Germany had relied on an influx of foreign immigrant workers for the post-World War II rebuilding of its destroyed infrastructure. 2001 celebrated forty years since the introduction of the *Gastarbeiter* program, in which Turkish immigrants were brought into Germany strictly for use as menial laborers. Some Germans continue to be openly hostile to immigration policies, especially since the events of 9-11. If advocates of restriction on the movement of labor are successful, it will likely have a negative impact on the long-term economical viability and growth of the powerful European Union. Integration by large numbers of immigrants to German society over the last three decades has clearly failed.

Anti-Semitic behavior and phobia still lurk as haunting reminders from Germany's dark past. Invariably, the message and threats of belligerent intolerance continue to come from radical German Skinhead and neo-Nazi factions. It would be incorrect to label every Skinhead as a racist, as many are from varying religious denominations that are nonracist and are not purveyors of hate crimes. Much of the bigoted violence in Germany has been directed against foreign workers, particularly poor and desperate Turkish immigrants. However, throughout the 1990s and into the new millennium, Jews and Turks became the Skinheads' target of choice. Year after year since, starting in 1990, there has been a steady increase in the number of hate crimes associated with Skinheads and attacks on members of Jewish and Turkish communities. They are most likely to be in their teens and in their early twenties. Skinheads usually operate in gangs and much of their hatred and violence is spewed after bouts of binge drinking. The gangs roam the streets looking for likely victims to attack. The collapse of the Communist regime in East Germany significantly affected the Skinhead situation. The emergence of the eastern Skinheads radicalized the movement in both numbers and militancy. Skins tended to move in with the extreme right-wing movements in Germany, namely Michael Swierczek's National Offensive, Frank Huebner's German Alternative, The National Front, and Christian Worch's National List.

German authorities were originally either slow or reluctant to respond to the right-wing threats being posed by the Skinhead's hate movement and propaganda; however, in the last decade or so, German authorities have banned some of the neo-Nazi groups and confiscated their propaganda materials. Skinheads have traditionally not aligned themselves with any particular political party, as they view the parties as being part of the "system."

Skinheads also view imprisonment as a badge of honor. Evidence indicates that Skinheads are receiving a thorough indoctrination in neo-Nazi ideology at "comradeship evenings" held in prison.

Much of this is provided by the Relief Agency for National Political Prisoners and their Dependants, a right-wing group that sends a steady stream of propaganda to incarcerated neo-Nazis and Skinheads.[31]

Germany in the Twenty-First Century

The unification of Germany, which was one of the most unexpected turning points in Germany's history, brought with it doubts about a new Germany's ability to cope with the depression and despair suffered by its people in the former East Germany. By the end of 1997, there were growing signs in German cities of right-wing neo-Nazi groups (Skinheads) fostering hate campaigns against foreign immigrants living in and coming to the new Germany. With most European communities lowering the barriers on movement between countries and with the fall of the Soviet Union, many thousands of ethnic groups surged westward for a "better life." What they found in Germany was a growing resentment, mainly by extreme right-wing groups, to the rising tide of outside ethnic groups seeking jobs in an already struggling economy. The Skinheads and others saw the immigrants as being responsible for the high rate of unemployment and the economic conditions. In many cities, extremists took the law into their own hands and, in shows of nationalist strength, set about abusing and intimidating immigrants.

By the spring of 1998, immigrants had virtually disappeared from some cities, having been frightened away by the fearsome onslaughts of neo-Nazism. No specific group or organized terror campaign is being sustained, although special police units are being utilized to break up obvious gangs of Skinheads. No one can predict how far—or if—Germany will regress toward a neo-Nazi influence, or whether this type of incident has been a mere pothole in the rough road to unification. What most observers are watching for from the German government is a signal that it fervently opposes the nationalist movements. However, with a growing number of incidents involving ethnic groups and neo-Nazi influences at various levels inside Germany's military, it is no surprise that there is a feeling of unease and terror in those who see the unsettling prospect of a rise in the nationalist movement all over again.

AL QAEDA IN GERMANY

Since 9-11 and its aftermath, Germany has come to the realization that it has become not only a safe haven but also a recruiting country for radical dissident Muslim youths. Imams in Germany's mosques were calling for a jihad against the United States. Students from North African and Middle Eastern countries were studying in university campuses throughout the country. Evidence points to Germany as being a staging post for Islamic extremists wanting to gain access to North America via forged travel documents, either directly or through Canadian ports of entry. This is a practice that has been ongoing for more than two decades. Many questions still remain, one of the most baffling being, "Why did the intelligence communities fail to detect the planning and steps toward 9-11?" Undoubtedly, that's a very difficult question, as we can now see that all the signs were there and the information on certain activities of groups and individuals was available. Clearly, it simply was not recognized as significant or it was ignored—or both. *The 9-11 Commission Report*, published in 2004, makes considerable mention of the involvement of the Hamburg cell and its growth and training in Afghanistan, its members' ability to freely move around Europe and the United States, and ultimately, its ability to plan and carry out, undetected, the largest terrorist event in recent history. A successful attack on the United States involving the members of the Hamburg cell would require complex planning and exceptional execution. *The 9-11 Commission Report* puts forward the following list that it believed al Qaeda would have required to fulfill:

- Leaders who were able to evaluate, approve, and supervise the planning and direction of the operation.
- Communications sufficient to enable planning and direction of the operatives and those who would be helping them.

- A personnel system that could recruit candidates, vet them, indoctrinate them, and give them necessary training.
- An intelligence effort to gather required information and form assessments of enemy strengths and weaknesses.
- The ability to move people.
- The ability to raise and move the necessary funds.

The information on the planes operation presented in *The 9-11 Commission Report* shows that by the spring of 2000, al Qaeda was able to meet these requirements. By late May 2000, two operatives assigned to the planes operation were already in the United States. Three of the four Hamburg cell members would arrive soon after.

Intelligence gathering and covert activities by Western governments was not at Cold War levels and, although the intelligence community and security services recognized the threat of al Qaeda, it undoubtedly underestimated the tactical capabilities of the group to strike deep into the heart of America. Germany had been more preoccupied with domestic issues and the revelation that planning for 9-11 had taken place within their country came as a surprise to most Germans. Two prominent members of the 9-11 hijackers, Mohammed Atta and Marwan Al-Shehhi, who are believed to have been the pilots that flew the aircraft into the two World Trade Center towers, spent a significant amount of time in Germany. Atta had studied at the Hamburg University for eight years; it appears that he attracted no suspicions from German authorities. He was not openly hostile and did not espouse radical or extreme Islamic views, at least not publicly. Since the fall of the Third Reich and Germany's rebuilding, the German government has been reluctant to interfere with individual rights and civil liberties. In Atta's case, subsequent investigations have revealed that he developed a small religious studies group that is now suspected of being a cover for his principal terrorist planning operations. In Germany, a religious freedom law forbids the government from banning or restricting any group that it recognizes as a religious group. Scientology is restricted under this law, as Germany has ruled that this is, in fact, a commercial enterprise, not a religion. As in the United States, German prosecutors must overcome a high standard of evidence to effect a prosecution. Germany's ability to gather and disseminate intelligence within its borders is also somewhat self-defeating. Law enforcement is decentralized, so police in one of Germany's sixteen states may not share information regularly with police in another region. Germany rarely conducts nationwide criminal investigations or passes information from international agencies to local police.[32]

The third pilot involved in the 9-11 attacks also spent considerable time in Germany. Ziad Zamir Jarrah was born in the infamous Bekka Valley in Lebanon, a stronghold of Hezbollah extremists. Jarrah and his immediate family were not religious fanatics by any means. His parents appeared genuinely shocked and surprised that their son would be involved in a suicide attack on the United States. Jarrah received a monthly allowance from his father that was more than adequate. However, Jarrah's involvement may have stemmed from his friendship with local radical Muslims in Aachen. Jarrah's transformation from an easygoing youth to an Islamic fanatic is puzzling to many. It appears that he drank alcohol and partied at college in Germany. His transformation to more radical ways evidently began around 1996 after he returned from a trip to Lebanon. He changed course in 1997 from dentistry to aircraft engineering for no specifically identified reason. At the same time, he was becoming more steeped in traditional Islamic ways. He grew a full beard and avidly read about jihad and debated the merits of Holy War with his friends. During the latter months of 1999, he told his girlfriend that he was planning to wage a jihad because there was no greater honor than to die for Allah. Radical Muslims in Aachen were involved in fundraising through local mosques for the Hamas terror group to aid suicide missions in the Middle East.[33]

As part of the coalition against terrorism, Germany has also banned a network of radical Islamic groups centered on the Kaplan organization based in Cologne. German police raided some 200 residences in seven separate German states in connection with the ban and seized the headquarters of the Kaplan group. Metin Kaplan, the Caliph of Cologne, is serving a prison sentence for

FIGURE 6-7 Islamic leader Muhammed Metin Kaplan, aka the Caliph of Cologne, stands in court in Dusseldorf in this photo taken on November 15, 2000. Germany outlawed 16 organizations linked to the jailed Turkish militant in September 2002, making use of anti-terror legislation passed after September 11, 2001, to crush a network of Islamic groups said to be part of the Caliphate State organization run by Metin Kaplan (Canadian Press).

calling for the murder of a rival religious leader. German authorities have characterized the Kaplan group as being anti-Semitic and anti-democratic, and have also banned Kaplan's associated foundation, the "Servants of Islam," as well as other groups totaling 1,100 members.[34]

Kaplan was extradited to Turkey in November 2004, but with his group's only 1,000 odd members, it was hardly able to influence the many Muslim immigrant workers in Germany. However, another more diverse group may well be a wolf in sheep's clothing. The **Milli Görüs**, which has a translation meaning of "National Vision," is the largest Muslim organization in Germany, with over 27,000 members. Its influence is felt within the tight-knit Muslim communities, particularly in the Turkish Muslim areas. German authorities believe the group to be the foreign wing for Islamist leader and former Turkish Premier Necmettin Erbakan, and that the group secretly seeks to dismantle Germany's democratic structures. Milli Görüs, however, describes itself as an apolitical, unaffiliated lobby for the interests of Muslims living in Germany. German domestic intelligence believes that despite all the public posturing from Milli Görüs, it is apolitical and seeks to help Muslims to integrate into German society, but it is in fact, indoctrinating Muslim youth. However, in an August 2007 interview, Erbakan made the following statement:

'When we look at the map of the world, we see about 200 countries painted in colors, and we think that there are many races, religions, and nations. The fact is that for 300 years, all these [200 nations] have been controlled from one center only. This center is the racist, imperialist Zionism. Unless you make this correct diagnosis for the illness, you cannot find the cure to it. You will ask, 'What is this belief, this racist imperialism that destroys happiness in this world?'

'Do you know what the safety of Israel means? It means that they will rule the 28 countries from Morocco to Indonesia. Since all the Crusades were organized by the Zionists . . . since it was our forefathers the Seljuks who stopped them, according to the Kabbala there should be no sovereign state in Anatolia. This is these people's [i.e. the Jews'] religion, their faith. You can't argue or negotiate with them. This is their religion, and it comes from the Kabbala.[35]

The activities of Milli Görüs have attracted the attention of Germany's Office for the Protection of the Constitution (BFV), one of three national intelligence services in Germany that is charged with gathering information on domestic as well as foreign extremist and terror groups. BFV considers Islamic terrorism poses the biggest security threat to Germany in modern times.[36] Islam is the third-largest religious denomination in Germany, but because it lacks a centralized structure like the Catholic and Protestant churches, it doesn't have the same rights and privileges as the Christian churches. Milli Görüs wants to be recognized as an Islamic church and, thus, unite the splintered Islamic community in Germany. The group has not been banned and neither has it been identified as being involved in crime and terrorism. The German intelligence agencies will, no doubt, continue to monitor the group's activities and development. According to a recent German report the fear within Germany is from Islamists who follow the model of jihad, or Holy War. Germans feel this is one of the most potent dangers to their

FIGURE 6-8 Containers of hydrogen peroxide displayed during a press conference in Karlsruhe, southern Germany, on September 5, 2007. German authorities arrested three suspected Islamist terrorists from a group nursing "a profound hatred of U.S. citizens" for plotting imminent, massive bomb attacks on U.S. facilities in Germany. Two of the three arrested were converts to Islam and had trained at camps in Pakistan and procured 700 kilograms (1,500 pounds) of hydrogen peroxide for making bombs (Canadian Press).

country. The report also mentioned the militant Islamist Abu Mussab al Zarqawi, whose al Qaeda-affiliated, Jordanian-based al Tawhid group was accused of carrying out attacks on Jewish targets in Berlin and Düsseldorf. Jihadists continue to focus their efforts on attacks in European centers and many use the justification that NATO countries are supporting and waging war in Afghanistan to legitimize their attacks. Apart from the Madrid attacks in 2004 there have been no spectacular attacks in Germany along the scale of Madrid. Germany has also become a fertile recruiting ground for homegrown converts to Islam to wage jihad. In late 2006, a man was spotted carrying out a surveillance operation on U.S. military installations in an around the city of Hanau. For almost a year German authorities kept the suspect under surveillance, which also led them to other conspirators. The Germans were convinced that an attack was being planned against a U.S. or British installation in Germany. The operation culminated in September 2007 when the German GSG-9 counter terror force raided a house in Oberschledorn and arrested the suspects who were planning to move a large quantity of hydrogen peroxide. The cell had been trained in Pakistan and had amassed almost 700 kilograms of chemicals to make explosives.

ITALY

After World War I, Italy's Mussolini had violently suppressed and oppressed the Italian Communists. By 1954, Italy was the most likely Western country to turn Communist. With the cessation of hostilities and the formation of a democratically elected government in Italy, the opportunity naturally presented itself for the Communists to come to the fore. A strong, Communist-indoctrinated, left-wing group with some fairly imaginative goals to steer Italy onto a different path than that established by the allied powers did rise up. As the new millennium arrived,

FIGURE 6-9 Map of Italy (Central Intelligence Agency, *The World Factbook*, 2008).

the transnational terrorism from al Qaeda and its associated cells became a frustrating reality for the Italian government and security services. Terrorist plots were to be planned and executed by foreign terror operatives residing in Italy.

Terrorism and Italy

The only significant terrorist movement to emerge from Italy has been the Red Brigade, which has its origins in the early 1970s and grew out of an established, left-wing political party, The Metropolitan Political Collective. The group's aim was to bring about a Communist revolution in Italy, which it believed would spread throughout Europe. At the other end of the spectrum was a smaller and little known group, the Ordine Nuove (New Order), which was an extreme right-wing, Fascist movement. In similar manner to the Red Brigade, Ordine Nuove embarked on a campaign of terror to establish its goal of a strong Italian state, supported by a powerful Fascist structure. Throughout the 1970s, both groups used bombings and assassinations as their modus operandi and it was not often evident which group was responsible for what specific acts of terror. Observers believed that some of the attacks, although credited to one group, could well have been done by the other. Italy, like Germany, France, and Spain, is also contending with Islamist threats, and, lest we forget, there are Italian troops in Iraq.

The Red Brigade (RB)

Like many other left-wing movements, the Red Brigade (RB) has its fundamental origins on the Italian university campuses in the latter half of the 1960s. The group might be considered as a fledgling of the World War II Volante Rosse, formed during the campaign against Nazi Germany as a Communist resistance movement. It continued its campaigns until the end of 1949 and had ongoing links to the Italian Communist Party, no doubt spawning the next generation of left-wing extremists to emerge on the campuses of the 1960s.

Following the end of World War II, Italy moved toward a governing style modeled on the political and economic example of the United States. During the years from 1950 to 1962, the industrial growth and success of the Italian government lay in the hands of coalitions of political parties—the Republicans, Liberals, Social Democrats, and Christian Democrats, all apparently trying to move beyond the Fascist past. While exploiting the need for industrial growth and foreign trade, Italy had neglected the social structure of the country. The bubble burst in 1968 with a cultural-style revolution in the universities and schools, and was quickly followed in 1969 with the worst union unrest in the industrialized north that Italy had ever experienced. The unions could not be placated and factories were seized and occupied by both workers and student demonstrators. Workers and management were intimidated and attacked. All of this became the fertile ground for the emerging RB.

The founding members of the RB, Renato Curcio and Margherita Cagol, came from the sociology department of Trent University.[37] The RB began to target the symbolic nature of the Italian state by attacking senior executives, politicians, and parts of Italian society perceived as being repressive by nature. RB did not burst onto the Italian scene but rather confined itself to incubation, largely in Milan's industrial heart. The period from 1969 to 1972 was a time of building, training, and testing of the RB's avowed objectives. Minor fire bombings and destruction of civil property were the order of the period. The RB support structure outside of Milan at this time was considerably weak. From 1972 to 1974, the RB entered a new phase of expanding to the adjacent areas of Turin and Genoa while experimenting in kidnapping and extortion. During this same time frame, Italian security forces were able to capture Renato Curcio after a gun battle in which his wife, Margherita Cagol, was killed. Observers predicted the imminent demise of the Red Brigade, but that was far from reality. The next generation of RB was on the scene and ready to continue the fight with the Italian government and society in general. The RB has, to some length, emulated the tactics laid out by Carlos Marighella in his *Mini Manual of the*

Urban Guerrilla, published in 1969. Attention to detail and technical knowledge, as well as logistical and intelligence information, became a hallmark of the RB. Contained in the *Mini Manual* is Marighella's definition of assaults:

- Assault is the armed attack, which we make to expropriate funds, liberate prisoners, and capture explosives, machine guns, and other types of arms and ammunition.
- Assaults can take place in broad daylight or at night.
- Daytime assaults are made when the objective cannot be achieved at any other hour, as for example, the transport of money by the banks, which is not done at night.
- Night assault is usually the most advantageous to the urban guerrilla. The ideal is for all assaults to take place at night when conditions for a surprise attack are most favorable and the darkness facilitates flight and hides the identity of the participants. The urban guerrilla must prepare himself, nevertheless, to act under all conditions, daytime as well as nighttime.

Kidnapping as a part of the terrorist arsenal was well demonstrated in Italy through the 1970s and perfected by the RB. Mainly symbolic in its action, the group did go beyond kidnapping prominent business personages when it kidnapped Genoa's Assistant Attorney General, Mario Sossi. The RB demanded the release of RB prisoners from jail and, in particular, Renato Curcio. Sossi was held captive for a month before his release. The concessions received from the government were the promised release of RB members. However, the Attorney General would not permit the release, which had been bargained under duress.[38] The RB also believed that the concessions they received had sufficiently undermined the state. On June 8, 1974, the RB struck down Genoa's Attorney General Francesco Coco in an armed ambush, which had a twofold effect. The first was a confirmation of the RB's retaliatory ability against the figure who had blocked the group's earlier attempts to free its colleagues; and, the second was that RB's threats to selected jurors in the Turin trial of Curcio led to a delay in the trial. Further attacks on members of the bar association had the desired effect of delaying the trial. The intimidating effect of terrorism was working well.

RB Structure

The RB based its operating habits on the cell structure to prevent infiltration and detection. Working from large industrial areas, it had widespread support among the working classes, who provided food and support to the group.

Total membership, either active or passive, has been hard to ascertain. It is believed there were more than 500 active members, with a support structure possibly in the thousands. It seems likely that by the last decade of the twentieth century, the RB was reduced down to around fifty active members.

As the twenty-first century dawned, it was not clear that the movement had not undergone resurgence as in late 2003 more than 200 pounds of high explosives and detonators were discovered during a police raid of a known RB house. Along with the explosives police discovered documents claiming responsibility for several attacks including the assassination of a government consultant in 2002. Some 140 of the original RB activists are still sought by Italy, many thought to be living in France.

With its Communist Marxist/Leninist ideology, its early support would have come from the Soviet Union, which in the Cold War years would have provided succor and support for such organizations operating in the West. After all, any activity likely to disrupt a democracy would be to the USSR's advantage.

Kidnapping

Italian terrorists perfected the art of kidnapping and, in fact, enhanced it. It enabled corporations to get kidnap insurance, turning the crime into a growth industry. This shortsighted provision made it possible for kidnappers to get their money and, for those who were kidnapped, to be released. Everyone went away content. The RB, on the other hand, kidnapped for different reasons and rarely for money. Two kidnappings stand out for their sheer audaciousness and the brutality with which they ended. These two kidnappings were significant watersheds for the RB. The first, which resulted in nothing more than the symbolic execution of the president-elect, Aldo Moro, was to turn public opinion against the RB. Several communiqués were issued prior to his murder and the RB made every effort to exploit the media coverage of this atrocity. During Aldo Moro's captivity, the RB showed its strength of purpose and its ability to continue with other operations and carried out two murders and six shootings in Rome, Turin, Milan, and Genoa, in spite of the massive police search and crackdown on the RB and any known members.[39] It was a significant demonstration of the RB's ability to conduct several simultaneous operations.

The second was the release of General James Dozier, the Italian Police force's first successful rescue of a kidnap victim from the RB. By the mid-1980s, the number of terrorist incidents committed by RB was down to single figures, following a significant decline in support from the left. By the mid-1990s, the group was distributing communiqués to indicate a cessation of all operations. How and what role RB will continue to play into the new century is at present unclear. However, at the end of 1998, the group was not functioning.

GAP AND NAP

Two other groups on the fringes of the Italian terrorism scene in the 1970s modeled themselves on the same style of clandestine activities and systematic violence as the RB. The **Partisan Action Group (GAP)** originated in Milan at about the same time (1969) as the RB. Their inception is believed to have involved the wealthy Italian publisher Giangiacomo Feltrinelli, who was the group's paymaster and sponsor. Feltrinelli believed that right-wing extremism was on the rise and a return to Fascism was a real possibility. He believed that the only way to confront the risk was to form an urban guerrilla movement. His approach was to form the GAP . . . a resistance/partisan movement modeled on the resistance fighters of World War II. This model differed from that of the RB, which probably accounts for the non-merging of the groups in the early days.[40] In the days of student and union unrest, which had also spread to Italy's prison system, another movement sprang up. The Armed Proletarian Nuclei (NAP) came to life from a left-wing prison movement—the Movement of Proletarian Prisoners and the Ongoing Struggle (Lotta Continua).[41] Unlike the RB, this group gained little acknowledgment. Coming from the ranks of Naples prison inmates, the membership immediately began the "armed struggle," financing its movement primarily by robbing banks. Its main base of operation started in Naples and spread to Rome. The group used explosives to bomb prisons and also attacked prison officials. Unlike the RB, all NAP members were easily traceable from their criminal records. Their modus operandi, coupled with their lack of attention to their own security, resulted in numerous arrests. With no ideological base, NAP'S recruitment of criminal elements led to its eventual downfall. The remainder of the group's membership joined the ranks of the RB. Throughout the terror campaigns, the majority of NAP targets were either political or paramilitary by nature. Indiscriminate attacks against the Italian populace were uncommon.

The Mancino Law

In 1993, the Italian government issued Decree No. 122 as an emergency measure to control, restrict, and limit attacks of a racial nature. Two months later, it was transformed into Law No. 205 by the then Interior Minister Nicola Mancino. The law enabled the state to prosecute individuals for "incitement to violence for a broad range of hate crimes" that included the use of symbols of hate.[42] Hundreds of youths have been charged under this legislation. Two Italian names have become associated with hate crimes in Italy: Maurizio Boccacci, a Skinhead organizer, and Dr. Sergio Gozzoli, an outspoken anti-Semite and a Holocaust denier.

Skinhead Organizations

The Italian Skinheads, following the example of the Germans, had by the early 1990s, organized themselves under the leadership of the Movimento Politico Occidentale (MPO, Political Movement of the West), founded by Maurizio Boccacci and headquartered in Rome. The group had links to other far-right Skinhead groups in France, Germany, and Great Britain. A notable incident that was bound to become a flash point was the painting of yellow stars on more than 100 Jewish businesses and shops in Rome. Jews attacked MPO skins as a result. The MPO has been banned by the government but has since renamed itself with the Fascist trappings of I Camerati, a term used by Mussolini to address his fascist followers.[43]

In its effort to become more politically acceptable, delegates at a convention of the neo-Fascist Movimento Sociale Italiano (MSI, Italian Social Movement) voted to move toward the mainstream political parties and to dissolve the MSI. They merged with Alleanza Nazionale (National Alliance), and it was hoped this would make the overall far-right movement more respectable. The delegates also agreed on a strong position against anti-Semitism. The extremists in the organization—many of them Skinheads—broke away from the alliance and reestablished their own version of the MSI.

Ideology

The Italian Skinhead ideology and that of the far-right extremists echo the sentiments of a past generation of neo-Fascists. Their ideology is loosely based on the following:[44]

- The denial of Nazi genocide against the Jews; "historical revisionism."
- Fear and hatred of foreigners, based on the myths of Aryan purity and supremacy,
- The fear and demonization of the Jews in a context of a sinister plot to rule the world.

With the breakdown of the symbolic, and all-too-real, Berlin Wall, the influx of Russian and Eastern nationals to the west—particularly Germany and Italy—has fueled the far right into action. Sporadic action between Skinheads of the Far Right and ethnic and minority groups continues in Italy into the new millennium.

International Terrorism

Italy has been no stranger to acts of terrorism, with the result that post-9-11 Italy, with its excellent police and intelligence services, has not only aided the U.S.-led War on Terror with its strong military contributions, but has had successes in tracking down and arresting suspected al Qaeda cells. International terrorism requires funding and, in the weeks after 9-11, the Italian government established the Financial Security Committee. This group comprised of Senior Ministry Officials from Finance, Justice, and Foreign Affairs, whose aim was to stem the flow of funding to terrorist groups in Europe. Even prior to 9-11, Italian security services had targeted such institutions as the Islamic Cultural Center in Milan because they suspected that an al Qaeda lieutenant, Sami Ben Khemais Essid, who had spent time training as a terrorist recruiter in Afghanistan, was active in Italy. The Italians were monitoring the Cultural Center to discover evidence of traffic in arms and explosives and discovered that Ben Khemais was, in fact, in contact with other extreme terrorist groups throughout Europe.

Among those seen at the Cultural Center were terrorists associated with the New York World Trade Center bombing in 1993, and the bombings of the U.S. embassies in Tanzania and Kenya in 1998. The apparent ease with which international terror groups, and particularly those associated with Osama bin Laden, have been able to operate with comparative freedom in Italy is a lesson that security services are now beginning to appreciate. Ben Khemais was sentenced to eight years in prison for his activities. His activities also give us an insight to what may be al Qaeda's next style of terror attack. During their investigation, Italian police intercepted Khemais conversation with another terrorist, which detailed the use of a deadly poison gas attack. The threat from Islamist terrorism is as significant a risk for Italy as it is for other western European states. Al Qaeda sympathizers and Euro converts to radical Islam will continue to attempt attacks. With a vast population of immigrant workers throughout Europe and with no solid border defenses the movement between countries by al Qaeda inspired cells will be a challenge for the foreseeable future. The presence of extreme thinking imams has also been at issue for Germany as it has been for the British authorities. In June 2003, the imam of the Rome mosque began inciting his own congregation to jihad in much the same manner as has taken place at London's Finsbury Park Mosque.

GREECE AND TURKEY

Terrorism is no stranger to these two countries; however, the actions of respective indigenous terrorist groups are restricted for the most part to actions within their countries, rather than out in the international arena. These two countries have had their own regional differences over the past several decades and have come close to all out war—and both countries are members of NATO. Their differences have revolved around territorial claims to a group of islands in Aegean Sea and the divided status of the island of Cyprus occupied by both Greeks and Turks. Turkey has for years aspired to join the European Union, and its application was actually supported by the Greek government. Their belief being that if Turkey could change its attitude and be accepted into "Europe" it would no longer pose a threat to Greece—however, Turkey's likelihood all but vanished when Cyprus joined the Union in 2004 and with its veto could effectively prevent Turkey from joining. The two countries are not currently in open conflict and that is probably as a result of two eastern bloc countries joining the European Union, Bulgaria and Romania. This means that Greece now has a land link to the rest of "Europe" proper without worrying about a hostile Turkey. To cement the lasting peace between the two countries, the Greek Prime Minister Costas Karamanlis visited Turkey on an official visit in January 2008—this being the first visit by a Greek minister to Turkey in almost fifty years!

FIGURE 6-10 **Map of Greece** (Central Intelligence Agency, *The World Factbook*, 2008).

GREECE

Revolutionary Organization November 17

After twenty-eight years, twenty-three assassinations, 345 bombings, and no arrests, the rest of the West views the Greek attitude and ability to prevent and deter terrorism with a large measure of cynicism. The European Union brought considerable pressure to bear on the Greek government for the security of the Olympic Games, held in Athens in 2004. Reacting to fears that Greek authorities could not prevent another Olympic Games attack, the Greek government arrested almost 75 percent of the believed membership of the November 17 group. In December 2003, fifteen members were convicted and sentenced: five members received life sentences and imposed sentences on the others that totaled 244 years.

The infamous November 17 group had operated in Greece with what seemed like total immunity until the arrests and convictions in 2003. Previously, police and security services had been unable, or unwilling, to identify or arrest any members of that organization. This group of left-wing extremists has to be considered Marxist-Leninist, anti-imperialist, anti-United States, anti-Europe, and anti-NATO. November 17's first action, and the first time it came to world attention, was the assassination of U.S. diplomat, Richard Welsh, in 1975. The group originates from the university campuses of Greece, much like other left-wing groups in the 1970s. The group's name, November 17, commemorates the date of the attack on the students, NTUA (National Technical University of Athens), on November 17, 1975. Greek military and police, under the control of the ruling colonels, killed several student activists and captured and tortured many more.

The Greek Military Junta was overthrown a few short months after the university incident. November 17's actual membership number is not known, but it can be assumed that it is a small group, with approximately twenty to thirty hard-core members. Unlike other groups, it did not take part in low-level operations to test its own ability; rather, it burst onto the world stage with a high-visibility terrorist attack on a diplomat from a major foreign power.

Like its Italian counterparts, November 17 group members are Marxist/Leninist in their ideology. In its early years, this group committed relatively few attacks; in fact, between 1975 and 1985, November 17 carried out only six attacks. Perhaps the length of time between operations was relative to the fact that police arrested no one. One of its earliest attacks was on the CIA Station Chief; Richard Welsh, who was shot outside his Athens residence several weeks after his identity had been published in the press.

The failure to track down November 17 was a sad reflection on the internal workings of the Greek government and its security services. Over the last twenty years, the group has carried out 345 bombings, resulting in 61 deaths and 250 injuries. Until 2003, no November 17 terrorist had ever been arrested and charged with offenses in connection with those incidents.

The group did expand operations after 1985, and by 1990 had carried out about forty attacks including bombings, assassinations, and shootings, often targeting U.S. military personnel stationed at NATO bases in Greece, Greek industrialists, and politicians. The group has been severely critical of the Greek government for its position in respect to U.S./NATO bases in Greece as well as Greece's membership of the EEC (European Economic Community). The largest number of attacks carried out by the group was directed at internal targets and foreign targets residing on Greek soil. To ensure that no other group claimed responsibility for November 17's terror acts, the group used handguns of the same caliber in consecutive attacks against Greek targets.

The group viewed itself as the people's vanguard and protector . . . to lead the fight on behalf of the working class and to take up the armed struggle. It makes its point with ideological communiqués and actions in support of its cause. Attacks are geared to making the subverted classes more abstractly aware of what is taking place in the political and economic processes in the country. The group fervently holds the United States responsible for complicity with Turkey over the Cyprus crisis, thus making the United States a legitimate military target in its relentless war for the oppressed. The group's early attacks were primarily symbolic; the first was against the United States and subsequent attacks were against the Greek police hierarchy and representatives of the Greek Military Junta. An example of the group's hatred toward the United States can be seen from the content of one of the November 17 communiqués: "The American military forces in our country are an occupation force, and we are going to hit anybody who is a member of it or an agent of its secret services. These actions are going to continue and are going to increase until the last Turkish soldier leaves Cyprus and the last American soldier leaves our country."[45]

In Greece's internal struggle with domestic terrorism, the break for Greek authorities came in 2002, with a botched bombing attack that seriously injured a terrorist bomber. As strange as this may seem, this was the first November 17 terror suspect that Greek authorities have been able to apprehend. The bomber in this instance was Savas Xiros, who was carrying a device that detonated prematurely as he approached the ticket office of a hydrofoil company in Piraeus. In the explosion, Xiros lost a hand and was blinded. The ensuing investigation found a 38 Smith and Wesson revolver in his possession, which had never been fired, but its rightful owner was a Greek police officer who was killed in a 1984 robbery. The bomber's fingerprints also matched those on the getaway car used in the assassination of a British/Greek tycoon. Greek police have had, and continue to have, a mutual assistance program with both the British police and the U.S. FBI as a result of the Greek government's signing of a joint memorandum on combating crime.

Espanastatikos Laikos Agonas (ELA)

The second-most destructive group operating on Greek soil, Espanastatikos Laikos Agonas (ELA, Revolutionary Peoples Struggle), is also committed to the overthrow of the Greek system and is a violent Marxist-Leninist organization. That is where any similarity between it and November 17 probably ends. It also grew out of the university campuses of the 1960s and early 1970s. Its fundamental aims and philosophy were directed at the state, imperialism, and capitalism. Most, if not all, of its targets for terror were of a symbolic nature. Unlike the secretive nature of November 17, which seeks to communicate its positions via communiqués or e-mail, ELA actually utilizes and operates an underground newspaper to forward its aims and political viewpoint. In May 1990, ELA announced that it had merged with another left-wing group, the revolutionary organization 1 May. Up to this point the strategy of the ELA had been to avoid death and injury to Greeks as well as foreigners on Greek soil. It had conducted a low-level style of campaign and had not ventured into the more dangerous world of remotely detonated bombs. A communiqué to the Greek government in 1993 appeared to be the turning point in ELA's violent methods in its dealings with the state. It perceived all police officers to be the "local representatives of the CIA."[46]

On September 19, 1994, the ELA remotely detonated a bomb alongside a police bus, killing one officer and injuring ten others, as well as a passerby. The ELA gave no warnings, which had previously been a signature for the group. Detonating the bomb without prior warning signaled a new and more virulent strain in Greek terrorist behavior. Successive and continuous failures by the Greek government to effect any cohesive response to domestic terror has allowed the organizations to continue to operate with impunity. While neighboring countries in Europe, Germany, Italy, France, and Belgium, had, for the most part, decisively dealt with left-wing violence and terrorist threats with a strong and dedicated response force established by powerful political mandate, it seemed to be lacking in Greece until 2001.

Much of the blame for the lackluster and feeble efforts of the Greek police must rest on the shoulders of those in political circles. The Pasok Party had held onto the reigns of power in Greece for the last two decades, up until the 2004 elections when their popularity had waned. The Conservative New Democracy Party had an easy victory in the 2004 general elections.

Revolutionary Cells/Revolutionary Nuclei (RN)

Revolutionary Cells, also known as Revolutionary Nuclei (RN), has its beginnings from a wide spectrum of anti-NATO, anti-United States, and anti-European Union left-wing groups in the mid-1990s. The group is believed to be the successor to the ELA. ELA has not been credited with any attacks since 1995, and many believe that RN (from the manner and style of its communiqués showing much of the same style as used by ELA) has now taken its place. RN's attacks in the 1990s were considered low level and were aimed mainly at companies that had NATO defense contracts as well as Greek government buildings. The RN has been most active in the Athens area and has also targeted European banks. The size of this terror group is believed to be relatively small, drawing support mainly from the Greek militant left.

Minor Terrorist Groups

The number of terrorist actions in Greece increased in 1998, not only against the state but also aimed at Jewish and anti-Semitic groups, foreigners, as well as politicians. The source of the terror appears to be previously unheard-of organizations operating in Greece. Firebombing has been the hallmark of the attacks, which have been aimed at vehicles and buildings. The government of Greece has indicated that these attacks are coming from various quarters—the New Group of Satanists, the Children of November, Anarchist Street Patrol, and Conscientious Arsonists, all previously unknown before 1998. With the ineptitude of the Greek security services already a well-established fact, only time will tell if their newly formed Special Task Force of more than 1,000 undercover police officers will be effective. As Greece depends heavily on its tourist trade for much-valued foreign currency, this style of attack, which seems so indiscriminate, will do a lot to drive that trade elsewhere.

CYPRUS

Situated in the Eastern Mediterranean Sea, this small island has a population of some 650,000 people, and consists of 78 percent Greek-Cypriots, 18 percent Turkish-Cypriots, and 4 percent Maronite and Latin-Cypriots. The Turks and Greeks lived together on the island for the last five centuries, and mosques and churches can be found almost side-by-side in many communities.

National Organization of Cypriot Combatants (EOKA)

Cyprus had long been under the control of the British Empire, which by the 1950s was well into its decline. The majority of the people of Cyprus were of Greek origin and, in the 1950s, were under the leadership of the Greek Cypriot Archbishop Makarios. Similar to the operations of the Stern Gang in Palestine, the **National Organization of Cypriot Combatants (EOKA)** terrorist organization and its followers began to strike at the occupying influences of Great Britain. EOKA was established in 1954 as an underground movement with the blessing and approval of Makarios. The revolt began in earnest with the bombing of the Cyprus Broadcasting Station on April 1, 1955. The British government had declared a state of emergency on the island and the Archbishop went into exile in the Seychelles. Makarios returned to Cyprus in 1959 and was elected president of the Cyprus Republic; the Founding Agreements made Turkey, Greece, and Great Britain "guarantor states" for Cyprus. Both the Turkish and Greek communities reached an agreement on a constitution for Cyprus, resulting in a Greek-Turkish Republic. Great Britain retained sovereignty over two military bases on the island. Within three years, Archbishop Makarios was preparing constitutional changes that would abrogate the power-sharing agreements that were contrary to the Constitution. The resulting inter-communal violence was to have a lasting effect on the island.

On July 20, 1974, Turkey invaded the island to "protect" the minority Turkish-Cypriot community. The international community quickly condemned the action. U.N. Resolution 353, adopted on the day of the invasion, called for all states to respect "the sovereignty, independence and territorial integrity of the

Republic of Cyprus." It further demanded an immediate end to foreign military intervention in the Republic of Cyprus. Turkey ignored the United Nations and the international community and seized control of at least one-third of the Republic's territory and since then has engaged in a type of terrorism that we now refer to as "ethnic cleansing." More than 1,600 Greek Cypriots are still unaccounted for, following the invasion, and more than 20,000 lost their homes and possessions. This was a constant and festering sore for the November 17 terrorist group, which continued to blame the United States for failing to act on behalf of the Greek Cypriots. Turkish forces enforced a partition of the island and Turkish Cypriots fled to the north into Turkish occupied Cyprus while Greek Cypriots fled south to the Greek side of the line. Since the 1970s, there has been little terrorist activity and plenty of political posturing with both Greece and Turkey claiming their side of the island as the legitimate Republic of Cyprus. In December 2004, Turkey agreed that it would recognize Greek Cyprus as a European Union (EU) member; however, the Turkish Prime Minister warned the EU that the Cyprus problem must be solved justly for both sides.

TURKEY

The history of the Turkish Ottoman Empire stretches back to when the Ottoman Turks invaded and captured Constantinople in 1453, bringing an end to the Byzantine Empire. The Ottoman Empire stretched across Eastern Europe and into regions of the Middle East, as we know it today. It stretched as far south as the western reaches of Saudi Arabia and to Yemen at the southern end of the Red Sea. Its conquests stretched through North Africa, from Cairo in the east and Algiers in the west. By the dawning of the eighteenth century, the Turkish Empire was commonly termed "the Sick Man of Europe," and was beginning to lose its huge territorial gains of the previous centuries. The Empire lost Algeria to French rule in 1830 and, by the end of 1880, Great Britain had taken control of Cyprus and Egypt. France seized Tunisia in 1881. With a crumbling empire, the Turks had to contend with disruptions on the home front as well, ruled by the dictatorship of Sultan Abdul-Hamid II. His rule was one of fear and violent repression of religious groups, and stimulated the first covert organization set up to oppose the dictator. The Young Turks, as they were known, were dissatisfied students and disaffected military personnel opposed to Hamid. The group staged a successful coup in 1908 with the aim of restoring democracy to Turkey. The replacement for Abdul-Hamid was his brother, Mohammad V. The Young Turks had envisioned returning the Ottoman Empire to its former greatness; however, the populace was less concerned with aspirations toward empire building and more concerned with its

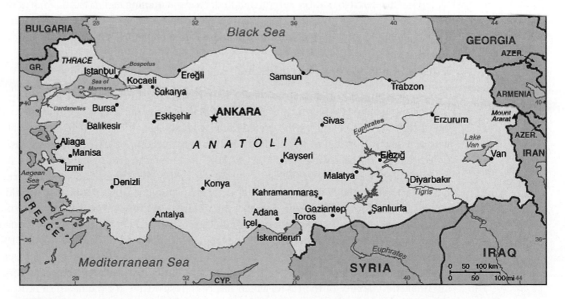

FIGURE 6-11   Map of Turkey (Central Intelligence Agency, *The World Factbook*, 2008).

own democratic rights and freedoms. With the Empire crumbling, Turkey entered World War I on the side of Germany in the hopes that it would win back much of its losses of the past half century.

Kemal Ataturk

As has been witnessed throughout history, many inspirational freedom fighters and military heroes with nationalist aspirations have risen to take control over and to form popular governments. Mustafa Kemal was one such leader. Kemal's origins in the Turkish military and his exploits as a natural leader of men brought him to the forefront of politics in Turkey. He formed the provisional government in 1920 after the invasion of the country by forces from Britain, France, and Greece. The Ottoman government was unable to protect the country, so the country turned to its nationalist leader, Kemal. The Sultan's powers weakened and the nationalists grew stronger and were able to forcibly evict the Greeks from Turkish soil. They then sued for peace with the allies. Turkey, as we know it today is formed around the boundaries outlined in the Treaty of Lausanne signed by the nationalists in 1923. The word "Ataturk" is the surname given to Kemal and means "Father of the Turks."[47] Kemal ruled as president of Turkey until his death in 1938. Turkey did not repeat its mistake of joining on the side of Germany at the outbreak of World War II and managed to keep out of the war. With Germany's defeat, Turkey joined the United Nations in 1946.

Turkey has witnessed many changes in government since the end of World War II, ably assisted by a strong military intent on keeping to the democratic principles that Kemal established so long ago.

Revolutionary Left (Dev Sol)

A left-wing Marxist group that has its origins in the Turkish Peoples Liberation Army split off in the late 1970s to form **Dev Sol.** This group is vehemently anti-NATO and anti-United States. The aims of this group are to foster an uprising or popular national revolution among the Turkish working classes. The group is financed primarily from armed robberies and extortion from businesses carried out in Turkey.

During the 1980s, the group restricted its area of operation to the domestic scene, mainly in Izmir, Istanbul, and Ankara. With the Middle East crisis and the Desert Storm Operation against Iraq, the group began attacks on the U.S. military personnel. The group launched a rocket attack at the U.S. Consulate in Istanbul in 1992. Since the early 1980s, the group has suffered from internal factional fighting and has carried out limited operations at home. From the training perspective, it is believed that the membership, which is considered to number several hundred, received training and indoctrination at radical Palestinian camps. By the end of 1998, this group was not particularly active in Turkey, but there are indications that it is beginning to resurface and may threaten U.S. commercial interests and Turkish government figures.

Kurdistan Workers Party (PKK)

The leadership and organization of the **Kurdistan Workers Party (PKK)** originated from the student movement at Ankara University. Abdullah Ocalan, the leader . . . now behind bars in Ankara but still the leader . . . set up the organization with the specific aim of liberating the Kurds. Ocalan was considerably brutal in his methods and used his version of terrorism on his own followers and fellow Kurds. By executing the dissenters, any dissent in the group was put down. It is believed that Ocalan killed more than 10,000 Kurds during the 1980s. His actions had some sobering effects on the Kurdish people—they showed them that PKK was strong and that the people should side with PKK in the struggle for freedom from Turkey. Any failure to actively support the movement was perceived as siding with the Turks. Operating in southeastern Turkey, this Kurdish terror group seeks to set up a Kurdish state fashioned on Marxist lines. Mainly composed of Turkish Kurds, PKK has been in operation since 1974 and has been involved in what would best be described as insurgent activities.

Large numbers of Turks migrated to Germany during the last forty years, and this, in part, adds to the financial viability of the PKK, which has been responsible for the death of at least 37,000 people since 1984. Turkey is home to 12 million Kurds; the neighboring countries of Iraq, Syria, and Iran have substantial but smaller Kurdish populations. To finance its operations, PKK uses a variety of tried-and-tested methods. It is involved in the lucrative trade in illegal immigrants from Iraq into European centers. In addition, the PKK also controls a lucrative portion of the drug traffic from the East into Europe. Its other levels of fundraising include extortion from Kurds residing in France, Germany, Belgium, and Romania. The PKK is also the recipient of aid from state sponsors, such as Iran and Syria. From Syria's perspective, the destabilization of the Turkish regime plays an important economic role.

It had been felt that the group was trying to become more mainstream politically, and has reformed itself with name changes—from the Kurdistan Freedom and Democracy Congress (KADEK) in 2000, and then to the Peoples Congress of Kurdistan (KONGRA-GEL). From a wider viewpoint, Turkey's support for the U.S. War on Terror has not endeared it to the Syrian regime; nor has its support of Israel. As the War on Terror continued, PKK was declared a "terrorist organization" by the European Union in May 2002. PKK continues to receive support from Iran and also maintains bases in the Bekka Valley, Lebanon. Abdullah Ocalan, imprisoned under sentence of death in a Turkish prison, declared in 2000 that his group, the PKK, which has for so long sought an independent Kurdish state through violent struggle, had changed its stance and would now seek, through a political campaign, only guarantees of Kurdish political, economic, social, and cultural rights in a democratic Turkey. Dormant but not dead, PKK membership, which probably ran to more than 5,000 in 1999 at the time of Ocalan's capture, was diminished down to around 1,000, with Kurdish fighters moving to neighboring Iraq following the U.S. invasion there. Small pockets of PKK, who had by spring of 2005 changed the name back to PKK from KONGRA-GEL, became active in southeastern Turkey. With the U.S.-led invasion of Iraq and Turkey acting a role of neutrality in the region, the United States was faced with Iraqi Kurds that actually supported the invasion. The Kurds designs for an autonomous region adjacent to the Turkish border area were a matter of national security for Turkey. This is a complex issue and the United States was not in a position to alienate Turkey, an old ally, and at the same time allow it a free hand to deal with the PKK in the north of Iraq. The United States most certainly wanted to protect the Kurds against any aggression from Turkey's military in the border region. The fact remains that the Kurds have been sheltering PKK separatists.

Restraining Turkey is in U.S. interests in Iraq but the attack in October 2007 by PKK just inside the Turkish border, which resulted in the death of twelve Turkish soldiers, began a build up of troops prepared to cross into the Kurdish region to root out the PKK. More than 300 troops—possibly Special Forces, crossed the border and it is believed they killed over thirty PKK separatists. In an effort to lower tensions the Kurdish Regional Government urged restraint on both sides and the Iraqi Prime Minister Talabani stated that his government might be prepared to hand over PKK members to Turkey. The problem for Turkey will persist with a strong almost autonomous Kurdish state on its doorstep.

Turkish Hezbollah

Also active in Turkey is Turkish Hezbollah, an extreme Islamic movement with two well-defined goals:

- Overthrow the Turkish secular government.
- Introduce a strict Islamic state inspired by Iran.

Hezbollah's radical ideals leave no room for competition. The group is secretive but it openly attacks the PKK and accepts no other ideology other than its own as being the true path of Islam. This violent terror group is believed to be fully funded by Iran, which has made for less-than-cordial relations between Iran and Turkey. There is wider concern for Turkey that the Iranians have been instrumental in trying to act as mediators between Hezbollah and the PKK.

Assassination has been Hezbollah's most common tactic, usually involving a daylight attack, often by pairs of young assassins using pistols of Eastern European manufacture.[48] The numbers killed in such attacks between 1992 and 1995 amount to over 1,000. Not only did Hezbollah attack the PKK, but by the end of the last decade it was targeting specific Senior Security officials who were responsible for arresting Hezbollah members. Hezbollah's vicious attacks mirror some of the torture and degrading attacks on the civilian expatriate population in Iraq in 2004. Hezbollah, apart from its normal tactic of assassination has also resorted to extreme levels of torture, including burning its targets while they are alive and burying them alive. The inability of the Turkish police to successfully tackle Hezbollah may be due to Hezbollah's ongoing war with its right-wing enemies in the PKK. Turkey continues to view PKK as a threat far greater than Hezbollah; however, a crackdown did eventually materialize and more than 1,000 Hezbollah members have been arrested. In concluding the future of terrorism in Turkey, the answers to its spread lie clearly with the government and its ability to improve the social economic well-being of young Turkish Islamists. If changes and improvements do not materialize, Turkey has a ready and waiting supply of young radicals who will consider other options that would likely see them embracing religious fundamentalism.

Armenian Terrorism

Like the Kurds, the ethnic Armenians of northeastern Turkey have, since 1974, been fighting for their own homeland and autonomy in the region. Two terror groups have come to the fore: the Armenian Secret Army for the Liberation of Armenia (ASALA) and the Justice Commandos of the Armenian Genocide. Both groups have targeted diplomats from Turkey in Europe and the United States as part of their terror campaign. Their attacks became more violent when they started to detonate bombs at airports in the 1980s. They set off a bomb at Orly Airport in France adjacent to the Turkish Airlines check-in counters, killing ten and wounding more than seventy in the process. The leader of ASALA, Hagop Hagopian, was shot to death on an Athens street in 1988 and since then the group has been silent.[49]

The Nationalist Threat

The Turkish Revenge Brigade is a previously unknown group that sprang up in 1998, in opposition to Kurdish movements. Considered to be ultra-nationalist, the group has targeted Kurdish and left-wing journalists who support the Kurdish movement. In May 1998, two members of the group attempted to assassinate a leading Turkish human rights activist, Akin Birdal. The motive for the attack is uncertain, but the head of the Human Rights Association claimed at the time that Birdal had received prior death threats and had asked for protection from the government, but to no avail. How the nationalist movement will develop and who is backing and financing its operations is unclear. No doubt, previous reports of Turkish death squads and their involvement earlier in the decade come back into question.

AL QAEDA IN TURKEY

Al Qaeda's presence in Turkey was likely a forgone conclusion after U.S. and British forces invaded Iraq. Both Britain and the United States are obvious and defined targets for al Qaeda and its splinter groups. In the first direct attack against Great Britain, an al Qaeda cell based in Turkey attacked the British Embassy compound in Istanbul in November 2003. In determining that al Qaeda was responsible, authorities looked at what was spread before them—simultaneous attacks, within seconds of each other; and the targets, the British Embassy and the HSBC Bank in Istanbul.

The method of attack in both instances was by suicide bombing. One has to speculate on what the terrorist cell hoped to gain by attacking during the holy month of Ramadan and killing mostly Muslims. Could it be that the cells involved believed that such an attack would radicalize the Muslim population and encourage others to join their apocalyptic fight against the Western democracies so long hated by al Qaeda? Or was this the start of a broader campaign being waged by al Qaeda against British interests in Europe? For the last two decades, Turkish authorities have concentrated almost exclusively on the PKK and turned a blind eye to any Islamic extremism fermenting in the provinces. The week prior to the British Embassy blast had seen suicide bombers target two synagogues in Istanbul. Authorities identified the bombers as Turks from Bingol.

BELGIUM

Belgium, and its involvement with terrorism, was of considerable internal concern during the 1980s. In this country, known for being a stable democracy and with a population of only 10 million, political violence had been unheard of in comparison to the troubles besieging its neighbors. Belgian terrorism was not widely publicized by the world press and probably received little or no mention in the U.S. press. Belgium has also received little or no mention by experts who review European terrorist threats. However, terrorist incidents have taken place on Belgium soil from external terror groups. Palestinian terrorists, from the Black September group, hijacked a Belgium state (Sabena) airliner to Israel in 1972, and PLO terrorists also attacked the Iraqi Embassy in Brussels in 1978.

The source for Belgium's internal troubles appeared to come from the direction of neo-Fascist terror gangs, who up until the 1980s had not been active but had aligned themselves with other terror groups in Europe. Considered to be more of a criminal gang element on the outer fringes of violent political struggle was the right-wing DARE, the New Force Party, and the West New Post. All were considered extreme Fascist movements, but they had been nonviolent in comparison to the activities of such groups in the rest of Europe.

Belgium is a country unfamiliar with violent armed robberies, so when an outbreak began in 1982, the country was gripped in panic. Terrorism in its ugliest form was on its doorstep! The Belgium press, who nicknamed the robbers the "Mad Killers," sensationalized the first attacks. Most of the early attacks were aimed at a supermarket chain and weapons were used. Timing and planning were a hallmark of the operation, and the gang readily killed numerous innocent bystanders. Armed with semiautomatic weapons and wearing bulletproof vests, group members escaped with limited amounts of cash, which gave the authorities grave concern as to the real motive for the attacks and killings. The Belgians were unable to determine where the threat was coming from—either from the left or from the right. Terror was causing a crisis in the government and panic

FIGURE 6-12   Map of Belgium (Central Intelligence Agency, *The World Factbook*, 2008).

in the country, with innocent bystanders being killed. After all, this was not the United States but a hitherto quiet, mainstream European country.

Revolutionary Front for Proletarian Action (FRAP)

The terms *revolutionary* and *proletarian* are often used as much by European neo-Nazis as they are by leftist groups. Contemporary Nazis also hate European links to the United States. The Revolutionary Front for Proletarian Action (FRAP) conducted its first action on April 20, 1985, a date universally celebrated by European Nazis as the birthday of Adolf Hitler. This was a bombing attack on the North Atlantic Assembly (NAA) in Brussels, and was followed the next day by an attack against the offices of AEG-Telefunken. The first reaction by authorities to these attacks and also from the media was that it was the work of an ultra-leftist group. The initial arrests were made from among members of leftist groups in Belgium. The attacks on these two establishments suggested that FRAP was as likely to be have been rightist as Communist, although the ambiguous circumstances of these attacks meant that it would be the left that would be stigmatized.[50]

Fighting Communist Cells (CCC)

The CCC came into being at about the same time as the so-called Mad Killers. How and where the group originated was a mystery and there was considerable speculation that its membership included members of the Belgium state security and agents of the far right. With no historical traditions for terrorism and violence, it seemed strange for this movement to emerge in Belgium so successfully. It was represented as a left-wing organization with affiliations with other left-wing European groups.

Like all its neighbors in Europe, Belgium has had to contend with the prospect of al Qaeda or al Qaeda inspired attacks. In 2003, Belgium authorities arrested and sentenced Nizar Trabelsi, a thirty-seven-year-old Tunisian to ten years in prison for planning to drive a car bomb into the cafeteria of a Belgian air base where about 100 U.S. military personnel were stationed. Trabelsi claims to have met Osama bin Laden and been trained in an al Qaeda camp in Afghanistan in the months prior to the 9-11 attacks.

Communist Combatant Cells (CCC)

Pierre Carette was the leader of the Belgian CCC group and became politically active when establishing a committee to gain the release of imprisoned members of the German Red Army Faction (RAF). In October 1984 CCC conducted a series of attacks on political and military targets, and Carette was subsequently arrested the following year. He was sentenced to a life sentence in 1988 for an attack on the Federation of Belgian Enterprises in Brussels in 1985, which resulted in the death of two fire fighters. He was released after fifteen years in 2003.[51]

Carette and the CCC began their short-lived campaign when, in October 1984, they attacked offices belonging to Litton Data Systems. Two months later, they followed with another attack on a NATO oil line near Brussels. Other attacks took place against symbolic property targets in Brussels and Antwerp. Carette's 1985 arrest spelled the end of the CCC. It is still not clear who or what was involved in the destabilizing attempt of Belgium. Was it all an attempt by the left, or was it some other form of terrorism with an as-yet undefined rationale? Whatever the case, there are some underlying aspects to the Belgium political structure that are relevant. One should not dismiss a theory that an agent provocateur may have been involved in the Belgian experience.

NETHERLANDS

The perceived or real threat that overpopulation from immigration may have on an otherwise liberal society is evidenced in the assassination of Pim Fortuyn and Theo Van Gough. Fortuyn was a blunt-speaking, anti-Muslim politician, who has become better known in death than he was in life. His

FIGURE 6-13 Map of the Netherlands (Central Intelligence Agency, *The World Factbook*, 2008).

comment, "The Netherlands is full" was one of his famous slogans. His viewpoint criticized the fact that the Netherlands was home to 1 million Muslims, the vast majority from Turkey and Morocco. He referred to Islam as a "backwards" religion that censored free thinkers and mistreated homosexuals and women. His assassination, the first to happen in Holland in 300 years, has generated widespread sympathy for his style of free speech. Perhaps surprisingly, it was not at the hands of a fanatical Muslim extremist that he met his death in a hail of bullets. His murderer was Volkert van der Graaf, an animal-rights activist; however, van der Graaf's motives for the assassination are not readily clear. The wake-up call for the Netherlands, and the knowledge of the presence of Islamic extremism there, was brought home to the populace with a broad-daylight assassination of Theo Van Gough on November 2, 2004, on an Amsterdam street. Mr. Van Gough, an avid and public critic of Islam—using his position as a film-maker, columnist, and television talk-show host as his platform—was attacked by a Moroccan with dual Dutch-Moroccan citizenship. The attacker, a member of an extreme Islamic group that has been named by the Dutch Intelligence Service as the Hofstadgroep, repeatedly shot Mr. Van Gough and then proceeded to stab him and slash his throat, to the point where his head was almost severed from his body. The Netherlands was shocked by this public display of Islamic fanaticism on its streets, in a country where radical extremist Muslims account for a very small minority of the 1 million Muslims who live there. The assassin, Mohammed Bouyeri, was sentenced to life in prison on July 26, 2005. After the killing, Bouyeri attached a note and his knife to the body of Van Gough. The note stated: "I surely know that you, Oh Europe will be destroyed." Once again, we see that the aim of the terrorist is not to make any deals or fathom any concessions from government, but to destroy a way of life. For the Islamic extremist, that includes (in this case) a non-Muslim critic of Islam. The Hofstadtgroep is also believed to be linked through its wider network with al Qaeda.[52] Soon after the attacks on 9-11, the Dutch Intelligence Services noted that the global recruiting of young Muslims was moving ahead in the

Netherlands. The Service believed that several dozen disenchanted Muslims had been recruited for suicide missions in the Middle East.

Dutch teenager Samir Azzouz was cleared of planning attacks on Amsterdam's Schiphol Airport, a nuclear reactor, and government offices. He had been found in possession of machine gun cartridges, mock explosive devices, electrical circuitry, maps and sketches of prominent buildings, and chemicals that prosecutors said could be bomb ingredients. Legal experts and security analysts said such cases raise a difficult question: In the absence of an actual attack, how close must a suspect be to detonating a bomb before prosecutors can demonstrate guilt?[53] The difficulty now for European countries is their inability to convict for terrorism offenses that are in the planning stage. No doubt, this will be seen as a win for the Islamic extremists. Police and security agencies will be sounding alarm bells as Europe gets set to become the new theater for attacks from Islamic groups with worldwide jihad in mind.

DUTCH CARTOONS—FREEDOM OF THE PRESS

The publication of a dozen cartoons depicting the Prophet Mohammed in the Dutch national paper *Jyllands Posten* resulted in at first localized protest then open street riots. The violence might have been contained in Holland if it had not been for imams taking a tour of the Middle East and stirring up Islamic fervor by distributing the same cartoons. The press will and do argue that political satire is what they do and many cartoons are seen in national papers on a regular daily basis. For the Muslim faith, Islam forbids any depiction of Prophet Mohammad. So when these cartoons appeared in late 2005 the tensions in the European Muslim communities were raised. To most observers the rioting and deaths that ensued seemed totally out of context from any message the cartoons may have been intending to portray to a wider audience. The Netherlands has a large Muslim immigrant population not dissimilar to other European countries, but it seems that any newspaper that prints any controversial commentary does so at its own risk.

Insulting a religion is despicable if that is what this is—or is it freedom of the press; however, in February 2006, more than three months after the original publication the imam of the Peshawar mosque in Pakistan, one Mohammed Yousef Qureshi, offered 1.5 million rupees (U.S. $30,000) reward for killing one of the cartoonists who portrayed the Prophet Mohammad. There was no outcry from western democracies or from the Dutch government for that matter. The way to resolve differences with the press has in western modern society rested with the courts. In October 2006, a Danish court dismissed a lawsuit brought by a group of Muslim organizations against *Jyllands-Posten*. "It cannot be ruled out that the drawings have offended some Muslims' honor, but there is no basis to assume that the drawings are, or were conceived as, insulting or that the purpose of the drawings was to present opinions that can belittle Muslims," said the city court in Aarhus. *Jyllands-Posten* called the decision a victory for freedom of the press, while the Muslim groups who jointly filed the lawsuit say they plan to launch an appeal.[54]

Summary

Terrorism has been synonymous with Europe for more than fifty years and, discounting the levels of genocide practiced by the Nazis in World War II, Europe has been the battleground for both the right and the left. While homegrown terrorism marked much of the 1960s era with groups such as Baader Meinhof, and the 1970s and 1980s with November 17 and ETA, a transformation has taken place. The cause of this change can be seen from two different angles. With the

fall of Communism came the influx of migrants from the former Soviet republics to Germany, Italy, France, the Netherlands, and Spain. From North Africa the inflow to Europe has seen migrants from the Muslim countries of Morocco, Tunisia, and Algeria, with universities accepting students from the wider swath of Islam from the oil-rich Persian Gulf states. The war on terror firmly rooted in a Western attack on the Islamic nations of Iraq and Afghanistan has led to young, disaffected migrants, many of whom are second-generation, taking up the call to jihad. These immigrants may have had no prior interest in their own Muslim faith but were drawn back into it by skilled Islamic recruiters for a worldwide Jihad against Western democracies. With the United States and Great Britain as the main targets, European nations will also have to contend with the broad specter of jihad in such metropolitan centers as Paris, Berlin, Brussels, Amsterdam, Madrid, and Rome as the second generation of marginalized youths from Islamic countries become the suicide bombers and terrorists of tomorrow. Europe's future security relies heavily on the network of security and intelligence agencies and their ability to identify the threats from Islamic extremism and the capacity and capability to prosecute to the full extent of the law. There can be no doubt that Europe is a target for Islamic extremism for recruiting, training, organizing, and prosecuting jihad. The Madrid train bombings of 2004 can be seen as a new beginning and a new front for terror against Western democracies. In Chapter 7, we will again see the threat of al Qaeda as radical Islam takes its toll in the East in Chechnya and the former Soviet Republics.

Web Sites

1. **Foreign Policy Association**—*http://www.fpa.org*
2. **Council on Foreign Relations**—*http://www.cfr.org*
3. **Washington Institute**—*http://www.washingtoninstitute.org*
4. **Militant Islam**—*http://www.militantislammonitor.org*
5. **Federation of American Scientists**—*www.fas.org/irp/eprint/calahan.htm*
6. **Danish Cartoons**—*http://www.militantislammonitor.org/article/id/1635*
7. **Executive Intelligence Review**—*http://www.larouchepub.com/other/1995/2246_eta.html*

Endnotes

1. U.S. Department of State Information Programs, usinfo.state.gov.
2. Intel Brief, courtesy U.S. Department of State archives on ETA, http://www.state.gov/s/ct/nls.
3. William Gutteridge, ed. "Contemporary Terrorism," an article by Peter Janke, the Institute for the Study of Conflict (1986), 152. Facts on File, Inc.
4. George Rosie. *The Directory of International Terrorism* (New York: Paragon House, 1987, p. 111).
5. Http://en.wikepedia.org/wiki/Batasuna.
6. "Spain: Move to Outlaw Separatist Party May Fail," *Strategic Forecasting* (July 5, 2002), www.stratfor.com/premium/analysis.
7. BBC World News—*ETA Declares Ceasefire*. http://search.bbc.co.uk/cgi-bin/search/results.pl?q=eta+ceasefire.
8. A History Written in Blood. http://www.telegraph.co.uk/news/main.jhtml?xml=/news/2006/03/23/weta223.xml.
9. Rosie. *The Directory of International Terrorism*, p. 135.
10. Pino Arlacchi. *Men of Dishonor* (New York: William Morrow and Co. Inc., 1993, p. 27).
11. Disk News Service. Spain Arrests al Qaeda Suspect with WTC Footage (July 16). http://news.bbc.co.uk.
12. Reuters Madrid. Prosecutor Seeks 220,000 Years for al Qaeda Suspects (February 14, 2005).
13. ZDF (German TV). Elmar Thevessen and Ulf Roller, "Das Netzwerk des Terrors," (October 24, 2001).
14. David Yallop. *Tracking the Jackal* (New York: Random House Inc., 1993, pp. 48–49.
15. Philip Jackson. "Under Two Flags: Provocation and Deception in European Terrorism." *Terrorism: An International Journal*, vol. II (New York: Taylor and Francis, 1988, p. 280).
16. Grant Wardlow. *Political Terrorism, Theory, Tactics and Counter-measures* (London: Cambridge University Press, 1982, p. 38).
17. Philip Jenkins. "Strategy of Tension: The Belgian Terrorist Crisis 1982–1986." *Terrorism: An International Journal*, vol. 13 (New York: Taylor and Francis, 1990, p. 299).
18. Yallop. *Tracking the Jackal*, p. 98.
19. Fighting Terrorism—Lessons from France. http://www.time.com/time/nation/article/0,8599,176139,00.html.
20. U.S. Department of State Web site, Patterns of Global Terrorism. http://www.state.gov.
21. TF1.Fr (French TV). "Gang de Roubaix: La Jeunesse de Dumont a l'Etude" (October 4, 2001); "Bin Laden's Invisible Network." *Newsweek*, International edition (October 29, 2001, p. 50).

22. Timeline—The Shoe Bomb Case. http//edition.cnn.com/2002/us/01/07/reid.timeline/index.html.

23. Adam Sage and Daniel McGory. "French Agents Knew of Hijack Suspect in 1994," *The London Times* (October 3, 2001, p. 4).

24. *BBC World* "Moussaqoui" (December 13, 2001); *CNN Inside Europe* (December 16, 2001).

25. Italy Anti-Semitism Worldwide 2003. http://www.ac.il.

26. *The World Book Encyclopedia.* vol. 9, S.V. "Reichstag." (1990), 254.

27. Richard Huffman. Motivations from an Internet article; Terrorist motivations (1997). www.Baader-meinhof.com.

28. Ibid.

29. Rosie. *Directory of International Terrorism*, p. 220.

30. Ibid.

31. Anti-Defamation League; A Worldwide Survey of Neo-Nazi Skinheads (New York: ADL, 1995), The Nizkor Project., www.Nizkor.org.

32. Donna Leinwand. *Germany Tightens Security in Sleeper Search, USA Today* (November 26, 2001), 13A.

33. Emerson Vermaat. "Occasional Paper" (Toronto: The Mackenzie Institute, 1993, pp. 129–131).

34. U.S. Department of State, *Patterns of Global Terrorism,* released by the Office of Coordinator for Counterterrorism (May 21, 2002), Europe Overview.

35. A Turkish Flash interview. http:// www.milligorusarsiv.com/videolar/file.php?f=5.

36. "German Intelligence says Islamists Present Major Threat," http://www.dw-world.de/dw/article/.

37. William Gutteridge, ed. *Contemporary Terrorism. A Challenge to Italian Democracy*, by Vittorfranco S. Pisano (London: The Institute for the Study of Control 1986, p. 167).

38. Ibid.

39. Ibid.

40. Ibid.

41. Ibid.

42. Anti-Defamation League Web site, *The Skinhead International*, a worldwide survey of Neo-Nazi Skinheads (New York: Anti-Defamation League, 1995), www.Nizkor.org.

43. Ibid.

44. Ibid.

45. Andrew Corsun. "Revolutionary Organization November 17 in Greece," *Terrorism: An International Journal*, vol. 14 (London: Taylor and Francis, 1991, p. 86).

46. G. Kassimeris. "Greece: Twenty Years of Political Terrorism," *Terrorism and Political Violence,* vol. 7 (London: Frank Kass, 1995, p. 81).

47. *World Book Encyclopedia*, vol. 19, S.V. "Kemal Ataturk," p. 511.

48. Human Rights Watch, "What is Turkey's Hizbollah?" (February 2000). http://www.hrw.org.

49. Ibrahim Cerrah and Robert Peel. "Terrorism in Turkey," *Intersec*, vol. 7 (West By Float, England: West By Float, 1997, p. 19).

50. Philip Jenkins. "Strategy of Tension: The Belgian Terrorist Crisis 1982–1986." *Terrorism: An Inter-national Journal* (London: Taylor and Francis, 1990, p. 304).

51. Http://en.wikipedia.org/wiki/Pierre_Carette.

52. Daniel Pipes. "Theo Van Gough and Education by Murder in Holland." New York: Sun (November 16, 2004).

53. Http://www.reuters.com (April 8, 2005).

54. CBC News Online October 26,th 2006: Muhammad cartoons: A timeline http://www.cbc.ca/news/background/islam/muhammad_cartoons_timeline.html.

CHAPTER 7

Eastern Europe and the Balkans

Terrorism has declared war on us, the people of Russia.

FORMER RUSSIAN PRESIDENT BORIS YELTSIN

Learning Objective

The study and review of this chapter will enable you to

1. Trace the history of Russian terrorism from the early twentieth century to the break up of the Soviet Union;

2. Discuss how Russia has managed and controlled the Chechen crisis;

3. Describe how the Balkan region became an area for ethnic cleansing;

4. Appreciate the difficulty in defining terrorism relative to events in the Balkans and Chechnya.

Terms to Remember

Archduke Franz Ferdinand	HEU	Partisans
Boevaya Oranisatsia (BO)	KGB	Pushkin Square
Bolshevik	Killer College	Russian Federation
Cheka	KINTEX	Sergei Kirov
FSB	Mehmet Ali Agca	Stalin
Gulags	Narodnaya Volya (NV)	

September 1, 2004—Islamic terrorists made up of Chechens, Arabs, Tartars, Kazaks, and Uzbeks take 1,000 hostages at School #One in Beslan. At the end of the standoff, the terrorists detonate their bombs and Special Forces attack the school. The resulting death toll accounted for 344 civilian deaths, including 137 children

August 13, 2007—The Nevsky Express train travelling at 80 mph between Moscow and Saint Petersburg was derailed by a powerful IED placed under the railways tracks, sixty people were injured.

January 17, 2008—A gun and grenade attack in Nazran, Ingushetia, reportedly targeted the home of the republic's prime minister. Russia's FSB director Nikolai Patrushev was attending a meeting of the National Antiterrorism Committee in Magas at the time of the attack.

OVERVIEW

Terrorism in the former Eastern Bloc and the now Soviet Republics is not a truly new phenomenon. The repression of the former Soviet Union, with its colorful and often sad history, was depicted in the stories by famous novelists of the nineteenth century, much as by the novelists of the twentieth century. Tolstoy, author and creator of War and Peace in 1869, captured the death and horror of the French invasion of Russia in 1812. Reforms made by Czar Alexander II were strongly opposed by his son Alexander III, who succeeded him after his assassination. It was this repressive approach that slowly nurtured the seeds of revolution in Russia, which were at first written about as themes of desperation, discontent, and bitterness by the many great novelists and intellectuals of that era.

This chapter reviews those early terror theories that were at work in Russia and the Slavic states, and also examines the manner in which the Soviet Union promoted state-sponsored terrorism on an international scale. Many of the nineteenth-century Russian writers, such as Maxim Gorky, wrote short stories and plays that reflected the theories of a Communist state in Russia. The early seeds of terrorism grew out of the appalling conditions in which the people of Russia existed under the cruel Czars, and out of a need for social change and the overwhelming hope of the people to have change occur. With the breakup of the Soviet Union in 1991, the new millennium has continued to witness unrest and the relentless abuses of human rights by Chechen rebels and Russian security forces. The widespread threat of Islamic extremism is not being checked and is spreading through the Russian republics seemingly like wildfire.

The chapter begins with a review of the most well-known historic events, and then examines other events that occurred in the central and eastern parts of Europe. Bringing this chapter into the twenty-first century, we will find how the War on Terror has played out in the Chechen Republic, and how the actions of so-called Chechen rebels are labeled as terrorism by the Russian government. The worldwide concern related to the availability of nuclear weapons, and their accessibility to terrorists through the Czech Republic, will also be carefully considered.

RUSSIA AND THE SOVIET UNION

Narodnaya Volya (NV) (1878–1881)

Roughly translated, **Narodnaya Volya (NV)**[1] means "the people's will." This highly effective terrorist organization was in existence for only four years. NV grew out of other disaffected Russian movements that were clandestine in nature and had been formed by the intelligentsia. Hard-liners from several of these groups formed the Narodnaya Volya. Like other terrorist organizations, the NV used terrorism as a means to a political end. Its aim was to cause the ruling Romanovs so much distress and turmoil that their actions would shake the Russian Empire's political foundation. NV drew its members from the ruling upper class of Russian society, and numbered probably no more than 500, with some fifty or more extremists. It set out to overthrow the tyranny of the Czars and declared a sentence of death to Czar Alexander II. The group made several unsuccessful attempts upon his life.

One of the most fanatical members of the NV organization, twenty-seven-year-old Sophia Perovskaya, succeeded in planting a bomb that killed Czar Alexander II in 1881. At the tender age of twenty-seven she was a fanatic, as well as the daughter of a Russian General; she was arrested along with five others and publicly executed. The NV was also responsible for the death of General Mezentsev, head of the third section of the Czarist OKHRNA (secret police), and also the Governor General of Saint Petersburg. NV members were hunted down and arrested by Czarist authorities, and terrorism in Russia diminished significantly over the next twenty years. However, the NV was to have a profound effect on Russian history.

The inspiration for Lenin to form the Social Democratic Labor Party was born from NV's theories. Lenin's views of, and appreciation for, NV had taught him an important lesson—that a revolutionary organization cannot be limited to terrorism, but must seize total autocratic and bureaucratic

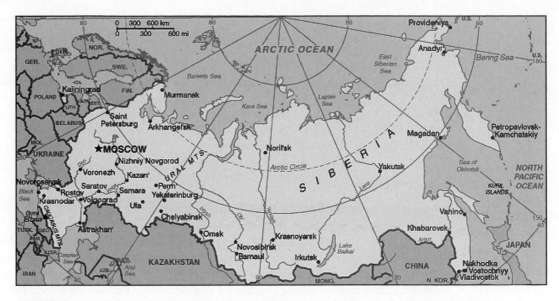

FIGURE 7-1 **Map of Russia** (Central Intelligence Agency, *The World Factbook*, 2008).

power. The NV symbolized the general social crisis that existed in nineteenth-century Russia, and later during the **Bolshevik** Revolution, which replaced the old order in Russia. Terrorism faded quickly with the passing of the NV, until the formation of the Social Revolutionary Party at the turn of the twentieth century. Members of NV took extreme care in planning and carrying out their assassinations to avoid killing any innocent citizens in the process. The targets for retribution were those deemed guilty of acts of corruption and other acts against the people.

Terror and revolution are two words that would be used frequently and interchangeably for Russians over the first twenty years of the twentieth century. In 1902, the Minister of the Interior was assassinated. The prime objective for terrorism in early twentieth-century Russia was to awaken the masses to the potential for revolution and social change. The philosophical view of this approach is seen today by struggles in other regions of nationalist conflict where the intent is to attempt coercion and motivate the masses to revolt and overthrow the existing authority.

Within the Social Revolutionary Party was a terrorist subgroup that was given autonomy under the party—**Boevaya Oranisatsia (BO)**, or the Fighting Organization. It can be argued that whereas the NV was more aligned with the educated Russian hierarchy, the BO appealed to a wider Russian audience. Within the revolutionary movement, widespread dissent continued over the use of terror tactics and, with the emergence of the class struggle, terrorism as a weapon of that period became redundant.

Mikhail Bakunin, the brilliant Russian orator, traveled widely throughout Europe promoting his ideals for revolutionary change. They were based on the destruction of the prevailing social order, as it existed in Russia. His approach to anarchy conflicted greatly with that of Karl Marx, and the two were bitter rivals. Bakunin put forward no useful or thoughtful ideas for a future social order. Marx saw him as a dangerous fanatic. Bakunin's view was that the state had to be overthrown, but Marx believed that it was capitalism that had to be purged. Marx's theory and ideology were that violence was necessary to transform the nature of the working class, and that violent insurrection was the only means by which society could be changed.

Opposition to the Bolsheviks' rule, following their rise to power in 1917, came from the intelligentsia, as well as from opposition newspapers. The Russian Republics were deeply involved in a civil war in the years from 1918 to 1921. In March 1918, Lenin dissolved the constituent assembly when it failed to recognize the leadership of the Bolshevik government. The protests from the socialist left went unheeded by Lenin, so much so that the group withdrew from the coalition.

The Bolsheviks then began a period of terror and repression against all groups that voiced opposition. Hundreds of artists and intellectuals were arrested, who were simply aghast at the attitude of the Bolsheviks and had expected a society based on freedom in the wake of the overthrow of the Czarist government. The Bolsheviks dealt with nationalists, social revolutionaries, as well as members of the intellectual levels of society (professors, writers, and artists) in the harshest of manners. The church in Russia also became a target of Communist terror and oppression. A systematic campaign by the Communists to deny the Russian Orthodox Church any voice in the Soviet Union started in the 1920s, and by 1939, all the clergy, and many of the church's followers, had been shot or sent to forced labor camps. Of the 50,000 churches in Russia, only about 500 remained open.

Joseph Stalin

To many, the very mention of the name "**Stalin**" conjures up scenes of sheer despotic terror. In the first quarter of the twentieth century, his name was synonymous with the word "terror." This chapter is not presented to teach the student the fundamentals of the Russian Revolution, but to explain that the intricate use of terror tactics, as practiced by Lenin's Bolsheviks, had the unspoken, but total, support of the Communist Party. Were the Bolsheviks considered to be terrorists, or were they merely revolutionaries fighting for their political beliefs to achieve a new Soviet Republic? In hindsight, and because popular movies such as *Doctor Zhivago* seemed to glory in the hostility and man's inhumanity to his fellow man, should we therefore consider the Russian revolution a result of effective terrorism? In later years, and specifically during the Cold War, the United States and NATO allies viewed the USSR as the prime exporter and sponsor of modern-day terrorism. The notorious terrorist "Carlos the Jackal" is believed to have received his indoctrination, training, and funding in the Soviet Union. Although there is some evidence that he did receive part of his university education there, no substantive evidence has ever been unearthed that shows the Soviet Union did, in fact, sponsor him.

   Josef Vissarionovich Dzhugashvili adopted the name "Stalin," a Russian word that means "steel." Following Lenin's death, Stalin became the "Absolute Ruler" of the Soviet Union, from 1929 until he died in 1953. As a young man, he earned a scholarship to study theology but was subsequently expelled for preaching Marxist ideologies. He was a strong political supporter of Bolshevism throughout Europe, and is credited with being the first editor of *Pravda*, the newspaper voice of the Communist Party. Stalin used extreme measures on the Russian populace to ensure absolute and blind obedience to his will. Anyone who opposed him was summarily dealt with, and either shot or sent to labor camps (**Gulags**) in Siberia. This form of state terrorism was carried out by his head of the secret police, Laurenty Beria. The very mention of Beria's name struck terror in the hearts of the Soviet citizens.

The Secret Police

In many states where suppression of the masses by deliberate terror takes place, there is a need for a sanctioned police force or other security network to do the bidding of a cruel dictator. Apart from Adolf Hitler, there have been few other world leaders who have slaughtered and sent to labor camps so many of their own countrymen. The Communist regime under Stalin viewed any dissent against the party as a repudiation of his proletarian struggle, and a violation of Marxist–Leninist ideology. Therefore, a threat to these guidelines was a threat to the very existence of the authority of Stalin and the state. To this end, the Bolsheviks, and then the Communists, relied heavily on strong, political secret police force to secure and maintain their rule. The original secret police, called the "**Cheka**," was formed in 1917, with the intention that it would be disbanded after the Bolsheviks under Lenin had consolidated power. The first chief of this secret police force was Feliks Dzerzhinski, who had the power under the Bolsheviks to investigate all or any "counter-revolutionary crimes."

   Much has been written of the Russian Revolution and few would argue that the results of the October Revolution would surely be felt for decades to come. Even though the Soviet Union has disappeared into the dustbin of history, the difficulty of defining what actions were really terrorism becomes murky. There is no doubt that the actions of the Social Democrats of the Lenin era were terroristic in attitude and nature. However, when reviewed and portrayed as a class struggle for worker rights, why are these struggles now termed as revolutionary actions? Is it the popular belief that where a common populace supports a cause, whether it be righteous or not, these activities are no longer referred to as merely terrorist acts, but rather a full-blown "popular resistance," or "revolution"?

In the latter decades of the twentieth century, Western governments have actively criminalized terrorism and created legislation to deal with specific "acts of violence" against the state, including the banning of terrorist-linked backed or supported groups. Might it therefore be reasonable to rationalize that a popular revolution exists within the borders of Spain (ETA) or in Northern Ireland (IRA)? As we strive to continually master what terrorism means in each specific category and, indeed, each country, it becomes less and less easy to define. In Afghanistan, following the Soviet invasion of that sovereign state, no doubt the rebels fighting for the freedom of their country out of the mountains around Kabul would most likely be termed as terrorists by the Soviet Union. It is equally fair to believe that to the Afghans these "terrorists" are better described as "freedom fighters"? It is now more than ironic that one of those freedom fighters, who were provided support in the form of training from both the United States and Great Britain, would turn and bite the hands that fed him. We are, of course, referring to Osama bin Laden. U.S. Special Forces and Britain's Special Air Service Regiment (SAS) trained Afghan freedom fighters and equipped bin Laden and his followers admirably for covert-style operations against their new "enemies" in the West. Some of those fighters, no doubt, were eventually involved in fighting alongside the Taliban and al Qaeda against coalition forces in Afghanistan.

The Great Terror

Throughout modern history, there have been many dictators who have purged their respective societies of all opposition, both from within and outside their own political structures. The murder of a senior Politburo member on December 1, 1934, was to set in motion a chain of events that resulted in the "great terror." **Sergei Kirov** was leader of the Communist Party in Leningrad, and an influential member of the ruling elite. Popular as he was in Leningrad, in support of workers' welfare, he disagreed with some of Stalin's policies. Although he was not thought to be a threat to Stalin, he had been approached by some Party members to take over as General Secretary.[2]

Did Stalin, who was having doubts about the loyalty of the Leningrad apparatus, possibly perceive Kirov as a threat? It seems entirely possible that the People's Commissariat for Internal Affairs (NKVD) could well have planned Kirov's murder on Stalin's instructions. Using the murder of Kirov as the excuse he needed to crack down hard and to purge the Leningrad party structure, Stalin introduced wide-sweeping laws that resulted in millions of Russians being arrested. This purge lasted for approximately four years and Stalin never again visited Leningrad. That four-year period saw millions of Russians sent to labor camps as well as summary executions and show trials. To say the Russian populace was terrified would be an understatement! In view of Stalin's terror tactics, his complete and total domination of the Russian people was further enforced by forcibly resettling more than 1 million people, primarily Muslims from the Northern Caucasus region and the Crimea. Ethnic Tartars, Chechens, Meskhetians, Kalmyks, as well as Bulgarians, Greeks, and Armenians from the Black Sea coast were also deported.

These deportations took place during and after World War II, with the excuse that all of these deportees were collaborators with the German occupying forces. The forced deportations took place with the use of cattle cars, reminiscent of German deportations of Jews and gypsies to forced labor and extermination camps. The destination for the deportees was Uzbekistan, Siberia, and Kazakhstan—names that today have a ring of familiarity. By the mid-1950s, Nikita Khrushchev denounced the forced deportations. However, many deportees were still not permitted to return to their native homelands until after the collapse of the USSR in 1991.

years, the FSB has undergone several structural changes as a result of political power struggles and was changed to reflect five separate departments and eight directorates:

- Counterintelligence Department
- Anti-terrorist Department
- Strategic Forecasting and Analysis Department
- Personnel and Management Department
- Operational Support Department
- Directorate of Analysis and Suppression of the Activity of Criminal Organizations
- Investigations Directorate
- Operational–Search Directorate
- Operational–Technical Measures Directorate
- Internal Security Directorate
- Administration Directorate
- Prison System Directorate
- Scientific–Technical Directorate

Organized crime was on the rise in the Russian Federation but the police force was ill-equipped to respond. Interpol, on the other hand, was hard at work, tracking the exploits of more than 400 Russian international criminals. The Office of International Criminal Justice estimated that at least 4,000 organized crime syndicates were operating in the Russian Federation by 1996.

With the breakup of the Soviet Union came the dissolution of the Soviet's intelligence service (KGB). Its agents, however, did not fade into quiet oblivion. Scratching the surface of Russian bureaucracy will uncover layers, like the little Russian dolls, of control dominated by former KGB operatives, many in local government and politics. Organized crime syndicates in the Russian Federation, in collaboration with former KGB officers, is probably a major factor in a booming trade in former Soviet-made weaponry, not the least of which are nuclear capability products.

The "Russian mafya's" links with former KGB operatives have led to the escalation of weapons sales to terrorist groups. The Russian mafya has moved from purely internal criminal activities to the exporting of terrorist weapons, some with the potential of mass destruction capability. Weapons of mass destruction have been placed on the market for sale to the highest bidder, and some of these sophisticated weapons have ended up in the hands of Third-World countries. The potential for global conflict from these sales, while yet to be realized, should not be ignored or minimized.

Russia continues to be at the crossroads on the road to reform—or possibly is taking the long and winding path to anarchy and corruption. Its nearby neighbors have been embroiled in revolutions throughout the first decade of the twenty-first century, however a new era of Russian dominance in the region is beginning to assert itself. This lawless society in Russia has led criminal elements to feed on the possibilities of controlling the state and reaping the rewards from corrupt politicians. With the criminal element playing so large a role in the proceedings of daily life in Russia, it is no wonder that these elements will stop at nothing to achieve their goals. On November 22, 1998, the staunch, pro-democracy parliamentarian, Galina Starovoitova, a vocal campaigner for human rights and against political corruption, was murdered in a scene reminiscent of a James Bond movie. She was shot three times in the head at close range as she entered her apartment building. Her campaign had been instrumental in exposing corrupt local politicians, and it is believed that this led to her assassination. Starovoitova was well respected but was among a minority of democracy reformers. The killing was done in a very professional manner and has all the hallmarks of a gangland-style execution. In a country where few women rise to the heights of local and national politics, her passing is something of a watershed for Russian politics. What the outcome will be is uncertain, but the grip of the underworld on Russia seems to be excruciatingly strong. "Democracy, free-market economy, and the rule of law" are not words or statements that go hand in hand with everyday life in Russia in the new millennium. The widespread corruption that continues to manifest itself in both private and public organizations is as rampant as ever. Organized crime covers vast areas of the economy, from diversion of collected revenues, a form of money laundering, and the defrauding of overseas aide donors. The illegal trade in arms dealing, and the concern that al Qaeda followers would like to acquire nuclear capability, suggest that Russia may be a possible prime source for such weaponry. It must be remembered that there are newspaper reports that handheld nuclear missiles are missing or unaccounted for! In either scenario, the threat from their mere existence will have, and should have, many governments concerned. Many terrorist organizations, not just the Chechens, would welcome having this type of capability, even if it was only for them to use as a threat.

The threat of nuclear terrorism and the desire of terror groups, in particular al Qaeda, to fashion a nuclear weapon requires discussion in relationship to the available materials needed to support such an operation. The Russian states have many sites that produced nuclear material during the Cold War years and beyond. Many observers and politicians, particularly those in the U.S. administration, believe the only probable method for a group such as al Qaeda to acquire material to produce such a weapon is through a rogue or hostile sponsor state. To this end, U.S. policy is fashioned to continuously target hostile states that pose a nuclear supply threat. Maybe this is a sound policy, or maybe it is not. What need concern the world at large are the nuclear stockpiles around the globe, and the poor security and accountability that characterize a great many of these sites. To consider fashioning a nuclear bomb, terrorist organizations and nations have different requirements. Countries developing nuclear weapons require facilities for research and development in the manufacture, control, development, and deployment for conventional means. For the terrorist, the word should be "unconventional." For Osama bin Laden and his al Qaeda-affiliated terror network, using a boat, truck, plane, or car as the means of delivering a nuclear weapon would be their conventional method. The Fatwa bin Laden sought and received from a Saudi cleric in 2003 for the use of a nuclear bomb would be permissible under Islamic law, indeed even mandatory, if it were used as a means to stop U.S. actions against Muslims. "*If a bomb that killed 10 million of them and burned as much of their land as they have burned Muslims' land were dropped on them, it would be permissible,*" the ruling held.[5]

According to the International Atomic Energy Agency (IAEA), since 1993 there have been 175 cases of trafficking in nuclear material and 201 cases of trafficking in other radioactive sources (medical, industrial, etc.). However, only eighteen of these cases have actually involved small amounts of highly enriched uranium or plutonium, the material needed to produce a nuclear weapon. IAEA experts judge the quantities involved to be insufficient to construct a nuclear explosive device. However, Mr. El Baradei, Director General of the International Atomic Energy Agency (IAEA), said: "Any such material being in illicit commerce and conceivably accessible to terrorist groups is deeply troubling." There has been a sixfold increase in nuclear material in peaceful programs worldwide since 1970. According to IAEA figures, there are 438 nuclear power reactors; 651 research reactors (of these, 284 are in operation); and 250 fuel cycle plants around the world, including uranium mills and plants that convert, enrich, store, and reprocess nuclear material. Additionally, tens of thousands of radiation sources are used in medicine, industry, agriculture, and research.[6] In respect to Russia in particular, the threat of theft of weapons-grade material such as highly enriched uranium (**HEU**), the compound needed to make a nuclear weapon, is still a major cause for concern. While treaties have been drawn up between the United States and Russia, much work in destroying the stockpiles and securing the existing ones must be addressed. The material for the terrorist to build his bomb is available and currently not that secure.

RUSSIAN SUITCASE N-BOMBS

After the collapse of the Soviet Union there was a global concern about suitcase-sized nuclear bombs, and attention to these portable nuclear devices peaked in 1997 following allegations by the late Governor of Krasnoyarsk and former Russian Security Council Secretary, General Alexander Lebed, that an unknown number of these weapons could not be accounted for. Interception of "suitcase bombs" is difficult along land borders and practically impossible along maritime borders.

At the same time, the political, psychological, and economic effects of a blast from a portable nuclear weapon would be far greater than, for example, those of a "dirty bomb."

The first and only reliable line of defense against the acquisition or use of "suitcase nuclear weapons" by terrorists lies in the countries that possess such devices or have the capability to produce them. Lebed's 1997 statements are particularly unnerving because the early 1990s represented the time of greatest risk with regard to nuclear weapons security in Russia. Governmental institutions were radically weakened, and a dramatic drop in the standard of living made individuals with access to these weapons extremely vulnerable to the temptation of easy, illegal profits on the black market. Official denials, including the denials that such weapons even existed, are not a sufficient reason for complacency.

Terrorist opportunities in the former Soviet state of Ukraine relate to the vast arsenal of weapons and missiles that resided in the country at the time of the breakup of the Soviet Union. In 1990–1991, the Soviet Union delivered 1,942 S-185 rockets to a military base west of Kiev, where they were to be dismantled. Since that date, only 488 have been accounted for. Additionally, in 2003, the Ukraine Ministry of Defense had no method of accounting for any inventories of military stock that it had inherited from the Soviet Union. The Minister ordered an audit and found that $170 million worth of military stock was likely missing and unaccounted for.[7]

UKRAINE

The former Soviet states of Ukraine and Kyrgyzstan have both experienced political unrest and felt the interfering hand of Russia in its attempt to steer both states away from democracy and a return to Communist ideals. Intelligence sources suggest that Russia used every means at its disposal to prevent the election of the pro-democracy, pro-West candidate Victor Yushchenko from succeeding in the Ukraine. Political and outspoken pressure was placed on the Ukrainian public with strongly worded support for the Russian favorite, Viktor Yanukovych. Russia reverted to its old tactics, not of invasion, which it has used so unsuccessfully in recent history, but of assassination. In this case, the popular Yushchenko was the target. Reports indicate that the hand of the Russian secret police was involved in supplying the dioxin poison that made the candidate so ill in September 2004.

FIGURE 7-2   Map of Ukraine (Central Intelligence Agency, *The World Factbook*, 2008).

CHECHNYA

A Mixed Background of Terror and Warfare

The Czars began a 300-year attempt to subjugate the northern Caucasus in 1560. By 1585, Chechnya and other areas of the Caucasus had been conquered by the Ottoman Empire and represented its northern reach into what has become modern Russia. Under Ottoman rule, the Chechens adopted Islam while Russia continued its attempt to capture the area and finally forced the retreat of the Ottomans by 1785.

After winning the Caucasian War (1817–1864), the Russians deported hundreds of thousands of Chechens. In 1877, 1920, 1929, 1940, and 1943, the Chechens made unsuccessful attempts to rebel against the Czars and then the Communists. While most of the Chechen males were fighting against Hitler in the winter of 1943–1944, Stalin ordered that Chechnya be obliterated. Villages were burned, 500,000 people were deported to Kazakhstan and Siberia, and their land was given to non-Chechens. In 1957, the Chechens were allowed to return to their homeland. Dzhokhar Dudayev seized power in Chechnya in August 1991, after a popular vote elected him president that November. Dudayev declared independence from the Soviet Union just a month before its collapse.

Problems in the Caucasus

In February 1994, Russian President Boris Yeltsin and President of the Republic of Tatarstan, Minitimir Shaimiev, initialed a treaty delineating a division of powers between the Russian national government and the government of Tatarstan. The treaty afforded Tatarstan a considerable amount of autonomy and was welcomed by Yeltsin's Nationalities Minister, Sergei Shakhrai, as a "breakthrough." Kabardino-Balkaria and Bashkortostan followed in short order. These treaties represented a fine-tuning of Russia's evolving federation relations, the basic framework of which had been established by the new Russian Constitution of December 1993. The consolidation of Russia's territorial integrity was essential to prevent another Afghanistan failure. The control of the vast group of Islamic states within and without the vast Russian borders was imperative. Above all, there was the explosive situation in the North Caucasus. There, among other problems, the breakaway republic of Chechnya continued to refuse to consider itself a part of the new Russian Federation.

Moscow's previous response to Chechnya's challenge amounted to a policy of benign neglect toward both the republic and its President, Dzhokhar Dudayev. Moscow allowed the republic to go its own way and even attempted periodically to enter into negotiations with Dudayev. The Russian government repeatedly asserted that under no condition would force be used to resolve its differences with the republic and expressed the hope that these treaties would serve as a model for finding a negotiated solution with Chechnya.

Even as words of encouragement were being spoken, Moscow began stepping up financial and military support for opposition forces to the government in Chechnya. Fighting in the republic intensified over the summer, leading to a major attack on Grozny by the combined forces of the Chechen opposition in an effort to overthrow Dudayev. Despite support from helicopters and aircraft with Russian markings, the attack failed. A little more than a week later, President Yeltsin issued a decree authorizing the government, including the military, to take all necessary steps to disarm "illegal armed formations" in the republic. Two days later, 40,000 Russian troops poured into Chechnya. It was a debacle and the Chechen rebels were able to send the demoralized Russian Army home in defeat.[8] In August 1994, the Russian government began military action to stop Chechnya's secession. Russian troops began aerial bombing and attacked the capital of Grozny in December and again in February 1995. Subsequently, the rebel Chechen government moved to the hills and Chechnya was put under armed Russian occupation.

Regardless of whether Russia had a right to use force to defend its territorial integrity against Chechen secession, it is now clear in hindsight that the invasion was a tactical error. The viciousness of the war made it inconceivable that Chechnya would ever become a "normal" member of the Russian Federation, even if it was granted considerable autonomy and a treaty-based relationship with Moscow, like that with Tatarstan. The hostility of the Chechen people toward Russia, deeply rooted before the conflict, has been immeasurably intensified by the brutality of the war and will not be ameliorated by Moscow's promises of financial aid to reconstruct the republic, assuming that Moscow is in a position to deliver on these promises, which it probably is not.

Moscow continues to make the full application of its constitution on Chechen soil as a condition of peaceful existence. With that caveat, the Chechen republic will remain a terrible burden on the Russian people, a political nightmare for whatever party is in power in Moscow, and a major and possibly decisive impediment to the preservation of Russian democracy.[9]

Current Situation

Chechnya continues to be a threat and a painful thorn in Russia's side. The fighting continues amid atrocities being committed by Russian troops in Chechnya. The Russian military, in May 2002, openly proclaimed that it was clamping down on the vicious attacks of its soldiers against Chechens; however, this proclamation seems not to have been heeded by the soldiers themselves. Two weeks later, Russian soldiers seized five young men and methodically knifed them to death.[10]

The Russian army has now managed to fight two separate wars in Chechnya, the last ending in 2000. Chechens remained undaunted and throughout 2000, the war was still being taken to the Russian public. Bomb attacks continued in Moscow—the **Pushkin Square** bombing on August 8, 2000, was detonated at the height of the evening rush hour, injuring more than ninety and killing twelve. Suicide attacks continued in 2004, with the simultaneous downing of two Russian passenger aircraft and train station attacks in Moscow. Whether the bombs came from Chechen militants or warring factions of the Russian Mafya has not become clear. Some speculate that the attacks were the work of the secret police as an excuse for the next invasion of Chechnya. The guilty party, from a Russian viewpoint, would necessarily be the Chechens. Chechnya suffers from a ferocious economic embargo from Russia, which has caused most of its infrastructure to be either destroyed or decaying; thus, Chechnya is barely functioning. How many times have we heard the expression, "The world has changed since 9-11"? Russia is now a staunch ally of the West, is friendly with NATO countries, and has provided logistical and tactical support to U.S. coalition troops engaged in fighting and deposing the Afghan Taliban regime. Even five years ago, that kind of cooperation with the Russians probably would have been unthinkable, let alone believable. Russia also plans to establish a regionally deployed "Rapid Response Force" in Kyrgyzstan, ostensibly to fight against extreme Islamic rebels/terrorists/fighters. Establishing such a response force will allow the Russian military to be deployed more widely and also to regain some of its self-respect. This Central Asian force, which will be located in the heart of Eurasia and likely staffed and commanded by Russian officers, will be supported by the other Eurasian signatories to the Collective Security Treaty of 1992, who agreed in May to coordinate their military tactical strength against the threat of insurgency from radical and extreme Islamic threats.

Assassinations

Akhmad Kadyrof, the Kremlin-backed President of Chechnya, was killed in a bomb attack in May 2004, along with twenty others when an explosion ripped through a VIP section of a stadium where he was celebrating the defeat of the Nazis in World War II. He was named as the head of Chechnya's civil administration in 2000, and the Kremlin had entrusted him with organizing a 2003 referendum that would approve a constitution, cementing Chechnya's status as an inseparable part of Russia.

Kadyrof was accused of siphoning funds destined for Chechen reconstruction. A former Imam, he had fought on the side of the Chechen separatists but later switched sides in an attempt to lead the republic to some sort of stability following two wars.

The Beslan school attack in North Ossetia in September 2004 was claimed as being an operation of Basayev's, but is more likely to have been promoted and supported by former Chechen president and warlord Aslan Maskhadov. Maskhadov was killed by Russian forces in a shootout in March 2005. He was formerly elected as president of Chechnya during its brief period of independence in the mid-1990s.

Shamil Salmanovich Basayev (January 14, 1965–July 10, 2006) was the right-hand man of the former Chechen President Dzhokhar Dudayev who was elected following the break up of the Soviet Union, in 1991. Basayev was to the Russians what Osama bin Laden is to the Americans. He was responsible for numerous guerrilla attacks on security forces in and around Chechnya as well as terrorist attacks on Russian civilians, including the Russian Theater siege in Moscow and the Beslan School massacre which resulted in 300 deaths of mostly school children. Basayev was killed by an explosion on July 10, 2006.[11] The two wars that have razed most of Chechnya since the 1990s have had a profound effect on its people. First, most Chechens believed themselves to be Russian and found it difficult to determine exactly how they should react. Terrorist actions led by Basayev were to have an immediate effect in ending the First Chechen war. In June 1995 Basayev led an eighty-plus team of Chechen fighters into Russia and attacked the southern city of Budyonnovsk where they stormed the police station, government buildings and the city hall. When Russian reinforcements arrived, Basayev and his group retreated and took over a thousand hostages at the local hospital—a bloody battle ensued resulting in the death of thirty hostages unable to escape the grenades being thrown into the hospital by the Special Forces. The unsuccessful attempt led to an eventual ceasefire—Basayev managed to negotiate his way out. In exchange for the hostages, the Russian government agreed to halt military actions in Chechnya—on June 18, 1995, Viktor. S. Chernomirdin, Prime Minister of the Russian Federation issued the following statement.

> *To release the hostages who have been held in Budenovsk, the Government of Russian Federation:*
>
> 1. *Guarantees an immediate cessation of combat operations and bombings in the territory of Chechnya from 05 AM, 19 June 1995. Along with this action, all the children, women, elderly, sick and wounded, who have been taken hostage, should be released.*
> 2. *Appoints a delegation, authorized to negotiate the terms of the peaceful settlement of conflict in Chechnya, with V.A. Mihailov as a leader and A.I. Volsky as a deputy. Negotiations will start immediately on the 18th June 1995, as soon as the delegation arrives in Grozny. All the other issues, including a question of withdrawal of the armed forces, will be peacefully resolved at the negotiating table.*
> 3. *After all the other hostages are released, provides Sh. Basayev and his group with transport and secures their transportation from the scene to the Chechen territory.*
> 4. *Delegates the authorized representatives of the Government of the Russia Federation A. V. Korobeinikov and V. K. Medvedickov to deliver this Statement to Sh. Basayev.*
>
> *Prime Minister of the Russia Federation*
> *V. S. Chernomirdin*
> *18.06.95*

However, by the time of the second Chechen war, the stark brutality of the Russian troops toward the civilian population—which has seen more than 250,000 killed, including around 45,000 children—the options became clear: Stay in the towns and be rounded up, kidnapped, or murdered or head for the forests and take up arms. A huge number chose the latter. As a Muslim population, Chechnya has been involved with affiliated terror groups from Muslim countries trained in Afghanistan during the Taliban regime. Suicide attacks by Chechen terror groups have struck in the heart of Moscow. The Riyadus Salikhin group, under the direct leadership of Chechen warlord Shamil Basayev claimed responsibility for the Dubrovka Theater attack in Moscow in 2002, which led to the deaths of more than 100 civilians. Basayev claimed responsibility for all five major suicide bombings in Russia in 2004 and had stated that he reserved the right to use chemical and toxic substances and poisons against the Russians. Basayev did not fit on the world stage as an "international terrorist" and did not pose a threat to the security of the United States. Many of his detractors, mostly Russian, considered that he was affiliated with the movement of Osama bin Laden's al Qaeda. We suggest that he was not and that his aims were purely within the realm of the domination and establishment of his own fiefdom in the North Caucasus region. As part of its political end-game with the Russians, the United States, through its then Secretary of State Colin Powell, made the following comment in 2003 in regard to Basayev: "He has committed, or poses a significant risk of committing, acts of terrorism that threaten the security of U.S. nationals, or the national security, foreign policy, or economy of the United States." This kind of response for a warlord/terrorist who had not likely left Chechnya in the previous ten years may seem somewhat bewildering and confusing. His death in 2006 has been claimed by the Russian FSB.

GEORGIA

The Pankisi Gorge area in Georgia is described, at best, as a lawless region and home to bandits, as well as Arab and Chechen terrorists. This area, over which the government of Eduard Shevardnadze or his successor exerts little control, could be a fertile region for terrorist training camps and for Chechen terrorists to launch attacks against Russian targets. British authorities suspect ricin production is established in this region. The government in Georgia remains among the least stable in the entire Eastern Bloc region. Controlling terrorism and the scourge of the Pankisi Gorge is a problem not easily solved. The mere threat and obvious presence of Islamic extremist terrorists functioning in the area does nothing to assist the United States in its wider War on Terror. As time passes, government attempts to crack down on this region have, at best, been weak and, at worst, downright pathetic.

FIGURE 7-3 **Map of Georgia** (Central Intelligence Agency, *The World Factbook*, 2008).

In the summer of 2002, Shevardnadze announced that his security forces would be cracking down on terrorists and others in the region of the Gorge; following that announcement, troops moved into the region. A further proclamation from the Ministry of the Interior was released that simply stated, "The information about the presence of a large number of armed terrorists is invalid." The Pankisi Gorge is tough terrain for troops and security forces, so it is highly likely that with the advance warning from the government, any terrorists have gone to ground. Human intelligence coming from this region indicates significant numbers of Islamic extremists operating in the Pankisi Gorge, so the Georgian claims may be out of line with the reality for this area. The presence of Islamic militants, particularly Chechens, has been an ongoing issue since the mid-1990s. The national TV station in Georgia announced in August 2002 that the Pankisi region was home to a few al Qaeda sympathizers, criminals, and bandits. This seems out of context with other intelligence coming from the region.

After 9-11, the Georgian president supported the U.S.-led War on Terror. Earlier in the year, the United States sent special operations troops to train in Georgia to ensure that local forces were able to respond to and root out terrorists in the Pankisi region. What has now turned out to be a fiasco can be blamed on many variables, including corrupt officials and the fear of reprisals from Chechen crime groups who are somewhat aligned with the Chechen extremists, and who are certainly capable of targeting officials in Georgia for reprisals.

With no serious outcome to the attempt by the Georgian security forces to crack down or otherwise disperse any terrorists, the region has become a prime location for Islamic militants to continue to regroup and train for future operations. The reality appears to be that al Qaeda can operate with impunity in the republic of Georgia. As for diplomacy and the need to trade off political hot potatoes, the government of Russia has sought to have a free hand in handling its Chechen problems without interference from the United States in exchange for Russia's support of the continuing American campaign in Iraq. However, Russia's August 2008 military incursion into Georgia has not been viewed along the same lines. Russia will no doubt continue to attempt to intimidate the former Soviet republics as it continues to widen its sphere of influence to combat the growth and independence of its former states.

YUGOSLAVIA

From World War I to Ethnic Cleansing

Yugoslavia was established as a nation by the League of Nations out of the union of territories dating back to the end of World War I in 1918. Bordered on the east with the Soviet Bloc countries of Romania, Hungary, and Bulgaria, the Communist State of Yugoslavia encompassed six separate republics mainly founded on their ethnic or religious background. The area in question has been populated for at least 100,000 years.[12] The first groups of Slavs moved to the area in around the fifth century. They migrated from regions now known as southern Poland and the republics of the Russian empire. Differing groups of Slavs formed their own enclaves and independent states. Serbians founded Serbia and Croats founded Croatia; however, from about 1,400 onward, the southern Slavs were ruled by foreign powers.

The Turkish Empire controlled Serbian areas, while Hungary and Austria ruled Slovenia and Croatia, respectively. As the centuries moved by, the desire for a united region became a goal of Slovenia and Croatia. The movement to unite sparked an incident that was to change the destiny of Europe and the fate of millions. On June 28, 1914, in Sarajevo, Gavrilo Princip, a Serbian terrorist from Bosnia, assassinated the **Archduke Franz Ferdinand** of Austria-Hungary. Because of pacts between European nations, this single terrorist act fueled the start of the Great War of 1914–1918. Yugoslavia was so named by King Alexander I, in 1929. The King ruled briefly as an absolute dictator; however, dissident Croat terrorists assassinated him in 1934.

FIGURE 7-4   Map of Kosovo (Central Intelligence Agency, *The World Factbook*, 2008).

To say that modern-day terrorism played a part in the structure of a nation such as Yugoslavia would not be far from the truth. Two resistance groups fought against each other, as well as against the occupying Germans during World War II. The partisans were led by Josip Tito and his Communist Party and the Chetniks who supported the monarchy under King Peter.

By the end of World War II, the **partisans** (terrorists?) under Tito established a Communist government and, on November 29, 1945, the region became the Federal Peoples Republic of Yugoslavia, thus abolishing the monarchy and sending King Peter into permanent exile. As will be seen throughout this sad tale, many dictators have felt the need to dominate and destroy all opponents of the regime. Yugoslavia under Marshall Tito was no different, with any and all opponents of the Communist government being imprisoned, killed, or exiled. Tito declared a one-party Communist state. Although a Communist state in its own right, Yugoslavia was not a puppet of the Soviet Union. In fact, after the late 1940s, Yugoslavia and the Soviet Union severed all ties to one another. During the Cold War, Yugoslavia became a moderate voice in the region.

Modern-Day Problems

The people of Yugoslavia were split along ethnic lines into six republics, with Slovenia in the north and Croatia on its southern border. To the south of Croatia was the often-disputed land of Bosnia-Herzegovina. Immediately to the east are Serbia and Montenegro. Civil strife among these ethnic regions has not, until recently, been cause for serious concern. Although nationalist tendencies have been in the forefront of Yugoslavia's political history for the last quarter of the twentieth century, they had not erupted into violent conflict until the civil war of the 1990s. Under the rule of Marshall Tito, the country and its republics had been forced to keep their nationalist feelings in check. Tito's aim was to do away with old ethnic divisions and create a united social revolution. When Tito died in 1980, the old nationalist desires of the various republics were reborn. Up to this time Serbs, Croats, and Muslims had lived side by side in a form of peaceful coexistence.

When tough economic times befell them, the Yugoslavs protested Communist Party policy and began to demand changes to a political system that had failed to permit any other political parties to participate. Nationalism was therefore again on the rise in the six republics of Yugoslavia.

Acts of political terrorism in the region have been mostly nonexistent. What had been occurring was a bloody civil war, pitching neighbor against neighbor—almost a Balkanized version of Northern Ireland. All sides in this conflict, however, have used different tactics from those used in the Northern Ireland conflict. Reports out of the various regions cite incidents of "ethnic cleansing," a sanitized term for such extreme measures as the extermination of whole villages (genocide).

The United Nations defines crimes against humanity as crimes committed in armed conflict, whether international or internal in character, and directed against any civilian population:

    a. murder;

    b. exterminations;

    c. enslavement;

    d. deportation;

    e. imprisonment;

    f. torture;

    g. rape;

    h. persecutions on political, racial and religious grounds;

    i. other inhumane acts.[13]

Article two of the United Nations Convention on the Prevention and Punishment of the crime of genocide states:

Genocide means any of the following acts committed with intent to destroy, in whole or in part, a national, ethical, racial or religious group, as such:

    a. Killing members of the group;

    b. Causing bodily or mental harm to members of the group;

    c. Deliberately inflicting on the group conditions of life calculated to bring about its physical destruction in whole or in part;

    d. Imposing measures intended to prevent births within a group;

    e. Forcibly transferring children of the group to another group.[14]

During the war in Bosnia-Herzegovina, the exact number of Muslims killed and displaced remains practically impossible to ascertain. But, by January 1993, between 200,000 and 250,000 people, 10 percent of the Muslim population, are thought to have died, and by early 1994, almost 2 million people were displaced.

This region of nationalist conflict and resulting civil war has not had the hallmark of terrorist activity as has occurred in other areas, like Palestine and Israel. One exception was the attempted assassination by bombing of Kiro Gligorov, the President of Macedonia, and an event that had the clear markings of terrorist action.

The hatred between the Albanians and Serbs was illustrated by the many reported atrocities committed by both sides. In all respects, the conflict had turned into a regional war. The lightly armed "freedom fighters," as they were termed (not "terrorists") were fighting against tanks and heavy artillery. Through the period of the last decade of the 20th century, the Serbian government of Slobodan Milosevic had been criticized for its treatment of ethnic minorities, especially in the minority-dominated areas of Vojvodina, Sandak, and Kosovo.[15] Milosevic came to power in 1989 and played a dominant role in the conflict in both Bosnia and Croatia, supplying both military and financial support to the Serb nationalist campaigns in the two republics. Milosevic supported proposals from the international community for a brokered peace plan in 1994; however, it was not well-enough-received by the Bosnian Serb leadership. This failure prompted Milosevic to close the border between the two republics. In 1995, Milosevic signed the Dayton Peace Accord with Bosnian President Alija Izetbegovic and Croatian President Franjo Tudjman. Full diplomatic relations were restored the following year between the former Yugoslavia, now the Federal Republic of Yugoslavia (FRY), and Bosnia Herzegovina. As for the region of Kosovo, it had resisted the Serbian government since the province lost its autonomy and the formation of the KLA in the mid-1990s began to target and attack the Serbian police. The response was swift, as the Serbian police and Yugoslav military attacked the ethnic Albanian community in early 1998, forcing nearly a quarter of a million people to flee from their homes. At this point, the representatives from the North Atlantic Treaty Organization (NATO) threatened to use force to curb the brutal assaults by Yugoslavian forces against the ethnic Albanians. Throughout much of 1998 and into early 1999, peace talks were attempted but failed, resulting in a NATO force, led by the United States, initiating a bombing campaign against Yugoslav military targets. This had the opposite effect on the Milosevic government, which hardened its position and intensified its campaign by burning entire villages and forcing the ethnic minority Albanians in Kosovo to flee to Albania, Montenegro, and Macedonia. Six hundred and fifty thousand people were forced from Kosovo between March 1998 and April 1999.[16] Many unsubstantiated reports of brutal treatment, rape, and torture of civilians in the Albanian region of Kosovo were beginning to emerge when, by June 1999, the Serbian government agreed to a peace plan for Kosovo. NATO's bombing campaign was suspended on June 10, 1999, and the United Nations Security Council authorized peacekeepers to enter the province. Milosevic lost the federal presidential election in September 2000, to the candidate of a coalition of opposition parties called the Democratic Opposition of Serbia (DOS). In December 2000, DOS won 176 of the 250 seats in Serbia's National Assembly. In March 2001, the Serbian government arrested Milosevic on charges of abuse of power and embezzlement. And, in June 2001, following pledges of economic support to the tune of $1 billion by Western governments, Milosevic was extradited to the International Criminal Tribunal for the Former Yugoslavia (ICTY) in The Hague, Netherlands, to stand trial for war crimes.[17]

The actions of the Serbian government almost mirror those of the Nazis during World War II, with the rounding up and arrest of those who have given, or were suspected of giving, any assistance to the so-called rebels. Those arrested were doctors, aid workers, lawyers, and journalists.

Kosovo remained a UN protectorate state; however, in March 2004 there were widespread ethnic clashes across the whole region. For more than five years, the region has made progress but the erupting violence certainly laid bare any inadequacies of the UN-led mission to Kosovo (UNMIK) and the NATO Peacekeeping Force (KFOR). Much of the violence returned the region to the levels not seen since 1999. Much of this was apparently orchestrated simultaneously by ethnic Albanian groups, possibly with the guidance or control of the Albanian National Army (AKSh), which is known to have launched attacks against ethnic minorities and security forces.

Since NATO intervened in 1999, Kosovo has become the crime capital of Europe. The illicit sex trade is flourishing. The province has become a major transit point for drugs en route to Europe and North America from Afghanistan. The demobilized Kosovo Liberation Army has not been disbanded or eliminated and is heavily involved in organized crime as well as political intrigue.[18] The majority of Kosovo Albanians saw UN involvement as the major obstacle to independence from Serbia. The geopolitics of the region has changed significantly since 1999—at that time there was no risk involved for a NATO and U.S.-led attack on Yugoslavia—Russia was not a force and was easily ignored. Boris Yeltsin was at the end of his reign and Russia was weak and in no position to challenge the United States and NATO. Putin is rebuilding the Russian sphere of influence in the former Soviet Union. He is meeting with the Belarusians over reintegration and at the same time is warning Ukraine not to flirt with NATO membership. He is reasserting Russian power in the Caucasus and Central Asia. His theme is simple: Russia is near and strong; NATO is far away and weak. He is trying to define Russian power in the region.

In total defference to Putin's prestige in Russia and the psychological foundations of his grand strategy, Kosovo declared its independence on February 18, 2008. Putin and the Russians repeatedly have warned that they wouldn't accept independence for Kosovo, and that such an act would lead to an uncontrollable crisis. Thus far, the Western powers involved appear to have dismissed this. Immediately the United States acknowledged Kosovo as an independenent state which over the coming months may be a problem for the Russian President.

Putin has two levers. One is economic. The natural gas flowing to Europe, particularly to Germany, is critical for the Europeans. Putin has a large war chest saved from high energy prices. He can live without exports longer than the Germans can live without imports.[19] Notwithstanding the geopolitics of the region, Kosovo is made up of about 2 million people of whom only 120,000 are ethnic Serbs, the remainder are ethnic Albanians. Kosovo is cherished by Serbs as home to celebrated Serb Orthodox monasteries and as the site of the battle of Kosovo in 1389 which resulted in the Serbs being defeated by the Ottoman Empire—the likelihood is that Serbia would retaliate but with political and economic sanctions only. While a majority of EU countries led by Britain, France, and Germany support the Kosovo independence move, some countries such as Spain and Greece are somewhat concerned with recognizing Kosovo as they have their own breakaway groups within their countries. The Albanian action could also spark the same sentiments in the northern region of Bosnia and see Serbs insisting on joining with Serbia. The short term is uncertain and Kosovo is in much need of support from the EU countries at a time where unemployment is running near 40 percent. It is possible that the declaration could be the cure for the outstanding issue of the Yugoslavia collapse and the signal for economic expansion in the Balkans; alternatively Kosovo's independence could again stir up conflict between the Albanians and Serbs and result in the destruction of Bosnia.

The International Criminal Tribunal for the Former Yugoslavia

The following is an extract from the indictment against Slobodan Milosevic before the International Criminal Tribunal for the former Yugoslavia:

> Beginning on or about 1 January 1999 and continuing until the date of this indictment, forces of the FRY and Serbia, acting at the direction, with the encouragement, or with the support of **Slobodan MILOSEVIC**, **Milan MILUTINOVIC**, **Nikola SAINOVIC**, **Dragoljub OJDANIC**, and **Vlajko STOJILJKOVIC**, have murdered hundreds of Kosovo Albanian civilians. These killings have occurred in a widespread or systematic manner throughout the province of Kosovo and have resulted in the deaths of numerous men, women, and children. Included among the incidents of mass killings are the following:
>
> **a.** On or about 15 January 1999, in the early morning hours, the village of Racak (Stimlje/Shtime municipality) was attacked by forces of the FRY and Serbia. After shelling by the VJ units, the Serb police entered the village later in the morning and began conducting house-to-house searches. Villagers, who attempted to flee from the Serb police, were shot throughout the village. A group of approximately 25 men attempted to hide in a building, but were

discovered by the Serb police. They were beaten and then were removed to a nearby hill, where the policemen shot and killed them. Altogether, the forces of the FRY and Serbia killed approximately 45 Kosovo Albanians in and around Racak.[20]

Milosevic conducted his own defense against the charges. He suffered from blood pressure and heart problems and died during the proceedings at The Hague in March 2006.

BULGARIA

State-Sponsored Terrorism

The debate on Moscow's level of effort in the arena of state-sponsored terrorism can be theorized at length; however, there is considerable belief that its Communist neighbor, Bulgaria, is active in this area, possibly on Russia's behalf. The extent of Bulgaria's involvement in state-sponsored terrorism is an issue worth discussion. During the Cold War, Moscow's attempts to destabilize the Western democracies involved the use of terror tactics against not only nations, but also symbolic personages. In Rome, Italy, on May 13, 1981, a Turkish nationalist attempted to assassinate Pope John Paul II in St. Peter's Square. The Pope was shot and his would-be assassin arrested. The ensuing investigation uncovered a link to Bulgaria. The Pope's assailant, **Mehmet Ali Agca**, is believed to have had an accomplice in place to aid in his escape from Italy. The accomplice, Oral Celik, escaped capture by leaving Italy in a Bulgarian Embassy diplomatic truck. The following year, a Bulgarian State Airline official was charged in Rome in

FIGURE 7-5   Map of Bulgaria (Central Intelligence Agency, *The World Factbook*, 2008).

connection with the assassination attempt.[21] Further evidence of Bulgaria's complicity to export terror is seen in the actions of Sallah Wakkas, a Syrian national operating out of Athens. He had purchased more than $50 million worth of Soviet-made weapons and ammunitions from a Bulgarian weapons company, **KINTEX**.[22]

Further Bulgarian involvement was uncovered when Greek customs seized a ship en route to North Yemen in 1984. The contents of a consignment of oil tankers revealed huge quantities of weapons and ammunitions. The ship's cargo of trucks had been consigned by the Bulgarian State cargo agency, Bulfracht, while the paperwork for the consignment was produced by Inflot, the Bulgarian state shipping agency. It must be assumed that this arms shipment was destined for the Palestine Liberation Organization's training camps in North Yemen. One must deduce that this is just an example of many other shipments that had not been intercepted. In addition, Bulgaria's involvement in drug trafficking has been fairly well-documented. Drugs, of course, can be used in the sale or barter for weapons and explosives. KINTEX of Bulgaria has also been known to be a supplier of heroin and morphine to Kurdish dissidents in Turkey, and these drugs have been used as trade for weapons.[23]

The Bulgarian tactics of inflicting terror on its own subjects and also striking out at dissidents in European locations came to sudden and painful light with two attacks on Bulgarian dissidents in Paris and London. On August 26, 1978, Vladmir Kostov, a Bulgarian defector to the West and a former well-known television personality, was jabbed with a poison-tipped umbrella, laced with the extremely lethal poison, ricin. He survived the attack. However, a similar incident in London against outspoken novelist and playwright, Georgi Markov, resulted in his death. The fact remains that both these men came from the ranks of the Bulgarian secret service, the Dazjavma Sigurmos, or DS, and were both broadcasting for Radio Free Europe, which was largely funded by the U.S. CIA. Although no one has ever been arrested or charged with either attacks it would seem most parobable to be the work of agents acting on behalf of Bulgarian Communist dictator, Todor Zhivkov.

Further evidence of Bulgarian attempts at destabilization revolves around the Red Brigade's shadowy involvement in the kidnapping of the American NATO General, James Dozier. From evidence deduced by the examining judge at the trial of the Red Brigade ringleader, Antonio Savasta, Bulgaria played a part in the interrogation of the general and offered logistical and training support to the Red Brigade.

CZECH REPUBLIC

The Czech Republic and, formerly, Czechoslovakia were well known for being the central clearing point for the arms trade in both Eastern and Western Europe. Although the republic is not synonymous with terrorism, its longstanding involvement in the arms business makes its exports and controls very intriguing to terrorist groups. The possibility for explosive materials to end up in the wrong hands is strong. Its Communist past and close ties with the Soviet KGB allowed it to have extensive networks in locations throughout the world, where it plied the arms trade effectively. The Czech Republic became a full member of NATO in 1999, but this did not necessarily curtail its arms disposal business to countries such as Yemen, which divert their weapons to third countries. The tracking of munitions across international borders, both legally and illegally, continues. *Jane's Intelligence Digest* reported in July 2004 that the Swedish Defense Ministry had shipped 328 tonnes of surplus plastic explosives. The material was similar to Semtex. The twenty-trailer convoy had traveled across Denmark and Germany before being intercepted by Czech Customs. What is probably most disturbing about this single shipment was that the material was unmarked (unscented), which would easily allow for it to be smuggled aboard a commercial airliner.

FIGURE 7-6   Map of Czech Republic (Central Intelligence Agency, *The World Factbook*, 2008).

Summary

Russia and the former Soviet republics, as we know them today, have undergone enormous changes. The Cold War is over and Russia and the United States are on modestly friendly terms in the War on Terror. No longer is Russia a Communist-dominated federation; no longer is it the "Great Bear of the East" that wielded so much power and influence in the world due to military strength and nuclear weapons. No longer does it have the respect of its neighbors or its enemies! Russia is, at the beginning of the twenty-first century, a country in turmoil. Its social and economic problems are clear for all who care to look. Its monetary system is in tatters and its ruined economy is being bailed out by the International Monetary Fund. The hopes and fears of a nation rest on how the political games are played out. Many questions are as yet unanswered. What is certain is that Russia is experiencing terrorism perpetrated against its citizens—not just in the streets of Moscow but in the air and in its neighboring republics. Organized crime infects Russian society; Russian Mafya-style syndicates permeate all levels of the Russian society. Drugs and weapons are freely available, and a dissatisfied and poorly paid military machine has ground to a halt. This military machine, however, has access to weapons of mass destruction. Some are missing; who has them and who controls them is open for discussion. The possibilities are endless for a criminal with access to this kind of weaponry. Chechnya remains an ongoing threat to the region's stability as Islamic extremists spread out to neighboring republics. Whether what we are seeing in Chechnya is terrorism or an all-out fight for a country's survival is an open question. Certainly, since the events of 9-11, Russia has seized the opportunity to use military excesses to press home any advantages it can against the rebel state, under the banner of "War on Terror." The region of Macedonia has been devastated by sporadic wars within its borders; the term *ethnic cleansing* is now used again to describe the mass murder of a particular ethnic group. The Kosovo Liberation Army lives to fight another day, and its Albanian support in the region is strong. In the years to come, if the direct fighting ends and some form of lasting peace can ever be achieved, there is no doubt that sporadic terroristic violence, bombings, and assassinations will be a pattern of daily life in these areas. Deep wounds from wars fought based on ethnic lines will take decades to heal. This conflict is an example of how poorly the United Nations has managed to control a region rife with ethnic violence— surely a good example to set for UN involvement in Iraq? For the future, the regions of the north Caucasus may well slip into lawlessness and drift away from Moscow's orbit. Following the disastrous interference in the Ukraine elections, Russia's president now talks of reconstituting the Russian empire. Russia is, in a sense, its own empire. The possibility that it may one day crumble in much the same manner as the former Soviet Union will be Putin's main fear.

Web Sites

1. **Center for Nonproliferation Studies**— *http://cns.miis.edu/pubs/week/020923.htm*
2. **International Criminal Tribunal for the Former Yugoslavia**—*http://www.un.org/icty/*
3. **The Heritage Foundation**—*http://www.heritage.org/ Research/RussiaandEurasia/em844.cfm*
4. **National Academies Press**—*http://www.nap.edu/ catalog.php?record_id=11801*

Endnotes

1. *The New Encyclopaedia Britannica*, vol. 8. (1985), 298.
2. "Secret Police," Revelations from the Russian Archives, Library of Congress (1996). http://leweb2.loc.gov/cgi-bin/query.
3. David Yallop. *Tracking the Jackal* (New York: Random House, 1993, p. 20).
4. Courtesy Russian Leadership Directory.
5. Mathew Bunn and Anthony Weir. *The Seven Myths of Nuclear Terrorism* (Philadelphia: Current History, Inc., 2005, p. 153).
6. International Atomic Energy Agency.
7. "Ukraine's Missing Missiles," *Jane's Intelligence Digest* (June 18, 2004).
8. Edward Walker. "The Crisis in Chechnya." *Center for Slavic and Eastern European Studies Newsletter* (Spring 1995).
9. Edward Walker. "What's Next in Chechnya." Association for the Study of Nationalities, http://www.nationalities.org.
10. "Putin's War," *U.S. News & World Report* (May 27, 2002), 26.
11. BBC News online—July 10, 2006, www.bbc.co.uk.
12. Araminta Wordsworth. "Sinking further in a morass of brutality," *Canada's National Post* (December 10, 1998, p. A15).
13. "The United Nations and Human Rights 1945–1995," *UN Blue Book Series*, vol. 7, 424.
14. Ibid.
15. Norman L. Cigar. *The Policy of Ethnic Cleansing* (College Station, TX: A&M University Press, 1995, p. 9).
16. Serbia History-Encarta online Encyclopedia. http://encarta.msn.com.
17. Ibid.
18. Ibid.
19. Stratfor—Geopolitical Intelligence Report—Russia: Kosovo and the Asymmetry of Perceptions December 18, 2007.
20. United Nations. www.un.org/icty/indictment/english/mil-ii990524e.htm.
21. Major General Lewis Mackenzie former commander of UN troops in Kosovo, 1992, "We bombed the wrong side," *The National Post* (April 6, 2004). The prospects for the region under the auspices of the UN are not exceptionally high.
22. Clare Sterling. "Bulgaria Hired Agca to Kill Pope," *New York Times* (June 10, 1984).
23. Philip Sherwell. "NATO planes strike on Kosovo," The Weekly Telegraph, The Telegraph Group Ltd., June 9–15, 1998, p. 19, issue #359.

CHAPTER 8

North Africa and the Middle East

*The time for peace has come, we, the soldiers who have returned
from battles stained with blood, we who have seen our relatives
and friends killed before our eyes, . . . we who have come from a
land where parents bury their children, we who have fought
against you, the Palestinians—we say today in a loud and clear
voice: Enough of blood and tears. Enough!*

YITZHAK RABIN (1922–1995)

Learning Objective

The study and review of this chapter will enable you to

1. Trace the history of terrorism in Israel;
2. Discuss the various terrorist groups currently shaping events in the Middle East;
3. Discuss the involvement of state sponsors effecting the political landscape in Lebanon;
4. Describe the spread of Islamic extremism through North Africa.

Terms to Remember

Abu Nidal
Al-Fatah
Ariel Sharon
Armed Islamic Group (GIA)
Balfour Declaration
Black September
Democratic Front for the
    Liberation of Palestine
    (DFLP)

Fedayeen
Hamas
Janjaweed
Mossad
Palestinian Islamic
    Jihad (PIJ)
Palestine Liberation
    Front (PLF)

Palestine Liberation
    Organization (PLO)
Popular Front for the
    Liberation of Palestine
    (PFLP)
UAV

January, 2007—Four people died when a Palestinian suicide bomber hit the Israeli seaside resort of Eilat. The bomber struck at a bakery in the town which is situated at the northern edge of the Red Sea. The Al-Aqsa Martyrs Brigade and Islamic Jihad both claimed responsibility for the attack.

July, 2007—Egyptian Police seized more than 1.1 tons of explosives in the northern Sinai Peninsula town of al-Roda, 62 miles from the Gaza border.

September, 2007—Anti-Syrian Christian lawmaker Antoine Ghanem is killed in a car bomb explosion in east Beirut.

March, 2008—A lone Palestinian gunman walked into a Jewish Seminary in the Kiryat Moshe neighborhood of Jerusalem and opened fire on high school–aged students, killing eight students and wounding scores more.

OVERVIEW

Peace and terrorism are two very familiar words when used in the context of the Middle East, especially when it involves the Israelis and the Palestinians. In stark contrast to Yitzhak Rabin's comment above, the late Yasser Arafat stated the opposite, "Peace for us means the destruction of Israel. We are preparing for an all-out war which will last for generations." The Peace Accords, and the innumerable sessions proclaiming a new round of talks to resolve the question of Palestinian statehood/homeland and Israeli security, will be examined in detail in this chapter. Resistance to the presence of Israeli settlers in Palestine, the effect this has on Israel's security, and the response by the men of terror in Palestine, will also be discussed. Israel's right to exist, and the threats and assaults it has had to withstand for over half a century, form much of the basis for terror attacks and extreme Islamic movements that have been spawned with the ultimate goal—the destruction of the Jewish State.

For the Palestinians, the conflict is about their perceived rights and freedoms, justice, as well as to their land. Palestinians have been depopulated and, for all intents and purposes, terrorized out of their homes to make room for Jewish settlers. This practice has persisted, contrary to clear International law, for over half a century. Syria has a role in this problem, under the relatively inexperienced son of the late President Assad. Although Syria has not been directly involved in terrorism, the country is a safe haven for various terrorist organizations that continue to ply their hateful trade, predictably and predominantly against Israel and the West. The Gaza Strip and the West Bank has become a flash point for internal fighting between Fatah and Hamas since the death of Yasser Arafat. The emergence of elements of al Qaeda surfacing in the region then does nothing for the overall stability, or security, in the area of the Middle East.

ISRAEL AND ITS RIGHT TO EXIST

The continuing violence, often referred to as, "The Middle East Crisis," is seen almost daily in the news and on television. The issues are the, "security" of the State of Israel and, "hope" for the Palestinians, in the words of President George W. Bush. Pro-Israel lobbyists in the United States contend that, "U.S. aid to Israel enhances American national security interests, by strengthening our only Middle East ally in an unstable, dangerous, and vital region of the world." The ongoing issue surrounding the Israeli settlements in the Palestinian Authority Areas continues. Since 1967, Israel has continued to create settlements in these territories. "The creation of a viable Jewish state, in an adequate area of Palestine instead of in the whole of Palestine would be acceptable," was stated by President Harry S. Truman in 1946.[1] The dual questions regarding Israel's inflexibility, and the Palestinian refugees having a safe homeland, clearly cannot be viewed as a new phenomenon. As far back as the creation of Israel, the United States has been fielding the criticism, and often the blame, for Israel's intransigence, her belligerence, and her arrogance for cold-bloodedness in her attitude toward refugees.[2] The question of a separate Palestinian State remains as much in focus today as it was over a half-century ago. In 1948, the United States and Britain, appreciated that the

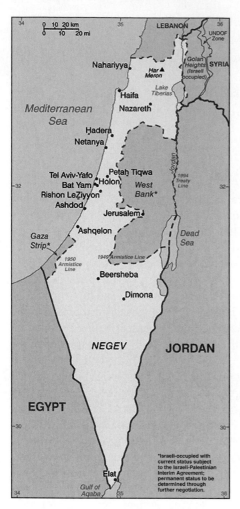

FIGURE 8-1 Map of Israel (Central Intelligence Agency, *The World Factbook*, 2008).

1947 UN partition plan had failed. They concluded that their best political solution, for both the United States and Britain, was to completely deny the Palestinians a State of their own. Under this U.S.-Anglo strategy, the Palestinians would simply disappear by being absorbed into their neighboring Arab states, mainly, Transjordan, as it was then known, now the Hashemite Kingdom of Jordan.[3] Land is not the only major issue surrounding the Palestinian/Israeli problem . . . but the retention of land seized beyond the UN mandate of 1947, and also following the Six-Day War, remains a continuing stumbling block along with the issues of civil rights, human rights, and freedom and liberty for Palestinians.

Early History

The Jewish people (known as "Hebrews"), settled in the region of Palestine about 1,200 years before the birth of Christ. From about 70 A.D. to 700 A.D., that region was under the control of the Romans, who dispersed most of the Hebrews from the region. With the collapse of the Roman Empire, the Ismaelites (Arabs) settled in the region and remained there until the Turkish (Ottoman) Empire subjugated them in 1516.

Political Considerations

To fully appreciate the complexities of this unique region, we must first look at what took place due to imperialist influences and designs on this region at the time of World War I. By the latter part of the 1800s, the Ottoman Empire, controlled by Turkey, was in total disarray and internal factional disturbances were continuing within the realm as Turkey's influences waned. The then Turkish Empire bordered Persia (Iran), which was then under the imperialistic controls of the Russians and the British. The dwindling Turkish Ottoman Empire comprised a significant section of the Arab territories of the Middle East, and this area was, by the start of World War I, an area ripe for the plucking. Britain most certainly had designs on the Arab lands, as did the French and Russians. As Turkey was fighting on the side of the German Empire against Britain and France, it suited Britain to turn the Arabs against the Turks. To sustain the Jews on the side of Britain, the British government issued the "**Balfour Declaration**," named after the highly respected British Foreign Secretary, Sir Arthur James Balfour. The Declaration read as follows "His Majesty's Government views with favor the establishment in Palestine of a national homeland for the Jewish people, and will use their best endeavors to facilitate the achievement of this objective, it being clearly understood that nothing shall be done which may prejudice the rights of non-Jewish communities in Palestine, or the rights and political status enjoyed by Jews in any other country."

This Declaration, at least from the British point of view, was to seek and win both financial and political support for the war from Jews in Europe and, more particularly, in wealthy Jewish neighborhoods in the United States. The Jews viewed this as tacit agreement for having their own homeland in Palestine. The Arabs, however, read a different meaning into the wording. The Arabs believed that they had been forced to agree to any terms put forward, before an agreement on self-determination of lands for the Jews had been realized. The Arabs fought in the belief that they were assured independence; the Jews in Palestine offered to raise troops to fight on the side of the British.

With the promise of independence to both Zionists and Arabs alike, the British government had unwittingly sown the seeds for an almost endless succession of Wars. In the decades to come, the Jews and Arabs would fight conventional wars that would then finally turn into what is now called "modern-day terrorism," a situation that endured for the remainder of the whole Twentieth Century. With the two groups focused on fighting the Turks, Britain had achieved its immediate aim of control of the region and was assured of support from both. But, it was a very shortsighted political decision, one that left the Middle East with the distinction of becoming a home base and fertile breeding ground for future generations of terrorists.

To many people, the very name, "Palestinian," is often seen as synonymous with "Terrorism." This view adequately portrays the immense problems that then beset this area of the Middle East. British strategic aims, at the end of World War I, were to solidify a friendly presence in Palestine to ensure protection of its routes into Africa and to the East into India. Of major importance in this plan would be the Suez Canal and the major shipping route from the Indian Ocean to the Mediterranean. The British set up Arab kingdoms after the war in such a fashion that strong, only traditional, family groups controlled them. Emerging from this were the three states of Saudi Arabia, Iraq, and Syria.

Settlements and Terror

Israel's history is founded on its struggle to exist in a hostile environment, and surrounded by unfriendly neighbors, and angry Arab refugees. Since the 1948 Arab-Israeli war, the areas that were occupied by Israel, have seen countless incursions by Arab refugees, and particularly, from Jordan and Egypt. Many of these incursions were raids by, "foraging Arabs," returning to their home villages, and stopping on route, to rob and steal. Many attacks on civilians in Jewish-occupied regions resulted, and it is from these early incursions that the Israelis initiated various response mechanisms. To prevent and deter such actions, the Israelis adopted a policy of destroying abandoned Arab villages along the border region and establishing Israeli Settlements in their place. With the numbers of dead Israeli civilians running into many hundreds by 1953, the Israeli government established "Unit 101," a special operations/commando type of retaliatory unit. Ariel Sharon, who led this unit in August 1953, was on orders from Prime Minister David Ben-Gurion. The unit drew much criticism due to its killing of innocent civilians, and in particular the Qibya operation, which left almost seventy civilians dead. However, its extreme decisive style of action developed into its later attacks against heavily guarded military objectives that became one of the fundamental cornerstones in the development of the Israeli Defense Force (IDF). The very brutal nature of the attacks, mainly against civilian targets, eventually led to the abandonment of Unit 101 in 1954, integrating it into the 202 Paratroop Brigade. Unit 101's belief was that the villages being attacked were hideouts for terrorists.

THE STERN GANG

The "Stern Gang" was an extreme, right-wing organization, founded by Avraham Stern in 1940, as a split-off group from the Irgun. Irgun was a Jewish terrorist group organized in the 1930s to defend the Jewish settlers from Arab attacks and, after World War II, used its skills to attack the British in Palestine. Irgun's vicious attacks then ended with the massacre of 250 Arab civilians at the settlement of Deir Yassin, outside Jerusalem in 1948. This single action prompted Israeli Prime Minister David-Ben-Gurion, to call for the Irgun to be disbanded and absorbed into the Haganah Army, which was the forerunner to the Israeli Defense Forces. Stern was killed by British forces in 1944, but the gang continued under the leadership of Israel Eldad, Natan Yellin-Mor, and Yitzhak Shamir, who became the Prime Minister of Israel forty years later. Two notable assassinations are credited to the Stern Gang. On November 6, 1944, it killed the British Resident Minister for the Middle East, Lord Moyne; and on September 17, 1948, the then UN Special Mediator for Palestine, Count Folke Bernadotte. The Deir Yassin massacre, in 1948, also involved the Stern Gang, but the much larger Irgun was the main perpetrator of that massacre. Both Stern and Irgun were in existence prior to the formation of the State of Israel and both sought the formation of the Jewish State through actions that are considered terrorism, and were mainly directed against the British mandate in Palestine. The Stern Gang's terror attacks were against the British, not the Arab communities. Discussion of Stern's approaches to the Nazis is controversial due to their very abhorrent nature; maybe it was a case that, in 1939, "his enemy's enemy was therefore Stern's friend." Stern could likely only consider this in terms of the total liberation of the region from British control.

Under the 1947 UN Partition Plan, Israel's original size had been limited to 5,900 square miles. Following the fighting in 1948, Israel's land total became 7,800 square miles. The 1967 Six-Day War dramatically altered the borders of Israel. After this brief war, Israel controlled some 20,870 square miles of newly acquired territory . . . nearly five times its original size.[4] Settlements continued to be created and Palestinians were being dispossessed of their land as Israel continued its expansionism. Condemnation of Israel for its actions came from the United Nations in the form of resolutions, which, in most cases, were vetoed by Israel's staunchest ally, the United States. However, in March 1976, the United States finally condemned these settlements as being both illegal, and an obstacle to peace. By the time of the U.S. declaration, there were already about sixty-eight settlements in the territories, not counting Jerusalem. In condemnation of the Israeli action, William W. Scranton, the U.S. Ambassador to the United Nations, informed the Security Council . . . "Next, I turn to the question of Israeli settlements in the occupied territories. Again, my government believes that international law sets the appropriate standards. An occupier must maintain the occupied areas as intact and unaltered as possible, without interfering with the customary life of the area, and any changes must be necessitated by the immediate needs of the occupation and be consistent with international law. The Fourth Geneva Convention now speaks directly to the issue of population transfer in Article 49. Clearly then, substantial resettlement of the Israeli population in the occupied territories, including East Jerusalem, is illegal under the convention and cannot be considered to have prejudged the outcome of future negotiations between the parties or the location of the borders of states of the Middle East. Indeed, the presence of these settlements is seen by my government as an obstacle to the success of the negotiations for a just and final peace between Israel and its neighbors."[5]

Israeli expansionism has continued in spite of these words spoken over thirty years ago. The Palestinians are under the control of Israeli military occupying forces in the West Bank. This, of course, does nothing to assure Israeli peace and, in the words of Scranton, the settlements are an obstruction to a peace accord. In February 1989, Israeli Prime Minister Yitzhak Rabin assured a "Peace Now," delegation that negotiations (with the Palestinians) were only but some "low-level discussions" that avoided any serious issues and granted Israel, "at least a year" to resolve the problem (presumably by force). Rabin further stated . . . "The inhabitants of the territories are now subject to both harsh military and economic pressure, in the end they will be broken."[6]

The peace accords of the 1990s, in particular the Oslo Peace Accords, have been so encumbered as to make it virtually impossible to determine what concessions, if any, Israel has made. This is due to the Israeli conditions, entailments, and qualifications, which were so one-sided that Palestinians felt no semblance of self-determination. It is not difficult to see why Palestinians then see terrorism as a tool—and likely their only tool—to make their views and issues clear, not only to the Israeli public, but to the world at large. The actions of suicide terrorists on 9-11 may have been seen as an opportunity for the Israeli government to bury the Intifada once and for all. In the week following 9-11, the Israelis took their War on Terror directly into Palestinian territory.

The Israeli army killed twenty-eight Palestinians, and mounted sixteen incursions into Palestinian Authority areas. The response to the swiftness of the Israeli attacks and incursion, forced Arafat to declare a ceasefire on all fronts, and express readiness to enlist in America's coalition for "ending terrorism against unarmed innocent civilians." Following this, the Palestinian Authority leader warned Islamic Jihad, Hamas, and others not to give "pretexts" that would aid Mr. Sharon's designs. Although these groups heeded the call from Arafat and ended the firing on Jewish settlements from Palestinian areas, they did not agree to end armed actions in their own defense of Palestinian towns still under occupation. These groups also affirmed that they would respond if Israel acted against them or their people. On September 24, 2001, the Israeli army established a twenty-mile "closed military zone" along the West Bank's northern border with Israel. This was ostensibly established to prevent suicide bombers from infiltrating any Israeli Territory.[7] A test of Israel's will came in the subsequent surprising events, which triggered the Second Intifada uprising . . . attacks by suicide bombers, and rioting that continued off and on through 2002. Israeli Prime Minister, Ehud Barak, dispatched a military force, led by the then Defense Minister Ariel Sharon, to the Al-Aqsa compound. Sharon strode into the Haram al-Sharif (The Noble Sanctuary) in what was designed to be a gesture to assert his rights as an Israeli, to visit this Muslim holy place. It was this single act that seems to have sparked the beginning of the Second Intifada. Sharon can hardly be described as a statesman whose actions were ever likely to endear him to Palestinians in general. His reputation was mainly due to his checkered career, in particular his questionable involvement in the Sabra and Shatila refugee camp massacres that took place in Beirut in 1982.

Throughout the latter half of 2001, and throughout 2002, the Israeli government then held the Palestinian Authority's leader, Yasser Arafat, "personally responsible" for terrorist and suicide attacks against Israel. Israel adopted the military option to attack specific "Terror" targets inside the Palestinian-controlled areas. In January 2002, the Israeli Air Force used U.S.-made F-16s to drop bombs on Arafat's compound in Ramallah. Most military actions had been in response to Palestinian suicide attacks against Israeli targets. Israel also used targeted assassinations to deter, destroy, and remove, Hamas militant leaders, with much success.

IRGUN ZEVA'I LE'UMI, NATIONAL MILITARY ORGANIZATION (NMO)

An armed Jewish underground organization, founded in 1931 by a group of Haganah commanders, who left the Haganah in protest against its defense charter. In April 1937, during the Arab riots, the organization split—about half its members returned to the Haganah. They carried out armed reprisals against Arabs, which were condemned by the Haganah. In the mid 1940s the NMO was led by Menachem Begin. The term "Special Night Squads" originates from an invention of the British Army in Palestine in 1938 when Orde Wingate set up plans using British soldiers, members of Haganah, and even the Jewish Settlement Police to combat nighttime incursions by Arabs into northern Palestine. Irgun operated exclusively in Palestine as a Jewish group for the establishment of a modern-day Israel. Their main targets were the resident Arab Palestinians and the occupying British Army in Palestine. Bombings were the order of the day and the two-pronged attacks were designed to have two legitimate aims for the Jews. The first was to destabilize the British presence in the region and make it costly for the British to retain a presence. The effect on the demoralized Palestinians was to produce a mass exodus from the area. Several notable members of Irgun played an important role over the following years in the development and political status of Israel. These included Menachem Begin, who would one day become Israeli Prime Minister, the charismatic Moshe Dyan, later to become Chief of Staff, and Ariel Sharon. The second, more obvious reason was to make life in Palestine extremely unpleasant for the Palestinians. With the agreement on partition by the United Nations, the terrorists of the Irgun began to immediately attack and kill Arab families and individuals who remained in the Jewish sector.

The Threat to Israel from Terrorism

The difficulties in realizing why peace cannot be achieved under the efforts of any of the peace agreements of the last decade, and those being lauded as this is written, is the credible threat of Hamas and its long-stated aim of the destruction of Israel. Maybe if the Hamas Charter was not so implicit, it could be a viable alternative to the Palestinian Authority to negotiate with Israel; however, it is inconceivable that Israel would desire to "sit down" and bargain for peace with a group whose avowed mission is Israel's destruction.

Ariel Sharon

Until his untimely and sudden illness that has kept him in a virtual coma since 2006 Ariel Sharon was viewed with passion by the Israelis, he joined the Haganah, which later became known as the Israeli Defense Force (IDF). After college studies he returned as a Major to head up the IDF's Unit 101. The unit was criticized for initially targeting civilians as well as the Arab armies, resulting in the widely condemned Qibya Operation in the autumn of 1953. More than sixty Jordanian civilians were killed in an ambush of Arab Legion forces. Shortly afterwards, Unit 101 was merged into the 202nd Paratrooper Brigade.

Sharon was a member of the Knesset from 1973 to 1974, and again from 1977 to the present. He served as the security adviser to Prime Minister Yitzhak Rabin and as Minister of Agriculture (1977–1981), and Defense Minister (1981–1983) in Menachem Begin's Likud government. During the Israeli invasion of Lebanon in 1982, while Ariel Sharon was Defense Minister, a massacre of several hundred Palestinians in Sabra and Shatila refugee camps in Beirut was carried out by the Phalanges, a Lebanese-Christian militia allied with Israel. It has been speculated that Ariel Sharon played a significant part in allowing the Christian militia a free hand in the camps and by security the perimeter for them to conduct atrocities within the two Palestinian camps. He was elected Prime Minister in February 2001 soon after the collapse of Barak's government. His Deputy Prime Minister Ehud Olmert assumed the role of prime minister on a permanent basis, on the declaration of Sharon's, permanent incapacity in April 2006.

MOSSAD

Israel found an immediate need to establish its own intelligence service and very early in its existence the very secretive and highly efficient Mossad agency was born. Mossad was the brainchild of Reuven Shiloah a close friend of David Ben Gurion who proposed setting up the agency in 1949. Mossad's immediate function was to coordinate the internal security and military intelligence organizations. Mossad started out under Foreign Ministry auspices. In March 1951, with a view to then enhancing its operational capabilities and to unifying all overseas intelligence gathering, Ben-Gurion authorized its final reorganization. An independent, centralized authority was set up to handle all overseas intelligence tasks. This was called the "Authority" and formed the major part of the Mossad. It included representatives of the other two services at HQ and field echelons. The Mossad broke free of the Foreign Ministry and reported directly to the Prime Minister, thus becoming part of the Prime Minister's Office. The Mossad adopted the following verse from the Book of Proverbs as its motto, guide, creative awakener, and ideology, but also as a dire warning: "WITHOUT GUIDANCE DO A PEOPLE FALL, AND DELIVERANCE IS IN A MULTITUDE OF COUNSELLORS"[8] *Proverbs XI/14.*

THE PALESTINIAN LIBERATION ORGANIZATION (PLO)

In May 1964, 422 Palestinian national figures met in Jerusalem under the chairmanship of Ahmad Shuqeiri and, following an Arab League decision, founded the **Palestinian Liberation Organization (PLO)**. The group laid down the foundations and structure of the PLO and, in the early years, followed pan-Arabic ideology. The PLO was set up as an umbrella movement for a large number of varied interest groups of the Palestinian people. This organization was regarded by many, the Israelis in particular, as a terrorist organization. The early PLO was not a cohesive organization and contained a broad spectrum of moderate-to-extremely radical viewpoints. The militant members of PLO were known as fedayeen (warriors), who were then prepared to die for Allah. With such diverse opinions, the PLO soon became splintered and factional. This internecine struggle was much like the many Republican factions in Northern Ireland.

The PLO's driving philosophy was the restoration of Palestine, the destruction of Israel, as a nation-state, and the re-creation of an Arab State in former Palestine. The PLO is now loosely organized under three headings: the Executive Committee, the Central Committee, as well as the Palestine National Council. The Executive Committee coordinates the major terror activities and the Central Committee acts as an advisory structure to the Executive Committee. During the 1960s, PLO guerrilla groups carried out sporadic attacks against Israel. However, the new organization then lacked a strong leader for its political and operational activities. During this period, the PLO operated from bases inside the Hashemite Kingdom of Jordan, ruled by British-educated King Hussein. There, Yasser Arafat laid the groundwork for his operations among the Palestinians in Kuwait. In 1964, Arafat began to take control of the PLO and turned it from a very weak political movement to one that would be recognized as the only one true body to represent all the Palestinian people. By 1974, the Arab nations had recognized the PLO as, "the sole, legitimate representative of the Palestinian people." In the same year, the United Nations (excluding Israel, of course) similarly recognized the PLO.

Like all good political and terrorist organizations, Arafat's PLO had a senior security advisor, Ali Hassan Salameh (aka Abu Hassan), the "Red Prince." The Israeli intelligence agency, Mossad, believed Salameh to be the PLO member responsible for planning the Munich Olympic Games massacre. Golda Meir, then Prime Minister of Israel, gave Mossad the task of tracking down the man responsible for the attack, wherever he might hide. The search lasted seven years. In their attempt to assassinate Salameh, the trackers killed an innocent Moroccan bartender in Lillehammer; such was their fervor to exact retribution on the PLO. Salameh met his end dying as he had lived, when a remote-controlled bomb detonated in a stationary vehicle as he drove by with his bodyguards. The attack took place in Beirut, Lebanon, on January 23, 1979.

Arafat worked tirelessly to steer the PLO toward legitimacy as a political organization and, in 1988, he took a monumental step in announcing the right of Israel to exist and renouncing the further use of PLO terrorism. This commitment, from the man who then spoke for the displaced Palestinians, moved Israel toward discussions on Palestinian self-rule. Young Palestinians, who were frustrated with the slow progress toward self-rule in a homeland of their own, then turned to Hamas or Hezbollah for their leadership.

On September 13, 1993 (in Oslo), the Declaration of Principles between the Israelis and the Palestinians was signed. Palestinian groups formerly under the umbrella of the PLO, such as the **Popular Front for the Liberation of Palestine (PFLP)**, and also the Democratic Front for the Liberation of Palestine-Hawatmeh (DFLPH), suspended their participation in the PLO in protest and continued their campaigns of violence not only against the Israelis but also Americans and members of Arafat's PLO. Arafat remained as the PLO leader in the region, until his death in 2004. Arafat had been the specific target of Israel almost unceasingly since 9-11. He endured house-arrest in his own compound for much of 2002 to 2004. Israeli raids into Palestinian areas such as Ramallah and Jenin, to rout out terrorists who were targeting civilians, still continued unabated in spite of international condemnation for the use of military hardware in the West Bank and Gaza regions. By the middle of 2002, Arafat was still hanging on as leader of the PLO, but he faced a mounting challenge from Hamas militants.

The likelihood that a Palestinian/Israeli accord could be brokered between Sharon and Arafat was always in question. Both men had a long history of serious mistrust for each other. Sharon's long-remembered direct or indirect involvement with Christian militias in the Sabra and Shatila camp massacres did nothing to ease the dangers for peace in the region.

Arafat tended to operate more as a dictator than a democratic leader. Some two years after an agreed deadline for democratic elections to be held, Arafat had blamed the delay on the Israeli occupation. He stated frequently that this must end before elections could take place.

The world held its collective breath following Arafat's death in a Paris hospital in 2004. Without any apparent and viable successor, the vacuum could well have been filled with warring factions that would have done nothing to promote peace in the region. By 2006 the warring and infighting between the various factions of Hamas and the PLO/Fatah became a long awaited reality. Arafat had been the main player in Palestinian politics and terror for over forty years and held a stranglehold on the PLO and its activities.

Arafat was Chairman of the **Palestine Liberation Organization**, the titular head of Fatah, then President of the Palestinian Authority (PA), and President of the State of Palestine as declared

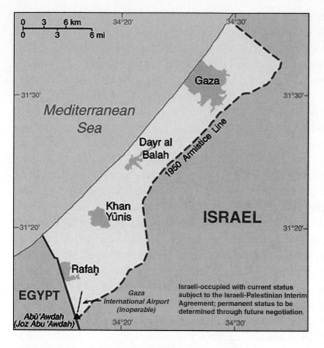

FIGURE 8-2   Map of Gaza Strip (Central Intelligence Agency, *The World Factbook*, 2008).

by the PLO in 1988. Fatah is the name used to describe the big **Palestinian National Liberation Movement** and is the largest constituent within the PLO. The elections held in early 2005 to elect Arafat's successor unfolded and saw the ascension of Mahmoud Abbas (a.k.a. Abu Mazen). He was elected on January 9, 2005, as President of the Palestinian Authority. Abbas and Israeli Prime Minister Sharon faced some daunting hurdles on both sides of their collective boundaries. Abbas will have to quickly and effectively try to reign in Hamas and, at the same time, gain some concessions from Israel. Abbas had opposed the Intifada that has lingered since 2000 and aims to support the U.S.-brokered "road map" to a peace settlement for the region. At an executive meeting on January 16, 2005, the PLO appealed for an end to armed attacks because they would provide excuses to the Israeli position of undermining Palestinian stability. With more than 5,000 deaths since the start of the 2000 Intifada, and two-thirds of that number being Palestinians, the hope is that Abbas will get much-needed support of the Arafat factions within the Fatah movement so that he will eventually have sufficient clout to control the various factions that seek only armed conflict with Israel.

ISRAELI DISENGAGEMENT PLAN

For Israel and former prime minister Sharon's designs to succeed, some serious balancing acts to somehow prevent extremist elements within Israel from disrupting the disengagement plans for the Gaza Strip were required.

The official document distributed by the Israeli Ministry of Foreign Affairs now contains the following:

GAZA STRIP

1. Israel will evacuate the Gaza Strip, including all existing Israeli towns and villages, and will re-deploy outside the Strip. This will not include military deployment in the area of the border between the Gaza Strip and Egypt.
2. Upon completion of this process, there shall no longer be any permanent presence of Israeli security forces or Israeli civilians in the areas of the Gaza Strip territory which have been evacuated.
3. As a result, there will be no basis for claiming that the Gaza Strip is occupied territory.

WEST BANK

1. Israel will evacuate an area in the northern Samaria area, including villages and all military installations, and will re-deploy outside the vacated area.
2. Upon completion of this process, there shall no longer be any permanent presence of Israeli security forces or Israeli civilians in the northern Samaria area.
3. The move will enable territorial contiguity for Palestinians in the northern Samaria area.
4. Israel will improve the transportation infrastructure in the West Bank in order to facilitate the contiguity of Palestinian transportation.

5. The process will facilitate Palestinian economic and commercial activity in the West Bank.
6. The Security Fence: Israel will continue to build the security fence, in accordance with relevant decisions of the government. The route will take into account humanitarian considerations.

Security situation following the disengagement:

GAZA STRIP

1. Israel will guard and monitor the external land perimeter of the Gaza Strip, will continue to maintain exclusive authority in Gaza airspace, and will continue to exercise security activity in the sea off the coast of the Gaza Strip.
2. The Gaza Strip will be demilitarized and shall be devoid of weaponry, the presence of which does not accord with the Israeli-Palestine agreements.
3. Israel reserves its inherent right to self-defense, both preventative and reactive, including where necessary the use of force, in respect of threats emanating from the Gaza Strip.

WEST BANK

1. Upon completion of the evacuation of the northern Samaria area, no permanent Israeli presence will remain in this area.
2. Israel reserves its inherent right to self-defense, both preventive and reactive, including where necessary the use of force, in respect of threats emanating from the northern Samaria area.
3. In other areas of the West Bank, current security activity will continue. However, as circumstances permit, Israel will consider reducing such activity in Palestinian cities.
4. Israel will work to reduce the number of internal checkpoints throughout the West Bank.

Under Sharon's "Disengagement" plan, Palestinians in the Gaza Strip continue to be subjected to the effective control of the Israeli Military. Although Israel will remove its permanent military presence, Israeli forces will retain the ability and inherent right to enter the Gaza Strip at will.[9] Israel will retain control over Gaza's airspace, sea shore, and borders.[10] Under the plan, Israel will unilaterally control whether or not Gaza opens a seaport or an airport. Additionally, Israel will control all border crossings; including Gaza's border with Egypt.[11] Israel will "continue its military activity along the Gaza Strip's coastline."[12] Taken together, these powers mean that all goods and people entering or leaving Gaza will be subject to Israeli control.

Finally, Israel will prevent Gazians from engaging in international relations. Accordingly, if it enacts the "Disengagement" plan as envisaged, Israel will effectively control Gaza, administratively and militarily.[13] Therefore, Israel will remain the occupying power of the Gaza Strip, as contrary to its own assertions. Israel's greatest battle is probably not against "terrorism," but against demography. Statistical analyses project that Palestinian Christians and Muslims will comprise the majority of persons in Israel and the occupied Palestinian territories by the year 2020.[14] If Israel wants to remain a "Jewish State," then it will be very difficult to maintain its Jewish identity if an ethno/religious minority continues to rule over an ethnic majority. Israeli journalist David Landau noted in a statement made to a British journalist that the Gaza plan represents "the simplest, crudest solution [to Israel's demographic time bomb]: to dump Gaza and its 1.3 million Arabs in the hope that that would 'buy' Israel 50 more years."[15]

For any success in the precarious region of Palestine, and for there to be any chance of any kind of settlement, let alone the realization of a separate state for the Palestinians Mahmoud Abbas must show that his administration will not tolerate corruption and, in doing so, establish the rule of law. Abbas will need to display significant results to the Palestinian people, by not only ending corruption but also by obtaining fundamental rights to freedom of movement and freedom from Israeli military interference in their daily lives. Probably more significantly, the leadership of the PA must display a prominent role in disengaging the Israelis from Gaza. The final disengagement and dismantling of Jewish settlements actually went ahead of schedule and for the region in a relatively calm manner. The expected militant Jewish backlash never came about and the militant Palestinian groups, Hamas in particular, celebrated the liberation of the Gaza Strip as being a victory for armed resistance. What will be the next scenario for this region and the West Bank in particular? With no settlements in the West Bank and militants convinced that this is the first step on their road to a full and independent Palestinian State, they have few targets to attack. Israel resides behind its secured Gaza fence line and the Hamas militants will have to focus more on infiltration operations. Since the August 2005 withdrawal from Gaza there have been sporadic rocket attacks and the more familiar bus/suicide bombings usually as a response to Israeli security operations.

AL-FATAH

Al-Fatah (or *Al-Asifa*), the fighting organization within the PLO, actually predated the PLO by six years. Under the leadership of Yasser Arafat, it took total control of the PLO after the debacle of the 1967 Six-Day War. It is considered the largest terrorist group under the PLO banner—estimated to have a force of up to 15,000 **Fedayeen**. The group is financed mostly by wealthy Arab states.

Al-Fatah, however, has never managed to prove itself as a military machine against the Israelis in spite of its size and support structure, not even in the occupied territories of the Gaza Strip and the West Bank region of Jordan. Fatah was unable to prevent the Jordanian army from forcibly removing the PLO from its Jordanian training camps around Ajlun and Jerash in 1970, nor could it prevent a repetition in Lebanon, when the PLO was swept out by an Israeli invasion force in 1982.

OPERATION BAYONET

In Chapter 6, we discussed how members of Black September had succeeded in breaching the Olympic Games security at the 1972 Munich Games and massacred eleven Israeli athletes. For the Israeli government there was to be retribution and the then Israeli Prime Minister Golda Meir, secretly ordered Mossad to track down and kill all those involved in the planning and execution of the raid in Munich. Mossad agents spread throughout Europe and the Middle East and tracked their targets and assassinated them—they made one error—in 1973 in Lillehammer, Norway, they killed an innocent Moroccan waiter who looked like their intended target Ali Salameh. Between 1979 and 1982 Mossad and Israeli military commandos killed more than a dozen members, effectively eradicating the entire group responsible for the planning and execution of the Olympic games attack.

Black September is the name of the al Fatah terror wing and takes its name from the month of the Palestinians eviction from Jordan; Black September is the operational military arm of Fatah.

In spite of the extensive Mossad operation in Europe, Black September rebounded to flourish as the defense arm of Al-Fatah, protecting it and Arafat from the extremist groups sponsored by Syria and Iraq, who were funding Abu Nidal's Black June.

During the 1960s and 1970s, Al-Fatah offered training facilities to a wide range of the Middle Eastern, European, Asian, and African terrorist organizations, as well as insurgent groups. In David Yallop's book, *Tracking the Jackal*, he confirms that one such terrorist movement of the early seventies included the notorious West German Baader–Meinhof Gang.[16] Then reciprocal arrangements within these groups allowed for terror operations to be carried out in each other's names, throughout the world. The arrangements also helped with the financial support required to allow the groups to maintain their operations.

Like the Palestinian people as a whole, Al-Fatah is spread throughout the Middle East but is primarily headquartered in Tunisia. Al-Fatah has been provided with aid from Saudi Arabia, Kuwait, and some of the other Arab states in the Persian Gulf region. Al-Fatah members have likewise received training from the former USSR as well as other former Communist, Eastern Bloc countries.

The tangled web of Middle East terrorism does not start and finish with the PLO. As time goes on and attitudes change, either the PLO will soften or harden in its fundamental approach to Israel and its supporters. The PLO, like most organizations that are divided over a wide area, will have many different points of political view. Sabri al-Banna was extreme in his belief that the enemy must be attacked on all fronts—and the enemy was Israel. Wavering from that belief was contemptible in al-Banna's eyes. Al-Banna and his supporters split from Fatah and he moved to Iraq in the early seventies.

ABU NIDAL ORGANIZATION

Abu Nidal is the cover name for Sabri al-Banna. The group also uses the following names:

- Fatah Revolutionary Council
- Arab Revolutionary Council
- Arab Revolutionary Brigades
- Black September
- Revolutionary Organization of Socialist Muslims

Similar to the splits in the Irish Nationalist movement, the ANO split from the Al-Fatah organization of the PLO because al-Banna believed Arafat's approach to dealing with Israel was softening. This was most definitely not to al-Banna's liking and, in 1974; he and his supporters left Al-Fatah and set up headquarters in Baghdad, Iraq. The Abu Nidal Organization was recognized as one of the bloodiest terror groups operating in the Middle East. It certainly became a truly international terror operation by expanding its horizons and ability to strike at its enemies wherever they might be throughout the globe.

Easily recruited, al-Banna was drawn to Baghdad most likely because of what is termed its "rejectionist" approach to those Middle East countries that favored a peace deal with Israel. "Rejectionism" is a Middle Eastern political term meaning unilateral refusal of any peaceful settlement with Israel. Iraq would have been considered one of the most extreme rejectionist states and one that would not sanction any such deals with Israel. This also had the effect of alienating those states in favor of moderation, such as Jordan and Egypt. Al-Banna's goals can be summarized simply: first and foremost, the destruction of Israel; and second, control of the PLO with the support of the rejectionist Iraqi government. It seemed to suit Iraq to have a terrorist group within its boundaries that would do its bidding in return for bases and logistical support. Al-Banna, under the protection and watchful eye of the Iraqis, trained about 200 fighters for their joint cause.

Al-Banna believed that by creating terror on a world stage—rather than just the Middle East—he could meet his goals. His ruthless approach to terrorist actions and atrocities focused the world media and political attention firmly on the regional problems. Abu Nidal has carried out attacks in at least twenty countries and is responsible for the deaths of over 900 people. The group has not just targeted Israel. The United Kingdom, the United States, France, and those moderate Palestinians with the temerity to seek a peaceful settlement with Israel have been hit as well. Many of Abu Nidal's attacks were spectacular in their audaciousness. The Abu Nidal group credits itself with the assassination attempt on the Israeli Ambassador outside the Dorchester Hotel in London, in June 1982. In broad daylight, a young Arab later identified as the nephew of Sabri al-Banna, walked up to the ambassador and shot him in the head at point-blank range. The ambassador, Shlomo Argov, was seriously injured. Members of the Metropolitan Police Diplomatic Protection Group also injured his assailant. This single terrorist attack precipitated another "eye for an eye—tooth for a tooth" revenge response from the Israelis.

The PLO, then still under Yasser Arafat, denied any involvement in the attack. However, from the Israeli viewpoint, this was sufficient cause to attack, as "terrorism begets terrorism." Israel's response was a military hard line. The Israeli Air Force mounted a bombing raid on Palestinian camps in Beirut, Lebanon, resulting in a death toll estimated at 50, with 200 injured. It has been speculated that this same act provided the Israelis with the excuse to conduct a full-scale invasion of southern Lebanon to purge the region of PLO fighters. The invasion commenced two days after the attack on Argov and was termed, "Operation Peace for Galilee." The action was aimed to destabilize Lebanon and force the PLO to flee the country to Syria, Tunisia, and Iraq. Many comparisons can easily be drawn to other assassinations that precipitated a war or invasion, and notably the death of the Arch Duke Franz Ferdinand, which started World War I. As the strength and notoriety of Abu Nidal increased, so too did the international flavor of the training camps in and around Baghdad. These training centers attracted radical European elements wishing to learn the trade of murder and mayhem.

SIGNIFICANT INCIDENTS

Abu Nidal was successful in attacking aviation targets. Two such attacks date back to 1985:

December 27, Rome Airport, 08:15—Leonardo Da Vinci Airport is situated on the outskirts of Rome and is the principal international airport in Italy. At 08:15, four young Arabs threw hand grenades at a line of passengers waiting in the check-in line for the El Al flight. El Al's check-in desks are flanked by those of TWA. The four Arabs then opened fire with Kalashnikov AK-47 assault rifles on the American and Israeli passengers waiting in line. Other passengers, including Greeks, Mexicans, and two Arabs, were killed in the attack. El Al has a record of being proactive in aviation security, and at Rome airport, its armed security staff returned fire, along with Italian police, and killed three and injured one of the terrorists. Fifteen passengers were killed and seventy injured.

Because the terrorists were Arabs, the PLO was immediately denounced as having orchestrated the attack. In this instance, Abu Nidal was the likely culprit; however, the incidents in Rome and Vienna (described next) were most likely aimed at discrediting Arafat and the PLO. Both Austria and Italy were well disposed to the Palestinian cause and this action would have been designed to turn those countries against Arafat.

December 27, Vienna Airport, 08:15—The Vienna attack was timed to coincide with the Rome attack. There were fewer casualties in Vienna than in Rome: two dead and forty-six injured. The terrorists used the same modus operandi as their colleagues in Rome. However, they were able to fight their way out of the airport and escape temporarily by car, pursued by Austrian police. A gun battle followed and one of the terrorists was killed and the remaining two surrendered. Again, informed experts attribute this attack to Abu Nidal and his attempt to discredit Arafat.[17]

The Abu Nidal group has shifted bases periodically from Iraq to Syria and has also had bases in Lebanon and Tripoli. Its presence has also been noted in the Sudan. Its support network and financial aid came primarily from Iraq and Syria and, more recently, from Libya. Reports of Sabri al-Banna's death came on August 19, 2002, through Middle East news reports that he died of gunshot wounds in Baghdad. He was reportedly suffering from leukemia and it is not known whether his death was murder or suicide.

Popular Front for the Liberation of Palestine (PFLP)

The PFLP was founded under the umbrella of the PLO in 1967. Its co-founders and leaders were George Habash and Wadi Haddad. George Habash was born in Lydda, Palestine, in 1925, of a wealthy family that followed the teachings of the Greek Orthodox Church. Wadi Haddad was born in Safad, Galilee, in 1939.[18]

When the British mandate on Palestine ended in 1948, Habash was studying medicine at the American University in West Beirut. He and his family became refugees overnight and fled to Jordan. After completing his studies, Habash set up a clinic with another Palestinian from the Greek Orthodox Church, Wadi Haddad, in Amman. It might seem strange that two committed doctors trained to save lives should organize a terrorist group. Both were committed to the belief in the 1950s that Gamall Abdel Nasser was the best hope for the liberation of Palestine. Both were extreme left-wing Marxists. In 1957, Nasser's supporters came close to toppling the Hashemite Monarchy of Jordan; however, King Hussein was able to defeat the uprising. Habash and Haddad fled and relocated their base of operations to Syria. The PFLP grew out of the Arab Nationalist Movement, which the two men had set up. Both viewed Yasser Arafat with total disdain and loathing for his involvement with the imperialist United States and for his efforts at appeasement of the Israelis. Their philosophy espoused pure terror and was born of the rationale that Israel won its prize by terror, so Arabs should gain Palestine back with similar terror tactics.

AL-AQSA MARTYRS BRIGADES

This group, unlike Hamas, does not strive for an Islamic state in Palestine but rather uses Islam as a weapon to inspire its struggle for an independent Palestine. The movement is linked to Yasser Arafat's Fatah faction and is responsible for many bombs and shooting attacks against Israelis, both in the occupied territories and in Israel itself.

FIGURE 8-3 Palestinian militants from the Al-Aqsa Martyrs Brigade, an armed wing of the Fatah movement, Hamas, and the Palestinian Front for the Liberation of Palestine (PFLP) hold their hands together during a news conference calling for the end to violence in the Gaza Strip in the West Bank city of Nablus on May 17, 2007 (Canadian Press).

Taking its name from the Al-Aqsa Mosque, one of the holiest of Muslim sites, the group is now allied with Fatah. Shortly after the death of Yasser Arafat, the group renamed itself, for a short time, to Brigades of Martyr Yasser Arafat. As a relatively new organization, it did not make it to the U.S. State Department's list of foreign terrorist organizations until after a deadly suicide bombing in Jerusalem in March 2002. Denials of its links to the PLO and Fatah have been commonplace; however, investigative journalists from Britain's BBC exposed documents in November 2003 that showed the Fatah organizations were in fact, paying Al-Aqsa Brigades $50,000 a month. Further confirmation came in 2004 from the Palestinian Prime Minister Ahmed Qurei, when he stated in an interview in *Ashraq al-Awsat*, a London-based Muslim newspaper: "We have clearly stated that the Aqsa Martyrs Brigade are part of Fatah. We are committed to them and Fatah bears full responsibility for the group." Some of the group's more vicious attacks have been centered on suicide attacks in Israel and, most notably:

- March 2, 2002—Beit Yisrael suicide bomber kills eleven.
- January 5, 2003—Twenty-two killed in southern Tel Aviv bus depot.
- April 17, 2006—Two suicide bombers are believed to have carried out the attack at Tel Aviv's Old Central Bus Station. There were at least 19 fatalities and 114 injured; 9 in serious or critical condition

The group's modus operandi is to employ a suicide belt for the individual bomber. The bomber wears a vest that covers the upper region of the body and is packed, not just with explosives, but also nails, ball bearings, and nuts and bolts to inflict widespread injury. Hiding this style of bomb requires a heavy layer of outer clothing as the bomb belt will likely weigh between 10 and 40 pounds, depending on the size of the bomber. Al-Aqsa has been using young teenagers for this activity and, like Hamas, has also used female bombers.

In early 2005, the Al-Aqsa group was respecting the ceasefire truce brokered by the new PA leader, Abbas. As noted earlier, Al-Aqsa is an offshoot of the Fatah wider organizational structure and has always remained committed to its central cause to end Israeli occupation of Palestine by armed struggle.

Year	Tool of Injury				Total
	LiveAmmunition	Metal Bullet	Gas	Miscellaneous[a]	
2000[b]	2,228	4,249	3,363	763	10,603
2001	1,441	1,233	1,489	2,232	6,395
2002	1,386	243	536	2,206	4,371
2003	1,011	327	215	1,441	2,994
2004	1,317	437	811	1,485	4,050
2005	236	232	174	350	992
2006	436	303	134	909	1,782
2007[c]	57	77	18	87	239
January	24	21	0	0	45
February	11	43	9	5	68
March	10	13	2	1	26
April	5	0	0	0	5
May	7	0	7	81	239
Total	**8,112**	**7,101**	**6,740**	**9,473**	**31,426**

[a]Miscellaneous include beating, torture, etc.
[b]Data Includes the period September 29, 2000–December 31,2000
[c]Data Includes the months listed only

FIGURE 8-4 Numbers of injured Palestinians in the Al-Aqsa Uprising (Intifada) from September 29, 2000 through May 2007 (Palestine Central Bureau of Statistics).

As the truce holds firm, there can be little doubt that Abbas is making moves to include, rather than alienate, the Al-Aqsa group to within his sphere of influence, which could include bringing it into the PA security structure. The issues for Fatah and the PA leadership will hinge on Al-Aqsa's demand that the group maintain its weapons and, no doubt, its continued distrust of the Israeli Prime Minister. Absorbing Al-Aqsa into the PA security services may be a sound method of integration, giving the PA some measure of control on the group and its leadership.

The Gaza Strip

The Gaza Strip[19] is an area of 140 square miles. It is home to over 830,000 Palestinians and between 4,000 and 5,000 Israeli settlers. The Palestinian population is concentrated in four cities and eight refugee camps. Ninety-nine percent of the population is Sunni Muslim. Although Gaza City is one of the oldest cities in the world, the borders of the area we know as the Gaza Strip were only created in 1949. With the end of the British mandate in Palestine and the resulting Arab-Israeli battles, eventually two-thirds of this area was claimed by Israel. Egypt claimed the remaining third. After the creation of the Gaza Strip, more than 250,000 Palestinians escaped from the fighting in other areas of the Middle East and came to settle there. Since that time, Israel has refused to allow those Palestinians to return home, in defiance of UN Resolution 141. Most of the current inhabitants of the Gaza Strip are descendants of this group.

The Suicide Bomber

The Palestinian terrorists have successfully used suicide bombers as a means to attack targets within Israel during the period of the Intifada. Since the signing of the Oslo Agreements in 1993, Palestinian terrorist organizations have sent over seventy suicide bombers on missions against Israeli targets. *Yediot Aharonot*, the Israeli daily newspaper, presents a profile of the typical suicide bomber:

- 47 percent of the suicide bombers have an academic education and an additional 29 percent have at least a high school education.
- 83 percent of the suicide bombers are single.
- 64 percent of the suicide bombers are between the ages of eighteen and twenty-three; most of the rest are under thirty.
- 68 percent of the suicide bombers have come from the Gaza Strip.

In a column published in The New York Times, William Safire wrote that, "the pride and joy of Arafat's arsenal was a weapon of mass terror that has no known defense: the human missile." Safire describes the suicide bombers as being "brainwashed" and considers the efforts necessary to enable the launching of these "missiles."[20]

HAMAS

The central figure in the establishment of the Hamas organization was Sheikh Ahmed Yassin, a wheelchair-ridden "cleric," whose spiritual ideology fueled current Palestinian terrorism. Many observers contend that Yassin preached only hatred and attacks on the Israeli state whereas his comments and ideology would say otherwise. He continually called for suicide terrorism as part of a Muslim's religious obligation and stated in 1998 that "the day in which I will die as a shahid (martyr) will be the happiest day of my life." Yassin most certainly was a target of the IDF on more than one occasion. He was finally assassinated in a helicopter gunship attack by Israeli forces on March 22, 2004. Yassin had long called for Islamic terrorists to join with Hamas in global jihad and to strike at Western interests everywhere if Iraq is conquered. A global jihad involving young and impressionable Muslims from throughout Europe is responsible for the upsurge in suicide bombings in Israel and terrorist attacks and insurgency in Iraq. Yassin would also have the dubious distinction of providing the first female suicide bombers for his attacks against Israel. It was, in fact, a British suicide bomber who was responsible for the attack on Mike's Place in Tel Aviv in 2003. Although the crippled Sheikh was as much a symbol of Palestinian resistance as was Yasser Arafat, Yassin was operating in a manner totally different from that of the Fatah organization. Yassin was active in sabotaging the peace accords of the 1990s and was hostile to the corrupt and secular PLO of Yasser Arafat. Under Yassin, Hamas aimed to replace the PLO with its own liberation of Palestine from the Jordan River to the Mediterranean Sea by means of violence and armed insurrection, and thus establish an Islamic Palestinian State from the ruins of the Israeli State.

Yassin joined the Muslim Brotherhood while studying at Cairo's Al-Azhar University and adopted the movement's belief that the rule of Islam should be imposed everywhere. After returning to Gaza, Yassin became actively involved in politics. In 1973, he founded the Islamic Center in Gaza, which soon controlled all religious institutions. In 1979, he founded the Islamic Organization; a body which Israeli military initially hoped would reduce the political influence of Yasser Arafat's Fatah movement. At the time, the Islamic Organization dealt mostly with welfare. But the ideology of the Muslim Brotherhood fueled Yassin's belief that the Israelis occupied an Islamic land whose ownership was not negotiable, and the sheikh gradually shifted from social and religious activity to clandestine activities against Israeli rule in the West Bank and Gaza.

Yassin was arrested in 1984 and sentenced to thirteen years in jail for possessing illegal arms, establishing a military organization, and calling for the annihilation of Israel. Yassin acknowledged that he founded an organization of religious activists with the goal of fighting nonreligious factions in the territories, and carrying out "jihad" operations against Israel. This organization used monies from Islamic activists in Jordan to acquire large quantities of weapons. He was imprisoned until May 1985, when he was released in a prisoner exchange deal between Israel and the terrorist organization of Ahmed Jibril.

During the first Intifada in 1987, Yassin transformed his Islamic organization into a new body called Hamas. An acronym for the Islamic Resistance Movement, *Hamas* means "zeal" in Arabic. In Hebrew, it means evil.[21]

Ahmad Rashad, a research associate at the United Association for Studies and Research, attributes Hamas's popularity to several factors:[22]

- Its call for the liberation of all of Palestine.
- Its reputation as an efficient organization.
- Its honesty and lack of corruption.
- Its resilience to Israeli crackdowns.
- Its daring and successful attacks against Israeli military targets.
- Its home-based leadership within the occupied territories, as opposed to the PLO's expatriate direction.

Whatever social or political aspiration Hamas may have for the people of Palestine must be then questioned in relation to its neighbor Israel. The Hamas charter speaks to its aims and concepts:

"Israel will exist and will continue to exist until Islam will obliterate it, just as it obliterated others before it."

"The Islamic Resistance Movement believes that the Land of Palestine is an Islamic War consecrated for future Moslem generations until Judgment Day. It, or any part of it, should not be squandered: it, or any part of it, should not be given up."

"There is no solution for the Palestinian question except through jihad. Initiatives, proposals and international conferences are all a waste of time, and vain endeavors."

"After Palestine, the Zionists aspire to expand from the Nile to the Euphrates. When they will have digested the region they overtook, they will aspire to further expansion, and so on. Their plan is embodied in the 'Protocols of the Elders of Zion,' and their present conduct is the best proof of what we are saying."[23] It is not difficult to see why Hamas is such a serious threat to Israel's continued security and why Israel would want to specifically target its leaders for assassination, as it has done so effectively since 2002.

Organization and Structure of Hamas

Hamas has been heavily involved in the local political scene in Gaza by putting up candidates for union representatives and the board of trade. Its political opponent is the PLO. Hamas dates back to the mid-1980s, when it identified itself as a wing of the Palestinian Muslim Brotherhood. The Brotherhood had been seeking to establish a political wing for its organization and in 1985 and 1986 it issued leaflets in Gaza to encourage a policy of civil disobedience. The leaflets were issued under names such as Harakat al-Kifah al-Musallah (Armed Struggle Movement), al-Murabitoon ala Ard al-Isra (The Steadfast on the Land of al-Isra), and Harakat al-Muqawama al-Islamiyya (Islamic Resistance Movement, IRM). As the tensions grew in the mid-1980s, these communiqués became more and more politicized and, by 1988, the name Hamas then began to appear.

The Military and Intelligence Wings of Hamas function independently; the Intelligence Wing gathers information and carries out surveillance operations on collaborators, drug dealers, and other antisocial activities and metes out punishments ranging from warnings to executions. It also distributes literature about Israeli recruitment policy and methods of collaboration and warns the populace about complicity. The Intelligence Wing also monitors crime in the region. The Military Wing has different, but well-defined goals and objectives:

- Establish usar (families) and underground cells.
- Gather information on Israeli Defense Force activities for use in planned operations.
- Carry out training programs in hand-to-hand combat.
- Carry out military-style operations against the IDF.

Hamas military strikes have continued, predominantly against Israeli settlers in the territories, and suicide attacks mainly against civilian targets in Israel. Tactics are of a hit-and-run nature—planting a bomb or a suicide bombing in populated areas of Jerusalem, for example. Despite the PLO agreements with Israel, the Hamas movement declared Arafat a traitor for his (what are now viewed as failed) agreements with the Zionist enemy. Hamas's response to these agreements has resulted in an increase in disputes with the PLO. Hamas receives its support from other Muslim countries, including Turkey, Iran, Afghanistan, Saudi Arabia and the Gulf States, Yemen, and even Malaysia. Hamas, although similar to the PLO, is willing to settle for a peace agreement with Israel, but has firm objectives that must be met before an agreement can be reached. In 1994, Hamas proclaimed that it was not opposed to peace; however, for it to. ". . . cease military operations in Gaza and the West Bank . . ." the following conditions would have to be met:

1. Complete Israeli withdrawal from the occupied territories.
2. Disarm the settlers and dismantle the settlements.
3. Place international forces on the "green line" established in the occupied territories during the 1948 and 1967 wars.
4. Hold free and general elections to determine true representation of the Palestinian people.
5. The Council, which will be composed of electoral victors, shall represent the Palestinians in any negotiations that determine their future and that of the occupied territories.

The removal of Israeli settlers and the pulling down of their settlements in the Gaza Strip in late 2005 and the opening of a border crossing with Egypt (now being controlled by the Palestinians) is hopefully a sign of more concessions and an opportunity for a road map to peace becoming a reality.

Many Palestinians lauded the Gaza-Jericho agreement of 1993, as they saw the new prospect of establishing their own legitimate Homeland. . . . however, the slow progress since the agreement was reached and the continued development of the occupied territories by Israeli settlers has led to disillusionment by many Palestinians. This has led to internal strife between PLO and Hamas, with pro-Arafat supporters being assassinated. Israel continued to wrangle over interpretation of sections in the agreement with the PLO throughout the remainder of the twentieth century. It is no surprise that acts of terror aimed at Israeli settlements and at targets in the West Bank and Gaza Strip continued almost unabated. As we know, no final accord has been brokered; even the current "road map to peace" remains in jeopardy. Hamas has been able to retain sufficient military strength to protect its interests against the Israelis and has a broad political constituency, especially among the young, due to the combination of its fundamentalist religious message and social welfare programs.

Hamas's social programs, such as establishing clinics and schools, are an effective alternative to the PA's own social infrastructure, which was crumbling from corruption and mismanagement even before much of it was destroyed by the Israeli military. The current Intifada, which has continued remorselessly since September 2000, has enabled Hamas to garner and maintain support from other Palestinian factions including Fatah, in what is becoming an unshakeable national consensus.[24] The Military Wing of Hamas, the Ezzedine al-Qassam Brigades, has continued to carry out suicide attacks against Israel in spite of massive security operations to block all such attempts. Hamas declared an "all-out war" on Israel in January 2002 as a result of an Israeli incursion into the West Bank city of Tulkarem, which saw Israeli commandos shoot dead four Hamas bomb makers and the West Bank leader of Hamas, Yousef Soragji.

Suicide, as a means to an end, has been used before against the United States in the Middle East. The Beirut attacks against the U.S. Marine Corps Barracks and the attack against the U.S. Embassy in West Beirut were the work of suicide attackers. The proximity of the Palestinians to the Israeli populous has made for somewhat easy pickings for the Hamas men of terror. Their targets have usually been civilian centers in Tel Aviv, Jerusalem, and other Israeli cities such as seaside resort towns like Netanya. Massive security clampdowns and numerous checkpoints on major arterial roads as well as street checks have not prevented repeated Hamas suicide missions. Each successful attack has resulted in a swift and ferocious response by Israel targeting "suspected" militants in refugee camps in Palestinian territory. The cycle of violence prevailed throughout 2004 and up to the "truce" in early 2005. Israel has also reverted to targeted assassination of "suspected" militants, mainly from Hamas. The method of the response has been to target residential buildings believed to house a specific suspect. On the night of July 23, 2002, an F-16 fighter aircraft dropped a one-ton bomb on the Gaza home of a Hamas leader. The collateral damage in this attack was fourteen civilians. This type of action by the Israeli forces could clearly be defined as a form of state terror. Israel claimed that it had not intended to kill innocent civilians; however, dropping a one-ton bomb in a residential neighborhood would likely have just that effect. In times of war, civilians are often involved in "mistakes." The direct targeting of civilians, as occurred in the World War II German bombings of London and the allies' carpet bombing of Dresden, can be deemed terror bombings and atrocities, as they have no specific military objective or significance. In targeting terrorists who hide or live in a civilian environment, such distinctions become difficult. From a Palestinian viewpoint, there is much to be gained in the propaganda war in showing dead civilians to eager news crews. What effect this style of reciprocal attack by Israel will have for peace is uncertain. Although calls for an investigation and wide criticism have ensued in the Israeli media, widespread condemnation has not been long lasting or particularly loud from the international community.

"HAMAS—STAN"

When Hamas won the general election in March 2006 it set itself on a collision course not only with Israel but also Fatah. Hamas had managed through its grass roots social programs and community involvement to cement its popularity in the Gaza Strip and have it recognized as a viable alternative to the corrupt Fatah dominated West Bank. This is not a new strategy and no doubt Hamas has watched and mirrored the evolving of Hezbollah to political power in Lebanon. The West's response to Hamas winning the election was the cessation of funds to the Palestinian National Authority. Hamas may have won the election; it had not won international recognition. Still listed as a terrorist entity, it was not going to be an easy transformation to an internationally recognized legitimate authority in the region. Hamas had assumed far more political responsibility than it was really capable of assuming in so short a time span, and with the rule of law on the streets effectively being the gun; internal battles were soon to follow. The Palestinian apparatus has always been at the center of power in both Gaza and the West Bank and taking control of that apparatus sparked the start of violence in 2007. Fatah and Hamas sparred in the political arena over control and attempted to come up with a power sharing agreement which included the Saudi Arabian brokered Mecca Agreement. The deal disintegrated with the battle over control of security forces. In its effort to effectively control Fatah, Hamas mounted an offensive in the Gaza Strip in June 2007.

Hamas believed by doing so, it would be able to negotiate from a position of strength in its negotiations with Fatah over the security forces. This had the effect of two separate states being controlled by differing and warring Palestinian factions, something that Israel would be quick to take advantage of. Hamas gunmen, in one week of June 2007,tore down the portraits of Yasser Arafat from office walls and removed the Palestinian flag, replacing it with the green banner of Islam. The forced removal of Arafat's Fatah movement in Gaza and the execution of key Fatah leaders in Gaza as well as taking control of Fatah compounds and their wealth of Western supplied weapons summed up a change that is spreading across a broad swathe of the Middle East. Secular nationalism of the sort Fatah has stood for is beginning to look like the weak force and radical Islam as the strong force.[25] Israel now has to contend with a radical Islamist state controlled by Hamas on the Mediterranean and a moderate Palestinian stronghold on its other flank, in the larger West Bank. Hamas in its rise to prominence at some stage would be required to recognize and negotiate with Israel something its grass roots leadership would be against. As early as January 2007, Hamas announced that it would never negotiate with Israel and would not be abiding by any of the treaties that Fatah had previously negotiated with the Israelis. The March 2007 kidnapping of a British Broadcasting Corporation (BBC) journalist Alan Johnson in Gaza by members from the shadowy group calling itself the Army of Islam provided the opportunity for Hamas to demonstrate to the international community its ability not to act and control events in Gaza. The Army of Islam is made up of ex-members of Hamas, so it is very likely that Hamas would be able to exercise a measure of influence to have the journalist released unharmed. The Hamas-brokered release of Johnson unharmed in July 2007 did little to deter the Israelis from making inroads with the Fatah controlled West Bank to further curtail Hamas in Gaza and prevent any reconciliation between Hamas and Fatah. The Israeli government of Ehud Olmert agreed to a meeting with Mahmoud Abbas and also granted a group of wanted exiled Palestinian leaders including the controversial figure, Nayef Hawatmeh, permission to enter the West Bank for the meeting. Hawatmeh had been the mastermind behind the tragic 1974 Maalot massacre which resulted in the death of twenty-three Israeli school children.

For the Israelis it was crucial to develop a dialogue of sorts with Fatah on the West Bank to prevent Hamas becoming the only Palestinian (Islamist) voice for the region. While Israel ponders an amnesty to Palestinian prisoners Olmert has to contend with the political fallout back home, as a very cautious public sees no advantage to releasing prisoners back to the West Bank with no guarantees they will renounce violence. The Maalot massacre maybe over thirty years ago but it is still fresh in Israeli memories and so is the name of the mastermind behind the attack. The other concern for Israelis is that any amnesty may also include the release of the "Nelson Mandela" of the West Bank and Fatah leader Marwan Barghouti who is serving life in prison for the murder of five people during the second intifada. The Palestinians of course want a large number exchanged for a captured Israeli soldier, Corporal Shalit. His release is also a precondition to any peace deal being worked out between Israel and the Palestinians.

WEAPONRY

The ability to strike at Israeli settlements is far easier from the West Bank than it is from the Gaza Strip which borders an area of Israel that is sparsely populated. The mini civil war that developed briefly over the summer of 2007 did not diminish Hamas's capabilities or their goals of attacking Israel. Hamas's arsenal contains the usual array of rifles and AK 47s, but they have also built up an array of improvised rocket devices, considered highly unstable, which will only get to perfection with more practise. The rockets they have developed are of the short range variety without any technical guidance system to support target identification. The rockets named as "Qassam Rockets" after the Syrian Cleric Izz al-Din al-Qassam, have been used extensively by Hamas and other groups against Israeli targets. These unstable devices are steel tubes with their stabilizing fins welded to their side using potassium nitrate fertilizer and sugar as the main propellant with TNT as the warhead. The longest range missile to have struck any target has been 12 kilometres. These missiles have a launch team of between five and ten people dependent on the type and size of the rocket being fired and this brings the operators into considerable risk of being spotted by Israeli drones in the skies above, or unmanned aerial vehicles (**UAV**'s).

Palestinian Liberation Front (PLF)

The Palestinian Liberation Front (PLF) split from the PFLP General Command in the mid-1970s and then again into pro-Syrian, pro-Libyan, and pro-PLO factions. Its membership cadre is estimated to be between fifty and hundred.[26] PLF based its operations in Iraq, having moved there from Tunisia after the attack on the cruise liner *Achille Lauro* in October 1985 and the murder of a wheelchair-bound U.S. citizen, Leon Klinghoffer. Abu Abbas, a longtime supporter of Yasser Arafat, led the PLF. Abbas, a renounced terrorist, was born in a refugee camp in Syria in 1948. He was a longtime Palestinian terrorist with a price on his head after the murder of the *Achille Lauro* passenger, Leon Klinghoffer. Abbas rose to prominence in the PLO and was elected to the powerful and influential Executive Committee of the PLO in 1982. Until 1985 he operated from Tunisia. After the *Achille Lauro* incident, Italian authorities briefly detained him until he was flown to Yemen.

Israel remained the prime target of Palestinian terrorist attacks during 1990. Escalating tensions resulted in a number of serious incidents during the year. On May 30, Israeli forces foiled an attempted seaborne assault against the Tel Aviv beachfront. Four terrorists were killed and twelve captured. The attack was carried out by the **Palestine Liberation Front**, led by Abu Abbas, with substantial assistance from Libya. PLO Chairman Arafat's failure to take concrete actions against the PLF, a constituent PLO member, led to the suspension of U.S. dialogue with the PLO.[27]

Abbas was an outspoken supporter of Saddam Hussein during the Gulf War. He was captured by coalition forces in Iraq in 2003 and died in custody from natural causes in March 2004. The PLF gets its support from Syria and has in the past received support from Libya. As well as with some presence in Gaza and the West Bank, it has also shown up in Lebanon.

Democratic Front for the Liberation of Palestine (DFLP)

The Democratic Front for the Liberation of Palestine (DFLP) is a strong and vocal opponent to the Israeli peace accord with the PLO. This Marxist group split from the PFLP in 1969.[28] DFLP believes the Palestinians can only achieve their goals by mass uprising. Its political position in the

FIGURE 8-5 Marilyn Klinghoffer is escorted by fellow Americans Neil and June Kantor as they leave the cruise ship Achllle Lauro at Port Said, Egypt, on October 10, 1985. Leon Klinghoffer was killed and thrown overboard during the hijacking of the ship. Abul Abbas, the Palestinian who planned the hijacking, died in U.S. custody in Iraq in March 2004 (Canadian Press).

early years of the 1980s was somewhere in between those of Arafat and the rejectionists. DFLP again split into two more factions in 1991—one pro-Arafat and one hardline group headed by Nayif Hawatmah. This group has suspended its membership in the PLO as it opposes the Declaration of Principles signed in 1993. The DFLP is estimated to have a membership totaling about 500 activists across both groups and has carried out its terror campaign mostly in Israel and the occupied territories. Since 1988, the DFLP has been involved only in cross-border raids into Israeli areas. It receives its funding and logistical support primarily from Libya and Syria.

Palestinian Islamic Jihad (PIJ)

The Palestinian Islamic Jihad (PIJ) has its roots among the Palestinian fundamentalists in the Gaza Strip dating back to the 1970s. Its goals differ from those of the PLO. Its aims are to achieve an Islamic Palestinian State through a holy war and a total commitment to the total destruction of Israel. It is a small factional terrorist organization operating under the guise of Palestinian resistance—its members are considered hard core and totally uninterested in a political solution in Palestine.

Ramadan Abdullah Shallah, Secretary General PIJ

Ramadan Abdullah Shallah was born in the Gaza Strip and spent five years at Durham University in northern England, where he reportedly coordinated the activities of Palestinian Islamic Jihad (PIJ) by sending and receiving orders to and from cells of the organization in Gaza and the West Bank. From 1990 to 1995, Shallah lived in Tampa, Florida, where he was a leading member of the Islamic Concern Project (also known as the Islamic Committee for Palestine). The organization distributed official PIJ literature used to indoctrinate followers by glorifying PIJ suicide bombers as martyrs. After PIJ leader Fathi Shaqaqi's death in October 1995, Shallah became the new leader of PIJ and a member of its Shura (consultative) Council.[29] The PIJ strikes at both Arabs and Jews alike and has not limited its area of operation to the territories and the Gaza Strip, like Hamas. It ranks the United

States alongside Israel as one of its prime targets. PIJ's acts of terror have been brutal and efficient. In 1991, the group attacked a tourist bus in Egypt, killing eleven passengers, nine of them Israelis. Its method of attack in Israel and the occupied territories has been suicide bombings of bus stations and markets.[30] PIJ continues to front attacks on Israeli targets both in Israel and the territories, although since the 9-11 attacks on the U.S. and Israel's erection of the security fence has certainly limited its activities. With respect to any disengagement plan that the Israelis have envisaged, the PIJ network in Northern Samaria has emerged as one of the most tangible threats to the implementation of the disengagement plan, as its leadership questions the value of sticking to the policy of calm (tahadiyah). The PIJ network, encompassing Jenin and Tul Karm and all of the villages in between, was responsible for a major attack within Israel—the suicide bombing at the Stage Club in Tel Aviv on February 25, 2005, in which five Israelis were killed and fifty more were wounded. One of its senior commanders, Luay Saadi, one of Israel's "Most Wanted" terrorists was killed by the Israeli Army in October 2005 in retaliation for his planning of The Stage Club bombing. After the attack, the PIJ leadership in Damascus engaged in evasive tactics designed to escape the flames of the Israeli response, as well as the unexpected fury the attack aroused among Palestinians who mostly want the calm to continue. Signs have been accumulating that indicate PIJ is back in action but they have only been credited with one attack in March 2007. Israeli intelligence sources also see evidence that the Military Wing in the northern West Bank has resumed planning major attacks.[31]

Kach and Kahane Chai

Kach is a Jewish ultra nationalist group operating in Israel and founded by the late Rabbi Meir Kahane founder of the Jewish Defense League (JDL), a U.S. organization dedicated to protecting American Jews. The JDL became increasingly militant, espousing violence and vigilantism to curb anti-Semitism. The Kach movement (Hebrew for "Thus") emerged from this international JDL office.

In 1984 the Kach and Kahane Chai organization was declared a terrorist organization by the Israeli Government under the 1948 Terrorism Law.[32] Binyamin Kahane, the son of Rabbi Meir Kahane, who was assassinated in the United States in 1990, leads this group. The aim of the group is to restore the biblical state of Israel and purge the land of all Arab settlers. The Kach and Kahane was an outspoken supporter of the terrorist attack on the al-Ibrahimi Mosque by Dr. Baruch Goldstein in February 1994. On several occasions over the last thirty years it has attempted, unsuccessfully, to turn itself into a political movement by running candidates for the Israeli Knesset; however, after the Goldstein attack the government banned the group from politics in Israel. The group has threatened and attacked Palestinians and Arabs in Hebron and the West Bank and is an embarrassment to the Israeli government. Its motto is "terror against terror." The group was violently opposed to Ariel Sharon's disengagement plan and the dismantling of Jewish settlements in both the Gaza Strip and the West Bank.

The 1993 Declaration of Principles—at its signing seen as breakthrough agreement—has staggered on with no outward resolution of the critical issues in the region; however, it is important to list its main points.

DECLARATION OF PRINCIPLES

ARTICLE VI: PREPARATORY TRANSFER OF POWERS AND RESPONSIBILITIES

1. Upon entry into force of this Declaration of Principles and the withdrawal from the Gaza Strip and the Jericho area, a transfer of authority from the Israeli Military Government and its Civil Administration to the authorized Palestinians for this task, as detailed herein, will commence. This transfer of authority will be of a preparatory nature until the inauguration of the Council.

2. Immediately after the entry into force of this Declaration of Principles and the withdrawal from the Gaza Strip and the Jericho area, with the view to promoting economic development in the West Bank and Gaza Strip, authority will be transferred to the Palestinians on the following spheres: education and culture, health, social welfare, direct taxation, and tourism. The Palestinian side will commence in building the Palestinian Police Force, as agreed upon. Pending the inauguration of the Council, the two parties may negotiate the transfer of additional powers and responsibilities, as agreed upon.[33]

The Declaration of Principles signaled a major breakthrough and a new hope for a definitive solution to the Palestinian question, even peace in the area that, of course, has not been realized. The full text of the Declaration of Principles is not included in this chapter; however, its contents form the basis and fabric for both the Israelis and the Palestinians to move toward the goal of a homeland for the displaced Palestinians. It has been a very bumpy road since 1993, and whether the two sides are able to fulfill the contents of the Declaration and meet all that is stipulated remains to be seen. There is considerable resentment in the territories and Gaza Strip of the slow pace toward meeting the goals of the Principles.

It is worthwhile to note that the Oslo strategy was to re-divide and subdivide an already fractured and fragmented Palestinian territory into three subzones: A, B, and C, in ways entirely devised and controlled by the Israeli side, because the Palestinians were, until very recently, a "map-less" society. At the negotiations, there were no Palestinian representatives with any geographical knowledge who could either argue or contest decisions.[34]

Recruitment and indoctrination into the terrorist cause is believed to continue unabated in the Gaza Strip as the next generation of terrorists are groomed and schooled in hatred aimed at their Israeli neighbors. Children as young as age seven are parading with automatic assault weapons and singing patriotic Palestinian songs that glory in the destruction of Israel.[35] This is hardly a harbinger of a peaceful settlement in the years to come. The core of mistrust between the Palestinians and the Israelis, in both words and deeds, runs deepest in the occupied territories.

JORDAN

The Kingdom of Jordan has been a "refuge" for thousands of displaced Palestinians from West Bank villages for the last four decades. Considerable support and sympathy for the Palestinian cause probably exists among Jordanians. Jordan became a safe haven for the Palestinians after the creation of Israel, but problems often arose with so many extreme elements actively embroiled in terrorist campaigns against Israel. The PFLP had training camps within striking distance of Jordan and, for the leadership of the PFLP, the King of Jordan himself became a target. There were open confrontations in the streets of Amman between Fedayeen members and the late King Hussein's troops. Wadi Haddad and George Habash were desperate to get the "Palestinian question" into the focus of world attention. Terror on a grand scale would do that for them. It is not certain whether the two men were actually in concert over the operation but, in July 1970, Haddad was in Beirut with Leila Khaled, a committed member of PFLP, planning what has been recorded as one of the most spectacular hijacking events of the twentieth century. The hijacking of international airliners to Dawson's Field in Jordan provoked a reaction around the world, and the traveling public experienced the start of passenger screening security at airports worldwide.

Hijacking of Airliners: A New Tactic?

Over the last forty-five years of the twentieth century, there have been so many attacks of a terrorist nature that it is sometimes hard to recall them. The spectacular ones seem to be held in our mind: the Munich Olympic Games massacre; the Iranian Embassy siege in London; the destruction of the U.S. Marine barracks in Beirut, Lebanon; the Oklahoma City bombing; Pan Am 103 over Lockerbie;

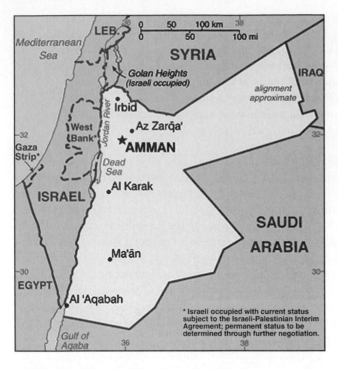

FIGURE 8-6   Map of Jordan (Central Intelligence Agency, *The World Factbook*, 2008).

the Air India bombing off the coast of Ireland; and, of course, the New York World Trade Center and the Pentagon attacks are etched in our memories. The hijacking of airliners and hostages-taking has the immediate ability to focus world attention through media coverage.

The actions of the PFLP almost led to a civil war in its adopted base of Jordan, and certainly led King Hussein to forcibly remove the PLO from the territory. The hijackings were audacious for their sheer nerve, daring, and lack of any respect for international convention.

The first hijacking took place on a TWA Boeing 707 at 11:50 A.M. on September 6, 1970. The plane was en route from Frankfurt, West Germany, to New York. The airliner had a full complement of crew and 145 passengers when it was seized in the skies above Belgium. The pilot was ordered to fly to Jordan. At about the same time, a Swissair DC-8 with a similar number of passengers and crew was seized over France and flown to the same location, Dawson Field, Jordan. At about 2:00 P.M., an attempt was made to hijack a third airliner, an El Al flight en route to Amsterdam from Tel Aviv. Due to confusion at check-in, the El Al hijack team was reduced to three members: Leila Khaled and Patrick Arguello, and the third, an Arab. When the pilot refused to obey their instructions, a violent fight ensued and a flight attendant was shot. An Israeli sky marshal killed the Arab hijacker. Khaled and Arguello were overpowered and the aircraft landed at London's Heathrow Airport. Arguello and Khaled were arrested and taken to a secure Metropolitan Police Station in South London. The remaining members of Khaled's group who had failed to make the flight hijacked a Boeing 747 operated by Pan American Airlines.

The airliner flew to Beirut, where it refueled and went on to Cairo. The PFLP blew the 747 up on the ground at Cairo Airport, after the crew and passengers were taken off. This action by the PFLP, though aimed at the international arena, was a statement to the Egyptian government about its acceptance of the Middle East peace agreement. With hostages numbering about 300 being held in Jordan, the PFLP laid out its demands to the international community. The hijackers demanded the release of the three members of the PFLP who had been jailed for an earlier attack on Zurich Airport, and who were presently languishing in a Swiss jail. They also demanded the same for terrorists being held in West Germany for the Munich Airport attack. Their third demand involved Leila Khaled's release from police custody for attempting to hijack an El Al airliner over Europe. The British government of conservative prime minister Edward Heath was in utter turmoil over how to deal with this problem, so the PFLP gave it another nudge by hijacking a BOAC VC-10 and adding 110 British passengers to the hostage list. After heavy pressure and diplomatic talks, the PFLP moved the hostages to the comfort of Amman, Jordan. Over the next two weeks, the hostages were moved around Amman in small groups before all were released on September 30, 1970. The PFLP had previously destroyed the British, Swiss, and American airliners at Dawson Field before the watchful lenses of the world's media.[36] Aerial terrorism had been born and imprinted on the air traveler's psyche.

The last British hostages were released on the same day that Leila Khaled was flown out of the United Kingdom and back to the Middle East. Israel has always steadfastly refused to negotiate with terrorists, and it strongly criticized the Western powers for giving in. Britain never made that mistake again.

FIGURE 8-7 Leila Khaled, who in 1969 successfully hijacked a TWA airliner to Damascus, Syria, totes a submachine gun at a Palestinian refugee camp in Lebanon in November 1970 (Canadian Press).

LOD (Israel) Airport Attack May 30, 1972

In May 1972 a daring attack led by Kozo Okomato, Yasuda Yasuki, and Okudeira Takushi from the Japanese Red Army, possibly acting on the behest of the Black September group, attacked Lod Airport. The team arrived at the airport near Tel Aviv and pulled from their luggage Czech made 7.62 machine guns. They opened fire indiscriminately in the terminal building and killed twenty-four instantly and injured seventy-seven others. Two of the attackers were killed by Israeli security and Kozo Okomato was tried by Israel and sentenced to life in prison but was released in May 1985 in a prisoner exchange with the PFLP-General Command. Kozo fled to Libya. In February 1997, he was arrested again, this time in Lebanon, but was deported and then he eventually disappeared. Today he is rumored to be living in North Korea.[37]

These events pushed the Middle East to the brink of war. The Bonn Summit conference of major Western powers met in 1978 and agreed to sanctions against states that aided and abetted the hijacking of aircraft. The countries agreeing were the United States, the United Kingdom, Canada, France, Italy, Japan, and West Germany.

Jordan in the Twenty-First Century

Jordan's wider role in Middle Eastern affairs is relevant for the fledgling Palestinian government of Mahmoud Abbas, who is considered to be pro-Jordanian. To assist in security, Jordan's King Abdullah has allowed Palestinian fighters to return to the West Bank. Most of these fighters have been trained by the Jordanian military and are pro-Jordan. Abdullah has also requested the Israelis to allow this action to take place. This is Jordan's opportunity to play a major role in the security of the West Bank, a region it considers part of its Hashemite Kingdom. At the same time, any attacks against the stability of the Abbas regime could be tempered with the presence of Jordanian-trained

Palestinian fighters. On its other flank are the problems of insurgents from Jordan fighting and supporting attacks against U.S. forces in Iraq. One such prominent fighter was Abu Musab al-Zarqawi, born in Jordan in 1966 of Palestinian parentage. He has been named as the link between Iraq and al Qaeda until his sudden death in a targetted bombing by the United States in June 2006. He had been involved with terrorist activities for many years and is thought to have been one of Osama bin Laden's chief supporters. He is believed to have been in Afghanistan in 1990–1991 and while the intervening years record little of his activities he did surface again in 1999 when he planned the Millenium attack on the Radison Hotel in Amman Jordan. The plot was discovered and so was his involvement—he was sentenced to fifteen years in prison in absentia. He returned to Afghanistan in 2000 and set up training camps that specialized in chem/bio weapons training.

When the Taliban were routed in 2001 he was suffering from a leg wound which took him to Iraq where his leg was amputated. During his recovery in Iraq he set up a base for his training operations, presumably with the blessing of the Iraqi regime. Zarqawi was linked to the assassination of a U.S. official in Jordan in late 2002. He returned to northern Iraq in 2003 and the fruits of his training were discovered in Britian when severel suspects, who had direct links to him, were arrested for plotting to put ricin toxin into the military food supply.

Zarqawi continued to focus attacks also on his homeland, Jordan. In November 2005 he dispatched suicide bombers to target three U.S. owned hotels in Amman, Jordan, killing fifty-seven and injuring hundreds, all the dead and injured were Jordanians.

LEBANON

Lebanon has been in existence for centuries and is occupied by both Christians and Muslims. The Christians settled mainly in the mountainous regions while the Muslims inhabited the coastal region. Like most of the Middle East, the area was under the rule of the Turkish Ottoman Empire until the end of World War I. After the war, the French began to prepare the region for independent status. The French assisted in the creation of the Lebanese Constitution. Lebanon gained its full independence in 1943 and, like its population; the government was designed to reflect the two majority religions, Christian and Muslim. From its very early days as an independent state, Lebanon had close links to Western powers. In the 1950s and 1960s, Beirut was affectionately called the "Riviera of the Middle East." Its hotels and restaurants and vibrant market scene made it a popular spot for tourists and the wealthy. Its location on the Mediterranean Sea helped it flourish as a port as well as a business center. Significant incidents brought about drastic changes in the Lebanese way of life, beginning with what must be termed an uprising. The first signs of trouble surfaced in 1958, when dissatisfied Muslims violently opposed the government's strengthening of ties to the West. The uprising was tempered when U.S. forces were sent to the aid of Lebanon, and all seemed to return to relative tranquility in short order.

Palestinians Come to Lebanon

With the PLO's reversal of fortunes in 1969—when it was forcefully evicted by King Hussein's Jordanian Army troops—its members spilled into Lebanon in dramatic numbers. King Hussein's actions were in response to the

FIGURE 8-8   Map of Lebanon (Central Intelligence Agency, *The World Factbook*, 2008).

rapidly growing number of confrontations between the PLO and Jordan's military. Support for the embattled King came by way of monetary contributions from the United States on a regular basis. The United States applied pressure on the Jordanian King, threatening to tighten the purse strings, and the eviction of the PLO was imminent.

The PLO was expelled from Jordan and it relocated primarily to Lebanon. This move, which took place in September, gave rise to the Black September terrorist group (which, as mentioned earlier, reached worldwide notoriety at the Munich Olympic Games in 1974). The Arab Muslim population in Lebanon swelled, but its people were treated, at best, as fourth-class citizens. Many lived in the shabby refugee camps around Beirut International Airport. Sabra and Shatila and areas of southern Lebanon that were in easy striking distance of Israel, remain in infamy as testament to the atrocities committed by Christian militias. PLO terror campaigns continued with strikes against Israel from these havens in south Lebanon. These actions further destabilized not only the government of Lebanon, but the country as a whole.

By 1975, the constant warring from the PLO incursions into Israel and the retaliatory strikes by the Israeli air force against these Palestinian camps brought the country to civil war. The PLO in Lebanon was widely supported by the predominately Muslim Arabs, but was opposed by the Lebanese Christians. To the casual observer, Beirut and all of Lebanon have seen a never-ending cycle of violence perpetrated by warring factions from within the country's borders and from unsympathetic neighbors such as Syria, Iran, Iraq, and Israel. What for many was an "Orchid in the Mediterranean" turned rapidly into a patch of thistles and thorns—a lawless society with a feeble government unable to restore order or control both internal and external elements bent on its destruction. The style and structure of terrorism to be played out in this theater of conflict can be viewed as political in nature. It is considered to be the oldest technique of psychological warfare— political terrorism may be defined simply as coercive intimidation. It is the systemic use of murder and destruction, or the threat of murder and destruction, in order to terrorize individuals, groups, communities, or governments into conceding to the terrorist's political demands.[38] While Syria had its own agenda and a desire to include Lebanon as a part of greater Syria, far more sinister notions were spreading outward from the Persian state of Iran.

The last decade of the twentieth century saw relative calm return to the streets of Beirut. However, the city continues to echo the problems of a bygone decade. In January 2002, a car bomb killed a Lebanese Christian warlord, Elie Hobeika, who had a dubious past and was a militia leader, armed and equipped by the Israeli military under the control of Ariel Sharon. Hobeika may have led the assault on the refugee camps of Sabra and Shatila near Beirut International Airport in 1982, massacring Palestinian civilians. All of this occurred with the knowledge and connivance of the Israeli military.

Hobeika had served as a Lebanese government minister until 1988, but as recently as 2001 he had agreed to give evidence against Ariel Sharon at the Belgian war crimes inquiry. Hobeika's record of involvement in the massacres is somewhat incomplete. Some say he directed operations of Christian fighters from outside of the camps. A 1983 Israeli investigation into the massacres concluded that Sharon bore indirect responsibility and that Hobeika did not enter the camps. Who profits from the death of Hobeika? Many would wish him dead, and not least of all, Palestinians. But the finger could equally be pointed at Israel for the embarrassment his testimony in Belgium would have caused the Israeli government. The group claiming responsibility for his death calls itself the "Lebanese for a Free and Independent Lebanon." However, the group has not been identified by any mainstream opposition groups in the country and could well be a cover name for some other organization.[39]

Political Assassinations

Assassination of anti-Syria politicians in Lebanon has been a feature of the political landscape for the last decade. Rafik Hariri a former Lebanese Prime Minister and outspoken opponent of Syria was killed in a massive car bomb attack in February 2005 and in June of the same year a leading anti-Syrian journalist was killed in a similar fashion. George Hawi the former Lebanese Communist Party leader was killed in a car bombing in June 2005 and the following month the Defence minister Elias al-Murr was seriously injured in an assassination attempt. In September an outspoken journalist from Lebanese Broadcasting was also injured in an assassination attack. In December another anti-Syrian Parliamentarian was killed in a car bomb attack and in November 2006 Pierre Gemayel, a Maronite Christian and very outspoken against Syria was assassinated when his car was ambushed by gunmen.[40]

ISLAM

Before we proceed to discuss the bloodbath that Beirut became, the student should understand some fundamental philosophies about the world of Islam. Islam is a religious faith much like any other. However, it is actually divided into two separate spheres of influence: the Sunni sect and the Shi'a sect. There are Five Pillars of Islam:

- Shehada—The statement in Arabic that says: "There is no god but Allah and Mohammed is Prophet."
- Salah—Prayer five times a day. Prayer in Islam is praise of God.
- Zakat—The paying of alms to the poor. This is traditionally calculated at 2.5 percent. Different Muslim countries have differing views on Zakat now that income tax is a reality for many.
- Ramadan—The month of holy fasting. During Ramadan, Muslims must not eat, drink, or make love from sunrise to sunset.
- Hajj—Pilgrimage to Mecca. This is an obligation of all Muslims who can afford it to make the trek to Mecca in Saudi Arabia once in their lifetime.[41]

Sunni Muslims account for about 90 percent of the world's Muslim population; the remaining 10 percent is Shi'a Muslims. Struggles between the two groups date back as far as the seventh century; both hold the Quran as their sacred text and Mohammed as the Last Prophet. The Shiites have and believe in their own version of Islamic law and their own theology. The Shiites believe in a chain of leaders, or Imams, who came after Mohammed, and in a structure of spiritual authority through mullahs and a religious establishment.[42] Iran has the largest population of Shi'a Muslims in the world.

So, with an unstable government and warring factions fighting openly in the streets of Beirut, the country was ripe for the radicals to move in. With the Shah of Iran deposed and an Islamic revolution underway, the actions of fundamentalists spread to the Middle East.

The Shi'a Sect in Lebanon

Imam Mousa el-Sadr, an Iranian-born cleric, was the undisputed leader of the Shi'a community in Lebanon by the end of the 1960s.[43] The Shi'a community was not, at this point, involved in any type of terrorist activity. Shiites were, however, aligned to politically defend and represent the poor of Lebanon. Together with Gregoire Haddad, a Catholic archbishop, they set up Haraket el-Mahroumeen, or Movement of the Deprived. This group's stated intention was to work within the Lebanese political system to achieve its political objectives. With the passing of time, the Imam found it no easy task to reach his goals for the poor and oppressed so he changed his doctrine and approach to the government. His party would become rejectionist and take up the sword to fight the injustices. The group was known by the acronym AMAL. In stark contrast to its near neighbors in Iran, the Shi'a sectarian movement continued to operate within the political system after the civil war of 1975. The Lebanese Shi'a community saw a significant ray of sunshine with the formation of a government out of the Iranian Revolution, particularly given the background and birthplace of the Imam. His contacts and involvement with the Iranian movement, as well as the leadership of AMAL, was to end with his abduction and disappearance in 1978. A natural vacuum now ensued and the AMAL became the Islamic AMAL, with headquarters in the Bekaa Valley of Lebanon under the new auspices of Hussein el-Musawi. Islamic Amal was now foundering. Musawi joined forces to bring AMAL under the umbrella of Hezbollah.

HEZBOLLAH

The origins and development of the Hezbollah movement in Lebanon represent the most important and successful example of Islamic Iran's efforts to export its pan-Islamic brand of revolution beyond its border.[44] Hezbollah is also known as:

- Islamic Jihad
- Ansarollah
- Organization of the Oppressed
- Party of God
- Revolutionary Justice Organization

The goal of Hezbollah was, and is, to establish an Islamic state in Lebanon.[45] The establishment of the Hezbollah in Lebanon was supported and financed by the revolutionary government of Iran; even members of the Revolutionary Guard were sent to the Bekaa Valley to join with the training cadres. It is widely accepted that the Hezbollah is controlled and directed by radical Shiite clerics under the more central control of Iran through contacts in the Syrian capital of Damascus. Up until his death in 1989, the supreme guardian of revolutionary causes was the Ayatollah Khomeini, who called on "all oppressed Muslims to replace their governments with Islamic Fundamentalist ones." His brand of terror stretched far and wide and with sweeping ferocity, he used terror as his instrument of punishment. His continued diatribes against the Great Satan,[46] his term for the United States, and his religious Fatwa (of death sentence) against the British author Salman Rushdie for writing a novel called the *Satanic Verses*, constantly stirred the boiling pot of the Middle East.

With Hezbollah's rise to prominence in 1982, the group became a further embarrassment to the Lebanese government. Prior to the Israeli invasion of Southern Lebanon, which led to the PLO retreating to Tunis, the streets of Beirut were governed by warring militia groups. These included the indigenous Druze populace of the hills around Beirut airport. It was not uncommon for rockets and mortars to be fired over the airport at the Palestinian positions nearby, causing chaos, damage, and destruction.

Hezbollah's main targets are the Israeli Jews, but it has also targeted non-Islamic influences in Europe, the United States, and Latin America. The United States is considered a legitimate target, as are other Western powers with U.S. alliances and its Middle East policies. With the withdrawal of the Israeli army from Southern Lebanon, Hezbollah has been able to prosper and recruit combatants for its "Holy War" against Israeli targets, most being military in nature. The Al-Manar TV network broadcasts a constant and objective view portraying the values of "martyrdom" (of suicide). This network is broadcast across a wide expanse and is viewed by 25 million viewers in the Arab world. It is also broadcast into the occupied territories and viewed by countless thousands of Palestinians. The intentional objective of this TV network is ". . . to encourage people to martyr themselves," in the words of Nayef Krayem, chairman of the network.[47] Beirut streets under the control of Hezbollah are marked with flags displaying the images of martyrs who have completed their missions. Nevertheless, Beirut is still the temporary home to thousands of Palestinian refugees who are denied the same rights as the indigenous population and continue to live in abject squalor. Hezbollah has managed to garner prestige from the Arab states by being responsible for the ultimate Israeli withdrawal from Southern Lebanon. The messages being sent to the Gaza region through such methods as the Al-Manar network may sow the seeds for more martyrs from the Palestinian population, but unlike Hezbollah, the Palestinians are unable to retreat away in the hills of Lebanon to escape the wrath of the Israeli military.

In any discussion covering Lebanese terrorism, there is always the specter of Syria to be considered. Syria has been involved in every aspect of Lebanon's existence for the last twenty-five years. Both Syria and Iran actively support the activities of Hezbollah, which is the best trained and equipped military force in Lebanon. Syria has always considered its presence in Lebanon a necessity to prevent civil war breaking out between Muslim and Christians. Syria's presence in the country for more than twenty-five years is testament to that action, but its involvement is crucial to its own economy. Therefore, the February 14, 2005, bomb attack that killed the former Lebanese

Prime Minister Rafik Hariri, an act laid at the feet of Syria by the international community, is somewhat difficult to fathom. Hariri has had a long hatred for the Syrian presence and interference in Lebanon and had been instrumental in calling for a Syrian withdrawal from the country. It is highly doubtful whether it will ever be established exactly who or which faction or state ordered the Hariri's assassination, but it was troubling to observe his bodyguard had been significantly reduced and along with it all his experienced protection specialists. Syria has vigorously denied that it had any involvement, and instead pointed the finger at Israel. Syria has been losing its grip on Lebanon since the death of the former Syrian President Hafez al-Assad in 2000. Its attempt to trample the Lebanese Constitution by extending the presidency of its hand-picked puppet, Emil Lahoud, by three years was greeted with outrage on the streets of Beirut. Assad died just one month after the final Israeli withdrawal from Southern Lebanon. The young son of the former president, and his successor, is not necessarily as competent to deal with his father's old guard, who would view any concessions as a sign of weakness. There is always the probability that, in a move to undermine the young Syrian president, forces from within the Syrian intelligence and security apparatus may have conspired to kill Hariri and set Assad up for the ultimate fall. There is no definite evidence to link the killing to Syria; however, the likelihood of it being any other is unlikely. The subsequent pullout of Syrian troops—at the demand of the United States and the wider international community—will cause problems at home for President Bashir Assad, in particular. With Hezbollah such an immense force in Lebanon, it is entirely probable that the U.S. demands on Syria to withdraw have a lot to do with the American and Israeli desire to nullify Hezbollah, a group that has been responsible for any number of embarrassing attacks against both countries.

Kidnapping

This is not a new tactic in the terrorist's arsenal, but the speed and efficiency with which Hezbollah conducted kidnappings and executions in Beirut took the Western world completely by surprise. The January 1987 kidnapping of Terry Waite, the Archbishop of Canterbury's special envoy to the Middle East, was remarkable in that it was carried almost live on the major news networks. Hezbollah believed, at the time, that Terry Waite was working for the CIA. However, news bulletins, which showed Waite leaving an aircraft in Cyprus several steps ahead of Colonel Oliver North, provided ample incitement for the kidnappers to justify their actions. The refusal of the British and the United States to deal with terrorists or acquiesce to their demands resulted in Terry Waite and others being incarcerated for several years in the suburbs of Beirut before their eventual release in 1991.

Structure and Development

From its original inception, Hezbollah operated like a "halfway house" for terrorists. It appears that Hezbollah received its direction from three different people within its hierarchy: Abu Musawi, Hassan Nasrallah, and Sheik Mohammed Hussein Fadollah, the last being the Hezbollah's spiritual leader. As a former fighter with the Islamic Amal, Nasrallah's role was to format a terrorist force for the Southern Lebanon region.[48]

As noted earlier, Hezbollah was intent on establishing an Islamic state in Lebanon. This would undoubtedly not be welcomed by the style of government established with the creation of Lebanon in the first quarter of the century, which assured that government would predominantly be in the hands of the Maronite Christian majority. As no census had been taken in the country for decades, it was probable that the Maronite Christians were no longer in the majority, a fact not lost on the Beirut militia commanders. With so many different groups fighting for control of the streets and the government, Hezbollah was not content to act like the PLO—as an umbrella for other groups. With the death of Musawi, Nasrallah turned his terrorist forces toward the same style of revolution as had occurred in Iran and effectively created a regional militia movement. Many other groups had, by 1991, laid down their arms and signed a peace accord. Hezbollah, on the other hand, remained the one major force against the Israelis in Southern Lebanon and has been waging a terrorist campaign ever since.

Hezbollah used the human bomb to great effect, as did the Islamic Jihad. Hezbollah is blamed for the suicide bomb attack on the U.S. Marine barracks in West Beirut in October 1983. A suicide bomber drove a truck loaded with explosives and detonated it as he crashed into the camp. The impact was devastating, taking the lives of 241 U.S. Marines. The outcry in the United States was loud and clear: "What are our boys doing over there?" In spite of the carnage and outrage, the suicide attacks continued with spontaneous irregularity and with the same devastating results. Intelligence on the group was scant, at best, and bringing any culprit to trial was almost impossible.

The terror tactics employed in Beirut significantly changed on March 28, 1986, when two British teachers were kidnapped in what had been considered, until this time, the "safe" area of West Beirut. The following month, Brian Keenan, a British national with dual nationality in the Republic of Ireland, was abducted. The following week, one of the Muslim militia groups operating in West Beirut announced that it had executed a British journalist, Peter Collett. The next day, the three bodies of the Americans—Peter Kilburn, Leigh Douglas, and Philip Padfield—were discovered, and another journalist, John McCarthy, was kidnapped. Beirut had become an extremely hostile place for Westerners. Hezbollah does not confine its attacks against the state of Lebanon exclusively to the Middle East theater; it is, in fact, a true international terrorist group with the ability to strike at Jewish targets throughout the world. Through local cell structures in South America, Hezbollah is believed to have been responsible for several large bomb attacks in Buenos Aires in 1994, and a car bombing in London.

Nazarallah, considered to be one of the shrewdest politicians in Lebanon as well as being the Secretary General of Hezbollah, has declared that his movement will not give up its arms, but with the withdrawal of Syrian troops, Hezbollah will continue to defend the interests of Syria. Syria's withdrawal poses the most serious challenge to the Shiite movement since the end of the civil war. If Hezbollah continues to defend the Syrian cause, it could well be on a collision course with a new Lebanese government and risks alienating its strong support among the country's 1.2 million Shiites, currently the largest single sect in the country. Nazarallah's ability to mobilize hundreds of thousands of Shiites, along with those from the thirty or so pro-Syrian factions in Lebanon, threatens to expose the deep rift within Lebanese society—the very crisis the Syrians always maintained their presence prevented. Lebanon's recent history has been one of constant bloodletting as well as of political opportunism by the various sects, who have repeatedly hired themselves out to regional powers to advance their sectarian interests. Syria was the last to play such a game.[49]

AT WAR WITH ISRAEL

During the summer of 2006 Hezbollah fighters made an incursion into Israel and captured two Israeli soldiers, and this set off a chain of events over the summer months that has had a lasting effect not only on the political fortunes of the Israeli government but also on the Lebanese. The naval blockade of Lebanon which the Israelis initiated after the raid and bombings of suspected Hezbollah strongholds in Southern Lebanon and the Bekaa Valley received a response that the Israeli's seemed ill prepared to handle. The Israeli strategy was a bombing campaign followed up by a conventional ground war with Israeli forces advancing as far as the Litani River. It became apparent that the Israeli government may have severely underestimated the abilities as well as the strength of Hezbollah who were well trained, equipped, and entrenched for the Israeli attack. They possessed a huge arsenal of rockets with which they targeted Israel even reaching the outskirts of Haifa. Although the Israeli response was probably not what the Hezbollah were expecting, while the Lebanese government were powerless to prevent it from happening. As long as there are Israeli troops occupying Southern Lebanon then there will continue to be a reason for Hezbollah to attack them. Hezbollah gained a certain notoriety and significant Arab sympathy and support for its actions. Hezbollah has a significant political foothold in Lebanon and is heavily involved in community programs. Any attempt by the Lebanese government to curtail the fighters would provoke the Shiite population and inflame many of the sectarian passions that were responsible for Lebanon's long civil war. For the West to have any effect on curtailing Hezbollah's popularity in Lebanon it will have to show and provide aid in significant proportions—as at the moment Hezbollah is filling that void exclusively.[50] What surprised most observers of the war with Israel was the fact that Hezbollah was in a position to operate at will without any hindrance from the Lebanese army. In addition, they were able to prosecute a conventional war thanks to state-of-the-art weapons and supplies they had received from Iran which included the latest shoulder launched anti-tank missiles as well as night vision equipment. Hezbollah was able to benefit from territorial control in southern Lebanon without having to be concerned with the obligations and vulnerabilities that come with governance. It used state-of-the-art missiles to not only target the Israeli military but it also rained missiles on Israeli towns. This was the first time a guerrilla army had managed to keep up a sustained bombardment on its enemy's territory and the psychological effect that this had on the Israeli public was enormous. Hezbollah had managed to maintain its foothold in the south after the Israeli withdrawal in 2000 and gave the rationale that it was the Lebanese resistance protecting the interests of the Shiite populous and they based this on the fact that in their opinion the Israelis continued to occupy a tiny portion of Israel, the border region of Sheba Farm.

While most of our attention is directed at the Islamic extremists from the Shiite sect, it also necessary to understand what is happening with the Sunnis in Lebanon. The western section of Beirut is the predominantly Sunni area of the city and since the assassination of al-Hariri in 2005, his son Saad al-Harir has begun to arm and lead the Sunni militia. They are getting support from Jordan and Saudi Arabia. The Sunnis are arming themselves out of a sense of preservation against Shiite aggression. During the Lebanese civil war the Sunnis looked to the PLO for protection and since the open warfare of 2006 between Hezbollah and Israel, the Sunnis have come to realize that they need their own militias to protect themselves.

The successes of Hezbollah are partly due to its fanatical and charismatic leader, Sheikh Hassan Nasrallah, rather than any inspiration from Tehran, but Nasrallah's stature has far exceeded Iranian expectations and is viewed with some skepticism for his accommodating approach to dealings with the Lebanese government. Israel has long sought to have him and others at the top table of Hezbollah assassinated, and the death of Imad Mugniyah in February 2008 indicates that Nasrallah although no longer openly appearing at public gatherings or party meetings is considered a definite target for the Mossad. Iran still holds the purse strings and has no doubt insisted that Nasrallah remain out of sight.

SYRIA

Syria has been a major player in the Israeli/Palestinian problems. This Muslim country has a population that is 90 percent Sunni Muslim. Syria gained independence from France in 1946, and by the mid-1960s the Baath party rose to power with Hafez al-Assad as its President. For years, Syria had been dominated by a succession of military governments. Assad, a former Air Force Colonel, died in 2001 and his power passed to his son, Bashar al-Assad, who continues much as his father did. Syria is a longtime supporter of the Palestinian cause and a sworn enemy of Israel. It has fought two unsuccessful campaigns against Israel and lost control of the Golan Heights on its southern border.

Although Syria both sponsors and harbors terrorists, it is likely that any terrorist acts perpetrated on its soil would be quickly suppressed. Assad himself shied away from the public eye and quietly assisted groups such as Islamic jihad and Hezbollah by allowing Iran to resupply them through Damascus. Assad's government was in open conflict with U.S. forces stationed in Lebanon and, in 1983, shot down an unarmed U.S. reconnaissance flight. Syria tries to maintain

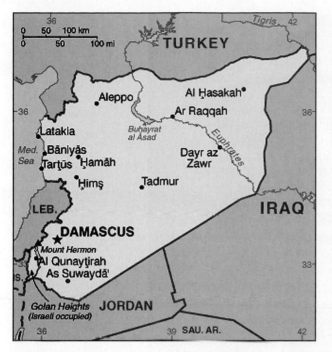

FIGURE 8-9 Map of Syria (Central Intelligence Agency, *The World Factbook*, 2008).

some measure of control over Hezbollah and its actions. It continues to hedge its bets and maintains a thriving business in support of training camps for expatriate terror groups such as the PFLP-GC, led by Ahmad Jibril, the Palestine Islamic Jihad; and the Japanese Red Army. Not far away in the Bekaa Valley are members of the Kurdish Workers Party (PKK), led by the university-educated Abdullah Ocalan, who spent time in Syria before his capture and death sentence in Ankara in 2000.

Syria does not permit homegrown terrorists to perpetrate actions against the state, and Assad's government violently suppresses any attempts, particularly by Islamic fundamentalists, to disrupt the workings of the state. Terrorists, fundamentalists and other political factions are suppressed in the one-party state of Syria. Despite this, the Muslim Brotherhood has attempted to raise its banner in Syria.

In 1982, an open revolt in the city of Hama by Islamic fundamentalists resulted in the Syrian army taking immediate and decisive action to crush the uprising, which resulted in many deaths and casualties. Syria does, however, continue to provide a safe haven for terrorist groups that are currently active. Among those groups that have headquarters and training camps in Syria are the Popular Front for the Liberation of Palestine General Command (PFLP-GC) under Ahmad Jibril, and Palestinian Islamic Jihad (PIJ). President George Bush included Syria in his list of countries forming an "axis of evil" in 2002. Al-Assad has openly expressed support for the U.S. War on Terror, but he has done little or nothing in support of it. Only time will tell whether al-Assad has the capability and fortitude to weather pressure from the United States and take some decisive steps against Hamas, the PFLP, and other groups that maintain close terrorist ties. The young president is often viewed as sitting on the fence and, although there is evidence of Syria's involvement in the U.S. practice of "extreme rendition," perhaps as a shrewd attempt to curry favor with the world superpower, he also has managed to disengage his military's visual presence in Lebanon and so far survive. No doubt, the humiliation of being pressured to move out will have far-reaching effects on Syria, as its own economy was tightly entwined with that of Lebanon.

Mossad Targeted Assassination?

A car bombing in Damascus on February 12, 2008, claimed the life of the legendary Hezbollah leader Imad Mughniyah nicknamed "The Wolf." He had managed to evade capture or death at the hands of the **Mossad** and the CIA for years. Mughniyah was the head of orperations for Hezbollah and was killed after leaving a Syrian intelligence office in Damascus. Israel is obviously the prime suspect in his death but quite naturally is not claiming any responsibility for any action in Syria. Mughniyah had strong ties to the Iranian Intelligence Service and was responsible for a vast number of terrorist attacks including masterminding the U.S. Embassy bombing and numerous airline hijackings. He would have been a major target for the Israeli Mossad.

In the wider events of the Middle East, Syria has become more of a U.S. target—its designation as being part of the "Axis of Evil" could well indicate it is next (after Iraq) for U.S. invasion. Syria enjoys, on its eastern flank, a border with Iraq. Prior to the Iraq invasion by U.S. and allied troops,

FIGURE 8-10 FBI "Most Wanted Terrorist" Imad Mughniyeh, killed in a Damascus car bombing on February 12, 2008. Mughniyeh, a Hezbollah military commander, was suspected for the bombing that killed 230 U.S. Marines in Beirut in 1983 as well as numerous plane hijackings and terrorist attacks (Canadian Press).

Syria was likely sending supplies and weapons into the region. Syria has long been a state sponsor of numerous terrorist groups throughout the last forty years and, with the presence of so many foreign troops on Muslim soil, Syria's willingness and ability to prevent insurgents going into Iraq would be questionable. The United States feels it has three main issues with Syria:

- Its ongoing support for Hezbollah.
- Border security, as it affects U.S. troop security within Iraq.
- Its support for Palestinian rejectionist groups.

Syria's close ties with Iran will also make for complex problems in the region. Iran's unabated nuclear program will only strengthen the Bush Administration's resolve to take some sort of punitive action against one or the other—or both—of these state sponsors. Syria remains a constant threat to Israel while continuing its close relationship with both Iran and its regional proxy Hezbollah. Syria which lies to the immediate south of Turkey has managed to establish a relationship with that government at it sees the country's anti-U.S. stance as positive for its relationship with Turkey.

Syria expelled PKK leader Abdullah Ocalan in 1998 after threats of military intervention from Turkey. Relationships have changed dramatically between the two countries. In October 2007, Syria openly supported Turkey's decision to mount cross border military operations to attack Kurdish rebels. The Syrians need the Turks more than Turkey needs Syria. Turkey of course has the respect of other Arab countries in the region and also Israel and the relationship with the United States will only be a temporary issue. Nevertheless Syrian–Iranian relations remain a source of intense concern to Arab countries. Syria also considers itself to be the main power broker on issues relative to Lebanon and its involvement in curtailing some of the insurgent activity in Iraq has achieved international recognition. While Syria takes one step forward it encumbers itself with two steps backwards in its ongoing activities with Hezbollah. Assad will also need to be certain that he can control any Jihadist threat at home and he has the security apparatus as well as his military to conduct any crackdown as necessary. Since the U.S.-led invasion of Iraq, the Syrians have facilitated the free flow of Islamist fighters across its border and into Iraq to fight against American troops.

THE REST OF NORTH AFRICA

Now that we have examined the core of the terrorism problems in the Middle East, we will continue with the next ring of terror in North Africa: Algeria, Morocco, Libya, Egypt, and others. The prospects for peace in the Middle East, which at one time looked promising, have turned ominously in the opposite direction since 1993, especially with extreme Islamic groups operating from Egypt and elsewhere.

MOROCCO

This North African country, neatly sandwiched between the Atlantic Ocean and Algeria, has been remarkably adept at keeping terrorism at bay. The Moroccan government has rigorously investigated all terrorist acts and threats and has been successful in countering any Islamic radicalism unrest within its borders. Morocco also arrested a member of the Algerian Islamic Salvation Front in December 1997.[51] Morocco gained its independence from French rule in 1955, after rioting broke out when the French sent the Sultan into exile. The uprising resulted in the Sultan being returned to his native Morocco. Sultan Mohammad V changed his title to that of "King" and established a constitutional monarchy to oversee and control all aspects of governing the country. On his death in 1961, his son Hassan assumed the mantle of King and also Prime Minister. Since its independence, Morocco has laid claims to regions of the Saharan Desert under Spanish mandate. Both Morocco and Mauritania had claims on the region and had to contend with the Polisario Front, an indigenous group operating in the Sahara region. The Polisario Front wanted self-determination and was not likely to accept being consumed by either Mauritania or Morocco. Mauritania dropped its claim to the desert region and, in its place, Morocco claimed the whole area. In its efforts to stave off Morocco, the Polisario Front received military support from Libya and Algeria.

On his death in 1999, Hassan was succeeded by his son. King Mohammed VI has been a strong U.S. ally in the War on Terror and although many Moroccans have been involved in al Qaeda-style attacks in Europe, the Moroccan regime has hit hard at Islamic extremists attempting to upset the status quo within the country. An attack by Islamic extremists in Casablanca in May 2003 killed more than forty-two, mostly Moroccan civilians, even though the bomb attacks were at five different locations—a Spanish social club, the Belgian Embassy, a Jewish cemetery, a resort hotel, and a Jewish community center. These simultaneous attacks came close after a string of similar events in Saudi Arabia and were likely the work of al Qaeda operatives within Morocco. The important issue here is that al Qaeda is far from being harried and chased out of its support bases in the Middle East. It seems capable of planning and setting up attacks of this scale in two Muslim countries at a time when George Bush was informing the world that al Qaeda might be a spent force—the reality is quite the contrary. For its part, the Moroccan King and his government have hit hard at suspected Islamic extremists within Morocco. Although severely criticized for

FIGURE 8-11 Map of Morocco (Central Intelligence Agency, *The World Factbook*, 2008).

human rights abuses while doing so, Morocco seems determined to hold down the terror factions within its borders and assist in the U.S. War on Terror. There is growing evidence of increased jihadist activity no doubt inspired by al Qaeda in this region and in spring 2007 a string of suicide attacks in Rabat had all the hallmarkings of an al Qaeda-inspired campaign. Both Algeria and Morocco are cooperating and exchanging intelligence information with Western governments and particularly, Spain, the United Kingdom, and the United States. Most of the attacks to date have not been particularly well planned or sophisticated in their operational execution allowing authorities to uncover caches of explosives. The stability of both Morocco and Algeria will depend heavily on how much material training these jihadists will get in the coming months. Whether there is capability for training and expertise available from any jihadists returning from actions in Iraq will no doubt dictate the level of effectiveness of attacks in the future. There is absolutely no doubt that the current batches of jihadists are willing to take the fight into the cities of Morocco.

EGYPT

The history of Egyptian contributions to modern society is fascinating. Egypt's feat of civil engineering, craftsmanship, and overall attention to detail in developing a dynasty before most of the world became civilized is a matter of historic record. The influences of the Egyptian people and the Pharaohs swept through Africa, the Middle East, and Mesopotamia, dominating societies for centuries. Even now, the study of ancient Egyptian writings occupies the dedication of countless professors and universities. It is believed that the first Egyptian pyramid was built 2,500 years before the birth of Christ. Egypt became a part of the Roman Empire in 31 B.C. and Roman rule dominated Egypt until approximately 395 A.D. when the country was overrun and ruled by Muslims from the Arabian Peninsula.

Twentieth-Century Politics

History sometimes repeats itself and that is the case with Egypt, which had been a country within the Ottoman Empire. The Muslim Brotherhood, which comprises a large percentage of native Egyptians, played a major part in the assassination of President Anwar Sadat in 1991. Sadat's readiness to make a peace deal with the Israeli government was as much about economics as anything else. Egypt was suffering from excessive military spending and Sadat had promised that this would be lessened with the signing of a peace treaty with the Israelis. At the latter part of the 1970s, Israel considered Egypt to be its most powerful enemy, as well as its next-door neighbor. A deal between the two countries was being brokered under the influence of U.S. President Jimmy Carter and, on March 29, 1979, in Washington DC, Menachem Begin and Anwar Sadat

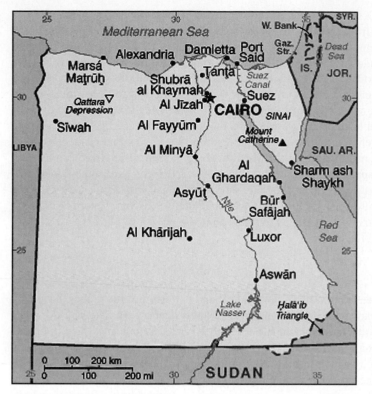

FIGURE 8-12 Map of Egypt (Central Intelligence Agency, *The World Factbook*, 2008).

signed a peace accord. In hindsight, this may have been the political action that led to Saddat's untimely assassination. Immediately after the signing of the historic treaty, a summit of Arab League nations was held in Baghdad. The result was that Egypt was ostracized, both economically and politically, from the Arab world. Under the terms of the treaty, the Israelis gave up the Sinai in return for a peace deal and financial support from the United States. Similarly, Egypt was now an outcast Arab state that was dependent on the United States for its aid. A large majority of Egyptians welcomed the accord.

The Muslim Brotherhood

Christians and Muslims have occupied Egypt for centuries. Egyptians who are born Christians are referred to as Copts, and number about 5 to 6 million. Formed in 1922 by Sheik al Banna, the Brotherhood stood solidly as President Nasser's most vitriolic of opponents in Egypt. There had been an attempt on his life by a member of the Brotherhood, which gave Nasser the excuse he needed to round up and jail the membership and proclaim a ban on the movement. The Brotherhood would see an about-face by the presidential office with the arrival of Sadat, and those factions of the Brotherhood willing to support Sadat against his extreme left opponents were themselves supported with large donations. The Brotherhood would eventually bite the hand that fed it, with considerable ferocity.

ANWAR SADAT, 1919–1981

Over time, Anwar Sadat's style of government became increasingly autocratic. Although he had suggested that Egypt would benefit economically from the Peace Accord, there was no immediate change regarding military spending. In fact, spending in this area increased. Sadat was not gaining any allies among his Arab neighbors as he continued to attempt to keep the Peace Accord with Israel alive. Israel's attentions, by 1981, were diverted to the Northeast and Lebanon. When the Israeli invasion of Southern Lebanon began in 1982, the peace process with Egypt became mired in the sand. On the homefront in 1981, Sadat was now facing increasing hostilities from the Muslim fundamentalists of the Brotherhood. Far from supporting Sadat, the Brotherhood was now actively challenging his rule. In June 1981, fighting erupted between Muslims and Christians in Cairo, which resulted in massive property damage and a large number of deaths. Sadat began to suppress the Brotherhood and arrested 1,500 members, including many of the organization's leaders.[52] Clearly out in the cold, Sadat's only close ally was the United States. This alliance fueled the Muslim Brotherhood's hatred of Sadat. This hatred was not aimed at the government, but at Sadat himself. President Nasser was, by all accounts, mourned by an entire nation; not so with the passing of Sadat. The Sadat government was seen as increasingly corrupt, with ordinary Egyptians suffering food shortages. Sadat's promise of a better life for Egyptians never seemed to materialize.

At a military review on October 6, 1981, Sadat was taking the salute when he was cut down by a burst of machine gun fire from his own troops in a bloody twenty-five-second rampage. The planning was meticulous and allowed the assassins to reach the dais. A three-ton military transport stopped in front of the grandstand and Lieutenant El-Sambouli and his co-conspirators opened fire on Sadat, killing him and six others in the grandstand instantly. Thirty others received serious injuries. There was no spontaneous eruption of violence, no revolution to carry the Muslim Brotherhood forward in Egypt, which had been the intention of the Muslim cell involved in the attack. Although Western world leaders and governments mourned his passing, Egyptians seemed to breathe a collective sigh of relief and, to some extent, regarded Lt. El-Sambouli as a hero. With Islamic fundamentalism on the rise throughout the Muslim world, it seemed probable that a revolt should occur, but this did not happen in Egypt. In elections in 1987, the Muslim Brotherhood allied with two political parties, won 17 percent of the vote, which translated into fifty-six seats in the Egyptian National Assembly.[53] In April 1982, El-Sambouli and his five co-conspirators were found guilty of Sadat's assassination and were executed for their crimes.

EGYPT'S ISLAMIC EXTREMISTS

Jamaat al-Islamiyya and Egyptian Islamic Jihad, both radical and extreme Islamic groups, have long been associated with Egypt and have made many attempts to violently attack and destabilize successive Egyptian regimes. Mohammed Atta, the supposed leader of the 9-11 attacks and an al Qaeda member, was an Egyptian, and many of the al Qaeda leadership come from this hot bed of Islamic extremism. The two groups gain much of their support from the slums of Cairo and the poorer regions of the state. Both have been responsible for the attacks against foreign tourists in Egypt that decimated the lucrative Egyptian tourism economy. Both groups have their roots going back to the Muslim Brotherhood and have been fighting for an Islamic state to replace the secular government of Hosni Mubarak.

Both groups are known to have sent members to Afghanistan for training with the mujahideen, who fought in Afghanistan against the Soviet Union. Many links exist between these two groups and al Qaeda. To this end, the Mubarak government has suppressed both of them. Claims of torture by human rights groups, and criticism from the United States on the topic, have not prevented extensive crack-downs on the extremist terror groups. The United States is a supporter of the Mubarak regime and pours considerable financial aid into the country. Of critical importance is the fact that Egypt continues to observe the terms of the 1979 Camp David accords, the first Arab peace treaty with Israel. Egypt's largest Islamic terror group is Jamaat al-Islamiyya, whose name means "the Islamic Group." Jamaat al-Islamiyya has a presence both in Egypt and worldwide. Its spiritual leader, the blind cleric Sheikh Omar Abdel Rahman, is serving a life sentence in the United States for his involvement in the 1993 attack on the World Trade Center. (In April 2002, the Justice Department charged that Abdel Rahman had tried to direct further terrorist operations from his cell in Minnesota.)

Following a violent campaign of attacks against the government, Christian, and other targets in Egypt, Jamaat al-Islamiyya has largely honored a March 1999 ceasefire with the Egyptian government. Exiled members of Jamaat al-Islamiyya are known to have joined al Qaeda and trained at its camps in Afghanistan.[54] The Islamic Jihad has close ties to bin Laden's al Qaeda and continues its assault on the Egyptian government. Due to the repressive nature of the Mubarak regime, the group has operated principally outside Egypt and has been turning its Islamic extremist campaign of terror toward U.S. targets. The philosophy of the fundamentalists is to overthrow the government and to replace it with a radical and extreme Islamic government similar to the former Taliban regime in Afghanistan. Over the last ten years, the Mubarak government's crackdown on the Islamic group has seen many militants either jailed or executed under military tribunals. Those held in jail are believed to number more than 14,000.

The Egyptian government continues to support, in principal, the U.S.-led War on Terror and is an ally of peace initiatives for the Middle East. However, arms continue to be supplied to Palestinian groups through the Sinai Peninsula. Egypt's crackdown on the extreme elements of the Islamic groups makes the leadership a prime target of bin Laden and his terror cells.

The United States had pointed out Egypt as a role model for democracy in the Middle East. It may be necessary to take a cautious view of a country that has cracked down hard on its Islamic radicals since the assassination of Anwar Sadat and has also seen little respect for human rights in prisons. Egypt's Mubarak is entering his twilight years and reforms to the political structure would surely be a legacy he would likely favor. His biggest threat still comes from the Muslim Brotherhood, even though it is banned from political activity or from participating in government elections, it has members that have stood as independents. Egypt's Parliament approved a constitutional amendment in May 2005 that opens presidential elections to multiple candidates, but opposition figures protested that its stringent conditions would make the September 2005 election a one-man referendum for President Hosni Mubarak. "This is a political trick which makes a mockery of democracy," said Mustapha K al-Sayyid, a Political Science professor at the American University of Cairo and a member of the fledgling opposition Kefaya movement, otherwise known as the Egyptian Movement for Change. "The amendment gives veto power to the ruling party to decide who will run in the elections."

Under the amended Article 76 of Egypt's Constitution, any independent candidate seeking to run would need the support of 250 elected politicians drawn from the People's Assembly, the Shura Council, or upper house, and the provincial councils in each of twenty-six governorates. The number had initially been set at 300 signatures, with a certain number from each body, but members of the governing National Democratic Party (NDP) lowered the requirement. Still, no independent could come close given the domination of NDP members. Moreover, recognized parties were granted entry into the presidential race but most of the leaders are elderly and not very well known. Meanwhile, the country's most visible young politician, Ayman Nour, would not qualify because his Ghad party was only approved in 2004.

The Muslim Brotherhood, although officially banned, still holds eighty-eight seats in the lower house of parliament. In the May 2007 elections for the Shura Council, not one MB member was elected. This in a region claimed by President Bush to be a model for democracy—some 800 MB members have been arrested since December 2006. In what has become a tradition on voting days in Egypt, riot police surrounded polling stations in districts where Brotherhood candidates looked likely to win. Some stations were simply sealed off, while in others the security cordon opened to let in busloads of government supporters. The two main legal opposition parties are far weaker than the Brotherhood boycotted the voting. Mubarak's National Democratic Party has held power for twenty-eight years.[55] Mubarak rules with the weight of the army behind him and will continue to do so as long as he is able to keep the MB at bay or in jail. U.S. military aid to Egypt runs to around $1.3 billion annually.

In the next presidential election, in 2011, only parties with 5 percent of the seats in Parliament can field a candidate. No group controls that many seats now except for the National Democratic Party.[56]

LIBYA

Libya is situated at the northern tip of Africa and has a northern border on the Mediterranean Sea. Its nearest neighbors to the east are Egypt and the Sudan, with Chad and Niger to the south and Algeria and Tunisia to the west and northwest, respectively. The country is made up of 97 percent Sunni Muslims or Arabian Berber tribesmen. In the 1930s, under Italian dominance, there was discrimination against Libyan Jews, who have been persecuted in Libya ever since. Libyans attacked the Jewish sector of Benghazi during World War II and deported about 2,000 Jews. By the time Libya had achieved independence in 1951, nearly all the remaining Libyan Jews had migrated either to Israel or Europe.[57]

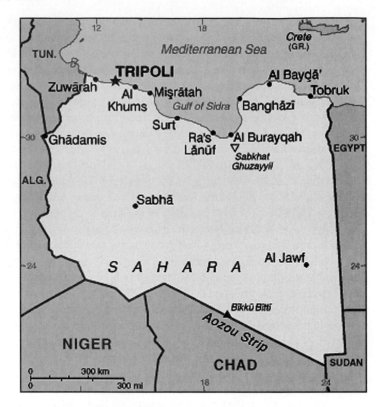

FIGURE 8-13   Map of Libya (Central Intelligence Agency, *The World Factbook*, 2008).

COLONEL MUAMMAR EL-QADDAFI

Muammar el-Qaddafi is a man driven by hatred for the state of Israel, the United States, and any foreign power that supports them. The United States was, for many years, on the Libyan leaders hate list, along with the United Kingdom. Up until the late 1990s, Libya did not limit itself to attacking foreign governments, but also sought out and killed Libyan opponents of the Libyan leader.

Qaddafi came to power following a military coup that deposed King Idris in 1969, and has now achieved dictatorial status as leader of the Libyan people. His views are anti-Israeli, anti-Zionist, and anti-Semitic, although in his public statements he makes no distinction among them. As a mark of his hatred for the Jewish people, he seized all Jewish-owned properties and businesses in 1971. He rules with an autocratic style and ruthlessly "removes" all dissenters. His control of the government is absolute through the setup of people's committees. As a former military student and officer, he had never been cast in the secular role that he seems to have adopted in the 1990s. Reports out of Libya indicate that several attempts on Qaddafi's life have taken place, by a group calling itself the Libyan Militant Islamic Group.

Support for Terror

The phenomenon of state-sponsored terrorism applies most appropriately to Libya, Iran, and Syria and forms part of what George Bush termed the "Axis of Evil." By far the most outspoken of the Arab world leaders, Qaddafi embarked through the 1970s and 1980s on what may be described as a reign of external terror against the United States and its citizens, specifically those in Europe. The Libyans have supported other terror groups in Europe and have allowed them to train on Libyan soil. Libya has also provided weapons to such groups as the Provisional Irish Republican Army (PIRA). In one notable incident, the Libyans supplied several tons of explosives and automatic weapons that were seized by security forces in the Irish Republic. To Qaddafi, the PIRA was fighting a guerrilla war of independence from the dominance of an imperialist power. Security experts have not taken such actions lightly. Libya has been a home and terrorist training ground for more than thirty terrorist organizations, such as Abu Sayeef from the Philippines. However, in order to get sanctions lifted (among other actions taken), Libya expelled members of the Abu Nidal organization in 1998.

There has been sufficient opposition to the Qaddafi regime to prompt him to unleash internal assassins to track down and coerce the dissidents into returning to Libya. Failure to return left only the option of death. In 1984 alone, more than thirty terrorist attacks were carried out by representatives of Libyan Revolutionary Committees on Libyans residing in Europe and the Middle East.[58] Not only did Qaddafi focus on his dissidents in Europe and the Middle East, he also sought them out in neighboring Chad and the sub-Saharan African states that were vociferously against his government.

Diplomatic Immunity

To circumvent the interference of foreign customs officials, Qaddafi used diplomatic privileges to move contraband weapons into and out of diplomatic missions in Europe. By the 1980s, Qaddafi had renamed the Libyan Embassies and was now referring to them as the Libyan People's Bureaus. The problems faced by the British government of Margaret Thatcher and public protests outside the Libyan People's Bureau in St. James's Park, London, would result in the severing of diplomatic ties between the two countries. The following are extracts from the Vienna Convention on Diplomatic Relation, 1961:

ARTICLE 22

1. The premises of the mission shall be inviolable. The agents of the receiving state may not enter them, except with the consent of the head of the mission.
2. The receiving State is under a special duty to take all appropriate steps to protect the premises of the mission against any intrusion or damage and to prevent any disturbances of the peace of the mission or impairment of its dignity.
3. The premises of the mission, their furnishings and other property thereon and the means of transport of the mission shall be immune from search, requisition, attachment or execution.

ARTICLE 29

The person of a diplomatic agent shall be inviolable. He shall not be liable to any form of arrest or detention. The receiving State shall treat him with due respect and shall take all appropriate steps to prevent any attacks on his person, freedom or dignity.

ARTICLE 31

1. A diplomatic agent shall enjoy immunity from the criminal jurisdiction of the receiving State. He shall also enjoy immunity from its civil and administrative jurisdiction.
2. A diplomatic agent is not obliged to give evidence as a witness.

ARTICLE 45

If diplomatic relations are broken off between two States, or if a mission is permanently or temporarily recalled:

a. the receiving State must, even in case of armed conflict, respect and protect the premises of the mission, together with its property and archives;
b. the sending state may entrust the custody of the premises of the mission, together with its property and archives, to a third State acceptable to the receiving State;
c. the sending State may entrust the protection of its interests and those of its nationals to a third State acceptable to the receiving State.

The BBC and ITN news networks in London showed the dramatic turn of events when gunfire erupted from the Libyan Peoples Bureau into the crowded street. The demonstrators were mainly exiled Libyan students protesting against Qaddafi. The gunfire killed a Metropolitan policewoman, Yvonne Fletcher. The incident, which took place in the heart of the diplomatic center of London on April 17, 1984, and accounted for a dozen injuries to the demonstrators, was not a random, maniacal act but a deliberate attack on the demonstrators. Intelligence intercepts of messages between Tripoli and the London Libyan People's Bureau revealed that those inside were ordered to fire on the demonstrators. On the home front, the Libyan-controlled press released a different story about the incident, stating that the police had stormed the building and described the episode as a "barbarous outrage." The standoff at the Libyan People's Bureau ended on April 27, when the occupants agreed to be taken to the Civil Services College in Berkshire to be interviewed by police. Under diplomatic privileges to which they were entitled, they refused to help in the investigation and were returned to Libya. The events at St. James's Square were the culmination of a series of bombings and attacks against dissident Libyans in London and the northwest of England.

Qaddafi and the United States

Qaddafi sees himself as a latter-day Abdel Nasser, with the ideology of leading and uniting the Arab nations. Fanatical and fundamentalist, he has targeted U.S. interests and personnel in Europe. It is believed the attack on the La Belle discotheque in Berlin on April 5, 1986, which claimed the life of one U.S. serviceman and injured several scores of others, was the work of Libyan agents. This incident did not yield a particularly high body count, but the United States was in no mood to trifle with the Libyan government of Colonel Qaddafi. American intelligence indicated that the disco bombing was planned and directed by "diplomats" from the East Berlin Libyan People's Bureau.

OPERATION EL-DORADO CANYON

International relations between the United States and Libya were at an all-time low by the middle of the 1980s. Behind the scenes at this time was the Soviet Union, which had been supplying weapons and aircraft to Libya. In a blatant effort to make the Libyans lose face, the United States began maneuvers with its Sixth Fleet in the Mediterranean off the north coast of Libya, in an area proclaimed by Libya as being an exclusion zone. The area in question was the Gulf of Sirte. These exercises began on March 24, 1986, and were calculated to intimidate the Libyan leader.

Far from intimidated, the result was the detonation of two bombs in Europe. The first, on April 2, 1986, exploded in the cabin of a TWA passenger jet in Greek airspace. Four Americans were killed in the blast; however, the aircraft landed without further incident. Four days later, a powerful explosion ripped through La Belle discotheque in West Berlin, killing an American serviceman. The deaths of U.S. citizens became the trigger the Reagan Administration was searching for to launch a previously planned U.S. air strike in Libya. On April 14, 1986, aircraft from U.S. bases in the United Kingdom and from the U.S. Navy aircraft carriers in the Mediterranean attacked and bombed targets inside Libya. One might argue that the United States had violated the UN Charter and international laws with such a preemptive strike against a sovereign state.

Over 100 aircraft took part in the raid in and around Tripoli and Benghazi, causing heavy damage and loss of life. It is believed that Colonel Qaddafi's adopted daughter was one of the fatalities. In all, more than 100 lives were claimed. Was the attack sending a message to other state sponsors of terrorism or was this strike designed to help topple or kill the Libyan leader and allow for a more moderate government to be formed in its place? This was the first time the United States had launched such aggressive military action at a specific country in retaliation for terrorist attacks. Would other terrorist groups heed the example of the attack on Libya and cease activities against the United States? On the political front, members of the United Nations, including France and Italy, the two countries that had refused over flight clearances for strike aircraft from U.K. bases, condemned the United States. Did the French and Italian governments fear some form of reprisal attack from the Libyan leader? The U.K. government, on the other hand, the strongest American ally at the time, had already severed diplomatic ties with Libya. Whatever analysts may think, a far more serious terrorist attack was not far away, indicating that preemptive military actions may not be successful against determined and fanatical terrorist movements. Some thirteen years later, under a different U.S. administration, spy satellites and long-range smart bombs would again target terrorist sites this time, but in Sudan and Afghanistan.

During the last decade, with the mounting pressure on his country from UN sanctions that were not lifted until 1999, the Colonel has had to reevaluate his position in the world. No longer does he have the support of the former Soviet Union. A period of appeasement was definitely the order of the day for Libya's survival. The concern to many is that Libya has small stocks of biological agents and the risk that those could fall into the wrong hands or, to be more specific, into the hands of al Qaeda, has been a pressing issue for the United States. In May 2002, the U.S. State Department added Libya to the list of countries that were developing chemical and biological weapons of mass destruction (WMD). Certainly, Qaddafi has no love for the Islamic extremists or al Qaeda, and since 9-11 he has reportedly provided intelligence on Libyan militants outside of the country. This action would be of pure benefit to Qaddafi as he has maintained an iron-fisted approach to Islamic extremist inside Libya.

PAN AM 103

One of the most appalling terrorist attacks of the last fifty years has been the destruction of a Pan Am 747–200 over Lockerbie, Scotland, on December 21, 1988. The subsequent trial and conviction of a mid-level intelligence officer in the employ of the Qaddafi government still leaves the obvious question as to the complicity of the leader of the Libyan government in this atrocity. In 1999, Libya fulfilled one of the requirements of the United Nations Security Council Resolutions (UNSCR) by surrendering two Libyans suspected in connection with the bombing for trial before a Scottish court in the Netherlands. One of these suspects, Abdel Basset al-Megrahi, was found guilty; the other was acquitted. Al-Megrahi's conviction was upheld on appeal in 2002. In August 2003, Libya fulfilled the remaining UNSCR requirements, including acceptance of responsibility for the actions of its officials and payment of appropriate compensation to the victims' families. UN sanctions against Libya were lifted on September 12, 2003.

On December 19, 2003, Libya announced its intention to rid itself of WMD and Medium To Close Range (MTCR) class missile programs. Since that time, it has cooperated with the United States, the United Kingdom, the International Atomic Energy Agency, and the Organization for the Prohibition of Chemical Weapons toward these objectives. Libya has also signed the IAEA Additional Protocol and has become a State Party to the Chemical Weapons Convention. In response, the United States has terminated the applicability of the Iran-Libya Sanctions Act to Libya and President Bush signed an Executive Order on September 20, 2004, terminating the national emergency with respect to Libya and ending IEEPA-based economic sanctions. This action had the effect of unblocking assets blocked under the Executive Order sanctions. Restrictions on cargo aviation and third-party code-sharing have been lifted, as have restrictions on passenger aviation. Certain export controls also remain in place and Libya remains on the state sponsors of terrorism list. U.S. diplomatic personnel reopened the U.S. Interest Section in Tripoli on February 8, 2004. The mission was upgraded to a U.S. Liaison Office on June 28, 2004. Libya re-established its diplomatic presence in Washington with the opening of an Interest Section on July 8, 2004, which was subsequently upgraded to a Liaison Office in December 2004.[59]

Libyan Islamic Fighting Group (LIFG)

Sunni Islamic militants have also been present in Libya but have not managed to engage any popular support for their cause. The LIFG has been in existence for several decades but only publicly announced its presence in a 1995 communiqué following a number of attacks against the Libyan regime. Over the course of 1995 and 1996, LIFG mounted assassination attacks against Colonel Qaddafi all were unsuccessful. The LIFG leader and its founder, Salah Fathi bin Suleiman was killed during a battle with Libyan military forces in September 1997. Unable to promote a popular uprising, the LIFG moved to exile in Sudan at a time when Osama bin Laden was setting up his organization in that country. The Libyan government brought significant pressure to bear on the Sudan government to kick out the LIFG members. Bin Laden, as a guest of the Sudan government, was compelled to remove the Libyan fighters from his camps. Many returned to Libya but did not stay long enough to be caught in Qaddafi's crackdown, but instead fled to Europe. Many rejoined al Qaeda in training camps in Taliban controlled Afghanistan and since 9-11 have gone on to prosecute a global jihad. Recruits from Libya have been heavily involved in the Iraq insurgency. In February 2006, the U.S. Treasury Department took significant steps aimed at nullifying LIFG's base in the U.K., designating five individuals, three companies, and one charity as terrorists for their ties to LIFG. In addition to labeling Birmingham U.K. resident Abdelrahman al-Faqih as a "senior leader for the LIFG" the Treasury Department also designated midlands resident Mohammed Benhammedi as a "key financier for the LIFG" and "a member of . . . . the LIFG economic committee" who is "believed to provide funds for LIFG through Sara Properties Limited, Meadowbank Investment Limited and Ozlam Properties Limited."[60]

The Sanabal Relief Agency was also described as a fund raising front organization for the LIFG and was designated as a Specially Designated Global Terrorist (SDGT) entity.

SUDAN

Sudan has been fighting an almost endless civil war between Muslims in the north and Christians in the south. Its government appears to have been devastated by the famine and poverty that have wrecked the nation. Sudan has, however, been on the U.S. State Department's list of countries that sponsor and support international terror groups. Safe haven and training grounds have been available to the Abu Nidal Organization, Hezbollah, Hamas, and the PIJ. The UN Security Council passed several resolutions concerning the role of Sudan in sponsoring terror groups; not all have been complied with. One name stands apart from all others at the end of this decade: Osama bin Laden. He was ordered to leave Sudan in 1997, but his legacy was to cause a military confrontation with the United States some twelve months later. Following the bombings of the U.S. embassies in the Kenyan and Tanzanian capitals, which claimed hundreds of lives, the United States struck back. In a reaction similar to that of Ronald Reagan, the Clinton Administration retaliated on the night of August 20, 1998. In his address to the nation on August 20, President Clinton stated, "Today I ordered our armed forces to strike at terrorist-related facilities in Afghanistan and Sudan because of the imminent threat they presented to our national security . . . In recent history they killed American, Belgian and Pakistani peacekeepers in Somalia. They plotted to assassinate the Pope and the President of Egypt. They planned to bomb six United States 747s over the Pacific . . . their (terrorist) mission is murder and their history is bloody. The most recent terrorist events are fresh in our memory. Two weeks ago, 12 Americans and 300 Kenyans and

FIGURE 8-14   Map of Sudan (Central Intelligence Agency, *The World Factbook*, 2008).

Tanzanians lost their lives. Another 5,000 were wounded when our embassies in Nairobi and Dar es Salaam were bombed." The attack against a factory believed to be developing chemical weapons was carried out by a sea-launched missile attack from U.S. naval ships in the Red Sea. The exact details of the strike were not confirmed; however, news reports seen on television indicated massive damage to the Al-Shifa Pharmaceutical Factory in Khartoum. This attack will, in all likelihood, only harden the radicals' resolve to continue the fight. Throughout the Middle East and Asia, there were spontaneous demonstrations against the United States, and the action has probably given significant impetus to the Islamic extremist movement in Afghanistan. As in the 1986 strike against Libya, this kind of response is not seen as an effective deterrent. To many analysts, it is seen as having precisely the opposite effect.

DARFUR

Recent memory of atrocities in Rwanda would make many observers wonder why nothing has occurred on an international scale to temper the actions of Sudan's proxy forces in the Darfur region of the Sudan. Much is made of the term *genocide* and whether this is taking place in this region or not. What is definitely taking place is the total destruction of entire villages, including the rape and murder of women and children. As recently as the end of 2004, the Sudanese government made a peace deal with rebels it has been fighting in the southern part of the country for a quarter of a century. The region of Darfur has been in turmoil since 2003, likely as a result of the Sudanese government's fear of being unable to fight two separate insurgent uprisings at the same time and originating in far-flung, impoverished regions of the country.

The National Islamic Front government came to power through a military coup in 1989 and gets its support from Sudan's wealthy and economic interest groups, which reflect only a small minority of the Sudanese population. The peace deal brokered and then signed on January 9, 2005, with the southern rebels from the Sudan Peoples Liberation Movement/Army (SPLM), gave considerable power-sharing concessions to the rebel movement. The Comprehensive Peace Agreement provides for:

- A new constitution
- Power sharing
- Wealth sharing
- Security throughout the country

New institutions will be created and a new Government of National Unity installed once the constitution is ratified. SPLM Chairman John Garang will become the First Vice President of Sudan and the new government of southern Sudan will be established. However, in Darfur, unlike the south, the problems began with the rise of two new movements to challenge the Khartoum regime—namely, the Sudan Liberation Movement/Army (SLA) and the Justice and Equality Movement (JEM). The region has been in conflict both at tribal and regional levels for decades and violent events were not uncommon, but the current levels of attack and counterattack by the government seem to be disproportionate to the problem. UN commissioners reported that the vast majority of attacks on civilians in villages have been carried out by government of Sudan armed forces and **Janjaweed**. The Janjaweed, or "evil horsemen," comprise mostly Arab ethnic militias. The attacks sponsored by the Khartoum government are aimed primarily at the African, rather than the Arab, population of Darfur.

The international legal definition of the crime of genocide is found in Articles II and III of the 1948 Convention on the Prevention and Punishment of Genocide. Article II describes two elements of the crime of genocide:

1. The mental element, meaning the "intent to destroy, in whole or in part, a national, ethnical, racial or religious group, as such," and
2. The physical element, which includes five acts described in sections a, b, c, d, and e. A crime must include both elements to be called "genocide."

Article III describes five punishable forms of the crime of genocide: genocide, conspiracy, incitement, attempt, and complicity.

EXCERPT FROM THE CONVENTION ON THE PREVENTION AND PUNISHMENT OF GENOCIDE

Article II: In the present Convention, genocide means any of the following acts committed with intent to destroy, in whole or in part, a national, ethnical, racial or religious group, as such:

    a. Killing members of the group;
    b. Causing serious bodily or mental harm to members of the group;
    c. Deliberately inflicting on the group conditions of life calculated to bring about its physical destruction in whole or in part;
    d. Imposing measures intended to prevent births within the group;
    e. Forcibly transferring children of the group to another group.

ARTICLE III: THE FOLLOWING ACTS SHALL BE PUNISHABLE:

    a. Genocide;
    b. Conspiracy to commit genocide;
    c. Direct and public incitement to commit genocide;
    d. Attempt to commit genocide;
    e. Complicity in genocide.

It is a crime to plan or incite genocide, even before killing starts, and to aid or abet genocide. Criminal acts include conspiracy, direct and public incitement, attempts to commit genocide, and complicity in genocide.[61] What is clearly taking place in the Darfur region is state terrorism being inflicted on a subgroup and, in this instance, it is the non-Muslim population. The Janjaweed may or may not be practicing genocide, but perhaps the term ethnic cleansing could be used to describe the terrible events taking place. To date, we have witnessed that the international community under the auspices of the United Nations will pass resolutions, recommendations, and some sanctions against the government of the Sudan; however, the numbers killed run into the hundreds of thousands with over a million displaced. For the future, it seems that only political and economic sanctions against the government will affect the outcome. The presence of UN and African Union peacekeepers in the region should push both sides to some agreement that will end the carnage in the region but so long as peace agreements continue to be torn up by the regime in Khartoum, there can be little prospect for any lasting peace in this region.

ALGERIA

The People's Democratic Republic of Algeria (Algeria) emerged from its French colonial era through a nationalist movement that pitted the FLN (Front de Liberation National) against French security forces, brutally aided by a pro-France terrorist organization known as the OAS (Organisation Armie Secrete). The terrorists' struggle lasted from 1954 to 1962; one million Algerians and 17,500 French occupation forces were killed before the Evian Agreement of 1962 ended the FLN's campaign of assassination, bombing, and sabotage and the French's ferocious counterinsurgency campaign of torture, death, and repression.[62] The FLN emerged as victorious revolutionary heroes whose primary sense of political legitimacy lay in throwing out colonial suppressors. Algeria emerged from an effective, two-pronged FLN campaign against the French: the guerrilla war in the cities and rugged countryside of Algeria, and a diplomatic campaign in European and African capitals. France agreed to a plebiscite in 1962 on the issue of independence;

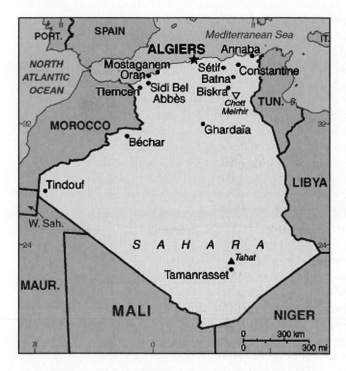

FIGURE 8-15 **Map of Algeria** (Central Intelligence Agency, *The World Factbook*, 2008).

99 percent of the votes were cast in favor of Algerian independence. Ahmed Ben Bella, an FLN political leader during the war of independence, became the first president of independent Algeria. The FLN was in power from 1962 to 1992, when the civilian government was dissolved in a political coup.

Algeria remained officially a one-party socialist country for the three decades of 1962 to 1992, assisted by the French in oil and gas technology, capital fusions, and foreign aid. Population growth increased the size of the nation from 9 million in 1962 to more than 28 million in 1995; 75 percent of Algerians are under the age of twenty-five.

The subsequent rise of a radical Islamic movement in Algeria, which won a round of the parliamentary elections in 1991, caused the FLN to abandon the election process and nullify the results. The party in question, the Islamic Salvation Front (FIS), was immediately banned by the FIS because of its radical Islamic goals. Following the ban, its military wing commenced a campaign of attacks against government and security forces.

Economic Crisis

It can be argued that the FLN was ineffective in governing Algeria from 1962 to 1992.[63] A rapidly growing number of young persons eager to secure economic positions and hoping for a brighter future encountered bureaucratic inefficiencies of a socialist state economy, coupled with corruption and rigid attempts to control entrepreneurship. A severe housing shortage emerged, along with declining agricultural and industrial production and a devastating drop in oil prices. The economic situation was complicated by a lack of consumer goods, high unemployment, and rising inflation. Servicing Algeria's huge foreign debt (more than $30 billion in 1995) requires almost all of the $9 billion in annual oil and gas revenues. In 1986, an austerity plan was imposed, in part to secure International Monetary Fund assistance.

October 1988 Riots

Algeria's deteriorating economic situation shattered social and economic expectations. Riots ensued and the military responded with excessive repression, firing on and killing hundreds of protestors/demonstrators. Thousands were arrested, and shortly thereafter rumors began to circulate that security forces were torturing dissidents. Algeria's older citizenry, freedom fighters three decades before in the 1960–1962 era, equated the military's torture to that of the "Colons" (the sometimes-brutal French leaders of colonial days), a similarity that struck a cord and captured some Algerian hearts.

In late 1988, then President Chadli Benjedid, undertook a democratic initiative. Referendums were held in 1988 and 1989, changing the constitution and including more respect for civil rights and a free press. Formation of political associations was permitted, and the one-party (FLN) system was abandoned. By February 1989, at least fifty new political parties were formed, including the Front Islamic du Salah (FIS), recognized as legal in September 1989 (Alexander). The FIS was organized through mosques and, by late 1989, had at least three million adherents. FIS political themes included criticizing the state bureaucracy, widespread corruption, and Western secular elites (French influences, primarily). Reflecting Islamic influences, subordination of women was advocated. The FIS sought an Islamic state governed by Islamic law; it proposed to discriminate against ethnic and other minorities

(Berbers, Jews, Christians, polytheists, etc.) and French-speakers ("the enemies of God"). Religious extremists sought imposition of Shari'a law into all aspects of politics and daily life in Algeria.

These earlier political pronouncements, especially the proposed imposition of puritan codes (drinking, dress, calendar, etc.), alarmed the educated, business people, and intellectuals. Minorities, French speakers, women, and the more educated staged counter-demonstrations. Many secular parties boycotted the elections in the fall of 1990. In the June 1990 elections for municipal, department, and provincial assemblies, the FLN was decisively defeated. The FIS won 54 percent of the popular vote cast, which totaled 65 percent to 75 percent of the eligible voters. Since no elections had been held for the national assembly, the FLN still controlled the national political scene and prepared for the June 1991 elections by gerrymandering to give more representation to FLN strongholds and districts. In this environment, one FIS leader (Abbassi Madani) called for a general strike, adoption of an Islamic state, and resistance through jihad and civil disobedience. The FIS was, interestingly, openly split over this call. Disruptive events occurred, but not mass revolution; the army declared a state of siege and elections were rescheduled for December.

There is some suggestion that the FIS might not have fared well in the fall 1991 elections, as it had not distinguished itself at local, urban, and municipal administration. It may have been that gerrymandering was an FLN provocation, and the FIS overreaction was triggered, in part, through infiltration of the FIS. In any event, the military declared a state of siege, banning meetings, publications, and demonstrations; suspending activities of political associations; and detaining civilian suspects. The military assumed local arrest authority and military tribunals conducted trials. FIS leaders were arrested en masse and detained in camps and jails. By fall 1991, the state of siege was lifted to permit elections, scheduled by Chadli Benjedid for December 1991 and January 1992.

DECEMBER 1991 ELECTIONS   In the December phase of the national election, the FIS won 189 of 231 National Assembly seats with 47 percent of the eligible vote; the rejection of the FLN was obvious. Faced with a certain FIS victory, the military pressured the president to resign. The National Assembly was dissolved, and the Haut Comite d'Etat (HEC) imposed. On January 11, 1992, the military coup was affected. The HEC banned the FIS (its principal opposition party), jailed almost all the known leaders, detained some 9,000 to 30,000 FIS members in five detention camps, and cracked down on the press. The latter included searching newspaper premises, expelling resident correspondents of European newspapers, arresting journalists writing for pro-fundamentalist papers, and jailing the editor of an independent weekly.

On January 22, authorities arrested the acting head of the FIS, radicalizing the movement and provoking widespread violence between FIS militants and security forces. A state of emergency was declared that continued until late 1995. By March 1992, the FIS leadership not in detention went underground or into exile, or migrated to adjacent countries. On May 5, military courts sentenced twelve FIS men to hang for the deaths of three army soldiers.[64] Five other Islamic extremist groups emerged and spread through Algeria: Armed Islamic Movement Group (an off-shoot of FIS), Armed Islamic Group, Hezbollah, Repentance and Emigration (*al-Takfir wa'l Hijra*), and Afghans (mostly veterans of the Afghanistan war). Actions were mostly decentralized acts of random terrorism and guerilla warfare. The volume of terrorist events increased sharply and included attacks on security forces, assault on the navy headquarters, and attacks on foreigners.[65] Bombings, assassinations, and attacks on government representatives expanded to include slitting the throats of captured foreigners, FLN members, and journalists. Disco dancers were killed by throat slitting and shooting. Petroleum workers were shot and plants were bombed. In the countryside, with its rugged terrain and desperately poor inhabitants, guerrillas controlled most of the mountain range. Satellite dishes were torn down, newspapers were banned, women were forced to wear traditional veils, men and women were segregated on buses, and Iranian-style enforcement of Islamic law prevailed. Eventually, an Air France airbus was hijacked, resulting in French security forces storming the plane, rescuing the hostages, and killing the hijackers.[66] Four nuns in Algiers were subsequently killed in retaliation. Iran and the Sudan provided arms and military training to the terrorists. To cut French support of the Algerian regime

($1.2 billion in annual aid to the Algerian government, intelligence, and training), a series of bombings in Paris and other French cities was undertaken, resulting in deaths and casualties and putting a considerable dent in tourism, as such attacks were widely reported by the media during 1995.

Algerian military undertook brutal and repressive actions in response to Islamic terrorism and violence. Military courts began to execute civilians convicted in the three courts that enforced the stringent antiterrorism law; executions began and a strict curfew was declared. Pro-government death squads patrolled both rural and urban areas, and anti-FIS vigilantes took the law into their own hands. Villages formed self-defense groups to ward off FIS terrorism. Riots within prisons were fostered by FIS and other resistance members and were brutally repressed, along with the wholesale slaughter of detained FIS leaders.[67] The army was expanded through conscription, with mandatory military service of eighteen months, and the military budget jumped 90 percent from 1992–1993 levels. The military elite argued that Islamic extremism could be stopped only by force.

By 1994, foreign investment had dwindled to a trickle, families of diplomats were evacuated, embassies had been closed, the official unemployment rate had risen to 20 percent, the Algerian dinar (money) had been devalued by 50 percent, and servicing the international debt was consuming most of the petroleum-generated income. Efforts toward "national reconciliation" by national dialogue were made but failed, primarily by government intransigence in meeting directly with FIS leaders, or FIS boycotting of dialogues in other international sites. Even "secret meetings" appeared to have no appreciable ameliorative effect. It was in this environment that the military regime replaced the HEC with retired General Liamine Zeroual as President, signaling the direct movement of the military into the political arena. The rise of armed Islamic groups came to fruition in 1992 when the military government voided the victory of the Islamic Salvation Front (FIS), the largest Islamic opposition party, in the first round of legislative elections held in December 1991. Islamists were aiming for a pure Islamic state and centered many of their attacks on the civilian population, inflicting countless massacres.

The Armed Islamic Group (GIA)

The **Armed Islamic Group (GIA)** is an FIS splinter organization that continued the fight against the Algerian military regime in 1992. Since this North African country plunged into a civil war in that year, the group has been linked to terrorist attacks in Europe and to the massacres of tens of thousands of civilians in Algeria. The government crackdown has been as fierce in Algeria as that witnessed in Egypt and, in a similar vein, the GIA seeks to overthrow the current regime and replace it with a radical Islamic one. Many GIA members have joined other groups in Algeria to continue attacks against the secular government. GIA is also credited with the audacious hijacking of an Air France airliner from Algeria to France in 1994, in which the terrorists had planned to set off explosives over the French capital, Paris. The GIA has targeted ex-colonial rulers in particular and has carried out limited bombing campaigns in France. France became the natural target as the Algerian government sought support from France to clamp down on GIA activists operating and raising funds for the overthrow of the secular Algerian government.

Rais Massacre, Algeria

In 1997, Algeria was at the peak of a civil war conflict that had begun after the military's cancellation of the 1992 elections, in fear that it would be won by the Islamic Salvation Front (FIS). The farming village of Rais had been supporting Islamist guerrillas in the region over a period of time but had recently stopped providing them food and money. The attackers arrived at the village in the early morning hours, armed with shotguns, knives, axes, and bombs. They killed the village's men, women, children, and even animals, until dawn, cutting throats and taking the time to burn corpses. They mutilated and stole from the dead and committed atrocities against pregnant women. Estimates indicate more than 400 were killed.[68]

The French government has continued to support the military government in Algeria, much to the opposition and ire of the GIA. Possible links to al Qaeda could relate to Ahmed Ressam, an

Algerian national who attempted to cross from Canada to the United States, with a bomb destined for Los Angeles International airport, in what is termed the "millennium plot." Although Ressam is Algerian and is believed to have met with al Qaeda operatives, this does not necessary widen the ties between the two groups. The GIA's aims are purely internal, as the group advocates the removal of the secular government, whereas the al Qaeda objectives are clearly now truly international.

Many Algerians, tired of the poor standards of living, yearn to leave their country. Most who have fled have gone to France, but many have fled to and sought refugee status in Canada. Their ability to speak French makes the Province of Quebec an ideal choice for settlement. In the aftermath of 9-11, there has been serious focus, not only on immigration policies, particularly in Canada, but also on those Algerians who currently reside inside the country and their possible involvement to al Qaeda. The relentless killings and massacres bought little internal support for the GIA and popular support diminished significantly by the end of the last decade of the twentieth century. The GIA officially rejected a 1999 amnesty law, but not so by its rank and file, who came down from their mountain hide-outs, renounced their ways, and returned to their old lives after surrendering their weapons. Although this has meant a significant drop in GIA violence, with over 85 percent of its members deserting, it has likely been eclipsed by a new subgroup. The Salafist Group for Preaching and Combat (GSPC), together with the GIA, both denounce the amnesty of President Bouteflika. Unlike GIA, GSPC has not concentrated its attacks on the civilian population. GSPC has also pledged it allegiance to al Qaeda.

Al Qaeda in the Land of the Islamic Maghreb-formerly GSPC

On September 14, 2006, the GSPC formally swore its allegiance to Osama bin Laden and renamed the GSPC "al-Qaeda in the Land of The Islamic Maghreb." With the demise of GIA, GSPC is taking the lead; however, there is again the probability that many within this movement, in similar fashion to the GIA, want to accept the government's amnesty proposals. This has led to factional fighting from within. In November 2004 the government was proposing a new ceasefire for GSPC and its members, which total around 500 although significant losses suffered through the relentless actions of the Algerian security apparatus has led to a slow but gradual collapse of this particular insurgency. GSPC had set up Islamic training camps in neighboring Chad and, in 2004, one of the group's significant figures, Amari Saifi, a former Algerian paratrooper, was captured by rebels from the Movement for Democracy and Justice in Chad (MDJT).[69] The MDJT had offered to hand him over to the Algerians, but as time passed, he was handed over to the Libyan government and then to Algeria. Libya's involvement in this incident is probably a direct desire of the Qaddafi regime to show its commitment to the U.S. War on Terror. The Libyans had, in fact, threatened to launch military strikes against the rebels in Chad if Saifi was not handed over. Al Qaeda and bin Laden, once staunch supporters of GIA, now have their own proxy in Algeria. In December 2006 and March 2007 the Islamic Maghreb launched its bombing campaign with roadside bomb attacks targeting foreign nationals in both attacks. This is a significant development and takes the focus away from the internecine warfare attacks carried out in previous years and the senseless massacre of civilians. With the new focus on oil exploration and foreign workers, the newly improved and equipped GSPC are seeking to intimidate the West as have the insurgents in Iraq, by attacking oil and gas lines. While the West seeks oil farther away from the Middle East, attention has gravitated to areas in Africa seen as oil rich. On April 11, 2007, the group launched a well orchestrated suicide attack on the capital Algiers with suicide truck bombings killing 30 and inuring over 200. The attempt at destabilizing the government is the main goal here.

GIA/GSPC's operational presence in Europe is also a consideration and this expansion was a result of the wave of crack downs against Islamist militants by the Algerian government in the early 1990s. The Islamists spread to Spain, France, Italy, Britain, and Sweden and beyond. Large numbers of Algerian fighters have turned up in Chechnya and Bosnia as well as Iraq and Afghanistan and have received training in Afghan training facilities—Ahmed Ressam, the millennium bomber captured crossing in the United States from Canada with explosives in his trunk, is Algerian. With Al Qaeda influencing events in Algeria we must expect to see more coordinated attacks of the scope being used by insurgents in Iraq.

Summary

Marked changes have taken place in the Middle East and North Africa over the last seventy-five years. Israel's statehood became a reality, and Palestinian statehood did not. In spite of the Oslo Accords of the last decade, peace seems no closer at hand since the death of Arafat in France in 2004. Israel remains the major power broker in the region and is prepared to use its military might whenever and wherever it sees fit to protect its nationhood. As for Palestine, the region remains locked in a time warp of refugees under strict controls from military doctrines of the Israeli government. However, the future may be brighter in this regard as the Israeli disengagement plan moves forward. The shadow of Osama bin Laden and his group hangs heavy over the region, particularly in Egypt where much of his support originates. The memory of Libya's involvement in the Pan Am disaster has faded to the extent that Libya is seen as a reluctant ally in the War on Terror. For the future, the Middle East will continue in turmoil, with particular emphasis on Lebanon and Hezbollah as a power vacuum emerges and Iranian influence expanding regime change, by fair means or foul. This could result in instability in Syria and democratization in Egypt, which surely will not go by without more threats from the Muslim Brotherhood.

Web Sites

1. **Muslim Brotherhood**—*http://www.ikhwanweb.com/*
2. **Political Analysis, Espionage and Terrorism**—*http://www.debka.com/*
3. **Palestine Facts**—*http://www.palestinefacts.org/pf_1991to_now_hezbollah.php*
4. **Jerusalem Center for Public Affairs**—*http://www.jcpa.org/*
5. **History of Jihad**—*http://www.historyofjihad.com/*
6. **HAMAS**—*http://www.hamasonline.com*

Endnotes

1. William Roger Louis. *The British Empire in the Middle East 1945–1951* (Oxford: Clarendon Press, 1988, p. 439).
2. Mark Ethridge, U.S. member of the Palestine Conciliation Report to State Department. Top Secret, NIACT (Beirut, March 28, 1949, FRUS 1949, pp. 876, 878).
3. Donald Neff. *Fallen Pillar, U.S. Policy towards Palestine and Israel Since 1945* (Washington, DC: Institute for Palestine Studies, 1995, p. 83).
4. The Foundation for Middle East Peace, Report on Israeli Settlement in the Occupied Territories, Special Report (July 1991); and Richard F. Nyrop, ed., *Israel: A Country Study*, 2nd ed. (Washington, DC: U.S. Government Printing Office, 1979), XIX: Epilogue, p. 185.
5. Jody A Boudreault, et al. (eds). *U.S. Official Statements: Israeli Settlements* (Washington, DC: Institute for Palestine Studies, 1992, p. 15).
6. Noam Chomsky. *The New Intifada, Resisting Israel's Apartheid*, edited by Roane Carey (London: Verso, 2001, p. 13).
7. "The beginning of the end of the Palestinian uprising?" *The Economist* (September 29, 2001, p. 50).
8. The State of Israel. www.mossad.gov.il/Eng/AboutUs.aspx.
9. Sharon's Gaza Disengagement Plan (May 28, 2004) section III, p. A3.
10. Ibid., section III, p. A1.
11. Ibid., section VI.
12. Ibid., section III, p. A1.
13. Claude Bruderlein. "Legal aspects of Israel's Disengagement Plan under International Humanitarian Law." Harvard University Program on Humanitarian Policy and Conflict Research (August 2004).
14. Jonathan Freedland. "A Gift of Dust and Bones: Sharon's Plan for a Pullout Owes More to Demographic Shifts than a Belated Conversion to Peace-Making." *The Guardian* (June 2, 2004).
15. Ibid.
16. David Yallop. *Tracking the Jackal* (New York: Random House Inc., 1993, p. 335).
17. George Rosie. *The Directory of International Terrorism* (New York: Paragon House, 1987, p. 290).
18. Ibid., p. 36.
19. Union of Palestinian Relief Committees Journal, "An Overview of the Gaza Strip," issue #25 (March 1997, p. 3).
20. Israeli Insider. http://israelinsider.com/home.htm.
21. PASSIA; IDF; Associated Press, and CNN.com (March 22, 2004); Gil Sedan. "Over the years, Sheik Yassin grew in status, violence and radicalism," Jewish Telegraphic Agency (March 23, 2004).
22. This material was drawn from an article by Ahmad Rashad, "The Truth about Hamas," http://www.rjgeib.com/biography/milken/crescent-moon/near-asia/palestine/palestine.htm.

23. Mid East Web for Coexistence R.A. http://www.mideastweb.org.

24. "Hamas has the peoples' heart." *The Economist* (December 1, 2001, p. 43).

25. "Martyrs and Traitors," *The Economist* (June 23, 2007).

26. MILNET, "Patterns of Global Terrorism" articles maintained by George Goncalves, *United States Department of State Publications* 10321 (1997).

27. Http://www.fas.org/irp/threat/terror_90/mideast.html.

28. MILNET, "Patterns of Global Terrorism," George Goncalves, 10321 (1997).

29. MIPT Terrorism Knowledge Base. www.tkb.org.

30. MILNET, "Patterns of Global Terrorism."

31. Http://www.haaretz.com/hasen/objects/pages/PrintArticleEn.jhtml?itemNo = 568735.

32. MILNET, "Patterns of Global Terrorism" articles maintained by George Goncalves, *United States Department of State Publications* 10321 (1997).

33. Israeli Ministry of Foreign Affairs—Main Points of the Declaration of Principles. http://www.israel.org/MFA/Peace+Process/Guide+to+the+Peace+Process/Declaration+of+Principles+_+Main+Points.htm.

34. Edward Said, "Palestinians Under Siege." *The New Intifada, Resisting Israel's Apartheid*, ed. Roane Carey (London: Verso, 2001, p. 33).

35. Tom Gross, "Children are indoctrinated into terrorism." *The Weekly Telegraph*, Issue no. 371. London, Telegraph Group Inc (September 1, 1998, p. 20).

36. Richard Clutterbuck. *Guerrillas and Terrorists* (Ohio University Press, 1980, p. 80).

37. Israeli Ministry of Foreign Affairs. www.mfa.gov.il.

38. Paul Wilkinson. *Terrorism and the Liberal State* (New York: New York University Press, 1979, p. 49).

39. Khaled Yacoub Oweis. "Slain Christian warlord had no shortage of enemies." Article by Reuters, *Daily Telegraph*, London (January 25, 2002).

40. Daily Telegraph, London—Lebanon's Victims-November 23, 2006.

41. "The Five Pillars of Islam." *Political Islam Glossary*. http://www.jihadwatch.org/islam101/.

42. "Sunnis and Shiites, the Great Schism." *Political Islam Glossary*, ibid.

43. Ayala Hammond Schbley. "A study of some of the Lebanese Shia's Contemporary Terrorism." *Terrorism: An International Journal* vol. 12, no. 4 (Basingstoke, England: Taylor andFrancis, 1989, p. 220).

44. Magnus Ranstrop. "Hizballah's Command Leadership." *Terrorism and Political Violence* vol. 6, no. 3 (London: Frank Cass, 1994, p. 304).

45. Yonah Alexander. *Hizballah: The Most Dangerous Terrorist Movement* vol. 4, no. 10 (New York Intersec, Three Bridges Publishing Ltd., October 1994, p. 393).

46. Edgar O'Balance. *Islamic Fundamentalist Terrorism* vol. 5, no. 1 (Intersec, Three Bridges Publishing Ltd., New York January 1995, p. 14).

47. Guy Lawson. "A Few Good Martyrs." *Time* (January 2002, pp. 89–93).

48. *Patterns of Global Terrorism: 1997*. U.S. State Department, Hellenic Resources Network. http://www.hri.org/docs/USSD-Terror.

49. "Hizbullah: The Real U.S. Target in Lebanon." *Jane's Foreign Report* (Coulsdon, Surrey: Jane's Information Group, Sentinel House, and March 10, 2005).

50. "In the spotlight"—Hezbollah (Party of God). www.cdi.org.

51. Jonathan. R. White. *Terrorism: An Introduction*, 2nd ed. (Wadsworth Publishing Co., Belmont, CA, 1997, p. 141).

52. Heather Blearney and Richard Lawless. *The Middle East since 1945* (B.T. Batsford Ltd. London, 1989, p. 37).

53. Ibid.

54. International Policy Institute for Counterterrorism. www.ict.org.

55. "Another flawed election." *The Economist* (June 16, 2007).

56. Neil MacFarquhar. "Egypt Limits Challenges to Mubarak, His Foes Say." *New York Times on Line* (May 11, 2005).

57. Http://www.tau.ac.il/Anti-Semitism/annual-report.html. Libya, Anti-Semitism World Report 1997.

58. "Patterns of Global Terrorism: 1984." *Terrorism: An International Journal* vol. 9, no. 3 (Basingstoke, England: Crane Russak & Company Inc., 1987, p. 419).

59. U.S. Department of State.

60. U.S. Treasury Press Release February 8, 2006. http://www.ustreas.gov/press/releases/archives/200602.html.

61. http://www.preventgenocide.org.

62. George Rosie. *Directory of International Terrorism* (New York: Paragon House, 1986).

63. Martha Crenshaw. "Political Violence in Algeria." *Terrorism and Political Violence*, vol. 6, no. 3 (1994, pp. 261–280).

64. Youssef Ibrahim. "Algeria Sentences 12 Militants to Hang," *New York Times* (May 4, 1992, p. A-3).

65. Rachid Khiari, "Downtrodden Algeria Ruled by Death, Fear," *San Francisco Examiner* (April 4, 1994, p. A-9).

66. Thomas Sancton. "Anatomy of a Hijack," *Time* (January 9, 1995, pp. 54–57).

67. Jesse Birnbaum. "The Prison of Blood," *Time* (March 6, 1995).

68. Rais Massacre. http://en.wikipedia.org/wki/Rais_massacre.

69. *Jane's Intelligence Digest* (November 12, 2004).

CHAPTER 9

The Persian Gulf

We suppose that humans are by nature wicked, the kindness and love need special explanation. If, on the other hand, we think that the depth of our soul knows only good, we must provide an account of wickedness and violence.

JOHN LACHS

Learning Objectives

The study and review of this chapter will enable you to

1. Discuss the methods used by Saddam Hussein to control the majority Shi'a in Iraq;
2. Describe the methods used by the Shah of Iran to control his people during his turbulent reign;
3. Discuss al Qaeda's presence in the Persian Gulf and their target selection criteria;
4. Discuss the Iraqi insurgency and differentiate between terrorism and insurgency.

Terms to Remember

Abu Abbas	Ba'athist regime	SAVAK
Abu Musab al-Zarqawi	Believing Youth Movement	Sayyid Qutb
Al Hassan al-Majid	Chemical Ali	Sharia
Al-Sabah dynasty	Insurgency	Tabun
Bahraini Hezbollah	Mahdi army	Wahhabis

May 2004—Riyadh, Saudi Arabia: Terrorists attack the offices of the Saudi oil company in Khobar, Saudi Arabia, take foreign oil workers hostage in a nearby residential compound, leaving twenty-two people dead, including one American.

January 2006—Baghdad, Iraq: Two suicide bombers carrying police badges blow themselves up near a celebration at the Police Academy in Baghdad, killing nearly twenty police officers. Al-Qaeda in Iraq takes responsibility.

April 2006—Baghdad, Iraq: At least 79 people were killed and 164 were wounded when suicide bombers wearing women's robes detonated their explosives at a Shia mosque in northern Baghdad.

Jalal Eddin al-Sagheer, the mosque's preacher and a leading Iraqi politician, said three people carried out the attacks as worshippers were leaving after the main religious service of the week.

March 2008—Baghdad, Iraq: A roadside bomb, followed shortly by a suicide bomb, killed fifty-five people in a shopping area in the Karrada district of Baghdad.

OVERVIEW

Recent historic events in the Persian Gulf, the body of water that is surrounded by a number of Arab and Islamic states, is now well known to most students. The oil crises, the exile of the Shah of Iran, the Iraq-Iran war of the 1980s, the hostages at the U.S. Embassy in Iran, the Gulf War of the early 1990s, the invasion of Iraq in 2003, and other headline events have made the "Persian Gulf" a household term. But little is really known about why this region of the world is the way it is today. Perhaps one of the most important areas of the world, especially when we consider state-sponsored terrorism, the Persian Gulf is surrounded by some of the biggest players on the field of terrorism. This chapter takes a fast-moving tour through the history and background of the major political and religious events in this fascinating region. We discuss how these countries are shaping the future of this region and how their past has influenced the present. These oil-rich countries have the power to bring modern technological societies to their knees simply by cutting off the supply of that most crucial commodity—oil. We begin our visit to the lands of the Arabian nights with the world's largest oil producer, Saudi Arabia.[1]

SAUDI ARABIA

The Kingdom of Saudi Arabia has borders with the Persian Gulf and the Red Sea, north of Yemen. The kingdom is slightly more than one-fifth the size of the United States, but only 2 percent of its land is considered arable. Bordering countries are Iraq, Jordan, Kuwait, Oman, Qatar, the United Arab Emirates, and Yemen. Most of the country is a harsh, dry, mostly uninhabited desert, with broad extremes of temperature. Despite these conditions, its petroleum, natural gas, iron ore, gold, and copper have made Saudi Arabia a very rich nation. The Saudis' extensive coastlines on the Persian Gulf and Red Sea provide leverage on shipping (especially crude oil) through the Gulf and the Suez Canal. Its population of only 20 million (which includes 5 million nonnationals) is able to build and support the infrastructure for the Kingdom in grand style. Ethnic groups are limited; 90 percent of the population is Arab and the remainder is Afro-Asian. One hundred percent are Muslim, and the official language is Arabic. As an Islamic monarchy, Saudi Arabia has no constitution. It is governed according to **Sharia** (Islamic law). In Western society, we need to understand what exactly Sharia Law means; a literal translation of the word means the "path" and is also described by theologians as "God's Law." Sharia is supposed to be interpreted and the law derived from four sources:

1. The Quran, Islam's holy book, viewed by Muslims as the literal word of God;
2. The *hadith*, or record of the actions and sayings and preaching of the Prophet Mohammed;
3. The *ijma*, the consensus of Islamic scholars; and
4. The *qiyas*, a reasoning that uses analogies to apply precedents established by the holy texts in the Quran to problems not covered by them; for example, a ban on narcotics based on the Quranic injunction against wine drinking.

The Sharia governs all aspects of Muslim life, and some aspects of it have formed part of the current Islamic legal codes. Where there is opportunity to interpret laws, as is the case in democratic legal forums, Sharia has developed through five separate schools since the death of the Prophet Mohammed, four in the Sunni sect and one in the Shia sect.[2]

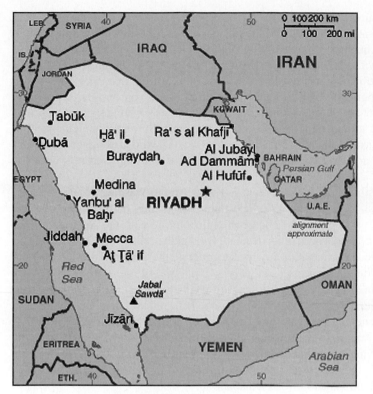

FIGURE 9-1 Map of Saudi Arabia (Central Intelligence Agency, *The World Factbook*, 2008).

King Abdul Aziz

The history of modern Saudi Arabia began in 1902, when Abdul Aziz Al-Sa'ud and a band of his followers captured the city of Riyadh, returning it to the control of his family. Abdul Aziz was born around 1880 and spent the early years of his life with his father in exile in Kuwait. After the bold capture of Riyadh, he spent the next twelve years consolidating his conquests in the area around Riyadh and the eastern part of the country, from where the Turks were expelled. The Arab tribes had never liked the Turks, and they were only too willing to listen to a new ruler, whose ambitions were assisted considerably by the troubles in the Ottoman Empire. In 1933, the lands under the control of Abdul Aziz were renamed the Kingdom of Saudi Arabia, and in 1936 a treaty was signed with Yemen marking it as the southern borders of the Saudi Kingdom.

Abdul Aziz's main preoccupations were the consolidation of his power and the restoration of law and order to all parts of his recently created Kingdom. To these ends, he developed a system whereby every sheikh was responsible for his own tribe under the authority of the King, who was empowered to intervene to impose law and order. It was clearly understood that internal anarchy within the Kingdom could quickly lead to foreign intervention. All were agreed that this was unacceptable. King Abdul Aziz died in 1953, after more than half a century as leader, and King Saud bin Abdul Aziz, his eldest son, succeeded him to the throne. After eleven years, King Saud abdicated in favor of his brother, Faisal, the Crown Prince. In March 1975, King Faisal was assassinated in Riyadh by one of his nephews. The transfer of power, however, went smoothly, and King Khalid bin Abdul Aziz took power, with Fahad bin Abdul Aziz being made Crown Prince. King Khalid continued most of King Faisal's popular policies. It was during King Khalid's reign that Saudi Arabia enjoyed the prosperity and enormous wealth of the "petrodollar" boom years.

King Khalid died in June 1982 and was succeeded by Crown Prince Fahad bin Abdul Aziz. King Fahad was well versed in the art of governing, as he had served as the country's first Minister of Education. King Khalid had been in poor health for much of his reign, so Fahad ruled in all but title. Continuing development within the country and the infrastructure marked King Fahad's reign. On the political front, Iran's open hostility toward Saudi Arabia led the government to strengthen its ties of defense with the United States, Britain, and France.

Within days of Iraq's invasion of Kuwait in 1990, King Fahad allowed U.S. troops into the Kingdom to help defend the country. In November 1990, he announced that plans were being made for the formation of a Consultative Council; there was some feeling that this was done in response to criticism that he had not consulted widely enough before allowing foreign troops into the Kingdom. In any case, in March 1992, the King announced that the Consultative Council would be appointed by year's end, and he made its duties clear. Like other such creations in the Gulf States, the Council is a purely consultative body with no legislative powers. Its formation, however, simply put an official stamp on the long-standing system of consultation, which has long been a mark of Arab politics and society. King Fahad suffered a stroke in 1995 and died on August 1, 2005. He is succeeded by his half-brother, Crown Prince Abdullah.

The U.S. administration under George W. Bush has a primary mission in the region, which is hunting down the al Qaeda in the Gulf States. President George W. Bush made some tough statements on June 24, 2002, when he outlined the new U.S. plan for peace in the Middle East and set specific terms for dealing with the Palestinians. He again called on Palestinians to reform and promised that, when the Palestinian people have new leaders, new institutions, and new security arrangements with their neighbors, the United States of America would approve and support the creation of a Palestinian State, whose borders and certain aspects of its sovereignty will be provisional until resolved as part of a final settlement in the Middle East. Since that statement, little has changed, and no positive recognition has come to the Palestinians, who are bogged down into infighting between Hamas, controlling the Gaza Strip, and the Fatah-dominated region of the West Bank.

Demanding that the Palestinians essentially replace Yasser Arafat, Washington had substantially improved Arafat's position. Anyone within the Palestinian community (at that time) who had demanded Arafat's resignation was open to the charge of collaborating with the Americans. The United States was aware of the consequences of its demand. By making reform and new leadership prerequisites for further American participation in a peace process, the United States created the framework for its withdrawal from that process.

The U.S. president was, in effect, washing his hands of trying to solve the Israeli-Palestinian conflict. Washington's challenge, however, was not aimed at the Palestinians but at the country that pushed for greater U.S. involvement in the peace process—Saudi Arabia. Riyadh tried to shift U.S. attention from its war against terrorists and al Qaeda by making clear resolution of the Israeli-Palestinian conflict a key prerequisite for Saudi cooperation in hunting down Osama bin Laden's associates and financiers. Bush's actions were a warning to the Saudis that the conflict between Israel and the Palestinians could no longer serve as a distraction.

By no longer taking responsibility for the Palestinians, Washington seems to be reaffirming its goal of destroying al Qaeda. To do this, it must strike at the network's center of gravity, Saudi Arabia. In response, the oil-rich Kingdom may now seek to create alliances to resist American pressure.

FROM THE PALESTINIANS TO RIYADH

Saudi Arabia inserted itself in the peace process when Crown Prince Abdullah used a column written by the *New York Times* writer Thomas Friedman, earlier in 2002, to publicize his own newly created Middle East peace proposal. Abdullah offered Israel complete normalization of ties with all the Arab States in exchange for Israel's full withdrawal to the 1967 borders. Though this was a promise Riyadh actually could not deliver, the tactic worked to buy time and direct the U.S. focus away, albeit temporarily, from Iraq and al Qaeda.

President Bush's Middle East policy seems to make the United States appear eager to expand its involvement in the Middle East conflict. It was clear that the Bush administration would be able to achieve reforms only if the Palestinians were willing to work with Washington. However, peace requires a new and different Palestinian leadership, and with Arafat's death in 2004, the way should have been cleared for the "road map" to take shape. President Bush has indicated that although Washington would continue to be engaged, its focus will change. Specifically, the Bush administration will try to segment its Middle East policy, placing the Israeli-Palestinian conflict in a box to freely adopt a policy to pursue its primary Middle Eastern goals—of destroying the al Qaeda, and its wider plans of establishing democracy in Iraq and the region. Containing Iran and its designs on nuclear weapons also figures into U.S. strategy for the region. The single most important piece of any U.S. strategy to annihilate bin Laden's terrorist network is to do something about Saudi Arabia. Since Riyadh continues to be a key U.S. ally in the Gulf, whereas the other regional power, Iran, is decidedly anti-American, Washington has resisted placing any blame for 9-11 squarely on the Saudis.

AL QAEDA AND THE SAUDI KINGDOM

Immediately after the events of 9-11, the United States considered that the efforts by the Saudi regime to curtail and track down supporters of al Qaeda were insufficient. It is important to note that the Saudi Royal family rules this oil-rich kingdom. This family has over 6,000 princes, including 45 ruling princes, and it should be no surprise to discover that there are splits within the family as to the support being given and offered to the United States. The ruling princes are mostly progressive in their attitudes toward the West but there are a growing number within the family who are much more conservative. Strong anti-Western sentiment, not just in the Middle East but also in Saudi Arabia, will pose difficulties for the dictatorial governance of the King. The decade of the 1980s was characterized by the rise of ultraconservative, politically activist Islamic movements in much of the Arab world. These Islamist movements, labeled *fundamentalist* in the West, sought the government institutionalization of Islamic laws and social principles. Although Saudi Arabia already claimed to be an Islamic government whose constitution is the Quran, the Kingdom has not been immune to this conservative trend.[3]

WAHHABI ISLAM

The term *Wahhabism* is an outsiders' designation for the religious movement within Islam founded by Muhammad ibn Abd al-Wahhab (1703–1792). Members describe themselves as muwahhidun ("unitarians"), those who uphold firmly the doctrine that God is one, the only one (wahid). This self-designation points to the movement's major characteristic—its opposition to any custom or belief threatening and jeopardizing the glorification of the one God. Wahabbiyyah is not a new sect within Islam but a movement whose purpose is to purify Islam of perceived heretical accretions. The **Wahhabis** claim to base their doctrines on the teachings of the fourteenth-century scholar Ibn Taymiyya and the rulings of the Hanbali School of Law, the strictest of the four recognized in the Sunni consensus. They believe that all objects of worship other than Allah are false, and anyone who worships in this way deserves to be put to death. To introduce the name of a prophet, saint, or angel into a prayer or to seek intercession from anyone but Allah constitutes a form of polytheism. Attendance at public prayer is compulsory, and the shaving of the beard and smoking are forbidden. Mosques should be architecturally simple, not luxurious or ornate. Prohibited are the celebrations of the Prophet's birthday, making offerings at the tomb of saints, and playing music. The injunctions of the Quran are to be taken literally.[4]

Osama bin Laden comes from a wealthy Saudi background and yet spent little time immersed in the teachings and preachings of the strict adherence to Wahhabism. From his behavior and comments, it would be more likely to assume he accepts the ideology of Sayyid Qutb. Bin Laden believes that the Saudi Royal family's support for Western interests is a betrayal of Islam. Although the strict adherence to Wahhabism continues in the Kingdom, the Saudi approach had always been to encourage those who wanted to spread the word of Islam, and violent jihad to do so wherever they wished—but not at home and within the Saudi Kingdom. This strategy worked well for the most part, with the Saudis exporting militants to Bosnia, Afghanistan, and Iraq. Recent attacks on Western interests in the Kingdom indicate clearly that the influences of the al Qaeda network are no longer confined to remote locations in Afghanistan and the Russian Republics. Fighters are returning to Saudi Arabia and are targeting the Western influences within the Kingdom. Al Qaeda's ultimate goals for the Kingdom are:

- Removal of the Royal family; and
- Removal of all Western influences in the Kingdom.

Owing to the massive U.S. presence in Iraq, anti-Western sentiment is growing quickly in Saudi Arabia. To effectively deal with al Qaeda operatives and sympathizers, the Saudis have to rely on their own security apparatus. Although Saudi security services have arrested many terror suspects, they have been unsuccessful at infiltration, garnering most of their intelligence from arrested suspects. Throughout 2003 and 2004, in almost every shootout that took place, involving terrorist attacks against Western targets and Saudi security forces, al Qaeda members were able to escape to fight another day. The availability of well-trained bomb makers returning from Iraq to set up operations in Saudi has had the desired effect on Western companies. So many have been targeted that it is having a negative effect on the oil economy of the Saudi Kingdom, which is almost totally reliant on Western expertise for its oil production. Al Qaeda's actual strength in the Kingdom may be small and limited to around 100 hardcore members, but it has the sympathy of about 50 percent of the population. This sympathy, coupled with any possible power struggle within the Saudi Royal family, could well lead to an eventual collapse of the existing pro-Western regime.

At the end of 2004, bin Laden was calling openly for attacks against his Saudi homeland. However, security forces in the Kingdom have been cracking down hard since the string of bomb attacks in 2003. Al Qaida's leader on the Saudi Peninsula, Fahd bin Faraj al-Juweir, is on record threatening not only Westerners but also the Saudi regime itself. He led a failed suicide attack on the Abqaiq Oil Refinery on February 24, 2006, and was subsequently killed three days later in a two-hour shootout with Saudi security forces. Two suicide attackers, both on a list of wanted militants, were killed in the refinery attack, which was the first significant strike by al Qaida militants on oil facilities in the region.

Sayyid Qutb

Sayyid Qutb joined the Brotherhood in 1951 and is probably the one man who could be considered the ideological grandfather of Osama bin Laden and the other extremists who surround him. Sayyid Qutb became radicalized on a trip to the United States back in the early 1950s. As Qutb traveled through America, he was shocked at the moral and spiritual degeneracy he observed, stating that "no one is more distant than the Americans from spirituality and piety."

In his home country of Egypt his outspoken behavior brought him into direct conflict with the pro-western government of the day. Like so many other young radicals, he was thrown in prison, where deprivation and torture were the norm. One of the most important things Sayyid Qutb wrote about was his explanation of how a Muslim might justly assassinate a ruler. For a long time, killing political rulers was expressly forbidden in Islam—even an unjust ruler was regarded as better than the anarchy of no ruler. Instead, the religious leaders of the *ulama* (Islamic scholars) were expected to keep the rulers in line. Qutb was hanged in Egypt in 1966.[5]

The Saudi wing of al Qaeda has been waging a violent campaign for more than four years aimed at toppling the pro-U.S. Saudi monarchy and expelling Westerners from the birthplace of Islam. Its most successful year would appear to be 2003, when suicide bombers attacked three Western housing complexes in Riyadh, but since then al Qaeda has been relatively contained. Throughout 2007 and into 2008 al Qaeda's relevance in Saudi Arabia has been insignificant especially by bin Laden's standards. In 2007, al Qaeda attacks were limited to just a single attack on February 26, allegedly, by Walid Mutlaq al-Rashadi, one of Saudi Arabia's most wanted terrorists. This was an attack against French and Belgian citizens traveling by car in the northwest of the country, killing four Frenchmen. In April 2007, the Saudis announced that they had arrested 172 suspected militants, 40 foreign nationals and 132 Saudi citizens. Historically, arrests by the Saudi security forces have involved shootouts and invariably loss of life to one or more of the militants. The likelihood is that this latest batch of militant arrests were part of the logistics and planning for a series of attacks and most likely none were front line actors—so no last-stand shootout or heroics. Looking forward it seems at the present that al Qaeda is having a difficult time trying desperately to maintain some level of relevance in Saudi Arabia. It has tried to appeal to all levels of society, including the security forces, with little or no success. Al Qaeda's leadership is clearly struggling to remain relevant in the ideological realm, a daunting task for an organization that has been rendered geopolitically and strategically impotent on the physical battlefield.[6]

KUWAIT

The State of Kuwait, a nominal constitutional monarchy, is slightly smaller than New Jersey, and lies between Iraq and Saudi Arabia, bordering the Persian Gulf. While its primary natural resource is petroleum, fish, shrimp, and natural gas are also plentiful. It is another Persian Gulf country with almost no arable land and no permanent crops (about 75 percent of its potable water must be distilled or imported). Kuwait has strategic value in its location at the entrance to the Persian Gulf. The small population of only 1,834,269 includes 1,381,063 nonnationals. The ethnic mix is 45 percent Kuwaiti, 35 percent other Arab, 9 percent South Asian, 4 percent Iranian, and 7 percent other. Muslims make up 85 percent of the religious followers, but are split: Shia 30 percent, Sunni 45 percent, and other 10 percent. Christians, Hindus, Parsi, and others make up the remaining 15 percent. While the official language is Arabic, English is widely spoken, as Kuwait only gained its independence from the United Kingdom in 1961.

The Chief of State is Amir Sheikh Saad Al-Abdullah Al-Sabah (since January 2006), and the head of government is the prime minister. While there are no official political parties and leaders, several political groups act as de facto parties (e.g., Bedouins, merchants, Sunni and Shia activists, and secular leftists and nationalists).

Kuwait has a small and relatively open economy with proven crude oil reserves of about 94 billion barrels, or roughly 10 percent of world reserves. Kuwait has rebuilt its war-ravaged petroleum sector; its crude oil production averages two million barrels per day. Petroleum accounts for nearly half of its GDP, 90 percent of export revenues, and 75 percent of government income. Kuwait lacks water and has practically no arable land, thus preventing development of agriculture. With the exception of fish, it depends almost totally on food imports. Because of its high per capita income, comparable with Western European incomes, Kuwait provides its citizens with extensive health, educational, and retirement benefits. The bulk of the workforce is non-Kuwaiti, who live at a considerably lower level of life than the natives. Per capita military expenditures are among the highest in the world. Kuwait's economy has improved moderately since 1994, with the growth in industry and finance. The World Bank has urged Kuwait to push ahead with privatization, including in the oil industry, but the government will move slowly on opening up the petroleum sector. Relatively low petroleum prices can have a serious impact on the Kuwaiti economy. The civil telephone network suffered some damage as a result of the Gulf War, but most of the telephone exchanges were left intact. By the end of 1994 Kuwait had restored domestic and international telecommunications to normal operation, and the quality of service is excellent.

In November 1994, Iraq formally accepted the UN-demarcated border with Kuwait that had been spelled out in Security Council Resolutions 687 (1991), 773 (1993), and 883 (1993). This formally ended Iraq's earlier claims to Kuwait and to Bubiyan and Warbah Islands. Saudi Arabia disputes ownership of Qaruh and the Umm al Maradim Islands.

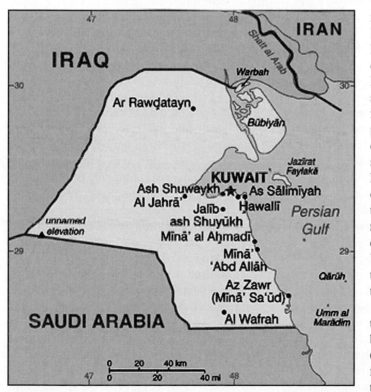

FIGURE 9-2   Map of Kuwait (Central Intelligence Agency, *The World Factbook*, 2008).

The present **Al-Sabah dynasty** was established in Kuwait in the mid-eighteenth century, about 1760. Kuwait was nominally a province of the Ottoman Empire, ruled from Constantinople. This was observed on paper but seldom in fact. In 1899, when the Turks threatened to take actual control of the country, the ruling sheikh sought and received British protection.

The Kuwait Oil Company discovered oil in Kuwait in 1938, but because of World War II it was not exported until 1946, after which time Kuwait's economy flourished. Kuwait remained a British Protectorate until 1961, when it became independent under Sheikh Abdullah Al-Salem Al-Sabah. However, when Iraq claimed the emirate in the early 1960s, it once again received British protection. In July 1961, Kuwait joined the Arab League and in 1963 became a member of the United Nations. In February 1963, the first legislative elections were held, and Sheikh Abdullah, the Emir of Kuwait, inaugurated the first National Assembly.

During the 1980s, Kuwait experienced several terrorist attacks by Shiite Muslim extremists, including one in 1985 that attempted to assassinate the emir. Kuwait, like most Arab States, supported Iraq in the Iran-Iraq war (1980–1988). Kuwait played a major role in establishing the Gulf Cooperation Council (GCC) in 1981, consisting of Saudi Arabia, Kuwait, Bahrain, Qatar, the United Arab Emirates, and the Sultanate of Oman. The Council held a firm position during Iraq's invasion of Kuwait on August 2, 1990, and its seven-month occupation of the Emirate.

When the oil industry was developed, Kuwait used the resources to tame the desert through construction and the planting of greenery. The oil resources were also used for the good of the Kuwaiti people and their brothers and sisters in developing countries around the world. Rather than befriend a tyrant, or surrender to Saddam Hussein in the Gulf War, Kuwait stood firm in the heart of all the battles it faced. The battle of resistance against aggression was followed by the battle of extinguishing the oil fires and of rebuilding a ravaged nation. During the period of the Iraqi occupation, from August 2, 1990, to Kuwait's liberation on February 26, 1991, the inhabitants of Kuwait once again gave evidence of their strength and fierce determination. After a decade, a whole generation is growing up with the memory of the Iraq invasion of Kuwait, but the younger teenage generation, with more fundamental, even radical views, seems to be sympathetic to the cause of the jihad in Iraq. Kuwait has a land border with Iraq, and it is one of the main staging points for U.S. troops en route to Iraq. It is also likely a returning point for insurgents escaping from areas such as Fallujah. Kuwait's proximity to the war zone—Iraq—has led to a spread of al Qaeda influence in the country. There are indications that Kuwaitis have been involved in suicide missions in Iraq against U.S. targets. It is also clear that Kuwaiti extremists were training in camps in Afghanistan during the Taliban regime, and the likelihood is that some may have returned to Kuwait to further attack U.S. interest there. Taped messages from the number one terrorist in Iraq, al Zarqawi, called on fighters in 2005 to return to Kuwait and attack not only U.S. interests but also Kuwaiti government officials.[7] The U.S. and coalition strike at Fallujah had the effect of galvanizing Islamic groups in Kuwait to lobby the government to condemn the actions. Many Muslim groups, particularly those in Kuwait, are still smarting from the Abu Ghraib prisoner abuse scandal and view it as part of the United States' overall plan to attack Islam and Muslims. Attacks in Kuwait, in comparison to those in Saudi Arabia, have been relatively minor. However, that has not discouraged the authorities from reactivating a 1984 law banning women drivers from wearing a veil covering their faces, on the premise that terrorists could disguise themselves. Unlicensed mosques that were constructed without the proper planning and consent were destroyed to prevent them from being used as militant hideouts. More extensive laws were introduced to search private premises and homes for weapons. Stricter control of extremist Web sites was also enforced.[8]

The Arab Gulf States, and this includes Kuwait, relies on foreign military support for their defense—as we saw in 1990 when Saddam Hussein invaded and occupied Kuwait. Kuwait's ruling family fled to the sanctuary of neighboring Saudi Arabia. That being said, we need to appreciate that these States need to contain the Shiite political influence in Iraq and prevent the spread of the Shiite militia groups, and they do this by providing a robust Sunni presence in the region. Iraq's Shiite militias are well trained and equipped by Iran's Revolutionary Guard Corps. The other factor that is in the hands of the Gulf States is the control of the world's oil distribution and by increasing the amount of oil being produced could seriously damage the Iranian oil industry, which utilizes outdated technology. As Iraq continues to be a melting pot for political antics and insurgency mayhem, the Sunni/Shia ethnic divide is a topic to be exploited by both the Saudi influence in the Gulf region and Iran. Iran has gone one up on the Saudis in this regard and has appealed to all Muslims (not only Shiites) to rise above nationalistic and sectarian divisions and called for pan-Islamic unity. This has not become a reality, but it does make the Saudi regime extremely cautious in its dealings with Iran. Saudi Arabia has always seen itself as the leader of the Islamic world and has on many occasions attempted to use the ethnic card to create a rift between Iranian Shia and those in the Gulf States.

IRAQ

Iraq is 97 percent Muslim (Shia, 60–65 percent; Sunni, 32–37 percent) and 3 percent Christian or other. The official languages are Arabic and Kurdish.

The Ba'thist regime, which held power over the last three decades of the twentieth century, engaged in extensive central planning and management of industrial production and foreign trade while leaving some small-scale industry and services and most agriculture to private enterprise. Iraq's economy has been dominated by the oil sector, which has traditionally provided about 95 percent of foreign exchange earnings. In the 1980s, financial problems were caused by massive expenditures in the eight-year war with Iran and damage to oil export facilities by Iran. This led the government to implement austerity measures and to borrow heavily and later reschedule foreign debt payments. Iraq suffered economic losses of at least $100 billion from the war. After the end of hostilities in 1988, oil exports gradually increased with the construction of new pipelines and restoration of damaged facilities. Iraq's seizure of Kuwait in 1990, and subsequent international economic embargoes and military action by an international coalition beginning in January 1991, drastically changed its economic picture. Industrial and transportation facilities, which suffered severe damage, have been partially restored. Oil exports were at only 25 percent of the prewar level because of implementation of UN Security Council Resolution 986 in December 1996. The UN-sponsored economic embargo had reduced exports and imports and contributed to a sharp rise in prices. The Iraqi government had been unwilling to abide by UN resolutions so that the economic embargo could be removed. The government's policies of supporting large military and internal security forces and of allocating resources to key supporters of the regime had exacerbated shortages. In accord with a UN resolution, Iraq agreed to an oil-for-food deal in 1996, under which it would export $2 billion worth of oil in exchange for badly needed food and medicine. The first oil was pumped in December 1996, and the first supplies of food and medicine arrived in 1997.

FIGURE 9-3   Map of Iraq (Central Intelligence Agency, *The World Factbook*, 2008).

SADDAM HUSSEIN (1937–2006)

Saddam Hussein was born in Auja, near Tirkit in 1937. He was president and prime minister of Iraq from 1979 to 2003. His political platform was a combination of moderate social democracy, close to the European model, amidst a struggle to keep the country of various ethnic and religious groups together. In the West, the image of Saddam Hussein went through a dramatic change, from being one of Europe's and the United State's favorites into the most negatively presented dictator in the world. UN officials confirmed that Iraq had contravened the Geneva Convention by using chemical weapons against Iran. Iraq also used "mustard gas" from 1983 and the "nerve gas **Tabun**" from 1985, as it faced attacks from "human waves" of Iranian troops and poorly trained but loyal volunteers. Tabun can kill within minutes. In 1988 Iraq turned its chemical weapons on Iraqi Kurds in the north of the country. Saddam Hussein's invasion and occupation of Kuwait would cast him as a complete pariah in the region. On the home front he presided over a secular state with relative freedom for the economic sector and freedom for women; there was also free education. He adopted a widespread and intricate system of secret police and spies to keep control on his people. Opposition to the Ba'ath Party regime was unheard of and those who were seen as plotting against his regime were arrested, tortured, and killed. He was responsible for the deaths of thousands of his own people. Saddam was a Sunni Muslim, and the minority Sunnis enjoyed benefits and positions in Iraqi society, but other groups, especially Shia, were denied these benefits. After the U.S.-led invasion of Iraq Saddam was eventually captured, tried, and convicted by an Iraqi court of crimes against humanity and his own people, the Kurds, the Marsh Arabs, and thousands of others who suffered under his rule. He was executed by hanging on December 30, 2006. One of Saddam Hussein's most senior officials, Ali Hassan al-Majid, also his first cousin, acquired the name "**Chemical Ali**" as well as the "Butcher of Kurdistan" for his role in leading the al-Anfal Campaign, during which he ordered a toxic gas attack on the Kurdish town of Halabja that resulted in the deaths of thousands of Kurds. He was the regional commander in southern Iraq and was responsible for suppressing the southern uprising of the Shiites. Ali was captured on August 21, 2003, and convicted of crimes against humanity and has been sentenced to death.

Iran and Iraq restored diplomatic relations in 1990 but were still trying to work out written agreements settling outstanding disputes from their eight-year war concerning border demarcation, prisoners of war, and freedom of navigation and sovereignty over the Shatt al Arab waterway. In November 1994, Iraq formally accepted the UN-demarcated border with Kuwait that had been spelled out in Security Council Resolutions. This formally ended Iraq's earlier claims to Kuwait and to Bubiyan and the Warbah Islands. There is still dispute over Turkey's water development plans for the Tigris and Euphrates Rivers. Ironically, the area of the Middle East we now call Iraq, which we have seen in recent decades as a major source for state-sponsored terrorism and constant wars, is also where, many scholars agree, recorded history as we know it began.

In ancient times, the landmass of Iraq formed a major portion of Mesopotamia, the land between the two rivers (Tigris and Euphrates). The Mesopotamian plain was called the Fertile Crescent. This region was the birthplace of the varied civilizations that moved us from prehistory to history. An advanced civilization flourished in this region long before those of Egypt, Greece, and Rome, for it was here, in about 4,000 B.C., that the Sumerian culture flourished. Land was cultivated for the first time in this area, early calendars were used, and the first written alphabet was invented there. Its bountiful land, freshwaters, and varying climate contributed to the creation of a deep-rooted civilization that fostered humanity.

Hammurabi was the King and a great lawgiver of the Old Babylonian (Amorite) Dynasty. His legal code was produced in the second year of his reign. Many new legal concepts were introduced by the Babylonians, and many have been adopted by other civilizations. These concepts included the following:

• Legal protection should be provided to lower classes;
• The state is the authority responsible for enforcing the law;

- Social justice should be guaranteed; and
- Punishment should fit the crime.

A copy of the code is engraved on a block of black diorite nearly eight feet high. A team of French archaeologists at Susa, Iraq, formerly ancient Elam, unearthed this block, during the winter of 1901–1902. The block, broken in three pieces, has been restored and is now in the Louvre Museum in Paris.

Abu Ja'far Muhammad ibn Musa al-Khawarizmi (680–750 A.D.), a great scholar and mathematician, originated algebraic equations. Some credit him with the invention of the concept of "zero." Al-Khawarizmi wrote ten math textbooks that have survived the test of time. His *Kitab hisab al'adad al-hindi* was an arithmetic textbook that introduced Hindu numbers to the Arab world; now they are generally known as Arabic numbers. Christian Europeans at first rejected the Arabic numbers and declared them the work of Satan. His major work is entitled *Kitab (al-jabr) w'al-muqabalah*, whose title gives us the word, "Algebra."

With a long and important history, Iraq developed into a major country on the Persian Gulf. In 1936, King Ghazi I formed the Pan Arab movement with the other Arab States, promising kinship and nonaggression. The first coup d'état in the modern Arab world came in 1936 as well, led by General Baks Sidqi. This marked a major turning point in Iraq's history, opening the door for further military involvement in politics. In 1945, Iraq became a founding member of the Arab League and joined the United Nations.

Iraq joined in the war with Israel in 1948, in alliance with Jordan, according to a treaty signed by the two countries during the previous year. The war had a negative impact on the Iraqi economy. Oil royalties paid to Iraq were halved when the pipeline to Haifa was cut off. The war led to the departure of most of Iraq's prosperous Jewish community. About 120,000 Iraqi Jews immigrated to Israel between 1948 and 1952. In 1961, Kuwait gained its independence from Britain and Abdul-Karim Qassim immediately claimed the Emirate as originally part of the Ottoman province of Basrah. Britain reacted strongly by dispatching a brigade to the country to deter Iraq. Qassim backed down. In 1963, Iraq finally recognized the sovereignty and borders of Kuwait (but this was not to be the last page of that story).

In the years leading up to 1979 Saddam Hussein was the power base behind the ailing President General Ahmed Hasan Al-Bakr. Bakr had appointed Saddam as his Vice President and when he stepped down due to ill-health Saddam Hussein took full control as President of Iraq, he immediately began a sustained purge of all his and the Ba'ath Party's political rivals to assure his position and total control of Iraq. Once more, the political situation flared into hostilities with Iran. The Iran-Iraq war, which began in 1980, lasted for eight years and had a crippling effect on the economies of both countries. It was a monumental disaster, and neither side gained any territory. But an estimated total of one million lives had been lost. In July 1988, Iran accepted the terms of UN Resolution 598, and the ceasefire came about. Before Iraq had a chance to recover economically, Saddam once more plunged into war, with the invasion of Kuwait in 1990.

The United States got involved and declared its interest in protecting Kuwaiti sovereignty. In the ensuing months, the UN Security Council passed a series of resolutions condemning the Iraqi occupation of Kuwait, and applied total, mandatory economic sanctions against Iraq. A coalition of NATO nations and Arab States subsequently provided support for Operation Desert Shield. In November 1990, the UN Security Council adopted Resolution 678, permitting member states to use all necessary means, authorizing military action against the Iraqi forces occupying Kuwait, and demanding Iraq's complete withdrawal by January 1991.

Saddam Hussein failed to comply with this demand, and the Gulf War, Operation Desert Storm, began on January 17, 1991. Allied troops from twenty-eight countries took part. The combined air forces of Great Britain and the United States launched an aerial bombardment on Baghdad to start the battle. The war, which proved disastrous for Iraq, lasted only six weeks, but 140,000 tons of munitions were dropped on the country, and as many as 100,000 Iraqi soldiers were killed.

Coalition air raids destroyed roads, bridges, factories, and oil industry facilities and disrupted electric, telephone, and water service. Finally, a ceasefire was announced on February 28, 1991. Iraq agreed to UN terms for a permanent ceasefire in April of that year, and strict conditions were imposed, demanding the disclosure and destruction of all stockpiles of weapons, including weapons of mass destruction (WMD).

Insurrections quickly broke out in southern Iraq and in Kurdistan in the north, where rebels took control of most of the region's towns. Units of Saddam's elite Republican Guard that had survived the conflict suppressed protest with extreme brutality to gain control in the Basrah, Najaf, and Karbala regions. In the southern cities, rebels killed Ba'athist officials, members of the security service, and other supporters of the Saddam regime. In Kurdistan, Iraqi helicopters and troops regained control of the cities taken by the rebels, and there was a mass exodus of Kurds to the Turkish and Iranian borders, fleeing from a possible repeat of the 1988 deadly chemical attacks. By the end of April 1991, 2.5 million refugees had fled from Iraq.

The United States, attempting to prevent the genocide of the Marsh Arabs in southern Iraq and the Kurds to the north, established air exclusion zones north of the 36th parallel and south of the 32nd parallel. The attempted assassination of former President George Bush in Kuwait prompted a swift military response on June 27, 1993. The Iraqi Intelligence Headquarters in Baghdad was targeted by twenty-three Tomahawk cruise missiles, launched from U.S. warships in the Red Sea and Persian Gulf.

In October 1994, Iraq again moved some Republican Guard units toward Kuwait, an act that provoked large-scale U.S. troop deployment to deter an Iraqi attack. The move was interpreted as a sign of Saddam's frustration with the continuation of stiff UN sanctions, but he backed down (establishing a pattern of behavior he continued using until the U.S. invasion of Iraq in 2003). He agreed to recognize the existence and borders of Kuwait. In the months that followed, Hussein's position appeared to become more precarious as dissatisfaction with his rule spread in the army and among the tribes and clans at the core of his regime.

In 1995, Saddam fired his half-brother, Wathban, as Interior Minister and in July demoted his notorious and powerful Defense Minister, Ali Hassan al-Majid, to give more power to his two sons, Udai and Qusai. It became clear that Saddam felt more secure when protected by his immediate family members. Major General Hussein Kamil Hassan al-Majid, his Minister of Military Industries and a key henchman, defected to Jordan, together with his wife (one of Saddam's daughters) and his brother, Saddam (also married to one of Saddam's daughters), and called for the overthrow of the regime. In response, Saddam promised full co-operation with the UN commission that was disarming Iraq (UNSCOM) in order to preempt any revelations that the defectors might make. Not surprisingly, when Saddam forgave the defectors and they returned to Iraq, other clan members murdered them both, soon after they crossed the border.

The weakening of the internal position of the regime occurred at a time when the external opposition forces were as weak as ever—too divided to take any effective action. At the same time, France and Russia were pushing for an easing of sanctions. The United States and Britain's determination to keep up the pressure on Iraq had prevailed, however. In any case, the apparent weakening of the regime was illusory. In fact, during 1996, the regime's grip on power seemed to have significantly strengthened despite Saddam's inability to end the UN sanctions. There was yet another major buildup of U.S. forces in the Gulf, as a result of Saddam's refusal to allow unrestricted UN inspections of suspected sites for storing weapons of mass destruction. In May of 2002, on the eve of signing a historic U.S.-Russian nuclear arms reduction treaty, President Bush spoke strongly to President Putin of the Russian Republic, "If you arm Iran, you're liable to get the weapons pointed at you." Bush considered Russia's dealings with Iran the single, greatest proliferation threat on the globe at the time. On a day that took him from the old East-West divide of Berlin to the heart of the former Soviet Union, a defiant Bush answered critics of his expanding antiterror war plans. He denounced anyone who would appease terrorists or ignore threats to Europe.

Bush and Putin met to sign a ten-year treaty binding the nations to reduce their nuclear stockpiles by about two-thirds—to a range of 1,700 to 2,200 each. The three-page treaty has a preamble and just five articles. Hundreds of Communists and leftists staged a noisy protest at the U.S. Embassy in the German capital. Bush responded to antiwar protesters who clogged city streets a day before—and to European leaders balking at his hopes of toppling Saddam.

President Bush came face to face with European opposition when three lawmakers from the ex-Communist party of Democratic Socialism, seated about 20 feet away, held up a banner reading: "Bush, Schroeder, Stop your wars." In a news conference before the address, German Chancellor Gerhard Schroeder declined to join Bush in pushing for a government change in Iraq. Separately, Defense Minister Rudolf Scharping suggested that Germany did not have the resources to participate in military action against Saddam. "We have no room for a new engagement," Scharping told German television. Nuclear proliferation is a sour point in a U.S.-Russia relationship that has flourished since 9-11. On another troubling issue, Bush said Putin understands that a loose nuke could affect his security and is doing what he can to prevent terrorists from getting nuclear materials from Russian stockpiles.

OPERATION IRAQI FREEDOM AND BEYOND

Saddam Hussein's reign came to an abrupt end in March 2003 following a demand by U.S. President George W. Bush that Saddam Hussein and his two sons, Uday and Qusay, leave Iraq immediately. Bush promptly provided a forty-eight-hour deadline for compliance. No one expected the Iraqi dictator to comply with such a demand, and the following day, U.S. spokesman Ari Fleischer announced that the United States would invade Iraq whether Saddam and his sons left Iraq or not. Fleisher stated that "the bottom line is, a coalition of the willing will disarm Saddam Hussein's Iraq, no matter what." The U.S. justification for the invasion has been widely debated and challenged. Most importantly, the United States and Britain's action did not have the explicit endorsement of the United Nations. Most scholarly and legal authorities have concluded that the action violated the UN Charter. With the invasion by land and attacks from the air, the Iraqi military machine crumbled away and, on May 1, 2003, George Bush announced an end to major combat. Most of the Iraqi military and the well-trained and equipped Iraqi Republican Guard had not fought or been captured, but had simply "gone home." They took their weapons and munitions with them, however, and would be the starting point for the years of insurgency to follow. Apart from the regular conscript army of Iraq and the Republican Guard, there was a third and vitally important paramilitary group that had been established in the mid 1990s—namely, the Fedayeen Saddam. This organization numbered around 40,000 to 50,000 members and was staffed by Sunnis and supporters of the Ba'ath Party regime of Saddam Hussein. This group had been variously under the control of both Uday and Qusay Hussein for periods of time. The Fedayeen was responsible for some of the most atrocious acts against Ba'athist opponents. It conducted widespread campaigns of assassination but was loyal to the Party. With the removal of Saddam Hussein, this force of fighters was adequately prepared and would have little to lose in fighting the United States and any Shiite-dominated government that came to power.

Deaths of Uday and Qusay Hussein—July 22, 2003

Lt. Gen. Ricardo Sanchez, Commander, Combined Joint Task Force Seven (CJTF-7) said:

> Today our coalition forces, associated with the 101st Airborne Division, Special Forces and Air Force assets, conducted an operation against suspected regime members. An Iraqi source informed the 101st Airborne division on today that several suspects, including Qusay and Uday, numbers two and three on the U.S. Central Command's most-wanted list, were hiding in a residence near the northern edge of the city. The six-hour operation began when the division's Second Brigade Combat Team approached the house and received small-arms fire. The division subsequently employed multiple

weapons systems to subdue the suspects, who had barricaded themselves inside the house and continued to resist detention fiercely. Four persons were killed during that operation and were removed from the building, and we have since confirmed that Uday and Qusay Hussein are among the dead. The site is currently being exploited.[9]

The minority Sunnis controlled Iraq for the last four decades of the twentieth century and had kept the large Shia majority firmly in check. Saddam's security apparatus—and it was a well-organized one—melted away in the face of the U.S.-led invasion. It has been able to immerse itself back into society to carry on attacks against both the invading coalition forces and the Iraqi Shiites. Much has been broadcast on news media and the Internet of Western hostages and their vile treatment, including torture and decapitation, but what has not been reported is that kidnappings of Iraqi citizens have far outnumbered those of Westerners. Basic law and order have been on the brink of total collapse and lawlessness is an everyday issue in Iraq. The numbers of insurgent organizations operating in Iraq have multiplied since the official end to hostilities in 2003. Both sides—Sunni and Shia—have developed fronts and insurgent forces to attack each other, but most frequently their goal is to attack U.S. and coalition troops. The Sunni fighters include the following insurgent groups:

The Iraqi National Islamic Resistance: This group wants to establish an Islamic Iraq free from external interference and the forcible removal of U.S. forces. Its activities have centered on Baghdad, and its attacks have been primarily launched against military targets in areas west of Baghdad. It takes account of its activities by distributing information outside mosques at Friday prayers.

The National Front for the Liberation of Iraq: This organization was formed soon after the invasion in 2003 and its influence is spread throughout the country. It consists of Islamists and nationalists and carries out attacks similar to those of the Iraqi National Islamic Resistance. In a statement sent to IslamOnline.net, the Front revealed that "after intensive contacts with a number of armed Iraqi groups and Arab volunteers who flocked to the country ahead of the U.S.-led invasion, a unified resistance command has now been forged." It indicated that the contacts made also included elements from Saddam Fedayeen and Ba'athists who were not loyal to Saddam Hussein.

The Iraqi Resistance Islamic Front (JAMI): This relatively new group, which formed in mid-2004, brings together a small coalition of resistance fighters. Its front of operations against the United States is located in the Ninwi and Diyali region. It takes the stand that by declaring jihad it has the duty to fight the invaders. According to statements issued by the front, JAMI's military wing, the Salah-al-Din and Sayf-Allah al-Maslul Brigades, has carried out dozens of operations against the U.S. occupation forces. The most prominent of these operations was in Ninwi Governorate, where operations included the shelling of the occupation command headquarters and the semi-daily shelling of the Mosul airport.

Imam Ali Bin-Abi-Talib Jihadi Brigades: This Shiite group appeared for the first time on October 12, 2003. It vowed to kill the soldiers of any country sending its troops to support the coalition forces, and threatened to transfer the battleground to the territories of such countries if they were to send troops. The group also threatened to assassinate all the members of the Interim Governing Council and any Iraqi cooperating with the coalition forces. The group also announced that Al-Najaf and Karbala were the battlegrounds in which it would target U.S. forces.

In addition to the groups resisting occupation, other armed groups have emerged and resorted to operations of abducting and killing foreigners as a method, in their opinion, to terrorize the enemy and as a political pressure card to achieve their specific demands.

The Black Banners Group: This group is a battalion of the Secret Islamic Army. The group abducted three Indians, two Kenyans, and an Egyptian who worked for a Kuwaiti company operating in Iraq. The aim was to compel the company to stop its activities in Iraq. The hostages were later released.

The Islamic Army in Iraq: This secret organization adopts the ideology of al Qaeda. The organization abducted Iranian Consul Feredion Jahani and two French journalists, Georges Malbrunot and Christian Chesnot.

Ansar al-Sunnah Movement: This group abducted and killed twelve Nepalese on August 23, 2004.[10]

Ansar al-Islam: Formed in 1998 as a breakaway faction of Islamist Kurds, splitting off from a group, the Islamic Movement of Iraqi Kurdistan (IMIK). Both Ansar and the IMIK were initially composed almost exclusively of Kurds. U.S. concerns about Ansar grew following the U.S. defeat of the Taliban and al Qaeda in Afghanistan in late 2001, when some al Qaeda activists, mostly Arabs, fled to Iraq and associated there with the Ansar movement. At the peak, about 600 Arab fighters lived in the Ansar al-Islam enclave, near the town of Khurmal. The leader of the Arab contingent within Ansar al-Islam was **Abu Musab al-Zarqawi**, an Arab of Jordanian origin, who reputedly fought in Afghanistan. Although early assessments indicated that Zarqawi commanded Arab volunteers in Afghanistan separate from those recruited by bin Laden, Zarqawi was linked to purported al Qaeda plots in the 1990s and early 2000s. He allegedly was behind foiled bombings in Jordan during the December 1999 millennium celebration, the assassination in Jordan of U.S. diplomat Lawrence Foley (2002), and reported attempts in 2002 to spread chemical agents in Russia, Western Europe, and the United States.

Although the United States and its Iraqi partners have, from the inception of the insurgency, conducted a broad counterinsurgency campaign, a major U.S. combat focus had always been on Abu Musab al Zarqawi, his network, and his successors. On March 15, 2004, Ansar al-Islam was named as a "Foreign Terrorist Organization" (FTO) under the Immigration and Nationality Act. On October 15, 2004, the State Department named the "Monotheism and Jihad Group"—the successor to Ansar al-Islam— as an FTO. The designation said that the Monotheism group "was. . .responsible for the UN headquarters bombing in Baghdad." Later that month, perhaps in response to that designation, Zarqawi changed the name of his organization to "al Qaeda Jihad Organization in the Land of Two Rivers (Mesopotamia—Iraq)," commonly known now as al Qaeda in Iraq, or AQ-I. The FTO designation was applied to the new name.[11]

Al Qaeda in Iraq: The most well-known and publicized group, this one was led by Abu Musab al-Zarqawi—the second-most-wanted terrorist on the planet, behind Osama bin Laden.

Zarqawi was first noticed in Iraq as the leader of the Tawhid and Jihad group, which was blamed for some of the early and most bloody insurgent attacks.

They included a truck bombing that killed twenty-three at the UN headquarters in Baghdad in August 2003 and another explosion in Najaf ten days later that killed a senior Shia cleric and more than eighty-five others. Tawhid and Jihad was also known for the brutal beheadings of foreign hostages. Zarqawi achieved notoriety and was also able to elude capture. Roadside bombings and beheadings, and posting gruesome videos of his atrocities on the Internet, were the hallmark of his insurgency operations.

He was a Jordanian Palestinian born in 1966 and had been sentenced to seven years in jail in Jordan in 1992 for plotting to overthrow the Hashemite Monarchy. He was killed on June 7, 2006, when U.S. forces bombed his safe house near the city of Baquba. On June 15, 2006, it was confirmed that Egyptian Islamic Jihad militant Abu Ayyub al-Masri would succeed Zarqawi as head of al Qaeda in Iraq.

Mujahideen Shura Council

In early 2006, al Qaeda in Iraq posted an Internet statement saying it had joined five other insurgent groups in Iraq to form a new umbrella organization, the Mujahideen Shura Council. Two of these groups—the Victorious Sect Army and the Islamic Jihad Brigade—were known, while three were

FIGURE 9-4   The leader of Al Qaeda in Iraq leader, Abu Musab al-Zarqawi, killed in a precision air strike on June 6, 2006, 30 miles northeast of Baghdad (Canadian Press).

apparently new groups. The Mujahideen Shura Council issues statements and posts videos on a Web site—including a video showing the executions of two Russian hostages in June 2006. Analysts say moves to build cooperation and a unified strategy among the disparate insurgent groups have had some success.

Mahdi Army

The Mahdi army is a Shia militia movement led by Muqtada Sadr, a young, radical Shia cleric, well supported by weapons plundered during the initial weeks of the U.S.-led invasion from Iraq's enormous weapons' stockpile. Analysts also believe that the movement is financed by Iran.

Sadr's brand of Shia nationalism, opposition to the U.S. presence in Iraq and hostility toward the powerful established Shia political parties, has proved popular among poor, disenfranchised Shia communities, and his key stronghold is the slum district of Sadr City, named after his father, a revered cleric murdered by Saddam Hussein's security forces. Mahdi fighters staged uprisings against U.S.-led forces in April and August 2004, but since then Sadr has become involved in the political process and holds thirty seats in the Shia bloc that dominates parliament.

As insurgent attacks have increasingly targeted Shia areas, the Mahdi army had become one of the major armed forces on the ground in Baghdad, controlling—and protecting—predominantly Shia areas. The Shia population in many of the Baghdad neighborhoods at first welcomed the Mahdi army as the national police and municipal officials were feeble at best, but they soon changed and began to display a serious appetite for sectarian violence as well as corruption and extortion. Whole areas were "cleansed" of Sunni civilians with many being summarily executed. The **Mahdi army** took over gas stations and mosques and extorted protection money from businesses. Al-Sadr was unable to control this rogue element within his movement, and they began to lose the grassroots support they had initially enjoyed. The 2007 military surge by the U.S. military into Baghdad further loosened the Mahdi army's control of the streets. Al-Sadr's reputation was severely damaged in August 2007 by

FIGURE 9-5   Shiite cleric Muqtada al-Sadr talks to the media in his home in the holy city of Najaf. He is the leader of the Shiite Mahdi Army in Iraq (Canadian Press).

fierce fighting in the holy city of Karbala when his men fought pitched battles and were fended off by the Badr Brigade militias of the Islamic Supreme Council of Iraq. While the two main Shia factions were fighting, this was not in the grand scheme of operations for the Iranians who want to have a united Shia movement, not a fractured one. The Sadr movement is pivotal to events, both political and military, in Iraq, and in early 2007 the U.S. Commander General David Petraeus called the Mahdi army the biggest single threat to Iraq.[12] Sunnis have accused its members of carrying out sectarian killings, although Mr Sadr denies the accusations.

Badr Brigade/Corps

This is a Shiite militia similar to the Mahdi army, composed of Iraqi military officers who escaped, defected, or were captured during and after the Iran-Iraq war, 1980–1988. The movement is supported by the Supreme Council for the Islamic Revolution in Iraq (SCIRI), the most powerful Shiite party in Iraq. The Badr Brigade waged a low-level war of ambushes, sabotage, and assassinations against the regime, using undercover cells in Iraq and bases in Iran when Saddam Hussein was still in control in Iraq. SCIRI's leader Abdel Aziz al-Hakim took over from his brother, Muhammad Baqir al-Hakim, after he was assassinated in a bombing in 2003, which some blamed on Zarqawi's Tawhid and Jihad group.

Its members were funded, trained, and equipped by the Iranian Revolutionary Guard Corps. During the U.S.-led-occupation government's crackdown on militia groups in 2003, the 10,000-strong militia changed its name from the Badr Brigade to the Badr Organization of Reconstruction and Development. The group operates mainly in the southern Iraq region, in and around Basra, where a number of regional governments are dominated by SCIRI representatives. SCIRI wants to create a separate Shiite-run region comprising nine provinces in southern Iraq. As an insurgent movement they continued to attack coalition troops from the British contingent based in the south.

INSURGENCY AND TERRORISM

As is often the case, commentators use the words insurgency and terrorism, so it is necessary to know what an insurgency is. **Insurgency** is a movement, basically a political effort with a specific aim. This sets it apart from both guerrilla warfare and terrorism, as they are both methods available to pursue the goals of the political movement. As we have witnessed in Iraq, the insurgency is aimed at challenging the government for control of specific areas and territory, and as is often the case external support is often a factor in supporting an ongoing insurgency. In the case of Iraq, we can see this support from Iran and Syria. Insurgency unlike terrorism does not require the targeting of noncombatants, although many insurgencies expand the accepted legal definition of combatants to include police and security personnel in addition to the military. Terrorists do not discriminate between combatants and noncombatants, or if they do they broaden the category of "combatants" so much as to render it meaningless. Deliberate dehumanization and criminalization of the enemy in the terrorists' mind justifies extreme measures against anyone identified as hostile. Terrorists often expand their groups of acceptable targets, and conduct operations against new targets without any warning or notice of hostilities. Terrorists use methods that neutralize the strengths of conventional forces. Bombings and mortar attacks on civilian targets where military or security personnel spend off-duty time, ambushes of undefended convoys, and assassinations of poorly protected individuals are common tactics.

Ultimately, the difference between insurgency and terrorism comes down to the intent of those players involved. Insurgencies can sometimes adhere to international norms regarding the law of war to achieve their goals, but terrorists are conducting crimes under both civil and military legal codes. Insurgents in Iraq have been responsible for some hideous atrocities. In 2004 a four-man private security detail from the U.S. company Blackwater were ambushed near Fallujah; they were killed and their mutilated bodies hung from a bridge over the Euphrates River.

FIGURE 9-6 Twenty-three Iraqis were killed in this four-vehicle suicide bombing in southern Baghdad. Suicide bombings were an almost daily occurrence throughout 2006 and 2007 (Canadian Press).

FIGURE 9-7   Private security contractors undergoing live fire training in the United States (Mike McGuire).

Terrorists routinely claim that were they to adhere to any "law of war" or accept any constraints on the scope of their violence, it would place them at a disadvantage vis-à-vis the establishment. Since the nature of the terrorist mind-set is absolutist, their goals are of paramount importance, and any limitations on a terrorist's means to prosecute the struggle are unacceptable.[13]

FIGURE 9-8   Private security contractors undergoing live fire training in the United States (Mike McGuire).

IRAQI INSURGENCY

The Iraqi insurgency may not have been something that the U.S. administration would freely admit that after the Iraq invasion it had planned for or even envisaged. That being said, the insurgency has been an ongoing problem for the security of Iraq and is now simmering especially with a Shiite-dominated Iraqi government. Al Qaeda's wider involvement and promotion of the insurgency is also worth considering. Bin Laden's declaration of Jihad in the early 1990s emphasized his desire to secure the withdrawal of U.S. and other foreign troops from Saudi Arabia, and he viewed the Saudi Royal family with disdain for inviting foreign troops to the Arabian Peninsula, which in his mind constituted an affront to the sanctity of the birthplace of Islam and a betrayal of the global Islamic community.[14] In 2004 bin Laden identified the Iraq conflict as a "golden and unique opportunity" for jihadists to engage and defeat the United States. He characterized the Iraq insurgency as the central battle in a "Third World War, which the Crusader-Zionist coalition began against the Islamic nation," he stated, "The whole world is watching this war and the two adversaries, the Islamic nation on the one hand and the United States and its allies on the other. It is either victory and glory or misery and humiliation. The nation today has a very rare opportunity to come out of the subservience and enslavement of the West and to smash the chains with which the Crusaders have fettered it."[15] His endorsement of the activities of the late Abu Musab al Zarqawi as an affiliate of al Qaeda is also representative of al Qaeda's need for a presence in Iraq. Bin Laden has also encouraged Muslim Iraqis and non-Iraqis of all ethnic stripes to cooperate in opposing the Iraqi government. His preferred and recommended methods of attack on both coalition forces and Government is the use of "martyrdom operations," or suicide attacks. "The Islamic State of Iraq" was born out of the death of Zarqawi and is based in Iraq's western Al Anbar Province. Since 2006 the group's leaders have released several statements outlining the policy and goals of the new "Islamic State" and attacking a number of other Iraqi groups. The Islamic State shares the same strict anti-Shiite sectarian views as al Zarqawi did.[16] Bin Laden and Zarqawi had based their calls for revolutionary change in Islamic societies on a stated belief in a model of governance where Muslim citizens would be empowered to choose and depose their leaders according to strict Islamic principles and traditions of consultation, or shura.[17] Iraq has been used as a training forum for many affiliated al Qaeda groups, so the question on the minds of many is will this change the focus of attacks on Israel and the Palestinian cause. Al Qaeda leaders have engaged in anti Israeli rhetoric with varying levels of intensity. While there has been very little evidence to suggest the presence of al Qaeda in the Palestinian territories, it remains a fact that the leadership continues to insist the aims of the preparations being made in both the east and the west include the removal of Israel from the Muslim lands of Palestine.

WEAPONS OF MASS DESTRUCTION (WMD)

It would be difficult to discuss the problems in Iraq without talking about WMD and possible links to the al Qaeda networks. The reason the United States and its allies are in the region in the first place was that Saddam Hussein was believed to have nuclear weapons capability. In the post-9-11 security environment, the argument goes, the Bush administration had little choice but to assume the worst. Many have charged that the White House either inflated or manipulated weak and otherwise ambiguous intelligence that showed Iraq as an urgent threat and thus make an optional war a necessity. In the two years that U.S. troops had been in Iraq, no sign to support the previous certainty that there were weapons of mass destruction had been uncovered. Large stockpiles of conventional weapons have been unearthed but none of the type that suggested there was an urgency in taking the War on Terror to Iraq itself. During the 1990s, when weapons inspection teams were attempting to uncover any evidence of a nuclear program, UN sanctions were in place and had a marked effect on the economy of the country. These sanctions also prevented any upgrade in conventional weapons, and that is likely one reason why the Iraqi army's resistance was so minimal in 2003. Sanctions were working. The Iraqi military and weapons program had, in fact, steadily eroded under the weight of UN sanctions. The unique synergy of sanctions and inspections eroded Iraq's weapons programs and constrained its military capabilities. These facts are contrary to the Bush administration's contention that Iraq was a "gathering" threat. The renewed UN resolve demonstrated by the Security Council's approval of a "smart" sanctions package in May 2002 showed that the system could continue to contain and deter Saddam Hussein.

Unfortunately, only when U.S. troops invaded in March 2003 did these successes become clear. The Iraqi military had, in the previous twelve years, been decimated by the strategy of containment that the Bush administration had called a failure in order to justify war in the first place.[18] Iraq has been the center and object—almost exclusively—for the U.S. "War on Terror," but your authors and, more widely, the media and politicians have used the term *insurgency* to describe the acts of violence in Iraq since the U.S. invasion in 2003. While the military has been fully engaged in counterinsurgency work, much of the security of foreign nationals has fallen to "global security providers," who have also become legitimate targets for insurgents. There is no doubt that many methods being employed by the factions in Iraq have involved terroristic-style attacks, but there is a distinction between what terrorism is and what insurgency is. Insurgency is better defined as being a movement—somewhat like a political movement with a specific goal in mind, as mentioned before in this text. Having said that, the ultimate goal of any insurgency is to challenge the existing government for control of its territory, or force political concessions in sharing political power. An insurgency requires the active or tacit support of at least a minority of the general population. This definition would certainly fit the events taking shape in Iraq involving the minority Sunni groups. While insurgents will frequently describe themselves as an insurgent or a guerrilla movement, terrorists have historically declined to call themselves "terrorists" and have preferred terms such as *freedom fighter.* Terrorists rely on the impact their activities have on the public at large and attempt to avoid the negative connotations of identifying themselves openly as terrorists.

Whether the spread of al Qaeda's influence in Iraq is a direct result of the U.S. presence there or whether there are fighters from the movement circulating throughout the country is unclear. However, the influential Strategic Survey conducted by the London-based International Institute for Strategic Studies quotes that a cadre of at least 18,000 individuals who trained in al Qaeda camps between 1996 and 2001 are today believed to be positioned in some sixty countries throughout the world.

SUPPORT FOR INTERNATIONAL TERRORISM

Prior to the invasion of Iraq, there were a large number of very senior U.S. politicians who could not accept that Iraq was involved in sponsoring terrorism or, for that matter, was a threat to U.S. security. Obviously, the world is a better place without Saddam Hussein; however, it is history that has determined his involvement in sponsoring terror groups. Many dissidents who escaped from Iraq during Saddam's regime claimed that he maintained terrorist training camps outside Baghdad. He had entertained and provided safe haven to **Abu Abbas**, a former Secretary General of the Palestine Liberation Front. It was Abbas who was responsible for the hijacking of the cruise ship *Achille Lauro* in 1985, in which an American citizen, Leon Klinghoffer, was killed. Abbas was briefly in Italian custody but was able to produce an Iraqi diplomatic passport, forcing the Italian authorities to release him. He may have arrived in Baghdad around 1995 and was caught there by U.S. forces in April 2003. He died while in custody in March 2004.

Saddam Hussein's support for the families of Palestinian suicide bombers is also well known and reasonably documented. Abu Nidal was responsible for terrorist attacks in more than twenty countries, the deaths of more than 400, and over 700 injuried. Nidal's terror group carried out simultaneous attacks in Rome and Vienna airports on December 9th 1985, killing nineteen.

Organization	Total Killed	Total Wounded	Americans Killed	Americans Wounded
Abu Nidal	407	788	10	58
Ansar al-Islam	114	16	1	—
Arab Liberation Front	4	6	—	—
Hamas	224	1,445	17	30
Kurdistan Workers Party (PKK)	44	327	—	2
Mujahedin-e-Khalq (MEK)	17	43	7	1
Palestinian Liberation Front	1	42	1	—
Total	811	2,667	36	91

FIGURE 9-9 Terrorist organizations that were provided funding, shelter, or training by the Ba'athist regime of Saddam Hussein (U.S. Department of State).

Sources: U.S. Department of State, Office of the Coordinator for Conterterrorism, "1968–2003: Total Persons Killed/Wounded—International and Accepted Incidents"; Ansar al-Islam Statistics: Jonathan Linday, "Islamic Militants Kill Senior Kurdish General," Knight-Ridder News Service (February 11, 2003); Catherine Taylor, "Saddam and bin Laden Help Fanatics, Say Kurds," *The Times of London* (March 28, 2002).

BAHRAIN

The State of Bahrain is on a scattered archipelago in the Persian Gulf, east of Saudi Arabia. These landmasses are small; totaling only 3.5 times the size of Washington DC. Bahrain has resources of oil, natural gas, and fish. It is close to primary Middle Eastern petroleum sources and located in a strategic position in the Persian Gulf. It has a very small population of 603,318 (including 221,182 nonnationals). Bahrain gained independence from the United Kingdom in 1971.

Bahrain's chief of state is Amir Isa bin Salman Al Khalifa (since 1961), and the head of government is Prime Minister Khalifi bin Salman Al Khalifa (since 1970). The cabinet is appointed by the Amir, who is a traditional Arab monarch. Political parties are prohibited. Political pressure groups and leaders comprise, and represent, several small, clandestine leftist and Islamic fundamentalist outfits. Following the arrest of a popular Shia cleric, Shia activists have fomented unrest sporadically since late 1994, demanding the return of an elected national assembly and an end to unemployment.

In Bahrain, petroleum production and processing account for about 60 percent of export receipts, 60 percent of government revenues, and 30 percent of GDP. Economic conditions have fluctuated with the changing fortunes of oil since 1985; for example, during and following the Gulf crisis of 1990–1991. With its highly developed communication and transport facilities, Bahrain is home to numerous multinational firms that conduct business in the Gulf. A large share of exports consists of petroleum products made from imported crude. Construction proceeds on several major industrial projects. Unemployment, especially among the young, and the depletion of both oil and underground water resources are major long-term economic problems. The Sultanate continued to be plagued by arson attacks and other minor security incidents throughout 1997, most perpetrated by domestic dissidents.

The State Security Court jailed thirty-six Shia Muslims accused of a pro-Iranian plot to topple the government by force, while acquitting twenty-three others. Unrest in Bahrain has led to at least twenty-eight deaths and hundreds of arrests since December 1994.[19] Shiites suffer from higher rates of unemployment and are barred from employment in the police or security services. The government maintains that the protests plaguing the country are organized by Hezbollah-Bahrain, allegedly backed by Iran.[20] Alleged members of the **Bahraini Hezbollah** were on trial. In all, fifty-four Shia Muslims in detention and twenty-seven others being tried in absentia are accused of fomenting violence and antigovernment activities.[21] The existence of Bahrain Hezbollah itself is questioned by

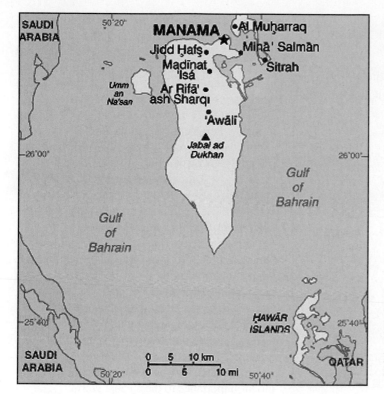

some who accuse the government of fabricating its existence in order to blame outsiders for the political unrest. Their jail sentences range from five to fifteen years. Some Bahraini Hezbollah members reportedly underwent terrorist training in camps in Iran and Lebanon.

The Sunni Muslim-led government in Bahrain is reforming the political system to pacify a vocal and increasingly discontented Shiite majority. However, these measures are limited in substance and may end up fueling more dissent and unrest in the country, which is a leading Persian Gulf banking center and U.S. naval headquarters.

In February 2002, Bahrain's leader, Sheik Hamad bins Isa Al Khalifa, proclaimed himself King and declared his country a constitutional monarchy. Hamad also dissolved Bahrain's appointed consultative council, paving the way for the establishment of a bicameral parliament following elections scheduled for later in the year. Kuwait is currently the only Persian Gulf state with an elected parliament.

The government's transformation from the emirate system into a constitutional monarchy has been heralded as a step toward democracy. The feeling in the rest of the world is that it is not. Instead, it reflects the latest battle in an unresolved power struggle between Bahrain's minority Sunni Muslim-led government and the majority Shiite Muslim community. In the near term, the shift will bring this struggle to the fore and could lead to another period of unrest in the tiny archipelago.

FIGURE 9-10 Map of Bahrain (Central Intelligence Agency, *The World Factbook*, 2008).

Instability in Bahrain could impact security and business in the entire Persian Gulf region. The country is not a major oil producer but does have a vital refining industry that imports crude from neighboring states. It is also an important financial hub for the region, with many foreign banks located in the capital, Manama. Moreover, Manama is also headquarters for the U.S. Navy's 5th Fleet and a center for U.S. military operations in the Gulf. Cooperation between Bahrain's two religious sects is critical to maintaining the island's calm. The situation in the country mirrors a historical contest between Islam's two largest sects throughout the Middle East, especially in the Persian Gulf. It also reflects the two distinct communities' struggle for control over Bahrain's valuable resources.

OMAN

The Sultanate of Oman borders the Arabian Sea, the Gulf of Oman, and the Persian Gulf, between Yemen and United Arab Emirates. It is a country slightly smaller than Kansas. Oman has a dry desert, but it is hot and humid along the coastal region. Although Oman is small, its natural resources include petroleum, copper, asbestos, some marble, limestone, chromium, gypsum, and natural gas. This parched nation has no arable land and no permanent crops. Oman is strategically located on the Usandam Peninsula and controls the Strait of Hormuz, a vital transit point for world crude oil. Seventy five percent of Oman's 2,264,590 population is Sunni Muslim, with the remainder Shia Muslim and Hindu. Oman is a sultanate, a monarchy that has been independent since 1650, when it expelled the Portuguese.

On November 6, 1996, Sultan Qaboos issued a royal decree promulgating a new basic law. Among other things, it clarified the royal succession, provided for a prime minister, barred ministers

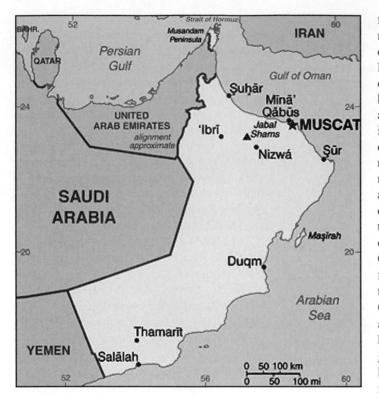

FIGURE 9-11 Map of Oman (Central Intelligence Agency, *The World Factbook*, 2008).

from holding interests in companies doing business with the government, established a bicameral Omani council, and guaranteed basic civil liberties for Omani citizens. The Sultan is the chief of state, the head of government, and a hereditary monarch. Oman's economic performance is closely tied to the fortunes of the oil industry. Petroleum accounts for 75 percent of export earnings and government revenues, and roughly 40 percent of GDP. Oman has proven oil reserves of four billion barrels, equivalent to about a twenty-year supply at the current rate of extraction. Agriculture is carried on at a subsistence level, and the general population depends on imported food. The earliest settlements in Oman, as in the Arabian Peninsula generally, date from some time in the third millennium B.C. At that time, and for some hundreds of years more, Oman was on the edge of the trade routes linking ancient Mesopotamia to the Indus Valley; however, it does not appear to have profited a great deal from its location. Some centuries later, however, what is now Oman became of paramount importance to the ancient world.

The southernmost region of Oman, modern Dhofar, was responsible for the area's importance. It is one of the few spots in the world where frankincense trees grow. Frankincense is an aromatic gum from certain species of trees that grow only in southern Oman, the Wadi Hadhramaut in Yemen, and Somalia. The incense burns well because of its natural oil content. In addition, it has medicinal uses; these two factors, plus its relative scarcity, made frankincense an extremely sought-after substance in the ancient world. (The gifts of the Magi to the Christ Child were gold, frankincense, and myrrh. At the time, gold was far less valuable than the other two.) Frankincense was vital to the religious rites of almost every civilization in the ancient world. The great temples of Egypt, the Near East, and Rome itself were all major consumers of the scarce commodity, not to mention the thousands of other temples found in every city, town, and village. Indeed, the writer Pliny, in the first century A.D., claimed that control of the frankincense trade had made the south Arabians the richest people on earth.

In the second century A.D., at the height of the trade, some 3,000 tons of frankincense were transported each year by ship from south Arabia to Greece, Rome, and the Mediterranean world. The center of the trade was in a place now called Khor Rouri, which the Greeks called Moscha. Although the trade went into a decline after the third century A.D., it still managed to keep south Arabia relatively wealthy for another three centuries.

The tribes in the northern part of Oman were converted to Islam during the first generation of the Islamic era, the middle of the seventh century A.D., and shortly thereafter came under the rule of the Umayyads, whose center was in Damascus. About a century later, the Omanis revolted against the Umayyads and expelled them from their country. The Umayyads themselves remained only a short time as the leaders of the Muslim world, for the Abbasids, whose capital was in Baghdad, soon overthrew them.

Oman managed to remain free of the Abbasids and continued its adherence to Ibadi Islam, which is still dominant in the country today. Because of Oman's remoteness from other Muslims, the Ibadis survived as a group long after they had vanished from other parts of the Muslim world.

By the end of the eighteenth century, the Omanis were in control of an extensive empire. At its height in the nineteenth century, the empire ruled both Mombasa and Zanzibar and had trading posts much farther down the African coast. (Oman's last colonial outpost—Gwadar, on what is now the coast of Pakistan—was not surrendered until September 1958, when Sultan Said bin Taimur allowed it to be reintegrated into Pakistan in return for a payment of £3 million.) In 1749, the first ruler of the present dynasty (Al-Busaid) gained power and, in 1786, the capital was formally moved from the interior to Muscat. About this same time, Al-Busaid adopted the title of "Sultan," which continues to this day.

The heyday of the Omani Empire occurred in the mid-nineteenth century under Sultan Said bin Sultan, who ruled from 1804 to 1856. He was responsible for bringing Dhofar under the Omani flag, and he also extended Omani influence and control quite a way down the East African coast. He had an army of 6,500 men and a navy consisting of fifteen ships. When he died, the empire split in two; one son became the Sultan of Zanzibar and the other, the Sultan of Muscat and Oman. In the very name of the latter, the perceived difference between the interests of the coast and those of the interior was acknowledged. In fact, they were regarded as two entities ruled by the same monarch, though the writ of the ruler in Muscat sometimes did not extend very far into the interior. Muscat's control depended very much on the regard for the Sultan held by the tribes of the interior. In the early twentieth century, the Sultan's power to control the interior of the country was felt to have decreased.

In February 1932, Sultan Said bin Taimur, father of the present ruler, came to power. When he tried to exercise his nominal control in the interior of the country in the early 1950s, the British, who believed the area had oil, backed him. And, in order to look for it, the British needed the Sultan to have actual control of the area and Oman's indefinite borders with Saudi Arabia and Abu Dhabi to be clearly defined and drawn. The ultimate result of this was a territorial dispute over the Buraimi oasis involving Oman, Saudi Arabia, and Abu Dhabi. With British help and his own bravado, Sultan Said, in the end, was the winner, and the Buraimi oasis is today firmly within the borders of Oman.

Sultan Said bin Taimur was, in the words of one British writer, an arch-reactionary of great personal charm. He wanted no change of any sort in Oman and did all that he could to isolate his country from the world. He issued all visas personally. He forbade travel to the interior by coastal residents and vice versa. Believing education was a threat to his power, he opposed it.

In general, Omanis were not allowed to leave the country, and those who did were seldom allowed to return. The Sultan's only contact with the outside world was through his British advisers and Muscat's merchant families. He allowed the latter to establish enormously lucrative monopolies for the import of goods, which he saw as crucial to his survival. In exchange, the merchants stayed out of politics and imported nothing that Sultan Said felt reeked of progress or the West (radios, books, eyeglasses). Through their customs receipts, the merchants provided the Sultan with most of the country's income. Aside from a few rich merchants, most of the population relied on agriculture and fishing.

Oman has been Islamic since the seventh century. In about 1507, the city of Muscat and its hinterland came under Portuguese control. The Portuguese maintained their control until 1650 when the Omanis revolted and extended their influence as far south as the island of Zanzibar, off the African coast. The country was under Persian control for a short time (1741–1749) and then, in 1798, a treaty of friendship was signed with Great Britain, but Oman retained its independence. From 1932 to 1970, Oman was controlled by Sultan Said bin Taimur, a reclusive and repressive ruler whose policies finally resulted in revolt in Dhofar in 1965. In 1970, his son, the British-educated Qaboos bin Said, overthrew his father and embarked on an ambitious modernization program. This small and tightly controlled country has been bypassed by most of the terrorism and violence in the region and is almost totally unknown in the rest of the world.

Oman, a key U.S. ally in the Middle East, is adjusting its budget to reflect its assistance to the War on Terror but the oil-rich sultanate is actually reducing defense funding and shifting the savings into social welfare programs. Unlike many other governments in the region, Oman's regime has faced relatively little domestic opposition to its relationship with the United States. This is largely due to strong oil revenues and an extremely tolerant local segment of Islam. Even so, it appears the Omani leadership is investing in preventative measures to keep a lid on unrest, knowing that

Washington will guarantee its external security. By addressing domestic security before it becomes an issue, Oman hopes to avoid the problems faced by neighboring Saudi Arabia, where extremist Muslims actively oppose the basing of U.S. military forces there. A pacified population will allow the Omani government to deepen its involvement with the U.S. military, which is likely reexamining its options in the antiterror campaign.

The U.S. military currently uses at least three air bases in Oman as part of operations in Afghanistan. The Navy runs P-3 Orion aircraft patrols out of the Masirah air base, where at least one squadron of AC-130 gunships is based as well. Oman also hosts several Air Force pre-positioning sites, with enough equipment and fuel to maintain three air bases and 26,000 support personnel. Its continuing support of the War on Terror makes Oman a key player in this global effort.

IRAN

One of the most controversial states in the Persian Gulf, the Islamic Republic of Iran borders the Gulf of Oman, the Persian Gulf, and the Caspian Sea, between Iraq and Pakistan. Iran is slightly larger than Alaska and has large resources of petroleum, natural gas, coal, chromium, copper, iron ore, lead, manganese, zinc, and sulfur. Its estimated population, 67,540,000, includes 917,078 nonnationals and a broad base of ethnic groups (Persian 51 percent, Azerbaijani 24 percent, Gilaki and Mazandarani 8 percent, Kurd 7 percent, Arab 3 percent, Lur 2 percent, Baloch 2 percent, Turkmen 2 percent, other 1 percent) and religious affiliations (Shia Muslim 89 percent, Sunni Muslim 10 percent, Zoroastrian, Jewish, Christian, and Baha'i 1 percent). This broad spectrum is reflected in languages as well (Persian and Persian dialects 58 percent, Turkic and Turkic dialects 26 percent, Kurdish 9 percent, Luri 2 percent, Balochi 1 percent, Arabic 1 percent, Turkish 1 percent, other 2 percent). Iran is a theocratic republic, and its constitution codifies Islamic principles of government.

FIGURE 9-12   Map of Iran (Central Intelligence Agency, *The World Factbook*, 2008).

Mujahedin-E Khalq Organization (MEK)

The MEK, also known as the National Liberation Army of Iran (NLA), the militant wing of the MEK, the People's Mujahedin of Iran (PMOI), and the Muslim Iranian Student's Society, was formed in the 1960s by the college-educated children of Iranian merchants. The MEK sought to counter what was perceived as excessive Western influence in the Shah's regime. In the 1970s, the MEK concluded that violence was the only way to bring about change in Iran. Since then, the MEK, following a philosophy that mixes Marxism and Islam, has developed into the largest and most active armed Iranian dissident group. Its history is studded with anti-Western activity and, most recently, attacks on the interests of the clerical regime in Iran and abroad.

The MEK directs a worldwide campaign against the Iranian government that stresses propaganda and occasionally uses terrorist violence.

During the 1970s, the MEK staged terrorist attacks inside Iran to destabilize and embarrass the Shah's regime; the group killed several U.S. military personnel and civilians working on defense projects in Tehran. The group also supported the

1979 takeover of the U.S. Embassy in Tehran. In April 1992, the MEK carried out attacks on Iranian embassies in thirteen different countries, demonstrating the group's ability to mount large-scale operations overseas. Several thousand fighters with an extensive overseas support structure are based in Iraq. Most of the fighters are organized in the MEK's National Liberation Army (NLA).

In the 1980s, the MEK's leaders were forced by Iranian security forces to flee to France. Most resettled in Iraq by 1987. Since the mid-1980s, the MEK has not mounted terrorist operations in Iran at a level similar to its activities in the 1970s. Aside from the attacks into Iran toward the end of the Iran-Iraq war, and occasional NLA cross-border incursions since, the MEK's attacks on Iran have amounted to little more than harassment. The MEK has had more success in confronting Iranian representatives overseas through propaganda and street demonstrations. Beyond support from Iraq, the MEK uses front organizations to solicit contributions from expatriate Iranian communities.[22]

Political pressure groups that generally support the Islamic Republic include Ansar-e Hizballah, Mojahedin of the Islamic Revolution, Muslim Students Following the Line of the Imam, and the Islamic Coalition Association. Opposition groups include the Liberation Movement of Iran and the Nation of Iran party. Armed political groups that have been almost completely repressed by the government include Mojahedin-e Khalq Organization (MEK), People's Fedayeen, Democratic Party of Iranian Kurdistan, and the Society for the Defense of Freedom.

Iran's economy is a mixture of central planning, state ownership of oil and other large enterprises, village agriculture, and small-scale private trading and service ventures. Under President Rafsanjani, the government adopted a number of market reforms to reduce the state's role in the economy, but most of these changes have moved slowly or have been reversed because of political opposition. In the early 1990s, Iran experienced a financial crisis caused by general financial mismanagement and an import surge that began in 1989. In 1993–1994, Iran rescheduled $15 billion in debt, with the bulk of payments due in 1996–1997. The strong oil market in 1996 helped ease financial pressures, however, and Tehran has so far made timely debt service payments. In 1996, Iran's oil earnings, which account for 85 percent of its total export revenues, climbed 20 percent from the previous year. Iran's financial situation remained tight through the end of the decade. Its continued timely debt service payments depended, in part, on persistent strong oil prices during the following years, a prediction that has failed badly as petroleum prices plummeted in 1998.

Iran is an illicit producer of opium poppy for the domestic and international drug trade. Iran continues to be a key transshipment point country for Southwest Asian heroin going to Europe.

THE SHAH OF IRAN

Mohammad Reza Pahlavi was restored to the Peacock Throne with the assistance of the Central Intelligence Agency in 1953. The CIA assisted in a coup against the left-leaning government of Dr. Mohammad Mossadeq, who had planned to nationalize Iran's oil industry. The CIA also provided organizational and training assistance for an intelligence organization for the Shah. With training focused on domestic security and interrogation, the intelligence unit was taxed with the mission to eliminate threats to the Shah. Formed under efforts of U.S. and Israeli intelligence officers in 1957, SAVAK became an effective secret agency. General Bakhtiar was appointed its first director, only to be dismissed in 1961. He was assassinated in 1970 under mysterious circumstances. His successor, General Pakravan, was dismissed in 1966, failing to crush the opposition from the clerics in the early 1960s.

In 1961, Iran initiated a series of economic, social, and administrative reforms that became known as the Shah's White Revolution. The core of this program was land reform. Modernization and economic growth proceeded at an unprecedented rate, fueled by Iran's vast petroleum reserves, the third largest in the world. Domestic turmoil swept the country as a result of religious and political opposition to the Shah's rule and programs, especially SAVAK, the hated internal security and intelligence service.

The Shah turned to his childhood friend and classmate, General Nassiri, to rebuild SAVAK to properly serve the monarchy. Mansur Rafizadeh, the SAVAK director in the United States throughout the 1970s, claimed that General Nassiri's telephone was tapped by SAVAK agents reporting directly to the Shah, an example of the level of mistrust pervading on the eve of the revolution. SAVAK increasingly symbolized the Shah's rule from 1963 to 1979, a period of corruption in the royal family, one-party rule, the torture and execution of thousands of political prisoners, suppression of dissent, and alienation of the religious masses. The United States reinforced its position as the Shah's protector and supporter, sowing the seeds of the anti-Americanism that later manifested itself in the revolution against the monarchy.

Accurate information concerning SAVAK is not publicly available. Pamphlets issued by the revolutionary regime after 1979 indicated that SAVAK had been a full-scale intelligence agency with more than 15,000 full-time personnel and thousands of part-time informants. SAVAK was attached to the Office of the Prime Minister, and its director assumed the title of Deputy to the Prime Minister for National Security Affairs. Although officially a civilian agency, SAVAK had close ties to the military, and many of its officers served simultaneously in branches of the armed forces.

Another childhood friend and close confidant of the Shah, Major General Hosain Fardust, was deputy director of SAVAK until the early 1970s, when the Shah promoted him to the directorship of the "Special Intelligence Bureau," which operated inside Niavaran Palace, independently of SAVAK.

Originally formed to round up members of the outlawed Tudeh, SAVAK expanded its activities to include gathering intelligence and neutralizing the regime's opponents. An elaborate system was created to monitor all facets of political life. A censorship office was established to monitor journalists, literary figures, and academics throughout the country; it took appropriate measures against those who fell out of line. Universities, labor unions, and peasant organizations, among others, were all subjected to intense surveillance by SAVAK agents and paid informants. The agency was also active abroad, especially in monitoring Iranian students who opposed Pahlavi rule.

SAVAK contracted Rockwell International to develop a large communications monitoring system called IBEX. The Stanford Technology Corp. (STC), owned by Hakim, had a $5.5 million contract to supply the CIA-promoted IBEX project. STC had another $7.5 million contract with Iran's air force for a telephone monitoring system, operated by SAVAK, to enable the Shah to track his top commanders' communications.

Over the years, SAVAK became a law unto itself, having legal authority to arrest and detain suspected persons indefinitely. SAVAK operated its own prisons in Tehran (the Komiteh and Evin facilities) and others throughout the country. SAVAK's torture methods included electric shock, whipping, beating, inserting broken glass, and pouring boiling water into the rectum, tying weights to the testicles, and the extraction of teeth and nails. Many of these activities were carried out without oversight. At the peak of its influence under the Shah, SAVAK had at least thirteen full-time case officers running a network of informers and infiltrators covering 30,000 Iranian students on U.S. college campuses. The head of the SAVAK agents in the United States operated under the cover of an attaché at the Iranian Mission, with the FBI, CIA, and State Department fully aware of these activities.

In 1978, the deepening opposition to the Shah erupted in widespread demonstrations and rioting. SAVAK and the military responded with widespread repression that killed 12,000–15,000 people and seriously injured another 50,000. Recognizing that even this level of state terrorism and violence had failed to crush the rebellion, the Shah abdicated the Peacock Throne and departed Iran in 1979. Despite decades of pervasive surveillance by SAVAK, working closely with the CIA, the extent of public opposition to the Shah and his sudden departure came as a considerable surprise to the U.S. intelligence community and national leadership.

The SAVAK organization was officially dissolved by Khomeini shortly after he came to power in 1979. However, it was no surprise that SAVAK was singled out as a primary target for reprisals. Its headquarters were overrun and prominent leaders were tried and executed by Khomeini representatives. High-ranking SAVAK agents were purged and 61 SAVAK officials were among 248 military personnel executed between February and September 1979.[23]

The 1979 Islamic revolution and the war with Iraq transformed Iran's class structure politically, socially, and economically. In general, however, Iranian society remains divided into urban, market town, village, and tribal groups. Clerics, called mullahs, dominate politics and nearly all aspects of Iranian life, both urban and rural. After the fall of Shah Pahlavi's regime in 1979, much of the urban upper class of prominent merchants, industrialists, and professionals, favored by the former Shah, lost standing and influence to the senior clergy and its supporters. Bazaar merchants, who were allied with the clergy against the Pahlavi Shahs, have also gained political and economic power since the revolution. The urban working class has enjoyed somewhat enhanced status and economic mobility, spurred in part by opportunities provided by revolutionary organizations and the government bureaucracy. The Shah went into exile and died in Cairo, in July 1980, where he was given a State funeral.

On February 1, 1979, exiled religious leader Ayatollah Ruhollah Khomeini returned from France to direct a revolution, resulting in a new, theocratic republic guided by Islamic principles. Back in Iran after fifteen years in exile in Turkey, Iraq, and France, he became Iran's national religious leader. Following Khomeini's death on June 3, 1989, the Assembly of Experts, an elected body of senior clerics, chose the outgoing president of the republic, Ali Khamenei, to be his successor as national religious leader in what proved to be a smooth transition. In 1989, an overwhelming majority elected Ali Akbar Hashemi-Rafsanjani, the speaker of the National Assembly, President. He was reelected June 11, 1993, with a more modest majority of about 63 percent. Some Western observers attributed the reduced voter turnout to disenchantment with the deteriorating economy. Iran's post-revolution difficulties included an eight-year war with Iraq, internal political struggles and unrest, and economic disorder. The early days of the regime were characterized by severe human rights violations and political turmoil, including the seizure of the U.S. Embassy compound and its occupants on November 4, 1979, by Iranian militants. By mid-1982, a succession of power struggles eliminated first the center of the political spectrum and then the leftists, leaving only the clergy. There has been some moderation of excesses, both internally and internationally, although Iran remains a significant sponsor of terrorism.

The Islamic Republican Party (IRP) was Iran's dominant political party until its dissolution in 1987; Iran now has no functioning political parties. The Iranian government is opposed by a few armed political groups, including the Mojahedin-e Khalq (People's Mojahedin of Iran), the People's Fedayeen, and the Kurdish Democratic Party.

Khomeini's revolutionary regime initiated sharp changes from the foreign policy pursued by the Shah, particularly in reversing the country's orientation toward the West. In the Middle East, Iran's only significant ally has been Syria. Iran's regional goals include its desire to establish a leadership role, curtail the presence of the United States and other outside powers, and build trade ties. In broad terms, Iran's Islamic foreign policy emphasizes the following:

- Vehement anti-U.S. and anti-Israel stances;
- Elimination of outside influence in the region;
- Export of the Islamic revolution;
- Support for Muslim political movements abroad; and
- A significant increase in diplomatic contacts with developing countries.

Despite these guidelines, however, bilateral relations are frequently confused and contradictory due to Iran's oscillation between pragmatic and ideological concerns. Iran's relations with many of its Arab neighbors have been strained by Iranian attempts to spread its Islamic revolution. In 1981, Iran supported a plot to overthrow the Bahrain government. In 1983, Iran expressed support for Shiites who bombed Western embassies in Kuwait and, in 1987 Iranian pilgrims rioted during the Hajj (pilgrimage) to Mecca in Saudi Arabia. Nations with strong fundamentalist movements, such as Egypt and Algeria, also mistrust Iran. Iran backs Hezbollah, Hamas, the Palestinian Islamic Jihad, and the Popular Front for the Liberation of Palestine-General Command—all groups violently opposed to the Arab-Israeli peace process.

Iran's relations with Western European nations have alternated between improvements and setbacks. French-Iranian relations were badly strained by the sale of French arms to Iraq. Since the war, relations have improved commercially but periodically are worsened by Iranian-sponsored terrorist acts committed in France. Another source of tension was Ayatollah Khomeini's 1989 call to all Muslims to kill Salman Rushdie, British author of "The Satanic Verses." Many Muslims consider this novel blasphemous to their Holy Scriptures. The United Kingdom has sheltered Rushdie, and strains over this issue persist. There are serious obstacles to improved relations between the two countries. The U.S. government defines five areas of objectionable Iranian behavior:

- Iranian efforts to acquire nuclear weapons and other weapons of mass destruction;
- Its involvement in international terrorism;
- Its support for violent opposition to the Arab-Israeli peace process;
- Its threats and subversive activities against its neighbors; and
- Its dismal human rights record.

The United States believes that normal relations are impossible until Iran's behavior changes. However, the United States has offered to enter into dialogue with authorized representatives of the Iranian government without preconditions. The Iranian government has not accepted this offer. The United States has made clear that it does not seek to overthrow the Iranian government but will continue to pressure Iran to change its behavior. Iran's continuing support of terrorists and terrorism creates continuing danger for Americans in Iran because of the generally anti-American atmosphere and the government's hostility to the U.S. government. American citizens traveling to Iran have been detained without charge, arrested, and harassed by Iranian authorities.[24]

IRAN AND NUCLEAR WEAPONS

The United States has cast Iran as being an integral part of the "axis of evil," and believes that it has been attempting to assemble the ingredients to manufacture weapons-grade nuclear material. This, of course, has not been confirmed. The Iranians can look at what has transpired since 9-11 and how the United States has reacted: The United States invades Iraq, which did *not* have nuclear weapons; the United States backed away from North Korea, which *does* have a nuclear weapons program. So, from a

FIGURE 9-13 Iranian President Mahmoud Ahmadinejad (Canadian Press).

survivalist standpoint, the need for Iran to have an active nuclear program could be viewed as a method of restraining U.S. aggression. A nuclear Iran under the leadership of President Mahmoud Ahmadinejad pronounced in 2006 that the solution to the Middle East crisis would be the destruction of Israel.

As we now know, the gathering and assessment of intelligence information is not an exact science and was clearly very lackluster when it came to dealing with the Iraq WMD question. As for the Iranians, the country's main opposition group, the National Council of Resistance (NCR), claimed in spring 2005 that the heavy water plant constructed near Arak should be capable of producing enough plutonium for a nuclear weapon by 2007. The reliability of this information has not been determined. However, in the recent past, NCR has exposed at least five nuclear facilities in Iran, forcing the Iranian government to notify the International Atomic Energy Agency (IAEA) of its activities. Iran's connections with and sponsoring of terror groups is well documented. Iran was intimately involved in the attack on the Khober Towers complex in Saudi Arabia and it has been supporting various Palestinian causes that hit at Israel's attempts at peace in the region. The obvious concern is that a nuclear Iran could supply the know-how to subgroups, or even the materials to construct a small nuclear device for delivery within Europe or the United States.

YEMEN

The Republic of Yemen was established on May 22, 1990, with the merger of the Yemen Arab Republic (YAR; Yemen Sanaa or North Yemen) and the Marxist-dominated People's Democratic Republic of Yemen (Yemen Aden or South Yemen). The newly formed republic borders the Arabian Sea, the Gulf of Aden, and the Red Sea, between Oman and Saudi Arabia. Yemen is slightly larger than twice the size of Wyoming, with borders to Oman and Saudi Arabia. There is an extraordinarily hot, dry, harsh desert on the east side of Yemen. Yemen has potential control of Bab el Mandeb, the strait linking the Red Sea and the Gulf of Aden, one of the world's most active shipping lanes. Estimates of its population run from 13.9 million to as high as 16.6 million people of Arab, Afro-Arab concentrations in western coastal locations, South Asians in the southern regions, and small European communities in the major metropolitan areas. Muslims, including Sha'fi (Sunni) and Zaydi (Shia), plus small numbers of Jews, Christians, and Hindus practice their brands of religion.

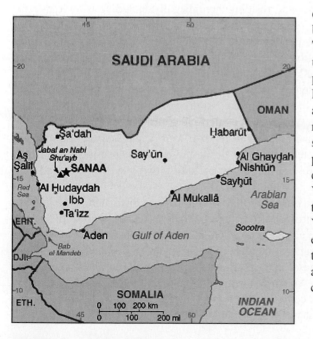

The former Aden (South Yemen) gained independence from the United Kingdom in 1967. North Yemen had become independent in 1918 from the Ottoman Empire. The northern city Sanaa became the political capital of a united Yemen. The southern city Aden, with its refinery and port facilities, is the economic and commercial capital. Future economic development depends heavily on Western-assisted development of the country's moderate oil resources. Former South Yemen's willingness to merge stemmed partly from the steady decline in economic support with the demise of the Soviet Union. The low level of domestic industry and agriculture has made northern Yemen dependent on imports for practically all of its essential needs. Once self-sufficient in food production, northern Yemen has become a major importer. Land once used for export crops such as cotton, fruit, and vegetables has been turned over to growing a shrub called "qat," whose leaves are chewed for their stimulant effect, but it has no significant export market.

British and Turkish Domination

FIGURE 9-14   Map of Yemen (Central Intelligence Agency, *The World Factbook*, 2008).

The British conquered Aden (Southern Yemen) in 1839, and it became known as the Aden Protectorate. The British also made a series of treaties with local tribal rulers in a move to colonize the entire area of southern Yemen. British influence extended to Hadhramawt by the 1950s, and a boundary line, known as the violet line, was drawn between Turkish Arabia in the north and the South Arabian Protectorate of Great Britain, as it was then known. (This line later formed the boundary between northern and southern Yemeni states in the 1960s.) In 1849, the Turks returned to Yemen, and their power extended throughout the whole of that region not under British rule. Local insurrection against the Turks followed, and autonomy was finally granted to the Zaydi Imam in 1911. By 1919, the Turks had retreated from Yemen for the last time, and the country was left in the hands of Imam Yayha, who became the country's king. Britain recognized Yemen's independence in 1925.

Separate States and Unification

In the late 1960s, the British presence in southern Yemen was minimal, outside of Aden itself. Intense guerrilla fighting throughout the mid-1960s resulted in British withdrawal from Aden in 1967. With the closure of the Suez Canal, Yemen's economy was on the verge of ruin, and the new People's Republic of South Yemen, which came into being in 1967, relied heavily on economic support from Communist countries. It became, in effect, the first and only Arab Marxist state. In 1970, the republic's name was changed to the People's Democratic Republic of Yemen, or PDRY.

Mutual distrust between the two Yemen's characterized the seventies, and tensions flared into a series of short border wars in 1972, 1978, and 1979. Two presidents of the YAR were assassinated during this period. But under the Presidency of Ali Abdullah Salah of the Hashid tribe, in the late 1970s and early 1980s, the stability of the YAR steadily improved. By the end of 1981, a constitution had been drafted to implement a merger between the two states. Attempts to consolidate, however, were delayed by political instability in the PDRY, and it was not until 1990 that the merger was made official.

The new country was named the Republic of Yemen. The border was opened and demilitarized, and currencies were declared valid in both of the former countries. A referendum sealed the unification of Yemen, and today's Yemen is probably more accessible than it has been throughout its history. Although there is no major tourist industry, visitors are now welcomed on a modest scale, and Yemeni society is fast becoming modernized.

Sanaa took major steps during 1997 to improve control of its borders, territory, and travel documents. It continued to deport foreign nationals residing there illegally, including Islamic extremists identified as posing a security risk to Yemen and several other Arab countries. The Interior Ministry issued new, reportedly tamper-resistant passports and began to computerize port-of-entry information. Nonetheless, lax implementation of security measures and poor central government control over remote areas continued to make Yemen an attractive safe haven for terrorists. Moreover, Hamas and the PIJ maintain offices in Yemen. A series of bombings in Aden in July, October, and November 1997 caused material damage but no injuries. No group claimed responsibility. The Yemeni government blamed the attacks on Yemeni opposition elements that had been trained by foreign extremists and supported from abroad possibly from Iran. A principal suspect confessed in court he was recruited and paid by Saudi intelligence, but this could not be independently verified. Yemeni tribesmen kidnapped about forty foreign nationals, including two U.S. citizens, and held them for periods ranging up to one month.

Yemeni government officials frequently asserted that foreign powers instigated some kidnappings, but no corroborating evidence was provided. All were treated well and released unharmed, but one Italian was injured when resisting a kidnap attempt. The motivation for the kidnappings generally appeared to be tribal grievances against the central government. The government did not prosecute any of the kidnappers. At the end of 2007 there was a growing Shiite revolt against the Yemeni government, led by the **Believing Youth Movement**. Attacks from this group and open fighting with the military were primarily centered in the northern region of the country in the Province of Sanaa. The attacks seem to emanate from a complaint that the government had cancelled a Shiite religious celebration.

FIGURE 9-15 April 2008—Yemeni security forces attend the scene of a bombing at a military checkpoint that killed three soldiers and injured four, not far from the site of the July 2007 suicide attack on a Spanish tour group's convoy. Al Qaeda has been active in Yemen despite government efforts to fight the terror network (Canadian Press).

Attacks against U.S. targets in the Gulf and surrounding states have been limited; however, the State of Yemen has experienced low levels of terrorism for some time. The attack on the U.S.S. *Cole* on October 12, 2000, in the Port of Aden while on a refueling stop, appears to have been a protest against American presence in the Middle East; it was not directed at any particular aspect of U.S. policy, such as Palestine or Iraq.

The al Qaeda attack in the Port of Aden was the first successful suicide attack on a U.S. Naval craft by terrorists. Eyewitnesses said an inflatable speedboat helping the destroyer moor exploded alongside the ship, opening a 20-foot by 40-foot hole at the waterline on the left side.

The use of suicide bombers suggests it was carried out by an armed Islamist group rather than a secular political organization. Seventeen American sailors were killed and thirty-nine injured in the seaborne suicide attack. The bomb is believed to have been made with a military grade C-4 plastic explosive, and around 400 pounds or more were used in the attack. The investigation has shown that the attack group in this case contained not only Yemeni but also Muslims from other Middle Eastern countries.

Southern Yemen, under Marxist rule, was classified by the United States as a "rogue state." The Marxist government provided the infamous Carlos the Jackal with a passport. The unification of North and South Yemen led to better relations with the United States and the states' subsequent removal from the list of rogue states.

Summary

The War on Terror, the invasion and containment of Iraq, and Iran and its designs on nuclear weapons are all subjects that will keep not just the United States but also the rest of the world focused on this region. Wider implications for the whole of the Middle East range from the proliferation of nuclear weapons to the threat of Islamic uprising in such friendly states as Saudi Arabia and even Yemen. With maybe tens of thousands of trained al Qaeda fighters at large and the presence of several hundred thousand U.S. and British troops based in Iraq, this region of the world continues to remain unstable. Iran's political and military posturing and desire to produce WMD will cause more extreme reaction from the United States, Israel, and Europe. The spread of extreme Islam in Iraq and consequences of its spread will have to be considered. Establishing democracies in parts of the world that have never experienced it may take many years, if ever, to reach fruition. Oil may be the prize that the United States seeks in the Middle East, and the removal of the United States from Muslim lands is the prize the extremists seek. It will be decades before we can look back at this time frame and determine what worked and what failed on the path to democratization and the successes of the "War on Terror" in this region of the world.

Web Sites

1. **CDI Terrorism Project**—*http://www.cdi.org/terrorism/menukes.cfm*
2. **Dudley Knox Library**—*http://www.nps.edu/Library/Research*
3. **Strategic Studies Institute of the U.S. Army War College**—*http://www.strategicstudiesinstitute.army*
4. **Belfer Center for Science and International Affairs**—*http://belfercenter.ksg.harvard.edu/publication/2110/*
5. **United States Institute for Peace**—*http://www.usip.org/pubs/specialreports/sr111.html*
   combating_terrorism_in_the_horn_of_africa_and_yemen.html
6. **Congressional Research Service**—*http://www.fas.org/sgp/crs/natsec/RL33110.pdf*

Endnotes

1. Most of the background data contained in this chapter were extracted from Web sites such as: The U.S. State Department of State, *Patterns of Global Terror Report*; The U.S. Department of State, *Country Reports on Human Rights Practices*; The U.S. Department of State Background Notes; *Geographic Entities and International Organizations*, http://www.state.gov; *The U.S. Central Intelligence Agency World Factbook*, http://www.cia.gov/ and other government sources.
2. Sharon Otterman, *Islam: Governing under Sharia Law*, Council on Foreign Relations. www.cfr.org/publications.
3. Country studies—Saudi Arabia. http://countrystudiesus/saudi-arabia/.
4. General information on Wahhabism. http://www.mb-soft.com/believe/txo/wahhabis.htm.
5. Austin Cline, *Your Guide to Agnosticism/Atheism.* http://atheism.about.com/od/islamicextremismpeople/a/qutb_p.htm.
6. Terrorism Intelligence Report—Fred Burton and Scott Stewart—al Qaeda in 2008 the Struggle for Relevance—Stratfor.com.
7. *Arab Times* (February 15, 2005).
8. *Kuwait Times* (February 20, 2005).
9. U.S. Department of Defense—Press Briefing (July 22, 2003).
10. *Al-Zawra*, Arabic weekly published in Baghdad by the Iraqi Journalists Association. An Inventory of Iraqi Resistance Groups Samir Haddad and Mazin Ghazi Al Zawra. "Who Kills Hostages in Iraq?" (September 19, 2004). http://www.indymedia.org.uk/en/2004/09/298084.html.
11. Federation of American Scientists. www.fas.org.
12. The Economist "The enigma of Muqtada al-Sadr," February 28, 2008.
13. Terrorism Research. http://www.terrorism-research.com/insurgency/.
14. Robert Fisk: "Interview with Saudi Dissident Bin Laden," *Independent* (London) July 10, 1996.
15. OSC Report—FEA20041227000762, December 2004.
16. Ibid.
17. OSC Report GMP20041216000222, December 16, 2004.
18. George A. Lopez and David Cortright "Containing Iraq, Sanctions Worked." George Lopez is Director of Policy Studies at the Joan B. Kroc Institute for International Peace Studies at the University of Notre Dame. David Cortright is president of the Fourth Freedom Forum and research Fellow at the Kroc Institute. *Foreign Affairs* (July/August 2004).
19. www.cidcm.umd.edu/mar/chronology (Reuters, March 29, 1997).
20. www.cidcm.umd.edu/mar/chronology (Middle East Review of World Information).
21. www.cidcm.umd.edu/mar/chronology (AFP, March 6, 1997).
22. Patterns of Global Terrorism: U.S. Department of State, April 1998.
23. The Federation of American Scientists. www.fas.org.
24. United States Department of State. Public Affairs Washington, DC (July 1994). http://www.state.publicaffairs.gov.

CHAPTER 10

Northeast, Central, and Southern Africa

Peace is not the absence of tension; it is the presence of justice.

—MARTIN LUTHER KING.

Learning Objective

The study and review of this chapter will enable you to

1. Examine the failed states that are ripe for exploitation by Islamic extremists;

2. Discuss the role played by Ian Smith in the creation of Zimbabwe;

3. Discuss why oil rich African states suffer from internal terrorist attacks;

4. Explain how political forces in Zimbabwe have managed to control both the white and black population since UDI.

Terms to Remember

Afrikaner Weerstandsbeweging (AWB)	Front for the Liberation of Mozambique (FRELIMO)	Ogaden National Liberation Front (ONLF)
Al-Ittihad	Great Trek	Robben University
Apartheid	Idi Amin Dada	The Bakassi Boys
Bureau of State Security (BOSS)	Mandela United Football Club	Unilateral Declaration of Independence (UDI)
Emperor Haile Selassie	Mau Mau	ZANPU
Front for the Liberation of Angola (FNLA)	MEND	ZANU
	Nelson Rolihlahla Mandela	ZIPRA

November 28, 2002: Mombasa, Kenya—Thirteen people (three Israelis and ten Kenyans) were killed and about eighty were injured when a car bomb rocked a hotel in Mombasa, Kenya, favored by Israeli tourists.

March 11, 2005: Kampala, Uganda—the Lord's Resistance Army (LRA) killed seven civilians in a raid near the Ugandan border with Sudan.

March 28, 2005: Darfur, Sudan—Ten security officials were arrested and charged with rape and murder in Sudan's western province. This is the first action taken by the Sudanese authorities to crack down on the escalating violence in Darfur.

OVERVIEW

This chapter introduces a different source of terrorism . . . one that evolves over time and turns a state against its ethnic, religious, and historic tribal enemies. Despotic leaders in the northeast, central, and southern regions of Africa have utilised any measures they saw fit to use, including genocide. This chapter delves into the rise and fall of some of the vilest rulers and the terror methods they employed . . . for example, the despicable, modern-day tactician, Field Marshall and President for Life, Uganda's **Idi Amin Dada**. We shall also examine the historical roots of African terrorism and its progression to modern times, in places like Mozambique, Zimbabwe, the Republic of Congo, and South Africa. Each country has its own significant and unique history. We start our safari for facts in "The Horn of Africa," Ethiopia.

ETHIOPIA

Ethiopia has undergone some major and dramatic changes since the 1974 overthrow of **Emperor Haile Selassie**, "The Lion of Africa." In 1935, the country became the object of Italian colonialism, and the Emperor fled the country to live in exile in England. During World War II, the British, with the help of the Ethiopians, evicted the Italians from the country and returned Emperor Haile Selassie to the throne.

Eritrea is a region that lies to the north of Ethiopia, along the Red Sea coast, which had been under Italian control and influence since the 1880s. The Ethiopian government took over control of Eritrea in 1961, and ever since has been fighting an unending battle with Eritrean Nationalists seeking independence. Extremely poor living conditions, coupled with resentment of the Selassie regime's autocratic methods and corrupt government, resulted in a military coup led by Lt. Colonel Mengistu Haile-Mariam in 1974. By 1977 he was the preeminent military ruler, seeking aid from the Soviet Union to establish a socialist People's Republic and was at first successful at fighting off incursions from Somali and Eritrean rebels. Elected to the Presidency in 1987 Soviet aid began to diminish as too did the economy of the country. He abandoned socialism and unable to mobilize the military resistance he fled south to Zimbabwe. Trouble also flared up in the south of the country in a region known as the Ogaden, which was claimed by neighboring Somalia. Many of the inhabitants of that region were Somalis, and the resulting invasion of the region by Somalia's military in 1977 has been an ongoing and festering sore between the two nations.

By the latter half of the 1980s, the military rulers were taking a turn toward elected civil government, under a new constitution. Although elections were held, the military leadership continued to control the country. On May 28, 1991, the Ethiopian People's Revolutionary Democratic Front (EPRDF) toppled the authoritarian government of Mengistu Haile-Mariam and took control in Addis Ababa.

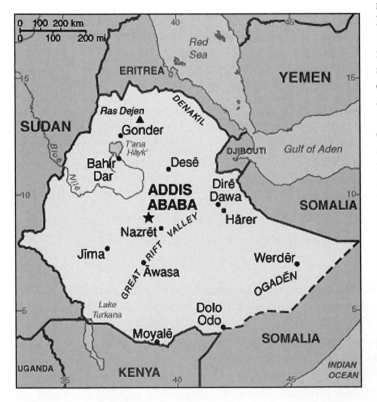

FIGURE 10-1 **Map of Ethiopia** (Central Intelligence Agency, *The World Factbook*, 2008).

A new constitution was promulgated in December 1994, and national and regional popular elections were held in May and June 1995. The main issue facing Ethiopia at the end of the decade was rebuilding the crumbling infrastructure of the country following years of civil war.

Ethiopia and Somalia still continue to squabble over the Ogaden region in the southern half of the country. The country is also a staging post for the transshipment of illicit drugs from Asia destined for Europe and North America, and cocaine for the markets of South Africa.

A region, such as the Ogaden which is a disputed area, has seen the rise to prominence of the **Ogaden National Liberation Front (ONLF)**. The group was formed as far back as 1984 and had not been of particular concern to the Ethiopian government until the regime's military invasion of Somalia in 2006 which targeted the Somali Supreme Islamic Courts Council (SICC) who aspired to create a Greater Somalia in the disputed Ogaden. There was obvious collaboration between the SICC and members of the ONLF. Since that invasion, ONLF have come out and attacked government forces and foreign oil installations. The government responses to ONLF activity have been broad sweeps by its counter insurgency troops and centering on villages that have supplied support to ONLF. The Ethiopian approach has seen its troops acting indiscriminately and has come under public pressure for its human rights abuses from the International Red Cross. Faced with mounting pressure to control the insurgency and to protect the oil resources in the Ogaden region, the Addis Ababa regime of Prime Minister Meles Zenawi must do all it can to destroy the ONLF. Zenawi is perceived as being dictatorial and no better than his predecessor, Haile Mengistu. In Somalia, Ethiopian soldiers ensure the security of a secular government led by Abdullahi Yusuf, who would be unlikely to survive the onslaught from SICC and Islamist fighters. Ethiopia's fate and that of Somalia lay in the hands of dictators attempting to destroy an Islamist surge in the Horn of Africa.

SOMALIA

Ongoing inter-clan feuding and a weakened military from the fighting in Ethiopia had left Somalia in desperate straits. In 1969, the clans within Somalia felt that the distribution of wealth only resulted in benefits to very few people. The control of the beleaguered country reverted to military rule, under the banner of the Somali Revolutionary Socialist Party, led by Major General Said Barre. All forms of the economy, i.e. banks, schools, and land, came under the direct control of the military government. This action coincided with one of the major famines of the twentieth century, and the ruling party did essentially nothing to aid the sick, starving, and dying, Somalis.

Resistance and uprisings finally came with the formation of the United Somali Congress (USC), which ousted Said Barre on January 27, 1991. However, since that date, the country has deteriorated even further, with no functioning government, anarchy throughout the land, and inter-clan fighting and banditry. This situation left one of the poorest countries in Africa to stumble around blindly with no functioning administration, as the various clans vied for power, until the transitional government of Ali Khalif Galaid was voted into power in 2000 . . . and just as quickly voted out by a no-confidence vote a year later. The interim government was recognized by the United Nations but was not held in high esteem by the Somali people. The country remains spilt down old tribal and sub-tribal clan lines, with warlords controlling the city of Mogadishu. Somalia is all about turf wars, and the possibility of any leader being able to bring the floundering country out of the Middle Ages seems somewhat remote.

After U.S. military successes in Afghanistan, speculation was that its next target against terrorism would be Somalia as it seemed to fit the bill of a lawless state that draws terrorists like a magnet. Sudan and Somalia remain the only regional countries not allied to the United States. Friendly relations with Kenya, Tanzania, Ethiopia, and Eritrea seem secure, despite some recent conflicts.

Since the U.S. missile strikes on Sudan . . . after the two U.S. embassy bombings (which resulted in Osama bin Laden being deported), and especially since 9-11, Africa's largest state has

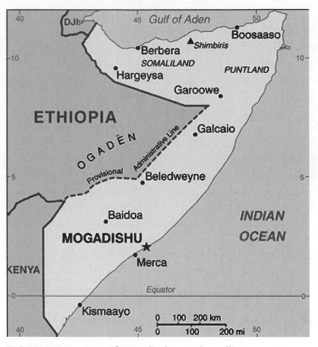

FIGURE 10-2 **Map of Somalia** (Central Intelligence Agency, *The World Factbook*, 2008)

been attempting to shed its image as a "sponsor of terrorism," and thus cut back the U.S. support for the southern rebels. The defining moment in relations between the two countries occurred in 1993 with the slaughter of eighteen American Marines and the deaths of hundreds of Somalis in the capital of Mogadishu. The Clinton administration subsequently evacuated and withdrew all U.S. forces from Somalia. This was portrayed as Somali rejection of a peacekeeping mission but, in fact, the deaths were a direct result of a seventh botched attempt to capture the notorious warlord, Mohammed Aideed. Aideed was killed several years later by a clan member. However, the hand of bin Laden was also at work as he had issued a "fatwa," calling for Muslims to attack the "soldiers of occupation." The United States has continued to strike at Somalia as it is viewed as a failed state and this makes the country a refuge for al Qaeda militants. In May 2008 Aden Hashi Ayro, al Qaeda's commander in Somalia, was killed in a U.S. air strike. Ayro had trained in al Qaeda training camps in Afghanistan and was leader of the Islamist group al-Shabaab.

Most reports claim that Ethiopia has long been Somalia's primary rival in the region, and its foreign policy is aimed at keeping Somalia weak and divided. Ethiopia had been urging the United States to extend its War on Terror to Somalia ever since 9-11. Ethiopia invaded Somalia in 1996 and 1999 (capturing or killing hundreds of Somalis). Ethiopia supported anti-government rebels such as the Rahanwein Resistance Army. In August 2000, a peace conference resulted in the closest thing that Somalia has had to a broad-based national government. However, Ethiopia, it seems, is actively trying to destabilize its ruined neighbor. Somalia can best be described as a defunct state with no functioning government or rule of law. The country nevertheless continues to function and has established clans and sub-clans with considerable inter-and sub-clan rivalry. Warlords still control various sections of the country. One may have expected that after the removal of the Taliban government from Afghanistan, Somalia would become a prime location for terrorist training camps and although it had been identified as being involved in the U.S. Embassy bombings in Kenya, it does not currently appear to be the "problem state" it most surely aspired to be. Its location on the Indian Ocean and, to the north, the Gulf of Aden gives it an easy launching platform to the Saudi peninsula. Somalia has a vast coastline, ideal for facilitating the movement of terrorists to operational hot spots in the Persian Gulf. Though mainly a Muslim Nation, much of what transpires in that country is not due to religious infighting but inter-clan differences.

The United States also declared the Somali Islamic Movement, al-Ittihad, a terrorist organization. **Al-Ittihad** emerged in 1991 as one of numerous warring militias; its aim was the establishment of an Islamic state. However, its military operations ended in defeat by invading Ethiopian troops in 1997. Since then, Al-Ittihad has become Somalia's leading provider of education and judicial, health, and welfare services—all scarce and badly needed in a country experiencing an extensive drought in the south, and facing severe food shortages elsewhere. The Somali government and the United Nations deny that al-Ittihad undertakes terrorist operations or has any links with al Qaeda.

But U.S. resolve was driven by its success in Afghanistan. After all, the United States found and courted enthusiasm for its war in Afghanistan among the Central Asian states, in particular, neighboring Uzbekistan and Tajikistan, which support anti-Taliban Afghan forces and are fighting their own Islamic insurgents. Thus, when one sees the regional gains made by the United States in its battles in Iraq and Afghanistan, it is not difficult to draw parallels to Somalia, and to understand the deep-rooted fear and suspicion in the Arab and Muslim worlds that behind the "War on Terror" is a strategy aimed at attaining regional dominance and compliant allies, regardless of consequences. The Somalis are basically distraught and mistrusting of the tribal politics that disrupt their country. The last government set a course to appease the warlords by offering olive branches in the form of cabinet posts. Some 15,000 militiamen were given positions as police officers. This has cost the government most of its treasury and it still dares not deploy the new policemen throughout Mogadishu, for fear they will return to the ways of their former warlord masters.[1]

The tracking of funds linked to terrorism has identified links between Sheikh Ahmed Nur Jimale the founder of a financial and telecommunications conglomerate with close ties to Osama bin Laden. The company founded in 1989 is involved in wire transfer services, telecoms, currency exchange, and internet services. The company is believed to operate over 127 offices outside Somalia and 60 within the country.[2]

Little has changed since 9-11. The transitional national government is now led by the recently elected Abdullahi Yusuf Ahmed, who was sworn into office in October 2004. He currently lives in Kenya, where most Somali government activity is conducted. Most sources now agree that the country has no terrorist bases or training camps currently in operation. The integration of the Al-Ittihad members into the social infrastructure, whether as teachers or preachers, means that they may be more difficult to monitor. There is no reason to suppose that they are not quite capable of reorganizing when the time suits them. Somalia is traditionally a country of Sunni Muslims and Islamic extremism is increasing rapidly. The country comprises two dominant clans and the Hawiye clan is the one that gave rise to the SICC, which went underground following the invasion and occupation by Ethiopian troops in late 2006. While the SICC remains underground, its two mouth pieces . . . Sheikh Sharif Ahmed, who at one time was leader of the now defunct Ittihad, and Sheikh Hassan Dahir Aweys, who leads the SICC's militant wing, have made noises to Ethiopia that they would consider brokering a peace deal. However, Somalia's current President Abdullahi Yusuf is from the other prominent Somali clan, the Darood. The likelihood that the Hawiye would actually agree to guarantee the security of the existing government is highly questionable. The Hawiye clan wants Ethiopian troops out of the region, who currently take some of the brunt of the attacks in the Somali capital Mogadishu from warring clans on the one hand and Somali and Islamist fighters on the other.

A peace deal in Mogadishu could also impact maritime shipping along the Somali coastline, an area that has seen a rapid increase in pirate activity. Somalia has experienced a rapid return to maritime piracy in 2007 with most attacks centered along the southern and central coasts. Practically no pirate attacks occurred under SICC control in the second half of 2006. Piracy is a means of generating income and not in this instance a case of terrorism. Suicide attacks which have been more frequently associated with attacks in Iraq and Afghanistan were also taking place in Somalia. The suicide attacks will not provoke any troop withdrawal but is an indication that the jihadist style of warfare is now present in the Horn of Africa and analysts believe that this gives credence to the viewpoint that al Qaeda or inspired al Qaeda operatives have a secure foothold in the area. This is also a reason for U.S. support to the regime in Addis Ababa and while Ethiopian forces have cleaned up the SICC in Mogadishu, none of the leadership has been killed or captured but have likely escaped or gone underground. In support of the regime, the U.S. launched airstrikes against SICC strongholds in the southern Somali town of Dobley on March 3, 2008, and was intended to target the SICC leadership. The presence of Islamic fighters in this region has continued to build and as African oil becomes a more precious commodity, we will continue to see U.S. support against Islamist insurgencies, particularly in this region where there is significant oil exploration.

While clan infighting will likely continue with an uncertain outcome for both Somalia and Ethiopia, the religious factor and the aims of the SICC are at odds with most Somalis. The SICC proclaims to want to unite all Muslims, however, Somalis being comprised mainly of Sunni Muslims do not subscribe to the strict Wahhabist and Islamist interpretations of Islam and many are concerned about the strict applications of Shari'a Law.

UGANDA

Located in Central East Africa and bordering on Lake Victoria in the south, Uganda, as we know it today, went through a long and turbulent period in its history. Uganda gained its independence from Britain in 1962 and elected Milton Obote to be its first prime minister. The country's president, Sir Edward Mutesa II, and Obote were at serious odds with each other on political issues. In 1966, Obote overthrew Mutesa, who fled to exile in Britain. Obote then established a new constitution that would encompass all the regions in the area including Buganda (a separate tribe, but from the same origins). Obote then assumed the role of president of Uganda, however, political stability did not last long in that turbulent African state and, by 1971, the Ugandan Army under the control of General **Idi Amin Dada**, led a military coup against Obote's government and forced him into exile.

For Ugandans, the 1970s were turbulent indeed—a time when Idi Amin Dada, Uganda's self-proclaimed "President for Life," might well have coined the modern phrase "ethnic cleansing." The sheer scope of the terrorism that this man committed on his own people during the very dark days from 1972 to 1979 is almost unbelievable in present times. His avowed praise of the work carried out by Adolph Hitler to exterminate the Jews, his open hostility and espoused demands for the destruction of Israel, spewed from the mind of this deranged psychopath! To try and understand any ideology that Amin may have had is an incredibly difficult task. He was extremely temperamental and prone to changing his mind quickly.

What is not in question is the length he went to purge that benighted country of Uganda of any and all opponents, both political and social. His first move was to cleanse the country of any foreign influence and return Uganda and its wealth to the native Ugandans (primarily to himself). The son of a witch doctor, Amin's appetite for wealth knew no boundaries or the incredible lengths he would go to get it. Obote made him responsible for military control of the northern region of Uganda.[3] To achieve his wealth, he engaged in smuggling and murder or, to put it the old-fashioned way, "rape, plunder, and pillage" were the order of the day.

One of the first actions Amin took on his route to terrorizing his own nation was the creation of a bureaucracy of state-sponsored terrorism to carry out his own bizarre, personal kinds of terror and torture. He established two secret state police organizations, the Public Safety Unit and the Bureau of State Research. The Public Safety Unit was empowered to shoot to kill anyone . . . on just mere suspicion. The Bureau of State Research carried out interrogations and torture, usually also resulting in the death of any hapless prisoner. The actual number of Ugandan citizens killed during Amin's reign has never been accurately documented or accounted for, but it is believed to be as many as 500,000 or more!

As is too often the case in other regions of the African continent, tribal rivalries and old hatreds play a large part in the business of selective "genocide." Under Amin (a member of the Lugbara tribe), Uganda set in motion the calculated elimination of all the Lugbaras' historical tribal enemies, especially the *Acholi* and *Langi* tribes. Handpicked secret police and vicious interrogation units from Amin's native *Lugbara* tribe were the implementers of this state-sponsored genocide.

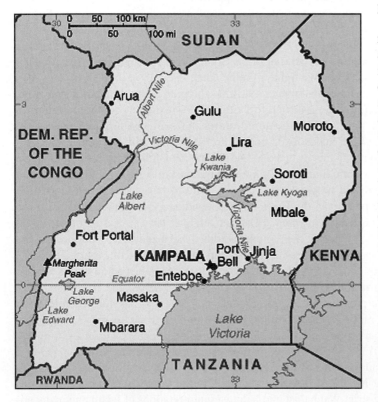

FIGURE 10-3   Map of Uganda (Central Intelligence Agency, *The World Factbook*, 2008)

On many occasions, Amin would observe or indulge in torture and other bizarre excesses personally. His presidential palace was linked by a series of tunnels connecting it to the Bureau of State Research in an adjoining building in the capital city of Kampala. He surrounded himself with a team of specially trained Palestinian bodyguards. When it came to executions, one of the methods employed was to provide a hammer to one prisoner who was then commanded, at gunpoint, to smash the skull of the prisoner next to him. This process of execution was then continued until the last prisoner was dispatched with a gunshot. Many executed prisoners were returned, in badly mutilated condition to their families, or dumped in rivers or in forests. Among other suspected atrocities practiced by Amin and his tribesmen was cannibalism. Killings by the army, where Amin's tribesmen were engaged in a systematic massacre of *Acholi* and *Langi* tribesmen, were the first signs to a watching public of the madness to follow. The expulsion of the Israelis, in 1972, was ultimately a result of their refusal to supply arms to Amin or Uganda. The Asian exodus was one of the most significant events in Uganda's history. The reason for the expulsion is not clear; certainly Amin was under significant internal pressure to "deliver the goods" of post-liberation euphoria and expectation, not just from the civilian population, but also from his army. Uganda is only now beginning to heal, after over a third of a century.

Airline Hijacking to Entebbe

The early 1970s saw an unprecedented number of airliner hijackings. One of the most notable was the hijacking of an Air France flight en route from Tel Aviv to Paris with 250 passengers and crew. The hijackers were made up of both German and Arab members of the Popular Front for the Liberation of Palestine. The aircraft flew first to Benghazi, Libya, and then on to Entebbe, Uganda. After negotiations began, the hijackers released 146 hostages but held onto the remaining 106 passengers, who were mainly of Jewish origin. They demanded the release of a large number of Arab terrorists being held in both Israeli and European prisons. As the negotiations dragged on it was clear to Israeli authorities that the Ugandan leader Idi Amin was helping the hijackers. The Israeli government quickly created a daring plan to release the hostages in Operation Jonathan. A force of Israeli commandos in three Hercules aircraft landed at Entebbe, much to the surprise of the hijackers and the Ugandan troops. The Israelis stormed the airport building killing seven of the eight hijackers as well as destroying Ugandan MIG aircraft on the ground. Three hostages were killed in the hour-long operation as well as the leader of the assault team Lt. Col Jonathan Netanyahu. One hostage, an elderly English woman, Dora Block, who had previously been taken to a local hospital suffering from the effects of the hijacking was subsequently murdered by the Ugandans as a reprisal for the attack on Entebbe.

Asians and the British owned and controlled over half of Uganda's wealth, and expelling them was Amin's shortcut to achieving what was expected. In addition, Amin bore some motives for revenge on the British and wanted to teach them a lesson they would never forget. According to Amin, the reason for expelling the Asians was revealed to him in a dream, wherein God decreed that if he didn't do it, the country would be ruined. Amin continued to exercise free license to murder anybody he perceived to be a threat. In 1978, Amin invaded Northern Tanzania in an effort to boost failing morale and wipe out more enemies. The retaliation was supported by expelled Ugandan troops, including the Front for National Salvation (FRONASA), which was led by Yoweri Kaguta Museveni. Museveni had been active since his student days at Ntare School, Mbarara; he studied political science and economics at the University of Dar es Salaam, graduating in 1970 with a Bachelor of Arts. The advance on Kampala was swift against the demoralized, though heavily armed, troops of Amin. The Tanzanian and Ugandan liberators arrived in Kampala in April 1979 under the banner of the Uganda National Liberation Army (UNLA). Once again, a chorus of jubilation echoed around the streets. After a short period of indecision, the Uganda National Liberation Front (UNLF) was formed from an amalgam of several Ugandan political and military groups. Not for the first time in Uganda's history, the people had united against a common enemy.

Milton Obote, who had then returned from exile, would contest elections as leader of the UPC (Ugandan Political Coalition). A third major political party emerged to do battle with the DP (Democratic Party) and UPC. It was the Uganda Patriotic Movement (UPM) and, once more, Yoweri Museveni was prominent in Ugandan affairs. Milton Obote won the election with a comfortable (though attained by dubious means) lead and he was sworn in as president on December 11, 1980. Obote's army, under Major General Tito Okello, returned him to power, anxious for revenge on those who supported Amin in 1979. Worst of all for Ugandans, Obote had no control over the army as senior officers systematically plundered government coffers and lower ranks looted and raped without restraint or punishment.

Dissatisfied with the election results, Yoweri Museveni and twenty-six young men retreated into the Luwero Triangle and started what was to be a long campaign of guerrilla warfare. The National Resistance Army (NRA) was formed under the banner of the National Resistance Movement (NRM). The turning point in the long bush war was the death of the UNLA commander, Oyite-Ojok, who was Obote's cousin. Ojok was a powerful figure and his death demoralized Obote's troops and caused a power struggle within the *Langi* and *Acholi* army factions. Obote's men continued to riot in the cities and towns, frustrated at the lack of success against the NRA. Obote consistently resisted appeals to negotiate with the NRA and he gradually alienated the *Acholi*, who felt they were fighting alone against the NRA. This up swell finally led to Obote being removed from power.

The constitution was suspended, parliament dissolved, and Major General Tito Okello was sworn in as president in July 1985, but violence and lawlessness remained. Gradually, the NRA gained more support and more control in crucial areas. Museveni and Okello met in Kenya and signed peace agreements for a new, equally represented government. Within a month of the agreement, the war intensified and the NRA moved closer to Kampala. Then, on January 26, 1986, the NRA forces overran Kampala.

Yoweri Museveni was sworn in as President of Uganda on January 29, 1986, and announced that his takeover represented a fundamental change in the affairs of Uganda and not a "mere change of guards." He proclaimed a ten-point program wherein NRM would "usher in a new and better future for the people of Uganda." The ten points included issues ignored or maligned by the previous seven presidents, such as democracy, security, and elimination of corruption. To mixed reactions, a large, broad-based cabinet was appointed with friend and foe alike. In an effort to unite every corner of Uganda under one government, Museveni included representatives of previously antagonistic political parties, tribal groups, and religious factions in the government of the day.

Museveni extended personal invitations to exiled Ugandans, offering key government advisory or corporate positions. A significant brain drain had taken place during the war years and Museveni was anxious that these individuals help rebuild a fragmented and broken country. When the NRA arrived in Kampala, it encountered no serious resistance. The victorious soldiers were disciplined and friendly; this army was within the law, not above it.

The task that lay ahead in 1986 was immense. The weird and violent policies of a whirl-wind of governments had left Ugandans without belief in their leaders. National pride and zidentity were essential to rebuild the battered country. One of Museveni's most painful and arduous tasks was to convince the people that a democracy would emerge from a military takeover. The country was in a mess and only a slow, systematic, and transparent examination of the damage might set wrongs to right again. The NRA re-established law and order everywhere in Uganda, except for the north and northeast, which had remained bastions of discontent and insecurity. The sporadic lawlessness in the north has been a constant problem to the NRA and until a national identity emerges, the issue will remain.

Uganda's infrastructure, including its judicial system, the constitution, road construction, agriculture, health care, education, and tourism, had broken down. Infrastructure redevelopment was the starting point for the new government. In addition, a system of local government through locally elected officials was put in place from the very beginning. Every Ugandan is a member of at least one legislative body that gives him or her a voice in everyday affairs. This was to be the primary foundation on which a new national identity would be built. The personification of Uganda's malaise has been the magnitude of the AIDS crisis. Uganda was one of the first countries in Africa to recognize and begin to deal with this terrible disease. The results have been very positive . . . education and awareness have been the key areas targeted.

Although Yoweri Museveni is a man with strong opinions and a keen sense of right and wrong, the reality of the chaotic situation he found in Uganda when he took power in 1986 meant that he had to accommodate people with views and attitudes that sometimes ran directly counter to his own.

As recently as August 2002, humanitarian agencies and Ugandan authorities were working out an emergency plan following a Lord's Resistance Army (LRA) attack on a refugee camp in northern Uganda, which forced thousands of Sudanese refugees to flee into the bush. The office of the UN High Commissioner for Refugees (UNHCR) said plans were in hand to move at least 24,000 Sudanese refugees who had fled from the camp to a safer location, following an LRA attack on the Acholi-Pii refugee settlement in Pader District. UNHCR's information officer for Uganda reported that Ugandan authorities had, at an emergency meeting between humanitarian agencies and senior government officials, agreed to relocate the refugees to a safer location yet to be agreed upon, preferably in Yumbe, Hoima, or Nebii districts, all in western Uganda.

The International Rescue Committee (IRC) for Uganda said it was also planning a response, which would involve transporting food to Rachkoko from neighboring Kitgum District. This was the second LRA attack in a week on the Acholi Pii Camp. The LRA group had first attacked the camp on July 31, 2002, but government soldiers repulsed the attackers, UNHCR said. Earlier, on July 8, LRA fighters had attacked the Maaji refugee settlement, in nearby Adjumani District, killing six refugees and putting another 8,000 into flight. The number of casualties incurred in the first attack remains unclear. Major Shaban Bantariza, the Ugandan army spokesman, told the BBC that about 200 LRA fighters had killed four soldiers and eight civilians, losing eleven of their own in the process. The magnitude of the attack was an indication that the Ugandan government was no longer able to guarantee security in northern Uganda, where humanitarian assistance was becoming increasingly dangerous as a result. The IRC had earlier withdrawn most of its staff from the camp, following the first attack, but re-deployed them there after receiving assurances from the Ugandan authorities guaranteeing their security. Since June 2001, the LRA has intensified attacks on northern Ugandan districts in response to the pressure exerted on it in southern Sudan. About 500,000 displaced Ugandans and some 155,000 Sudanese refugees live in camps in northern Uganda, according to the refugee agency.

THE LORD'S RESISTANCE ARMY (LRA)

The Lord's Resistance Army (LRA) is one of the largest terrorist organizations in the world. It has killed more people than many other violent groups, yet few Westerners have ever heard of it, since nearly all its violence is perpetrated in the border region between Uganda and Sudan in East Africa.

On a continent plagued with endless guerrilla warfare, where war crimes are standard fighting fare, the LRA stands apart as an especially odious group. LRA crimes against humanity are so repulsive that its only former ally, the Islamic government of Sudan, jettisoned its relationship with the LRA to improve Sudan's international relations. What began in 1986 as a rebellion against the Ugandan government has metamorphosed into a military millenarian cult. Its reason for existence is to perpetuate the power of its leader, a ruthless witchcraft practitioner named Joseph Kony.[4] The LRA under Kony had a fearsome reputation for its brutality against the people of Northern Uganda, and it is believed the group has managed to abduct and indoctrinate over 20,000 children into its ranks since it was first established in 1987.[5]

Since Museveni came to power in 1989, one of his most significant challenges has come from the Lord's Resistance Army, which formed out of the Ugandan People's Democratic Action party in

1989. Its leadership cadre is located in bases inside southern Sudan. In more than fifteen years of fighting with Ugandan forces, it has failed in its attempts to overthrow the government. LRA attacks and atrocities are invariably centered on the civilian population and involve the standard African tribal approach . . . looting, raping, and burning villages. One of the more unsavory factors about the LRA is its propensity to forcibly recruit child soldiers as young as age twelve to either carry out attacks or to be used as sex slaves. Human rights groups believe the LRA's ranks consist of 85 percent child soldiers. A large percentage of the children are kidnapped and forced to commit atrocities against their own families, and young girls are held as sex slaves and "wives" for local commanders. Recent attempts by the government to eradicate the LRA have included well-organized operations centered in southern Sudan, with the approval of the Sudanese government. However, there are claims that both sides have used extrajudicial methods to suit their needs. Ugandan People's Defense Forces (UPDF) is also reportedly using and abusing children. The operation inside Sudan, code named "Iron Fist," has displaced more than 1.2 million inhabitants from northern Uganda and seen over 60,000 children being used as soldiers. The phenomenon of "night commuters" has also emerged—an estimated 20,000 children flee their homes each night in fear, seeking refuge from possible abduction by the LRA, and searching for places to sleep in churches and hospitals.[6] Uganda has deployed approximately 8,000 of its troops in the Democratic Republic of Congo (DRC). Again, this is a consequence of the rich reserves of timber and diamonds. A form of trade was developed in the border regions, with shipments transferred through Uganda under the control of the Ugandan military. There is no vested interest for the Ugandans to see any ceasefire or peace within the DRC. Much of the spoils in this conflict originate in the northern city of Kisangani.

As the Ugandan government makes headway in peace talks with the Lord's Resistance Army, it emerged that it may ask the International Criminal Court to scrap indictments for the LRA's top five leaders as part of a final agreement with the rebels. Any attempt by the government to have the indictments against LRA leader Joseph Kony and his top four lieutenants nullified will cause international controversy since it was Ugandan president Yoweri Museveni who himself triggered international statutes in the first place to compel The Hague-based ICC to act. The warrants against Kony, Vincent Otti, Raska Lukwiya, Okot Odhiambo, and Dominic Ongwen were historic, since they were the first issued by the fledgling ICC, which began work in 2002. Lukwiya was killed in August 2006 during a fight between the LRA and Ugandan military forces. The war in northern Uganda has been raging since 1987, when the LRA under Kony, a self-declared mystic, began its attacks across the north, mainly in ethnic Acholi areas, ostensibly in an attempt to overthrow the Museveni government so that Uganda could be ruled in accordance with the Bible's Ten Commandments.

With great fanfare, in January 2003, Museveni invited the ICC to indict the LRA's leaders for crimes against humanity and war crimes, arguing that his country's own justice system was unable to deal with cases of such legal magnitude.[7] The LRA have suffered from regional political influences as they were often used as pawns, particularly in the conflict between Sudan and Uganda. The LRA was funded and supplied by the government in Khartoum and the Ugandan government were sponsoring attacks by the Sudan Peoples Liberation Army (SPLM), but since 2005, SPLM plays an official role in government so that source of financial and material aid has dried up.

ZIMBABWE

Many Black African states were looking to shed the yoke of the British Empire in the 1960s and 1970s. White rule in Rhodesia, under Ian Smith, ended in 1980 when the country gained its independence and Robert Mugabe became the country's first prime minister. However, Mugabe and his government faced violent opposition mainly from the region of Matabeleland. Mugabe's ruling party, the **Zimbabwe African National Union (ZANU)**, was also strongly opposed by the **Zimbabwe People's Revolutionary Army (ZIPRA)** and the **Zimbabwe African People's**

FIGURE 10-4   **Map of Zimbabwe** (Central Intelligence Agency, *The World Factbook*, 2008)

Union (ZANPU). Mugabe used what can easily be termed *state terror* on the peoples of Matabeleland to ensure his own position in Zimbabwe. To do this he used the Zimbabwe Army Fifth Brigade as a vehicle to control, repress, torture, interrogate, and execute all armed opponents in Matabeleland.

UNILATERAL DECLARATION OF INDEPENDENCE (UDI)

November 11, 1965, is the date on which Ian Smith declared a **Unilateral Declaration of Independence (UDI)** for Rhodesia. If one were to look to the north about the same time, as scenes were being played out in the name of independence, the view was far from gratifying. Millions were dead in Nigeria and the Congo, more than 500,000 in the Sudan and over 200,000 in Rwanda and Burundi. In nearly all instances, it was Black man killing Black man, and the countries were in the hands of blood-crazed total dictators.[8]

Unfortunately for the rebel government of Ian Smith, the rest of the world, including Britain and the United Nations, would not recognize the new breakaway state, and instead enforced strong economic sanctions on the country. In the years preceding the UDI, most forms of terrorism and violent criminal actions were well under the control of the authorities. In that era, when there was a perception of weakness and an opportunity arose to destabilize a region in Africa, the undertones of Communist involvement were never far away. So, too, it was with Rhodesia. Many of the young Blacks were lured out of the country on promise of "scholarships" in Zambia and Tanzanyika. In fact, these young men were being sent for Communist indoctrination and weapons training in camps in North Korea and the former USSR. They were returned via such ports as Dar es Salaam

REWARD NOTICE

Substantial rewards will be paid by Government to any person who volunteers information, to the Security Forces, which leads to the death or capture of terrorists or their supporters, or to the recovery of terrorist weapons. This information will be kept secret.

Rewards can be paid in cash, or into a Post Office savings account, bank savings account, or building society savings account. The payment of such reward money will be kept secret by Government.

LISTED BELOW ARE THE REWARDS:

$5 000 — Not less than $5 000 FOR INFORMATION LEADING TO THE DEATH OR CAPTURE OF A SENIOR TERRORIST LEADER.

$2 500 — Not less than $2 500 FOR INFORMATION LEADING TO THE DEATH OR CAPTURE OF A TERRORIST GROUP LEADER.

$1 000 — Not less than £1 000 FOR INFORMATION LEADING TO THE DEATH OR CAPTURE OF ANY TRAINED TERRORIST.

$500 — Not less than $500 for EACH anti-vehicle mine, heavy weapon of war.

$300 — Not less than $300 for EACH full box of small arms ammunition, grenades, anti-personnel mines, OR EACH light personal weapon.

A substantial reward will be paid for INFORMATION LEADING TO THE ARREST of any person who voluntarily houses, feeds, associates with or helps terrorists.

These rewards will not be payable to a civil servant who is engaged on duties concerned with anti-terrorist activities or to a member of the Security Forces, unless he obtained the information while he was off-duty.

BY ORDER OF THE GOVERNMENT OF RHODESIA

FIGURE 10-5   Reward poster dropped by air over Rhodesia (Glenn Ross).

on the coast of Africa and then infiltrated back into Rhodesia to fight against the Smith government. Ian Smith, was prime minister of Rhodesia and a powerful advocate of White minority rule; his unilaterally declared independence (UDI) from Britain in 1965 would result in a fifteen-year campaign against Communist backed African nationalists fighting for an independent African state later to become Zimbabwe. The campaign would cost the lives of 40,000 people.

Smith never once backed down from his position that there should never be Black majority rule in Rhodesia. The white South African government withdrew its support for Rhodesian UDI and this was a turning point for Smith. By 1972 the armed African nationalists under Joshua Nkomo and Robert Mugabe were raiding white farms at will. Ian Smith died on November 21, 2007, aged 88.[9]

With so many ways to define terrorism, would the likes of Nkomo and Mugabe be viewed as terrorists, insurgents, freedom fighters, or just violent criminals? The answer to this question is not easy. From the Rhodesian standpoint, they were certainly seen as terrorists, so the Smith government used the Rhodesian Special Air Service Regiment to good effect in destroying these "terrorists." The task from the military standpoint was almost hopeless, given the makeup of the borders that surrounded the country. The only friendly region lay to the south with the South African government. The numbers of terrorists and insurgents continued to grow in the same manner as that faced by the United States when it fought an impossible-to-win war in Vietnam.

The politics of the day did nothing to inhibit the violence in Rhodesia. On the contrary, to most people in Rhodesia, both Black and White, it seemed that the terrorist forces had the tacit support of the British government in the name of African nationalism. The two leaders of the terror groups, Joshua Nkomo and Ndabaningi Sithole, were openly supported in Britain even though they were leaders of the two parties banned by the Smith government. The Black nationalists, Robert Mugabe being one of them, formed ZANU as a result of a split with the Nkomo leadership. Nkomo formed the opposing ZAPU movement. Formed along tribal lines, Nkomo's support came principally from the Ndebele tribes of Matabeleland in the west, while Mugabe's support lay in the tribes of Mashonaland in the east of the country.

As a result of the serious voting irregularities during the 2002 general election witnessed by the Commonwealth Observers, an announcement from London was that Zimbabwe was to be suspended from the Commonwealth for twelve months. The leaders of South Africa, Australia, and Nigeria made the decision on behalf of the fifty-four-nation group, after studying an observer mission report on Zimbabwe's appalling presidential elections. Announcing the decision in London, Australian Prime Minister John Howard said he hoped the international community would encourage reconciliation in Zimbabwe between the main parties. At a summit held before the Zimbabwe election, Howard and the presidents of South Africa and Nigeria, Thabo Mbeki and Olusegun Obasanjo, were appointed to decide what action, if any, the Commonwealth should take against Zimbabwe. The ballot in Zimbabwe saw the re-election of incumbent President Robert Mugabe amid allegations of violence, terrorism, and intimidation against the opposition Movement for Democratic Change, led by Morgan Tsvangirai. Western governments have severely criticized the fairness of the election, while African governments have been less willing to condemn Mugabe.

The Commonwealth Observer Group accused Mugabe of using state powers and institutions to steal his victory. The United States, Britain, and the European Union condemned the elections as "unfair and not free." Before leaving Australia for London, Howard said, "This is quite a moment of truth for the Commonwealth . . . it's not something that can be swept under the carpet."

Mbeki and Obasanjo held talks with Mugabe, to try and seek a compromise. Among the proposals speculated on was a Government of National Unity, but both Mugabe and Tsvangirai cast doubt on the plan. Tsvangirai said: "We arrived at the conclusion that the objective conditions do not exist for meaningful discussion because Mugabe's party . . . ZANU-PF, is embarking on mass retribution against our members in the rural areas."

Mugabe, who has been in power since 1980, was sworn in for another six-year term. He took the victory as a mandate to pursue his land reform program. Zimbabwe's main Labor Federation called for a three-day general strike to protest what it called post-election harassment of workers.

The Harare meeting came on the same day that a White farmer was shot dead by suspected ruling party militants. Terry Ford was the first White farmer killed since Mugabe was re-elected and the tenth killed since militants began often-violent occupation of White-owned land two years earlier. Denmark, which is not a member of the Commonwealth, announced it was closing its Harare Embassy and ending further developmental aid to the country, and stated that reports from national and international observers clearly showed that the election was neither free nor fair. Denmark withdrew its Embassy staff from Harare that summer.

Zimbabwe continues to reel under the effects of Mugabe's dictatorship, with millions facing certain death from disease, starvation, and state-sponsored violence, yet Mugabe's message to the nation was a promissory note for more misery and death. The annual National Heroes' Day in 2002 proved to be no exception. The illegitimate ZANU-PF government has routinely turned this somber national occasion into an indecent partisan junket to spread a message of violence and hatred.

Mugabe fails to connect with the primary concerns of the people of Zimbabwe, which are food, jobs, health, and an end to poverty. He instead concerns himself primarily with rhetorical nationalism. In fact, Zimbabwe now is a country where everything is in short supply except misery, starvation, and death. The regime has reduced innocent citizens to the levels of scavenging animals.

Where Zimbabweans expect a message of hope and decisive leadership to confront the problems bedeviling the country, they are told that their daughters and sons will be forcibly drafted into the

FIGURE 10-6 Zimbabwean President Robert Mugabe attends a church service in Bulaweyo, 300 miles north of Harare, in March 2008 (Canadian Press).

so-called National Youth Service and be transformed into killing machines for the perpetuation of Mugabe's dictatorship. Change in Zimbabwe is inevitable, no matter how many innocent citizens are slaughtered by his regime. Evidence at hand demonstrates, beyond any reasonable doubt, the regime's culpability in widespread and systematic incidences of murders, tortures, rape, abductions, arsons, and many other forms of well-organized political violence that have taken place with impunity over the first decade of the twenty-first century. The partisan public media has never exposed nor condemned ZANU-PF violence, but has instead defended it. The police force, on the other hand, has mastered the art of selective harassment, arrests, and prosecution of the opposition, while ruling party criminals who are guilty of heinous crimes are walking scot-free. As the 2008 elections came around there was the real prospect that Mugabe now over eighty years old would relinquish his control and fade into obscurity. On the contrary the March 2008 elections were a well rigged affair by the Dictatorship—thugs from Mugabe's ZANU-PF party roamed the countryside at will attacking and intimidating voters. True democracy is still not being felt in what was once the bread basket of Africa.

In addition to the acts of barbarism that have been perpetrated with state sanction and impunity, the regime has sought to legalize the harassment of political opponents, and to control what the people read, hear, and see through the enactment of legislation with severe democratic deficits, like Jonathan Moyo's Access to Information Act and John Nkomo's Public Order and Security Act. What is blatantly disturbing and unacceptable about the regime is that at a time when the nation has an avalanche of political and economic crises on its hands . . . for which the regime is responsible . . . its ministers, such as John Nkomo, Joseph Made, and Jonathan Moyo, are busy trying to outdo each other in their daily television appearances. The regime's ministers have become obsessed with little things at a time when they should be answering questions about more serious things, like the supplying of salt for Zimbabwean families.

The United Nations has condemned Zimbabwe, Uganda, and Rwanda for actions in the DRC. These three countries initially intervened in the DRC to stabilize the area in the aftermath of Laurent Kabila's overthrow of Mobutu Sese Seko and the subsequent chaos that took place in the eastern half of the former Republic of Zaire.

Both Uganda and Rwanda support the rebels in the east and Zimbabwe supports the government. However, the UN report accuses Zimbabwe, Uganda, and Rwanda of perpetuating the war for their own financial gain, as they exploit the country's rich mineral resources. The DRC is one of the richest countries in the world in minerals. It has gold, copper, diamonds, cobalt, coltan (a metal ore for use in aerospace telecommunications industries), and timber.

In the rebel-controlled areas, Rwanda is accused of exporting coltan, which it mines inside the DRC; Uganda is accused of gold-smuggling activities; and Zimbabwe allegedly engages in joint ventures with DRC government officials, which benefit only the ruling elite back in Harare. The armed forces of the DRC have been pushed into the western half of the country, unable to penetrate the areas held by the Tutsi-backed rebels in areas where these three countries' armies are operating, despite receiving military aid from Zimbabwe, Angola, and Namibia.

The governments of Rwanda and Uganda reject the claims that they are prolonging the war for their own gain. Although a UN-monitored ceasefire has been established, there is still fighting between rival armed groups. The result, as is the usual case in Africa, is paid for in civilian suffering and lives. Infant mortality stands at 40 percent. There are reportedly 2 million displaced persons and 16 million people classified as not receiving the basic nutritional levels as stipulated by the United Nations.

ZANU-PF 5 BRIGADE

The PF-5 Brigade came into existence under Prime Minister Mugabe's command. In October 1980, Mugabe signed an agreement with North Korean President Kim Il Sung that arranged for North Korean training of Zimbabwean troops. Koreans were sent to train this new brigade which Mugabe said would be used to "deal with dissidents and any other trouble in the country." The 3,500 ex-ZANLA troop members that made up the 5 Brigade were supplemented by some ZIPRA troops, which were withdrawn before the end of the training stage. The training lasted until September 1982. At deployment, the 5 Brigade was different from any other army units: it answered only to the Prime Minister and did not follow the standard military chain of command. It had unique codes, uniforms, radios, and equipment that were not compatible with standard-issue Zimbabwean army tools. The 5 Brigade's most distinguishing feature was their red berets.

The 5 Brigade was deployed twice into Matabeleland—once in Matabeleland North in late January 1983, then in Matabeleland South in January 1984. After this, they were retrained, deployed again, and then in 1986 finally withdrawn, to undergo a conventional training period under the British Military Advisory Team. In late 1986 the 5 Brigade was disbanded and its soldiers spread out between other regular army brigades.

The deployments of the 5 Brigade into Matabeleland in the early 1980s were marked with a reign of terror, with actions meant to draw out anti-government "dissidents." Within the first weeks of the first deployments, 5 Brigade troops had murdered more than two thousand civilians, beaten thousands more, destroyed property, and burned houses. Civilians seemed to be specifically targeted during those weeks; hundreds of civilians were rounded up, marched at gun point to a central area, like a school or village well, beaten with sticks, and made to sing Shona songs praising ZANU-PF. These gatherings would then end with public executions.[10]

In the clinical sense, starvation has not yet set in Zimbabwe. But the signs are there . . . people with stick-like arms and legs and swollen bellies. AIDS is wiping out a whole generation of parents. Thousands upon thousands of small children barely exist with no food, no family income, no medicines, and no answers. Over a third of these children have HIV or AIDS. It is not life they are living—they are just waiting to die. Zimbabwe is now facing a major famine that may decimate half of the country's population.

Zimbabwe's 1992 Land Acquisition Act is at the heart of the redistribution of land owned by white farmers and arbitrarily handed over to blacks. The Act was intended to speed up the land reform process by removing the "willing seller, willing buyer" clause. This empowered the government to buy land compulsorily for redistribution. From Harare, the word of Zimbabwean officials is that: "White

Farmers will live to regret their defiance of government orders to abandon their land." This follows nearly 3,000 white farmers being ordered to leave their property as part of a plan to seize white-owned lands and turn them over to poor blacks. No serious measures have yet been taken against farmers who have defied the deadline, which changes quickly and often. But, Co-Vice President Joseph Msika, head of Zimbabwe's Land-reform Task Force, told state television about the farmers refusing to leave their land: "Those who are not going to work within the laws of Zimbabwe have nobody to blame but themselves. The law will take its course." A powerful local government minister said: "All the excuses by the farmers show what an arrogant and racist bunch they are. It shows they want to derail the land-redistribution program by any means . . . they will not succeed," according to the state-run Herald newspaper. Vice President Simon Muzenda warned that authorities would act firmly against farmers opposing the, "irreversible" land program. "You are told by government what we want done and you simply do that," he told state radio. In Washington DC, the U.S. State Department denounced Zimbabwe's attempt to evict the farmers and thousands of farm workers as "a reckless and reprehensible act."

While Robert Mugabe continues to rule supreme in Zimbabwe, he continues to target all opposition and, in May 2005, he targeted the urban centers that failed to support him during his re-election campaign in March 2005. The country languishes in abject poverty and real fears of famine exist. In late May 2005, Mugabe ordered a "cleanup" that sparked rioting in Harare. Three thousand police supported by the Zimbabwe military destroyed informal settlements and street markets and arrested almost 20,000 hawkers. The government-sanctioned destruction has left tens of thousands homeless with nowhere to repatriate. The opposition Movement for Democratic Change claims that this action is purely a pretext for the government to announce a "state of emergency." Today the Mugabe brand of politics, intimidation, murder, rape, and forced removals of his own people mark the standard for a failed state that the rest of the world, although condemning it, does little to correct.

SOUTH AFRICA

For the last half of the twentieth century, South Africa operated under a white dominated apartheid government, using "**apartheid**," as an official method to control the actions, activities, and opportunities of native black colored, and African-Asians in the Republic of South Africa. The main political party that was set up to fight apartheid was the African National Congress (ANC). Strangely, that party started on a political platform and moved eventually toward armed confrontation with the South African government.

Color alone, by no means, carries with it a unity of belief, purpose, or ambition. The most virulent and persistent of hatreds in Africa is often those between people of the same color. The black population of South Africa is divided into at least seven distinct ethnic groups, each with its own written language and home area, and each resolved to retain its own identity. That way the groups could develop separately and still remain apart. In the forty years up to the early 1990s, the South African governments set out to regulate this "problem" by the establishment of separate, self-governing "homelands" for each group.[11] To most people, from the outside looking in, apartheid has always had an evil connotation. Although this text is not intended to be a forum for debating the pros and cons of segregation of ethnic groups in South Africa, it is relevant to the South African experience with terrorism.

Britain's involvement in the Cape colony dates back to over three centuries, when the region along the Cape was very important as a refueling and trading post for shipping to and from the Orient and India. The Cape colony was also home to Dutch

FIGURE 10-7   Map of South Africa (Central Intelligence Agency, *The World Factbook*, 2008).

migrants from Europe who had settled the Colony in 1652. From the middle of the sixteenth century, the Dutch East India Company had executive powers over the Colony, and all its inhabitants, but allowed Dutch settlers to leave the company and start their own farms. These people became known as "Boers." With the migration inland, the white farmers fought the tiny, "San Tribes," people (Bushmen), and either killed or enslaved them for work on their farms.

The Dutch government formally turned the Colony over to Britain in 1834. The first British settlers had arrived in the Cape in 1820, and with control going to Britain, an unpopular decision was made to end slavery. Britain established English as the official language of the Cape to the extreme resentment of the Boers living in the Colony. Unhappy with British rule, the Boers began to move north and settled in regions farther away in the Transvaal, the Orange Free State, and Natal. The move north became a historic event for the Boers and is generally referred to as the **Great Trek**.

With the discovery of diamonds in the Kimberley region, and gold in the Johannesburg areas, Anglos and Boers would eventually fight the first Anglo-Boer War. Overwhelming force of arms allowed the British to defeat the Boers by 1902, thus bringing about the Orange Free State, Transvaal, and Natal, all under firm British rule. This rule, not surprisingly, included all the Black tribes, most of which submitted peacefully to their new masters. As in most matters, there is always an exception to a rule, and the South African exception was the "Zulus." This warlike tribe would submit to nobody and, in 1879, defeated and destroyed a well-trained British regiment at Isandhlwana. Overwhelming superiority of forces and firepower eventually defeated the Zulus and, by 1888, none of the black African tribes retained independence.

Afrikaner Nationalism

Two famous Boer generals, Louis Botha and Jan Smuts, had a great part to play in the rise of Afrikaner nationalism in South Africa. General J. Hertzog formed the Nationalist Party, which had the ideology that the Boers had a right to rule South Africa and to unite the Anglos and Afrikaners. With a nationalist government coming to power in South Africa for the first time in 1922, nationalists began the changes that would shape the United South Africa of their dreams. This included the recognition of Afrikaans, alongside English, as the official language and also the development of industry less dependent on Great Britain. With the outbreak of World War II, South Africa was already an independent nation within the British Commonwealth and there was considerable debate as to which side, if any, to support. Hertzog favored neutrality while the Boer General Smuts sided with the British against Germany.

Apartheid

During the war years, the Nationalist Party underwent a rebirth and change of direction under the inspiration of D.F.D. Malan, a strong supporter of the nationalist South African cause. Under his guidance, the adoption of segregation along racial lines (**apartheid**) was developed and instituted as part of government policy, with sweeping police powers of enforcement. The government had created the power to direct the masses as to where to live and where to work. The struggle against apartheid, or racism, as some observers prefer to call it, became a part of the South African struggle and terrorism for over fifty years. However one significant incident in March 1960 marked the turning point in the attitude of the international community toward the apartheid government of South Africa and caused the sting of economic sanctions against it. One of the requirements of the apartheid laws was for all blacks to carry ID cards. In protest, Blacks went to police stations without their cards and waited to be arrested. The same scene was played out in many locations; however, in Sharpsville, the police opened fire with automatic weapons, and killed 67 and wounded over 200 blacks. From this one incident the ANC formed its military wing, the Umkonto We Sizwe (Spear of the Nation).

Extreme Right-Wing Afrikaner Movement

Extremism in South African politics emerged at the end of the 1960s from splinter groups that broke off from the National Party and called themselves the Herstige Nasionale Party (HNP). By 1971, all the hard-liners of Afrikaner Nationalism had been forced out from the National Party and thus formed the **Afrikaner Weerstandsbeweging (AWB)**, The Afrikaner Resistance Movement. The AWB became known principally for its menacing, but flamboyant, leader, Eugene Terre'Blanche. Likened to Adolph Hitler, his speech-making skills were legendary. This ability allowed Terre'Blanche to attract large crowds of supporters to his meetings. Not only was he a consummate politician and orator, but an accomplished sportsman. He served in the South African Police Service as a Warrant Officer. After leaving the police service, he went on to form the AWB in July 1973 with another former police colleague, Jan Groenewald. The early movement was extremely small, and the meetings were secret for fear of drawing the attention of the **Bureau of State Security (BOSS)**.

When the group first came out to public view, it portrayed all the same trappings and uniform style, complete with swastika, as the German Nazi Movement. Albert Hertzog, a former cabinet member of the National Party and founder of the HNP, was at this time outside of the party hierarchy, following the party's disastrous showing in the general election, and was looking for a cause to support. That support, together with his great business acumen, went to Terre'Blanche and the AWB. Although the 1970s were the formative years for the AWB, no specific acts of terror can be attributed to the organization. With the dismantling of the apartheid system in South Africa, that would change over the following seventeen years.

Many observers labeled the AWB as a neo-Nazi organization. Although the leadership of the AWB vehemently denied the label, the group's flamboyant uniforms did not easily dispel this viewpoint. Still searching for its true identity, the AWB went through several different scenarios, usually linked to storm trooper and motorcycle gang-style images with fearsome-sounding names like the Lightening Falcons or Storm Falcons. Most were burly and surly men outfitted with jackboots and helmets.

The first signs of violence came in 1985, when Terre'Blanche proclaimed that the AWB would form into units of guards. These groups were called the "Sentinels" or "Brandwag" and were formed up along the Northern Transvaal border with Zimbabwe. The white farmers in the border areas formed Brandwags to protect against incursions from across the border with Zimbabwe. The AWB equipped itself with its own bodyguard of heavies to "control" and monitor meetings. Most of the white farmers in the more remote regions of the Transvaal were also local commando (army) members, so it was not surprising that they would be well-armed with sophisticated weapons. With the extreme right-wing's sympathy, and now sophisticated weapons in its members' hands, the aims of the AWB were to make sure black groups and political organizations would not become targets for action. What made the AWB so popular was its belief in preserving its claims to land and demands for an Afrikaner nation to be formed out of the former Boer Republics.

By the end of the 1980s, it became clear that the enemy of the AWB, apart from left-wing politicians, was also the African National Congress (ANC). Over the years that led up to the first ANC-elected government and the ending of the apartheid system in South Africa, AWB members and supporters carried out various terrorist acts to destabilize the ANC and the elected government. The AWB had hoped to escalate the violence into a full-scale civil war. As we now know, that was never to be the case. However, the bomb attacks were directed mainly at black civilian targets as were the indiscriminate use of bombs in the major cities. The bombing campaign resulted in many AWB arrests and convictions. In 1996, the AWB, still under the control of Terre'Blanche, announced that the movement would now operate underground.

The AWB symbol is the eagle. The group's official guidebook details that: "This emblem enables the AWB to give its full acknowledgement to the symbolism of the eagle which epitomizes the protection of the Lord: Like an eagle that stirs up its nest that flutters over its young, spreading out its wings, catching them, bearing them on its pinions." (*Deuteronomy* 32:11)

The Future

In April 1994 the African National Congress gained over 60% of the vote in the country's first free elections bringing an end to apartheid and white minority rule. With the public's general acceptance of the new government, UN recognition, and the rapid lifting of international sanctions, it is difficult to see the AWB or a similar nationalist movement emerging in South Africa in any significant fashion for the near future. As long as Afrikaner nationhood is alive and well, however, there will always be the opportunity and threat for a different generation to take up where Terre'Blanche left off.

The African National Congress (ANC)

The quasi-political African National Congress (ANC) movement dates as far back as 1912, and has consistently, along with other liberal groups, opposed the nationalists and their apartheid policies. Garnering support for any action, given the overwhelming numbers (75 percent of the population is black and 14 percent white, with the balance being made up of Asians), would not be difficult. Probably the most famous name connected to the movement is that of the first black President of South Africa, **Nelson Rolihlahla Mandela**. Born in 1918, the son of a tribal chief, Mandela received an excellent education and became a lawyer. Toward the end of World War II, he joined the African National Congress. Mandela, an outspoken opponent of apartheid, led protests and demonstrations against apartheid and police brutality during the 1950s, for which he was arrested and charged with treason. The charge was not proven, however, and he was acquitted. He was arrested again in 1962, charged with terrorist offenses, and sentenced to life in prison. His release thirty-two years later would become the harbinger and beginning of the new South Africa and a black majority government. The role of the ANC and various acts of terrorism in South Africa are intertwined. The ANC contention is that it had been driven to acts of criminal violence, bombings, shootings, and murder because it lacked any political alternative. With apartheid firmly in place and its leader firmly in jail, the ANC members embarked on a terror campaign aimed at the state, the white minority, and their own black brothers who failed to support them. Intertribal fighting has been a hallmark of fighting in the south. Some of the forms of brutality the ANC used are quite gruesome to describe. One favored method in killing recalcitrant blacks was the "rubber necklace" . . . a badly beaten victim was placed in a stack of used car tires and then set on fire.

The ANC received external support in its campaign from Communist sources outside South Africa's borders. This led to the government reducing and diminishing the effects of apartheid on the Black and Colored communities. The ANC had a military wing that advocated revolutionary violence. It further advocated the kind of Communist revolution that swept into Russia at the start of the twentieth century. A 1987 quote from Winnie Mandela, then wife of the imprisoned Nelson Mandela, clearly defined the Communist goals for the ANC: "The Soviet Union is the torchbearer for all our hopes and aspirations. In Soviet Russia, genuine power of the people has been transformed from dreams into reality." Since the middle of the 1980s, the Republic of South Africa has undergone drastic political changes, and with those changes came the fruition of the dream of the overthrow of the regime and the system of apartheid.

Having been banned since 1961, the ANC had been headquartered outside South Africa, in neighboring Zambia. To this extent, one may assume the Zambians gave material support to ANC terrorists crossing into South Africa. The South African police and military were very effective in patrolling and controlling border incursions from neighboring African countries, especially those hostile to the apartheid regime. The neighboring countries of Lesotho, Mozambique, and Botswana have been, at varying times, the locations for terrorist training bases for the ANC and were supported by Russian technicians. The external locations did not prevent the South African security forces from taking preemptive actions against the training base locations in those countries. The ANC also aided in defining the term *terrorism* by declaring in the 1980s that the South African government was a terrorist government and that the ANC was acting in self-defense.

Robben Island University (Isle of Purgatory)

Many historic landmarks have formed central points for penal servitude around the world. Well-known among those landmarks are Wormwood Scrubs in London, England; the Island of Elbe; Devil's Island;

and Alcatraz. Not so well-known to the world is Robben Island, situated off the southern coast of Africa at Cape Town, with a splendid view of Table Mountain. This island had served as a dropping off point for Cape traders in the sixteenth century. It has been a leper colony, a hospital for the insane, an armed garrison, and the long-time residence of Nelson Mandela and other banned and convicted members of the ANC. Today it is a national monument and tourist attraction. The island was turned over to the South African Department of Prisons when the South African Artillery School vacated it in 1959. The first African political prisoners arrived at the prison to serve their sentences in 1962, along with members of the Pan-African Congress activists, as well as soldiers from an armed group called "Poqo." Members of the ANC, including Nelson Mandela, arrived soon afterward. Many arrived in a state of general illiteracy. However, "B Section," which housed Nelson Mandela and his cohorts, became known as **Robben University**. Here, many inmates were able to learn and further their political debates and beliefs. The ANC "students" observed a prison code that required they maintain their commitment to changing South African society, and to find positive development through their term of imprisonment. The code also required that none of them were to leave the prison without some education. The last prisoners left the island in 1991, after the ANC finally received political recognition.

Winnie Madikizela-Mandela

Winnie, the estranged wife of Nelson Mandela, the first black president of South Africa, has been described as the "Mugger of the Nation." During the political build-up to her husband's dramatic release from his life sentence on Robben Island, in true charismatic fashion, Winnie surrounded herself with a phalanx of bodyguards. As the ex-wife of the former president, her actions and those of her bodyguard have been questioned. Winnie Mandela, her bodyguards, and a group of tough youths from the Soweto Township became known as the **Mandela United Football Club**. Jerry Richardson, who was a convicted murderer, was the group's leader. They were involved in beatings of Blacks in the townships. Winnie herself was convicted of kidnapping in 1991.[12]

Is South Africa out of the shadow of terrorism? Apart from the Planet Hollywood bombing in 1998, the country has been relatively free of terror attacks. The passage of time and the removal of the apartheid South African government have not seen any sudden improvement in everyday living conditions, hoped for by the millions of black South Africans. Questions are now coming to the table about corruption and incompetence of the highest order under the current government. Weak governments on the African continent have been susceptible to terrorism. However, until recently, South Africa had a strong democratic system of government and had control of its borders and an effective security force. It seems probable that the rainbow of nations in South Africa and their neighbors may someday pale. As Whites leave the country in ever-increasing numbers for a safer life outside the Republic, the fabric and wealth of South Africa may suffer from instability.

ISLAM IN SOUTH AFRICA

People against Gangsterism and Drugs (PAGAD)

People against Gangsterism and Drugs (PAGAD) was established in 1996 as a community anti-crime force. It originated in a network of hitherto disparate and isolated anti-drug, anti-crime groups and neighborhood watches frustrated by their inability to tackle problems whose roots extended far beyond their individual localities. Predominantly, but by no means exclusively, Muslim, PAGAD began with a loose organizational structure and an informal, collective style of leadership. It was open to approaches from other anti-crime groups and prepared, at least, to consider working with the police. Many of the more violent actions taken against drug dealers, such as the attack on Rashaad Staggie in August 1996, were neither planned nor formally sanctioned by the organization as a whole. PAGAD's development since these early days cannot be seen simply as the unfolding of a master plan conceived and executed by a small group of Islamic radicals. Rather, it has to be viewed as the outcome of the interplay between many internal and external forces . . . of action by PAGAD and its constituent elements and reaction by the state and its agencies in the specific political, social, and economic context of the Western Cape.

The state's view of PAGAD has changed dramatically over the last four years. From a popular anti-crime movement, it has become first a violent, and therefore illegitimate, vigilante organization and then, since 1998, an urban terror group threatening not just the state's monopoly on the use of coercive force but the very foundations of constitutional democracy. In line with these altered perceptions, the state's response to PAGAD has changed from constructive engagement to demonization and repression.[13]

PAGAD has become rabidly anti-Western, as well as anti-government in its activities. It views the current South African regime as a threat to Islamic values. The group is led by Abdus Salaam Ebrahim. PAGAD's G-Force (Gun Force), operates in small cells and is believed to be responsible for carrying out acts of terrorism and targeting mainly synagogues and nightclubs in the Cape region of South Africa.[14]

PAGAD's activities seem at odds with its value structure. The group's Web site lists the following as its goals:

- To propagate the eradication of drugs and gangsterism from society;
- To cooperate with, and to coordinate the activities of people and people's organization, having similar aims and objectives;
- To make every effort to invite/motivate/activate and to include those people and people's organizations that are not yet part of PAGAD;
- To raise funds to realize the foregoing aims; and
- PAGAD is a non-profit-making movement. All its assets, income, and contributions shall be used to achieve these objectives of PAGAD.[15]

Boeremag (Boer Force)

Since the end of the apartheid regimes, South Africa has had to contend with a small outbreak of extreme right-wing nationalism in the form of the Boeremag movement. This group seeks to overthrow the current South African government and drive the black population north into central Africa and create a Boer (white) homeland. Boeremag's activities in the first four years of the millennium have been to place a number of bombs around buildings and bridges, most often where there is a large concentration of blacks. Bombs went off in the township of Soweto and the group expected the black population to rise up in a race war against the whites. Eighteen of the group's members have been arrested as it continues to demand a separate Afrikaner Homeland.[16]

Both the South African and United States governments have officially designated PAGAD as a terrorist organization. South African police efforts and court prosecutions severely damaged the group in the early 2000s. Since 2001, PAGAD has demonstrated a significantly weakened operational capability.

KENYA

Myriad tribal groups, spread throughout the land, have populated Kenya for untold centuries. The Kikuyu is one of the largest tribes of the region, and it works the land alongside the Kamba, Masai, and Luo tribes. The beginnings of colonialism in the nineteenth century saw the erosion of the tribal rights in Kenya. Britain was granted title over the lands now called Uganda and Kenya. Uganda became a British Protectorate in 1885, and Kenya followed shortly after in 1893. Britain, in those

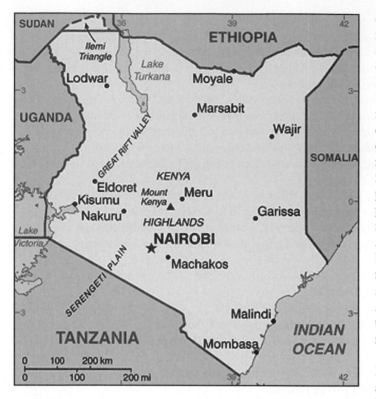

FIGURE 10-8   Map of Kenya (Central Intelligence Agency, *The World Factbook*, 2008).

days, was interested primarily in the rich natural resources of Uganda, and constructed a railway system between Kampala and Mombassa. Much of the work was done by imported labor from the Indian subcontinent. Most of the merchants of Kenya and Uganda are the descendents of these railway workers. By 1915, British settlers had claimed the fertile highland regions for growing crops for export and displaced the tribes of those regions. Africans and Asians were prohibited from being landowners.[17] The British, unprepared to deal with the native issues in Kenya, permitted the growth of Black Nationalist movements and, in 1929, one of the most prominent African leaders of the 20th century, Jomo Kenyatta, went to England to negotiate for land rights on behalf of the Kikuyu Central Association. With the onset of World War II, Africans were conscripted, thus providing a trained cadre for what became the Mau Mau terrorist group.

Unlike its near neighbors, the population of Kenya has been relatively free of terrorist activity and atrocities. Insurrections and uprisings in Kenya have been perpetrated in living memory by what is still considered one of the most shadowy and frightening organizations to gain a foothold on the African subcontinent . . . the **Mau Mau**. This almost mythical, shadowy, and mysterious organization in Kenya came to prominence again as a result of what may be construed as a colonial land grab. In fact, the tribes of Kenya were land farmers and cattle herders who considered the land "everyone's land." But much of their area was "owned" by white families. Kenya became part of Britain's far-flung empire, bringing with it taxation as well as education to the natives of the region. Britain and the settlers were of an unshakable belief that the land was the sole property of the tribal government, and therefore the colonial government had rights to the land. Naturally, such an assumption did not sit well with the tribes of Kenya. The land grab instigated a rebirth of the Mau Mau. Although the specific aims of the organization have never been detailed, the group flourished in the tribal lands of Kenya.

One of the best-educated tribes of the region was the Kikuyu, and it was from this environment that the Mau Mau found its roots. The Kikuyu, like the other tribes, had been reduced almost to the levels of third-class citizens or serfs in their own country. In a region of the world where superstitions and magic have a considerable foothold, the groundswell of support for a secret society, to fight for the people, quickly became apparent. The Mau Mau had sworn an oath . . . that the Kikuyu took extremely seriously . . . for the total removal of all whites and those that had supported the colonial British government. In the early 1950s, the Mau Mau began attacking White settlers on their farms in Kenya. The attacks came to a full-scale rebellion in 1956 and were finally forcibly crushed by the British. Many tribesmen were sent to detention camps or were hunted and killed. The Mau Mau leader at the time was Dedan Kimathi, who was executed for leading the uprising. The Mau Mau campaign had a softening effect on the British and sincere efforts were made to stabilize the country; however, from 1956 to 1960, the country was under a "state of emergency." The Kenyan African Union (KANU), led by Jomo Kenyatta, sought independence for the country. In 1963, Britain granted full independence to Kenya. Kenyatta became the country's first president.

INTERNATIONAL TERRORISM IN CENTRAL AFRICA

With the emergence and spread of Islamic fundamentalism throughout the Middle East, and also into regions of Northern and Southern Africa, it is not surprising that a "soft" target, such as an embassy of a foreign super power, would suffer the brunt of a terrorist attack.

That attack came against the U.S. Embassy in Nairobi, Kenya, in early August 1998. The U.S. Embassy in Nairobi certainly did not have the levels of security protection afforded to other U.S. legations, particularly in the Middle East. The embassy was considered below the acceptable standards for security, particularly after the bombing of the U.S. Marine Corps barracks in Beirut in 1984, which claimed the lives of 242 marines. Recommendations to tighten U.S. security had not included Kenya; presumably, the threat assessment was considered low for this region of the world. With lax security and the location of the building being in the center of Nairobi, it became too good a target for the determined terrorist to pass up. A massive car bomb decimated the embassy building and caused extensive damage to the surrounding buildings. The bomb claimed 170 lives, mostly Africans, and wounded several thousands. The object of the attack was the U.S. administration, and not Kenya. This attack demonstrated how determined terrorists can attack at will and without warning and drive home their vengeful message to a nation.

The prime suspect in this attack was Osama bin Laden, the Saudi Arabian dissident with operational training bases in Somalia, Pakistan, and Afghanistan . . . a man whose name would always be associated with infamy in regard to the 9-11 attacks on the United States.

Politically Expedient Response

The attack in Nairobi will always be viewed as history repeating itself in almost the same vein as similar catastrophic terror events. At the time of this action, the terrorists caught the Clinton administration almost totally unprepared for a problem of such magnitude, and at a time when the president was facing serious personal and legal problems of his own. The outrage that this attack caused had the same kind of political and military response as the Libyan attack on U.S. servicemen in Germany. That incident quickly resulted in President Reagan ordering an attack on Libya, even though there was no verifiable evidence that the Libyans were, in fact, responsible.

If retribution or retaliation is to be meted out, and it seems to have been in this case, governments must be cautious about the levels of violence and the message that they are sending, not only to a small group of determined terrorists but also to whole nations that become the target.

The effects of retaliatory attacks against the Sudan and Pakistan have been determined, in this tit-for-tat approach, to be marginal at best. Do these counterattacks result in a diminished number of terror attacks against the United States and other Western governments? Since 9-11, it is fair to wonder. The answer to this question is not simple, nor is it easy to quantify.

The police crackdown after the IRA bombings on the British mainland in the early 1970s, and its success in bringing the supposedly wrong people to trial for the Guildford Pub Bombings, did not deter whole generations from becoming immersed in terrorist activities, both on the U.K. mainland and in Northern Ireland. The attacks against Libya did not deter the bombers from destroying a Pan Am airliner over Lockerbie, Scotland, in 1988. On the other hand, the suicide attack against the U.S. Marines in Beirut did not deter President Reagan from ordering his marines to invade the tiny Caribbean Island of Granada a very short time later, responding to fears of an alleged Cuban takeover of the island.

ANGOLA

Angola had been Portugal's prize jewel in Africa for more than 500 years. Portuguese navigator Diego Cam landed in Angola in 1482 and left his mark in the traditional Portuguese shape of the cross. Over the centuries, the Portuguese exploited little, if any, of the natural wealth of the country, which was rich in mineral deposits. With colonial development happening all around, Angola languished in quiet slumber. All of this was to change on March 15, 1961, when gangs of

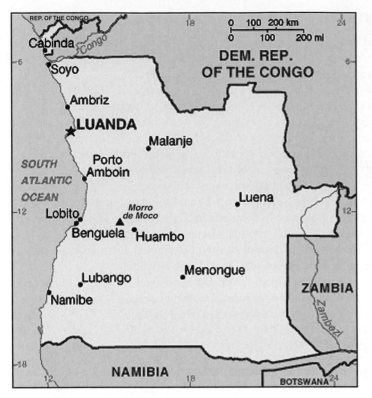

FIGURE 10-9 **Map of Angola** (Central Intelligence Agency, *The World Factbook*, 2008).

guerrillas loyal to Holden Roberto raided villages in Northern Angola in a cross-border incursion. They killed many villagers and committed atrocities on both the living and the dead. At one location, the victims were put through a sawmill while they were still alive.[18] They attacked men, women, and children, hacking limbs from bodies and heads from torsos. Over the next decade, this one act spurred Angolan economic development to a fever pitch. It also brought with it Communist factions bent on controlling the country and removing the Portuguese influence.

Popular Movement for the Liberation of Angola (MPLA)

The Popular Movement for the Liberation of Angola (MPLA) started in the late 1950s in the Angolan capital of Luanda and, by 1961, had begun to fester into a civil war throughout the country. In the northern region of Angola, the **Front for the Liberation of Angola (FNLA)** was formed and, in 1966, the National Union for the Total Independence of Angola (UNITA) appeared. The warring factions continued sporadic fighting over the years. However, the Angola military's overthrow of the Colonial Portuguese government in 1974 led to Angola's eventual independence a year later. With the guerrilla army's spread throughout the country, neither of the sides could agree as to which would eventually lead the new government, and fighting resumed. The MPLA was receiving considerable aid from the USSR, as well as Cuba. The Russians supplied weapons, training, and support, while Cuba supplied the fighters to help with the guerrilla war.

By 1976, the battles were over, and the Marxists dominated and influenced the MPLA. With a Marxist government so close to the northern border of Namibia, formerly Southwest Africa, the South African government continued to provide support and weapons to the UNITA rebels fighting against the Marxist government forces of the MPLA. Many of those fighting with the UNITA were South African mercenaries as well as former British soldiers. A ceasefire eventually came into effect in May 1991 and lasted until October 1992.

At that time, UNITA refused to accept the election results and fighting resumed between UNITA and the MPLA government. Sporadic fighting continued over the next two years and, finally, in 1994, it was agreed that UNITA guerrillas would merge with the Angolan army. All of this took place under the watchful eye of UN peacekeepers, and although the transition was slow, the new government of National Unity came into office in April 1997. Since that time, UN forces have pulled out of Angola.

However, the ongoing decades of violence since Angola's independence from Portugal have now seen a dramatic shift in the fortunes of one of the main protagonist groups, namely the ongoing battle with the National Union for the Total Independence of Angola (UNITA). In February 2002, government troops engaged in a fierce firefight with UNITA rebels led by their patriarchal leader, Jonas Savimbi. During this single action, Savimbi was killed when troops attacked his stronghold in the southern region of the country. The short- and long-term effects of his death will likely mean that there will be a vacuum and those insiders will likely concentrate on a power struggle, thus fracturing UNITA. Whether this means the end of UNITA, it is still too early to say. Much of the funding support for UNITA came from its illegal trade in diamonds. It is probable that the illegal trade will continue and arms will still be traded for them. Savimbi's movement has not benefited from the end of the Cold War when much of its support network came from the Democratic Republic of the Congo, headed up by Mobuto Sese Seko.

MOZAMBIQUE

Sandwiched between Tanzania and South Africa, this other legacy of Portuguese colonialism bears the ravages of civil war, and is today one of the poorest nations in Africa. Many of Mozambique's problems stem from its nearby neighbors, South Africa and Zimbabwe, the former Rhodesia. Organized along the lines of a one-party state, the current Mozambique government moved out of the realm of a guerrilla/terrorist organization and become a political party. In the early 1960s, many inhabitants were becoming increasingly frustrated with the Portuguese rule, and the **Front for the Liberation of Mozambique (FRELIMO)** was formed.

FIGURE 10-10 Map of Mozambique (Central Intelligence Agency, *The World Factbook*, 2008).

The movement carried out operations against the Portuguese until 1974, when the country was finally granted independence. FRELIMO was a strong Marxist regime, opposed to the White minority rule (apartheid) of South Africa in the 1980s and also of the Ian Smith minority independence government of Rhodesia (Zimbabwe). When independence was declared, FRELIMO closed its western border with Rhodesia and many dissidents from Rhodesia set up bases in Mozambique to attack the Smith government, assisted by the Russian supported FRELIMO. As the ideological focuses of the surrounding states changed, so did Mozambique. The Samora Machel government in Maputo supported the banned ANC movement in South Africa and supplied weapons, training, and support to terrorists fighting cross-border battles with the South African security forces. Mozambique also had its own internal strife at this time, and South Africa supported the Mozambique National Resistance Movement (RENAMO) in its guerrilla war with the Marxist government. By 1984, South Africa and Mozambique reached an agreement to stop supporting terrorists and guerrillas in each other's country. However, this did not stop RENAMO from continuing its war against apartheid with the FRELIMO. RENAMO's tactics were aimed at totally destabilizing the country and it began to destroy even schools and medical facilities with over 1,800 schools and 500 health centers destroyed. Close to 100,000 people were killed in countryside villages.

Death of Samora Machel

In 1986, President Samora Machel met his death in an untimely fashion when his Russian-made Tupolev aircraft (with a Russian crew), crashed into a hillside on the South African side of the border. What is uncertain about this crash is the manner in which it occurred. Was it an accident or a planned assassination? There has been much speculation since the crash that there was a high-level South African plot to eliminate Machel. Evidence from the crash suggests that external influences somehow tampered with the directional systems of the Tupolev 134A-3 aircraft. Because it was so wildly off course, it is suspected that a decoy navigational beacon was activated to misdirect the aircraft onto a crash course into a hilltop. South Africa covertly supported the increasing number of

RENAMO raids into Mozambique and had increasingly angered Machel. Whether South Africa was involved or not, it is known that there were raised tensions in the previous weeks before the crash, including threatening signals from the SA Defense Ministry. This led to extreme tension between the two countries and continuing distrust on both sides.

By 1992 the two sides reached an uneasy peace and called for an election process that would include RENAMO on the ballot. When voting took place in 1994, FRELIMO had 44 percent of the vote and RENAMO 33 percent

RWANDA

A small, landlocked African state, Rwanda had become infamous with the unexplained murder of Diane Fossey, the famed naturalist and expert on silver-backed gorillas. In the 1960s, others knew of Rwanda for its fabulous pictorial postage stamps that graced many a philatelist's collection. But, in 1994, it became a killing field for the native Hutus, who eventually massacred well over 500,000 Tutsis.

Rwanda had for centuries been a land of farmers occupied by the Hutu tribesmen and Pygmy hunters. In the thirteenth century, the warrior Tutsis invaded and took control over the Hutus. To the casual onlooker, it might seem logical to assume that the Hutus and Tutsis were sworn enemies. That could not be further from the truth; in fact, Hutus and Tutsis had lived side by side and intermarried for hundreds of years.

There are few differences in the physical characteristics of the two tribes. They look the same, pray to the same Gods, and had peacefully coexisted for centuries. So the question one has to ask is: What happened to cause the genocide that took place in 1994? One must first look at the role played by the colonial forces of Belgium who ruled up to the early 1960s. The Belgian authoritarian control in Rwanda decided to organize and institutionalize the ethnic stereotypes in the country. As it was impossible to physically distinguish between Hutu and Tutsi, the Belgians decreed a system that sounds like it came out of the Dark Ages in order to define in which ethnic group a person belonged. Amazingly, it used these following criteria: If a farmer owned nine cows or less, he was issued an identity card stating he was a Hutu; if he owned ten or more cows, he was a Tutsi. The Belgians had over night created a class structure dependent on the details of an identity card, and this had been the basis for a social division of the two tribes since the 1930s.

Now that the Belgians had created a minority elite, they gave them privileges and positions on the Belgian colonial administration structure. The Belgians ruled by the grace of the Tutsi minority in Rwanda, who had been schooled and educated by the Belgians. As they grew more powerful, they sought to throw off the mantle of colonialism and demanded independence for their country. To counter the Tutsis' demands, the Belgians began to switch their allegiance to the Hutu majority, producing enough hatred against the Tutsis to start a popular uprising. The uprising brought the Hutu into government and over 100,000 Tutsis were killed. A similar number of Tutsis, fearing further atrocities, fled to neighboring Uganda in the north, where they remained in exile. It was this exiled group and their descendents who returned to begin the civil war in 1990. In exile, the group formed the Rwandan Patriotic Front (RPF), which was made up of displaced Tutsis and Hutus dissatisfied with the Hutu government. The aims of the RPF were to replace the oppressive and repressive government with a new democratically elected government.

The Hutu-dominated government of President Habyarimana, was determined not to be removed from power. To achieve that end, it planned to eradicate the Tutsis in methods not dissimilar to the Nazi genocide perpetrated against the Jews in Germany. The tool of the trade, in this instance, was propaganda. As most of the Hutus were illiterate farmers, the government began to systematically bombard the population with radio announcements that were deliberately and openly anti-Tutsi. It went beyond just denouncements of the Tutsis, but actively demanded that civilian Hutus kill any and all Tutsis they came across. Terror and threat, terror and threat, were repeated over and over in efforts to sow the seeds of total annihilation for the Tutsis. In a format reminiscent of South American death squads, the Hutu

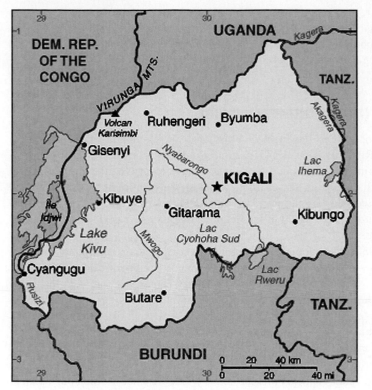

FIGURE 10-11   Map of Rwanda (Central Intelligence Agency, *The World Factbook*, 2008)

government set up civilian militia, training them in weaponry, hand-to-hand combat, and methods to quickly kill their enemy, the Tutsis. This organization was called the Interahamwe, which means "those who attack together." The Hutu militias began killing Tutsis wherever they found them, and soon it became apparent that to kill a Tutsi would not be considered a crime in that country . . . it was just eliminating a form of vermin. However, after three years of the civil war and slaughter, a cease-fire was finally reached between the two sides in 1993. Then, under the auspices of the United Nations in 1994, the devastated country prepared to set up some form of transitional government. However, the Hutus continued to arm and train its civilian militia openly, right under the noses of UN observers. It is still not clear to the international community as to why the United Nations made no effort to report these facts or to seek any clarification on how to handle the issues.

Death of a President

Uprisings often need to have a "trigger mechanism" to set them off. In April 1994, the plane carrying President Habyarimana was shot down as it approached Kigali, the Rwandan Capital, killing the president. This single incident became the "green light" for the genocide to begin once more in earnest. Within hours of his death, the attacks and killings of Tutsis commenced, and within a single month nearly half a million Tutsis lay dead and the rest were scattered throughout the country. Those who were able to escape fled to neighboring countries. The United Nations simply stood by and observed the genocide, and has been criticized for its failure to intervene and stop the massacres.

It was through the death of President Habyarimana, that the world came to hear about the genocide being perpetrated on the Tutsis, as graphic and horrifying pictures and accounts in newspapers emerged worldwide. Two months into the killings, the United Nations finally passed a resolution to send in a UN peacekeeping force of around 5,000 troops. With the killings all but over, and the RPF advancing from the north, many of the Hutu militia and military escaped across the border to Tanzania and to refugee camps set up inside the border. The point may have been missed in newspaper articles in regard to the goings-on in Rwanda, and the need for urgent humanitarian aid for the refugees. But most of the refugee camps held only the murderous members of the Hutu, as nearly all the Tutsis had been caught and killed in the preceding six-week period. A long rebuilding process has begun for the Tutsis who survived, but how long the scars and hatred will take to heal is anyone's guess.

The country's demand that the Hutus and Tutsis reintegrate within Rwanda is unique in world history. Genocide, civil war, refugee flight, abundant hate propaganda, a culture of impunity, and ongoing insurgency and atrocities—these are the stories in Rwanda. The most telling and difficult question is whether the people of Rwanda can rewrite a social contract that will be acceptable to any functioning society. Can they overcome their mutual suspicion and live as neighbors and fellow countrymen again? The Hutus returning to Rwanda must fear retaliatory actions being meted out against them, the same as to the Tutsis in 1994.

In recent history, such a reintegration has never happened. It certainly did not take place in Germany, causing the international community to create Israel, a sovereign Jewish state. Fleeing from the killing fields, the people of Cambodia resettled in other countries. Rwanda today is still a dangerous and suspicious place; terror and atrocities continue to take place; as old and not-so-old scores are settled.

DEMOCRATIC REPUBLIC OF CONGO (DRC) FORMERLY ZAIRE

The Democratic Republic of Congo (DRC) is located in the center of Africa and straddles both the equator and the mighty Congo River. Its population is around 40 million. The DRC is rich with mineral resources of gold, copper, zinc, and diamonds, to name but a few. Henry Stanley discovered the region now called the DRC in the 1870s, and was asked to set up Belgian trading posts along the Congo River in 1878 by King Leopold of Belgium. The King ruled this African country as his own private fiefdom and it only fell under the control of the Belgian government in 1908. At that time, it was called the Congo Free State.

By the last years of the 1950s, the colonial Belgian rule was coming to an end and, on June 30, 1960, the Belgian Congo became the independent Republic of Congo. The first president of the new Central African Republic was Joseph Kasavubu, with the legendary Patrice Lumumba as his prime minister. Unluckily, for the young, Communist-inspired Lumumba, his position was extremely tenuous in the eyes of the West, particularly the United States.

The 1960s was the height of the Cold War and the CIA was intent on reducing and eliminating any Soviet involvement in mineral-rich central Africa. The CIA conspired with factions that were anti-Communist to overthrow the Lumumba government and install a pro-West regime. This was achieved by infiltrating mercenary elements into the country. The CIA had worked out a plan to poison Lumumba; however, prior to his assassination, the army mutinied. The army at this time was led by a young Zairian office Joseph Desire Mobutu. In July and again in September 1960, Mobutu, a colonel in the army, announced the suspension of all political parties and took control of the country. In November 1960, Lumumba was arrested and handed over to rebel forces, and was executed on January 17, 1961. For the next four years the government was in turmoil, until the military coup of Desire Mobutu. The next thirty-two years saw Desire Mobutu rule the country with an iron fist and in a somewhat African tradition plundered the country's central bank for his own personal use and gains, buying homes, villas, and castles in Europe. His leadership was violently anti-Communist and strongly pro-West, which suited the world situation in the Cold War years and the particular interests of the U.S. Mobutu received vast sums of "development" aid, aimed at preventing the spread of any Communist influences. In the 1970s he began a period of "Africanization" and changed his name to Mobutu Sese Seko with a literal translation meaning "He the all powerful warrior". Names of cities were changed; Leopoldville was changed to Kinshasa, and changing the country's name to the Democratic Republic of Zaire, from Congo. Mobutu has plundered his country to such a state of deprivation that when the Hutu and Tutsi fighting in neighboring Rwanda spilled over into Zaire he had no military to stop the incursions. The Rwandans were led by an old friend of Patrice Lumumba, namely Laurant Kabila.

Mobutu Sese Seko

Mobutu's tyrannical reign was all about ancient methods of pillage and plunder in a twentieth-century format. He was estimated to be one of the five richest men in the world, and was president of one of the poorest nations and lowest standard of living in Africa, or even the entire world for that matter.

In a country of such enormous mineral wealth, it is not very difficult to establish where the wealth had gone. Mobutu and his cronies lived a lavish lifestyle in Africa, and had plush villas throughout Europe. One of the earliest uprisings against the Mobutu regime came in 1964, in the area of the eastern Congo. It was led by a young rebel of Marxist trappings, Laurent-Desire Kabila, who would later return to lead the civil war against the Mobutu regime. Much of what took place in the Congo was a result of outside influences and internal disputes between the many ethnically diverse tribes that had settled in the region. Refugees from rebel actions and atrocities in neighboring countries also were factors.

Hutus and Tutsis differences over the genocide in Rwanda played a significant part in the eventual rebellion and civil war that overtook the DRC. Insurgent rebellion was prevalent throughout the long dictatorial reign of Mobutu, but he had always managed to put down the uprisings, either by force or by proclaiming presidential or legislative reforms. The country existed as a one-party state under Mobutu, so challenges to his rule were frequent. Citizenship issues and land rights also added to the tensions of the DRC. The complications of the various regions of the DRC are interwoven within the ethnic groups, who vie for power. The principal groups are located in the province of Kivu, which has a long history of ethnic violence; these groups are the Hunde, Nande, and Banyarwanda.

Banyarwandans are a collection of displaced Rwandans who arrived in the region to work the land, courtesy of their colonial Belgian masters; they are comprised of both Hutus and Tutsis. Members of this group were not considered to be citizens of Zaire under Mobutu's rule, and that has not changed with the transition to Kabila's government in 1997. The local chiefs in Northern-Kivu Province had rented to the Banyarwandans most of the land they occupied. By 1993, the Banyarwandans were pushing for reforms and an end to the injustices carried out against them. What was to complicate the situation in Zaire was the massive and sudden exodus of Hutus from Rwanda. Included in this exodus was the local Militia Interahamwe, which had been involved in the genocide in Rwanda after the death of the Rwandan president.

An uprising in 1993 escalated into yet another, full-scale ethnic battle. Most of those killed were Banyarwandans. The situation was not improved by the arrival of the Hutu refugees from the fighting and killing in Rwanda. The uprising spread and soon became a national movement to overthrow Mobutu. The rebel forces consisted mainly of Tutsi warriors, and soon Laurent Kabila became their revolutionary leader.

Widespread disillusionment in the Zairian army led to the eventual capitulation of the Mobutu government. On May 16, 1997, with only his personal bodyguard remaining in Kinshasa and the rebel forces on the doorstep, Mobutu left quietly for the safety of Morocco, where he lived in exile until his death in September 1997, from prostate cancer. However, since Kabila came to power, the ethnic violence between the factions has not ceased, and with unprotected borders, the DRC has seen an increase in rebel attacks from outside. From within, the fighting and massacres have continued, particularly in the North and South Kivu provinces. Hutu and Tutsi continue to kill each other, and an end to this violence is not expected anytime soon. Much of Kabila's support comes from the army, which has been dominated by Rwandan Tutsis.

The Congo can be viewed in much the same vein as Somalia as it, too, is defined as a failed state. Since the start of the ceasefire in 1999, the most contentious issues are still unresolved. The country is variously occupied by six foreign armies and roving bands of militia. Hundreds of thousands of residents have been displaced in the war years and have not yet been repatriated.

The Congo is home to many non-Congolese groups and one, in particular, is the Hutu-dominated Liberation Army of Rwanda (ALiR), which fled from that country after the genocide it perpetrated in Rwanda in 1994. The ALiR continues to be supported by the government in Kinshasa, as the Congo has no effective military force to deal with the occupying forces of Rwanda and Uganda. The Tutsi-dominated regime in Rwanda, afraid of renewed Hutu attacks, maintains its own occupying forces in eastern Congo, refusing to withdraw until the Hutu groups are disarmed. And, for reasons of their own, Angola, Zimbabwe, Namibia, Uganda, and Burundi all maintain a strong military presence in the Congo as well. President Joseph Kabila and his backers, Angola and Zimbabwe, refuse to consider power-sharing through the dialogue with anti-government rebels without guarantees of Rwanda and Uganda's full withdrawal. The rebels and their sponsors, on the other hand, refuse to consider withdrawal until a transitional government is established through dialogue and Rwanda's border security is guaranteed. These external demands have to be addressed as part of the Congo's political transition. In total, these challenges appear to present a near-impossible "catch-22." But they can be resolved if the international community, and especially the United Nations, is prepared to make a greater commitment to completing all three parts of the peace process.[19]

NIGERIA

The rise of Islam in Nigeria is not something that should necessarily be a surprise, particularly to the Nigerian public. The country has been subjected to years of government squandering and corruption, so much so that Muslim regions have turned to the strict Shari'a to enforce laws. After 9-11, there were sporadic outbreaks of violence between Muslims and Christians, including burning and looting of Christian-owned shops and restaurants that served alcohol in retaliation for a Christian attack on a mosque. In the many decades since the retreat of colonial powers, Africa has been an unsettled and volatile land. So, it is not surprising that radical Islamic fundamentalism would have a significant foothold in areas of Nigeria as well as other underdeveloped nations in Africa. Does the rise of Islam also mean that there is likely to be an increase in fundamentalist attitudes toward Western democracies and values? Certainly, a minority would seek to use religion as a cover for subversive operations against either the host state or to assist in propagating the fundamentalist movement.

Lawlessness and crime are an everyday problem for most nations of the world; however, the activities noted in Nigeria lend a new twist to the meaning of crime fighting. **The Bakassi Boys** are a group of young men who have taken some measure of control over the lawless southern city of Onitsha. The Bakassi Boys operate a terror subculture working outside of the established law. The Boys' brand of terror is to snatch victims, usually suspects in some crime or wrongdoing, and subject them to interrogation and, in many cases, instant execution. The Anambra State Governor, Chinwoke Mbadinuju, has financed the group and provided it with weapons and even police vehicles. Quite clearly, law and order has broken down, and regional southern states have turned to vigilante operations to suppress crime. This can quickly lead to wider regional implications for the formation of private armies to do the bidding of their financial backers. Nigeria is Africa's most populous nation, with more than 125 million people and over 200 distinct ethnic groups, so it is not unusual to have clashes on religious, ethnic, and communal grounds. The violent outbreaks have claimed thousands of lives since the election in 1999 of President Olusegun Obasanjo, following sixteen years of military rule. That period of military rule was able to contain ethnic and religious violence. More than 900 people died in 2004 and there are many claims that the Nigerian police and military did nothing to prevent the killings from taking place.

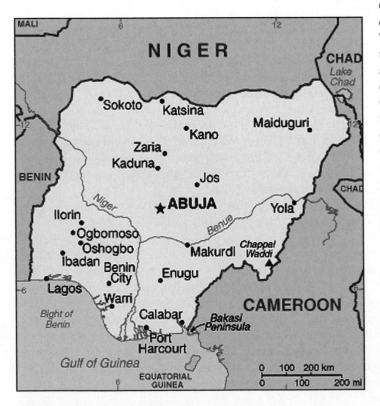

FIGURE 10-12   Map of Nigeria (Central Intelligence Agency, *The World Factbook*, 2008)

In a report on two waves of killings in Plateau and Kano state in February and May 2004, Human Rights Watch said the government's failure to punish the killers was feeding the cycle of violence. Central Nigeria lies on a religious fault-line, dividing the mainly Christian south and the predominantly Muslim north. Tension has been heightened by the adoption of the strict Islamic law, or Shari'a, by several state governments elected with the ending of military rule in 1999.

In rural areas, the divide between Muslims and Christians often coincides with a conflict over land use. Violence in Plateau dates back to 2001 when around 1,000 people were killed in less than a week in September during religious riots in the state capital, Jos. Over the next two years, there followed a series of tit-for-tat attacks by Muslim and Christian communities in the hinterland that escalated into large-scale violence again in 2004.[20]

Nigeria, in recent years, has also become oil rich and has seen such companies as Shell Petroleum Development company to have an almost 50 percent stake in the oil reserves of the country. Most of the pipeline and development activity is centered around the Niger delta and it's in this area that a shadowy and violent group has emerged to attack pipelines, kidnap workers, and generally harass and disrupt the supply of crude oil. The Movement for the Emancipation of the Niger Delta (**MEND**), operates in fast inflatable boats along the Niger and began operating in late 2005 with attacks on the oil infrastructure. The Nigerian President Olusegun Obasanjo had attempted to make electoral reforms that would allow him to preside for a third term, and a vote in the Senate supported by Vice President Atiku Abubakar rejected his attempt to make the necessary amendments. Oil wealth and government corruption continue to be the order of things in Nigeria and

FIGURE 10-13   MEND—the Movement for Emancipation for the Niger Delta—a militant group that patrols the creeks of the Niger delta area of Nigeria. Most of the crude oil in Africa's largest oil producer is pumped from beneath this region, which nonetheless remains mired in poverty. Citizens and this group, MEND, are behind a spate of attacks and kidnappings that have driven oil prices up worldwide and now warn that violence aimed at enhancing the region's share of oil revenues controlled by the federal government will only increase (Canadian Press).

with oil at $100 plus per barrel and with production set at around three million barrels per day, would see revenue of around $100 billion. Controls being as weak as they are in Nigeria, it was not surprising that Abubakar would want Obasanjo out of power and it was he who helped set up the MEND militia organization.[21] Attacks against the oil infrastructure have gone on for several decades, however, the activities of MEND were somewhat different as they focused on political change rather than an all out assault on the oil patch. Their systematic approach had the desired effect and the third term in office for Obasanjo failed to materialize. May 2007, as part of a new crackdown on the mismanagement and corruption in Nigeria's oil industry, saw a new President in office, Umaru Yar'Adua took office pledging drastic changes and reforms. His Vice President was Goodluck Jonathan, an ethnic Ijaw from the Niger Delta Province, turned out to be an official spokesman for MEND.

MEND immediately had concerns that revenues would not be flowing in the manner that they demanded and set about disrupting the pipeline operations and the flow of crude. Many attacks are committed against oil interests and many are attributed to MEND, but in fact are carried out by other like-minded militants operating under MEND's umbrella. As the years have passed MEND has become more of a loose affiliation of gangs . . . some operating independently of MEND's authority. To combat MEND, the Nigerian government has used the country's counter insurgency troops from the Nigerian Joint Military Task Force. MEND continues to be a force in the area despite the heavy military presence to counter their activities.

Summary

The turbulent passage to independence for many northeastern, central, and southern African countries has led to widespread violence. The establishment of an apartheid-free South African Nation under the Presidency of Nelson Mandela had its share of violence perpetrated by both sides. South Africa is still considered one of the richest and most powerful nations in Africa and its influence over its neighbors over the coming years will be of considerable interest worldwide.

The troubles plaguing the regime of Robert Mugabe and the struggle that brought him to power in Rhodesia/Zimbabwe were all typical of states gaining nationhood in southern Africa. Many of the fledgling countries that fought for independence have suffered under the hammer of tyrannical dictators, whose only real interests were to use capital and foreign investment in their respective countries for bankrolling their personal lifestyles. The influences of Communist involvement in the region over the past fifty years have been considerable and destabilization seems to continue in one form or another. This extremely vast geographical area is at the same time rich in resources but impoverished in the human sense. The devastation caused by intertribal wars, genocide, and revolutions has been supplemented and exacerbated by the devastation caused by AIDS and famine. This region of the world holds great promise and will grow in importance as we move deeper into the twenty-first century. In the following chapter, we will examine the rise of terrorism on the Indian subcontinent and beyond.

Web Sites

1. **Political Islam in sub-Saharan Africa**—*www.usip. org/pubs/specialreports/sr140.html*
2. **Lord's Resistance Army**—*http://www.globalsecurity. org/military/world/para/lra.htm*
3. **World Defense Review**—*http://worlddefensereview. com/pham062107.shtml*
4. **The Triumph of Evil**—*http://www.pbs.org/ wgbh/pages/frontline/shows/evil/*
5. **The National Security Archive**—*http://www.gwu.edu/ ~nsarchiv/NSAEBB/NSAEBB53/press.html*
6. **Human Rights Watch ZANU**—PF *http://www.hrw.org/ english/docs/2008/04/19/zimbab18604.htm*

Endnotes

1. "Somalia's Government and Warlords—A Patchwork of Fiefs." *The Economist* (November 3, 2001).

2. The White House, Office of the Press Secretary, November 7, 2001. http://www.whitehouse.gov/news/releases/2001/11/20011107–11.html.

3. Bruce Quarrie. *The World's Secret Police* (London: Octopus Books Ltd., 1986, p. 104).

4. Deliver Us from Kony *Why the children of Uganda are killing one another in the name of the Lord.* J. Carter Johnson in Kitgum, Uganda. www.christianitytoday.com.

5. Buteera, Richard. The Reach of Terrorist Financing and Combating It–The Links between Terrorism and Ordinary Crime. International Society of Prosecutors. Washington, DC (August 12, 2003).

6. Coalition for Human Rights and Justice Institute for Northern Uganda.

7. Institute for war and peace reporting (AR No. 121, July12, 2007), http://www.iwpr.net/.

8. Douglas Reed. *The Siege of Southern Africa* (Johannesburg, South Africa: Macmillan, 1974, p. 45).

9. Telegraph.co.uk Buteera, Richard. The Reach of Terrorist Financing and Combating It–The Links between Terrorism and Ordinary Crime. International Society of Prosecutors. Washington, DC (August 12, 2003).

10. Breaking the Silence, Building true peace. A Report on the Disturbances in Matabeleland and the Midlands 1980–1989.http://www.hrforumzim.com/members_reports/matrep/matreppart1a.htm.

11. Reed, *The Siege of Southern Africa*, p. 95.

12. Peter Hawthorn. "Mugger of the Nation." *Time, Canada Limited* (December 8, 1997, p. 37).

13. Bill Dixon and Lisa-Marie Johns "Gangs, Pagad & the State: Vigilantism and Revenge Violence in the Western Cape." *Violence and Transition Series*, vol. 2 (May 2001). Bill Dixon is a Senior Lecturer in the Department of Criminal Justice, University of Cape Town, and a researcher at the Institute of Criminology.

14. http://en.wikipedia.org/wiki/People_Against_Gangsterism_and_Drugs.

15. http://www.pagad.co.za/aims.htm.

16. SCG International Risk—Terrorist Group Profiles. http://www.scgonline.net/index.htm.

17. Kenya, Capsule History. http://www.africanet.com.

18. Reed. *The Siege of Southern Africa*, 25.

19. "Disarmament in the Congo: Preventing Further War." International Crisis Group Report. http://www.intl-crisis-group.org/projects/showreport.cfm?reportid=519.

20. Ibid. UN Office for the Coordination of Humanitarian Affairs, NIGERIA: Rights group accuses government of letting religious killers off hook.

21. Stratfor.com Global Market Brief, May 10, 2007.

CHAPTER 11

Southern and Southeast Asia

Extremist groups have in their sights all those committed to democratic processes in Pakistan

DAVID MILIBAND—UNITED KINGDOM FOREIGN SECRETARY 2007

Learning Objective

The study and review of this chapter will enable you to

1. Discuss how the Taliban have been able to maintain a foothold in Afghanistan;
2. Describe the threat posed to the Pakistan leadership by Islamic extremists;
3. Discuss how drug smuggling and insurgency are intricately connected;
4. Debate why the Pakistani ISI is so closely linked to terrorist activities.

Terms to Remember

Dal Khalsa
Harakat-ul-Ansar
  (HUA)
Inter Services Intelligence (ISI)
International Sikh Youth
  Federation
Khmer Rouge
Khmer Royal Armed Forces
  (KRAF)
Lashkar i Jhangvi (LJ)

Liberation Tigers of Tamil
  Eelam (LTTE)
Madrassas
Mujahideen
Mullah Omar
Pol Pot
Shiromani Gurudwara
  Prabandhak Committee
  (SGPC)

State Law and Order
  Restoration Council
  (SLORC)
State Peace and Development
  Council (SPDC)

June 18, 2007: Paktika, Afghanistan—A U.S. airstrike on a mosque and religious school killed seven children as well as several suspected al Qaeda militants. The attack took place near the Pakistan border shortly after a suicide bomber killed at least thirty-five people onboard a police academy bus in Kabul.

January 10, 2008: Lahore, Pakistan—Twenty-three people were killed, most of them policemen, and seventy injured in a suicide motorcycle bomb attack. The bomb was detonated at a checkpoint where a large number of police had been deployed for a protest rally.

November 26 & 27, 2008—Twenty Islamic terrorists launched a coordinated attack in the heart of Mumbai targeting western tourists and businessman at the Oberio, Taj Mahal and Trident Hotels and at a Jewish Center, St Georges Hospital and Mumbai railway terminus killing over 120 and injuring more than three hundred.

OVERVIEW

In this part of the world, the splits between religions and factions within the same religions are longstanding and deep. To add to that delicate situation, two of the region's major powers—Pakistan and India—both have nuclear weapon programs. This is one of the most mysterious and misunderstood parts of the world to both Americans and Westerners. The region is continuously faced with terrorism and violence. This chapter will introduce some of the major problem areas in the most troubled countries, from the vastness of India, to Pakistan, to tiny Sri Lanka. The chapter discusses ongoing battles for autonomy and freedom, fought largely by terrorism and insurrection and shows how difficult it is to separate the problems of this vast region into neatly defined categories. In addition, we will take a critical look at the potential threat of the Islamic efforts to unite into a global power stretching from the Persian Gulf to the eastern states of the Russian Republic. We will start with South Asia, beginning with the long history of ancient, mysterious India.[1]

INDIA

It is important for the student to now have some historical background of the vast Indian subcontinent and its bordering states, which have long been the crossroads of Southern Asia. In some ways, this area is like the Balkans, with many cultures passing through on their way to the East and West. The Indian subcontinent has had a civilization since 2,500 B.C., when the many inhabitants of the Indus River Valley developed a culture based on commerce and sustained by their agricultural trade. But during the second millennium B.C., pastoral, Aryan-speaking tribes migrated from the Northwest into the subcontinent and then settled in the Middle Ganges River valley. The history of this region includes religious discord, violence, and terrorism. The map of ancient and medieval India was made up of many kingdoms with often-changing boundaries. In the fourth and fifth centuries A.D., northern India was unified under the Gupta dynasty. During this period, known as India's Golden Age, Hindu culture reached up to new heights.

Islamic influences spread across the subcontinent over a period of 500 years, starting in the tenth and eleventh centuries. Turks and Afghans invaded India and established sultanates in the areas around and near Delhi. Then descendants of Genghis Khan swept across the Khyber Pass in the eleventh century, and established the Mogul Dynasty, which lasted from the eleventh to the fifteenth centuries. During this long period, there were two major cultural and religious systems . . . those of the Hindus and the Muslims. These cultures had centuries of mutual contact, trade, and lasting influences on each other. The British appeared on the subcontinent in 1619 and, by the middle of the 1800s, controlled most of present-day India, Pakistan, and Bangladesh. In 1857, a bloody rebellion in north India was led by mutinous Indian soldiers, resulting in the transfer of all political power to the British Crown, which then began administering most of India directly and controlled the rest through treaties with local rulers. By the late 1800s, India had taken its first steps toward self-government. The British viceroy established provisional councils comprised of Indian members to advise the Crown. The British subsequently widened Indian participation in such legislative councils. By 1920, the Indian leader, Mahatma Gandhi, had then transformed the Indian National Congress political party into a powerful movement against British colonial rule.

Following Gandhi's concepts of non-violent resistance, the party used both parliamentary means and non-cooperation, to finally compel the British to award India its independence. In 1947, India was awarded Commonwealth status and Jawaharlal Nehru became India's the first

FIGURE 11-1 **Map of India** (Central Intelligence Agency, *The World Factbook*, 2008).

Prime Minister. A period of continuing and escalating bloody conflicts between the Hindus and Muslims finally led to the British partition of India. This division, created on the basis of incompatible religions, then resulted in forming East and West Pakistan, where there were Muslim majorities. These groups were forcibly moved . . . Muslims to the north and Hindus to the south . . . creating anger as well as animosity that still continue to the present day. After partition, India became a full member of the Commonwealth, and a republic, on January 26, 1950.

Present-day relations between India and Pakistan took a downward plunge when both acquired nuclear weapons capability. Recent tests seem not more calculated to divert attention from economic and international issues, but rather than to "rattle their nuclear sabers." India has long complained about continuing foreign interference from Afghanistan and Pakistan, and the menace of escalating terrorism in the region. For years, the most ruthless of the Islamic and other terrorist organizations have been known to use Afghanistan as a base for recruiting, training, and harboring terrorists to carry out operations abroad.

GANDHI FAMILY ASSASSINATIONS 1948–1991

January 30, 1948—Mohandas (Mahatma) Gandhi, spiritual leader of the Indian independence movement, was shot to death by a fanatical young Hindu.

October 31, 1984—Indira Gandhi, the Prime Minister of India, was assassinated by members of her own Sikh bodyguard as revenge for the Indian Army attack on the Sikh Temple at Amritsar in June 1984.

May 21, 1991—Rajiv Gandhi, President of the Indian Congress Party, while campaigning, was assassinated by a female suicide bomber from the LTTE (Tamil Tigers)

Aircraft hijackings have also been a popular modus operandi for Pakistani terrorists. In 1999 an Indian airliner was hijacked on Christmas Eve and continued to fly between India, Pakistan, Afghanistan, the United Arab Emirates until December 31 at which time they surrendered to UAE authorities. Their demands were for the release of terrorists held in prisons and also a large sum of money. During the stand off they killed one passenger in an attempt to press their demands. When the ordeal ended it was determined that the terrorists had links to Pakistan's **Inter Service Intelligence agency (ISI)**.

On many occasions, India has drawn attention to the presence of training camps in neighboring Kashmir and Afghanistan. Terrorists are trained and equipped to carry out operations in India, particularly in the states of Jammu and Kashmir. Many hundreds of thousands of refugees from Afghanistan's war against the Russians were readily recruited by their protectors in Pakistan and used to foment terrorism and to pressure India into granting even more territory in the Kashmir region.

SPECIAL ECONOMIC ZONE

Although fighting between Muslims and Hindu's within the country is not uncommon, the Indian Government has considerable exposure to internal troubles due to rapid business expansion in its Special Economic Zone . . . a swath of land stretching almost across the country that has seen phenomenal growth and wealth to the booming IT industry. Land grabs by many unscrupulous politicians have led to large numbers of displaced tribesmen in these areas. India faces militant threats primarily from three sources

1. Maoist rebels known as Naxalites;
2. Tribal-based ethnic separatists;
3. Islamist militants fighting in the name of Kashmir.

Most militant activity is in the Jammu and Kashmir regions, and the northeastern part of the country. The Naxalites have made direct threats against multinational corporations, though they primarily focus their attacks on police stations, locally owned factories, and Indian government officials. The Naxalite movement has created a single command center for the revolution, which clearly means more attacks are to come.

The Naxalites still have a host of problems to deal with, however. India has at least ten Naxalite splinter groups that have broken away from the main movement due to differences over ideology and militant strategy, along with general disillusionment with the movement and war fatigue. Indian media also reports Naxalite defections on a nearly daily basis, though these incidents often are exaggerated and in some cases stage-managed by the police. This was most recently illustrated in January 2008, when reports came out that as many as seventy-nine Naxalites in Chhattisgarh had defected. Soon enough, allegations emerged that innocent tribal people were forced to "surrender" as Maoist rebels.

ISLAM AND INDIA

Most Islamist attacks have centered in India and militants have traditionally not been exported from India, and those operating within the country have likely come from and been sponsored by Pakistan. Al Qaeda seems to have paid scant attention to India as a center for targeting attacks but its internal security apparatus and lack of security infrastructure would make certain sectors and particularly the affluent Special Economic Zone a prime, "soft," target for Islamist militant attacks. Osama bin Laden has made mention of India in previous proclamations, when in 2006 he called on the Kashmiri Muslims to rise up against India. However, al Qaeda appears to have no base as such and would most likely depend on Kashmiri jihadists to do its bidding in India. Successful attacks have been carried out by Kashmiri militants and the devastating railway bombings in Mumbai in 2006 are a good example of the spread of the jihadist threat. The November 2008 attacks in the heart of Mumbai carried out by Islamist militants had all the hallmarks of an al-Qaeda inspired if not sponsored attack. The attacks were aimed at western targets in the bustling center of Mumbai carried out by a group calling itself the Deccan Mujahedin which is likely a cover name for either Lashkar Tayyiba or Jaish Muhammad. The coordinated nature and the ruthless sophistication of this attack caught intelligence authorities completely by surprise. The attack is likely the work of Islamists with scores to settle in regards to the disputed region of Kashmir with the attack coming just days after Pakistan's President Zadari announced that he would end the decades old dispute over Kashmir. Determining why this area became a target is less easy to define, however India is a significant contributor and supporter of the Hamid Karzai government in Afghanistan and is seen a power base in the region. One likely outcome of this mayhem may see Hindu retaliation attacks against Muslim targets in India. Whatever the motive for this coordinated attack it created worldwide media attention on terror, India, and Muslim extremism! For the past two decades, at least, successive Indian governments have concentrated counter terrorism efforts in combating escalating Sikh and Tamil terrorism.[2]

THE PUNJAB AND SIKHISM

The northern Indian state of the Punjab has seen politics and religion mix with deadly results. In 1984 it led to the assassination of then Prime Minister Indira Gandhi by her own Sikh bodyguards who believed she had used the politics of religion for her own political gains and to the benefit of the Congress Party in the Punjab. Violence continued in the Punjab for years after her assassination. In May 2007, there were clashes between mainstream Sikhs and followers of the Dera Sacha Sauda. The Dera had openly supported the Congress Party in the State Assembly elections in March 2007; however, Akali Dal, the main Sikh political party, won and since then has encouraged open protests against Dera. The flash point for recent violence was the heretical behavior of the Dera leader, one Ram Rahim Singh who dressed up as Gobind Singh, the Sikh's most revered "guru." The weak apology by Singh has done little to tone down the acts of violence that have followed. A Dera is a temple that conducts educational and social activities and there are literally thousands of Deras in the Punjab; however, it appears that Mr. Singh may have outgrown the organization with more than 400,000 thousand followers, both Sikh and lower caste Hindus. As the Akali Dal and Congress continue to play religion and politics, the likelihood of sectarian attacks is very real. This is also exacerbated by the economic hardship in the Punjab due to over-farming and the falling water table.[3]

PAKISTAN

Pakistan remains a strong supporter of the U.S. War on Terror, despite ongoing conflicts with its nuclear neighbor, India, over the disputed province of Kashmir. The Bush administration's diplomatic contacts with both of these nuclear powers have been a major effort to keep the peace, while still fighting the battles in Afghanistan and Iraq.

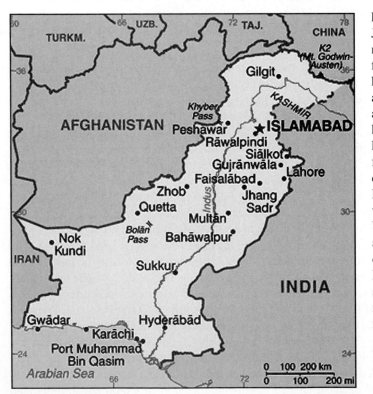

FIGURE 11-2 Map of Pakistan (Central Intelligence Agency, *The World Factbook*, 2008)

America has followed India's concern over Pakistan-sponsored, cross-border terrorism in Jammu and Kashmir carefully. The U.S. government has expressed continuing concern over the fate of the four remaining Western hostages kidnapped in Kashmir in 1995: Keith Mangan and Paul Wells (U.K.), Donald Hutchings (U.S.A), and Dirk Hasert (Germany). Of the six original hostages, one managed to escape and another was killed in captivity. But the fates of the remaining four remain unknown. The kidnappings did, however, reveal and highlight the involvement of the Pakistan-sponsored, Harakat-ul-Ansar (HUA), which was listed as a terrorist organization by the U.S. government in 1997, under the Anti-Terrorism and Effective Death Penalty Act of 1996. It is difficult to separate the issues of terrorism between India and Pakistan and external terrorism by surrounding Muslim states. Therefore, we shall now make an examination of some of the most important and prevalent of these issues.

In November 1997, four U.S. employees of Union Texas Petroleum and their Pakistani driver were murdered in Karachi when their vehicle was attacked near the U.S. Consulate. Shortly after the incident, two separate groups claimed responsibility for the killings, the Aimal Khufia Action

Committee, a previously unknown group; and the Islami Inqilabi Mahaz, a Lahore-based group of Afghan war veterans. Both groups cited the motive for the attack as being the conviction of Mir Aimal Kansi, a Pakistani National who was tried in the United States in November for the murder of two CIA employees and the wounding of three others in 1993. Kansi was found guilty and sentenced to death. Ramzi Ahmed Yousef, who was extradited from Pakistan to the United States in 1995, was also convicted in New York in November 1997 for his role in the 1993 World Trade Center bombing in New York City.

BENAZIR BHUTTO

Benazir Bhutto, until her assassination in December 2007, was portrayed as being Pakistan's last great hope to bring a level of democracy to the country. Unfortunately, any hope of that ever happening died with her, when a gunman and suicide bomber attacked her, killing her instantly. Ms. Bhutto had only recently returned to Pakistan from her self-imposed eight years in exile, following President Pervez Musharraf's dropping of the corruption charges against her.

Before her return to Pakistan, she had clearly criticized the government of Pervez Musharraf for failing to reign-in and defeat the Islamic militants of al Qaeda and the Taliban. "Pakistan is in a crisis and it's a crisis that threatens not only my nation and region, but could possibly have repercussions on the entire world."[4] Benazir Bhutto was returning to Pakistan almost as a symbol of hope for the country. She had previously been elected prime minister in 1988, and immediately ran afoul of the powerful military machine, and the Inter Services Intelligence Agency, who both have enormous control and influence throughout Pakistan. Within two years of taking office, she was dismissed by the military on charges of corruption and misrule. She regained power in the 1993 general election at

FIGURE 11-3 Former Pakistan Prime Minister Benazir Bhutto was killed in a Rawalpindi in December 2007. Benazir Bhutto had earlier claimed that four suicide bomb squads, including one led by a son of Osama bin Laden, would attempt to kill her (Canadian Press).

about the same time as the Taliban regimes were coming into power in Afghanistan. Her party, the Pakistan Peoples Party, is a left-leaning party that eschews religious extremism but had recognized in the Taliban the new opportunity to secure trade routes across southern Afghanistan. Her difficulty with confronting her own military was also a problem and she agreed to provide covert aid to the Taliban regime, but denied to the United States that Pakistan was funding or arming the Taliban. In 1996, she was again removed from power by the very powerful military, and she sought exile in London, and then Dubai in the UAE where from a distance she then remained involved in Pakistani politics.

On October 18, 2007, Bhutto returned to Pakistan, and the first attempt on her life took place at just after midnight on October 19, 2007. Her entourage was en route from Karachi International Airport to the tomb of Muhammad Ali Jinnah, the founder of the country, when it was attacked most probably by suicide bombers in the dense crowd around Bhutto's armored bus. Reports then indicated that there were two explosions shortly after one another and that around 140 people were killed as a result—how many were killed by the bombings and how many by the stampeding masses as they tried to escape the carnage has not been made clear by Pakistani authorities. What is clear is that the moment she set foot in Pakistan she would become a target either for the Musharraf supporters or Islamist militants. Prior to her return, she had already pledged to take on the Islamists and went so far as to say, if she were prime minister she would permit the United States to send troops into Pakistan if the situations in the tribal areas were to further deteriorate. It was then that Musharraf ordered troops to storm Islamabad's Red Mosque and Ms. Bhutto came out in strong support of the action.

There has been plenty of speculation that the attack on Bhutto was in fact part of a government conspiracy; however, on December 27, 2007, after attending a political rally in Rawalpindi, she was shot by an assailant as she stood in the well of her vehicle, her head and shoulders exposed through the sun roof, when the assailant then detonated an explosive vest killing twenty people to include Benazir Bhutto.

While Pakistan continues to be a theoretic supporter of the U.S. role in both Afghanistan and Iraq, its military is coming under continuous attacks from Islamist militants in the rugged Northwest Frontier Provinces (NWFP). Pakistan's military is a very formidable force and most certainly one to be reckoned with. In the past where assassination attempts against government officials have taken place, swift and violent retribution has been meted out by the military.

The Lal Masjid (Red Mosque)

Religious schools, or **Madrassas**, as they are known in Pakistan, are a familiar site. The Red Mosque in the Pakistani capital Islamabad has been in place since 1965, and home to fundamentalist teachers with links to global terrorism and jihad in the interviewing decades. The mosque leadership had been openly opposed to the government. After the London bombings of July 7, 2005, Pakistani police went to the mosque to investigate links between one of the bombers, Shehzad Tanweer, and the mosque. The police were confronted and repulsed by baton wielding women from the self-styled vigilante, Lal Majid Brigade.

By the summer of 2007 the mosque leadership had become more and more extreme and speeches from the leadership became far more menacing. The Pakistani authorities were of the belief that the Mosque had become home to Jihadists from the Tribal region that is bordering Pakistan and Afghanistan, and had turned the fundamentalist religious institution now into an armed military camp. The Chinese government was a significant supporter of Musharraf and his regime, and had a large number of its nationals in Islamabad. When the Lal Majid brigade kidnapped seven Chinese nationals from a massage parlor, this raised the stakes for the mosque to a significant level. The Chinese government demanded that the Pakistani authorities take action to release the kidnapped Chinese. Islamabad is a heavily fortified city, so when President Musharraf proclaimed "surrender or die" as his final message to the inhabitants of the mosque, the ensuing daylong battle was unexpected in its ferocity. Far from being a bastion of education, it turned out that the Red Mosque was heavily fortified and occupied with trained fighters and militants from banned religious groups and fighters linked to both the Taliban and al Qaeda militias operating in the tribal regions. The weeklong stand-off at the mosque was followed up by 200 commandos storming the enclave resulting in more than 100 deaths, including another dozen soldiers and the head of the extremist Abdul Rashid.

FIGURE 11-4 Pakistani religious students react over the army operation against Islamic militants holding Islamabad's Lal Masjid (Red Mosque) in July 2007. Troops engaged in fierce fighting, which resulted in the death of fifty militants and eight soldiers at the Red Mosque (Canadian Press).

Pervez Musharraf

As Chief of the Army General Musharraf has been in power since the military seized control of Pakistan in 1999 and has been a supporter of the U.S. "War on Terror." This has made him a target for Muslim fundamentalists as well as opposition parties. In November 2007 there were challenges to the validity of his re-election as President. His suspension of the Pakistani Constitution did nothing to curry favor with the powerful state judiciary, and his jailing of several key ministers including the Chief Justice Minister would cause a political backlash amid attempts to impeach the embattled President. It was with this backdrop that Musharraf decided to resign as President in August 2008 rather than face impeachment. The vacuum that this has created will pose many issues for the region. In September 2008 the widower of Benazir Bhutto was sworn in as President—Asif Ali Zardari who until his wife's assassination was not in the political limelight and in fact was better known for his conviction and imprisonment for corruption. He has little or no political experience and only time will tell on his ability to handle the army which has been and will remain the power base of Pakistan's politics. More importantly with dwindling support for U.S. action in Afghanistan his relationship with the United States will be critical both to his survival and ability to handle the Taliban insurgency that threatens the very survival of Pakistan.

Pakistan, Afghanistan, and Islam

Religious differences and a long history of violence and hatred among former brothers and fellow countrymen still separate India and Pakistan. Sponsoring international terrorism, separatist subversion, and insurgency are not new to either side. Since the 1970s, Pakistan has also trained many rebel Sikh and other Indian separatist movements. **The Shiromani Gurudwara Prabandhak Committee (SGPC)** is the major Sikh terrorist organization in India. It began to establish a tight control over the culture and economy of the Indian State of Punjab in the early 1980s. The SGPC forced Sikh traditionalism and conservatism on Punjabi society. Pakistan was quick to recognize this as an opportunity to exploit any further divisions in India. The Sikh struggle for an independent state attracted Pakistan's attention. Pakistan had long held its own claims to Kashmir and saw some possible benefit from encouraging the formation of a Sikh state, Khalistan, located in the Punjab, as this would weaken India's defense of the remaining portion of Kashmir. Then Pakistan hoped to exploit the tensions in Kashmir in order to destabilize India. Pakistan began to provide training and military assistance, and terrorist actions of the Sikh militants increased. The Sikhs began to represent such a potential threat that India, in July 1984, launched an assault on the Golden Temple at Amritsar, one of the holiest places for Sikhs. That event started an unprecedented bloodletting between Sikhs and Punjabis, with casualties far exceeding those of all Sikh terrorism efforts combined to that point. Ultimately, the escalation of Sikh separatist terrorism resulted in the assassination of Indira Gandhi, the prime minister and daughter of Jawaharlal Nehru, India's first prime minister. The Sikhs' armed insurrection escalated as high quality weapons became available. The arsenal included sophisticated bomb-making techniques and better training for Sikh terrorists of the Dal Khalsa separatist movement in the Afghanistan mujahideen camps. The long reach of Sikh terrorism further resulted in the bombing of the Air India jet from Toronto that blew up over the coast of Ireland, killing 329 passengers.

A corresponding ideological development in Indian Kashmir then occurred. Almost overnight, the prevailing popular sentiment in Indian Kashmir was the belief that because the targets of Indian security forces were Muslims, Islam was in danger. This had a galvanizing effect on the fanatical Islamic youth of the Kashmir region, and they formed new cadres of terrorists. The extent of Pakistani and Afghan influence on the Islamist transformation of the Kashmir insurgency was profound and deadly.

Pakistan's **Inter Services Intelligence (ISI)** then assumed quite a different role from its behind-the-scenes maneuvers. It seemed to be taking over direct control of the Sikh movement. The ISI made the city of Darra, Pakistan, the primary source of weapons for the Sikh, Tamil, and Kashmiri liberation movements. The escalation of terrorism by the Karachi-based organizations rejuvenated the domestic Darra market and the Pushtan population in Karachi became the storefront for the regional arms market.

The availability of weapons, which had primarily been long supplied by America, to the Afghan resistance fighters, turned the major cities of Pakistan into shopping centers for international weapons-dealing. Suspected "shoppers" included Palestinians and people from India, Nepal,

FIGURE 11-5   Pakistani soldiers stand near the Red Mosque in Islamabad in July 2007 after the building was stormed by Pakistani military forces (Canadian Press).

Afghanistan, Burma, Thailand, Sri Lanka, the Philippines, and Africa. These weapons-dealers were Muslims who lived in Karachi, providing manpower for the planning and development of terrorist operations. Having witnessed the initial impact of the Islamist message in Indian Kashmir, Pakistan began to broaden its horizons and set its sights higher. In 1986, with growing experience in training, organizing, and operations with the Afghan mujahideen, and with military supplies available, Pakistan began expanding its operation to sponsor and promote separatism and terrorism, primarily in Kashmir, as a strategic, long-term program. Among the most crucial activities of the ISI were the following:

- Religious radicalism was propagated in small, but lethal, doses to promote separatism and communal outlook.
- Training and indoctrination of selected leaders from the Kashmir Valley was arranged to create militant cadres.
- A large number of youths from the Kashmir Valley and Poonch sector were given extensive training in the use of automatic weapons, sabotage and attacks on security forces.
- Automatic weapons and explosives were issued to these people.
- Special teams were trained to organize disruption and engineer incidents to damage the myth of a democratic and secular image for India and Kashmir.

The Harakat-ul-Ansar (HUA)

The **Harakat-ul-Ansar (HUA)**, an Islamic militant group based in Pakistan and operating primarily in Kashmir, was formed in October 1993 when two Pakistani political activist groups, Harakat ul-Jihad al-Islami and Harakat ul-Mujahedin, merged. Faroogi Kashmiri is currently leading this group. His predecessor, Fazlur Khalil, supports the al Qaeda doctrine of attacks against the West, and the United States in particular. Khalil is the secretary general of the organization.

The HUA has carried out a number of operations against Indian troops and civilian targets in Kashmir. It has been linked to the Kashmiri militant group, Al-Faran, which kidnapped five Western tourists in Kashmir in July 1995; one was killed in August 1995 and the other four reportedly were killed in December of the same year. The HUA has several thousand armed supporters located in Azad, Kashmir; Pakistan; and in southern Kashmir and the Doda regions of India. These areas are composed of mostly Pakistanis and Kashmiris, but include Afghans and Arab veterans of the Afghan war. The HUA uses light and heavy machine guns, assault rifles, mortars, explosives, and rockets.

The HUA is based in Muzaffarabad, Pakistan, and members have participated in insurgent and terrorist activities primarily in Kashmir. The HUA trained its militants in Pakistan and in Afghanistan during the Taliban regime, prior to the U.S. airborne attacks of 2001. The HUA collects donations from Saudi Arabia and other Gulf and Islamic states, and from Pakistanis and Kashmiris. The source and amount of its military funding is unknown. Khalil was detained by Pakistani forces in 2004 but released later that year. One of HUA's associates is Ahmed Omar Sheik, who was convicted for the abduction and murder of Wall-Street Journal journalist, Daniel Pearl. HUA began to use a different name in 2003, calling itself Jamiat ul-Ansar (JUA).[5]

The head of the ISI Political Section developed a long-term program called K-2, aimed at castigating the Kashmiri and Sikh subversive efforts by making them appear to be under one umbrella of Sikh and Kashmiri extremists and Muslim fundamentalists. These groups would clearly not become allied with each other because of long-held hatred among them. This program would then intensify acts of violence in Punjab, Jammu, Kashmir, and the Terai region of Uttar Pradesh. Escalation of terrorism and subversion since the early 1990s is widely believed to have been a direct outgrowth of the ISI's implementation of the K-2.

Sikh terrorists were increasingly smuggling weapons from the Jammu and Kashmir areas or from Ganganagar in Rajasthan, where the ISI had its own bases. Clandestine ISI support for the Sikh terrorists continued to improve. Eventually, Sikh terrorists in Punjab were reportedly receiving instructions from Pakistan-based leaders for an intensification of terrorist operations, which, as pointed out before, seems highly improbable. More likely, the support was from Pakistan. Sikh terrorists received additional explosives and small arms from Pakistani stockpiles, as well as anti-aircraft guns and recoilless rifles, sniper rifles, and "the latest weapons" for special operations. These weapons now dominate the insurgency in the Rajasthan area. By 1992, the ISI was operating thirteen permanent, eighteen temporary, and eight joint-training camps for Kashmiris in Pakistan and Kashmir alone. Thus, while these Kashmiris failed to incite or stir up a popular war, they did establish wide, and solid enough, popular backing to embark on the second phase . . . a direct and violent confrontation with the Indian security forces, whom they consider to be occupiers. That would not have been possible without Pakistani and other Islamist support.

Many of the factions involved in the Afghanistan civil war included large numbers of Egyptians, Algerians, Palestinians, and Saudis. Many of these factions continue to provide haven to terrorists by facilitating the operation of training camps in areas under their control. The factions remain engaged in a struggle for political and military supremacy over India. The Indian and Pakistani governments both claim that the intelligence service of the other country sponsors bombings on its territory. The government of Pakistan acknowledges that it continues to provide moral, political, and diplomatic support to Kashmiri militants, but denies allegations of providing any other assistance. Reports continued from Indian intelligence and, in 1997, Pakistan officially announced its support to militants fighting in Kashmir. In Pakistan, deadly incidents of sectarian violence, particularly in Sindh and Punjab provinces, continued throughout 1997. Pakistan accuses India of being the instigator of these incidents. There continues to be credible reports of official Pakistani support for Kashmiri militant groups that engage in terrorism, such as the HUA (Harakat-ul-Ansar).[6]

Lashkar-e-Toiba (Army of the Pure)

LeT is an Islamic terrorist organization, active in Jammu and Kashmir. The outfit is the terrorist arm of the Markaz Dawa-Wal-Irshad, an Islamic fundamentalist organization. It came to notice in 1997 during Nawaz Sharif's second term as Pakistan's prime minister. LeT uses "suicide attacks" where small groups of fidayeen (suicide squads) would storm a security force camp and kill as many personnel as possible. The outfit is reported to have changed its name to Pasban-i-Ahle Hadith following their inclusion in the U.S. State Department's Foreign Terrorist Organization list. One of its main goals is the destruction of India and the establishment of an Islamic state. Lashkar-e-Toiba was launched during the last days of Afghan resistance against Soviet occupation. Though Lashkar-e-Toiba's entry into Jammu and Kashmir was first recorded in 1993, it came into the picture of Kashmir militancy only in 1997. Its induction to Kashmir is believed to be the result of deteriorating Harkat-ISI relations.

The pan-Islamic militancy was introduced in Kashmir to infuse a fresh lease of life into the otherwise dwindling local militancy. And the best choice available then was Harkat-ul-Mujahideen—the militant wing of Moulana Fazlul Rehman Khalil's Jamiat-e-Ulemai Islam, Pakistan. The group was powerful and had a huge network of madrassas, which it ran across the Pakistan-Afghan border. The group, however, became extremely powerful after its Talibs (students) took over Afghanistan. This Lahore-based group is the militant wing of a purely religious group—Markaz dawah-ul-Irshad led by Prof Hafiz Mohammad Sayeed and had absolutely no stakes in Pakistan's domestic politics.

Lashkar's militant activities soon outshone those of Harkat. The group would first use local Kashmiri militants only as helpers and guides, keeping both the armed operations as well as leadership with non-local cadre, generally Punjabis from Pakistan. Today, the outfit is the largest group active in the Valley with a dedicated *Fidayeen* unit (suicide squad) that changed the landscape of militancy in Kashmir.

LeT has 2,200 offices across the country and an estimated two dozen launching camps along the Line of Control, an unmarked border between India and Pakistan in Jammu and Kashmir.

Two LeT training camps are located at Muzaffarabad, the capital of Pakistan-held Kashmir. The training is divided into two phases—Daura Aam (basic phase) and Daura Khaas (special phase). During the first phase, a twenty-one-day period, students are motivated to internalize jihad as an exclusive life-long mission, mainly through intensive exposure to semi-mythical stories glorifying the lives and exploits of Islam's historical martyrs. The second phase lasts for three months and involves weapons training, ambush, and survival techniques.[7]

However, what really drives the organization's ideological indoctrination and the rigors of its jihadi training is a concept evolved by Hafiz Saeed. His unique approach has been to merge Islamic education with modern curricula, thus ensuring a balance between religious and secular training.[8]

LeT has also become a focus for the Pakistan ISI to use it in its campaign against India. LeT played a major role in the planning and execution of the bomb attacks on a train station in the Mumbai financial district in July 2006, when powerful bombs ripped through seven commuter trains killing 174, and wounding nearly 500 others. Like HUA, the LeT is used to pit Mulsims against Hindus, and placing bombs and targetting either of the religious groups they hope to succeed in their objective. However, to date with attacks on the increase throughout India, there is no indication that Muslims and Hindus are likely to stage a popular uprising.

Sikh Terrorism

Sikh terrorism is mainly sponsored by expatriate and Indian Sikh groups, with designs to create an independent Sikh State called Khalistan (Land of the Pure) from Indian territory. Active groups include Babbar Khalsa, International Sikh Youth Federation, **Dal Khalsa**, and the Bhinderanwala Tiger Force. A previously unknown group, the Saheed Khalsa Force, claimed credit for the New Delhi marketplace bombings in 1997. Sikh attacks in India are usually against Indian officials and facilities, other Sikhs, and Hindus. They include assassinations, bombings, and kidnappings. These attacks have dropped markedly since 1992. Indian security forces killed or captured many of the senior Sikh militant leaders and extremist groups. Many low-intensity bombings that might have been due to Sikh extremists occur without subsequent claims of credit. Sikh militant cells are active internationally, and extremists gather funds from overseas Sikh communities. The Sikh expatriates have formed a variety of international organizations that lobby for the Sikh cause overseas. Most prominent are the World Sikh Organization and the **International Sikh Youth Federation**.[9]

KASHMIR

Over the decades, there has been a continuous cycle of declared and undeclared wars between India and Pakistan, with an ever-increasing enmity between the two countries. Protagonists of each country are emphatic about their separate claims to Kashmir and stubbornly proclaim that they will never give up that claim.

The Kashmir problem was created toward the end of British rule in India, and still lies at the heart of the instability between Pakistan and India. This issue even affects Afghanistan. In the last years of British rule, all parties agreed to divide India into a Hindu-majority country called India, and a Muslim-majority country called Pakistan. Pakistan took its first form as East Pakistan (now Bangladesh), and West Pakistan, about 1,100 miles apart on either side of India.

The State of Kashmir was close to the heart of Jawaharlal Nehru, the first prime minister of independent India; he did not wish to give it up to Pakistan, in spite of its Muslim majority. The departing British, under Lord Mountbatten, made no secret of their dislike for the nascent state of Pakistan and for its leader, Mohammed Ali Jinnah. Britain's Viceroy, The Earl Mountbatten joined Nehru in persuading the Hindu Raja of Jammu and Kashmir to accede to India. To afford India with a contiguous connection to Kashmir and make it defensible, the British granted the adjoining Gurdaspur district to India, instead of Pakistan as was originally planned.

The Muslim majority of Kashmir has been unwilling to accede to Indian rule over Kashmir and has been involved in a steady escalation of resistance to India since independence in 1947. As a result, India has had more troops and other security forces per capita in Kashmir than any other nation has had anywhere. The George W. Bush administration has referred to all Kashmiri Resistance Fighters as "Terrorists." Had it not been so tragic, it would have been considered funny that Bush, and Russian President Putin, stood side by side as they jointly told Pakistan's President Musharraf to stop aiding terrorists in crossing the ceasefire line into Indian Kashmir. George Bush was obviously ignoring the record of his companion, Putin . . . a man responsible for the killing of almost 100,000 Chechens, and counting. It is also a sad fact that the United States only defines "terrorism" as something done by individuals and groups, and not by nations, unless, of course, the nation has the misfortune to be on the U.S. list of nations to despise. In Kashmir, the fact is that Indian forces have long prevented a reign of terror. Kashmiri Muslims disappear after being "detained" by Indian security forces. If they are lucky enough to ever return, it is only after suffering severe torture. Many are killed either "while resisting arrest," or while "attempting to escape"; euphemisms applied with impunity by the occupying forces.

No sooner had India and Pakistan become independent than hostilities began between them for the possession of Kashmir. It is said that the Kashmir dispute has been the cause of two wars between India and Pakistan. In fact, the Kashmir dispute has been the cause of a long, sixty year war between India and Pakistan . . . the two nuclear-armed nations have hardly ever had a week without an exchange of some kind of deadly weapons fire along the ceasefire line that exists between Indian Kashmir and Pakistani Kashmir. Huge numbers of soldiers have been killed and wounded in this game of "keep-away," but each side carefully keeps their losses a closely held secret. Billions and billions of both side's currency's have been spent in pursuit of continuing warfare between the two nations attempting to get an upper hand in the battle for Kashmir. At the same time, millions of people constantly face death by starvation and preventable diseases (or even nuclear war!).

The only problem in Kashmir that gets any attention is the human rights situation there, but that is far more complex. India regards Kashmir as a part of India and, therefore, pride and honor are involved; for Pakistan, it is a matter of "survival" because the only major river in Pakistan now originates in Kashmir.

At the time of independence, there were six major rivers flowing through Pakistan. All, except for the Indus River, flowed through the province of Punjab ("five waters") in North Eastern Pakistan. The Ravi, Sutlej, Beas, and Chenab rivers all flow from Indian East Punjab, and the Jhelum flows from Kashmir. In the 1950s, India drew up plans to divert the flow of some of the rivers that passed through Pakistan. After over nine years of negotiations, an agreement was then made that resulted in the "Indus Waters Treaty" of 1960. This treaty gave up three of the rivers, the Ravi, Beas, and Sutlej, for India's exclusive use, while the Indus, Jhelum, and Chenab were determined to be shared with Pakistan.

The mighty Indus, which was used for fishing as well as for river commerce, is no longer mighty. In fact, during the dry months it becomes almost stagnant in the south, permeating the air with the smell of rotten vegetation. Over 100 miles upstream, one may cross this now slow river on foot without ever dampening one's knees. It is small wonder that Pakistan feels insecure if India should control the headwaters of the Indus, the Jhelum, and the Chenab.

Currently, Pakistan is accused of supporting the "terrorists" in Kashmir. These are all largely Kashmiris supported by Pakistanis who are struggling to remove Indian rule from Kashmir. And Pakistan does support them by giving them protection, shelter, and some military support. This is no different from Indian support of rebels in areas of Pakistan like Baluchistan, the North-West Frontier Province, etc. In fact, the largest support India has now given to any rebel movement in Pakistan (which pales in comparison with anything Pakistan has done in India), was then to the Bangladesh Freedom Fighters. This support first began in 1971 when India began providing some shelter to the Mukti Bahini, the Bangladesh Liberation Army. Support then continued to escalate until, finally, war was declared between India and Pakistan, resulting finally, in the independence of Bangladesh. In hindsight, this was a just war for India to be involved in, as the Bengalis were oppressed and near-genocidal action was being taken against them by the (Western) Pakistani Army. One could make a similar argument for the Kashmiris of today, and for support of their liberation movements.

Since independence, India has dissolved at least three popularly elected state governments of Kashmir. The Muslim governments of Kashmir failed to toe the Indian line by demanding more and more autonomy, so India imposed presidential rule over them, each time lasting for years. During the last sixty years of war and terror between India and Pakistan, only a few voices have been heard demanding Kashmir for Kashmiris . . . and both sides ignored them. Why did they not vacate Kashmir and leave it for the Kashmiris to rule? Such a step would have led to the first rapprochement between the two warring nations. It would also have allowed the beleaguered Kashmiris their first opportunity to attempt to live and prosper in peace.

In such a scenario, Kashmir would be a neutral independent state. In the beginning, both India and Pakistan could provide a tiny fraction of their military billions and help build a more viable economic infrastructure in Kashmir, with help from the West. A Kashmir with open borders would give people from India and Pakistan opportunities to meet, promote mutual understanding, and invest there in joint ventures. With the elimination of tensions in Kashmir, would come a scaling back of arms and, perhaps, demilitarized borders. From there, it may only be a small step toward a closer relationship and, perhaps, even the initiation of a loose federation involving India, Pakistan, and Bangladesh. All three nations spring from the same source; families have been split among the three sides and even culturally, the similarities far outweigh the differences. Is there really a reason why these three countries cannot follow the European Community model to come together?

Resolving the Kashmir issue may be the first and greatest step in preventing many future wars and separatist movements in South and Central Asia. The removal of tension may even help bring democracy to Pakistan, where "security" is the catchword for all sorts of repression by successive governments—civilian and military.[10]

Nuclear Proliferation Threats

There has been much worldwide commentary on whether or not Islamic terror groups . . . such as al Qaeda, are searching for the means to develop weapons of mass destruction (WMD). Pakistan has had a thriving, albeit secret, nuclear program operating since the 1970s and under the direct control of a Pakistani scientist. It has come to light that the scientist in question, Dr. Abdul Qadeer Khan, has, since the 1970s, provided much-needed assistance to the Iranian nuclear program. Through the support and financing of the Pakistan government, Khan was in control of the Khan Research Laboratories. The U.S. CIA is of the firm belief that this man may have been peddling his nuclear technology to unfriendly countries and possibly even to terrorist groups like al Qaeda. Whether this will ever be confirmed is another matter, as Khan is currently under house arrest in Pakistan and the government refuses to allow either UN or U.S. investigators to interrogate him. A vast majority of Pakistanis view Khan as a celebrity figure who donated money to charities throughout the country. How far-reaching his black market activities have spread, and how much this activity has spread the threat of nuclear weapons proliferation, is not yet clear. The threat is certainly clear in this case, and whether the threat will emanate from such rogue states as North Korea or Iran, we will have to wait and see.

ISLAMIC MILITANCY

Since 9-11 and up until his resignation in August 2008 President Pervez Musharraf had pledged support to the War on Terror and had gone on record to state that he would deal with Islamic terrorists who reside within Pakistan's borders. Most of the arrests of al Qaeda-linked suspects have occurred in the vast metropolis of Karachi. Official reports target Karachi as being home to more than 417 well-known terror cells and operatives from differing sectarian and militant outfits. Karachi has a population in excess of 14 million with more than 1,000 religious schools and 10,000 mosques. And many former Taliban fighters fled from the Afghan war to the border towns of Pakistan's northwest frontier and spread into Karachi, a rich and fertile breeding ground for recruiting misguided youths for jihad. President Musharraf finds himself on very dangerous ground and has to be continually mindful of threats to his own safety and his government from Islamic extremists. His fears are well founded . . . there have been attempts at his assassination on numerous occasions. When the Taliban controlled Afghanistan, a large number of Pakistanis trained for jihad in Taliban-supported training camps and the numbers, which cannot be confirmed, are thought to be over 30,000 such fighters over the years. Following the fallout of 9-11, the Pakistani government also cracked down hard on militant fundraising and focused more specifically on those groups supporting jihad in Kashmir. One such terror organization is the **Lashkar i Jhangvi (LJ)**, an extreme Sunni group that has its roots in a sectarian movement calling itself Sipah-I-Sahaba Pakistan. With sectarian violence the group's goal, its main subjects for attack have been mostly those from the Shia religious sect. The group had ties with the Taliban regime in Afghanistan and aided many fighters returning through the northwest frontier cities of Peshawar and Rawalpindi. It was this terror group that had made attempts on former President Musharraf's life.

The **Jaish-e-Mohammed** (**JEM**, the Army of Mohammed), is an Islamic extremist group based in Pakistan that was formed by Masood Azhar upon his release from prison in India in early 2000. Azhar's release resulted from the hijacking of an Indian Airlines flight, which had similar modus operandi to the attacks that took place on 9-11. In the Indian Airlines hijacking, the terrorists slit passengers' throats with knives smuggled onto the flight and then stormed the cockpit. Masood Azhar was released from prison in India in exchange for the 155 passengers on board the flight

JEM's aim is to unite Kashmir with Pakistan. It is politically aligned with the radical political party, Jamiat-I Ulema-i Islam Fazlur Rehman faction (JUI-F). In October 2001, the United States announced the addition of JEM to the U.S. Treasury Department's Office of Foreign Asset Control's (OFAC) list, which includes organizations that are believed to support terrorist groups and have assets in U.S. jurisdiction that can be frozen or controlled. In December 2001, JEM was added to the U.S. list of Foreign Terrorist Organizations. The group is located primarily in Peshawar and has its operations in Kashmir. Most of its support members come from Pakistani or are former Taliban/Afghan fighters. The leadership of JEM has threatened to kill India's Prime Minister in its bid to rid Jammu and Kashmir of Indian forces. JEM's extensive organization in Pakistan has set up schools for Jihad at its offices throughout the country and with its external links to the former Taliban regime in Afghanistan as well as Sunni terror cells in Pakistan JEM will continue to be a threat in the region. JEM uses fidayeen (suicide terror) attacks as well as more conventional attacks with light weapons and improvised explosive devices. Although banned in Pakistan since 2002 the group appears to operate openly in many areas of Pakistan.

NEPAL

Nepal is a region of the world that we have come to know for its rugged terrain, for Sir Edmund Hillary's conquering of Mount Everest, and for the heroic deeds of mountain-faring Sherpas, rather than a hotbed for political violence and insurgency. The insurgency in this poverty-ridden kingdom comes from a Maoist movement looking to replace the monarchy with a Communist state. Fighting has been going on in Nepal for almost a decade and the Maoists claim to control approximately 40 percent of the country. Democratic reforms seem unlikely . . . the King Gyanendra announced a state of emergency in February 2005, following his dismissal of the government and has become increasingly reliant on the Royal Army, which has been less than effective in fighting the rebel insurgents. The King had also relied on political collaboration with India, which feared that the insurgency could spread there with support from left-wing groups. However, in May of 2008 the end finally came to the 240-year reign of the Nepal Royal family. In recent months, the Nepalese government had reached a peace accord with the Maoist rebels, in a country desperate for peace.

Nepal was declared a republic by the constitutional assembly which voted to abolish the Hindu monarchy, which has been in control of the country for over two centuries. King Gyanendra

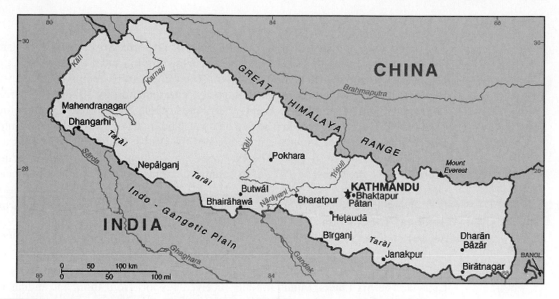

FIGURE 11-6   **Map of Nepal** (Central Intelligence Agency, *The World Factbook*, 2008).

came to the throne soon after a large number of the Royal family was massacred in 2001. Conspiracy theories abounded about his involvement which would only sour his relationship with his subjects. His sacking of the government and his embarking on a period of autocratic rule can have only hastened his demise.

FIGURE 11-7   Maoist rebels on the march in Dhankutta, 250 miles east of Katmandu, in February 2006. Emboldened by a string of recent setbacks to the absolute rule of King Gyanendra, the Maoists eventually toppled the 200-year-old monarchy through political means in May 2008 (Canadian Press).

SRI LANKA

The Democratic Socialist Republic of Sri Lanka (short form, Sri Lanka) is an island in the Indian Ocean, south of India. It is slightly larger than West Virginia and was known as Ceylon until 1972. Sri Lanka was the center of Buddhist civilization in the third century B.C. and still has a strong Buddhist majority (69 percent), with minority representation by Hindus (15 percent), Christians (8 percent), and Muslims (8 percent), distributed among an estimated population of more than 18,700,000. The Portuguese first settled on this island in 1505, followed by the Dutch in 1658. The British arrived in 1796 and made it a colony of the British Empire in 1853. Sri Lanka was finally granted independence in 1948. The Ceylonese government resisted an insurrection by terrorists attempting its overthrow in 1971. The country commands a strategic location near major Indian Ocean sea lanes.

There have been hostilities between the Sri Lankan government and the armed **Liberation Tigers of Tamil Elam (LTTE)**, and other smaller Tamil separatist groups since the mid-1980s. Several hundred thousand Tamil civilians have fled the island and, as of late 1996, about 63,068 were housed in refugee camps in southern India; another 30,000 to 40,000 lived outside the Indian camps. More than 200,000 Tamils have sought political asylum in the West, many in Canada. The Sri Lanka Tamils initially received support from India and Indian Tamil groups in South India.

Drought, slow economic reform, and civil war in 1996, have exacted a heavy economic toll. Insufficient monsoon rains caused power cuts that hurt industrial and agricultural production, and the stepped-up LTTE insurgency reduced foreign investment and tourism, Sri Lanka's two key sources of foreign exchange. Meanwhile, the government counterinsurgency efforts caused defense expenditures to overrun budget targets by 42 percent.

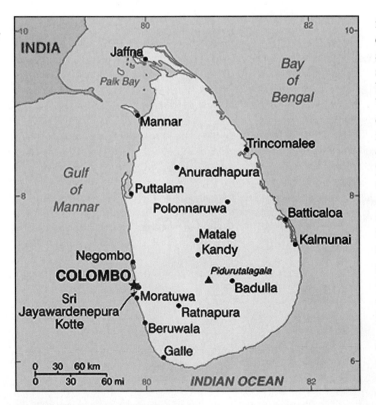

FIGURE 11-8   Map of Sri Lanka (Central Intelligence Agency, *The World Factbook*, 2008).

The LTTE continued its terrorist activities in 1997, attacking government troops and economic infrastructure targets, and assassinating political opponents. The LTTE's most spectacular terrorist attack in 1997 was a truck bombing directed at the newly opened Colombo World Trade Center on October 15, 1997. The explosion injured more than 100 people, including many foreigners, and caused significant collateral damage to nearby buildings. Eighteen people including LTTE suicide bombers, hotel security guards, and Sri Lankan security forces, died in the explosion and aftermath. Sri Lankan authorities shot two of the terrorists as they tried to escape, and another three killed themselves to avoid capture. One of the bombers lobbed a grenade into a monastery as he fled the scene, killing one monk. In two separate incidents in June, in the Tricomalee area, the LTTE assassinated two legislators and nine other civilians.

During the summer months of 1997, naval elements of the LTTE conducted several attacks on commercial shipping, including numerous foreign vessels. In July, LTTE rebels abducted the crew of an empty passenger ferry and set fire to the vessel. The Captain and a crewmember, both Indonesian, were released after only three days. The LTTE stormed a North Korean cargo ship after it delivered a shipment of food and other goods for civilians on the Jaffna Peninsula, killing one of the vessel's thirty-eight North Korean crewmembers in the process. The ship's North Korean captives were freed five days later and eventually returned to the vessel. Sri Lankan authorities charged the LTTE with the July hijacking of a shipment of more than 32,000 mortar rounds bound for delivery to the Sri Lankan military. In September, the LTTE used rocket-propelled grenades to attack a Panamanian-flagged, Chinese-owned merchant ship that had been chartered by a U.S. chemical company to load minerals for export. As many as twenty people, including five Chinese crewmembers, were reported killed, wounded, or missing from the attack.

Lack of a Peace Process

Any likelihood of a peaceful settlement to the ongoing Sri Lankan/LTTE insurgency would have to have the approval of Velupillai Prabhakaran who controls the activities of the LTTE from a secret jungle base in the northeast of Sri Lanka. He has a reputation as a fearless and ruthless guerrilla leader, and under his leadership, the LTTE, or "Tamil Tigers," have become a highly disciplined and highly motivated guerrilla force. His organization shows no sign of being defeated militarily by the Sri Lankan army, even though it is vastly outnumbered. Mr. Prabhakaran is reputed to wear a cyanide capsule around his neck, to be swallowed in the event of his capture. He expects the same dedication from his troops, many of whom the Sri Lankan government says are either women or children. He has also been accused by India of playing a key role in the murder of its former Prime Minister, Rajiv Gandhi, in 1991.[11]

An affiliate of the Tigers calling itself the Internet Black Tigers (IBT) claimed responsibility for e-mail harassment of several Sri Lankan missions around the world. The group claimed, in its Internet postings to be an elite department of the LTTE specializing in "suicide e-mail bombings," with the goal of countering Sri Lankan government propaganda disseminated electronically. The IBT stated that the attacks were only warnings. The Sri Lankan government has strongly supported international efforts to address the problem of combating terrorism. It was the first nation to sign the International Convention for the Suppression of Terrorist Bombings in January 1998. The government was quick to condemn terrorist attacks in other countries and raised terrorism issues in several international venues, including the UN General Assembly and the Commonwealth Heads of Government meeting in Edinburgh. There were no confirmed cases of attacks on U.S. citizens by LTTE, or other terrorist groups in Sri Lanka from 1997 up to the deadly tsunami in 2004.

The LTTE shows no signs of abandoning its campaign to cripple the Sri Lankan economy and continues to target government officials. The group retains its ability to strike at the heart of their nation's capital, Colombo, as demonstrated by an October 1997 bomb attack on the Colombo's World Trade Center in the financial district, similar to the January 1996 truck bomb attack that destroyed the Colombo Central Bank.

The United States designated LTTE a Foreign Terrorist Organization, pursuant to the orders of the Antiterrorism and Effective Death Penalty Act of 1996.[12]

Known Sri Lankan terrorist front organizations include:

- The Liberation Tigers of Tamil Eelam (LTTE)
- World Tamil Association (WTA)
- World Tamil Movement (WTM)
- Federation of Associations of Canadian Tamils (FACT)
- The Ellalan Force
- The Internet Black Tigers (IBT)[13]

Of all of these organizations, the LTTE is by far the most powerful Tamil group in Sri Lanka. The LTTE group's elite "Black Tiger Squad" conducts suicide bombings against any important targets, and all rank-and-file members carry a cyanide capsule to kill themselves rather than be caught. The LTTE is very insular and highly organized, with its own intelligence service, naval element (the Sea Tigers), and women's political and military wings. The LTTE has integrated a battlefield insurgent strategy with a terrorist program that targets key government and military personnel, the economy, and public infrastructure. Political assassinations include the suicide bomber attacks against Sri Lankan President Ranasinghe Premadasa in 1993, and Indian Prime Minister Rajiv Gandhi in 1991 (the group's only known terrorist act outside Sri Lanka). The LTTE has detonated two massive truck bombs directed against the Sri Lankan economy, one at the Colombo Central Bank in January 1996, and another at the Colombo World Trade Center as mentioned previously. The LTTE also has attacked infrastructure targets such as commuter trains, buses, oil tanks, and power stations. It prefers to attack vulnerable government facilities and then withdraw before reinforcements arrive, or to time its attacks to take best advantage of security lapses on holidays, at night, or in the early morning. The LTTE is also known to have recruited approximately 10,000-armed combatants in Sri Lanka, with approximately 3,000 to 6,000 members that form a trained cadre of fighters. The group also has a significant overseas support structure for fundraising, weapons procurement, and propaganda activities.

The Tamil Tigers control most of the northern and eastern coastal areas of Sri Lanka but have conducted operations throughout the island. Headquartered in the Wanni region, LTTE leader Velupillai Prabhakaran has established an extensive network of checkpoints and informants to keep track of any outsiders who enter the group's area of control. The LTTE's overt organizations support Tamil separatism by lobbying foreign governments and the United Nations. They also use its international contacts to procure weapons, communications, and bomb-making equipment. The LTTE exploits large Tamil communities in North America, Europe, and Asia to obtain funds and supplies for its fighters in Sri Lanka. Information obtained since the mid-1980s indicates that some Tamil communities in Europe are also involved in narcotics smuggling. The LTTE has clearly learned well from the tactics employed by the IRA in Northern Ireland.

Throughout 2006 and 2007, fighting escalated between elements of the LTTE and the Sri Lankan military in spite of an agreed cease-fire. The Tamil leader, Velupillai Prabhakaran, announced the commencement of the Fourth Eelam War in November 2006, while the Sri Lankan Government only made the announcement in January 2008 that the ceasefire was at an end.

Actions by the Sri Lankan military throughout 2007 have done little to cause the LTTE to waiver in their demands for a Tamil homeland. While the Sri Lankan military gained the upper hand in the Eastern Province and overran rebel positions at Sampur, just south of the port of Trincomalee, plus gaining control of two key coastal towns, which greatly restricted the LTTE's ability to resupply and reinforce its eastern forces from its stronghold in the north. The military then launched Operation Definite Victory, clearing the LTTE from the Ampara district before moving on to other rebel controlled towns. The LTTE seemed powerless to respond after their camps were overrun one after the other.[14]

The ebb and flow of success in insurgent operations is a reality in this theater of war as in any other and the Tamils continue to attack government forces and use new methods of attack to undermine the government as much as to publicize their presence. In March 2007, the LTTE launched its first aerial attack using light passenger aircraft to carry bombs and successfully attacked an air force base outside the capital Colombo. In October, they launched a spectacular commando raid on an air base north of Colombo and while all the commandos were killed, they managed to destroy a large number of Sri Lankan Air Force aircraft on the ground, including two attack helicopters.

According to the FBI, more than 4,000 people have been killed by the Tamil Tigers in the two years from 2006 to 2008 and are considered one of the most well-organized and deadly of terrorist organizations. They have perfected the use of suicide bombs and vests and also the use of females in their attack scenarios. More than 70,000 have died since the conflict started in 1983.

The success of the Tigers is in many ways due to their fundraising abilities abroad, with a flourishing and loyal Tamil Diaspora in western countries, including Canada, U.S.A., Australia, and Great Britain. Vast numbers of Tamils have fled as refugees to the West, and are "taxed" by the LTTE, who also engage in criminal activities for fund raising including widespread credit card fraud. Most weapons brought into the area originate from dealers in Southeast Asia and then are invariably smuggled in by a small flotilla of ocean-going ships operated by the LTTE. There seems little appetite for conciliation on either side, so this terrorist group and actions against the government and its military will continue into the foreseeable future.

AFGHANISTAN

The Taliban

The Taliban ("Students of Islamic Knowledge Movement"), ruled Afghanistan from 1996 until 2001. A grotesgue movement that supressed women and operated like a feudal society. They came to power during Afghanistan's long civil war. Although they managed to hold 90 percent of the country's territory, their policies—including their treatment of women and support of terrorists—ostracized them from the world community. In the context of Afghan history, the rise of the Taliban, though not their extremism, is unsurprising. Afghanistan is a devoutly Muslim nation . . . 90 percent of its population are Sunni Muslims. Religious schools were established in Afghanistan after Islam arrived in the seventh century and *taliban* became an important part of the social fabric: running schools, mosques, shrines, and various religious and social services, and serving as **mujahideen** when necessary.

After the 9-11 attacks the U.S. government pressed the Taliban to turn over bin Laden and al Qaeda who had sanctuary in the mountainous regions of the country. To no one's surprise, the Taliban refused to give him to the U.S. Their refusal was the signal for the aerial bombing of Taliban military sites. By November 21, the Taliban had lost control of Kabul and by early December had been completely routed. In 2008, more than five years as Afghanistan's leader, President Hamid Karzai came to power he still had only marginal control over large swaths of the country. The Taliban continues to fund its insurgency through the drug trade. An August 2007 report by the United Nations found that Afghanistan's opium production doubled in two years and that the country supplies 93 percent of the world's heroin.

Islamic extremists from around the world, including large numbers of Egyptians, Algerians, Palestinians, and Saudis, used Afghanistan as a training center and home base from which to operate. The dreaded Taliban, as well as many of the other combatants in the Afghan civil war, facilitated the operation of training and indoctrination facilities for non-Afghans in the territories they controlled. Several Afghani factions provided logistic support, free passage, and sometimes passports, to

FIGURE 11-9   Map of Afghanistan (Central Intelligence Agency, *The World Factbook*, 2008).

members of various terrorist organizations. Many of these individuals, in turn, were involved in fighting in Bosnia and Herzegovina, Chechnya, Tajikistan, Kashmir, the Philippines, and other parts of the Middle East.

The Saudi-born terrorist-financier, Osama bin Laden, a man originally recruited by the CIA in its efforts against the Soviet occupation and war in Afghanistan, relocated from Jalalabad to the Taliban's capital of Kandahar in early 1997. There, he established a new base of operations and continued to incite violence against the United States, particularly against U.S. forces in Saudi Arabia. Osama bin Laden called on Muslims to retaliate against the U.S. prosecutor in the Mir Aimal Kansi trial for disparaging comments he made about Pakistanis, and praised the Pakistan-based Kashmiri group, HUA, for being listed on the U.S. Foreign Terrorist Organization list. According to the Pakistani press, following Kansi's rendition to the United States, Osama bin Ladin warned the Americans that if it attempted his (bin Laden's) capture, he would "teach them a lesson similar to the lesson they were taught in Somalia."

That the Taliban was a ruthless organization is beyond question, and the tribal warlords on the other hand were often as equally vicious. One such leader was Mullah Dadullah, who was many times described in the reports as being the military mastermind of the Taliban insurgency. Dadullah had until his death in 2007, been front and center of the military activities of the Taliban. Dadullah traveled to Pakistan to raise money and arms for the insurgency and focused his attention on the madrassas in Karachi to recruit his fighters. In 2003, Mullah Omar released a tape naming him as a member of the new ten-man leadership council that would "confront the occupation". He led the Taliban's day-to-day operations in the south and southwestern Afghanistan but more importantly, he was one of the closest links between the Taliban insurgency and al Qaeda. As part of his fundraising efforts he was responsible for the increase in kidnappings in the region, which

FIGURE 11-10 Ayman al-Zawahri poses with Osama bin Laden in this 1998 photo in Khost, Afghanistan (Canadian Press).

provided a good level of income for the Taliban such as the estimated $1.5 million paid for two French hostages.[15]

He was also the Taliban's spokesman for the progress of the insurgency and was at ease dealing with the news media, especially when it came to detailing his involvement in the training of the suicide bombers, executing suspected collaborators, and beheading hostages. On many occasions in 2006, he was listed as killed in actions against U.S. and Afghan forces. He was a ruthless fighter and particularly so in battles against the Northern Alliance when the U.S. war to remove the Taliban started in 2001. He had been sentenced to life in prison in absentia by a Pakistani Court for attempting to assassinate Maulana Shirani, then a member of the Pakistan Parliament. Mullah Dadullah lost a leg when he trod on a landmine in 1994; however, this did not deter him from his personal involvement in the fighting with the then Afghan government forces and also against the Northern Alliance. He was killed in a clash with British and U.S. Special Forces in Helmand Province on May 13, 2007. He was a close friend and ally of the Taliban leader Mullah Omar and his loss was a serious blow to the Taliban.

The realities of the War on Terror and the Afghanistan campaign that filtered out after the ousting of the Taliban may have punctured the mood that prevailed in October 2001. The idea that the Afghanistan campaign was a possible new strategy for warfare, based on the employment of massive, precision-guided airpower with little commitment of ground troops, is now being revisited. Large numbers of Afghan civilians died, owing to less-than-precise bombing, and scores of people allied to the United States were targeted and killed by U.S. forces, acting on sometime faulty intelligence. Relying on Afghan mercenaries to do the fighting on the ground resulted in Osama bin Laden's escape from the Tora Bora Mountains. And when U.S. troops did engage in close-quarters fighting with the Taliban/al Qaeda forces in the Gardez area near Pakistan in early March 2002, an enemy that was assumed to be on the run bloodied them.

Most of the Taliban's leaders were educated in Pakistan, in refugee camps where they had fled with millions of other Afghans after the Soviet invasion. Pakistan's Jami'at-e 'Ulema-e Islam (JUI) political party provided welfare services, education, and military training for refugees in many of these camps. They also established religious schools in the Deobandi tradition.

Though the United States has not achieved its prime objective of capturing Osama bin Laden, or successfully dismantling the al Qaeda network, Washington thinks it has the strategic initiative. It seems to be the case, however, that America has launched itself into a multi-front war of attrition . . . and it cannot consolidate victory on any front. The momentum is also being lost on the political front.

As the military campaign lessened in intensity in Afghanistan, the United Nations was brought in to broker a political settlement that would usher in representative democracy; meanwhile, the European Union was then dragged in to police the peace via a British-led armed contingent. It has become clear, however, that the narrow, centralized Taliban authority has given way to a return of warlords' taking their power roles to different parts of the country. The role of the security force is increasingly to keep the ex-partners in the Northern Alliance from being at each other's throats. The current Karzai government seems to be losing support because it is perceived more and more as a front for U.S. control. This became more suspicious when American forces replaced the Pashtun security forces which were guarding Karzai.

ISLAMIC EMIRATE OF AFGHANISTAN

In early 2008, **Mullah Omar** still reigned supreme over the Taliban, who had changed their official name to the "Islamic Emirate of Afghanistan" in communiqués. He has managed to avoid capture, but has found a way to appear in videos released to the Middle East media. In December 2007, rifts in the al Qaeda organization started to become public when Mullah Omar sacked Mansour Dadullah, the brother of Mullah Dadullah. Mansour was commander of the southern area of

Afghanistan. Although it is unclear why he was removed, his references to "worldwide jihad" reflect an ideology akin to that of al Qaeda, rather than the more traditional Taliban focus on Afghanistan. He also was an advocate of extreme and controversial tactics seen as unpopular in Afghanistan. Dadullah was captured by Pakistan security forces as he and five others attempted to cross into Pakistan's southwestern Province of Baluchistan.

The prestige of Islamic extremists among the population is now probably greater than before the 9-11 events. Saudi Arabia is seething with discontent, and Washington faces the unpleasant prospect of having to serve ultimately as a police force between an increasingly isolated Saudi elite and a restive youthful population that regards Osama bin Laden as a hero or a prophet.

Washington's continued tilt toward Israel has not helped in shoring up the legitimacy of its Arab allies (including Egypt's Hosni Mubarak) among their people. Israel is the great spoiler of the U.S. effort to manage the Middle East, and Israel can get away with it because it can rely on massive support in the U.S. Congress to blunt pressure from the U.S. Executive Branch. The brazen Israelis even moved to destroy the Palestinian Authority in defiance of Washington.

Indeed, the Afghan fiasco and Israel's continued intransigence, can be argued, have combined to make Washington's strategic situation in the Middle East and the Persian Gulf worse rather than better. There have been no political or military gains in Southeast Asia, with Indonesia maintaining its distance from Washington and the U.S. buildup in the Philippines becoming more controversial by the day. The introduction of U.S. forces in some of the Central Asian republics . . . the so-called "Stans," may, on the surface, seem to be a strategic plus, especially when one takes into consideration the energy reserves of the area. However, with the failure to achieve decisive military or political victory on any front, Washington's Central Asian deployment may actually be a case of overextension.

The impressions (real or imagined), that the United States is now actually working to undermine Islam is being strengthened by U.S. support of regimes in Uzbekistan and Turkmenistan. These regimes, like America's other ally, Turkey, are brutal in their suppression of Muslims and any practice of Islam. As the negative image of the United States grows throughout non-extremist Islam, so do acts of terrorism against Americans and U.S. facilities in Islamic regions.[16]

Drugs and the Taliban

The big question surrounding opium production in Afghanistan, in terms of international drug control efforts, was how to prevent the massive opium poppy harvest in Afghanistan from reaching global drug markets. And the more important question that follows is one of how to end decades of Afghanistan's dependency on opium growing at all. To fully understand the importance of the issue, one only needs to know that as recently as 2004 Afghanistan accounted for a huge proportion of the global production of opiates as well as for most of the heroin found in European markets.

Taliban authorities finally issued a ban on opium poppy cultivation, declaring it "non-Islamic." This ban resulted in a considerable decrease of opium production in 2001. There are plenty of theories as to the motivation of that oppressive regime's decision. Some believe that the Taliban wanted to escape a threat of new sanctions, while others speculate that it wanted to please the international community and relax its isolation. Many have said that the reason for the ban was that the Taliban simply wanted to increase the price of existing stockpiles from the record harvest in 1999, which was 4,600 metric tons, and "next-to-the-best harvest" in 2000 of 3,300 metric tons. Whatever its motivation, the Taliban's ban was effective. In 2001, the areas under opium poppy cultivation were reduced by 91 percent. If the ban had been maintained for another year, the existing stockpiles (estimated to amount to two or three years of production) would have melted down with all the predictable consequences . . . a gradual shortage of heroin in European markets, increase in prices, decrease in purity of the heroin offered, and even a higher demand for treatment. That historic opportunity in international drug control efforts is now in danger of being missed or, at least, delayed.

The period following the events of 9-11, and the subsequent fall of the Taliban regime, coincided with the opium poppy planting season in southern and eastern Afghanistan. Since the Taliban has been removed from the government of Afghanistan, the amount of land now used for opium

FIGURE 11-11   A Taliban militant is seen with an AK-47 at right as farmers collect resin from poppies in an opium field in Naway district of Helmand Province in April 2008. Helmand province is one of the world's top opium poppy-producing regions (Canadian Press).

production is larger than the corresponding total for coca cultivation in Latin America (Colombia, Peru and Bolivia combined). In 2007, Afghanistan produced 8,200 tons of opium, 34 percent more than was produced in 2006, thus accounting for 93 percent of the global opiates market! No other country has previously produced narcotics on such a massive and deadly scale. Quite clearly, opium production in Hilmand and Kandahar provinces is being fuelled by the ongoing insurgency, with Hilmand accounting for almost 50 percent of the production. In 2007, the Taliban controlled large swathes of Hilmand and Kandahar provinces as well as along the border with Pakistan.[17]

Present and Future Challenges

Afghanistan's present and future challenges are tied directly to the issue of drug control. In terms of the country's drug trade, some people wonder if Afghanistan would be better off if the Taliban were still in power. The answer is clearly "no"! It was the Taliban regime that profited from the drug business for years and made Afghanistan a safe haven for international terrorist masterminds and created conditions for drug trafficking in the first place.

The Taliban regime seized control of the major opium-producing areas of Afghanistan in 1996 and regularly collected taxes from the drug business (10 percent from producers and 20 percent from traders). It is difficult to imagine that in such a tightly controlled society, producing, selling, and stockpiling of literally thousands of tons of opium could have gone on throughout the 1990s without the complicity of the Taliban. Further proof of the regime's involvement in the growth of opium production over the past decade is the fact that there were no recorded drug seizures in that country, while 90 percent of global seizures of heroin took place in neighboring Iran.

On January 17, 2001, Afghanistan's new interim authority head, Dr. Hamid Karzai, issued a ban that was even more comprehensive than the one issued by the Taliban. His decree banned not only cultivation, but also processing and illicit use, smuggling, and trafficking of opium. At the time of the ban, most opium poppy fields had already been sown.

Afghanistan's interim authorities are committed to drug control, but the fact is, after decades of devastation of the country, the interim government still does not have the capability to enforce its ban.

That is why the international community needs to assist the country in building that power. In the short term, the challenge for the international community is how to assist Afghanistan's authorities in preventing the poppy harvest from reaching the world markets. Answers range from destroying the opium poppy crops to compensating farmers by buying their harvest and then destroying it. Proponents of the second option argue that buying opium from producers (at farm-gate prices, which average about $30 per kilo) is much less expensive than allowing it to get into the hands of the traffickers (who sell it, depending on the region, for $230–$300 per kilo). Whatever course of action is finally decided, destroy, buy, or something else, it is a decision that needs to be made on the ground, in full coordination and cooperation with Afghanistan authorities and international representatives. This short-term strategy also needs to include a tightening of the security measures against drug trafficking countries like Iran, Pakistan, Tajikistan, and Turkmenistan. The basic conditions for establishing lasting drug control in Afghanistan are being put in place . . . a cooperative government committed to drug control and an international community engaged in the UN-coordinated reconstruction of the country. There is an emerging consensus among all involved that unless effective drug control is actually exercised, everything else being done in Afghanistan might be in vain. The illicit trade in opium is likely centered along the border with Pakistan and also involves trafficking in weapons and manpower. The presence of state of the art weapons has not been as evident in Afghanistan as in Iraq. There is little use of missiles or surface to air missiles (SAM's) in the volatile Hilmand province or around Kandahar. In addition, the numbers of fighters facing NATO troops has not increased and British military estimates the Taliban insurgents to number in the 5,000–6,000 range.

The Taliban have been fully engaged by NATO forces in both the cities and the country; however, there have been several key attacks on areas that were thought to be too well guarded and therefore out of reach of Taliban insurgents. In January 2008 four suspected Taliban militants wearing suicide vests and armed with grenades and rifles attacked a heavily guarded luxury hotel in the Afghan capital, Kabul, killing at least six people. Six other people were wounded in the gun and bomb attack. One of the attackers blew himself up and another was shot dead by security staff. The Taliban have also directly targeted Hamid Karazi. In April 2008 in an eerily similar attack reminiscent of the assassination of Anwar Sadat of Egypt in 1981, six Taliban fighters infiltrated a military parade in Kabul and fired at the grand stand containing Afghan President Hamid Karzai who narrowly escaped injury. Even though they failed at their attempt to assassinate Karazi, the Taliban were able to clearly demonstare that they can infiltrate secure areas almost at will.

BURMA (MYANMAR)

Burma is a mysterious Southeast Asian nation that most people know very little about. Veterans of World War II will recall the Burma Road and the Flying Tigers, but most of us probably know little or nothing of today's Burma. Images of shining pagodas, elephants, and flying fish at play along the mighty Irrawaddy River, from Rudyard Kipling's famous poem "Road to Mandalay" may come to mind. But Burma's reality today has little in common with such romantic legends. For most of its modern history, following its independence from Britain in 1948, Burma has been run by a military-controlled socialist regime that has isolated the country, wrecked its economy, and totally repressed its many diverse ethnic populations.

A massive and peaceful "people power" demonstration movement demanded an end to the military dictatorship in 1988 and again in 2008. The army leadership reacted violently and swiftly to repress and quell this movement. To maintain the status quo, a new military junta, the **State Law and Order Restoration Council (SLORC)**, seized direct power to quell any kind of movement toward democracy. Crowds of peaceful protesters were machine-gunned down by SLORC troops, and thousands were killed. For a few days, events in Burma captured world headlines but were soon replaced by sound bites about other world events in some more familiar locales. Global attention briefly picked up again, however, in December 1991, when Daw Aung San Suu Kyi, the

FIGURE 11-12 **Map of Burma** (Central Intelligence Agency, *The World Factbook*, 2008).

long-detained democracy advocate and leading voice of freedom for Burma, was awarded the Nobel Peace Prize.

Still, most of the world has little interest in Burma. To further confuse the situation, the SLORC generals changed the country's long-standing official name (by decree and without public consultation), to Myanmar, a transliteration of the country's Burmese language name. And Burma's democratic opposition and powerful generals outright rejected the name and refused to recognize it. More confusion came in November 1997, when the generals renamed their own junta the **State Peace and Development Council (SPDC)** in hopes of improving their rapidly deteriorating and well-earned bad international image.

The people of Burma continue to suffer under one of this planet's most brutal and repressive regimes. The United Nations, world religious leaders (including the Pope in Rome, and the Dalai Lama of Tibet), many governments, and human rights groups, have urged an end to the many oppressive human rights violations in Burma. The military regime's response so far has been intensified abuse, such as murder, torture, rape, political imprisonment, and forced labor. There is absolutely neither expression nor freedom of association in Burma, and the Junta does not allow Burmese citizens any voice in the shaping of their nation's future.

Their cruel military regime allows, and probably participates in, the growing explosion of heroin production in Burma. Ceasefires with several ethnic opposition armies that have long traded in drugs, have allowed an estimated increase of nearly 400 percent in Burma's heroin production since the junta took power in 1988. Around the world, this flood of cheaper and purer heroin is causing a vast new wave of addiction. In recent years, approximately 60 percent of the heroin reaching the United States has been of Burmese origin. And, in Burma itself, an estimated half million addicts are spreading an AIDS epidemic at a rate that has been seen only in some areas of Central Africa.

Burma plays a pivotal role in South Asia's security, due to its strategic position linking South and Southeast Asia and bordering the continent's two most populous countries, China and India. But Independent Burma had long pursued a policy of neutrality. To the alarm of many countries, the military regime is now increasingly dependent on China as a political ally and arms supplier. Fear of Chinese military influence in Burma is helping to spur a costly regional arms race that diverts funds desperately needed for their human development.

People who argue that trade and tourism can help promote respect for human rights are pressing for increased international involvement with the Burmese military regime. Some claimed that "constructive engagement" might convince the junta to fight drug trafficking and to reduce its reliance on China.[18] A few simply declared that business and human rights are separate issues that should not be mixed. The junta itself, backed by a few Asian autocrats, asserts that it respects human rights in an "Asian" or "Burmese" context and such internationally recognized standards do not apply in Burma. Among these critical human rights issues is the SPDC's continuing detention of opposition figures.

Resolution of the political impasse in Burma will eventually require real, substantive dialogue with the democratic opposition, including Aung San Suu Kyi and representatives of the ethnic groups. Arbitrary detentions are unjustifiable and will only worsen rather than solve the political crisis.

The United States has protested the policies of the Burmese government through its embassy in Rangoon, and will continue to work with like-minded countries to press the Burmese government to take positive action, including the release of political prisoners and the initiation of a genuine dialogue with Aung San Suu Kyi and other NLD leaders.

The 1997 explosion of a parcel bomb at the house of a senior official in Burma's military-led government was the country's most significant terrorist event. In his visit to Burma, Bishop Tutu spoke of the blast that killed the adult daughter of Lieutenant-General Tin Oo, Second-Secretary of the ruling State Law and Order Restoration Council. No group or individual claimed responsibility for the attack, but the government of Burma attributes the act to Burmese anti-government activists in Japan. The package containing the bomb bore Japanese stamps and post-marks. The Burmese expatriate and student community living in Japan denies any involvement in the incident.[19]

Afghanistan is the world's leading producer of illicit opium, accounting for about 90 percent of Southeast Asian production, and about half of the world's supply. Recent reports suggest a massive increase in methamphetamine production and distribution from Burma as well. Although the Burmese government has expanded its counter-narcotics efforts over the past few years, the impact has been limited at best. While part of the problem is that the Burmese government does not control many of the ethnic groups that traffic in drugs, the government also does not make sufficient effort at interdiction. There is also some evidence of corrupt elements in the military that may be aiding the traffickers, and there are signs that the Burmese encourage traffickers to invest in a multitude of development projects throughout the country.[20]

The United States remains concerned about the limited commitment of the Burmese government to fight narcotics and about the potential damage that opium cultivation in Burma can inflict on the United States and the rest of the world.

Burma is a poor country, with an average per capita GDP of approximately $406, at a weighted exchange rate, perhaps double that in terms of purchasing power parity. Progress on market reforms has been mixed and uneven. Beginning in 1988, the Burmese government partly opened the economy to permit expansion of the private sector and to attract foreign investment. Though modest economic improvement ensued, since 1993 the pace of economic reform has slowed and major obstacles to further reform persist. These include disproportionate military spending, extensive overt and covert state involvement in economic activity, state monopolization of leading exports, a bloated bureau-cracy prone to arbitrary and opaque governance, a poor education and physical infrastructure. In addition, due to international opposition and to the SPDC's unwillingness to cooperate fully with the International Monetary Fund (IMF), SPDC access to external credit from the IMF, World Bank, and Asian Development Bank continues to be blocked by sanctions. In September 1998, the World Bank announced that Burma had defaulted on its loan repayments. Some analysts think the laundering of drug profits in Burma's legitimate economy is extensive.

At the ASEAN meetings in Manila in July 1998, then U.S. Secretary of State Albright, with Foreign Minister McKinnon of New Zealand, led a discussion of the political impasse in Burma. The meetings included representatives from Austria, Australia, Canada, Germany, Korea, Japan, Great Britain, and Burmese Foreign Minister Ohn Gyaw. The ministers expressed their concerns over the deteriorating conditions in Burma and demanded a speedy, peaceful resolution to the situation. They pressed for the immediate commencement of an SPDC dialogue with the democratic opposition, to include Aung San Suu Kyi. Secretary Albright continued to actively promote interna-tional constructive engagement with the SPDC toward an improved human rights climate.

It is clear that the SPDC is not eager to release its chokehold on the Burmese people, and the world's attention is often drawn away from such remote areas. It remains to be seen whether or not worldwide preoccupation with problems in Bosnia, Israel, and Iraq will distract prompt diplomatic action by the major powers to right the situation in Burma.

In South Asia, many of the factions involved in the Afghanistan civil war, including large numbers of Egyptians, Algerians, Palestinians, and Saudis, continued to provide haven to terrorists by facilitating the operation of training camps in areas under their control. The factions remain engaged in a struggle for political and military supremacy over their countries and regions.

CAMBODIA

Cambodia is located on the Gulf of Thailand, between Thailand and Vietnam. It is a tiny country, slightly smaller than Oklahoma. The country is a land of rice paddies and forests and is dominated by the Mekong River. It has a population of about 11 million, ethnically composed of Khmer (90 percent), Vietnamese (5 percent), Chinese (1 percent), and other (4 percent). The religious preference is overwhelmingly Theravada Buddhist (95 percent). Cambodia was called "Kampuchea" under the disastrous dictatorship of the Khmer Rouge.

The Cambodian economy has been virtually destroyed by decades of war, but it is slowly recovering. Government leaders are moving toward restoring fiscal and monetary discipline and have established good working relations with international financial institutions. Growth, starting from a low base, was strong between 1991 and 1996. Despite such positive developments, the reconstruction effort faces many tough challenges because of internal political divisions and the related lack of confidence of foreign investors.

Rural Cambodia, where 90 percent of about 9.5 million of the Khmer live, remains mired in poverty. The almost total lack of basic infrastructure in the countryside hinders development and contributes to a growing imbalance in growth between urban and rural areas over the near term. Moreover, the government's lack of experience in administering economic and technical assistance programs and rampant corruption among officials, slow the growth of critical public sector investment. The decline of inflation from the 1992 rate of more than 50 percent is one of the bright spots in Cambodia's return to a peacetime period. In a somewhat interesting and unusual move, the **Khmer Royal Armed Forces (KRAF)** was created in 1993 by the merger of the Cambodian People's Armed Forces and the two non-Communist resistance armies (KRAF is also known as the Royal Cambodian Armed Forces, or RCAF).

FIGURE 11-13 **Map of Cambodia** (Central Intelligence Agency, *The World Factbook*, 2008).

Offshore islands and sections of the boundary with Vietnam remain in dispute and the maritime boundary with Vietnam is not clearly defined. Also, parts of the border with Thailand are now in dispute, as its boundaries are also not clearly defined. In the Golden Triangle, where Cambodia, Thailand, and Vietnam have mutual borders, heroin is being routed to the West, giving Cambodia the possibility of becoming a major money-laundering center. High-level, narcotics-related corruption reportedly involves the government, military, and police. There are small-scale opium, heroin, and amphetamine production operations in Cambodia and a larger production system of high-grade marijuana for the international market.

Hard-liners based in the Khmer Rouge stronghold at Anlong Veng regularly launched guerrilla-style attacks on government troops in several provinces. Guerrillas are also suspected in two deadly attacks against ethnic Vietnamese civilians in Cambodia, but they have denied playing a role in the disappearance of two Filipino and two Malaysian employees of a logging company in 1997.

The death of former **Khmer Rouge** leader **Pol Pot** (Saloth Sar) on April 15, 1998, in the

Thai-Cambodian border area, brought an end to one of the most chilling and bloody chapters of the twentieth century. During Pol Pot's three and a half years of rule over Cambodia, from 1975 to 1978, the Khmer Rouge was suspected of killing as many as 2 million people through mass executions, starvation, and slave labor.

The genocide in Cambodia was the outcome of a complex historical development in which the pernicious ideological influence of Stalinism came together with the military bloodbath carried out against the people of Indochina. Pol Pot will be little mourned by the people of Cambodia.

The fate of British mine-clearing expert Christopher Howes, allegedly kidnapped by the Khmer Rouge in March 1996, remains unresolved. Unconfirmed reporting suggested Howes was with forces loyal to Pol Pot, and some Cambodian officials expressed fears publicly that he had been killed. In May 1996, Khmer Rouge leader Khieu Samphan denied any knowledge of Howes' whereabouts.

Incidents of terrorism in East Asia continue to increase. Continuing defections from the Khmer Rouge to Cambodian forces reduced the threat from the terrorist group, but guerrillas in the Cambodian provinces have been responsible for deadly attacks on foreigners. The unstable political situation in Cambodia has led to marked political violence. In October 1997, the Secretary of State designated the Khmer Rouge as a foreign terrorist organization pursuant to the Antiterrorism and Effective Death Penalty Act of 1996.

Pol Pot

The political activity of Pol Pot (Saloth Sar), began in post-World War II France, when Cambodia was part of its Indochina colony. The son of a relatively well-off peasant family, Pol Pot received a government scholarship in 1949 to study in Paris, where he gravitated with a number of his friends to the Stalinist circles around the French Communist Party. He returned to Phnom Penh in 1953, worked as a teacher, and was involved in the start of the embryonic Communist Party in Cambodia. Police repression under the government of Prince Norodom Sihanouk, the country's first post-colonial ruler, forced the party leaders to flee the capital in 1963 and seek sanctuary in the remote rural areas of the country.

It was only after the American intervention in Cambodia during the Vietnam War that Pol Pot and the Khmer Rouge began to get wider support. From a badly organized force of less than 5,000 men in 1970, the Khmer Rouge expanded to an army of around 70,000. In April 1975, the Lon Nol dictatorship

FIGURE 11-14 Skulls in Phnom Penh (the "killing fields") in April 1981. Authorities say the victims were tied together by rope before being executed by followers of Premier Pol Pot, who was ousted from power in 1979 (Canadian Press).

collapsed and Pol Pot came to power. The peasant-based army and Khmer Rouge leaders carried out policies of an anti-working-class character, which had far more in common with fascism than socialism. With an economy in shambles, Pol Pot was unable and unwilling to organize the feeding of the cities; he ordered the evacuation of Pnomh Penh and other towns. The entire urban population of workers, intellectuals, civil servants, small shopkeepers, and others was driven into the countryside to harsh labor on irrigation schemes and other grandiose projects aimed at elevating agricultural production.

Under Pol Pot's leadership, the Khmer Rouge conducted a campaign of genocide in which an estimated 2 million people were killed during its four years in power in the late 1970s.[21]

The Khmer Rouge is a Communist insurgency that is trying to destabilize the Cambodian government. It is still engaged in a low-level insurgency against the Cambodian government, although its victims are mainly Cambodian villagers, the Khmer Rouge has occasionally kidnapped and killed foreigners traveling in remote rural areas. One to two thousand members of the Khmer Rouge operate in outlying provinces in Cambodia, particularly in pockets along the Thailand border.

The Khmer Rouge may not be considered by many as a serious threat to destabilization of Cambodia yet again. But, some seventeen years and three Cambodian regimes later, the National Army of Democratic Kampuchea, as the Khmer Rouge military is known, continues to wage warfare and terrorism from scattered jungle bases of operation in an attempt to regain control of Cambodia and resume its utopian experiment. Although there have been large-scale defections from the Khmer Rouge to Cambodian government forces since 1996, and the group suffered a significant split in 1997, it still may be considered dangerous.

THAILAND

The ancient Kingdom of Thailand sometimes referred to as "Siam" lies southeast of Burma and borders the Andaman Sea and the Gulf of Thailand. It is slightly more than twice the size of Wyoming. This country has a population of almost 60 million; the ethnic groupings are Thai (75 percent), Chinese (14 percent), and other (11 percent). Religious affiliations are Buddhism (95 percent), Muslim (3.8 percent), Christianity (0.5 percent), Hinduism (0.1 percent), and other (0.6 percent); All religions seem to live harmoniously. Thailand has had independence since 1238 A.D. and has never been colonized. A new constitution was approved in 1991 and amended in 1992.

History Timeline—Thailand

Some significant dates:

- June 24, 1932: King Prajadhipok falls in a bloodless coup, and a constitutional monarchy and parliament are introduced. A succession of military dictators retains power for most of the period until 1973.
- October 14, 1973: 400,000 student-led protesters topple the military rulers, leading to a brief period of unstable democracy.
- October 6, 1976: A bloody crackdown on student protesters ends with the military returning to power.
- March 1980: Moderate military ruler Prem Tinsulanond survives several coup attempts.
- July 1988: General Chatichai Choonhavan wins general elections.
- February 1991: General Sunthorn Kongsompong stages a coup and topples Chatichai's civilian government.
- May 1992: Junta member General Suchinda Kraprayoon assumes the prime minister's post, drawing hundreds of thousands of protesters into the streets of Bangkok demanding a return to civilian rule. The king intervenes and General Suchinda agrees to resign.
- September 23, 1992: Democrat party leader Chuan Leekpai is elected prime minister.

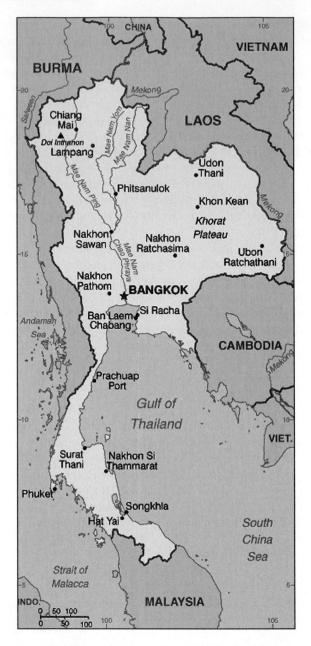

FIGURE 11.15 **Map of Thailand** (Central Intelligence Agency, *The World Factbook*, 2008).

- October 11, 1997: The king signs the country's 16th "People's Constitution" into law, in a major development for political reform and democracy.
- March 4, 2000: The first senate elections are held under the new constitution.
- January 6, 2001: Telecommunications magnate Thaksin Shinawatra wins elections in a landslide to become the twenty-third prime minister.[22]

Thailand is one of the more advanced developing countries in Asia. It depends on exports of manufactured goods, including high-technology goods, and the development of the service sector to fuel the country's rapid growth, averaging 9 percent since 1989. Most of Thailand's recent imports have been for capital equipment and raw materials, although imports of consumer goods are beginning to rise. Thailand's 35 percent domestic savings rate is a key source of capital for the economy, and the country is also benefiting from rising investment from abroad.

THAILAND'S INSURGENCY

Since 2001, the level and intensity of Thailand's insurgency has started to increase, with the main problem areas being the southern Thai Provinces of Pattani, Yala, and Narathiwat, home to the majority of the country's Malay Muslims. Statistics from the Thai Ministry of the Interior show that in 2001 there were fifty terrorist-related incidents across the three affected Provinces, with nineteen police officers killed. In 2002, guerrillas attacked several police stations, seizing huge quantities of arms and ammunition. Between January and November 2004, some 573 people were killed and 524 injured.[23] There are no significant signs the Thailand's insurgents are being exported to other conflicts around the globe and that their focus is purely on their domestic political grievances. However, as Malay Muslims are known to practice a more moderate form of Islam, but Wahhabi teachings and the increase in religious schools in the south being sponsored and supported by states in the Middle East is a cause for concern to the Buddhist government. The sharp rise in insurgent attacks in 2007 and the types of attack being carried out point to a level of expertize that was not evident over the last four years. This leads analysts to believe that the increased insurgency may be due to the presence of foreign trainined fighters. Thailand has been ruled by a Buddhist dominated government for decades and is kept in power by a powerful military with unwavering support for the Thai monarchy. The south is home to the poorest of the population in Thailand and the Malay Muslim grievances go back decades which stem from discrimination against the ethnic Malay Muslim population and attempts at forced assimilation by successive ethnic Thai Buddhist governments. The presence of insurgent groups date back to the late 1960s and early 1970s and some were created to defend against Communist influences spreading across Thailand's borders. In 1971, the Thai Royal family sponsored and continue to sponsor the Village Scouts . . . a right wing ultra nationalist group that were established not to be involved in politics but as a group to do the bidding of the Royals. Today they continue to have the support of the Thai Royal family as well as the Royal Thai police and military. In the 1970s and 1980s, the most effective of the groups operating was the Pattani United Liberatioin Organization (PULO), which were then calling for an independent Islamic state in Thailand.

The Thai government managed to stem the unrest with political and economic reforms that undercut support for armed struggle, and hundreds of fighters accepted a broad amnesty. The insurgency looked to be all but over by the mid-1990s.

But new strains then appeared, with four particularly significant groups emerging or re-emerging, with major violence erupting early in 2004. The major groups active today include:

- BRN-C (Barisan Revolusi Nasional-Coordinate, National Revolutionary Front-Coordinate) the only active faction of BRN, first established in the early 1960s to fight for an independent Patani state. Thought to be the largest and best organised of the armed groups, it is focused on political organizing and recruitment within Islamic schools.
- Pemuda, a separatist youth movement (part of which is controlled by BRN-C), is believed to be responsible for a large proportion of day-to-day sabotage, shooting and bombing attacks.
- GMIP (Gerakan Mujahidin Islam Patani, Patani Islamic Mujahidin Group), established by Afghanistan veterans in 1995, is committed to an independent Islamic state.
- New PULO, established in 1995 as an offshoot of PULO and the smallest of the active armed groups, is fighting for an independent state.

In an effort to understand the current violence and who is involved, this report focuses in detail on three relatively recent major outbreaks. The first, on January 4, 2004, involved carefully coordinated attacks in which militants raided an army arsenal, torched schools and police posts, and the following day, set off several bombs.

The second, on April 28, 2004, involved synchronized attacks on eleven police posts and army checkpoints across Pattani, Yala and Songkhla, and ended in a bloody showdown at the Krue Se Mosque, when the Thai army gunned down thirty-two men inside. By the end of the day, 105 militants, 1 civilian and 5 members of the security forces were dead.

The third, on October 25, 2004, began with a demonstration outside a police station and ended with the deaths of at least eighty-five Muslim men and boys, most from suffocation after arrest as a result of being stacked five and six deep in army trucks for transport to an army base.

There are several explanations, none mutually exclusive, for why violence has escalated. Two of the most plausible are the disbanding of key government institutions, and the fear and resentment created by arbitrary arrests and police brutality, compounded by government failure to provide justice to victims and families. Rapid social change has also contributed to insecurity and frustration in Malay Muslim communities and a feeling that their way of life, values, and culture are threatened.[24]

In the south of the country separatist rebels have continued to wage a bloody insurgency and by 2008 more than 3,000 had died. The government has had little success in putting down or negotiating a peaceful settlement with the insurgents.

The simmering differences between the Thai military and the government will do nothing to resolve the situation in the south. On the contrary, while politicians and generals continue their infighting and political power struggles, it will give the insurgents more opportunity to attack and destabilize the government. The heavy-handed response to the insurgents by both the military and police is fueling the current insurgent attacks.

VIETNAM

The Socialist Republic of Vietnam is a Communist state made up of the former North and South Vietnams, after ten years of the Vietnam War. This country, war-torn for many decades, is in Southeastern Asia, bordering the Gulf of Thailand, the Gulf of Tonkin, and the South China Sea, between China and Cambodia. It is slightly larger than New Mexico. After consolidation at the war's end, Vietnam has a population of over 75 million. The ethnic population distribution is Vietnamese (85 percent to 90 percent), Chinese (3 percent), with Muong Tai, Meo, Khmer, Man, and Cham making up the ethnic balance. Religious affiliations are (in descending order) Buddhist, Taoist, Roman Catholic, indigenous beliefs, Islam, Protestant, Cao Dai, and Hoa Hao. Vietnam won its independence from France in 1945 when the French colonial forces were defeated. Its new constitution was approved in 1992.

Vietnam is a poor, densely populated country that has had to recover from the ravages of decades of war, the loss of financial support from the former USSR, and the rigidities of a centrally planned economy. Substantial progress has been achieved over the past ten years in moving forward from an extremely low starting point. Economic growth continued at a strong pace with industrial output rising by 14 percent during 1996; real GDP expanded by 9.4 percent. Foreign direct investment rose to an estimated $2.3 billion for the year. These positive numbers, however, mask some major difficulties that are emerging in economic performance. Many domestic industries, including coal, cement, steel, and paper, reported large stockpiles of inventory and tough competition from more efficient foreign producers. While disbursements of aid and foreign direct investment have risen, they are not large enough to finance the rapid increase in imports. It is widely believed that Vietnam may be using short-term trade credits to bridge the gap. That is a risky strategy, one that could result in a foreign exchange crunch in the near term.

Meanwhile, Vietnamese authorities continue to move very slowly toward implementing the structural reforms needed to revitalize the economy and produce more competitive, export-driven industries. Privatization of state enterprise remains bogged down in political controversy, while the country's dynamic private sector is denied both financing and access to markets. Reform of the banking sector is proceeding slowly, raising concerns that the country will be unable to tap sufficient domestic savings to maintain current high levels of growth. Administrative and legal barriers are also causing costly delays for foreign investors and are raising similar doubts about Vietnam's ability to maintain the inflow of foreign capital. Ideological bias in favor of state

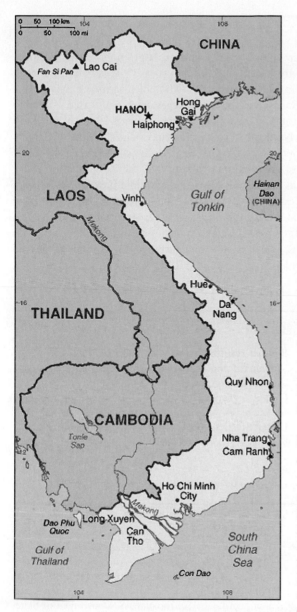

FIGURE 11-16 **Map of Vietnam** (Central Intelligence Agency, *The World Factbook*, 2008).

intervention and control of the economy is slowing progress toward a more liberalized investment environment.

Vietnam has disputes over maritime boundaries with Cambodia and is involved in complex negotiations over the Spratly Islands in the South China Sea. These are ongoing with China, Malaysia, the Philippines, Taiwan, and possibly Brunei. There are also unresolved maritime boundaries with Thailand and with China in the Gulf of Tonkin, and disputed ownership of the Paracel Islands in the South China Sea, which are occupied by China but claimed by Vietnam and Taiwan. Offshore islands and sections of boundary with Cambodia are in dispute as well. Key growing areas in Vietnam cultivated 3,150 hectares of poppy in 1996, producing 25 tons of opium, making it a major opium producer and an increasingly important transit point for Southeast Asian heroin destined for the United States and Europe. Vietnam has a growing opium addiction problem, plus possible small-scale heroin production in country. While there is little known terrorism in Vietnam, a Vietnamese court sentenced two persons to death and three others to life in prison for carrying out a grenade attack on the waterfront in Ho Chi Minh City in 1994, in which twenty persons, including ten foreigners, were injured. The five were part of the Vietnam Front for Regime Restoration, an anti-government exile group based in the United States.

Ho Chi Minh

The affectionate name given to him by his countrymen, "Uncle Ho," gives rise to an image as a kindly, humble man. Yet Ho was a life-long revolutionary, who used any and all means to achieve his ends. Ho first led an insurrection against Japanese occupiers. In 1945, Ho's commandos took Hanoi, the Vietnamese capital. In one of the ironies of history, Ho Chi Minh paraphrased a future enemy's benchmark of freedom—the U.S. Declaration of Independence—while addressing an enormous crowd after the success against the Japanese. Ho proclaimed: "All men are born equal. The Creator has given us inviolable rights: life, liberty, and happiness!"

Ho again led revolutionary forces against outside control, fighting an eight-year war that led to the division of Vietnam into two countries, North and South Vietnam. An election that was meant to be held in 1956 to reunite the country under a democratically elected leader was never held. South Vietnam, backed by the United States, refused to participate in the elections, fearful Ho would win.

Ho's regime in the North became rigidly totalitarian. After the defeated French exited, the United States escalated its involvement, supporting a series of weak governments in South Vietnam.

Vietnamese independence was finally achieved, just six years after Ho's death in 1969 at age seventy-nine. The victory came at a staggering price: an estimated 3 million North and South Vietnamese were killed in the struggle.[25]

Summary

The terrorism and violence generated in Southern and Southeast Asia span a large menu of very complicated and diverse scenarios. These range from individual acts (assassination of two prime ministers named Gandhi), religious hatred (the Hindus, the Muslims, and the Sikhs), political genocide (Khmer Rouge), state terrorism (Burma), up to conventional and nuclear war possibilities. This complex region, one little understood in the Western world and often mysterious, holds huge potential but many problems. Thailand alone stood somewhat calm until 2001, but increasing insurgent problems in the south and an influx of Islamic extremists is giving rise to concerns. The former Indochina tries to recover from decades of suffering from wars, terror, and destruction for over four decades and is beginning to make some progress, but with fits and starts. The situation between India and Pakistan, the two nuclear-armed giants of this region, seems to be the biggest problem to face. Added to that mix is the significant presence of Islamic fighters in the Northwest Frontier Provinces and the flow of fighters either entering or leaving Afghanistan. Time will tell if these great nations will survive, facing a situation every bit as dangerous as any in the Middle East. The incredibly long histories of most of the nations in the region have created long memories, great hatreds, and grudges. The next chapter discusses many of the same issues and problems, which have been exacerbated by serious economic problems, on the Pacific Rim.

Web Sites

1. **History Politics**—*http://www.sscnet.ucla.edu/southasia/ History/Independent/Indira.html*
2. **Liberation Tigers of Tamil Eelam**—*http://www.ict.org. il/inter_ter/orgdet.cfm?orgid=22*
3. **Jane's Islamic Affairs Analysis**—*http://www.jiaa.janes. com/public/jiaa/index.shtml*
4. **South Asia Analysis Group**—*http://www. southasiaanalysis.org/*
5. **Benazir Bhutto**—*http://www.benazirbhutto.org/*
6. **Musharraf and Terrorism (Archives)**—*http://www. southasiaanalysis.org*
7. **Global Terrorism Analysis**—*http://www.jamestown. org/terrorism/news/article.php?articleid=2370192*
8. **United States Institute for Peace**—*http://www.usip. org/fellows/reports/2005/0603_swami.html*

Endnotes

1. The U.S. Department of State, *1997 Patterns of Global Terrorism Report*; The U.S. Department of State, *Country Reports on Human Rights Practices*; The U.S. Department of State, *Background Notes: Geographic Entities and International Organizations*; The U.S. Central Intelligence Agency, *World Factbook*.
2. India: Rural Development and the Naxalite Threat, www. stratfor.com.
3. The Economist, India's Sikhs, *Heresy and History*, July 7, 2007.
4. Macleans. December 3, 2007, p. 30.
5. Patterns of Global Terrorism—U.S. Department of State, 2005.
6. U.S. Department of State, *Patterns of Global Terrorism*, 1997 (Washington, DC, 1997), http//www.state.gov.
7. The Jamestown Foundation. http://www.jamestown.org/ publications_details.php.
8. Saeed Shafwat, *The Rise of Dawat ul-Irshad and Lashkar-e-Toiba in Pakistan: Nationalism without a Nation*, ed. Christopher Jaffrelot (New Delhi: Manohar Publications, 2002).
9. Patterns of Global Terrorism, U.S. Department of State, 1998.
10. The authors are grateful, again, to our friend and consultant, Jafar Siddiqui, who provides us with a different view of these regions.
11. BBC News—South Asia. http://www.news.bbc.co.uk/ 2/hi/south_asia/212361.stm.
12. U.S. Department of State, *Patterns of Global Terrorism*, 1997 (Washington, DC, 1997), http://www.state.gov.
13. Press Statement by James P. Rubin, spokesman (September 8, 1998), http://www.state.gov.
14. Tigers Suffer Setback—Janes Terrorism and Security Monitor, London, January 2008.

15. Hekmat Karzai, *Center for Conflict and Peace Studies, Taliban: Why Dadullah's Death Matters*, May 22, 2007.

16. Walden Bello (April 29, 2002), http://www.state.gov.

17. UN Office on Drugs and Crime—Afghanistan Opium Survey, 2007 Report.

18. Editors. "Afghanistan's 2002 Opium Harvest." *Intersec* (March 3, 2002, pp. 78–81).

19. Irrawaddy News Magazine Interactive (Archives), http://www.Irrawaddy.org.

20. The White House. Office of the Press Secretary (October 27, 1998), http://www.state.gov.

21. The Death of Pol Pot, http://www.wsws.org/news/1998/apr1998/plpt-a18.shtml.

22. Http://australianetwork.com/news/infocus/s1745603.htm.

23. Janes Intelligence Review, May 1, 2005.

24. Southern Thailand: Insurgency Not Jihad—Asia Report #98, May 18, 2005, www.crisisgroup.org/home/index.cfm?id=3436.

25. PBS. www.pbs.org.

CHAPTER 12

The Pacific Rim

I support Osama Bin Laden's struggle, because his is the true struggle to uphold Islam, not terror . . . the terrorists are America and Israel

ABU BAKAR BASHIR

Learning Objective

The study and review of this chapter will enable you to

1. Explain how Islamist separatist groups have been linked to al Qaeda;
2. Examine why Falun Gong is perceived by the Chinese authorities as a threat;
3. Discuss how terrorism has shaped Indonesia's political landscape;
4. Why Australia is a target for terrorism.

Terms to Remember

Abu Sayyaf Group (ASG)
Antiterrorism and Effective Death Penalty Act of 1996
Aum Shinrikyo
Democratic Progressive Party (DPP)
Falun Gong
Fiahs

Japanese Red Army (JRA)
Jemaah Islamiyaah (JI)
Keiretsu
Moro Islamic Liberation Front (MILF)
Moro National Liberation Front (MNLF)
New People's Army (NPA)

People's Consultative Assembly
People's Republic of China (PRC)
URAJ
Xinjiang Uighur Autonomous Region (XUAR)

October 12, 2002: Bali—A remotely detonated bomb attack destroyed Paddy's Bar, killing 202 tourists and injuring more than 200.

September 9, 2004: Jakarta, Indonesia—Armed militants detonate a car bomb outside the Australian Embassy, killing 10 people and injuring 182 others. **Jemaah Islamiyaah** claimed responsibility.

October 30, 2005: Sulawesi, Indonesia—Three Christian schoolgirls were beheaded by local militants in the Poso region while walking to school.

OVERVIEW

The Pacific Rim contains those countries that sweep in a long arc from Australia to Japan. Many of these countries have been suffering serious financial crises. As major trading partners to the United States, and the European Economic Community, many of these countries have brought the world great turmoil; through wars, insurgencies, corrupt governments, and with right and left-wing terrorists. These problems have a major impact on the other countries of this region. Their financial and political chaos creates opportunities for terrorist groups to take advantage of the turmoil to enhance and forward their own causes. This chapter builds upon the previous analysis of Southern and Southeast Asia, and discusses how individual countries are reacting in terms of their backgrounds and sad histories of terrorist actions. We shall start with the biggest country, in terms of population, China.

CHINA

Our examination of the Far East and the Pacific Rim cannot begin without first discussing the **People's Republic of China (PRC)**. Following the fall of the Soviet Union, the PRC has now become the world's second-greatest superpower.

China is bordered by a coastline of over 10,000 miles that includes the East China Sea, Korea Bay, Yellow Sea, and the South China Sea. The country is only slightly smaller than the United States. Its land borders are over 14,700 miles long, and include the countries of Afghanistan, Bhutan, India, Kazakhstan, North Korea, Kyrgyzstan, Laos, Macau, Mongolia, Nepal, Pakistan, Russia (Northeast), Russia (Northwest), Tajikistan, and Vietnam. China is the world's fourth largest country (after Russia, Canada, and the United States), with a population of approximately 1.3 billion. The ethnic makeup of this world giant is: Han Chinese 91.9 percent; Zhuang, Uighur, Hui, Yi, Tibetan, Miao, Manchu, Mongol, Buyi, Korean, and "other" make up the remainder. While China is officially atheist, it is traditionally pragmatic and eclectic. Daoism (Taoism), Buddhism, and Muslim religions are unofficially practiced by 2–3 percent of their population, and Chinese Christians number only about 1 percent. But, remember, these are percentages of 1.3 billion people . . . and 1 percent still represents a very large number!

China was an ancient, and widely scattered, society until it was unified under the Qin, or Ch'ing, Dynasty in 221 B.C. The Ch'ing Dynasty, the last of the dynasties, was replaced by the Chinese Republic in 1912. The People's Republic of China was later established in 1949. Beginning in late 1978, the Chinese leadership began trying to move the economy from a sluggish, Soviet-style, and

FIGURE 12-1 Map of China (Central Intelligence Agency, *The World Factbook*, 2008).

centrally planned economy, to one that is more market-oriented, but still within a rigid political framework and firmly under Communist Party control. To this end, the authorities switched to a system of household responsibility in agriculture in place of the older collectivization. It increased the authority of local officials and plant managers in industry, permitted a wide variety of small-scale enterprises in services and light manufacturing, and opened the economy to increased foreign trade and investment. The result has been a quadrupling of China's GDP since 1978. Agricultural output doubled in the 1980s, and industry also posted major gains, especially in coastal areas near Hong Kong and across the Straight in Taiwan, where foreign investment helped spur output of both domestic and export goods. On the darker side, the leadership then often experienced in its hybrid system the worst results of socialism (bureaucracy, lassitude, and corruption) as well as those of capitalism (windfall gains and stepped-up inflation). Beijing, thus, has periodically had to backtrack, re-tightening central controls at intervals. From 1992 to 1996, annual growth of GDP accelerated, particularly in the coastal areas, averaging more than 10 percent annually, according to official Chinese figures. In late 1993, China's leadership had approved additional long-term reforms, aimed at giving still more play in their market-oriented institutions, and at strengthening Beijing's control over the financial system. State-controlled enterprises would continue to dominate many key industries in what was then termed "a socialist market economy." From 1995 to 1996, inflation dropped sharply, reflecting tighter monetary policies and stronger measures to control food prices. At the same time, the government struggled to:

- Collect revenues from provinces, businesses, and individuals.
- Reduce corruption and other economic crimes.
- Keep afloat the large, state-owned enterprises, most of which had not participated in the vigorous expansion of the economy and many of which have been losing the ability to pay full wages and pensions.

It is estimated that from 60 million to 100 million surplus rural workers were then adrift, between the villages and the cities, many subsisting on part-time, low-paying jobs. Another long-term threat to continued economic growth was the deterioration of the environment . . . notably, air pollution, soil erosion, and the steady dropping of the water table, especially in the north. China still continues to lose arable land, because of erosion and economic development. Furthermore, the Chinese government gives insufficient priority to serious agricultural research. The next few years might see increasing tensions between a highly centralized political system and an increasingly decentralized economic system.[1]

China is also a major transshipment point for heroin produced in the Golden Triangle, and is beginning to experience a rapidly growing domestic drug abuse problem.

Terrorism in China had matured long before the 9/11 tragedy, with February 5, 1997, marking the beginning of active terrorism in the country. These activities have three separate yet interrelated dimensions. First, the insurgent movement has a well-defined political program, aimed at achieving independence through ethnic struggle. More concretely, this program contains a mixture of ideas including the Pan-Turkic movement that spread to Xinjiang at the beginning of the last century. In the 1930s, when Xinjiang was at the height of turmoil, the Uighurs established an East Turkistan Islamic Republic. Although it existed for only three months, its legacy died hard. In the early 1980s, the spirit of independence based on Turkish ethnicity was rekindled, inspiring many Uighurs who resented Chinese domination of local affairs. Ethnic self-determination works in tandem with Pan-Turkism as another motivating factor. Under the banner of human rights and equality, the dissidents use both peaceful means of lobbying in the international arena and violent means by way of protest within China. The movement has generated sympathy from a range of Uighur communities in remote Xinjiang. Second, Jiangdu activists have built base networks both at home and abroad, with extensive foreign connections revolving around three centers of activity, each of them interconnected: Activists launch anti-China campaigns under the name of promoting human rights and ethnic equality in the West. Dozens of Islamic organizations comprised of Chinese exiles were legally registered in Central Asia during the mid-1990s, such as the East Turkistan Liberation Movement in Kazakhstan.

Although most of them were later outlawed, they continued to engage in covert operations that pose a security threat to Beijing. The third center used to be in Afghanistan, where Xinjiang insurgents received indoctrination and military training from al Qaeda. One Chinese source revealed that more than fifty known terrorist organizations existed in Central Asia, and that more than 500 Xinjiang insurgents had been trained in Afghanistan.[2]

Reports from China on terrorist events have been limited and most events since 1997 have been attributed to separatist attacks by Uighurs who continue to wage a campaign of violence. The Uighurs are a Chinese-Muslim ethnic minority group, and concentrated in the Xinjiang autonomous region in far western China. In February 1997, Uighur separatists conducted a series of bus bombings in Urumqi, which killed nine persons and wounded seventy-four. Earlier Uighur rioting in the city of Yining resulted in as many as 200 deaths. Uighur exiles in Turkey claimed responsibility for a small pipe bomb that exploded on a bus in Beijing, killing three persons and injuring eight. In another incident, Uighur separatists were blamed for killing five persons, including two policemen. The Chinese government quickly executed several individuals who were involved in both the rioting and the bombings. Beijing claims that support for the Uighurs is coming from neighboring Muslim countries, an accusation that has been strongly denied.

The government has tightly controlled the practice of Islam, and official repression in the **Xinjiang Uighur Autonomous Region (XUAR)** targeted at Uighur Muslims tightened in some areas. Regulations restricting Muslims' religious activity, teaching, and places of worship continued to be implemented forcefully in the XUAR. The government continued to repress Uighur Muslims, sometimes citing counterterrorism as the basis for taking action that was repressive. Chinese authorities detained and arrested persons engaged in unauthorized religious activities. The government reportedly continued to limit access to mosques, to detain citizens for possession of unauthorized religious texts, imprison citizens for religious activities determined to be "extremist," and force Muslims who were fasting, to eat during Ramadan, and confiscating Muslims' passports in an effort to strengthen control over Muslim pilgrimages. In addition, the Uighur government maintained the most severe legal restrictions in China on children's right to practice religion. In recent years, Uighur authorities detained and arrested persons engaged in unauthorized religious activities and charged them with a range of offenses, including state security crimes. Xinjiang authorities often charged religious believers with committing the "three evils," . . . terrorism, separatism, and extremism. Uighur authorities prohibited women, children, Chinese Communist Party (CCP) members, and government workers from entering mosques.[3]

The East Turkestan Islamic Movement (ETIM)

The Uighurs are an ethnic minority group of approximately 8 million. Their ethnicity, language, and culture are more similar to the Turkic peoples of neighboring Central Asian republics. Although the ETIM seeks to establish an independent Islamic regime, the majority of Uighurs are Sunni and do not support an Islamic state. ETIM is a small but extreme group founded by the Uighurs, whose mandate is an independent state called "East Turkestan." From the Chinese government perspective, it is quite convenient to have this group operating here as it is close to the center of Islamic extremism in Afghanistan and Pakistan, and allows the Chinese to claim that they are fighting the "War on Terror" in their own backyard. This allows them to put pressure on the U.S. Administration to "ignore" Chinese human rights issues. In 2002, the U.S. State Department deported two ETIM members to China from Kyrgyzstan for allegedly plotting attacks on the U.S. embassy in the Kyrgyz capital of Bishkek, as well as other U.S. interests abroad.[4]

The ETIM is a separatist group that has been operating since the mid 1990's, and with the approach of the Summer Olympic Games in 2008 the Chinese were keen to curtail any terrorist activities. In January 2007 the government announced that it had conducted raids on a suspected ETIM training base in the Pamir Mountains in Xinjiang Province, an area of rugged mountains bordering Afghanistan and Tajikistan. China claims that ETIM members were being trained, funded and supported at the base by al Qaeda.

President George W. Bush met with The President of China in October 2001 during the President's visit to Shanghai. During an exchange of views and mutual support on matters confronting the global threat of terrorism George Bush stated " . . . the government of China responded immediately to the attacks of September 11th. There was no hesitation, there was no doubt that they would stand with the United States and our people during this terrible time. There is a firm commitment by this government to cooperate in intelligence matters, to help interdict financing of terrorist organizations. President Jiang and the government stand side by side with the American people as we fight this evil force."[5] The meeting between the two heads of state in October 2001 signalled that China would make the most of controlling those groups that were considered subversive and internal enemies of the state. On January 21, 2002, the Information Office of the State Council (China's cabinet) issued a report arguing that terrorist forces from Xinjiang "jeopardized . . . social stability in China, and even threatened the security and stability of related countries and regions." The report cited four waves of terrorism during which Uighur activists were allegedly responsible for explosions, assassinations, attacks on police and government institutions, and poison and arson attacks both inside China and abroad. From 1990 to 2001, the combined efforts resulted in over 200 incidents, 162 deaths, and more than 440 injuries. During those years, Xinjiang police reportedly broke up 487 terrorist groups and identified 253 major violent terrorist crimes. The most serious threat purportedly came from organizations operating from neighboring countries, such as Afghanistan and Uzbekistan, but the report also alleged that other groups, operating from bases in Turkey, Germany, and the United States also sponsored terrorist activities.

Much of the State Council's report and a subsequent one in September 2002 focused on the East Turkistan Islamic Movement (ETIM), dozens of whose members allegedly trained in Afghanistan.[6]

Falun Gong

While there has been limited reporting on terrorism in China, members of the "Falun Gongs" spiritual group have created cracks in the tight controls of mainland China's aging leadership. The government's anti-Falun Gong propaganda . . . a new phase in the battle between this group and the government could possibly pose a bigger threat to the Communist Party, if that country's rate of urban unemployed were to rise up in support of the **Falun Gong**. The Falun Gong has hacked into Chinese government television broadcasts in Yantai, Shandong Province, and briefly aired a message saying, "Falun Gong is good." The incident was one of a string of broadcast station hackings that hit six cities in six months, primarily in the country's northeastern "rust belt," where unemployment and labor unrest are growing. The group was trying to counter the government's massive anti-Falun Gong propaganda campaign, which centers on the January 2001 self-immolation attempt by a group of Falun Gong followers in which two had died. These new tactics revealed the Falun Gong's technological savvy, and may even have pointed to a shift in focus. Since most of the Falun Gong broadcasts were focused on China's northeast, the government fears groundwork may be underway for a new showdown with the group, one that could draw on the urban unemployed. By hacking into state television, taking its case directly to the Chinese people, the Falun Gong is also confronting China's central leadership, a strategy that has thus far used peaceful demonstrations, appeals for dialogue, and attention from foreign media, to try to convince Beijing to lift its ban of the movement. The government's inability to crush the group has only reinforced Beijing's perception that the Falun Gong is a serious threat to its authority. Although the group could simply have gone underground after the government outlawed it in 1999, it chose to fight for its rights, which has led it down the path toward confrontation.

The Falun Gong first emerged as a semi-religious exercise group in the early 1990s, and grew rapidly, crossing all socioeconomic classes, and seemed to be filling a spiritual void in China at a time of rapid change. In April 1999, after a run-in with a local government, the Falun Gong then confronted Beijing directly . . . in perhaps one of the most impressive displays of civil action in China since the 1989 incident in Tiananmen Square, when more than 10,000 followers and students, converged along the street outside the government compound in Beijing, in a daylong silent vigil.

This Gandhi-inspired peaceful demonstration, which faded quietly into the night, unfortunately had precisely the exact opposite effect on the Chinese Government. Rather than persuading China's leaders to legitimize the Falun Gong, it sparked confusion among the country's elite. The protest showed the Falun Gong's very well-developed command and communications structure could be massive and pervasive across Chinese society. After a brief respite, Beijing then banned the group, and began a massive crackdown . . . rounding up and detaining thousands of the Falun Gong's members. The Falun Gong quickly began to appeal for international help. It turned to foreign supporters and drew international media attention at a time when China was petitioning for entry into the World Trade Organization (WTO), and bidding seriously to host the 2008 Summer Olympic Games (which it won). Falun Gong then began appearing in Tiananmen Square in peaceful protest. The heavy-handed crackdown by Chinese security forces that followed was captured on foreign media and broadcast worldwide.

In January 2001, the group's strategy fell apart after a group of alleged Falun Gong practitioners arrived in Tiananmen Square and set themselves on fire! Whether these were simply overzealous members of the Falun Gong, or a group of people misled by government infiltrators to take extreme measures, the self-immolation proved a propaganda coup for the Chinese Government.

Whereas previous government claims that the Falun Gong was evil and dangerous were more often brushed aside by many Chinese who felt Beijing was overreacting, the pictures of half-burnt young girls on national television gave credence to the government's argument. Once again, the Falun Gong altered its strategy. Foreigners, rather than Chinese followers in Tiananmen Square, increasingly carried out protests. Also, wherever the Chinese leaders traveled in Europe or Asia, supporters of the Falun Gong were also there. In January 2002, the Falun Gong began a new tactic of pirate attacks on government television. The first incident took place on January 1 in Chongqing, Sichuan Province, and was followed later on February 16 in Anshan, Liaoning. In Anshan, three Falun Gong activists tapped into the local cable line but were caught in the process, and security forces shot at least one.

On March 5, Falun Gong activists managed to hack into eight channels in Changchun, Jilin Province, the hometown of Falun Gong Founder, Li Hongxi. They broadcast two twenty-minute films contradicting the self-immolation story and extolling the virtues of the Falun Gong. On April 21, they struck in Harbin, Heilongjiang Province, reportedly airing pro-Falun Gong material for more than an hour.

Two recent cases, in Laiyang and Yantai, both in Shandong Province, were shorter broadcasts, simply relaying the message that "Falun Gong is good." But, in these cases, rather than hacking into cable lines, the Falun Gong managed to hijack the government satellite broadcasts, according to Chinese security officials, cited by the *South China Morning Post*, something quite a bit more sophisticated than splicing a VCR into cable lines.

The most recent Falun Gong activities have three key characteristics: First, they all suggest that what appeared to be a headless organism does have a centralized planning and organization structure. Second, the attacks indicate sophisticated technological savvy, particularly if the group managed to pirate into the state's satellite system. The similarity of the attacks and their dispersal also suggest there is an active training network inside the Falun Gong. Finally, the TV hijackings primarily took place in China's northeast rust belt. Heilongjiang, Jilin, and Liaoning Provinces have been the sites of active labor protests for months, and large-scale demonstrations have rocked Daqing and Liaoyang, and broken out in Fushun and Anshan. Although this could be a coincidence, the area is the traditional support base of the Falun Gong; it also could be an attempt to bridge the gap between the group and the large pool of unemployed former state workers there.

There appears now to be a realization among the Falun Gong leadership that the Chinese government will not, and perhaps cannot, change its position on the group now, particularly after a three-year nationwide campaign denouncing it as an evil cult and a socially destabilizing element. There is no way to regain the rights to practice Falun Gong through persuasion or dialogue with the current regime.

The following is a brief chronology of the reported manner in which China treated a Falun Gong practitioner. A brief chronology of Ms. Gao's suffering under the Chinese government's persecution:

- July–December, 1999: Arrested five times in Shenyang and Beijing for petitioning the government to stop persecuting Falun Gong. Suffered beating and force-feeding in jails.
- February 2000–January 2001: Arrested and detained in Masanjia Labor Camp. Suffered various torture.
- June 20–July 7, 2003: Arrested and detained in Shenyang Detention Center. Suffered electric baton shock, beating, and forced-feeding.
- July 8, 2003: Sentenced to three years of forced labor in Longshan Labor Camp. Suffered various torture.
- May 7, 2004: Handcuffed to a steel pipe and shocked on the face by two policemen with three electric batons for seven hours. Face was disfigured.
- July 7, 2004: Ms. Gao's photos published on a Falun Gong Web site (http://www.minghui.ca/).
- May 8–October 4, 2004: In police custody at a hospital.
- October 5, 2004: Escaped police custody.
- March 6, 2005: Rearrested.
- June 6, 2005: Sent to a hospital's emergency room.
- June 12, 2005: Parents informed to come to the hospital.
- June 16, 2005: Died in the hospital.[7]

HONG KONG

Hong Kong was returned to its former status as a province of China on July 1, 1997. High-flying Hong Kong businesspersons and others fled from the island in droves when this move was first announced several years ago. Many are now returning back to be, "where the action is," in Asia. In a joint declaration, China promised to respect Hong Kong's existing social and economic systems and

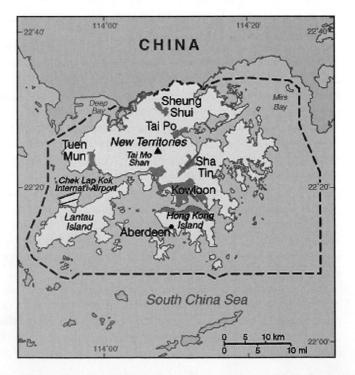

FIGURE 12-2   Map of Hong Kong (Central Intelligence Agency, *The World Factbook*, 2008).

lifestyle. Hong Kong borders the South China Sea and mainland China, about six times the size of Washington DC, and is scattered over more than 200 islands. The six and a half-million people are an unbalanced ethnic mix of 95 percent Chinese and 5 percent other. They practice religion in an eclectic mix of 90 percent local religions and 10 percent Christians.

Hong Kong has long been the major and most dynamic business and financial center of mainland Asia, and a bustling free market with few tariffs or nontariff barriers. Natural resources are severely limited, and food and raw materials must be imported. Manufacturing and construction account for about 18 percent of GDP. Goods and services exports account for about 50 percent of GDP. Real GDP growth averaged a remarkable 8 percent. A shortage of labor continues to place upward pressure on prices and the cost of living. Prospects remain bright, but only as long as major trading partners continue to be reasonably prosperous . . . and they probably will, as long as investors feel China will continue to support free market practices. While terrorism has been virtually nonexistent there, Hong Kong is a major hub for the Southeast Asian heroin trade and is involved with transshipment of drugs and money laundering. There is also an increasing problem with the indigenous population's amphetamine abuse.

TAIWAN (REPUBLIC OF CHINA)

The Republic of China (usually referred to as Taiwan since the 1970s) on the island of Taiwan has experienced at least twenty terrorist events since 1979, including thirteen aircraft hijackings and five bombings. Factors responsible for the relatively small burden of terrorism on Taiwan in the past include tight military control over political dissent until 1987, a warming relationship with the People's Republic of China in the 1990s, political inclusion of major internal cultural groups, geographic isolation, and a lack of other significant international enemies.

The Republic of China borders the East China Sea, the Philippine Sea, the South China Sea, and the Taiwan Strait. It is north of the Philippines, on a large island off the southeastern coast of China, and is slightly smaller than Maryland and Delaware combined. The population of approximately 21,699,776 is composed of Taiwanese (84 percent), mainland Chinese (14 percent), and aborigine (2 percent). Religion in Taiwan is based on a mixture of Buddhist, Confucian, and Taoist (93 percent), Christian (4.5 percent), and "other" (2.5 percent). Political pressure groups include the Taiwan independence movement and various environmental groups. Debate on Taiwan independence has now become acceptable within the mainstream of domestic politics in Taiwan. Political liberalization and the increased representation of the opposition **Democratic Progressive Party (DPP)** in Taiwan's legislature have opened public debate on the island's national identity. Advocates of Taiwan independence, including those within the DPP, oppose the ruling party's long-time traditional stand that the island will still eventually be reunited with mainland China. Goals of the Taiwan Independence Movement include establishing a sovereign nation on Taiwan and entering the United Nations. Other organizations supporting Taiwan independence include the World United Formosans for Independence and Organization for a Taiwan Nation.

Taiwan has a dynamic and capitalist economy, with considerable guidance of investment and foreign trade by government officials, and partial government ownership of some large banks and industrial firms. Real growth in GDP has averaged about 9 percent a year over the past three decades. Export growth has been even faster and has provided the impetus for industrialization. Inflation and unemployment are very low. Agriculture contributes less than 4 percent to GDP, down from 35 percent back in 1952. Traditional labor-intensive industries are steadily being moved off shore and replaced with more capital and technology-intensive industries. Taiwan has become an active major investor in China, Thailand, Indonesia, the Philippines, Malaysia, and Vietnam. Tightening of labor markets has led to an influx of foreign workers, both legal and illegal.

Taiwan is involved in long-standing and complex territorial disputes with China, Malaysia, the Philippines, Vietnam, and (possibly) Brunei over the Spratly Islands. The Parcel Islands are occupied by China, but are claimed by both Vietnam and Taiwan. China and Taiwan also dispute claims over the Japanese-administered Senkaku-shoto (Senkaku Islands/Diaoyu Tai). The island nation is tightly controlled, and there is very little terrorism of any great scope. Taiwan is considered an important heroin transit point and there seems to be a fast-growing problem with domestic consumption of methamphetamine and heroin.

JAPAN

The ancient kingdom of Japan is a constitutional monarchy that became an independent state in 660 B.C., through the efforts of Emperor Jimmu. It is located in Eastern Asia and is an island chain between the North Pacific Ocean and the Sea of Japan, east of the Korean Peninsula. Japan is slightly smaller than California and has a population of over one and a quarter million. The appetite of the Japanese for fish is contributing to the depletion of this resource, in Asia and elsewhere. Ethnic diversity is literally unknown in Japan, where 99.4 percent of their large population is Japanese, and only 0.6 percent is, other (mostly Korean). Religions are also similarly broken out: Those who observe both Shintoism and Buddhism comprise 84 percent, and other comprise 16 percent.

Japanese government–industry cooperation, a strong work ethic, their mastery of high technology, and a comparatively small defense allocation (roughly 1 percent of GDP), have helped Japan's economy advance with extraordinary rapidity to become one of the most powerful in the world. One notable characteristic of the Japanese economy is the working together of manufacturers, suppliers, and distributors in closely knit groups called **keiretsu**. A second basic feature has been the guarantee of lifetime employment for a substantially large portion of the urban labor force. But, sad to say, this guarantee has been slowly eroded. Industry, the most important sector of their economy, is heavily dependent on importing raw materials and fuels. The much smaller agricultural sector is highly subsidized and protected, with crop yields that rank among the very highest in the world. Usually self-sufficient in rice, Japan must import about 50 percent of their requirements of other grain and fodder crops. Japan maintains one of the world's largest fishing fleets and accounts for nearly 15 percent of the global catch.

FIGURE 12-3   Map of Japan (Central Intelligence Agency, *The World Factbook*, 2008).

For over three decades, overall real economic growth had been spectacular: a 10-percent average in the 1960s, a 5-percent average in the 1970s, and a 4-percent average in the 1980s. Growth slowed considerably from 1992 to 1995 largely because of the aftereffects of overinvestment during the late 1980s, and contradictory domestic policies intended to wring speculative excesses from the stock and real estate markets. Growth picked up again in 1996, largely a clear reflection of fiscal and monetary policies as well as low rates of inflation and social disorder. As a result of the expansionary fiscal policies and declining tax revenues due to the recession, Japan currently has one of the largest budget deficits, as a percent of GDP, among all the industrialized countries. The crowding of habitable land area and the aging of the population are another two major, long-term problems.

Aum Shinrikyo was the group responsible for the Sarin gas attacks on the Tokyo subway system in 1995. The trial and after-effects of the group's leader have created an ongoing discussion as just how to define "terrorism" in Japan. A government panel decided not to invoke the Anti-Subversive Law, and ban Aum Shinrikyo, concluding that the group still posed no future threat, although the group continued to operate and to recruit new members. The U.S. Secretary of State designated Aum Shinrikyo as a, "Foreign Terrorist Organization," pursuant to the **"Antiterrorism and Effective Death Penalty Act of 1996."** In addition to the murder charges stemming from the March 1995 Sarin nerve gas attack on the Tokyo subway system, Shoko Asahara faced sixteen other charges, ranging from, kidnapping and murder, to illegal production of drugs and weapons. Nine former Aum Shinrikyo members pled guilty or received sentences from twenty-two months to seventeen years for crimes they committed on behalf of Asahara. One Aum Shinrikyo member was acquitted of forcibly confining other cult members. Shoko Asahara claimed to be a reincarnation of the Hindu god Shiva, and promised to lead his followers to salvation when impending Armageddon arrived. He was not arrested until 1995 on Mount Fuji and his case came before the courts the following year and he was eventually convicted and sentenced to death in 2004. His final appeal was dismissed in 2006 and he waits execution.

Despite the legal proceedings against Aum Shinrikyo, Asahara and other members, of what had remained of Aum following the 1996 arrests, continued to exist, operate, and even recruit new members in Japan. The government panel ruled that Aum Shinrikyo posed no future threat to Japanese society because it was financially bankrupt and most of its followers that were wanted by the police had been arrested.

Several members of the **Japanese Red Army (JRA)** terrorist organization were arrested in 1997. Five members were convicted in Lebanon on various charges related to forgery and even illegal residency, and sentenced to three years in prison. Another member, Jun Nishikawa, was captured in Bolivia and deported to Japan, where he was indicted for his role in the 1977 hijacking of a Japanese Airlines flight. Four of the five JRA members arrested remain in custody in Lebanon The Japanese government is seeking extradition of the five to Tokyo to face terrorism and other serious charges.

Tsutomu Shirosaki was captured in 1996 and brought to the United States to stand trial for the offenses arising from a rocket attack against the U.S. Embassy in Jakarta, Indonesia, in 1986. He was convicted in Washington DC, of assault with the intent to kill, attempted first-degree murder of internationally protected persons, and attempted destruction of buildings and property in the special maritime and territorial jurisdiction of the United States. He was also convicted of committing a violent attack on the official premises of internationally protected persons. In February 1998, he was sentenced to thirty years in prison. Seven hardcore JRA members remain at large. The battle against Aum Shinrikyo is a hard, uphill one. Thousands of young Japanese had attended Aum Shinrikyo meetings; some had paid up to thousands of yen for joining fees. The cult may also be active in Russia, where it is banned. It is possible that young people are still joining Aum Shinrikyo because all the factors that created Aum Shinrikyo's membership in the first place still exist. Japan remains a rigid society that stifles individualism, and Aum Shinrikyo exploits this, as it does the general sense of unease generated by Japan's stagnant economy.

It seems remarkable that Aum Shinrikyo's revival is based on selling exactly the same product as it did before. Armageddon remains as the cult's pivotal concept, "We are now living in an age when, 'evil of all kinds thrives'," Araki explains. "This evil will be shed in a huge 'catastrophic discharge' made manifest through wars and natural disasters, such as the Kosovo conflict, or a storm in Sydney in 1999 with hailstones the size of golf balls." Could Aum Shinrikyo ever again develop the potential to give this so-called catastrophe a nudge? In 1999, Japanese police had unearthed "Sarin precursor chemicals," hidden by Aum Shinrikyo in mountains north of Tokyo, then raising the question, "What else was the cult hiding?" A few months before that, a self-declared Aum Shinrikyo member threatened to release gas at eleven Moscow subway stations.

In its continuing crackdown, police have confiscated more than half a million leaflets. Aum Shinrikyo has never apologized or expressed remorse for its past actions. An apology is vital if the cult expects any chance of normal relationships with Japanese society, but the cult's six leaders have not come to the same conclusion. The Japanese authorities could have outlawed Aum Shinrikyo using a draconian 1952 law against subversive activities, but it decided that the sect did not pose an "immediate and obvious threat," to public safety. And, meanwhile, clumsy policing and political paralysis may continue to provide the conditions for Aum Shinrikyo to rise and thrive once more.

Taro Takimoto is one person dedicated to putting the brakes on Aum Shinrikyo's current new resurgence and growth. He runs a support network for more than 100 ex-Aum Shinrikyo cultists called the Canary Group, named after the canaries used by police as Sarin detectors during raids on the cult's compounds in 1995. Fifty of the group's members now have jobs or even college placements, says Takimoto, while the rest are still recovering from years of physical and mental abuse, "Only a handful have really gotten over it," he says. Takimoto himself narrowly escaped assassination in 1994 when a teenage Aum member injected Sarin into his car.[8]

UNITED RED ARMY OF JAPAN (URAJ)

This is the alternate name that was used by the "Japanese Red Army." The group was small and fanatical in nature and had direct links to the Palestine Liberation Organization in the 1970s as well as other west European terror groups. The group had grown out of the tough period of student unrest in the 1960s, adopting a violent Marxist ideology mixed-in with traditional Japanese militarism as the hallmark of **URAJ** movement. Their first actions were then the hijacking of a Japanese airliner and, more prominently, they were responsible for the Lod Airport massacre in Israel in 1972, when three of its members opened fire in the terminal building with automatic weapons killing twenty-seven people and injuring another sixty-nine. One of the three terrorists was Kozo Okamoto who was captured and later exchanged for Israeli soldiers held in Lebanon, his two accomplices were killed.[9]

NUCLEAR JAPAN

By some estimates, the country has enough weapons-grade plutonium from fast-breeder reactors to build as many as 6,000 nuclear weapons, and there is little doubt about Japan's technical ability to build such weapons. A nuclear program in Japan, then, is not limited by technology, as it may be in countries like Pakistan and North Korea, but by political will. And the resistance to changes in Japan's defensive posture is clearly fading fast.

An international outcry that followed comments by the former Vice Minister of Defense Shingo Nishimura in a 1999 interview, when he said, "If Japan armed itself with nuclear weapons it may be better off." The minister was then forced to resign, and the public outcry nearly broke apart the fledgling coalition between the ruling Liberal Democratic Party and Nishimura's Liberal Party. Other "provocative" statements by Japanese politicians have been similarly received. Japanese Defense Agency Chief Fukushiro Nukaga resigned in 1998, ostensibly over an agency procurement scandal. His statement that a preemptive strike on North Korean missile sites could be considered as "defense" under Japan's Constitution, but did little for his political longevity. Japanese politicians have suggested that Japan's constitution would be a form of U.S.-imposed pacifism that would force Japan to remain defenseless.

With the 1998 North Korean missile launch over Japan, and East Timor's referendum for independence from Indonesia a year later, Japan's military policy slowly began to evolve.

The 9-11 attacks and the U.S. global anti-terrorism campaign have accelerated this ever-growing evolutionary change.

The changing shape of Japan's military in the twenty-first century world now bears watching carefully. But, even more frightening, is the thought that fanatical groups like the Japanese Red Army, or the Aum Shinrikyo, or terrorists from rogue states may find ways to up the ante on their terrorism and get at the stockpiles of enriched plutonium to build a dirty bomb. The world continues to change in the wake of 9-11.

THE TWO KOREAS

The Democratic People's Republic of North Korea

Following World War II, Korea was split into two and its northern half had come under Soviet-sponsored Communist domination. North Korea tried to conquer the U.S.-backed Republic of South Korea in the Korean War (1950–1953), but failed. North Korea's President, Kim Il-sung, then adopted a policy of diplomatic and economic "self-reliance" as a check against excessive Soviet or Communist Chinese influences. Kim Il-sung set out to mold North Korea's political, economic, and military policies around his eventual objective of reunifying the two Koreas under his control.

Kim's son, the current ruler Kim Jong-Il, was officially designated as Kim's future successor in 1980, and assumed a growing political and managerial role until his father's death in 1994, when he assumed full power without opposition. After decades of sad economic mismanagement and resource misallocation, the North, since the mid-1990s, has relied heavily on international food aid to feed its population while continuing to expend resources to maintain an army of about 1 million. North Korea's long-range missile development and research into nuclear, chemical, and biological weapons,

FIGURE 12-4 Map of North Korea (Central Intelligence Agency, *The World Factbook*, 2008).

and massive conventional armed forces, are still a major concern to the international community. In 1994, North Korea signed an agreement with the United States to freeze and ultimately dismantle its existing plutonium-based nuclear program. The International Atomic Energy Agency (IAEA) was monitoring North Korea to assure its compliance with the agreement. North Korea later was found to be in violation of that agreement, when the world learned that it was pursuing a nuclear weapons program based on enriched uranium. In 2002, North Korea expelled the IAEA monitors and in 2003, declared its withdrawal from the International Nonproliferation Treaty. In mid-2003, Pyongyang announced it had now completed their reprocessing of spent nuclear fuel rods (to extract weapons-grade plutonium), and was now developing a "nuclear deterrent." Since August 2003, North Korea has participated in six-party talks with the United States, China, South Korea, Japan, and Russia to try to resolve the stalemate over its nuclear programs.

The Republic of South Korea

South Korea has experienced thirty suspected terrorism-related events since 1958, including attacks against South Korean citizens in foreign countries. The most common types of terrorism used have included bombings, shootings, hijackings, and kidnappings. Prior to 1990, North Korea was responsible for almost all terrorism-related events inside of South Korea, including multiple assassination attempts on its presidents, regular kidnappings of South Korean fisherman, and several high-profile bombings. Since 1990, most of the terrorist attacks against South Korean citizens have occurred abroad and have been related to the emerging worldwide pattern of terrorism by international terrorist organizations or deranged individuals. The September 11, 2001, World Trade Center and Pentagon attacks and the 2001 U.S. anthrax letter attacks prompted South Korea to organize a new national system of emergency response for terrorism-related events.

Korea was an independent kingdom under Chinese Suzerainty for most of the past millennium. Following its victory in the Russo–Japanese War in 1905, Japan occupied Korea; five years later it formally annexed the entire peninsula. After World War II, a Republic was then set up in the southern half of the Korean Peninsula while a Communist-style government was installed in the north.

FIGURE 12-5 Map of South Korea (Central Intelligence Agency, *The World Factbook*, 2008).

During the Korean War (1950–1953), U.S. and other UN forces intervened to defend South Korea from North Korean attacks that had been supported by the Chinese. An armistice was signed in 1953, splitting the peninsula along a demilitarized zone at about the 38th parallel. Thereafter, South Korea achieved rapid economic growth, with per-capita income rising to roughly "eighteen-times" the level of North Korea. In 1987, South Korean voters elected Roh Tae-woo to the Presidency, ending twenty-six years of military dictatorship. South Korea today is a fully functioning, modern democracy. In June 2000, a historic, first North–South summit took place between the South's President Kim Tae-chung and the North's leader Kim Jong-II.

The United States planned to withdraw one-third of its 37,000 troops from South Korea by the end of 2005, according to a South Korean government official. The withdrawal of more than 37,000 troops, the first pullback since 1992, included 3,600 American soldiers scheduled to deploy from South Korea to Iraq in summer 2005, stated Kim Sook, head of the North American Division at South Korea's Foreign Ministry, at a press briefing in Seoul. He said the South Korean government was informed of the plan. The American decision to cut troops in South Korea . . . the only major American military presence in the Asian mainland . . . caught South Koreans by surprise. President Roh Moo Hyun, speaking at an event honoring South Korea's war dead, promised to "properly nurture the South Korea-U.S. alliance." In an address for the opening of a new session of the National Assembly, he made no reference to the alliance.

The cutback appears to be part of a wider-planned rearrangement of American troops to be in the Pacific. In Tokyo, the newspaper *Asahi Shimbun* reported that the United States is sounding out Japan about moving some of the 14,000 U.S. Marines stationed in Okinawa to a Japanese base in Hokkaido. On a stopover in Okinawa in 2004, the U.S. Secretary of Defense, Donald H. Rumsfeld, endured a scolding from the local governor, who complained about the disproportionate burden of the American forces on his crowded island.

Separately, Australian radio reported that Mr. Rumsfeld and his Australian counterpart, Defense Minister Robert Hill, might sign an agreement to build a major military training center up in northern Australia, either in Queensland or in the Northern Territories. The joint training center was discussed at a meeting in Singapore between the two defense chiefs.

Australian radio reported that the United States would not pre-position equipment at the center, which would be used for joint air, land, and sea exercises. With Washington's concern growing about monitoring and patrolling international sea lanes in the region, the United States is already investing tens of millions of dollars in expanding Air Force and Navy facilities on Guam, an American island in the Western Pacific. According to the South Korean News Agency, Yonhap, South Korea wanted the troop reduction to be phased over ten years. Fifteen years ago, the United States agreed to move its headquarters, with about 7,000 soldiers, out of the Yongsan base in downtown Seoul.

But it was only in 2004, after years of anti-American demonstrations outside Yongsan that South Korea finally came up with an out-of-town site. Although South Korea originally agreed to pay for the move, some members of the new, liberal-dominated National Assembly are now objecting to the cost. In a retort, some American conservatives say that South Korea, now with the world's eleventh largest economy, can afford to defend itself against its impoverished northern neighbor.

"The South Korea lobby in Washington is dying," a conservative American lawyer, John E. Carbaugh, said, referring to the fact that there are no longer any Korean War veterans in the U.S. Congress. On the peninsula, Communist North Korea has 1.1 million soldiers, and South Korea has 690,000. The American contingent of 37,500 troops, about one-tenth the size of the U.S. forces at the peak of the Korean War, is largely symbolic. For years, some American soldiers served in border posts as "trip wires" . . . deployments designed to re-awaken American public opinion in the event of a repeat of North Korea's 1950 invasion of the south. Discarding the "trip wire" strategy, U.S. Secretary of Defense Rumsfeld announced that by 2006, all American troops would be shifted to areas south of the Han River, and out of artillery range of the North. The United States has promised to spend $11 billion over the next five years to upgrade its military firepower in Korea. But some South Korean conservatives complain that this is merely a repackaging of planned spending programs.[10]

THE PHILIPPINES

The Republic of the Philippines is situated in Southeastern Asia, on a long archipelago between the Philippine Sea, and the South China Sea. It is east of Vietnam and is slightly larger than the State of Arizona. The scattered population of more than 76 million has an ethnic mix of Christian Malay (91.5 percent), Muslim Malay (4 percent), Chinese (1.5 percent), and other (3 percent). The major religions are Roman Catholic (83 percent), Protestant (9 percent), Muslim (5 percent), Buddhist, and other (3 percent).

The Philippine economy is primarily a mixture of agriculture and light industry. It continued its fourth year of recovery in 1996, led by growth in exports and investments. Officials targeted 7.1 percent to 7.8 percent growth for 1997, after achieving an estimated 5.5 percent growth in 1996. The government is continuing its economic reforms to enable the Philippines to move closer to the development of the newly industrialized countries of East Asia. The strategy includes improving infrastructure, overhauling the tax system to bolster government revenues, and moving toward further deregulation and privatization of the economy.

In the Philippines, implementation of peace agreements with insurgent groups has reduced the fighting with government forces, but former members of these insurgent groups and members of Philippine terrorist organizations continued some attacks. Foreigners number among their victims. In 1998, the U.S. Secretary of State designated one of these terrorist organizations, the **Abu Sayyaf Group (ASG)**, as a foreign terrorist organization pursuant to the new Antiterrorism and Effective Death Penalty Act of 1996. In Indonesia, separatist violence, not targeted against foreigners but having the potential to claim foreigners as collateral victims, continues.

The Philippine Government began implementing terms of a peace agreement signed with the **Moro National Liberation Front (MNLF)**, in 1996, and continued efforts to negotiate a peace agreement with the **Moro Islamic Liberation Front (MILF)**. The government began the process of integrating former MNLF rebels into the Philippine military. A ceasefire with the MILF reduced the fighting that peaked in the first half of 1997, but the two sides failed to agree on a more comprehensive arrangement. The MILF and the smaller Abu Sayyaf Group continue to fight for a separate Islamic state in the southern Philippines.

Abu Sayyaf (ASG)

ASG is a relatively new group that became very active in the 1990s, and has aims at promoting an Islamic state along the Sulu Archipelago. It has become well known for its kidnappings, mainly of foreign tourists, usually for ransom, bombings, and extortion. ASG's trail of terror stretches back to its first bombing attack in 1995, when it carried out an attack on a small town in Mindanao Province. Its most prominent attacks came in 2000, when an armed group of ASG members had attacked an upscale resort complex in Malaysia and kidnapped twenty-one tourists. The following year, it continued its campaign of striking high-profile locations and targeting foreign tourists. In 2001, ASG again kidnapped more Westerners from a Philippines' resort complex and subsequently murdered several hostages, including an American citizen, when security

FIGURE 12-6 Map of Philippines (Central Intelligence Agency, *The World Factbook*, 2008).

forces attempted a rescue operation. A similar fate occurred during a rescue attempt of U.S. hostages in June 2002, which also resulted in the death of another U.S. citizen.

Continued attacks in 2004 included the bomb attack on a ferry in Manila Bay that killed 132 passengers and is believed to have been the work of a faction loyal to ASG. ASG was formed from a breakaway faction and in late 2004–2005, took on a somewhat Islamic character in its attacks. The group's successes were limited when the United States sent troops to the Philippines to train the army in counterinsurgency techniques. The military onslaught against the ASG reduced its numbers to around 450 by early 2005. However, like so many other insurgent terror groups, ASG managed in February 2005 to launch simultaneous bomb attacks in Manila, General Santos City, and Davao, killing 11 people and wounding more than 100. With the peace agreement between the government and the Islamist Moro Islamic Liberation Front gaining pace, it seems highly likely that the smaller ASG would want to create a level of instability and try to attract hard-line, dissident members of MILF who have little sympathy for the peace deal. The regional extremist group, **Jemaah Islamiyaah (JI)**, whose strongest ally until the 2003 peace deal was MILF, has possibly the most to lose in this probable outbreak of peace. JI yearns for an Islamic caliphate in the South Asia region and had maintained a presence in the ASG training camps. The Philippine government continued its strong support for international cooperation against terrorism and actively sought to build a multilateral approach to counterterrorism in some regional and other forums. The government cooperated in providing additional personnel to protect likely targets and to identify, investigate, and act against likely terrorists. The government quickly responded when a U.S. company experienced what appeared to be a **New People's Army (NPA)** attack on one of its subcontractors in Quezon, and officials at the cabinet level met with company executives to discuss what could be done to improve security.

The Moro Islamic Liberation Front rebels handed over an Italian priest, Luciano Benedetti, to Philippine government officials several hours after he had been kidnapped by MILF forces.

The guerrilla arm of the Communist Party of the Philippines (CPP) is an avowedly Maoist group formed in December 1969. Its aim is the overthrow of the government through protracted guerrilla warfare. It is the longest running Communist insurrection in the world and is still the most active conflict in the Philippines. Although primarily a rural group, the NPA has an active urban infrastructure to carry out terrorism and it uses city-based assassination squads called sparrow units. It derives most of its funding from contributions of supporters and so-called "revolutionary taxes" extorted from local businesses. NPA is in disarray because of a split in the CPP, a lack of money, and successful government

FIGURE 12-7   A police agent arranges bomb-making materials (C-4, clock, cell phones, and blasting caps) seized in a raid of an alleged terrorist group east of Manila in February 2007 (Canadian Press).

operations. With the U.S. military gone from the country, NPA has engaged in urban terrorism against the police, corrupt politicians, and drug traffickers. The NPA has an estimated strength of several thousand members who operate throughout the Philippines. It is unknown whether it receives any external aid. The CPP-NPA remains a designated terrorist organization by both the United States and Europe. In an interview between The Communist Party of the Philippines spokesman Ka Roger and Janes Terrorism and the Security Monitor, it was evident that the CPP had no intention of laying down arms or coming to any deal with the government and its posture is still to replace the existing government with a Leninist style peoples' revolutionary government. It views the current ruling system as semi-colonial, semi-feudal, and dominated by foreign capitalist countries. The CPP also accuses President Arroyo, of "fixing" the 2004 vote. Ka Roger also went on to explain how the CPP would set up a mass people's militia, reorganize the military, set up a pro-people program, complete the land reform, and nationalize strategic industries and fast track a national industrialization program. Over 40,000 people have died as a result of the Communist-inspired insurgency.[11]

The Philippines has had a long and complex dispute with China, Malaysia, Taiwan, Vietnam, and possibly Brunei over the Spratly Islands. It has also laid claim to the Malaysian state of Sabah. Philippine growers export locally produced marijuana and hashish to East Asia, the United States, and other Western markets and it serves as a transit point for heroin and crystal methamphetamine to Western countries.

Who is Abu Bakar Bashir?

An elderly Indonesian cleric, stately, if frail in appearance, Abu Bakar Bashir (also spelled Ba'asyir), hardly strikes the eye as one of the world's most fearsome men. His inflammatory rhetoric, however, has commanded widespread concern. Bashir was released from Indonesian prison on June 14, 2006, after serving out a twenty-five-month sentence. He was found guilty by Indonesian courts in 2003, of being part of an "evil conspiracy" to commit the 2002 Bali suicide bombings, though all charges directly linking him to the attacks were subsequently dropped.

If Bashir's involvement in coordinating the Bali bombing is debatable, as many experts have said, it is also somewhat beside the point. Indonesian officials say a striking number of the more than 200 Jemaah Islamiyaah (JI) militants arrested in the aftermath of the Bali attacks cited Bashir as their inspiration, the ideological general of their "holy war." Bashir has accordingly been labeled the "spiritual leader" of JI by a number of news sources.[12]

INDONESIA

Indonesia, the former Dutch East Indies, is situated in Southeastern Asia on an archipelago in between the Indian Ocean and the Pacific Ocean. It has a varied population of almost 210 million in a land area slightly less than three times the size of Texas. Independence from the Netherlands came in 1949 and the combined islands of Indonesia have the largest Muslim population in the world.

Indonesia enjoyed a decade and a half of peace in the 1950–1960 timeframe, but its political fortunes shifted significantly in 1965, following a leftist coup attempt against President Sukarno, the republic's first leader. Within days, the army executed the leaders of the coup, but its aftermath brought a wave of violence. Rightist gangs, encouraged by their military commanders, killed tens of thousands of alleged Communists. By 1966, an estimated 500,000 people had been killed in the violent unrest. The events of 1965 and 1966 left the then President Sukarno severely weakened. In 1966, he was forced to transfer key political and military powers to General Suharto, who led the military defeat of the coup. In 1967, the legislative assembly named Suharto acting president, removing Sukarno from power.

With the backing of the military, Suharto quickly proclaimed a "New Order" in the Indonesian politics, concentrating on policies of economic rehabilitation and development. Using advice from Western-educated economists, Indonesia grew steadily, transforming itself from an agricultural backwater to a highly diversified manufacturing and export-driven state. Per-capita income levels rose

FIGURE 12-8 Map of Indonesia (Central Intelligence Agency, *The World Factbook*, 2008).

from $70 in 1966 to $900 in 1996, while the proportion of the population living below the poverty line declined from 60 percent to an estimated 11 percent over roughly the same period. The government instituted further economic reforms in the early 1980s, liberalizing trade and finance and expanding foreign investment and deregulation. Trade and investment boomed as a result; Indonesia's economy grew more than 7 percent annually from 1985 to 1996.

Suharto, his family, and his friends benefited greatly from the economic expansion. Critics claim the president regularly used his position to provide subsidies, and regulatory relief, for those companies of his children and friends. Suharto's family controls an empire valued anywhere from $16 billion to $35 billion in industries ranging from hotels and transportation to banks and automobiles.

The country's economic prosperity, however, did little to affect the political freedom of all the average Indonesians. Beginning with the 1965 coup, Suharto's security forces jailed hundreds of activists for speaking out against the government; many were eventually tortured and died in prison.

In the mid-1970s, Suharto moved quickly to stop what he saw as a leftist move, to then force the colony of East Timor to be independent, after Portugal abandoned the territory. Fearing creation of a state that could destabilize surrounding provinces, Suharto sent in troops to crush that movement, and annexed East Timor. Thousands of people died during the fighting, or later starved to death.

The United States cut off some military assistance to Indonesia in response to a November 1991 shooting incident in East Timor, involving security forces and peaceful demonstrators. In 1996, government forces swept through East Timor again, this time after a series of guerrilla attacks on security personnel. The Government takeover of the Indonesian Democratic Party's East Timor headquarters, in July of that year, triggered serious rioting in Jakarta. Human rights officials say that 5 died and 149 were injured in the attack. Twenty-three other people were reported missing.

Despite the corruption and human rights abuses, Suharto continued to stay in power into 1998. His grip on power started deteriorating the year before, however, when Thailand announced the devaluation of the baht in July 1997. This move caused the value of Indonesia's currency, the rupiah, to drop as much as 80 percent at one point. Foreign investors fled and many companies that were adversely affected by the currency devaluation went bankrupt. Like other Asian countries, Indonesia's banks were hit especially hard; by January 1998, sixteen banks had their operations suspended. As the country negotiated with the International Monetary Fund over the terms of its $43 billion bailout package in early 1998, riots began to erupt over rising food prices, gradually intensifying despite violent police efforts to put them down.

The **People's Consultative Assembly**, a legislative body that was largely appointed by the president himself, reelected Suharto to a seventh term. Student protests broke out, amid calls for him to step down. In May, riots and looting turned violent as tens of thousands of students demonstrated in Jakarta and other parts of the country. Hundreds perished in clashes with security forces in Jakarta. In a show of resistance, students then began to occupy the country's Parliament grounds, demanding the president's resignation. On May 21, Suharto bowed to the pressure and resigned from his office, naming Vice President B.J. Habibie as his successor.

Within days, Habibie pledged to lift restrictions on political parties and hold open elections as part of a package of reform measures intended to liberalize life in Indonesia and revive political activity that had been stifled for more than four decades. The moves, however, did little to quell the unrest. Throughout the summer of 1998, student demonstrators continued to demand the resignation of President Habibie as well, claiming that the Government had done little or nothing to stem the country's economic crisis or spiraling high prices.

In November 1998, massive student-led protests for greater democracy in Jakarta turned violent after a harsh crackdown on demonstrators killed at least five students and two others. As rioting ensued, demonstrators burned shops across the city and set cars ablaze. At least sixteen were killed over a period of several days.[13]

To add to the mounting problems in this troubled country, 1,000 fires were burning at the end of February 1998 in the parched rainforests of East Kalimantan, the Indonesian part of the island of Borneo. It was only three months since monsoon rains finally put out the last set of devastating fires on the island. Those fires burned from July to November 1997, destroyed 15,000 square kilometers of forest, and covered a huge area of Indonesia, Malaysia, Singapore, and Brunei with thick choking smog. The pollution forced schools and airports to close and made thousands of people ill with breathing problems. Every one of these fires had been started deliberately. It was clearly a man-made disaster . . . but by whom, and why?

The United States welcomed the Indonesian government's newly established broad-based fact-finding team in 1999 to investigate the causes of the May riots and the rapes of ethnic Chinese women. In November, the team, which included representatives from the government, the Indonesian military (ABRI), the police, and nongovernment organizations, released its report. Despite the "reservations" of some members, and the fact that investigators, victims, witnesses, and family members faced anonymous death threats and other forms of intimidation, the fact-finding team issued a credible, balanced report under difficult circumstances.

The report determined there were three types of riots; (1) some were local and spontaneous, (2) some were aggravated by provocateurs, and (3) others were obviously deliberate, to include an involvement by elements of the military. The report called for further investigations and even had recommended that Lt. Gen. Prabowo and all others involved in cases of kidnappings of political activists be brought-up before a military court. The report also verified that eighty-five acts of violence targeted against women occurred during the riots, including rapes, tortures, sexual assaults, and sexual harassment, mostly being against ethnic Chinese.

To restore credibility and confidence, it was crucial that the Indonesian government implement the team's recommendations, including further investigation of military leaders and others alleged to be involved in fomenting or participating in the violence. It was further strongly urged that the Indonesian government take steps to prevent intimidation and threats of violence against investigators, witnesses, and their families and that those responsible for these acts should be held accountable.[14]

Portugal and Indonesia are now in a dispute over the sovereignty of Timor Timur (East Timor Province). The United Nations does not recognize Portugal's claim. Those two small islands are in ownership dispute with Malaysia. Indonesia continues to be an illicit producer of cannabis, largely for domestic use, but has a possible growing role as a transshipment point for Golden Triangle heroin. Separatist groups in East Timor apparently continued to target noncombatants and were involved in several bomb-making activities in 1997. In Irian Jaya in April 1997, an alleged attack by the separatist Free Papua Organization against a road surveying crew left two civilians dead. If Indonesia cannot get its economic situation straightened out, it is a powder keg for escalating violence and terrorism between the state and opposition groups.

Indonesia has more Muslims than any other region in the world. It is little surprise that Islamic extremism would find a base and sympathy here among some radical minorities. Islamic terrorism has been extensive throughout the region and is led primarily by an al Qaeda "proxy organization," Jemaah Islamiyaah (JI). This shadowy Islamist terrorist organization has developed economic and military assets through the use of cells (**fiahs**), operating throughout Southeast Asia. Guided by its objective of creating an Islamic state ruled by shari'a (Islamic law), JI wishes to create an Islamist theocracy (JI's conception of Dawlah Islamiyyah, or Islamic state) which would unify Muslims in Thailand, Malaysia, Indonesia, Brunei, and the southern Philippines. JI shares a common philosophy with, and has links to, the al Qaeda network, both before, and after, the attacks of September 11, 2001. The JI has emerged as the most extensive transnational radical Islamist group in Southeast Asia. Since its inception, the JI has been responsible for a series of bank robberies, hijackings, and the bombing of civilian targets.

It has been active for several years and became synonymous with attacks planned against not only Western interests, but also against Christian churches in Indonesia. The government of Singapore had discovered in 2001 that JI was planning to attack the British and U.S. embassies, as well as Australian interests in Singapore. The JI attack on the island of Bali in October 2002 is often referred to as "Indonesia's 9-11." The attack targeted European, American, and Australian tourists, resulting in over 200 deaths. The bomb attack against the Marriott Hotel chain in Jakarta in August 2003 is also likely the work of JI extremists.

AUSTRALIA

Six separate statements issued by bin Laden himself or his deputy Ayman al-Zawahiri specifically threatened Australia:

- On November 3, 2001, bin Laden said, "The Crusader Australian forces were on the Indonesia shores . . . they landed to separate East Timor, which is part of the Islamic world."
- In an interview released in mid-November 2001 concerning the war in Afghanistan, bin Laden said, "In this fighting between Islam and the Crusaders, we will now continue our Jihad. We will incite the nation for Jihad until we meet God and get his blessing. Any country that supports the Jews can only blame itself . . . what do Japan or Australia or Germany have to do with this war? They just support the infidels and the Crusaders."
- Bin Laden made further reference to Australia in a videotape released in the United Kingdom in May 2002 in which he said, "What has Australia in the extreme south got to do with the oppression of our brothers in Afghanistan and Palestine?"
- On November 12, 2002, bin Laden made a statement that gave much more prominence to Australia than any other non-U.S. Western country, and reaffirmed Australia to be a terrorist target: "We warned Australia before not to join in [the war], in Afghanistan, and [against] its despicable effort to separate East Timor. It ignored that warning until it woke up to the sounds of explosions in Bali. Its government falsely claimed that they were not targeted."
- On May 21, 2003, in an audiotape, Ayman al-Zawahiri said: "O Muslims, take matters firmly against the embassies of America, England, Australia, Norway and their interests, companies and employees."

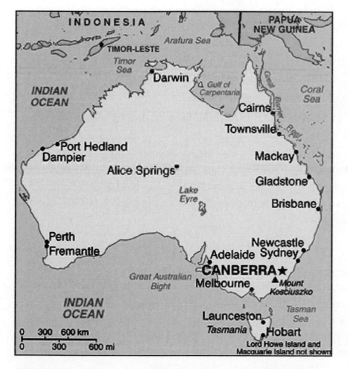

FIGURE 12-9 Map of Australia (Central Intelligence Agency, *The World Factbook*, 2008).

- On October 18, 2003, in an audio message addressed to the American people concerning the war in Iraq, bin Laden stated that, "We maintain our right to reply, at the appropriate time and place, to all the states that are taking part in this unjust war, particularly Britain, Spain, Australia, Poland, Japan and Italy."[15]

The Commonwealth of Australia is located on the Oceania continent, and is slightly smaller than the United States. It is the world's smallest continent, but its sixth-largest country. Its population (estimated at about 18,438,850) is concentrated along the eastern and southeastern coasts. The ethnic makeup is Caucasian (95 percent), Asian (4 percent), and Aboriginal (1 percent), and some other. Religious affiliations are Anglican (26.1 percent), Roman Catholic (26 percent), other Christians (24.3 percent), and the balance unknown. Australia became an independent member of the Commonwealth in 1901 and it has a prosperous, Western-style economy. Per-capita GDP is above the levels in many highly industrialized West European countries. Rich in natural resources, Australia is a major exporter of agricultural products, minerals, metals, and fossil fuels. Commodities account for about 60 percent of the value of total exports, so a downturn in world commodity prices can have a big impact on the Australian economy. The government is pushing for increased exports of manufactured goods, but competition in international markets continues to be severe.

In May 2004, an Australian citizen Jack Roche pleaded guilty to charges of conspiracy to commit offences against the Crimes (Internationally Protected Persons) Act 1976. Roche was sentenced to nine years' imprisonment. Roche was associated with Jemaah Islamiyaah in Australia, trained in Afghanistan, and met with and took direction from Hambali and other extremist identities, including Khalid Sheikh Mohammed. Roche videotaped the Israeli embassy in Canberra and the Israeli consulate in Sydney in June 2000 as a preliminary measure to support a possible future terrorist attack in Australia.

Australia is considered a safe country. Only a few terrorist acts have been carried out over the past sixty years:

1975—A letter bomb that originated in the Middle East injured a press secretary at the Queensland State Premier's office.

1978—A bomb explodes outside the Hilton Hotel in Sydney where the Commonwealth heads of government were staying.

1980—Turkish Consul General, Sarik Ariyak was assassinated in Sydney by two members of the "Justice Commando of the Armenian Genocide."

1990—Gasoline bomb attack on a Jewish College in Sydney.

1996—A premature explosion of a parcel bomb in a Melbourne mailroom was believed to be intended for a major pro-Yugoslav supporter.

2002—Jack Roche, a British-born convert to Islam, was charged with plotting bomb attacks on the Israeli embassy in Canberra and the Israeli consulate in Sydney. Roche claimed to have been al Qaeda-trained in Afghanistan. In May 2004, he pleaded guilty to charges of conspiracy to commit offenses against the Crimes (Internationally Protected Persons) Act 1976 and was sentenced to nine years' imprisonment.

INTERNATIONAL TERRORISM

Australia has been a staunch ally in the forefront of the War on Terror and is an outspoken supporter of both the United States and Great Britain. It has supported the war in Iraq with a contingent of Australian forces. Regionally, its proximity to Indonesia makes it a target for Islamic extremists. Australian nationals were targeted in the Bali attack, so the threat remains a serious one for Australia. Indications are that Australia must reckon on a sustained campaign over many years to diminish that threat. Regionally, terrorist groups like JI show themselves to be capable of adapting to the setbacks following the arrest and prosecution of most of those responsible for the Bali bombing.

JI and al Qaeda retain a potent capacity to inflict harm on Australian interests in Southeast Asia. The Australians cannot discount the possibility of a threat emerging from splinter groups inspired by the jihadist ideology of al Qaeda and JI. The very anti-Western nature of these groups will focus more likely on locations outside the country, where Australians travel for vacations. Areas such as Bali and Bangkok, Thailand, are havens for not only Western tourists, but also for Australians.

Summary

China continues to be the fastest growing economy as it embarks on a five-year program to spread the wealth more equitably among its poorer citizens throughout the country. While the Falun Gong is considered hostile in the minds and attitudes of the Chinese Political apparatus, China continues to react with extreme sanction against the movement by using physical methods to "reeducate" practitioners bordering on torture. Japan has seen limited terrorist activity; however, the release of Sarin gas on the Tokyo subway system by Aum Shinrikyo could be a forerunner for a chemical or biological attack on a similar target by al Qaeda-affiliated groups. Islamic extremism has surfaced in Australia and foreign groups have used the country as the launching pad for attacks and assassinations. The spread of Islamic extremism throughout Indonesia in the shape of Jemaah Islamiyaah will continue to pose a terrorist threat to mainly Western interests in those regions.

Web Sites

1. **International Crisis Group**—*http://www.crisisgroup. org/home/index.cfm?id=3630*
2. **Parliamentary Library of Australia**—*http://www.aph. gov.au/library/pubs/CIB/2001–02/02cib06.htm*
3. **South Asia Analysis Group**—*http://www. southasiaanalysis.org/%5Cpapers16% 5Cpaper1596.html*
4. **DEBKA**—*http://www.debka.com/section.php?cid=15*

Endnotes

1. U.S. Department of State, Secretary Albright, "Meeting the Far East Crisis: What Should Governments Do?" http://www.state.gov.
2. Dr. You Li—China's Post 9/11 terrorism Strategy. http://www.asianresearch.org/article/2047.htm.
3. Country Report on Human Rights Practices—2007— U.S. State Department. http://www.state.gov/g/drl/rls/ hrrpt/2007/100518.htm.
4. Council on Foreign Relations. http://www.cfr.org/ publication/9179/east_turkestan_islamic_movement_ etim.html_terrorist_organizat-ions.
5. U.S. China Stand Against Terrorism, Remarks by President Bush and President Jiang Zemin in Press Availability Western Suburb Guest House (Shanghai, People's Republic of China), White House Press Release October 19, 2001.
6. In the Name of Counter-Terrorism: Human Rights Abuses Worldwide—A Human Rights Watch Briefing Paper for the 59th Session of the United Nations Commission on Human Rights March 25, 2003. http://www.hrw.org/un/ chr59/counter-terrorism.
7. Falun Gong Human Rights Working Group. http:// www.flghrwg.net/index.php?option=content&task=vie w&Itemid=50&id=1272.
8. Andrew Marshall and David Kaplan. *The Cult at the End of the World: The Incredible Story of Aum* (London: Arrow Books, 1996).
9. George Rosie, Directory of International Terrorism, Paragon House London.
10. James Brooke. *The New York Times* (June 7, 2004).
11. Janes Terrorism and Security Monitor, October 2007.
12. Council on Foreign Relations. http://www.cfr.org/ publications/10219.
13. Tim Ito. Washingtonpost.com (October, 1998).
14. George Wehrfritz. *Newsweek* (April 13, 1998, pp. 24–30).
15. Transnational Terrorism the Threat to Australia— Australian Government Department of Foreign Affairs and Trade. http://www.dfat.gov.au/publications/terrorism/.

CHAPTER 13

Latin America and South America

Individually and collectively we will deny terrorist groups the capacity to operate in this hemisphere. This American family stands united.

DECLARATION BY THE ORGANIZATION OF AMERICAN STATES, SEPTEMBER 21, 2001

Learning Objective

The study and review of this chapter will enable you to

1. Discuss how death squads have been allowed to operate with impunity in Central America;
2. Describe the rise of the peasant revolt and its causes in Mexico;
3. Discuss why the Tri-Border area is strategically important for terrorist organizations;
4. Examine the history and development of FARC in Colombia.

Terms to Remember

Anti-Terrorism Assistance
  Program (ATA)
Cali cartel
Chiapas
Contra
GAULA
Morazanist Patriotic Front
  (FPM)
Monsignor Juan Gerardi
  Condera

Montoneros (Movimiento
  Peronista Montonero)
Movimiento Revolucionario
  Tupac Amaru (MRTA)
North American Free Trade
  Agreement (NAFTA)
Popular Revolutionary Army
  (EPR)
Rebel Armed Forces (FAR)

Revolutionary Armed Forces
  of Colombia (FARC)
Sandinistas
The Shining Path
United Self-Defense Forces of
  Colombia (AUC)
Zapatista National Liberation
  Army (ELZN)

February 1, 2005: Iscuande, Colombia—An attack by FARC on a naval base kills fifteen people and injures twenty-six.

June 25, 2007: Buenaventura, Colombia—A man and a three-year-old girl were killed when guerrillas detonated a bomb at a beach in Colombia's main port city. FARC detonated the bomb as a tractor moved through the beach area.

November, 2005: Colombia—FARC kidnapped sixty people, holding them hostage until the government decides to release hundreds of their comrades serving prison sentences.

OVERVIEW

Modern-day Latin America remains a region not easily understood. The term *Latin America* covers a wide variety of people and places. Geographically, Latin America includes the landmass extending from the Rio Grande border between Texas and Mexico to the southern tip of South America, plus some Caribbean islands. Latin America's total landmass is two and one-half times the size of the United States. Brazil alone is larger than the continental United States.

The physical features of this vast expanse present sharp differences: The Andean mountain range, which stretches the full length of South America, and has peaks as high as 20,000 feet; the dense, tropical forest of the Amazon basin; the arid desert plains of Northern Mexico; the fertile, deep grasslands of the Argentine pampas.

The people of Latin America contain elements and mixtures of three primary racial groups: native indigenous Indians, white Europeans, and Black Africans. Spanish is generally spoken everywhere, except for Brazil (Portuguese), the Andes (Quechua and other uniquely Indian languages), Guatemala (over twenty Indian languages), the Caribbean (French, English, and Dutch), and Mexico (scattered pockets of Indian languages). By early 2005, the total population of this vast area came to 365,384,570 compared with 295,267,054 million in the United States.[1] Latin American society displays startling contrasts between rich and poor, city and country, learned and illiterate, powerful lords of the hacienda and the deferential peasants, the wealthy entrepreneurs and desperate street urchins. Politically, Latin America includes twenty-six nations, large and small, whose recent experiences range from military dictatorships to electoral democracy. Economically, Latin America belongs to the "developing" world, having been beset upon, and battered by, historical and contemporary obstacles to rapid economic growth. Here, too, there is diversity . . . from the one-crop dependency of tiny Honduras to the industrial promise of dynamic countries such as Brazil, Chile, and Mexico.

Throughout their modern history, Latin Americans have sought, with greater or lesser zeal, to achieve political and economic independence from colonial, imperial, and neo-imperial powers with only one goal: wealth for the winners. Thus, it is a bitter irony that the name "Latin America" was coined by mid-nineteenth-century French, who thought that since their culture, like that of Spanish and Portuguese America, was "Latin" in context (i.e., Romance language-speaking), it was destined to assume leadership throughout the huge continent. As these observations suggest, Latin America resists easy categorization. It is a region rich in many paradoxes:

1. Latin America is both young and old. Beginning in 1492, its conquest by the Spanish and Portuguese created a totally new social order based on domination, hierarchy, and intermingling of European, African, and indigenous Indian elements. The European intrusion profoundly altered the Indian communities. Compared with the ancient civilizations of Africa and Asia, these Latin American societies are relatively young. On the other hand, most nations of Latin America obtained political independence from Spain and Portugal in the early nineteenth century, more than 100 years before successful anti-colonial movements in other Third-World countries. Thus, from the standpoint of nationhood, Latin America is actually relatively old.
2. Throughout its history, Latin America has been both tumultuous and stable. Its tradition of political violence has erupted in coups, assassinations, armed movements, military interventions, and (more rarely) social revolutions. Ideological encounters of liberalism, positivism, corporatism, anarchism, socialism, communism, fascism, and strong religious teachings of every doctrinal hue have sharpened the intensity of struggle. Despite the differing forms of political conflict, old social and economic structures have persisted.
3. Latin America has been independent and dependent, autonomous and subordinate. The achievement of nationhood by 1830 in all but parts of the Caribbean basin represented significant growth and achievement. Yet, this nationhood continued to be affected by new forms of colonization originating from Britain and France, and ultimately, the United States.

4. Latin America is both prosperous and poor. Ever since being conquered by the Europeans, the region has been described as a fabulous treasure house of natural resources: first, the lust for silver and gold and, today, the urge may be more likely for petroleum, gas, copper, iron ore, coffee, sugar, soybeans, or for expanded trade in general. But the image of endless wealth lingers. In startling contrast, there is also the picture of great poverty: peasants without tools, workers without jobs, children without food, and mothers without hope.

To understand Latin American history and its many experiences with terrorism, political violence, and insurgency requires a flexible, broad-based approach. This chapter draws on the works of numerous scholars, presents authors' own opinions and interpretations, and their present alternative viewpoints.

LATIN AMERICAN TERRORISM

The terrorism that has occurred in Central and South American countries tends to be significantly different than the terrorism that has taken place in Western Europe, Asia, and the Middle East. Many of the Latin American countries have suffered from "state terrorism," including the use of death squads by extreme rightwing, authoritarian governments. A definition of "terrorism" worth considering once more is that put forward by the U.S. Department of Defense:

> The calculated use of violence or the threat of violence to inculcate fear intended to coerce or to intimidate governments or societies in the pursuit of goals that are generally political, religious, or ideological.

This definition was carefully crafted to distinguish between terrorism and other kinds of violence. The act of terrorism is defined independently of the cause that motivates it. People employ terrorist violence in the name of many causes. Insurgency, freedom-fighting, or just plain terrorism from both the left and the right continues unabated in Colombia. The tendency to label as terrorism any violent act of which we do not approve is erroneous. Terrorism is a specific kind of violence. It therefore begs the question: Is state involvement in systematic abuse of human rights and a government's tacit support of military junta and the use of unofficial death squads in many Central and South American countries terrorism? The so-called banana Republics, joked about in the early part of the twentieth century, became serious problems when they experienced revolutions and insurgencies in the 1970s and 1980s. The former Soviet Union and other Communist causes often backed efforts to destabilize the area and break the U.S. support of dictators.

This chapter will start with the most prominent terror movements in Central America, from their developmental stages after the Mexican Revolution of 1910, to the changes in typical terror tactics in South America. Drug dealings by Colombian, Mexican, and other drug cartels (referred to as narco-terrorism), and the oppressive regimes in Uruguay, El Salvador, Argentina, and other countries will be discussed. The horrors associated with Latin American death squads will be explored, along with the conditions, tactics, and distinctive characteristics of Latin American terrorism.

MEXICO

We start with the United States' closest neighbor to the south, Mexico. For several decades after its independence, this developing nation's political life was a prototype of chronic political instability. National governments came and went at gunpoint, threatening the new nation's territorial integrity. By the mid-nineteenth century, Mexico was heading toward a liberal government that would have greatly reduced the power of the church and the corresponding burden of its colonial legacy. Political liberalism, however, gave way to the dictatorship of Porfirio Diaz from 1876 to 1880 and

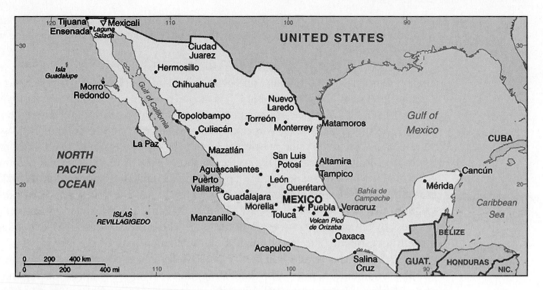

FIGURE 13-1 Map of Mexico (Central Intelligence Agency, *The World Factbook*, 2008).

again from 1884 to 1911 and, thus, was confronted by the Mexican Revolution . . . the first of the world's great twentieth-century revolutions. Out of that revolution, a stable political system arose that has been unmatched anywhere in Latin America. The Wars for Independence left Mexico in abject shambles, disorder, and decay. Actual fighting was widespread and protracted, leaving a severely disrupted economy. Gold and silver mines, once the pride of Spain's overseas Mexican empire, had fallen into disrepair. Insurgents and royalists had made it a point of killing technicians, while thousands of miners had gone off to war, leaving the mines to fall into ruins. Roads had been neglected as well, so the country lacked a workable system of transportation and/or strong communication capability. Travel by stagecoach was difficult and hazardous, and transport, often by pack saddle, was costly and slow. This was a serious obstacle to economic integration or progress. It was once estimated that over 30 percent of the entire adult male population in Mexico was unemployed, often angry, and usually well armed. They posed not only an economic problem, but a social and criminal threat as well. Some of these veterans did find work while others turned to crime (highway robbery being a particular favorite). Some stayed on in the military while others drifted into unofficial, quasi-military police units that provided support for local political bosses, generally known as *caudillos*, who were soon to play a dominant role in Mexico's political scene.

There were two institutional power bases in Mexico after independence . . . the Catholic Church and the Mexican military. The church had come through the independence wars with most of its wealth intact. It was estimated the Catholic Church may have once controlled nearly one-half of the nation's land and earned regular income from rents on its vast real estate holdings. Its investments were everywhere and it was, by far, the largest banking operation in all Mexico. The second power base was the military, which dominated national politics during the forty-year period from 1821 to 1860. Mexico had at least fifty separate presidencies, each lasting an average of less than one year! Army officers led thirty-five of these ill-starred regimes. The usual means of winning the presidential office was through a military coup to get rid of the sitting president. Looming through this period was the powerful figure of General Antonio Lopez de Santa Ana, who held the presidency on nine separate occasions and who installed figureheads at other times. Santa Ana was one of Mexico's most famous caudillos. These strongmen assembled their armed followers (miniature armies), who were primarily seeking wealth. Once they fought their way into national power, they participated in the further draining of national reserves, until the next reigning caudillo, armed with new followers, fought his way into power. The caudillos themselves did not bother too much with the job of governance. That was left up to a cadre of lawyers and professional advisors, many who described themselves as *licenciados*, meaning licensed, degreed, or in some way considered to be certified individuals.

General Porfirio Diaz assumed power after the death of Benito Juarez in 1872, who had himself overthrown Maximilian von Hapsburg of Austria (1863–1867). The Diaz Era (1876–1911) signaled progress, but at a stiff price. For the thirty years of his reign, Diaz proved himself to be a master of political intrigue. He began by creating a broad coalition of his military colleagues and followers. Building his army was one of his major goals and he forged ahead while maintaining control of a vast countryside, where the large majority of Mexicans lived. Diaz relied heavily on a force of guardias rurales, or rural police. In short, Diaz patiently built up the power of the federal government where it counted, in military and police power. A shrewd politician, Diaz avoided ever presenting himself as a corrupt dictator. He simply had the constitution amended, time and time again so that he could be re-elected to the presidency. The Mexican government made economic progress by building a vast network of railroads whose costs were partially supplemented by private foreign investment. The government took to seizing much of the railway land in the interest of nationalizing. These regular seizures of land also involved private homes, businesses, villages, and farming communities, many who were struggling economically under this regime.

Emiliano Zapata emerged as a rock-hard leader of former landowners and landless peasants in the southwestern state of Morelos. Zapata's groups were the country dwellers who had seen their traditional land rights taken away by the smooth-talking lawyers and a myriad of licenciados using the new laws of "liberal" inspiration. These Zapatistas (as they inevitably became known), saw the rebellion as a chance to restore justice. That meant regaining their lands. At the end of World War II, Mexico looked to industrialization as a way out of poverty. The man to lead the way was Miguel Aleman, the first civilian president since the Revolution. One of Aleman's first acts was to reorganize and rename the official political party, now called the Partido Revolucionario Institucional (PRI). Adding the word "institutional" signaled a turn toward pragmatism, which has also been described as leftist in its leanings. The party was made up of three sectors: peasant, worker, and popular. The format is still retained. PRI emerged as a dominant official party, different from any other in Latin America. This era signaled a start of what became Mexico's legacy of political dominance through a one-party system. In 1964, Mexico's other political party, known as Partido Autonomista Nacional (PAN, a right-wing-oriented party), began to win seats in the Mexican congress, although it was still overwhelmingly outweighed by PRI representation. Throughout history, the PRI has actually annulled mayoral and congressional elections won by PAN candidates in order to maintain its legacy.

In 1971, guerrillas appeared on the scene, calling for violent action against the PRI. They staged a series of bank robberies and kidnappings. The latter reached into the diplomatic corps, and their victims included the U.S. Consul General in Guadalajara and the daughter of the Belgian Ambassador. In 1974, the father-in-law of the president was seized and held for ransom by militant guerillas. In the state of Guerrero, an ex-school teacher, Lucio Cabanas, led a guerrilla army that began to strike at will. Cabanas had turned revolutionary soon after his 1962 election as General Secretary of the Federation of Socialist Peasant Students in Mexico. He eventually fled the city for the Guerrero mountain region where he led his Army of the Poor and Peasant's Brigade against Injustice. It kidnapped the official PRI candidate for governor and defied the army by direct attacks on isolated outposts. It took a 10,000-man army more than a year to hunt down and kill the rebels and their leader. Despite predictions on the left, Cabanas had no successor in Guerrero or elsewhere, as the guerilla threat soon faded. To avoid capture Cabanas committed suicide.

In the late 1960s, student-initiated protests in Mexico shook the Western world. The precipitating factor was Mexico's hosting of the summer Olympic Games in 1968. The Mexican government went all out to "sell" Mexico to the world. The Mexican Left, always strong among students in Mexico City, was upset that the government might succeed in this public relations venture. There began a test of wills. A secondary school clash in Mexico City in 1968 was met by brutal force from the riot police.

Protest spread to the national university in August, culminating in a strike. The government thought it was a "subversive conspiracy" bent on disrupting the Olympic Games. President Diaz Ordaz responded by sending army troops onto the campus, thereby violating its historic sanctuary status. The battle was quickly joined. Could the student left stop the Olympic Games? The tragic pattern of confrontation between students and troops continued. On October 2, 1968, a rally of students in the Mexico City section of Tlateloco drew an unusually heavy contingent of security forces. An order to disperse was not observed and the police and paramilitary forces moved in. Later they claimed to have taken sniper fire from surrounding buildings. They began shooting and the crowd was caught in a murderous crossfire, as hundreds fell dead and many more wounded. The massacre at Tlateloco sent a shudder throughout Mexico. There was no inquiry and no convincing explanation from the military or civilian authorities responsible for the slaughter. Many critics said the massacre proved the bankruptcy of the PRI monopoly on power. By the same token, the brutal show of force convinced everyone that mass challenges to authority would only bring more death and destruction. The effect was then very chilling.

On January 13, 2005, Special Prosecutor Ignacio Carillo announced that Mexico would be bringing charges of genocide against two dozen former officials for the 1968 leftist dissident student massacre at Mexico City's Tlatelolco Plaza, just days before the Olympic Games opened there. Ex-President Luis Echeverría, who was interior minister at the time, was under investigation for his role in the tragedy. In July 2004, the prosecutor sought to bring genocide charges against Echeverría and twelve others in a different case, a 1971 attack on students that left at least a dozen dead. The charges were dismissed based on the statute of limitations, and the Supreme Court is reviewing Carillo's appeal. He pledged to file charges in the Tlateloco case even if the Supreme Court has not ruled in the 1971 killings, though the High Court's decision is seen as crucial to establishing a framework for prosecuting similar cases.

In June 2006, eighty-four-year-old Echeverría was charged with genocide in connection with the massacre. He was placed under house arrest pending trial. The following month he was cleared of genocide charges, as the judge found that Echeverría could not be put on trial because the statute of limitations had expired.

President Vicente Fox, of the Partido de Accion Nacional (PAN), took office in 2000, ending seventy-one years of single-party rule by the PRI party. He has pledged to expose Mexico's repressive, secret past. From the 1960s to the 1980s, 100 or more Mexicans are reported to have died at the hands of government security forces in a so-called "dirty war against dissidents." Rights groups hailed Fox's appointment of Carillo in 2002 as an unprecedented step toward ending official impunity. But limited resources, court maneuvers, and resistance by police and military have hampered the prosecutor. Of eleven "dirty war arrest warrants", just three suspects have been arrested and face trial. Genocide, normally associated with slaughters like the Nazi killing of the Jews, is increasingly being used in human rights cases around the world. In Mexico, genocide can apply if victims were targeted as members of a group, such as a student movement.[2]

North American Free Trade Agreement (NAFTA)

Mexico's emergence from a colonial past has been conditioned by one factor that no other Latin American nation shares: a 2,000-mile border with the United States. That proximity has produced benefits and liabilities. Harvard-educated economist Carlos Salinas de Gortari, at the age of thirty-nine, was elected president of Mexico in 1988. He quickly moved toward an economy based more on free market principles than on state control, and toward better economic relations with the United States. He is, perhaps, best known for his role in negotiating the **North American Free Trade Agreement (NAFTA)**. Salinas was a técnico, a competent technocrat with little, or no, grassroots political experience. Technically, he was highly qualified to deal with the nation's problems. Politically, however, he had to define himself on the campaign trail. Salinas won with only 50.4 percent of the vote . . . his victory marred by allegations of fraud. As president, he worked to revive Mexico's economy by curbing inflation and reducing government regulations.

He became the major promoter of NAFTA, and in signing the accord (in 1992), reversed Mexico's historical resistance to foreign investment and to U.S. involvement in its affairs. Although Salinas's administration was praised for its economic reforms, it lost some of its luster when his brother, Raúl, was arrested in 1995 for the 1994 murder of a PRI official and was later (1996) accused of massive financial misappropriations. After Carlos Salinas responded by criticizing the Mexican government, he was pressured into de facto exile, only returning to Mexico in 2000. All the optimism resulting from the NAFTA accord promptly came under assault. On January 1, 1994 (the day after NAFTA came into effect), a guerilla movement in the poverty-stricken state of Chiapas rose up to denounce the free trade accord, the Salinista economic model, and the undemocratic character of the political regime.

Zapatista National Liberation Army (ELZN)

A major issue facing the Mexican government has been the land dispute surrounding the **Chiapas** region in southern Mexico. Mexico has experienced almost unprecedented economic growth in the past few decades, but there has been a clear failure to equitably distribute that wealth due to a lack of social reform. As a result, Mexico remains a country of "haves and have-nots." In addition to Chiapas, other regions have experienced guerrilla warfare or, as the Mexican government portrays it, terrorist movements. These are located in the regions of Oaxaca, Hidalgo, Vera Cruz, and Puebla. Immortalized from the days of the revolution, Emilio Zapata who had been conscripted into the army and served for seven years fought passionately for restoration of confiscated land; his Plan of Ayala, called for the seizure of all foreign owned land, all land taken from villages, confiscation of one-third of all land held by "friendly" hacendados and full confiscation of land owned by persons opposed to the Plan of Ayala. Zapata, who was killed in an ambush in 1919, is still lauded by the peasants of southern Mexico as their true hero. Using Zapata as a symbol of revolutionary righteousness, the Zapatista movement continues to wage an armed struggle for land rights in the Chiapas region. This group, called the Zapatista National Liberation Army (ELZN), appeared violently on the world scene in 1994, when it fomented an armed uprising against the Mexican government, to protest the distribution of land in the region. This movement better fits the definition of a guerrilla war group than a subversive terror organization. The group uses many different terror tactics to achieve notoriety and influence political aims.

The ELZN burst onto the national scene as a result of the political and economic alliance forged among Mexico, the United States, and Canada. In the latter two countries, the pros and cons of NAFTA were hotly debated. In Mexico, however, some went to war over it.

As we have seen in so many similar conflicts, the primary issue that influenced the uprising was land. Mexicans who farmed the land and eked out their living in that fashion had long been granted land for their families. This ended with NAFTA, when the Mexican government stopped its Land Distribution Program. Angry and well-armed men from Chiapas then came out of the hills and attacked the cities. The response from the Mexican government to this localized and popular uprising was to send in the military. Chiapas became a region that was patrolled and controlled by the Mexican army. Many of the problems facing Mexico revolved around the stumbling economy in 1994 and the very slow rate of recovery. The erosion of the ruling Institutional Revolutionary Party's (PRI) power has not helped and continues to contribute to the continuing unrest. In 1995, 30,000 Mexican soldiers, intent on the destruction of the ELZN guerrillas, invaded the region of Chiapas. The military exercise was an abject failure. ELZN simply disappeared into the hills of Chiapas, much like the Viet Cong did in Vietnam. The soldiers continued to surround Realidad, believed to be the center of Zapatista operations. To appeal for the farmers' rights to the land and a cessation of the violence, Bishop Samuel Louis Garcia acted as a mediator among the ELZN, the people of Chiapas, and the Mexican authorities. Chiapas is still a region of ongoing conflict and one of the main reasons for the fall of the long-ruling PRI in Mexico. The PRI lost both the presidency and the governorship in the province of Chiapas in 2000. Vincente Fox began his term with the intention of bringing an end to the ELZN rebellion in that region. The talks between Fox and the ELZN foundered and the zones controlled by the Zapatista rebels, although much quieter now, continue to remain off-limits to government control.[3]

The Zapatistas, relying on the classic tactic of surprise attacks, and blessed with considerable communications skills, initiated a public relations extravaganza. As the premier online guerilla group, it carefully disseminated many of its official documents and communiqués to a global audience on the Internet. While the group enjoyed some crucial successes, it has also been saddled with some considerable political and military limitations. This predicament stands in sharp contrast to the context of the group's famous hero, Emilo Zapata, who also marched to the rhythm of global politics and, subsequently, achieved broad revolutionary goals.

The Chiapas regional conflict does not garner much press, but the issues of land grabs and unchecked violent attacks continue. Massacres of farm workers are not uncommon and the police do little to prevent such actions.

Right-Wing Violence

An extreme right-wing movement called "Peace and Justice" has been carrying out disturbing attacks against the ELZN and its supporters. This group pledges its support to the Institutional Revolutionary Party and operates as a death squad in the Chiapas region. The viciousness of the right-wing attacks seems to have the support of the military, as well as the local police authorities, and this has led to beatings, murders, and the mass evacuation of entire villages. Active units, pledging support for the government and finding support from the police, appear to have the same goals seen in state-sponsored terrorism: "the systemic and purposeful creation, by a political regime, of fear by violent means, and/or by the threat of such violence." The purpose of the systematic exercise of such publicly visible violence is to maintain, legitimize, or strengthen the social and administrative control of the state. The activities of the Peace and Justice Group seem destined to be part of the fabric of Mexican society for this region. By generating significant fear, this right-wing group is able to influence the predominantly Mayan Indian population of Chiapas.

Popular Revolutionary Army (EPR)

The Popular Revolutionary Army (EPR) probably ranks second in strength to the Zapatista movement. With its base and origins in the southern states of Oaxaca and Guerrero, it gains support from the poverty-stricken villages of those regions. The topography of the regions . . . forested mountains and rugged terrain . . . makes an ideal home base for a guerrilla force. The EPR is a left-wing group, considered by the Mexicans to actually be several different movements operating under a single banner. EPR attacks have been sporadic and often without defining a clearly understood objective. Armed ambushes against federal police and military convoys are EPR's primary tactics. Their strength and size has yet to be precisely determined, but the group claims to have over 20,000 guerrillas operating in the southern states. Support for the group has also come from an unknown outside source that may well be responsible for arming it with modern, Russian-made weaponry. In response to the logistics and training it has received from Peru's Marxist-oriented Shining Path, the EPR set up a Mexican support committee for the popular war in Peru. Sustained operations have been difficult and it is questionable if the group has the ability to employ any effective tactics to disrupt or alter government policy. Some EPR attacks on the outskirts of Mexico City have occurred and communiqués have been issued to its members to target the "fat cat" capitalist businesses located there.

Other movements are surfacing in the poorer regions of Mexico as a result of the country's economic woes and the perception that the poor are getting poorer and the rich are getting richer. Such groups as the Revolutionary Army of Popular Insurgence and the Armed Front for the Liberation of the Marginalized People of Guerrero may be following the Zapatista uprising as a means for gaining concessions from the government. It is unclear whether the Mexican military can contain more than one guerrilla army at a time. Currently it is fully occupied with the Chiapas region and it would seem incapable of handling yet another battlefront.

Mexico in the Twenty-First Century

As Mexico entered the New Millennium, the growing discontent and trouble from insurgent groups, especially in the poorer regions of the country, cannot be discounted. Unrest has begun to reach the cities where the abuses of paramilitary police produce the same results as those the Zapatistas have seen in the rural areas. Mexico currently has neither an effective means to deal with violence and corruption within the ranks of its police force. Situated conveniently between Colombia and the U.S., Mexico is rife with a healthy drug trade, and associated with that comes the inevitable violence with cartels settling scores among them. Much of the killings tend to be within the cartels, but bribery of police and judiciary is also commonplace. New challenges confronting Mexico include the emergence of new and even more powerful drug cartels. These cartels operate at will and often target police and the judiciary with assassination. It has been said that the power of the drug cartels is so significant that it could possibly lead to situations of ungovernability. The most dangerous of these cartels were involved not so much in marijuana or heroin (traditional products of Mexico), but in transshipment of cocaine from Colombia. With an estimated over $7 billion in annual profits, these groups could easily spend as much as $500 million per year on bribery alone . . . more than twice the total budget of the Mexican Attorney General's Office! By the mid- to the late 1990s, Mexico had about a dozen drug organizations of truly international scope in Tijuana, Sinaloa, Ciudad Juarez, Guadalajara, and in the state of Tamaliupas (where traffickers operated a flourishing cocaine pipeline along the Gulf of Mexico). Drug cartels were implicated in a wave of violence that swept through Mexico, including the assassination of a Roman Catholic Cardinal in 1993. Former prosecutor, Eduardo Valle Espinosa, proclaimed that the country had fallen under the heel of drug traffickers and, like Colombia, could actually become a "narco-democracy."

Mexico elected Felipe Calderon to the office of President in December 2006—he took over the office from Vicente Fox also a conservative politician.

GUATEMALA

Guatemala has a long history of "strong man rule." After Rafael Carrera died in 1865, Justo Rufino Barrios established a twelve-year-long dictatorship (1873–1885), and Manuel Estrada Cabrera followed with a twenty-two-year, iron-fisted regime (1898–1920), the longest uninterrupted one-man rule in Central America. In 1931, General Jorge Ubico came to power and immediately launched a campaign to crush the fledgling, but growing, Communist Party.

Outside Communist influences in Guatemala during the last forty-five years have done much to further the violations of human rights of any individuals opposed to the many dictatorships and juntas that have managed to come to power. During the Cold War years, this influence was particularly strong. The United States assisted in the military overthrow of Guatemala's Communist regime in 1954, but the series of extreme right-wing military governments that followed did nothing to initiate reforms in the region. Rather, they focused on campaigns against Communist infiltration. With so much oppression in the country, the peasantry began to retaliate with such movements as the **Rebel Armed Forces (FAR)**, which began to take shape in the early 1960s, and was the precursor to the Guatemalan National Unity (URNG), established in 1982. The military had little success in repressing such movements and, with the arrival of URNG, embarked on a vicious campaign of state-sponsored terror.

The military was then unleashed and clandestine death squads were formed, while military and security police openly committed murder and torture. The resulting exodus from the region gradually gained international attention. Military leaders in Guatemala, however, were becoming desperate to remain in power, and to this end they increased the tactics of state-sponsored terror and murder against their own people. A "scorched earth" policy was employed in many instances and whole villages, as well as their lands and crops, were destroyed. Torture of suspected Communists was commonplace and the methods of torture were gruesome to the extreme, and usually fatal. Human rights in Guatemala, and past U.S. support for the regime, are issues to ponder, as are questions regarding the level of involvement of the U.S. government in such political murders, torture, and human rights abuses.

FIGURE 13-2 Map of Guatemala (Central Intelligence Agency, *The World Factbook*, 2008).

The Bishop of Guatemala—Monsignor Juan Gerardi Condera

Guatemala and its rebels signed a peace deal in 1996 but did little to eradicate the violence that permeated the country. In April 1998 Condera released his report "Guatemala Never Again" concerning human rights abuses and violations mainly perpetrated by the Guatemalan Army, and two days later was beaten to death as he returned to his home. Condera was the coordinator of the Archbishop's Human Rights Office (ODHA) and was the driving force behind the project for the Recovery of Historical Memory (REMHI), which had been created to shed light on the war's human rights violations. It seemed likely that his death was the work of a Guatemalan death squad. Death squads had killed with impunity during the thirty-six-year conflict.[4]

Impunity

The abuses and atrocities perpetrated by, and in the name of, the Guatemalan state had rested on a system of impunity, which can be defined as "freedom from accountability for criminal wrongdoing, or freedom from other legal sanctions." The impunity system in Guatemala was conducted by several simple mechanisms. First, the state denies any state-sponsored violence, and second, those who would have made claims of torture and rights abuse had simply "disappeared." Such disappearances made it difficult to bring any judicial action against Guatemala. In the sixteen years leading up to 1990, it is estimated that over 100,000 Guatemalans were killed, and possibly another 40,000 disappeared without a trace! The government has a very thin veneer of democracy, but its ability to control the powerful military is doubtful, especially when it comes to human rights abuses. The peace accord, finalized in 1996, brought an end to thirty-six years of internal fighting, and Guatemalans began returning to their shattered villages from neighboring countries. One such village that will likely never recover from atrocities committed by the military is the remote mountain hamlet of Plan de Sanchez where the army slaughtered more than 200 people, mostly Mayan women and children. On July 18, 1982, soldiers on anti-insurgency duties overran the hamlet, then raped and tortured villagers, herded them into a building and blew it up. No one has been prosecuted for the Plan de Sanchez massacre and few have faced justice for other rights abuses during the war. In 2005 the Inter-American Court of Human Rights in Costa Rica awarded 317 family members close to $25,000 each to be paid by the Guatemalan government.[5]

State-sponsored terrorism in Guatemala has fostered a populace with a shared set of experiences of systemic human rights violations. It is a populace not only cynical of the formal, institutional applications of justice, but one that has experienced extralegal "justice" in the fight for social control and social transformation of Guatemalan society.[6]

The Civil War

The first thorn in the side of successive oppressive military governments was the Rebel Armed Forces (FAR), which began limited guerrilla operations as far back as 1962. Over the years, the movement grew among the indigenous groups and expanded to include the Guerrilla Army of the Poor (EGP) in 1972 and the Organization of People in Arms (OPRA). With the merging of these three guerrilla movements, all with the same causes and complaints, the Guatemalan National Unity Group (URNG) was formed. The military conducted operations in which they destroyed villages and killed entire populations. In some of these operations, their actions, which were collectively called "pacification," typified those used in the Vietnam War. They employed a scorched earth policy. By targeting the civilian population in the Guatemalan countryside, the military assumed it would stop support of the guerrilla army.

Since the signing of the 1996 Peace Accords, there have been many attempts to bring justice to Guatemala. Amnesty International has been prominent in detailing human rights abuses believed to be perpetrated by the military and the death squads. This has led to attacks against prominent Catholic Church leaders in Guatemala to try to silence their criticism.

By the end of 1998, climatic changes in the region prompted the government to suspend parts of its Constitution. Following the distinctive impact of Hurricane Mitch, which decimated several Central American countries, including Guatemala, the government of Alvaro Arzu suspended two articles of the country's Constitution . . . Articles Six and Twenty-Six. This is believed to be a direct result of the looting and violence in the cities following the hurricane and the government's fear of a resurgence of terrorism.[7] Article Six protects Guatemalans from detention or imprisonment without cause or in the absence of a court order, while Article Twenty-Six guarantees the right of freedom of travel. Such severe measures threaten to return Guatemala to a repressive government. This volatile country should be watched carefully over the next decade.

HONDURAS

Honduras has undergone the least turmoil of all the Central American republics. Rivalries between the Liberal and Conservative parties persisted to the mid-twentieth century, popular agitation has been minimal, and power has rested in the hands of a triangular alliance—landowners, foreign investors (mainly United Fruit), and the military. Because of its economic and political weakness, Honduras has been especially vulnerable to outside influence. Honduran history reveals a fundamental fact of Central American political life—the emergence of the military as an autonomous caste and as a supreme arbitrator in national affairs. A career in the Honduran Armed Forces offers chances of upward mobility to middle-class young men. The aristocracy controls land, universities are restrictive, and there is hardly any industrial development. An ambitious person of middling origin has almost no alternative. As a result, recruits and cadets take immense pride in the honor and dignity of the military as an institution, and officers tend to look down on politicians and civilians.

FIGURE 13-3   Map of Honduras (Central Intelligence Agency, *The World Factbook*, 2008).

Strife with neighboring countries has played an important part in Honduran history. During the 1960s, for example, tensions with El Salvador mounted steadily. There have been long-standing, although minor, territorial disputes. El Salvador is a densely populated country; Honduras is just the opposite. Consequently, people from El Salvador looking for jobs in Honduras create resentment. A 1963 law prohibited companies from employing more than 10 percent foreigners (read Salvadorans), and a 1968 decree prevented Salvadorans from gaining title to Honduran land.

As has been evidenced throughout most of Central America, the paranoia that gripped the United States during the Cold War years of the 1960s was played out in its support of countries ripe for Communist influence. Honduras has benefited from decades of military support from the United States, and was involved, throughout the 1980s, in fighting the invading **Sandinistas** and in hunting down rebel Contra bases. Geography made it inevitable that Honduras would be drawn into the U.S.-sponsored War against the Sandinistas. The United States rapidly transformed Honduras into a launching pad for Contra attacks against neighboring Nicaragua. Thousands of regular U.S. military and National Guard units rotated duty in Honduras, inundating the economy with hundreds of millions of U.S. dollars. All of these activities just reinforced the power of the Honduran military.

Morazanist Patriotic Front (FPM)

The Morazanist Patriotic Front (FPM) is a small, extreme left-wing terror group that was violently opposed to U.S. intervention and support of the right-wing political government in Honduras. FPM targeted the United States for attacks. The group, small and not particularly well organized, is believed to have been supported by Cuba. It carried out bomb attacks on military buses carrying U.S. service personnel and, in 1989, claimed responsibility for just such an incident, in which three U.S. servicemen were wounded. Since then, FPM attacks have been sporadic and ineffectively executed.[8]

EL SALVADOR

As in Mexico, the natives of El Salvador have been engaged in an ongoing demand for land reform and rights, dating back nearly seventy years. Much of El Salvador's economy was based on its coffee production and export, which was controlled by a select and influential group of families. The first sign of protest dates back to the first quarter of the twentieth century and to a campaigner from the Central American Communist Party, Augustin Farabundo Marti. His goal, like that of the Chiapas of Mexico, was not the overthrow of the government, but the redistribution of wealth from the land on an equitable basis. By 1930, the country was under the military control of General Martinez, who sided with the society elite and coffee growers. Augustin Farabundo Marti Martinez was arrested in a military crackdown on his movement and was subsequently executed by a firing squad. The peasants were not organized in sufficient numbers to mount any sort of insurgent response. The military sought to purge the country of peasant "subversives" and went on a massive killing spree, which accounted for more than 30,000 deaths. In 1981 alone, there were 12,501 murders reported in El Salvador.

In the late 1960s and 1970s, El Salvador provided yet another example of extreme right-wing terror used as a governmental tool to eradicate opposition. Again, death squads became the norm and two specific groups were formed, one covert and the other overt, to protect wealthy landowners and to spread fear among the peasants. In 1968, the commander of the El Salvador National Guard[9] formed the ORDEN. This was an intelligence-gathering organization formed to amass information. It went beyond information gathering, however, and included kidnapping and murdering peasants. In attempting to analyze and define terrorism, some scholars believe that the actions of death squads are not terroristic in nature. However, the subversive actions of a terrorist or guerrilla organization spread fear, disorder, and uncertainty within the ruling government and

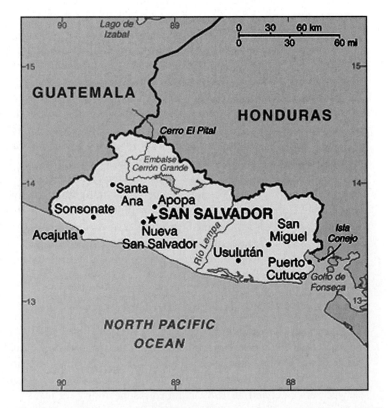

FIGURE 13-4 Map of El Salvador (Central Intelligence Agency, *The World Factbook*, 2008).

the country as a whole. Repression by death squads or paramilitary groups has the identical impact. Periods of relative peace were interrupted by violence against the peasantry mainly by the death squads, which operated both clandestinely and openly. The violence was brought to a halt in 1992 with a peace agreement. Liberal views made anyone a target for death squads, and even priests and nuns became targets and were murdered. Also targeted were outspoken labor leaders as well as politicians. Throughout the 1980s, fear was the pervasive mood throughout El Salvador.

NICARAGUA

This small Central American country of 4.5 million has been embroiled in what can best be described as a struggle between superpowers. Nicaragua has had a leadership that boasts close ties to the United States and its military training institutions for the better part of the twentieth century. This country has also been involved in the sale of drugs for weapons, and brought into disrepute the dealings of the U.S. Central Intelligence Agency (CIA). The National Guard of Nicaragua was modeled after and trained by the U.S. military in the years prior to World War II. The United States provided support to the regime of Anastasio Garcia and successive generations of his family, up until 1979. It seemed of no particular concern to U.S. administrations, as to what political ideology was being espoused, so long as it was not Communism. In fact, Garcia held power with corrupt associates and used repression to great effect. He was also an avid anti-Communist, which very much appealed to the United States during the Cold War years.

Garcia's corrupt government, and a Communist-inspired revolutionary movement called the Sandinistas, eventually ended the use of the repressive tactics. The Sandinistas National Liberation

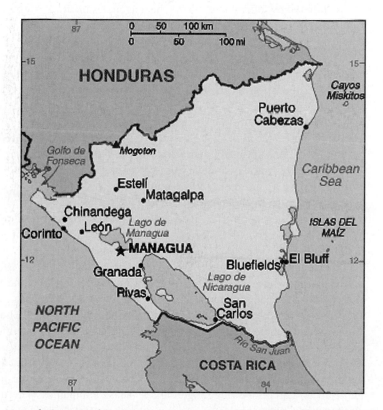

FIGURE 13-5 Map of Nicaragua (Central Intelligence Agency, *The World Factbook*, 2008).

Front (FLSN) had been waging a guerrilla war against Samoza Anastasio since the start of the 1970s. The Cold War was not a distant memory for the United States, and military assistance was provided to the Anastasio government to fight the Sandinistas. The Sandinistas, with Soviet assistance, seized power from Anastasio in 1979. Now the stage was set for the United States to support what the Nicaraguan government would call "rebels," while the Soviet Bloc would support the Sandinista government. The Reagan administration was committed to eliminating any Communist influences on its doorstep and promptly poured aid into the rebel **Contra** movement in its attempt to dislodge the Sandinistas.

Fund-raising

Aside from the problems of the guerrilla war in Nicaragua, a far bigger scandal was unraveling in the halls of the Pentagon. Questions arose concerning the level of U.S. involvement in drug trafficking in exchange for weapons to the Contras. There have been many sensational journalistic pieces that pointed a finger at the CIA and the Reagan administration. The Kerry Committee Report of April 1995 holds some interesting facts in its findings. The subcommittee found that the Contra drug links included:

- Involvement in narcotics trafficking by individuals associated with the Contra movement.
- Participation of narcotics traffickers in Contra supply operations through business relationships with Contra organizations.
- Provision of assistance to the Contras by narcotics traffickers, including cash, weapons, planes, pilots, air supply services, and other materials, on a voluntary basis.
- Payment to drug traffickers with U.S. Department of State funds authorized by the Congress for humanitarian assistance to the Contras, in some cases after the traffickers had been indicted by federal law enforcement agencies on drug charges, in others while traffickers were under active investigation by these same agencies.[10]

There is no doubt that those involved in these drug schemes on the U.S. side hoped to expunge any pending legal indictments in return for assistance to the rebel Contras. The level of exploitation by the drug traffickers was purely self-serving and certainly not ideologically driven.

When examining the infrastructure that was in place in the 1970s for the movement of illegal narcotics through Central America to the United States, it was a simple shift of purpose to include weapons into this operation's mix. This was a method the Sandinistas used to bring Cuban weapons into Nicaragua. Supply and staging areas abounded along the Nicaraguan border with Costa Rica, and most of the neighboring governments, which supported the actions of the Sandinistas, offered them safe haven and the opportunity to transfer drugs and weapons for their cause. When the Sandinistas finally gained power, the gun-running did not cease. In fact, all that changed was the end-user. The suppliers now had El Salvadoran rebels as customers, and not the Sandinistas.

One name has become synonymous with the Contras in the 1980s . . . U.S. Lieutenant Colonel Oliver North, who at the time "managed" Contra operations on the Southern Front. Evidence in the Kerry findings relates also to a U.S. national living in Costa Rica . . . John Hull, an Indiana farmer who moved to Costa Rica and bought up large tracts of land. The area, known as Hull's Ranch, happened to include six airstrips, ideal for drugs and weapons smuggling. Hull helped the CIA with military shipments to the Contras and was also heavily involved in transshipment of drugs from Colombia. Added to this was the fact that the U.S. State Department was actively signing contracts with companies and their principals; companies that were either under investigation or had been indicted on narcotics-smuggling charges. These companies were used to make military hardware drops to the Contra rebels.

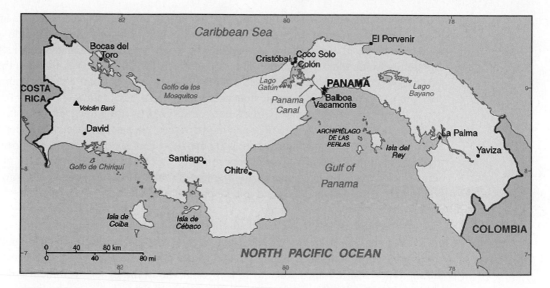

FIGURE 13-6   Map of Panama (Central Intelligence Agency, *The World Factbook*, 2008).

PANAMA

Formerly under Spanish rule, this tiny strip of land between the Pacific and the Atlantic first became a province of Colombia, before gaining its independence in 1903. Famous for the Panama Canal, which was under the control of the United States until the late 1970s, Panama has been a largely rural nation. The country has seen many varied forms of military governments over the past century or so, but the most notorious was that of General Manuel Noriega, who became president in 1983. From the time he came to power, he ran a corrupt government, made millions of dollars from drug trafficking to the United States and from diverting aid funds. Noriega controlled the public with strong-arm tactics and death squads. In 1988, a Florida grand jury indicted him on charges of racketeering and drug running. Up until 1989, Noriega continued to act with impunity. However, after the death of a U.S. Marine officer and Noriega's overturning the results of a democratic election, President George H. Bush gave the almost unprecedented order for U.S. troops to invade Panama and restore the elected president. The paratroopers also seized Noriega and handed him over to U.S. marshals. He then stood trial and was sentenced to forty years in federal prison, where he still languishes today. Some think the effort to restore democracy in Panama was more about trying to stem the endless flow of drugs into the United States and to bring Noriega to trial for his drug trafficking.

CENTRAL AMERICAN GANG PROBLEMS

Today, gangs are Central America's number one crime problem. Violent young men experienced in gunplay and in evading law enforcement efforts are being sent back to countries they haven't seen since they were children. Some are dropouts; many can barely speak Spanish. Gangs enlist teenagers who are abandoned, unemployed, and devoid of hope and teach them what they know best i.e., robbing, stealing cars, selling drugs, and killing. In the mid-1990s, the United States stepped up deportations of Central American criminals; many of them gang members from the 18th Street, or Mara 18, and its chief rival, Mara Salvatrucha 13.

An estimated 150,000 gang members, or Mareros, control the streets of Central America, at times outgunning local police in El Salvador, Honduras, and Guatemala. These gangs are extremely violent and their crimes are cold-blooded. Salvadoran officials say gangs are responsible for

80 percent of the homicides in that country. According to regional leaders, gangs are becoming the most destabilizing threat since the civil wars in Central America ended, a decade or so ago. Some have been involved in extortion and mass murder, others linked to organized crime. As a whole, they threaten not only their rivals and public safety in general, but they even threaten the success of the Central American Free Trade Agreement (CAFTA). It is a fact that better economic and political conditions did not deter the explosion in the number of gangs throughout the 1990s. Across the board, Central America experienced economic growth after decades of debilitating internal conflicts. Yet, gangs grew in number and in viciousness, in part because of U.S. deportation policies that returned to the region thousands of gang members convicted of crimes, but primarily because of inaction or impotence of regional governments. In December 1994, leaders of the thirty-four democracies, meeting in Miami during the first Summit of the Americas, recognized the threat of youth marginalization and the need to take practical steps to counter it. As yet, however, no unified regional strategy has been adopted.

At the highest levels, the Bush administration has been thinking about the security impact of gangs. Former U.S. Secretary of Defense, Donald Rumsfeld, warned of an "antisocial combination" of terrorists, drug traffickers, and gangs that is increasingly seeking "to destabilize civil societies" in the region. When it comes down to figuring out who in the U.S. government will take the lead to address this security threat, however, most security officials seem averse to even recognize that they are discussing it. Perhaps the reason for this is obvious. All security threats and gang violence, in particular, cannot be met by force alone. Addressing this issue will require a mix of law enforcement, prevention, rehabilitation, parental involvement, and after-school programs—a whole web of social initiatives that developing countries generally lack. While it may be hard to pinpoint just how far the Bush administration will pursue security to achieve opportunity and prosperity, there are signs that a broader vision might inform future action. Helping Central America get a grip on its gang problem would require a significant investment of time and resources from different agencies in the U.S. government. The Department of Justice and the U.S. Agency for International Development would have much larger roles than would the Pentagon or other security agencies.

In the rush to confront the problem, gang experts say, U.S. officials failed to anticipate how other countries would be affected by the deportation of unwanted gang members: "The world is too global to export a problem and not expect it to come back," said David Brotherton, a professor at the John Jay College of Criminal Justice in New York, who has written two books on gangs. "In El Salvador, Guatemala, Honduras, and Mexico, there's a whole new inner-city youth subculture that originated in the First World. We've created an insoluble problem, and these countries just can't respond. There's no social work infrastructure. There's no rehabilitation. There's no money. They have enough trouble just providing basics for their own people." The U.S. Immigration and Customs Enforcement (ICE) launched a nationwide gang enforcement program in 2005 and began Operation Community Shield a national law enforcement initiative that targets violent transnational street gangs through the use of ICE's broad law enforcement powers, including the unique and powerful authority to remove (deport) criminal aliens, including illegal aliens and legal permanent resident aliens.

In May 2005, it expanded Operation Community Shield to include all transnational criminal street gangs and prison gangs.

Results

Since inception, ICE agents across 100 field offices, working in conjunction with hundreds of federal, state and local law enforcement agencies nationwide, have arrested a total of 7,655 street gang members and associates, representing over 700 different gangs.

These apprehensions include 2,444 criminal arrests and 5,211 administrative immigration arrests. One hundred-seven of those arrested were gang leaders. More than 2,555 of the arrested suspects had violent criminal histories. Through this initiative, ICE has also seized and removed from the streets 287 firearms.

In all, Operation Community Shield arrests are up 533 percent since fiscal year 2005 and 134 percent over fiscal year 2006.

Under Operation Community Shield, ICE:

- Partners with federal, state and local law enforcement agencies, in the United States and abroad, to develop a comprehensive and integrated approach in conducting criminal investigations and other law enforcement operations against violent street gangs and others who pose a threat to public safety.
- Identifies violent street gangs and develops intelligence on their membership, associates, criminal activities and international movements.
- Deters, disrupts and dismantles gang operations by tracing and seizing cash, weapons and other assets derived from criminal activities.
- Seeks prosecution and/or removal of alien gang members from the United States.
- Works closely with our attaché offices throughout Latin America and foreign law enforcement counterparts in gathering intelligence, sharing information and conducting coordinated enforcement operations.
- Conducts outreach efforts to increase public awareness about the fight against violent street gangs.[11]

Meanwhile, Central American governments are desperately searching for strategies to combat gangs. The Honduran Congress unanimously passed one of the hemisphere's toughest anti-gang laws in 2003, setting a maximum twelve-year prison sentence for gang members. El Salvador followed with its own version of what has become known as the *mano dura,* or firm hand, which locks up any young man who bears gang tattoos. In May 2004, Mexico's southernmost state of Chiapas approved five-year prison sentences for anyone who simply belongs to a gang. Human rights activists complain that gang members are being hunted down and killed by police, but the crackdowns continue, especially against the 18th Street and MS 13, which are Central America's largest and most violent gangs. The gangs have proven to be resilient. Every time they're uprooted, they resurface in another neighborhood, another city, and another country. They move with the assurance that no matter where they go, fellow gang members will feed them, house them, orient them, and possibly even provide them with weapons.

In a report released in 2004, a UN panel on illegal executions concluded the rate of youth slayings by security agents in Honduras was among the highest in the world and chastised the government for appearing to tolerate the slayings. The report was issued nearly a year after Hondurans elected President Ricardo Maduro on a tough, anti-crime platform. Maduro has conceded that security forces were behind some of the killings and declared that one of his top priorities was to end the slaughters. Maduro created a special unit to investigate the youth slayings, but child welfare advocates contend it is inadequate—in nearly two years, they note, the unit has referred only thirty-five cases for prosecution. Although thirty-two police and security officials have been named as suspects, not one person has been convicted in a youth murder since 1988.

In April 2004, sixty-eight inmates, most of them gang members, were killed during an uprising in El Porvenir prison in the northern region of the country. A government report concluded that the security forces had executed most of the inmates. Abuses by security forces have been a problem in Honduras since the 1970s and 1980s, when government-backed paramilitary groups tortured and murdered citizens suspected of Communist leanings. Many of these groups cruise through poor neighborhoods in unmarked vans, gunning down young people with automatic weapons pointed out of darkened windows. Their ranks include current and former members of the police and military, as well as organized crime members. Government officials and child advocates agree that the slayings are, in part, a reaction to soaring crime rates and booming populations of young people. Half of Honduras' nearly 7 million inhabitants are age eighteen or younger and have almost no prospects in a country mired in poverty and unemployment. In El Salvador, more than half the population is under age twenty-four. Increasingly, the gangs work with Honduras-based drug traffickers and are blamed for rampant robbery, rape, and other violent crimes. With police and courts poorly equipped to fight the crime wave, some police and civilians have felt justified in taking justice into their own hands.[12]

COLOMBIA

Colombia was one of the three countries that emerged from the collapse of Gran Colombia in 1830 (the others being Ecuador and Venezuela). Colombia's history has been shaped by spatial fragmentation, which has found expression in economic challenges and cultural differentiation. The geography of Colombia has had a significant effect on its history and on the evolution and development of what is often described as a fragmented and divided society. Colombia is bordered on the northwest by Panama, on the east by Venezuela and Brazil, and on the southwest by Peru and Ecuador. Through the western half of the country, three Andean mountain ranges run north and south. The eastern half is a low, jungle-covered plain, drained by spurs of the Amazon and Orinoco rivers, and inhabited mostly by isolated, tropical-forest Indian tribes. The fertile plateau and valley of the eastern range are the most densely populated parts of the country. The country's historically most-populated areas have been divided by its three mountain ranges. In each mountain range are many small valleys. The dispersion of much of the population into isolated mountain pockets has long delayed the development of transportation, adequate means of communication, and the formation of integrated national markets. Due to these geographic and spatial limitations, Colombia has developed local and regional cultures. Politically, this dispersion has created regional antagonism and local rivalries that were expressed in the nineteenth century in civil war, and in the latter part of the twentieth century in intercommunity violence.

FIGURE 13-7   Map of Colombia (Central Intelligence Agency, *The World Factbook*, 2008).

Over the last two centuries, Colombia has suffered through virtually continuous warfare. The country has been characterized by a pronounced fractured dispersion of power, further manifested by extreme levels of localism and regionalism. This problem is then paired with a variety of dispersed political identities and political truths. It is not too surprising that all of this contributes to disproportionately high levels of violence in Colombia. One of the most severe challenges to any U.S. policy toward Colombia derives from issues involving human rights. Political and extrajudicial actions involving government security forces, paramilitary groups, and members of the guerilla forces result in the deaths of thousands of civilians. Paramilitary forces are responsible for the great majority of these deaths. Hundreds of thousands of Colombians are forced to leave their homes. Others are displaced by rampant and uncontrolled violence. The homicide rate is considered to be one of the highest per capita in the world. Government security forces are frequently involved in many of the abuses, including extrajudicial killings, and they sometimes collaborate directly and indirectly with paramilitary forces. And, although the government has worked to strengthen its human rights policy, the measures adopted to punish officials accused of committing violations, and to prevent paramilitary attacks, are insufficient. In the meantime, paramilitary forces have increased their social and political support among the civilian population in many parts of the country.

To most students, the name "Colombia" conjures up several simple words . . . drugs, kidnapping, rebels. The U.S. Department of State has characterized the country as one of the most dangerous in the world to visit. That is still a fact even now, well into the new millennium. Marijuana, cocaine, and kidnappings have been products of Colombia for the past forty or more years, but the market for drugs did not take off until the wealthy and middle classes in the United States began abusing them.

Cocaine became the drug of choice, and the opportunity for expansion into a North American market was huge. Drugs in Colombia are controlled in two regions of the country . . . Medellin and Cali. The Medellin and **Cali cartels** control nearly 80 percent of Colombia's distribution of drugs. Terrorist groups in Colombia have been fully involved in the sale and supply of narcotics for financial support in their bitter fight against successive Colombian governments. Violence and intimidation in Colombia have focused around the drug trade. Terrorism, therefore, becomes a by-product of the drug trade and a means of control and power. Extortion, kidnapping, and murder are all hallmarks of the drug cartels. In a country where economics are dictated by drug barons, anarchy is never too far away. It is difficult to appreciate the enormous wealth that comes from the machinations of the drug trade. Drug barons are known to have utilized outside "sources" to assist their own internal security services. The economy of Colombia seems to be drug dependent, and eradicating drugs from the region would be simpler if there were a legal economy that was able to produce an income similar to that of the drug trade. Several have been attempted, but the demand for drugs makes growing coca a better alternative. Colombia also has to contend with an insurgent group of left wing rebels/revolutionaries/terrorists that have plagued the state for close to forty years with little or no sign of resolution.

A forty-year insurgent campaign to overthrow the Colombian government escalated during the 1990s, fueled in part by funds from the drug trade. Although the violence is deadly and large swaths of the countryside are under guerrilla influence, the movement lacks the military strength and popular support necessary to overthrow the government. An anti-insurgent army of paramilitaries has grown to over several thousand strong in recent years, challenging the insurgents for control of territory and illicit industries such as the drug trade and the government's ability to exert its dominion over rural areas. While Bogota steps up efforts to reassert government control throughout the country, neighboring countries worry about the violence spilling over their borders. In August 2000, the U.S. government approved "Plan Colombia," pledging $1.3 billion to fight drug trafficking. President Andres Pastrana, elected in 1988, used the plan to undercut drug production and prevent guerrilla groups from benefiting from drug sales. In August 2001, Pastrana signed "war legislation," which expanded the rights of the military in dealing with rebels. Alvaro Uribe of the Liberal Party easily won the presidential election in May 2002. He took office in August, pledging to get tough on the rebels and drug traffickers by increasing military spending and seeking U.S. military cooperation. An upsurge in violence accompanied his inauguration, and Uribe declared a state of emergency within a week. In his first year, Uribe beefed up Colombia's security forces, with help from U.S. Special Forces troops, launched an aggressive campaign against the drug trade, and passed several economic reform bills.

In May 2004, the United Nations announced that Colombia's thirty-nine-year-long drug war had created the worst humanitarian crisis in the Western Hemisphere. More than 2 million people had been forced to leave their homes, and several Indian tribes are now close to extinction. Colombia now has the third-largest displaced population in the world, with only Sudan and the Congo having more. Uribe has produced some impressive results in fixing his country's ills, however. According to his defense minister, during 2003, more than 16,000 suspected leftist guerrillas and right-wing paramilitary vigilantes had surrendered, were apprehended, or were killed. The U.S. Office of National Drug Control Policy has announced that coca production has declined by 30 percent, but Colombia still continues to produce 75 percent of the world's cocaine.

Terrorism in Colombia

Colombia's democracy and its forty-plus million inhabitants have been under assault since the early 1960s and 1970s by three Marxist, "narco-terrorist" groups: the **Revolutionary Armed Forces of Colombia (FARC)**, the National Liberation Army (ELN), and the **United Self-Defense Forces of Colombia (AUC)**. These three groups were capable of providing over 25,000 well-trained combatants. FARC and AUC have had a pronounced involvement at all levels of the drug trade and derive a considerable income from it . . . some estimates run as high as $300 million annually. In 2001, the AUC killed two Colombian legislators and FARC kidnapped six; and the three groups accounted for the assassinations of twelve mayors.[13]

The numbers of kidnappings according to the Colombian government have dropped dramatically from the peak year in 2000 when 3,500 people were taken, down to 521 in 2007. As part of the U.S. government's Plan Colombia, which was focused on reduction of the flow of cocaine, the United States has provided some $5 billion worth of aid and a fraction of that amount has gone toward the **Anti-Terrorism Assistance Program (ATA)**. The Colombian government gives credit to a little-known program, run by the U.S. State Department's Bureau of Diplomatic Security, which has trained more than 600 **GAULA** members. (GAULA is the Spanish acronym for Unified Action Groups for Personal Liberty.) The DS training, offered under its Anti-Terrorism Assistance program, has focused in particular on rescuing hostages.[14]

The Revolutionary Armed Forces of Colombia (FARC) terror group is widely accepted to be the largest, best equipped, and best trained of the terror organizations in Colombia. An extreme left-wing, Communist-inspired movement, FARC aspires to the overthrow of the Colombian government, and little else. It first came to notice in 1966 as a military wing of the Colombian Communist Party. Formed along military lines, its members engage in a broad scope of activities. In a country where kidnapping is as commonplace as drinking a cup of coffee and might be considered the largest growth industry, the FARC targets the government, military, locally elected municipal mayors, police, and civilians. Much of FARC's income is derived not only from drug trafficking, but also robbery, kidnapping, and extortion. FARC is rabidly anti-United States and its campaign resembles that of Cuban-style revolution. Its campaign against the Colombian government has not specifically detailed or promoted attacks outside of the country. For foreign visitors, particularly American businesspeople, a trip to Colombia is one to be avoided at all costs. FARC's membership of active terrorists is believed to number around 16,000 at its peak in the 1990s and has dwindled down to approximately 9,000 in 2008, but still manages to gains some support in rural areas from the indigenous population.

FARC's central demands are not considered realistic. Most observers do not consider FARC's control demands as realistic, i.e. their demands for the ending of privatization and reduction of the 20 percent unemployment rate and other reforms seem hopelessly futile. On the political front, the Colombian government of President Andreas Pastrana had made slow headway in negotiating a peace deal with FARC. In 2001, the year leading up to the elections, negotiations became bogged down and the Pastrana government threatened to end the deal that had created a demilitarized zone (DMZ) in southern Colombia, an area approximately the size of Switzerland, which had long been occupied by FARC. Since the events of 9-11, the Colombian government has been fortified with U.S. aid and military hardware for the express purpose of combating the drug trade in Colombia. This aid has given significant impetus to the Colombian military to go on the offensive against FARC, something of a novelty for Colombia's military, which has traditionally fought in defensive mode against FARC. Operation "Black Cat" commenced in February 2002. This military offensive was directed against FARC with the use of aircraft and helicopters. At the same time, Pastrana annulled the FARC's political status and issued arrest warrants for its leaders. In the February 2002 campaign, the Colombian military struck so far into FARC territory that the group was taken totally by surprise. The area attacked was the town of Barrancomina in eastern Colombia, an area where the 16th Front of FARC had been able to operate with complete impunity. The significance of the attack showed that the Colombian military had the skill and the intelligence support, as well as the military know-how, to attack FARC. In future campaigns, this will no doubt be a deciding factor in peace talks, if they ever resume. FARC's resilience has never really been in question and the organization has been a proven survivor. FARC cannot be called a truly Communist inspired movement, even though committed Communists are included in its membership. FARC is also involved in the drug trade, although it cannot be considered a drug cartel, but it is definitely involved in narco-terrorism. Because FARC flourishes in the deep rural and jungle regions of the state, it could be considered a peasant army. In some respects, this may be true but, because of its wide-ranging terror attacks, it cannot be termed as the vanguard of the peasant populace. FARC's appeal to the peasantry could be rationalized, as it offers a level of employment when there is no prospect elsewhere. After thirty-eight years, a new leadership will become self-evident. The failures of the group's participation in government representation may spawn an organization that will feed off the lucrative trade in drugs, kidnappings, and extortion.

FARC will likely continue to become even more marginalized as it sees itself up against the U.S.-backed Colombian military and an ever-growing number of paramilitary forces. In this context, it is expected that now that it has been hit systemically in areas where it once operated with complete freedom, it will have to reconsider its actions and adapt to survive in this new environment.

FARC and ELN (National Liberation Army) have become bitter enemies. Agreements between the two on sharing the spoils in kidnapping ransoms have been violated and FARC is again licking its wounds. FARC's ability to strike against both the local political apparatus and the civilian population is well documented and this is exactly what has happened since February 2002. With the arrival of the new president, Alvaro Uribe, who has committed himself to destroying FARC during his term of office, there is little doubt that further attacks will continue. The new president also has some unfinished business with the rebels, who have tried on at least fifteen occasions to kill him. But more than that, the FARC rebels killed his father in a botched kidnapping in1983. The new president hails from the Antioquia Province where he was the governor from 1995 to 1997. During his term as governor, he promoted the "self-defense" groups, some of which evolved into paramilitary groups that, like the rebels they battle, are blamed for numerous civilian massacres.

The National Liberation Army (ELN), formed in 1963, is a smaller and less organized operation than FARC, and has carried on a long-term campaign against the Colombian government. It is predominately a Marxist-inspired group and has a membership of about 3,000 fighters. Similar to FARC, the ELN is anti-United States, and frequently engages in the profitable tactic of kidnapping.

The target is usually a businessman from a foreign company working in Colombia. In addition, ELN targets U.S. and foreign installations for bomb attacks. ELN's operations are focused on Colombia's northwestern border with Venezuela . . . regions that produce cannabis and poppy opium. ELN and FARC have both systematically targeted Colombia's oil facilities and, in 2001, the government suffered nearly $500 million in lost revenues. To this end, the United States has supplied $6 million in foreign military funds (FMF) to train Colombian military units to protect the Cano Limon pipeline, which has been repeatedly bombed by both groups. ELN continues the practice of kidnappings for ransom.

Peace Talks?

Peace talks between successive Colombian Governments, FARC and ELN have been a part of the political/insurgent process since the 1980s and any likelihood that peace will break out is unlikely. FARC has previously had little external support for its insurgent activities against the government; however, in 2006 FARC announced its conditions for agreeing to any bi-lateral peace accord hostage/prisoner exchange. Since then little has developed and FARC continues to hold approximately 700 hostages. However with the presence of the ubiquitous Hugo Chavez in neighboring Venezuela, who it is alleged has supplied millions of dollars of aid to FARC, will certainly complicate any strides the Colombians make toward peace. Experts estimate that FARC takes in $200 million to $300 million annually, at least half of its income, from the illegal drug trade. The FARC also profits from kidnappings, extortion schemes, and an unofficial "tax" it levies in the country-side for "protection" and social services. About sixty-five of the FARC's 110 operational units are involved in some aspect of the drug trade, according to a 2005 International Crisis Group report, but evidence from that period indicates they primarily managed local production.[15]

The right-wing death squads, which rose to prominence in Colombia, appear to have had the tacit support of both the government and the military. Many of these defense groups sprang up in the 1960s and 1970s in response to FARC's terrorist activities against wealthy landowners. Over the years, the groups, which tended to operate in select areas, moved from defensive to offensive strategies. They began to attack suspected members of FARC and intimidated peasant villagers believed to be helping the FARC.[16]

In regions such as central Magdalena, drug cartels began buying up rich tracts of land, and this was directly responsible for transforming the self-defense units into right-wing death squads.[17]

For the Colombian drug lords, the end justifies the means. This is the real issue in the rise of death squads and the necessary need for terrorist actions in this country. In a country so heavily dependent on the production and export of drugs, the methods used to terrorize the populace are not intended as means to overthrow or replace a political system. These efforts are aimed at maintaining the status quo and fear, for the groups' own benefit, and for dissuading police, judges, and politicians from strict legal approaches in dealing with drug traffickers. The rise of the right-wing death squads and paramilitaries dates back over thirty years, when rich landowners, farmers, and the drug cartels adopted their own small and very private protection forces. These have grown into a sort of loose coalition known as the United Self-Defense Forces of Colombia (AUC). AUC and FARC have been responsible for more than 5,000 kidnappings and the deaths of more than 4,000 Colombians. AUC has publicly stated that it gains most of its support and income from the lucrative drug trade. Allegations of human rights abuses by the AUC abound. It has been linked on more than one occasion to senior members of Colombia's military elite. The AUC's methods of intimidation have resulted in more than 340,000 Colombians being forcibly evicted from their homes and land, bringing the total number of displaced persons to more than 2 million in just the last decade.

The ticket of Alvaro Uribe, which swept to a landslide victory in the 2002 presidential elections, is unable to exert much control outside the large urban centers. Uribe has had ongoing talks with AUC, which was formed in 1997, but the group continued to indiscriminately slaughter leftist guerrillas, politicians, activists, union leaders, as well as civilians until 2003. Information from the Colombian National Police states that between January and October 2000, the AUC carried out 804 assassinations, 203 kidnappings, and 75 massacres in which 507 people died. Uribe's decommissioning of AUC began in earnest in 2003 and the number of attacks and assassinations has dropped considerably and this now allows the Uribe government to continue pursuing FARC and ELN in the countryside. One of the major problems facing the Colombian government is AUC's deepening involvement with drugs. Since 2003, some thirty thousand paramilitaries have been disbanded, however, this does not mean that they have been arrested but have more likely become involved in the lucrative drugs trade.

As for international links, America's most-wanted terrorist, the Saudi dissident millionaire Osama bin Laden, is not, at this point, known to have provable links with Latin American terrorist groups. However, one of his associates, Mohammed Abed Abel, a member of Egypt's largest militant group, Jammaa Islamiyya, was arrested in Bogotá, Colombia, in early November 1998. He was subsequently released by the Colombian authorities and deported back to Ecuador, his country of origin. Why would such a high-ranking and high-profile terrorist be in Latin America? It may be assumed that he was either studying the U.S. Embassy as a potential target, or negotiating meetings with FARC or ELN to set up trade deals involving drugs for weapons. FARC and its connections to Irish paramilitary groups came dramatically to a head when the Colombian authorities arrested several senior IRA members in 2001. Prior to their arrest, Colombian authorities revealed that the IRA men had been involved in training members of FARC in military tactics, the use of explosives, and the manufacture of arms. General Tapias, Chairman of the Joint Chiefs of Staff for the Armed Forces of Colombia, made these claims in testimony before the U.S. House of Representatives International Relations Committee in April 2002. The types of attacks the FARC mounted in 2002 showed a higher level of sophistication than had previously been the case. The attacks' level of sophistication was similar to those of the IRA. The reason and background for IRA involvement is not yet clear but, of course, there is plenty of speculation from the various security organizations. In Britain, the suggestion is that the FARC paid the IRA $2 million for the training in explosives and, of course, the U.S. concern is that it may be a hint of a much broader coalition of international terror relationships, but there is no hard evidence for this. The official response to the arrests from the IRA came from Gerry Adams, the leader of Sinn Féin. While Adams refused to testify before the U.S. House International Relations Committee, he did respond in writing to the chairman of the committee, Henry Hyde. Adams wrote: "Let me state again that neither I, nor anyone else, in the Sinn Féin leadership were aware that the three men were traveling to Colombia."[18]

Of course, the careful wording in this statement cannot be construed that Sinn Féin was not aware of their involvement, no doubt a good enough reason not to testify. It seems highly probable that FARC is delving deeper into drug trafficking in exchange for military hardware and much-needed cash reserves for its continuing fight.

From Counter-Narcotics to Narco-Terrorism

During the past several years, U.S. foreign policy toward Colombia has undergone significant changes. The events of 9-11, combined with the definitive rupture of the Colombian government's peace process with the rebels in February 2002, have converted this country into the primary training theater for U.S. counterterrorism operations in the Western Hemisphere today. Washington's traditional counter-narcotics policies have been based on repressive, prohibitionist, and hard-line language. The manner in which Colombia itself has addressed the drug problem derives substantially from the U.S. approach, with most of Bogotá's measures to fight the drug trade the result of bilateral agreements or the unilateral imposition of specific strategies designed in Washington DC. It has been theorized that these approaches have produced countless negative consequences for Colombia, aggravating the armed conflicts that continue to escalate and forcing urgent national problems such as the strengthening of democracy, the defense of human rights, the reduction of poverty, and the preservation of the environment to become secondary to countering the drug trade.[19]

Between 1996 and 2001, U.S. aid to Colombia (in the form of military and other government assistance) has increased approximately fifteen-fold, from $67 million to over $1 billion.[20]

At conceptual and practical levels, it is difficult for the United States to separate the war on drugs from its counterinsurgency efforts. Given that the global War on Terror has targeted the links that exist among terrorism, arms, and drugs, a new term has been coined . . . "narco-terrorism" . . . to describe players such as the FARC, former AUC, al Qaeda, and others that fund terrorist-related activities with drug money.[21]

In 2003, President Bush asked the Congress for an additional $600 million for Colombia with the majority being in the form of military aid and to rebuild and train the stagnating Colombian military. The request included line items to train and equip two new Colombian army brigades to protect the Cano Limon-Covenas oil pipeline, in which the American firm, Occidental Petroleum, is a large shareholder. Dubbed "Plan Colombia," the infusion of millions of dollars aimed at destroying the coca crops that so easily produce the cocaine for the cartels and FARC. FARC's significant control of the drug industry in Colombia is how it derives most of its financial support—estimated to be $1.3 billion per year. FARC has also been implicated in providing training to the kidnappers of former Paraguayan President Raul Cuba's daughter, Cecilia, who was abducted in September 2004 and found dead in February 2005.

The drug trade drives Colombian terrorism from both the left and the right and there is little evidence to suggest that the price of cocaine and its demand has dried up. The Colombian cocaine trade was estimated at $35 billion in 2000, which is vastly more than the earnings of some well-known multinational companies.

The assistance given to the Colombian military by the United States has been rewarded by the death of one of their most wanted—Raul Reyes had been, until his death the one and only spokesman for the FARC.

Luis Edgar Devia Silva a.k.a. Raul Reyes (September 30, 1948—March 1, 2008)

Also known publicly as Raul Reyes, the central figure and spokesman for the FARC in almost all communications with the group was killed on March 1, 2008, when the Colombian Air Force launched a bombing raid on an FARC camp located about 2 miles from the Colombian border just inside Ecuador. Reyes had been formally sentenced in absence for the deaths of thirteen policemen and eighteen soldiers, eighteen kidnappings and the deaths of a judge, a physician, three judicial auxiliaries, the ex-minister of Culture Consuelo Araújo, Congressman Diego Turbay and his mother, Catholic monsignor Isaías Duarte, Governor of Antioquia Guillermo Gaviria, the Colombian ex-minister Gilberto Echeverri, eleven members of the Valle del Cauca Assembly, and at least four other persons. Most of these persons were kidnapped before their deaths.[22]

The success of the Colombian military has pushed the FARC to its limits and with the deaths of many of its key players has meant that its force of around 18,000 fighters is now likely less than 8,000. In May 2008 FARC was dealt another significant blow to its already flagging morale when it was announced that Manuel Marulunda, who had led the FARC for four decades, had died of an apparent heart attack in March 2008.

FARC had also sought support from Venezuela and reports after the death of Raul Reyes that the Colombian military had found a number of files on his computer that indicated that the Venezuelan government of Hugo Chavez was prepared to back FARC did nothing for regional stability. The claims were swiftly denied by the Venezuelan leader.

FIGURE 13-8 Manuel Marulanda (center), the founder and leader for the Revolutionary Armed Forces of Colombia (FARC), talks to his rebel commanders in Los Pozos, southern Colombia, in February 2001. FARC reported that Marulanda died of natural causes in March 2008 (Canadian Press).

FIGURE 13-9 March 2008—Ecuadoran soldiers look at weapons and equipment found near the border with Colombia where Colombian military forces killed the top commander of FARC, Raul Reyes. Reyes' computer files were recovered at the scene and revealed that senior Venezuelan officials attempted to help arm the FARC (Canadian Press).

PERU

Any understanding of Peru must begin with its geography. Located on the Pacific coast of South America, and approximately twice the size of Texas, the country has three geographical regions: coastal, sierra, and mountain ranges. As in other regional countries, these disparate geographical features have created separate regional economies, ethnic variations, and cultures. Ancient Peru was the seat of several prominent Andean civilizations, most notably that of the Incas, whose empire was captured by the Spanish conquistadors in 1533. Peruvian independence was declared in 1821 and the remaining Spanish forces defeated in 1824. Several other ethnic and culture variations exist with the native Indians; also included in this mix are Spanish, Blacks, and Asians. Not surprisingly, this mix of ethnic backgrounds has led to widely divergent interpretation of Peruvian history and society.

Peru is often remembered only for its fabulous Inca villages, Machu Picchu, and the high Andes Mountains. History indicates that an Inca chief named Tupac Amaru and his Inca followers overcame their colonial Spanish masters in the latter half of the seventeenth century. The country has been under the control of military juntas throughout much of the twentieth century, but civilian rule returned to Peru in the 1980s. Peru suffers from two sources of indigenous terrorism . . . the Sendoro Luminoso (**The Shining Path**) and the Tupac Amaru Revolutionary Movement (MRTA).

Sendero Luminoso (The Shining Path)

The movement has its origins in the university city of Aucayacu, in the upper Huallaga region. Abimael Guzman, who received his indoctrination and training in China in 1965, at the start of the Chinese Cultural Revolution, then created and led The Shining Path. His trips to, and training in China, taught him how to set up and organize clandestine political and terrorist activities against the democratic state. On his return home, he became the leader of the pro-Maoist faction of the

FIGURE 13-10 Map of Peru (Central Intelligence Agency, *The World Factbook*, 2008).

Peruvian Communist Party. Guzman was working high in the Andes Mountains as a university lecturer studying the exploitation suffered by Peru's Indians. He had no trouble drawing parallels with the Chinese peasants who had fought for Mao Zedong three decades earlier. He recruited his students into the Maoist Party and sent them to agitate in the Indian villages.[23]

Students comprised the group's largest sector of membership, a reflection of the leadership's organizational strategy of tapping into the existing state-organized network of education to recruit Sendero devotees. His movement went underground in 1976 and began preparations for its campaign of terror and insurgency in 1980. Sendero derived much of its power by relying on ethnic factors and by resurrecting the feeling of historical greatness associated with the Inca civilization. A second and related story, from Peruvian history since the Spanish conquest in the early 1500s, concerned the effects of its subjugation, first to Spain, then to England, and most recently to the United States. It describes a legacy of exploitation, debt, and generally bad development that provided ready-made fuel for Sendero Luminoso to create and promote a radical and isolationist ideology.

Sendero burst onto the scene by brutally assassinating any village leaders who resisted the group's call to smash authority and establish an egalitarian utopia. Many local police crumbled before the group, which issued no manifestos and maintained absolute silence about its structure and leadership. Mounting Sendero violence in the highlands forced the Peruvian government to authorize a military offensive, which left its own wake of brutal repression. Peruvian military tactics failed to eliminate Sendero. On the contrary, the movement spread to other highland provinces and to Lima. More massacres in the Sierra and blackouts (from dynamited power lines) in greater Lima demonstrated growing Sendero strength. Sendero forced the government into greater reliance on the police and the military. Government forces killed indiscriminately, prompting the firing of numerous commanders for atrocities in the field and for the slaughter of numerous prisoners who had surrendered after a massive prison riot.

In 1976, while the Peruvian government was trying to restore the democratic processes and the economy of the country, Guzman and his Sendero Luminoso followers were training with automatic weapons. He and his followers were of the belief that Peruvian society had to be torn down, and a classless society designed to replace it. Guzman and his followers started out as the saviors of the poor of Peru. That was to quickly change as Guzman's Marxist style became similar, in his approach to the natives, to that of the Khmer Rouge in dealing with the Cambodians. In merging the extreme teachings of Chairman Mao with the philosophy of Che Guevara,[24] a dangerously violent hybrid emerged. Like the Khmer Rouge, Guzman and his guerrillas set about the destruction of the country by intimidating villagers into either joining the movement or die. Those who refused were promptly killed. The group quickly became a cult of mass murderers, feared for their savagery throughout Peru. Guzman's aim was to overthrow the Peruvian democratic government and replace it with a Marxist dictatorship, built in his own image. Over the next fourteen years, the group's reign of terror took the lives of 25,000 Peruvians and resulted in over $20 billion in damage to the country's infrastructure. Sendoro terrorists included a number of female operatives who have been known to use small children to deliver suicide bombs to public buildings and police stations. Guzman's philosophy and ideals spread farther than just Peru, however. He had goals of resurrecting the old Inca Empire; his terrorists threatened not only Peru, but Ecuador, Colombia, and Bolivia. Guzman's supporters believed him to be invincible and they called him the "Fourth Sword of Marxism" because of this belief.[25]

Fortunately for Peru, this belief was to be rudely upset by his capture in September 1992. During the 1980s, terrorist activity had been so prevalent that villagers were fleeing to the urban slums of big cites, such as Lima, to escape the ravages of The Shining Path. International observers feared that the democratic government in Peru would not be able to deal with the onslaught from Guzman's follower's depredations. Following Abimael Guzman's capture in 1992, the movement staggered, lost fervor, and began to disintegrate. The Peruvian government of President Fujimori was determined to overcome both narcotics trafficking and terrorism in

Peru and seemed to have the overwhelming support of the people. Prior to Guzman's capture, several other key members of The Shining Path were behind bars. No doubt, information gathered during their interrogations assisted in Guzman's apprehension. Fujimori's democratic administration and revival of the country's economy had done much to defeat the terrorist threat, which, considering the meager level of counterinsurgency training available to the poorly equipped security police is quite surprising. Following Guzman's capture the void was temporarily filled by Oscar Durand the group's strategist on military matters until he himself was captured by the Peruvian authorities in 1999.[26]

The Shining Path, in spite of the setbacks of the late 1990s, is still a credible and deadly force and a problem for Peruvian authorities. In the 2001 U.S. State Department *Patterns of Global Terrorism Report*, it indicates that in that year alone, the number of Shining Path terrorist acts in Peru was 130. Little has been heard of from Shining Path in the first decade of the twenty-first century, although their focus and determination to overthrow the government remains a core objective. What has taken place in the last few years is that Sendero had moved into the drugs trade and uses proceeds from drug trafficking to fund its insurgency operations. Indifference or outright antipathy on the part of the peasantry also undoubtedly contributes to Sendero's resilience. In a country where 54 percent of the population was estimated to be below the poverty line in 2003, that puts Peru on a par with locales such as Afghanistan (53 percent), The Republic of Georgia (54 percent) and Turkmenistan (58 percent). Sendero's cocaine production enterprise must be counted as a major employment attraction in the area. They are, in effect, a government within a government, ruling over thousands of square miles of Peru virtually unchallenged.[27]

Tupac Amaru: Movimiento Revolucionario Tupac Amaru (MRTA)

The second of Peru's terrorist movements takes its name from the previously mentioned legendary Inca leader, Tupac Amaru II, a revered Indian rebel who led an uprising during the late eighteenth century against Spanish colonial arrangements. **Movimiento Revolucionario Tupac Amaru (MRTA)**, considered in part a rival to Sendero, was actually less powerful, but still a very deadly Peruvian guerrilla organization during the late 1980s and early 1990s. The original rebellion by the Inca leader, Tupac Amaru II, was ultimately suppressed, but it remained a symbol of ethnic-political unity and hinted at prospects for more successful uprisings in the future. The greatness of the Inca Empire has remained alive in the hearts of many of Peru's indigenous population.

With the country heading toward elections in 1993, the levels of terrorism began to pick up and, by 1996, both MRTA and Sendero were resorting to campaigns of terror once again. Sendero was not able to deliver the same number of guerrillas to the campaign as it had previously, however, and the numbers of combatants were also significantly lower.

Victor Polay formed the Tupac Amaru in 1985. A traditional Marxist/Leninist movement, its goal was the overthrow of perceived imperialism in Peru. The group had no external support and its membership was considerably less than that of Sendero. Polay, however, was captured in 1992 and sentenced to life in prison. In a spectacular display of support and solidarity for Polay, Tupac Amaru terrorists attacked the Japanese ambassador's residence in Lima during a diplomatic Christmas celebration in December 1996. They took hundreds of guests, mainly diplomats, as hostages. In front of the world's press and television corps assembled outside, Tupac Amaru demanded the release of Polay. With the strong support of the Peruvian population, Fujimori stood his ground and did not give way to the threats from the terrorists. Through pressure from the government of Japan for a quick resolution to the impasse, everyone settled down to wait. The assault on the ambassador's residence took place when about 400 guests were seated for a meal. The celebration was short-lived, as more than a dozen heavily armed guerrillas stormed the grounds, firing weapons into the air. The attackers were calling themselves the Edgar Sanchez Special Forces, commanded by Comrade Edigirio Huerta. The assault began at about 8:00 P.M. on December 17, 1996. The situation was delicate, as a large number of foreign dignitaries and ambassadors were being held hostage, including the ambassadors of Austria, Brazil, Bulgaria, Cuba, Guatemala, Panama, Poland, Romania, South Korea, Spain, and Venezuela . . . a truly significant group. The government of President Fujimori would be put to the test, as it had steadfastly refused to negotiate with the terrorists. Both political and economic implications would rest on the outcome.

The Tupac Amaru terrorist demands were as follows:

1. They would shoot hostages unless their demands were met.
2. Release of their imprisoned comrades, totaling up to 500.
3. Transfer of freed prisoners and hostages to a jungle hideout, with the last hostage to be released at the final destination.
4. Payment by the Peruvian government of a "war tax" of an unspecified amount.
5. An economic program to aid the Peruvian poor.[28]

The End of the Crisis

After dragging on for four months, the drama was eventually brought to its climax when the Peruvian special security forces tunneled into the compound and rescued the hostages. Up until the middle of March, negotiations had been proceeding well, and the numbers of hostages had dwindled down to seventy-one, as concessions and counter-concessions were made. However, Fujimori would not budge on the terrorists' main demand, which was for the release of the imprisoned members of Tupac Amaru. At 3:20 P.M., April 22, 1997, the rescue began. The Peruvian government had authorized a rescue mission: tunneling, which had taken weeks, was now completed, allowing security forces to gain entry for a surprise strike. Explosions and gunfire were heard from inside the compound and plumes of smoke curled up from the residence windows. Within forty minutes, the 140-man rescue team had secured the residence, all fourteen Tupac Amaru guerrillas were dead, and twenty-five hostages were injured. Two members of the rescue team died in the operation. This incident brought worldwide congratulations to Fujimori for his stance against terrorism. But the attack was also a harsh reminder of the vulnerability of political leaders to terrorist attacks.[29]

In overall terms, the Peruvian authorities have seen some considerable success go their way in the war on domestic terrorism. In 2001, they had captured more than 259 suspected terrorists, and since the 9-11 attacks, Peru presented itself as a strong regional leader in the fight against terrorism and has participated in the U.S. State Department Antiterrorism Training Assistance program.

BOLIVIA

Bolivia, named after independence fighter Simon Bolivar, broke away from Spanish rule in 1825; much of its subsequent history has consisted of a series of nearly 200 coups and counter-coups. It has been a land-locked country ever since the war of 1879–1884 when Chile seized the Port of Antofagasta and the surrounding area. As a result, Bolivia's relations with Chile have been troublesome throughout its history. Comparatively democratic civilian rule was established in 1982, but leaders have faced difficult problems of deep-seated poverty, social unrest, and drug production. During the last months of 2001, the country witnessed several corruption scandals involving government officials, growing crime rates, and evidence of a criminal network that had infiltrated national police authorities. Current goals include attracting foreign investment, strengthening the educational system, resolving disputes with coca growers over Bolivia's counter-drug efforts, and waging an anti-corruption campaign. Bolivia is the world's third-largest cultivator of coca (after Colombia and Peru), with an estimated 8,450 hectares under cultivation in 2003, a 23 percent increase from 2002. Intermediate coca products and cocaine exports go mostly to or through Brazil, Argentina, and Chile to European and U.S. drug markets.

FIGURE 13-11   Map of Bolivia (Central Intelligence Agency, *The World Factbook*, 2008).

Eradication and alternative crop programs have not been able to keep up the pace with farmers' attempts to increase cultivation. Money-laundering activities related to narcotics trade, especially along the borders with Brazil and Paraguay, have flourished.[30]

In August 1971, Colonel Hugo Banzer overthrew the leftist popular regime of Juan Jose Torres. The majority of the military, and the business class, supported the new regime. The Banzer administration could best be described as a return to an openly authoritarian state. He repressed all social groups opposed to his regime, especially workers and peasants. Between 1971 and 1978, around 19,140 Bolivians were exiled, including Juan Lechin Head of the Bolivian Workers Union and four ex-presidents.[31]

Thousands were detained at different times and were subjected to numerous kinds of torture. However, the number of persons actually killed by the state was relatively low. The universities were frequently closed and all union activity was forbidden. One particularly grisly event gained special notoriety: the so-called massacre in the Cochabamba Valley in January 1975. In protest against the prices fixed by the government, the peasants in that central region blocked the roads. In retaliation, the military harshly repressed them. Many died or disappeared.[32]

When a military coup toppled the Bolivian government in 1980, the usual array of journalists, opposition politicians, and trade unionists were detained by the secret police, the Servicio Especial Seguridad (SES). However, most detainees were only held for a short period of time. Politically motivated assassinations have also been a hallmark of political unrest in the region. An outspoken member of the Socialist Workers Party was kidnapped in January 2002, and his tortured and bullet-riddled body was found two days later. Many of the violent gang activities are laid at the door of former groups involved in urban guerrilla activities in Chile. One of the main protagonists in Brazil's gang problems is Mauricio Norambuena, a leading figure in the Manual Rodriguez Patriotic Front (FPMR), which is now believed to have its base in Montevideo, Uruguay.

BRAZIL

Brazil has become a seething hotbed for kidnappings and extortion, some of which may be clearly politically motivated. Although Brazil has a subversive and anti-Western group called the Tupac Katari Guerrilla Army (EGTK), the group's actions have been extremely limited. Brazil has a democratic constitution that prohibits the inhumane treatment of prisoners and detainees. Brazil is famous in international terrorist circles for the pamphlet, *Mini-Manual of the Urban Guerrilla*, which was written by Carlos Marighella in 1969. On Tuesday, November 4, 1969, Carlos Marighella was assassinated in Sao Paulo. On that day, two missions were simultaneously interrupted. The first was the life of a man who, for nearly forty years, had been shaping theories in the struggle against the dominant system. The second was that of a determined urban guerrilla. Marighella was killed in an ambush as he was about to begin rural guerrilla warfare, the next step in his liberation cycle. He had the unique position of having made valuable contributions to the revolutionary cause in both theory and practice. During the last year of his life, as a parallel to the action he undertook, he wrote intensively to support his theories about the liberation of Brazil.

The *Mini-Manual of the Urban Guerrilla* has special importance. The work examines the conditions, characteristics, necessities, and methods of guerrilla warfare by the urban guerrilla, and demonstrates Marighella's sense of detail, organization, and mental clarity. It also shows, in passing, that Marighella was endowed with inexhaustible confidence and a youthfulness that belied his fifty-eight years. The *Mini-Manual of the Urban Guerrilla* became one of the principal books for every man who, in the inevitable battle against the bourgeoisie and imperialism, takes the road of armed rebellion.[33]

FIGURE 13-12   Map of Brazil (Central Intelligence Agency, *The World Factbook*, 2008).

The Mini-Manual of the Urban Guerrilla

The chronic structural crisis characteristic of Brazil today, and its resultant political instability, is what has brought about the upsurge of revolutionary war in the country. The urban guerrilla is a man who fights the military dictatorship with arms, using unconventional methods. A political revolutionary and an ardent patriot, he is a fighter for his country's liberation, a friend of the people and of freedom. The area in which the urban guerrilla acts is in the large Brazilian cities. There are also bandits, commonly known as outlaws, who work in the big cities. Many times, assaults by outlaws are taken as actions by urban guerrillas. The urban guerrilla, however, differs radically from the outlaw. The outlaw benefits personally from the action, and attacks indiscriminately without distinguishing between the exploited and the exploiters, which is why there are so many ordinary men and women among his victims. The urban guerrilla follows a political goal and only attacks the government, the big capitalists, and the foreign imperialists, particularly North Americans.

Another element just as prejudicial as the outlaw and also operating in the urban area is the right-wing counterrevolutionary who creates confusion, assaults banks, hurls bombs, kidnaps, assassinates, and commits the worst imaginable crimes against urban guerrillas, revolutionary priests, students, and citizens who oppose fascism and seek liberty. The urban guerrilla is an implacable enemy of the government and systematically inflicts damage on the authorities and on the men who dominate the country and exercise power. The principal task of the urban guerrilla is to distract, to wear out, to demoralize the militarists, the military dictatorship and its repressive forces, and also to attack and destroy the wealth and property of the North Americans, the foreign managers, and the Brazilian upper class.

The urban guerrilla is not afraid of dismantling and destroying the present Brazilian economic, political, and social system, for his aim is to help the rural guerrilla and to collaborate in the creation of a totally new and revolutionary social and political structure, with the armed people in power. The urban guerrilla must have a certain minimal political understanding. To gain that, he must read certain printed or mimeographed works such as:

- Guerrilla Warfare by Che Guevara
- Memories of a Terrorist
- Some Questions about the Brazilian
- Guerrilla Operations and Tactics on Strategic Problems and Principles
- Certain Tactical Principles for Comrades Undertaking Guerrilla Operations
- Organizational Questions
- O Guerrilheiro, newspaper of the Brazilian revolutionary groups

Personal Qualities of the Urban Guerrilla

His bravery and decisive nature characterize the urban guerrilla. He must be a good tactician and a good shot. The urban guerrilla must be a "person of great astuteness to compensate for the fact that he is not sufficiently strong in arms, ammunition, and equipment." The career militarists or the government police have modern arms and transport, and can go about anywhere freely, using the force of their power. The urban guerrilla does not have such resources at his disposal and leads a clandestine existence. Sometimes he is a convicted person or is out on parole and is obliged to use false documents.

Nevertheless, the urban guerrilla has a certain advantage over the conventional military or the police. It is that, while the military and the police act on behalf of the enemy, whom the people hate, the urban guerrilla defends a just cause, which is the people's cause.

The urban guerrilla's arms are inferior to the enemy's, but from a moral point of view, the urban guerrilla has an undeniable superiority. This moral superiority is what sustains the urban guerrilla. Thanks to it, the urban guerrilla can accomplish his principal duty, which is to attack and to survive. The urban guerrilla has to capture or divert arms from the enemy to be able to fight. Because his arms are not uniform, since what he has are expropriated or have fallen into hands in different ways, the urban guerrilla faces the problem of a variety of arms and a shortage of ammunition. Moreover, he has no place to practice shooting and marksmanship. These difficulties have to be surmounted, forcing the urban guerrilla to be imaginative and creative, qualities without which it would be impossible for him to carry out his role as a revolutionary.

The urban guerrilla must possess initiative, mobility, and flexibility, as well as versatility and a command of any situation. Initiative, especially, is an indispensable quality. It is not always possible to foresee everything. And the urban guerrilla cannot let himself become confused, or wait for orders. His duty is to act, to find adequate solutions for each problem he faces, and not to retreat. It is better to err acting than to do nothing for fear of erring. Without initiative there is no urban guerrilla warfare.[34]

URUGUAY AND PARAGUAY

In comparison to other Latin American states, Uruguay seemed to have an advantage with a prosperous economy built upon its sugar crop and its large export market. However, as has been evidenced in other regions of the world, the onset of severe economic downturns have led to the rise of worker parties, student revolts, and general unrest. This was the scenario in Uruguay when its economy crashed in the late 1950s. With the collapse came unrest, high unemployment, and inflation. The sugar workers had already organized labor unions to speak on their behalf, and by the end of the 1950s, the union was being led and influenced by extreme elements demanding social reforms and justice. Confrontation was the ultimate result.

FIGURE 13-13   Map of Uruguay (Central Intelligence Agency, *The World Factbook*, 2008).

FIGURE 13-14   Map of Paraguay (Central Intelligence Agency, *The World Factbook*, 2008).

National Liberation Movement (MLN): The Tupamaros

The Tupamaros movement grew out of the disillusionment of unionists, who marched on Montevideo, Uruguay's capital, in 1962. The confrontations with police ended in numerous arrests. The government was unsympathetic to union demands, and rather than listen to its claims, portrayed the unionists as insurgents and guerrillas. Raul Sendic, a law student who was arrested during one of the clashes, rose to form the MLN. Sendic emerged from a brief spell in prison, bitter and determined to fight back. The government imposed more restrictions on rights and freedoms, which forged the beginnings of terrorism in Uruguay. Largely an agricultural country, to mount an effective campaign, the group decided that its base and battleground would be the streets of Montevideo. The aim of the MLN was not to replace the government, but to force issues and change policy for the redistribution of wealth. Although the MLN espoused Marxist theories, it did not engage in rhetoric at the expense of public support. By the end of the 1960s, the Tupamaros had grown significantly and were believed to number more than 2,000. The combatants had no doubt studied the *Mini-Manual of the Urban Guerrilla* as their approach and their tactics tended to mirror Marighella's teachings. For support and supplies, the MLN depended on bank robberies and kidnapping officials for ransom. The group's methods became an example for other terror groups operating in urban centers of the world. The police in Uruguay were unable to stop the growing surge of the Tupamaros. With the democratic fabric now in tatters, the police resorted to torture to extract information and to deter would-be Tupamaros. Many suspected members of the MLN ended up in the country's top-security prison, the Penal de Libertad, under the control of the country's secret police, the *Organismo Coordinador de Actividades Anti-Subversivas*.[35]

Methods of torture were cruel, inhuman, and effective and included rapes, sensory deprivation beatings, burning, electrical shocks, and sleep deprivation.

The end for the Tupamaros came about unexpectedly. The chaos they had brought to the cities forced the government into a more vigorous application of repressive measures. In other words, in classic fashion, the Tupamaro's brand of terror forced the government to respond with its own brand of terror. However, the Tupamaros sought respectability and began to align with left-wing political movements to replace the government at the polling booth. This was a disaster, as left-wing constituents did not favor terrorism, and the bid for a socialist ticket failed. As socialists, they should have expected support from the working classes, but MLN was made up mainly of middle-class Uruguayans. With the failure of the political movement, a strong right-wing military government came into power. The populace endorsed its draconian measures in curbing the Tupamaros. The result was mass arrests and the end of MLN. The kidnapping of the British Ambassador, Sir Geoffrey Jackson, in Montevideo in 1972 ultimately shattered the myth that the Tupamaros were invincible. Shortly after Jackson's release from captivity, a general election was held, and the *Frente Amplio* (Broad Front), a strong political supporter of the Tupamaros, was decimated at the polls. The government was returned to office with a clear mandate to try to end terrorism.

The Tupamaros served as an example of how to organize an effective strike force of terrorists in an urban environment, using the city for cover and following the advice of the *Mini-Manual of the Urban Guerrilla.* Other such terror groups have profited from this example in Northern Ireland and in West Germany. The tactics employed by these middle-class terrorists, as saviors of the poor of Montevideo, did not translate into popular support for the movement. To some extent, this organization was built on small independent units and a cell-like structure, also a hallmark of the Irish Republican Army.

Internationally, South American countries could become havens for Middle East and North African terrorist groups: not just a sanctuary, but also a fertile recruiting, logistical, and financing region. Uruguay does not figure on the world map of terrorism but is an outspoken supporter of antiterrorism conventions in the region. The presence of al-Said Hassan Mokhles, a suspected Armed Islamic Group (GIA) member, was discovered in Uruguay and his presence immediately brought a request for extradition to Egypt where he was wanted on terrorist offences. GIA does have links with al Qaeda and many Algerians have migrated to North America, in particular Canada, over the last two decades. Uruguay has also become a home base for the Chilean Urban Marxist Guerrilla movement, the Manuel Rodriguez Patriotic Front.

The terrorist organization Hezbollah has been active in the tri-border region where Argentina, Paraguay, and Brazil converge. Little has been done about Hezbollah's presence particularly in Brazil as that country does not recognize any issues with Hezbollah and appears unwilling or unable to confront the problem. The main issue here is that the Hezbollah are actively raising funds for terrorism activity elsewhere. Tracking terrorist fund raising and financing is not a finite art and Brazil has not had any success in this area. In addition, most South American countries with the exception of Argentina have not suffered from any Middle Eastern influenced violence and are thus not motivated enough to go after Hezbollah.

ARGENTINA

Argentina has suffered through systematic human rights violations under the political will and control of strict military juntas since the mid-1970s. To escape the problems at home, the Argentine military government called on the historic claims of the nation to the Malvinas Islands (Falkland Islands) deep in the South Atlantic. Argentina had, for the past century, claimed title to the islands, which were populated by British families. Before the battle for the Falklands (1982), Argentine's military had attempted to "remove" all political opponents to its regime. This was achieved by clandestine arrests, which were followed by the complete disappearance of those arrested. Brutalized and tortured bodies that had been dumped in the ocean were pulled up in fishing nets.

Before World War II, Argentina had close ties to Germany. However, in 1945 the new government of General Farrell severed its links and joined the allies in the defeat of Germany. Two of the most celebrated names associated with South American politics are Colonel Juan Domingo Peron and his

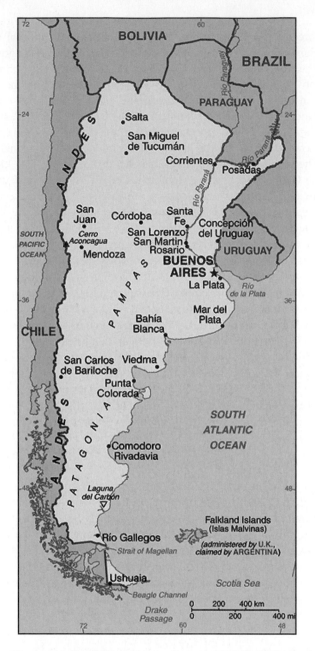

FIGURE 13-15   Map of Argentina (Central Intelligence Agency, *The World Factbook*, 2008).

equally famous wife, Eva. Peron was almost certainly responsible for initiating the use of what is now termed "death squads" in Argentina. His vision on coming to power as president in 1946 was to industrialize the nation at the expense of the agricultural industry, which had been Argentina's economic mainstay for most of the century. With industrialization and heavy government spending, came inflation at a staggering rate never before seen in Argentina. Left-wing political opposition to Peron's activities mounted, and as the 1950s dawned, Argentina was sliding down a dangerous slope, where food shortages and protests were the order of the day. In response, Peron nationalized the press and took total control over what was printed in the media. In 1949, he had created his own secret police force known as the CERT. CERT and its later version, the Division de Informacion Politicas Antidemocratic (DIPA), hid within its ranks a group designed for torture and repression called the Triple A, or the Argentine Anti-Communist Alliance. Peron was deposed in 1955, three years after the death of his famous wife, Eva.

The Triple A (AAA)

The AAA was an extreme right-wing death squad that functioned clandestinely at the beginning of the 1970s and consisted of members of the Argentine military and police. Many people suspected of being left-wing sympathizers were abducted, usually in the very early hours of the morning. The captors would explain that they were government agents. Death camps were set up apart from the normal prison structures of the country, making it almost impossible for relatives to locate those taken, let alone establish what kind of agency had detained them. There were forty-seven of these secret camps, which were similar to the concentration camps built by the Nazis, in World War II.[36]

FIGURE 13-16   Rescue workers comb through the rubble of the Jewish Community Center in Buenos Aires on July 18, 1994, after a car bomb rocked the building. Imad Mughniyeh, the legendary Hezbollah military commander, is believed responsible for planning this attack that killed 95 (Canadian Press).

As the years of unceasing military repression grew, so did the pressure from the Red Cross and Amnesty International who accused the military junta as accountable for those missing. In a remarkable piece of legislation passed by the Argentine government in 1979, those who were missing were presumed to be "legally dead" unless it could be proven otherwise!

International Terrorism in the Tri-Border Area (TBA)

The relatively lawless TBA region, the area where the borders of Paraguay, Brazil, and Argentina meet has been an area that has seen the development of international terrorist activity and which first came to notice with two bombings in Buenos Aires by Hezbollah in the early 1990s, the first attack was a bombing of the Israeli Embassy which killed 29 people and this attack it is believed was aided by Iranian diplomats. The second attack was on a Jewish Community Center where 85 people were killed. In both instances the finger is clearly pointed at Hezbollah who may well have been acting on behalf of Iran.

Fundraising and recruitment for terrorist activities has gone relatively unchecked in the TBA and has for years drawn attention as a center for contraband smuggling, drug trafficking, and large-scale money laundering, in part because all of the countries whose borders are involved profit from the illicit trade. It is also an easy place to hide and move money. Estimates of the amount of drug money alone laundered through the two main urban centers in the TBA, Foz do Iguacu and Ciudad del Este, range as high as $12 billion a year. Hezbollah is not the only extreme Islamist group believed to operate in the Central American region as Intelligence Services have documented the presence of Hamas and al Qaeda.[37]

Montoneros

One of the military junta's main targets was the **Montoneros (Movimiento Peronista Montonero),** and its supporters. Set up as a left-wing Peronista movement after the death of Juan Peron, this group was active from 1975 to 1979. The Montoneros were violently opposed to the military takeover of the Argentine government. They attempted to organize the union movement as a cohort in their activities, but a brutal crackdown by the junta prevented any effective action in the cities, and the group had to settle for actions in the countryside. Their tactics were hit-and-run, using bombings and shootings. By 1979, the group had been totally destroyed.[38]

This is yet another example of how an extreme right-wing military government resorted to terrorism of its own to remain in control . . . by using torture, murder, and widespread intimidation.

CHILE

As a sad century of military dictatorships in central, southern, and Latin America drew to a close, the only active terror group in Chile was a splinter group called the Manuel Rodriguez Patriotic Front (FPMR). The Lautaro Youth Movement, which was a mixed bag of disillusioned youths, leftist elements, and criminals, was active in the 1980s.

General Augusto Pinochet, a military dictator of strong Fascist principles was one of the most significant influences in Chile over the past twenty years. He is today, considered by many in Chile, the elder statesman of the country. Few dictators ever successfully reach happy retirement, but Pinochet is an example of one who has "gone the distance," despite the appalling acts during his tenure. Pinochet swept to power in 1973 during a bloody military coup that removed the Marxist regime responsible for the mismanagement of the country and its economy over a three-year period.

The Marxist leader Salvador Allende was the first democratically elected Marxist president to head any nation in the Western Hemisphere. Allende came to power in 1970 on a ticket promising social programs for Chileans. His government took immediate control of the country's copper mines and banking system. His huge increase in the minimum wage structure and attempts to keep

FIGURE 13-17   Map of Chile (Central Intelligence Agency, *The World Factbook*, 2008).

the cost of consumer products at a low level fueled runaway inflation. Between 1971 and 1973, inflation rose by nearly 400 percent! The government was besieged on all sides. Violent protests began in the streets of Santiago. The military, assisted by the U.S. CIA, overthrew the Allende government on September 11, 1973. Allende was arrested and died in custody. Reports on the circumstances of his death vary from torture, execution, to suicide.

The Pinochet Years

The Chilean military takeover, followed by the installation of yet another junta, was not widely popular. Fighting broke out between right-wing supporters of Pinochet and the extreme-left Communist elements. The junta cracked down hard on all opposition by dissolving congress, restricting the freedom of the press, and privatizing what had formerly been nationalized industries. Pinochet banned all political opposition parties and ran the country as a dictatorship. The trigger point for the attempted coup was not a momentary aberration on the part of Pinochet, in fact, many of the high-ranking military generals actually served in the Allende cabinet. What caused the problems for the military was the inclusion of left-wing extremism into the fabric of Chile's society. Allende had placed Communist reactionaries in the armed forces to incite rebellion, and over 14,000 foreign agitators moved into Chile. These included Cuban DGI agents, who were in Chile to reorganize internal security for Allende, as well as Soviet, Czech, and North Korean military instructors and arms suppliers, and hard-line Spanish Communist Party members. Their intent was to organize revolutionary brigades to take on the established military. The 1970s were a decade of change for Central and South America, and insurgent terror groups and guerrilla movements were on the move from Montevideo to Managua.[39]

To stem the flow of left-wing subversives, the Pinochet junta carried out mass arrests and used torture to gain both information and confessions. The military junta arrested not only Chileans, but also foreign subversive elements. These are the actions for which the international communities wanted Pinochet held accountable. Executions were commonplace in Chile, and the targets were leftist politicians, trade unionists, and other activists. Many simply disappeared, never to be heard from again. The junta engaged a semiofficial death squad organizations to do some of its dirty work. The Avengers of the Martyrs was a fascist paramilitary movement comprised mainly of military and police/security personnel. To make sure the security and paramilitary groups could conduct business in an unfettered manner, the military passed a decree to effectively denude the legal process and protection of the public. The Decree Law on Amnesty gave all security forces total and unequivocal immunity from arrest and prosecution.

The Pinochet military regime laid the foundation for a vibrant South American economy and passed it on to a democratic government that followed. Pinochet had turned Chile from a second-rate, Third-World country into a strong market economy, one that was being emulated in the 1990s and into the twenty-first century. Military dictators usually leave in the same violent manner by which they arrived in power, but General Pinochet is considered by many in Chile to be a hero of the people, and to a great many others, a despot and murderer.

In 1998, on a visit to Britain for back surgery, General Pinochet was arrested in his hospital bed and there were requests for his extradition. The highest court in Britain dealt a stunning blow to Pinochet, and in a stand for international law and justice, the British have hammered a nail into a portion of his coffin. Pinochet and the democratic government of Chile claimed he had diplomatic immunity as a former head of state and was therefore not subject to arrest and extradition. In the majority decision handed down in November 1998, Britain's Lord Nicholls commented: "The Vienna Convention on diplomatic relations may confer immunity in respect of acts performed in the exercise of functions, which international law recognizes as functions of a head of state, irrespective of the terms of his domestic constitution." Lord Nicholls further commented: "It hardly needs saying that the torture of his own subjects, or of aliens, would not be regarded by international law as a function of a head of state."[40]

Santiago's reactions to the decision led to waves of protest, as well as outpourings of relief. Whether the democracy that Pinochet had resurrected in Chile can survive remains to be seen. Certainly, any frailty of the system may invite left-wing advances on the power base of government and a return to Marxism. Pinochet subsequently returned to Chile and stood trial in what was termed the "Caravan of Death." Pinochet orchestrated political killings soon after he swept into power in 1973 and unleashed death squads to systematically execute political prisoners and subversives throughout the country. A ruling came down in March 2001 that was then appealed to the Chilean Supreme Court, which, in July 2002, accepted the earlier ruling that the former dictator was mentally unfit to stand trial. To many, his death on December 10, 2006, was a fitting end to his regime's horrendous abuse of civil liberties. On the international terror front, Chile experienced two terror-related incidents. In the wake of the 9-11 attacks, the U.S. Embassy received a functional letter bomb, and an anthrax-laced letter was sent to a doctor's office. However, the composition of the anthrax did not match with those strains used in the U.S. attacks. In a wider investigation, the government of Chile began to take a serious interest in the activities of Lebanese businessman Assad Ahmed Mohamed Barakat. It is suspected that Barakat was involved in financial holdings and money transfers for the Lebanese Hezbollah terror group.

VENEZUELA

Venezuela was once considered a democratic oasis in a desert of military dictatorship, but not anymore. Unlike much of Latin America, this country has had a history of democratic government since 1958, with lessening interference by the military. Venezuela suffers incursions by Colombian terrorists in the border villages and towns. Kidnapping and extortion are the main activities of both the National Liberation Army (ELN) and the Colombian People's Liberation Army (EPL).

Since the independence movement led by Venezuela's favorite son, Simon Bolivar, in the early 1800s, the country had been the home to a succession of military dictators. Venezuela began to prosper with the discovery of petroleum, which became its main source of revenue.

FIGURE 13-18 Map of Venezuela (Central Intelligence Agency, *The World Factbook*, 2008).

Mismanagement and corruption ended the military dictatorship of General Gomez in 1935, when the democratic movement, supported by the army, overthrew him and established a democratic government. The country has been ruled by two parties since 1958 . . . the Accion Democratica (AD) and the Christian Democratic Party (COPIE). Each has had its share of periods in office. However, economic downturns have stalled government action on behalf of the many poverty-stricken Venezuelans. Although there is no active terror movement in the country, there are definite signs that reforms will be needed if democracy is to endure. The government has utilized severe measures to control the country in tough economic times. The former leader of the 1992 military coup, Lieutenant Colonel Hugo Chavez, has made a successful leap into the current political system. General elections were held in December 1998, and Chavez won the presidency with a plurality of 56.5 percent, for a five-year term.[41]

Many of the problems facing the existing government involve corruption at the highest levels as well as drug smuggling and money laundering. The United States is one of Venezuela's main import and export partners and has, on the surface, made some effort to deter the drug traffic. Poverty is widespread and, with little light at the end of the economic tunnel, a different style of government has emerged. There are also problems associated with cross-border incursions from Colombia and the probability that the Venezuelan government has been turning a blind eye to such actions. For the landowners and ranchers in the border regions, this has meant reliance on vigilante squads and support from AUC in Colombia to combat the FARC incursions into Venezuela. The embattled President, Hugo Chavez, had to contend with a coup attempt in April 2002, which briefly saw him ousted from power. A general strike in November 2002 shut down Venezuela's oil industry. Noticeably, the U.S. television news coverage had failed to note that this strike was not being led by the working-class masses but by the middle-class management population! In its attempt to unseat Chavez, the opposition party has attempted to illicit support for a coup from the United States; however, the Bush government was more concerned with global issues involving Iraq and North Korea and paid little attention to Venezuela. Chavez has managed to retain control of the military and will likely continue to do so as long as the government does not attempt to use force against the strikers. Chavez has become more and more rabidly anti-American with every speech he makes. He is intent on stirring up trouble with the U.S. administration. Much before 2006, Venezuela's Chavez was little known to the U.S. public but his outburst at the UN General Assembly in September 2006, speaking the day after U.S. President George W. Bush, he stated "Yesterday the devil came here. Right here and it smells of sulfur still today." He has made many odorous comments and called the U.S. president a drunkard and a terrorist, and Condoleezza Rice (Secretary of State), a sexually frustrated and illiterate female; his goals are a direct challenge to the United States. To this end, he has sought alliances with most of the world's more extreme leaders, i.e. Mahmoud Ahmadinejad of Iran, Bashar al-Assad of Syria, and Kim Jong-IL of North Korea. Iranian factories are being constructed in Venezuela and there are direct flights between Caracas and Tehran. President Chavez has been outspoken for his support of Hezbollah and been openly hostile to Israel for its Lebanon attacks in 2006. Clearly he thinks he is a force to be reckoned with. Venezuela is oil rich and the current climb in oil prices has no doubt emboldened him, as his government reaps the riches from the soaring price of a barrel of oil. He has often threatened to cut off the supply of oil to the United States, however, that may not be a reality in the short term as Venezuela exports approximately 50 percent of its oil to the United States.

Chavez has also been involved in indirect talks with the FARC in an effort to have some of the numerous hostages released. In February 2008, the FARC released three hostages who had been held for more than six years. President Chavez caused considerable displeasure to the Colombian government by speaking directly with FARC, an action not sanctioned by the Colombians.

ECUADOR

Ecuador is not a region well known for terrorism and insurgency. In the past decade, it has remained relatively calm with the exception of the October 12, 2000, kidnapping of eight oil rig workers by armed men that lasted into early 2001. The hostage-takers executed Ron Sander, one of the U.S. hostages. A little-known group calling itself the Revolutionary Armed Forces of Ecuador has taken credit for two bombs that exploded in the coastal city of Guayaquil. The FARE could be a front for the Revolutionary Armed Forces of Colombia (FARC) or a stand-alone group. Either way, its emergence suggests that the Colombian conflict soon will affect U.S. personnel and assets outside Colombia. In August 2002, a bomb attack on a McDonald's restaurant was claimed to be the work of an unknown terror group calling itself the FARE. FARE states that it is a prodigy of the Revolutionary Armed Forces of Colombia (FARC), and it threatened more violence and assassination. At this juncture, very little is known about the group, its makeup, or its aims. However, there is a probability that it could actually be a breakaway faction of the FARC, and could be setting up in Ecuador to make the politicians wary of being aligned with the U.S. war on narcotics in the region. Elections held in October 2002, were a focal point for the FARE in its wish to influence any political outcome. Authorities have previously reported the presence of FARE, but no terror attacks have been previously attributed to the group, which authorities say may number several hundred members from both Ecuador and Colombia. The FARE does not appear to be linked to drug trafficking; however, if it is actually FARC by another name, narcotics trafficking may soon be on its agenda. The leftist governments of both Venezuela and Ecuador continue to lash out at their neighbor Colombia mainly for its pro U.S. stance. In early March 2008, when Colombian aircraft crossed into Ecuador and killed Raul Reyes, a senior member of the FARC leadership, it raised the possibilities of a military

FIGURE 13-19   Map of Ecuador (Central Intelligence Agency, *The World Factbook*, 2008).

confrontation between the three. Ecuador has been tolerant of the presence of FARC rebels residing inside its territory and the March 2008 raid was roundly condemned by the main leftist governments in South America and this has fuelled Latin America's ideological divisions. Colombian President Alvaro Uribe is a conservative who has received vast sums for his campaign against the drug trade and FARC terrorists, and what was originally hailed as a major victory for the Uribe government has become the focus of open hostility from Ecuador and Venezuela. Both countries view Colombia as a pawn of the United States. On the other hand, the Colombian military claimed to have discovered evidence that FARC was attempting to obtain materials to build a dirty bomb.

Summary

Central and South America have been mostly under strong right-wing military rule for many decades of the twentieth century, and into the twenty-first. They have also suffered the ravages of death squads. In studying the causes of terrorism and guerrilla activity throughout Latin America, there are trends that become apparent. In Mexico, El Salvador, Chile, and Uruguay, much of the activity was related to land claims, where the few wealthy landowners had immense influence on the ruling political and military governments. In protecting those interests, the extreme-right death squads operated with impunity. Violations of human rights and the prosecution of those responsible continue to the present. Argentina is recovering from the stringent rule of the military juntas of the 1980s and crushing humiliation and defeat in the Falkland Islands at the hands of the British. The loss of loved ones to death squads will continue to plague the citizens of new democracies as they strive to move forward. After four decades, Colombian terrorism seems likely to continue with an upsurge in attacks by FARC. The possibility that they would seek to use and even build a dirty bomb, will give much cause for concern, as will the Hezbollah presence in the tri-border regions. South American countries still lead the way in kidnappings and extortion. The presence of Lebanese Hezbollah and Hamas members as well as the GIA will prompt U.S. power-brokers to keep close watch on developments to ensure that international terrorism, with aims of attacking the United States and its interests, is not played out in the region.

Web Sites

1. **The Council on Foreign Relations**—*http://www.cfr.org/region/242/mexicol*
2. **Human Rights Watch**—*http://www.hrw.org=south_america*
3. **FBI Columbia Joint Terrorism Task Force**—*http://Columbia.fbi.gov*
4. **Plan Columbia and Beyond**—*www.csmonitor.com/2006/0928/p01s03-woam.html*
5. **U.S. Department of Defense**—*http://www.defenselink.mil/news*
6. **The Transnational Institute**—*http://www.tni.org*

Endnotes

1. U.S. Census Bureau. http://www.census.gov/main/www/popclock.html.
2. "Mexico, Post Rebellion Pains." *The Economist* (January 12, 2002, p. 35).
3. Reuters News Service. http://www.reuters.com/.
4. Piet van Lier: *War called Peace, Death of a Bishop* (1997) http:zena.securforum.com/znet/LAM/zGuatemala.html.
5. www.Boston.com/news Mica Rosenberg, February 9, 2006.
6. Frank M. Afflitto. Abstract from a paper presented at the Conference of the American Society of Criminology, San Diego, CA (November 20, 1997).
7. Global Intelligence Update. http://www.stratfor.com/standard/analysis.
8. U.S. Department of State. *Patterns of Global Terrorism*, Publication 10321, http://www.strafor.com.
9. Jonathan R. White. *Terrorism: An Introduction* (Belmont, CA: Brooks Cole Publishing, p. 157).

10. The Kerry Committee Report (April 19, 1995).
11. U.S. Immigration and Customs Service. www.ice.gov/pi//investigations/comshield/index.htm.
12. Edwin Early. *The History Atlas of South America* (New York: Macmillan USA, 1998).
13. U.S. State Department International Information Programs. "Grossman Outlines Terrorist Threat to Colombia." Testimony by Ambassador Marc Grossman, Undersecretary of State for Political Affairs before the Senate Committee on Foreign Relations Sub-Committee for Western Hemisphere Affairs (April 24, 2003), http:///usinfo.state.gov/topical/pol/terror.htm.
14. Kevin Whitelaw—The State Department is helping train elite police units to go after kidnappers and rescue hostages. www.USNews.com Inside Colombia's War on Kidnapping. February 27, 2008.
15. Council on Foreign Relations—FARC, ELN: Colombia's Left-wing guerrillas http://www.cfr.org/publication/9272/.
16. Stan Yarbo. *The Christian Science Monitor* (November 18, 1998).
17. Ibid.
18. U.S. Department of State International Information Programs. "U.S., Colombia Investigate Expansion of Terrorist Alliances." Charlene Porter Washington, File Staff Writer (April 25, 2002), http://usinfo.state.gov/topical/pol/terror02042500.htm.
19. Colombia Basic Information. http://www.infoplease.com/ipa/A0107419.html.
20. Noam Chomsky. "On the War on Drugs." Interviewed by Week Online *DRCNet* (February 8, 2002), http://www.chomsky.info/interviews/20020208.htm.
21. Mike Gray. *Drugs & Terrorism.* http://www.narcoterror.org/mike_oped.htm.
22. U.S. Department of State Briefing Note 2008.
23. Sam Dillon "As Peru Votes, Insurgents Mystique Casts Shadow." *Miami Herald* (June 10, 1990, pp. 1A, 26A).
24. White. *Terrorism: An Introduction*, p. 82.
25. "The Shining Path Comes Back." *The Economist* (August 17, 1996, p. 35).
26. Armed Conflict Reports—Peru 1980. http://www.ploughshares.ca/libraries/ACRText/ACR-Peru.html.
27. Jamestown Foundation—The Jamestown Foundation—Global Terrorism Analysis vol. 4, no. 28 (September 11, 2007), http://www.jamestown.org/terrorism/news/article.php?articleid=2373637.
28. Gabriel Escobar. "Peruvian Guerrillas Hold Hundreds Hostage." *Washington Post*, Foreign Service (December 19, 1996).
29. CNN Interactive World News. "One Hostage Killed in Daring Peru Rescue." CNN (April 22, 1997), http://www.cnn/world19704/22/peru.update.late.
30. *CIA World Fact Book*—Country Reports, http://www.cia.gov/cia/publications/factbook/geos/bl.html.
31. San Jose State University, Economics Department, http://www2.sjsu.edu/faculty/watkiins/bolivia.htm.
32. "La Massacre del Valle de Cochabamba." *La Paz Cadernos* "Justicia Y Paz," 1975.
33. N.A. Keck, CPP. ASIS Presentation Paper (May 16, 1996).
34. Carlos Marighella. *Mini Manual of the Urban Guerrilla* (Pamphlet, 1969, pp. 1–2).
35. Bruce Quarrie. *The World's Secret Police* (London: Octobus Books Ltd., 1986, p. 48).
36. Quarrie. *The World's Secret Police.*
37. Douglas Farah—Hezbollah's External Support Network in West Africa and Latin America—International Assessment and Strategy Center, August 4, 2006, www.strategycenter.net/research/pubID.118/pub_dctail.asp.
38. White. *Terrorism: An Introduction*, pp. 48, 49.
39. Arnaud de Borchgrave. "Demonized for Killing a Left-Wing Plot." *The Washington Times* (October 1998, p. A-15).
40. International News, *The Globe and Mail, Canada* (November 26, 1998).
41. Steven Gutkin. Associated Press (November 28, 1998).

PART THREE

The War on Terror

CHAPTER 14

Countering Terrorism

We are not fighting so that the enemy may offer us something.
We are fighting to wipe out the enemy.

HUSSEIN MUSSAWI, FORMER HEZBOLLAH LEADER.

Learning Objective

The study and review of this chapter will enable you to

1. Discuss why the SAS was so feared by the Provisional IRA during the "Troubles";
2. List the counter terror units established by western governments to tackle terrorism;
3. Discuss why intelligence is such a key ingredient in the fight against terrorism;
4. Discuss how the threat of chemical and biological warfare can easily pose a threat to any democracy.

Terms to Remember

Al Jazeera
Emergency Provisions
European Civil Aviation
  Conference (ECAC)
General Staff Reconnaissance
  Unit #69
Grenzschutzgruppe 9 (GSG-9)
Groupment d'intervention de
  la Gendarmerie Nationale
  (GIGN)

Grupo Especial de
  Operaciones (GEO)
Human intelligence
  (HUMINT)
Interpol
Joint Task Force 2 (JTF-2)
Major Criminal Hijack
  (MCHJ)
Man Portable Air Defense
  Systems (MANPADS)

Nerve agents
Signals intelligence (SIGINT)
Special Air Service
  (SAS)
Special Boat Squadron (SBS)
Vesicants

April 30, 1980: London, UK—Armed men stormed the Iranian Embassy in London, taking twenty-six people hostage. Six days later, the SAS ended the siege, killing five terrorists and capturing one.

January 25, 2000: Ratchaburi, Thailand—Thai commandos rescued 700 hostages from a besieged provincial hospital in a dawn strike, killing ten gunmen from a radical Myanmar guerrilla faction headed by twelve-year-old twins.

August 11, 2006: London UK—A major plot to "commit mass murder on an unimaginable scale" by destroying passenger jets in mid-air had been foiled. The targets were as many as nine flights leaving British airports destined for America. U.S. officials said the plan bore some of the hallmarks of an al Qaeda plot.

OVERVIEW

Since September 11, 2001, the world has had to take stock of the way it counters what has evolved into a global threat. The threats are emanating not only from al Qaeda, but also are from religiously motivated Islamists while al Qaeda has transformed itself into something akin to a very virulent cult following for extremist, ideological Islamists. During the last four decades of the twentieth century, the emphasis for countering terrorist attacks was very much focused upon the specific terrorist groups that were targeting specific areas within many defined regions or countries. Modern urban terrorism was an unfamiliar topic for the security forces of most countries until the 1970s. Significant incidents . . . such as the Munich Olympic Games massacre showed the world how totally unprepared many security/police forces were at handling such situations. Individual countries had thus established highly elite counter-terror units for both domestic and foreign deployment. No day passes without mention of terrorism or an insurgency in some area of the world and clearly the democracies of the world have been and are being challenged continuously to fight against it. In the United States, Americans have seen legislation enacted that is often draconian in its measures and application, and also, some would say, attacks the civil liberties of a nation . . . laws that are barely raising a whimper from the public. The entire structure and makeup of U.S. security has been radically transformed, as a result of the attacks on September 11, 2001. The emphasis now is on protecting vital areas of national infrastructure, food sources, the material supply chain, roads, railways, aviation, bridges, dams, and computer systems. The government and its intelligence services are looking to the future on how to hopefully protect, prevent, deter, and detect the next major terror event.

This chapter looks at the unconventional forces that have been established to counter terror and discusses what may have changed since 9-11, particularly in the United States and Europe. We discuss attitudes aimed toward countering the scourge of terrorism. We will review the most effective and recognized response units for countering terrorism from around the world, some well known, and others maybe less so.

We discuss the needs of nations to develop a trained and specifically designated organization that can be held responsible for responding to any terrorist incidents while maintaining all civil liberties on a scale that would be acceptable to the public in general. Aviation still continues to present itself as a target of choice for terrorists, so we will look at the protection of aviation to both facilities and aircraft in flight. Should we develop and implement new efforts and systems to prevent hand-held missile attacks against civilian airliners? How do we propose to prevent and respond to chemical and biological threats?

If the primary objective of countering terrorism is the protection of democratic institutions and the rule of law, how far can we expect to go in reaching that objective? Can we solve the issue of political violence, if governments and dictatorships are prepared to sacrifice all considerations of basic humanity and to then totally ignore constitutional and judicial rights?[1]

THE ROLES FOR COUNTERTERRORISM

Are the actions of subversive groups, insurgents, and terrorists considered criminal behavior? Throughout this text the issue continues to surface, whether the issue of terrorism is in the Far East, Near East, Middle East, Europe or North America and how best to legislate against those bent on terrorism. In many countries, legislation has been enacted not only to ban membership in terror organizations, but to sometimes allow for certain suspensions of civil rights to facilitate law enforcement and intelligence activities. To implement such actions successfully in a democratic society requires that the government ensure that such legislation requires review and renewal on a regular basis. In the United Kingdom, the legislation restricting the Irish Republican Army and other terrorist groups required the government to regularly justify its need for such drastic powers because, without such justification, it would automatically lapse.

The terrorist tactics that strike fear in the public for political gain are well documented. Terror and insurgent groups operating in Iraq used a new tactic in 2004 and 2005 . . . the Internet. At the touch of a computer mouse, millions were witness to the grizzly decapitation of Western hostages. The political gain the terrorists seek, in this instance, is to place enormous pressure on government to respond in a specific manner—to either act or react in a determined manner. This has been clearly shown in the United Kingdom, where the Provisional IRA has waged a continuous campaign of indiscriminate violence against authorities and innocent civilians. One of the earliest terror incidents in Great Britain was an attack on the Parachute Regiment Officers' Mess in Aldershot, southern England, which is located about 50 miles southwest of London. The bomb attack took place on February 22, 1972, and killed five female kitchen attendants, a padre, and injured nineteen others. The public viewed the attack as reprisal for the "Bloody Sunday" massacre by British paratroopers in Northern Ireland that had claimed the lives of thirteen civilians three weeks prior to the Aldershot bombing.

The reaction depicted in local and national press coverage and on the television news was complete outrage at such a senseless act. Immediately after the bombing, there were sporadic incidents against local Irish families, who were intimidated and even assaulted. The same reaction occurred after Irish republican terrorists struck at public houses in Guildford and Birmingham, killing and injuring indiscriminately. Calls for restraint from both sides of the British political and religious spectrum went out quickly and diffused a major outpouring of hatred against the several million Irish citizens who have coexisted peacefully alongside their British counterparts.

In the same manner, the events of 9-11 allowed a frantic American public to then think that every Muslim or Arab was a terrorist in waiting. The way we regarded our ethnically and religiously different neighbors suddenly changed. It would most certainly be incorrect to cast a suspicious eye at every "Muslim-looking" person. Government intelligence and security forces have been criticized for "racially profiling" specific ethnic and religious groups. On 9-11, the attackers were of Middle East and North African origin, but does the color of the skin determine a person's political and ideological status in society? We think not. Intelligence, of course, is not the sole domain of their governments . . . in nearly all instances, the planning for any major assault, or a terrorist attack has involvement in the gathering of intelligence by the terrorist group, individual, or organization. In the case of 9-11, there was ample time and opportunity for the terrorist groups to openly view and study the methods used at security checkpoints of the targeted airports and, no doubt, they conducted dummy runs. In the theater of Northern Ireland, the Provisional Irish Republican Army (PIRA) has always used intelligence gathering successfully to execute operations and has used tactics designed to strike at security forces as they respond to a bomb attack. We are seeing insurgents in Iraq and Afghanistan using this same tactic as they detonate one car bomb, and then a second when rescue workers and security personnel arrive on scene.

In the same way, we cannot characterize any group purely by their religious beliefs. Not every Catholic is, by any stretch of the imagination, therefore a supporter of the Provisional Irish Republican Army and neither must one now make the mistake that every Middle Eastern person is therefore an Islamic extremist. Immigration must come under specific scrutiny in both the United States and Canada, and review method and process by which students and visitors visas are issued and how checks are made.

The problem for Americans, if, in fact it is to be considered a problem, is that they enjoy a free and open democracy, and value their freedom of speech, their freedom of association, and an ability to travel without undue hindrance. This concept is in stark contrast to many countries, where such liberties are not accepted. The events of 9-11 were clearly perpetrated by people who took advantage of those freedoms and liberties that we all hold dear, and they will continue to attempt to destroy those values and freedoms wherever they can.

Maintaining Order

The past examples of the, "Irish Troubles," have been remarkable in many respects. In Britain and Northern Ireland, the role of the policeman had always been very public, and the typical British "Bobby" was always on hand to assist. During the terrorist bombing campaigns of mainland Britain, from the late 1960 to 2000, the police had not resorted to a system of rigid rules and control. As has been evidenced in many Latin American countries, terrorist threats, and very harsh intimidation, have too often been met by even harsher measures inflicted by military and paramilitary police. In the British experience, terror against the public, in general, reached almost epidemic proportions in the 1970s. But order and calm prevailed, and any public outrage was contained. Rather than form vigilante groups to hunt down suspected terrorists, the British public and media were fully supportive of the police actions. TV news coverage showed the police as the front-line troops, always the first on the scene of whatever new atrocity the PIRA . . . or others, had perpetrated. In the 1970s, London became a virtual battleground, but sound police tactics and investigative techniques did far more to bring the criminal terrorists to justice than the suspension of any civil liberties might have done.

In many countries throughout the world, armed and aggressive police forces are a reality. That was not the case in Great Britain, where police were predominately unarmed throughout the PIRA crisis. The police adhered to their role of identifying, tracking down, and apprehending the terrorists, just as they would any criminal. Police investigations are all about the necessity to gather information, intelligence, and, ultimately, solid evidence. Britain's Special Branch, which deals with terrorists, took the lead in gathering intelligence on subversive Irish groups operating in Northern Ireland and Great Britain. Success for such efforts, however, must be as a result of cooperation among police, the public, and the media. As evident in the United States, such cooperation among agencies can often be strained. Some police agencies jealously guard not only sources, but information as well. The public is usually the last to know the true story. There is no simple right or wrong answers with the tactics in combating terrorism. There are, however, many examples of (how and how not) to deal with any terrorist situation.

The most open display of police weaponry up until the terrorist attacks in 2005 was at London's Heathrow Airport, which has been the site of numerous false alarms, as well as actual terrorist bombings and mortar attacks carried out by Irish terrorists. The message is clearly sent that the police are ready to respond with overwhelming force. Since the London subway attack the sight of armed police in the capital is now as common as it is in the USA.

Racial Profiling

Profiling has long been an issue and certainly not since the terrorist attacks of September 11, 2001. In a world where we not only have to be seen to be politically correct but also to actually apply that correctness to such issues as national security is a considerable challenge. Clearly the overall reliance on race as the predetermining factor when there are many other avenues or tools for law enforcement to use is incorrect. However the mere mention of the word profiling gets politicians and rights groups in an uproar. The ultimate solution, one that would most effectively strike a balance between the preservation of civil liberties and the need for heightened security has been elusive. Increased polarization of perspectives about the role and effectiveness of racial profiling are now, even more than ever, at the forefront of discussions regarding new legislation that will ultimately shape and determine law enforcement's proactive response to terrorism. There are two kinds of glaring mistakes that we could potentially make in regards to terrorism, one is failing to identify terrorists because we don't want to offend anyone, and two, investigating someone who resembles the profile of a terrorist and therefore upsetting them as a result if the person is not a terrorist.[2] An extreme example of what can go wrong relates to the London Underground bombing threat in 2005 where anti terror police had a suspect under surveillance at an apartment block in the capital. A male was seen leaving the premises was challenged by police but did not stop. The police had a new "shoot to kill" policy if they "suspected" a suicide bomber. The unfortunate man was wearing a back pack and ran down into the Stockwell Tuber station at which point he was shot five times in the head at point blank range. It turned out that Jean Charles de Menezes, twenty-seven, was not involved in terrorism but was a migrant worker possibly working illegally in the country.

Repression

To determine whether a state's repressive actions against terror are effective, one only has to examine the Soviet Union . . . before the fall of the Communist regime. Very few, if any kind of terrorist attacks were neither recorded or reported in the former Soviet Union, which had a thriving community of secret police, and thousands of informers inside of every sector of business and society. This made it very difficult, if not impossible, for subversive ideas to ever become reality. The KGB would almost always snuff out such plots before they could be executed. Yet, with the breakup of the Soviet Union, we have witnessed criminal activity and terrorism on a significant scale. Why did this happen in the USSR? The fall of the Soviet Union was so sudden and the Russian Federation of States underwent such rapid change, that it eventually brought about the collapse of the state, and of the well-structured and supported police service. In a vast empire that had relied on the state police for all forms of investigations and tactics, both overt and covert, there was now only chaos and a vacuum. The vacuum was filled by criminal and subversive elements that filled the void vacated by established authority.

The drastic reduction in the need for nuclear weapons capability created a ready illegal market in which radical, rogue governments could acquire nuclear technology and even create devices, especially if they could afford to bid at the highest prices. While no terror group has actually used a nuclear device so far, there is an obvious concern that the ingredients to make a "dirty bomb" could well come out of the former Soviet states where controls are weak and the tracking of such materials is difficult and suspect.

Great Britain, since the 1990s, is a very different battleground altogether. With ever-increasing demands on civilian police forces, they have adopted a significant "Big Brother" approach to their duties, maintaining a watchful eye on the communities they serve. Closed-circuit television cameras that monitor the heart of the major cities, as well as the network of the major motorway systems, have aided in the search for serious criminals and terrorists. Civil libertarians and the extreme left-wing agitators may argue that it is an invasion of privacy, but the London police have had indisputable success in tracking down terrorists who abandon vehicles packed with vast quantities of explosives.

To many observers, it would have been an acceptable solution in the wake of the PIRA bombing campaign to unleash the army against what were perceived to be vicious and callous terrorists. One must keep in mind that an army's main role is that of national defense, not policing. The use of the U.S. Marines in Somalia demonstrated the futility of having policing done with a military combat unit. In Northern Ireland, when the local (formerly) Royal Ulster Constabulary was unable to protect Catholics from Protestant violence, the army was called in to "assist." That assistance to the Catholic community was also the rallying call for the under-equipped Irish Republican Army of the day. As matters further deteriorated at the end of the 1960s, the army was brought into a policing role that involved searches of houses for weapons. At the very least, the army's actions were heavy-handed, and the soldiers became the objects of hatred and scorn for the local Catholics they were attempting to protect.

Military responses to terror events have also been graphically emphasized by the Israeli use of heavy armor, helicopters, and fighter aircraft to attack elements of Hamas in the West Bank and Gaza regions. Winning the war in Iraq is a point in question, winning the peace has been something else altogether. While military tactics have been used in attempts to "pacify" large areas of Iraq, there has been little consideration given to the ethnic, religious, clan, and social structures that fuel the counterinsurgency campaigns. Israel mounted a campaign in 2002 to identify locations where suspected terrorist leaders were, and then hit them with extreme force. The problem was that Israel was actually targeting areas where civilians lived. Collateral damage can always occur where terrorists are concerned; however, firing rockets into densely packed apartment buildings with the express intent to kill one suspected terrorist will invariably result in the deaths of many innocent civilians. We see and hear daily how many American soldiers are killed and injured in Iraq but little or no figures are available on the significant casualty figures for the Iraqi population when troops target a civilian area where insurgents are hiding. The international community questions Israel's actions but has not done so of the United States in regard to Iraq. Of note here is that Israel's military actions have not been successful in curtailing the never-ending cycle of violence in Israeli cities and in the Palestinian areas of the West Bank and Gaza Strip, nor has U.S. policy in Iraq quelled the insurgency there. From Israel's perspective, its intelligence network has become so efficient in targeting suspected terror elements that it will continue targeting civilian areas as a means of routing out terrorists.

NORTHERN IRELAND

Without using the ultimate weapon of imposing martial law in Northern Ireland, the British government used a statutory instrument to control the lawlessness of the terror groups operating against the security forces in the province. Special powers to deal with "The Troubles" came into effect in 1973. The Northern Ireland (**Emergency Provisions**) Act empowered the military to have a greater impact in dealing with the urban terrorists. "No go" areas sprang up in areas of Belfast and Londonderry during the Troubles enabling terrorists to remain in their 'safe houses' within the communities they were fighting to protect. The Emergency Provisions gave sweeping powers to the military to search houses at any time without the necessity of warrants from the civil courts. The security forces could detain and question anyone for up to four hours. These methods allowed the military to build up a significant database of information about the people of Northern Ireland. From 1972 to 1976, the army searched nearly 250,000 houses, and uncovered 5,800 weapons and 661,000 rounds of ammunition. Added to these powers was the internment of active members of terrorist organizations. Hundreds of Irishmen were interned in the 1970s and, in hindsight, brought the Provisional IRA to the brink of defeat. Nearly all its executive and operations groups were either serving prison sentences or interned.[3] The IRA's call for a Christmas truce in 1974 was made from a position of extreme weakness. After all, there was no way IRA demands for the swift total withdrawal of the British from Northern Ireland and general amnesty for all convicted terrorists would be met. It would be another twenty-four years before the IRA terrorists would walk out of prison as part of the Good Friday Agreement of 1998.

Legislation

Many operational methods and legislated practices can be put into place, but for a true and solid democracy it must ensure that civil liberties are not abrogated to such an extent that the public is duly affected by their restrictive nature. Over the past thirty years, there have been significant pieces of legislation and internationally recognized conventions aimed at curbing the activities of terrorists and countering their actions. The first major terror attacks that attracted attention on a global scale involved PLO hijackings of commercial airliners. Those significant hijackings coupled with the ineptitude of most governments in handling such crises, prompted international anti-hijacking legislation to be drafted. The hijackings also prompted a more fundamental approach by one of the target states . . . Israel.

Israel was one of the first states to provide trained and armed "sky marshals" on all of its aircraft around the world. On all El Al flights, specially trained staff carry out stringent physical and profile security checks on every passenger boarding the flight. So effective was the El Al approach to handling security issues that the terrorists had to find a "soft underbelly" to attack. This, in several instances, was a ground-level attack at airport check-in counters. There were also attempts to shoot down aircraft by means of RPG-7 rockets, as was the case with the failed attack by Black September terrorists at Orly Airport in France. The RPG-7 is a reloadable, shoulder-fired, muzzle-loaded, recoilless antitank and antipersonnel rocket-propelled grenade launcher that launches fin-stabilized, oversized rocket assisted HEAT grenade from a smooth bore 40mm tube. The launcher with optical sights weighs 15.9 pounds and has a maximum, effective range of 300 meters against moving point targets and 500 meters against stationary point targets and therefore ideal for use in an around airports and airfields.

The fundamental principle of international legislative instruments, such as that of the Chicago Convention and, in particular, Annex 17, was that they required member states to safeguard global air transportation from acts of unlawful interference. The Convention applied a common set of standards for the security of international civil aviation.

TERRORISM AND AVIATION

Attacks against airliners has long been a choice target for terrorists dating back to the 1970s, however, 9-11 laid bare the blatant incompetence of airport security that Americans had become used too in their daily travels in North America prior to that fateful date: the inadequacies of the airline security program to protect, to any degree, passengers flying out of international airports in the United States was totally exposed. Although aviation security was thrust to the forefront when terrorism struck in 2001, the problem of lax airport security had been around for decades. In 1968 there were twenty-seven hijackings and attempts to hijack commercial airliners to Cuba. In 1969 Palestinian terrorists were responsible for a large majority of the eighty-two hijackings worldwide as they attempted to publicize their cause and to put pressure on the Israeli government to release Palestinian prisoners. It would be grossly unfair to be critical of only U.S. aviation when the problem is systemic across all countries, with the possible exception of Israel. The Federal Aviation Administration (FAA) has the responsibility for the safety of U.S. civil aviation. Although it has an excellent staff with immense expertise, it is severely hampered in its ability to implement the changes needed to protect civil aviation from terror attacks inside the United States. This is, in part, because the FAA lacked the funding for research and development of new technology. Also, a powerful aviation lobby had been successful in blocking some of the necessary changes. There are international conventions that cover protocols for dealing with hijackings, aside from the criminal statutes that nation-states have promulgated to deal with individual criminal acts. The enacting of international treaties covers the issue of international terrorism and the hijacking of aircraft. There are twelve significant conventions developed over the last sixty years related to terrorism as follows:

1. Convention on Offenses and Certain Other Acts Committed on Board Aircraft ("Tokyo Convention," 1963—safety of aviation):
   - Applies to acts affecting in-flight safety;
   - Authorizes the aircraft commander to impose reasonable measures, including restraint, on any person he or she has reason to believe has committed or is about to commit such an act, when necessary to protect the safety of the aircraft;
   - Requires contracting states to take custody of offenders and to return control of the aircraft to the lawful commander.

2. Convention for the Suppression of Unlawful Seizure of Aircraft ("Hague Convention," 1970—aircraft hijackings):
   - Makes it an offense for any person on board an aircraft in flight [to] "unlawfully, by force or threat thereof, or any other form of intimidation, [to] seize or exercise control of that aircraft" or to attempt to do so;
   - Requires parties to the convention to make hijackings punishable by "severe penalties";
   - Requires parties that have custody of offenders to either extradite the offender or submit the case for prosecution;
   - Requires parties to assist each other in connection with criminal proceedings brought under the convention.

3. Convention for the Suppression of Unlawful Acts against the Safety of Civil Aviation ("Montreal Convention," 1971—applies to acts of aviation sabotage such as bombings aboard aircraft in flight):
   • Makes it an offense for any person unlawfully and intentionally to perform an act of violence against a person on board an aircraft in flight, if that act is likely to endanger the safety of that aircraft; to place an explosive device on an aircraft; and to attempt such acts or be an accomplice of a person who performs or attempts to perform such acts;
   • Requires parties to the convention to make offenses punishable by "severe penalties";
   • Requires parties that have custody of offenders to either extradite the offender or submit the case for prosecution.

4. Convention on the Prevention and Punishment of Crimes against Internationally Protected Persons (1973—outlaws attacks on senior government officials and diplomats):
   • Defines internationally protected person as a Head of State, a Minister for Foreign Affairs, a representative or official of a state or of an international organization who is entitled to special protection from attack under international law;
   • Requires each party to criminalize and make punishable "by appropriate penalties which take into account their grave nature," the intentional murder, kidnapping, or other attack upon the person or liberty of an internationally protected person, a violent attack upon the official premises, the private accommodations, or the means of transport of such person; a threat or attempt to commit such an attack; and an act "constituting participation as an accomplice."

5. International Convention against the Taking of Hostages ("Hostages Convention," 1979):
   • Provides that "any person who seizes or detains and threatens to kill, to injure, or to continue to detain another person in order to compel a third party, namely, a State, an international intergovernmental organization, a natural or juridical person, or a group of persons, to do or abstain from doing any act as an explicit or implicit condition for the release of the hostage commits the offense of taking of hostage within the meaning of this Convention."

6. Convention on the Physical Protection of Nuclear Material ("Nuclear Materials Convention," 1980—combats unlawful taking and use of nuclear material):
   • Criminalizes the unlawful possession, use, transfer, etc., of nuclear material, the theft of nuclear material, and threats to use nuclear material to cause death or serious injury to any person or substantial property damage.

7. Protocol for the Suppression of Unlawful Acts of Violence at Airports Serving International Civil Aviation, supplementary to the Convention for the Suppression of Unlawful Acts against the Safety of Civil Aviation (extends and supplements the Montreal Convention on Air Safety, 1988):
   • Extends the provisions of the Montreal Convention (see No. 3) to encompass terrorist acts at airports serving international civil aviation.

8. Convention for the Suppression of Unlawful Acts against the Safety of Maritime Navigation (1988—applies to terrorist activities on ships):
   • Establishes a legal regime applicable to acts against international maritime navigation that is similar to the regimes established against international aviation;
   • Makes it an offense for a person unlawfully and intentionally to seize or exercise control over a ship by force, threat, or intimidation; to perform an act

of violence against a person on board a ship if that act is likely to endanger the safe navigation of the ship; to place a destructive device or substance aboard a ship; and other acts against the safety of ships.

9. Protocol for the Suppression of Unlawful Acts against the Safety of Fixed Platforms Located on the Continental Shelf (1988, applies to the terrorist activities on fixed offshore platforms):
   • Establishes a legal regime applicable to acts against fixed platforms on the continental shelf that is similar to the regimes established against international aviation.

10. Convention on the Marking of Plastic Explosives for the Purpose of Detection (1991 provides for chemical marking to facilitate detection of plastic explosives [e.g., to combat aircraft sabotage]):
    • Designed to control and limit the used of unmarked and undetectable plastic explosives (negotiated in the aftermath of the 1988 Pan Am 103 bombing);
    • Parties are obligated in their respective territories to ensure effective control over "unmarked" plastic explosive (i.e., those that do not contain one of the detection agents described in the Technical Annex to the treaty);
    • Generally speaking, each party must, among other things: take necessary and effective measures to prohibit and prevent the manufacture of unmarked plastic explosives; prevent the movement of unmarked plastic explosives into or out of its territory; exercise strict and effective control over possession and transfer of unmarked explosives made or imported prior to the entry-into-force of the convention; ensure that all stocks of such unmarked explosives not held by the military or police are destroyed or consumed, marked, or rendered permanently ineffective within three years; take necessary measures to ensure that unmarked plastic explosives held by the military or police, are destroyed or consumed, marked, or then rendered permanently ineffective within fifteen years; and, ensure the destruction, as soon as possible, of any unmarked explosives manufactured after the date-of-entry into force of the convention for that state.

11. International Convention for the Suppression of Terrorist Bombing (1997, UN General Assembly Resolution):
    • Creates a regime of universal jurisdiction over the unlawful and intentional use of explosives and other lethal devices in, into, or against various defined public places with intent to kill or cause serious bodily injury, or with intent to cause extensive destruction of the public place.

12. International Convention for the Suppression of the Financing of Terrorism (1999):
    • Requires parties to take steps to prevent and counteract the financing of terrorists, whether direct or indirect, though groups claiming to have charitable, social or cultural goals or which also engage in such illicit activities as drug trafficking or gun running;
    • Commits states to hold those who finance terrorism criminally, civilly or administratively liable for such acts;
    • Provides for the identification, freezing, and seizure of funds allocated for terrorist activities, as well as for the sharing of the forfeited funds with other states on a case-by-case basis. Bank secrecy will no longer be justification for refusing to cooperate.[4]

The task of applying an acceptable level of aviation security is well documented, and was graphically detailed in a statement before the House of Representatives, Government Activities and Transportation Subcommittee in September 1989 by Homer Boynton, one year after the Pan Am disaster over Lockerbie, Scotland. Homer Boynton, Security Director of American Airlines, stated to the Subcommittee that, "In 1988, ICAO estimated that worldwide, 1.1 billion passengers flew on board 1,100 commercial aircraft, on 38,000–40,000 flight segments. During this period one explosive device caused the awful aviation disaster over Lockerbie, Scotland. If one looks at these statistics in their totality, security personnel were seeking one explosive device carried by one passenger among 1.1 billion passengers."[5]

Taking Boynton's comments in the context of the tragic 9-11 events seems to underscore the point that even though security agents are on the job, they are not necessarily going to find everything. Unfortunately, the U.S. system has been so deplorable for the last two decades; it is surprising that such an event had not happened earlier. In addition, Boynton's comments would seem to point the finger at security screeners missing a bomb in baggage, when, in fact, that was not the specific case in Pan Am 103; there were more factors to the inherent risk that passengers were taking by flying Pan Am in 1988. The President's Commission on Aviation and Terrorism concluded in 1990 that Pan Am was basically an accident waiting to happen and the Lockerbie disaster was preventable. What are the undisputed facts in this case? A terrorist was able to place a bomb in a suitcase that went on board Pan Am 103. The bomb detonated at 31,000 feet, killing 259 persons on the aircraft and 11 on the ground. If this was preventable, perhaps it is important to understand how easy it was in 1988 for human elements to come into play. After the FAA inspected Pan Am's operation at Frankfurt, West Germany, it was concerned with the airlines lack of a verifiable tracking system for interline bags (i.e., bags transferring from other airlines) and the confused state of its passenger screening process. The FAA inspector wrote, "The system, trying to control approximately 4,500 passengers and 28 flights per day, is being held together only by a very labor-intensive operation and the tenuous threads of luck." The inspector then went on to condone the actions by adding: "It appears the minimum FAA requirements are being met." Luck, however, was not on the side of passengers of Pan Am 103. Among the many questions being asked after Lockerbie, Scotland was, "How did the interline bag get onto the flight?" It seems the answer to that is "with ease," given the vagaries of the systems at that time. Reconciliation of passengers with their baggage is a central issue—the requirement being that an aircraft on an international flight will only carry bags for the passengers it has checked in for the flight. Having stated that, there is obviously a weak link that is ready to be exposed by the current Islamic extremist terrorists prepared to die for their beliefs. The terrorist strategy for 9-11 was to identify the weaknesses of aviation security and exploit them in order to carry out the suicide mission. Purely ensuring that passengers fly with their baggage will not prevent a suicide attack.

Looking ahead, the old ways of doing things are gone forever. The U.S. Department of Homeland Security is implementing next-generation technology to identify many multi-faceted threats, not only to aviation, but a whole gambit of possible targets, in the fields of mass transit, ports, airports, and railways. Looking back at Pan American Airlines in 1988, one of the main problems was that the screening process for interline bags was by X-ray detection. Even with the X-ray technology in place, the system was incapable of detecting the trace elements of the Semtex explosive used in the Lockerbie explosion. What could have been detected were the sources used to detonate the explosive. Thus, human error played a part in the bombings, as well as a lack of sufficient technology to detect the specific explosive. In Pan Am's defense, it informed the President's Commission that the FAA Director of Aviation had given the airline verbal approval to X-ray interline bags rather than searching or reconciling them with passengers, which, not surprisingly, the FAA denied.

There are some eerie similarities between the intelligence failings in 1988 and what went wrong, thirteen years later, on 9-11. Prior to the bombing of Pan Am 103, the intelligence community had received warnings that trouble was brewing in Europe. A total of nine security bulletins that could have had relevance to the Pan Am tragedy were issued between June and December 1988. One bulletin described how a Toshiba radio cassette player, containing a fully primed bomb with a barometric trigger, was found by the West German police in a vehicle belonging to a member of the PFLP-GC. The FAA cautioned airlines that the device found by the West German authorities "would be very difficult to detect via normal X-ray," and informed U.S. airlines that passenger/baggage reconciliation procedures "should be rigorously applied." That specific threat was received by the U.S. Embassy in Helsinki on December 5, 1988, detailing a threat that a woman would carry a bomb on board a Pan Am flight from Frankfurt in the following two weeks, was released by the FAA and then redistributed by the U.S. State Department to U.S. embassies around the globe. The U.S. embassy in Moscow made the information public to the country's 2,000-member community of U.S. citizens, including alerting Moscow news media.[6]

Although there has been no solid evidence to link these specific threats with the actual bombing, it is surprising that Pan Am management and security were then not paying specific attention to baggage reconciliation at this juncture. In view of the FAA's threat assessment, there were some significant lapses in adherence to the careful application of the reconciliation process at Frankfurt on that fateful day in 1988. It is also important to appreciate just how impotent the FAA was in dealing with Pan Am's security problems. Even after the Lockerbie disaster, the FAA found numerous security discrepancies with Pan Am, at both Frankfurt and London's Heathrow Airport. Almost six months after Lockerbie, the FAA found major discrepancies at Pan Am's Frankfurt operation. The inspector's report on June 9, 1989, stated, "The posture of Pan Am is considered unsafe, all passengers flying out of Frankfurt on Pan Am are at great risk."[7]

Concerning the attacks on the World Trade Center and the Pentagon, an awakened and anxious public is now fully aware the plot to attack aviation was brought to the attention of the FBI from flight-training academies inside the United States and from reports from its own agents. The clear failure of any resource to follow up on such intelligence is but one issue that led to the tragic destruction on 9-11.

Security improvements in the 1990s, particularly in the light of the aforementioned President's Commission, fell woefully short. The viewpoint of the FAA was basically that "it won't happen here." Hijacking aircraft was not yet a North American problem as it was seen by U.S. authorities to be a European and Eastern European aviation issue. After all is said and done, no one had been injured by an act of terrorism against airliners flying within or from the United States. Admiral Cathal Flynn stated that in the decade since (Pan Am 103) amid attacks on other carriers, no U.S. aircraft has been successfully attacked and not one person harmed on U.S. flag flights anywhere in the world, despite terrorist's determined efforts. "This owes a great deal to strengthened intelligence and law enforcement efforts and to international cooperation in fighting terrorism, both airport and carrier programs have been key factors."[8] Since these comments were made it has been clear that the intelligence process has failed and both airport and air carrier programs have been shown to be completely inadequate to protect the traveling public and aviation facilities from terrorist attacks.

Passenger screening at airports

There are many issues surrounding passenger screening, and the related training of the security operatives. In the United States and Canada, in the decades leading to 9-11, aviation regulations had made the airlines responsible for security of passengers and baggage screening. In many other regions of the world, governments have made the airports responsible. As was shown after 9-11, passengers were able to board aircraft with small-bladed knives that were used to gruesome effect to disable pilots and eventually crash aircraft into the World Trade Center and the Pentagon. The need to apply screening processes developed as a result of hijackings by Middle East and European terror groups in the late 1960's and early 1970's. In the late 1960s, the threat posed was from gun, and explosives-toting terrorists who were gaining access to aircraft. Their intent was not specifically to kill just anyone, but to use their hostages as bargaining chips for the release of prisoners held in jails, primarily in Israel and Europe. The training and equipment for passenger screening had not changed that much since those early days. The message was clear to terrorists in the past and still is today: as long as aviation security measures are not in place, aviation is a lucrative, media grabbing, and sensational target.

Tombstone Technology

When the body count becomes too much for an administration to bear, the cost of fixing most existing problems gets the necessary funding it should have had in the first place. We like to refer to this as, "tombstone technology," The fact remains that 9-11 could have been . . . and most probably should have been, detected in advance and therefore prevented. This may be a very bold assertion but it is an assertion we are definitely not alone in making. In North America, all the airlines were tasked (up until 2002), with the security of passengers. Costs are always an issue for airlines and, in the United States, security companies were required to bid on security-screening contracts. The successful bid was almost always given to the lowest bidder. Our security was entrusted to low-paid, low-skilled, often untrained, poorly motivated individuals, and in many instances, new immigrants. Not only were they poorly paid, but a proportion of them were, in fact, illegal immigrants. This is, and has been, the case in the United States for the last two decades of the twentieth century. The level of training and the types of test items that the staff used for training were totally out of context with the types of weapons and cutting devices available on the market. So, it is correct to state that there were significant holes in the screening process, both in the United States and elsewhere. Inconsistency is also another issue. Different items attract attention at one airport, but perhaps not at another, and this problem continues.

A major flaw in the process, and one most noticeable in the United States, had been that passengers and the general public could go through security screening, but all this did was raise the obvious prospect of breaches and banned items getting through the security screening process. The Security screeners, working at minimum wage and poorly trained, have had only about seven seconds to determine what they are viewing on the X-ray monitor. Added to this, most passengers (before 9-11) took the view that security was a hindrance. The abuse suffered by low-paid screeners from irate passengers and airline staff is legend. In many cases, the decision on whether a passenger could take a specific item on board was referred to an airline supervisor for a decision. Most of the decisions were made in favor of the fare-paying passenger. This did little for the morale of the screeners and even less for security. The problem is underscored in such documents as the 1994 U.S. Government Accountability report to Congressional Committees on Aviation Security. In that report, which disseminated the President's Commission Report, the Commission raised concerns about screeners' efficiency, mail and cargo, and the coordination of security between law enforcement and airport personnel. Little changed in the intervening years . . . "shutting the barn door after the horse has bolted" is a phrase that adequately describes what has taken place since 9-11. Responsibility for airport security has now been passed to the Department of Homeland Security's Transportation Security Administration (TSA). Now all airport security screeners are federalized, creating a long-awaited, consistent level of training, for all of those employees. Added to this is the requirement to screen all hold baggage. The 100 percent screening of hold baggage has been a reality in the United Kingdom since 1998, but North America and some European countries were far behind. Since 9-11, funds have been budgeted and are being provided to support the security functions at U.S. airports and seaports; however, this may be too little, too late. Prior to 9-11, the opportunity existed for terrorists to openly observe the screening processes at U.S. airports, to assess where the weakest points were, to see how the screeners searched and what items they took from passengers. It is not improbable to suggest that they had done dummy runs with similar objects, and even if they had been detected, the outcome would not have brought them to the attention of the authorities.

An early attempt at a proxy suicide bombing involves the interesting case of Nazer Hindawi a Jordanian Palestinian with the support of Syria had spent a considerable amount of time in Ireland and befriended a young Irish girl whom he managed to get pregnant and on August 17, 1986, he sent her back to the Middle East to meet his family and the route he chose for her was via an El Al Israeli Airline flight from London's Heathrow Airport. By the spring of 1986, the world was well accustomed to the specter of airport delays caused by security checks with Heathrow being no exception. The traveling public was subjected to waiting in monotonous lines for hand luggage to be searched, blissfully ignorant that the suicide or mule bomber even existed. There had, at this juncture, been no recorded attempts to destroy an aircraft by suicide bombing. This was to change dramatically on that April day. Terminal One at Heathrow International was the hub for British Airways European and domestic arrivals and departures. However, on several days of the week, it was also the terminal used by Israel's El Al Airlines for its Boeing 747 flight to Tel Aviv, Israel. At mid-morning, with the El Al 747 at departure Gate 23, passengers for that flight began to come through the pre-boarding security checks. All passengers leaving the United Kingdom in 1986, and specifically those with checked baggage, were asked a series of questions:

- Is this your baggage?
- Did you pack it yourself and are you taking any packages for somebody else?
- Have you left your baggage unattended at any time?

After answering the questions, the passengers would proceed to an immigration desk for passport inspection, not far from the watching eye of Metropolitan Police Special Branch officers.

On this particular day, a young woman from the Republic of Ireland answered all the questions. Her passport was checked and her hand luggage and hold baggage were screened by X-ray. The girl proceeded to the El Al boarding gate with her single piece of carry-on baggage. The bag was of nylon construction with an expanding compartment at the base, a type of bag used by millions of travelers. El Al prides itself on being one of the most secure airlines in the world (with good reason), always conducts its own secondary, manual security check and questioning of every passenger. The young lady, who was pregnant with her boyfriend's baby, was apparently going to visit his family in the Middle East; he, however, was not traveling. The El Al security staff thought this was an unusual story, and while doing the physical check on the bag, noticed that even when it was empty it seemed overly heavy for its construction. At that point, a police explosive search dog reacted to the bag. Further inspection revealed several sheets of plastic explosive wired to a calculator and battery. The bomb was in a false bottom of the bag. The boyfriend, Nazer Hindawi, had befriended the young woman, gotten her pregnant, and was sending her to her death. Hindawi was a Jordanian Palestinian, sponsored by Syria. He had gone to remarkable lengths and considerable planning to pull this attack off. He was sentenced to forty-five years in prison. The plan was for the bomb to detonate approximately two hours after departure. After the failed bombing, Hindawi sought refuge at the residence of a Syrian Diplomat in the UK.

The Global Threat to Civil Aviation

The 1970s and 1980s were the decades of hijackings . . . preferred mode of attack for terrorists at that time. As effective security was moved against that threat, the terrorists shifted their attention to other areas of aviation that they considered to be weak. Pan Am 103 is one example. To many people, the attacks against civil aviation tend to get lost in the mists of time. Few remember the specific threats and attacks, particularly when they occur in far-away regions of the globe. We list here some specific examples where the threat is from explosive devices, either placed in the hold or carried on as cabin baggage. A Pan Am 747 had a bomb explode on board on a flight from Tokyo to Honolulu in August 1982, and also the same year an improvised explosive device (IED) was discovered on a Pan Am 747 at Rio de Janeiro airport. In December of the same year, a piece of checked luggage was removed from an Alitalia (Italian Airlines) flight when the passenger who checked the luggage did not board the aircraft. The passenger was checking the bag through to a Pan Am flight to New York. Police discovered a bomb inside the bag.[9]

The terrorist hijackings by Palestinian groups in the late 1960s and 1970s (and, subsequently, many other terrorist groups with connections to the Middle East) changed the face of aviation for the next thirty years. For the terrorists, a hijacked aircraft became a way to attract the worldwide media coverage that the group craved. This allowed them to present an agenda or message about their cause instantly and universally. For the respective governments and the traveling public, the

Blue "Trolley Bag"

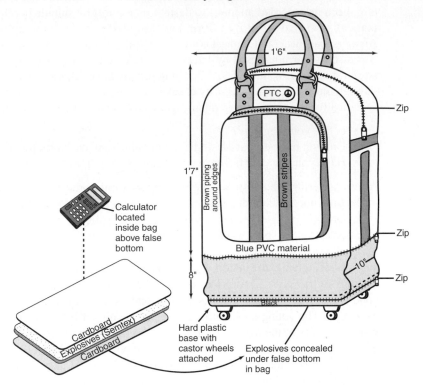

FIGURE 14-1   Trolley bag bomb intended to blow up on an El Al flight at London's Heathrow Airport in 1986. The explosive device was hidden in the false bottom of the carry-on bag (Jeremy R. Spindlove).

horror became too much to deal with. Measures to counteract these depredations were hastily drawn up and passenger screening for hand-carried baggage was born. Security is, in many ways, a reactive function and this has been clearly demonstrated in the aviation industry.

Six years prior to 9-11 al Qaeda planned an attack targeting U.S. flights from Manila in the Philippines. Operation Bojinka was planned in 1995 and was uncovered by Philippine authorities—they stumbled by accident on a bomb making factory in an apartment block that had caught fire and discovered sulfuric acid, nitric acid, sodium trichlorate, ammonia, silver nitrates, and nitrobenzoyl, and a document written in Arabic that detailed how to construct liquid bombs. They also found twelve forged Norwegian, Saudi, and Afghan passports. The apartment was rented by Ramzi Yousef and details of the Bojinka plot were found on the hard drive of his lap top detailing flight schedules and detonation information. Yousef is currently serving 240 years in prison for the 1993 World Trade Center bombing.

Five years after 9-11, in 2006, a group of British Muslims allegedly planned suicide missions on at least seven international flights from London's Heathrow to North America. On this occasion, intelligence work was able to prevent the attacks being carried out. The attacks were to use items that could be legally carried on board an aircraft, hidden inside containers of liquid. The result being that the carriage of liquids and aerosol quantities is currently restricted. These items were never detected in the passenger screening process, but their intention was to get items that could be assembled into improvised explosive devices onto an aircraft for a suicide mission.

Airports are busy and often-cramped locations designed and built in the decades before security of passengers and aircraft became such a significant issue. Even newly built facilities in the United States over the last five years of the twentieth century failed to factor in hardening of the facility for security purposes, especially the screening areas, or incorporating sophisticated detection devices into the baggage sorting/conveyor systems. A demand had now added an additional layer of baggage security to an already overburdened system. The problem facing the airlines was, "Who is going to pay for all this added security?" In the long run, it would, of course, be the traveling public, as it always is. After the bombing of Pan Am 103 in 1988, it was important to develop effective explosive-detection equipment that could handle the heavy volume of baggage. Throughput was also part of the immediate challenge for airports and aviation security experts. Screening hold baggage had not been a priority for North America in spite of the President's Commission Report in 1990. Since the 9-11 attacks and the advent of the Transportation Security Agency (TSA) in the U.S., 100 percent screening of checked baggage at long last became a reality. As we move forward, the government (TSA) intends to continue research into more effective ways to scan baggage for explosive substances and devices by funding programs to efficiently inculcate the airport/airlines' baggage systems with state of the art technology to screen checked baggage. The remaining gap in screening now reverts to the cargo hold and the amount of unchecked mail and freight. So as governments continue to find ever more sophisticated methods to prevent the next unthinkable attack, the very sobering message we now get from the terrorists is that they want nothing from us except our destruction! Hussein Mussawi, former Hezbollah leader stated, *"We are not fighting so that the enemy may offer us something. We are fighting to wipe out the enemy"*; this also meets exactly with the goals of Osama bin Laden's al Qaeda terrorist organization.

Airport Facilities

Airports are, by their very nature, open and public places. As a result, the opportunity for terrorists to leave bombs in such public places is always present. Only awareness, vigilance, and response by the public and police can help to avert disasters. What about security in the other sectors of the aviation industry? What about mail and airfreight carriers? How secure are they? Airlines move millions of tons of freight throughout the world and a large percentage travels without any serious screening in the holds of passenger aircraft. At the present time, this area of airline operation is open to serious risk and exposure. Furthermore, access to the aircraft by catering facilities, airport workers, etc., must receive serious attention if the sterility of the aircraft is to be maintained. It is of little benefit to any operation if the passengers are fully screened for weapons, but airport workers are allowed almost unrestricted access without checks. Without stating the obvious, the opportunity exists for airport workers to secrete weapons or even bombs on an aircraft. A comprehensive system must be employed to assure the integrity of all those persons who have access to restricted areas of the airport and also the bags and items that they carry in with them. Although measures are in place to verify freight by known shipper, this is a far cry from a totally secure cargo hold. In 2008, the security of airlines is focused on the freight hold of the aircraft and how the millions of tons of freight can be screened before loading, who will pay for this and what will it do to such industries as the courier companies that rely on the "just in time" philosophy for the cutting edge of their business. By inserting heavy duty screening equipment and bomb detection dogs into this mix will delay freight operations but will it deter a would be terrorist? No doubt we may have to wait for the first bomb in a freight hold to learn the answers to some of these questions.

As already evidenced in Europe, threats can also extend to passengers waiting in line at check-in counters. For airports and security, these areas require consideration and attention. Attacks can occur even at times of heightened security and the United States most certainly was on guard on July 4, 2002, the United State's Independence Day, when a man of Middle East descent opened fire on passengers at the El Al check-in desks at Los Angeles International airport. The vehicular attack on Scotland's Glasgow airport by two men driving a bomb laden vehicle are prime examples of how easy it is for the determined terrorist in these cases to launch an attack. What do we learn from such events as this? El Al, the Israeli national airline, is a model for all to observe. El Al prides itself on its stringent security systems and its passenger profiling. Other methods of terror attack, such as a suicide truck or car bomb targeting the front of an airport terminal, must also be addressed.

For example, with the amount of glass in airport terminals, how can passengers be protected and the risk of injuries be reduced from blast damage to those facilities with large areas of partitioned glass? El Al does not restrict its security activities solely to the airport and the perimeter areas of airport faciliites but also includes hotels where its crews stay on international flights. The June 2008 information that was being gathered by a group from Hezbollah in Toronto, Canada was specific to the location where the El Al crew were staying. El Al immediately changed its security procedures as a result fearing an imminent attack against its personnel and operations.

Attacks on airports have been relatively few but always have taken authorities by surprise. The attacks on Heathrow Aiport in 1994 and the Scottish attack in 2007 are good examples of the lengths to which a group of committed individuals will go to in order to cause death and mass confusion and fear.

Heathrow Airport Attacked by Terrorists

FIRST ATTACK: On Wednesday March 9, 1994, between 5:00 P.M. and 5:30 P.M., using a recognized code word, telephone calls were received by various news organizations warning of:

- Bombs at Heathrow;
- In terminals and runways in one hour.

Just before 6:00 P.M., there was an explosion in a car in the parking lot of the Excelsior Hotel, on the north side of the airport. Several cars were engulfed in flames and four mortars were found near the northern runway.

- None had exploded on impact.
- No damage or injury occurred.
- The hotel parking lot had in the past been utilized as an evacuation point.

SECOND ATTACK: On the following day between 5:30 P.M. and 9:45 P.M., a number of similar calls were received. At midnight, four more bombs were fired from wasteland beyond the perimeter on the southern side of the airport near Terminal Four. Again there was no explosion, damage, or injury. The launcher was a freestanding, purposely built apparatus, placed in undergrowth and concealed with plastic sheeting and branches.

THIRD ATTACK: Three days later on Sunday, March 13, 1994, there were again a series of similar calls between 6:00 A.M. and 6:40 A.M. Flights were diverted from the southern runway and just after 8.00 A.M., rockets were again fired toward Terminal Four, from the opposite direction. One landed on the terminal without causing damage.

FOURTH ATTACK: Between 6:45 P.M. and 7:30 P.M. on that same Sunday, coded calls were received, giving the same unspecific information, stating that bombs had been placed at Heathrow and Gatwick. Contingency plans were implemented at both airports, but this was found to be a hoax. It is properly described as an attack because the disruptive effect was equal to that at earlier incidents.[10]

While the type of device used by the PIRA in this attack was crude and unsophisticated had they had the opportunity to use **Man Portable Air Defense Systems (MANPADS)** they would surely have hit targets that they chose. There are an estimated 500,000 Man Portable Air Defense Systems (MANPADS) currently in existence. Some of the simpler systems are available for as little as $1,000 on the open market. The MANPADS used thus far in terrorist attacks, such as the Russian-made SA-7, suggest that terrorist groups currently do not have access to more sophisticated systems, although general small-arms proliferation trends suggest that it is only a matter of time before they acquire more advanced systems. Many of the MANPADS are unaccounted for, including at least forty Stinger missile systems missing after the 1991 Gulf War, as well as hundreds of

U.S.-made MANPADS shipped to foreign nations and then left untracked, with thousands of systems built by France, China, and Russia.[11]

In the Heathrow Airport attack this was the first time police and intelligence had to be concerned not only with the airport facility and its protection, but also had to evaluate the threat from areas surrounding the airport. The better use of closed circuit television systems (CCTV) and better intelligence on who owns the lands and buildings in close proximity to airport facilities now had to be viewed in the overall risk assessment for an airport. Following the terrorist attacks on 9-11, there was considerable concern about the use of and the availability of Stinger missiles against U.S. and UN targets. While there is no evidence to suggest that any Stinger missiles are in the United States, it is important to note that a U.S. military fact sheet details the Stinger in this manner: "The missiles' complexity can be accommodated by almost any potential user nation or group."

The "Stinger missile" is five feet long and weighs thirty-four pounds. It was and is manufactured by Raytheon and can be fired from a distance of five miles and has a vertical range of 10,000 feet. A Stinger would be a lethal weapon when used against a conventional civilian airliner. Stingers were originally sent to Afghanistan as part of the campaign to arm the local mujahideen against the Soviet invasion. At the time of the transfer, there were advocates against such a move, with the outright fear that the Islamic fundamentalist who dominated the Afghan mujahideen had about as much love of the West as they did for the Soviets. The opportunity for some to be traded to terrorist organizations was a genuine and highly conceivable proposition. Other countries that have Stinger missiles include Somalia, Iraq, United Arab Emirates, Qatar, Zambia, and North Korea.[12] Attacks by shoulder-fired missiles have been an ongoing concern since the November 2002 attack in Kenya against an El Al flight taking off from Mombasa. There are earlier recorded attacks, but the underlying worry is the existence of these systems in such large numbers.

In June 2007, a full frontal attack using a vehicle as a means to deliver an incendiary bomb took place at Glasgow International Airport in Scotland when two men of Middle East appearance drove a Range Rover SUV loaded with propane tanks and soaked in gasoline at the main doors of the terminal. The attack was thwarted by the reinforced doors to the building to prevent such attacks, the vehicle and its two occupants caught fire and were both arrested by members of the public and airport police. However this is an example of the vulnerability of public locations to this type of uncoordinated but nevertheless deadly style of attack. Had they succeeded in breaching the doors the resulting mayhem and death would have been considerable.

A People Issue

Prior to the events of 9-11 a problem in U.S. and European airports had been the vast number of people having access to the restricted areas of airports. What measures can be taken to ensure that airport workers, baggage loaders, refuelers, aircraft cleaners, and the like have undergone sufficient background checks to assure authorities of their integrity? News reports out of the United Kingdom in early September 2002 indicated that at least fifteen illegal aliens were employed cleaning aircraft at London's Heathrow Airport.

The FAA studied weapon-detection rates at the twenty-five largest airports in the United States and found that the lowest rates were at Boston's Logan International; Newark, New Jersey; and Dulles Airport in Washington DC. After the loss of TWA 800 off Long Island, New York, in 1996, the Gore Commission made many recommendations in regard to airport security, including positive bag-matching for passengers on domestic flights. The airlines insisted that the resulting cost in delays was unacceptable and came up with a proposal to use Computer-Assisted Passenger Profiling. This would permit the airlines to identify from a set of parameters those passengers who might pose a threat. The four hijackings of 9-11 have shown how devoid of any value that system turned out to be. Since 9-11, we have been led down a path . . . Americans falsely believe that the TSA has tightened airline security by federalizing all security screeners. However, as we approached the one-year anniversary of 9-11 in 2002, the new TSA reported that all was not well. It revealed that screeners at thirty-two of the largest U.S. airports failed to detect weapons and explosive devices in approximately 25 percent of the tests it carried out in June 2002. Granted tests are designed to show weakness in the system, however, 25 percent is higher than was likely expected, and in airports such as Cincinnati, Jacksonville, and Las Vegas, the newly monitored screeners failed to detect at least half of the tests, and at Los Angeles International, the failure rate was 41 percent.[13]

The following statistical information was provided by the U.S. Transportation Security Agency:
During 2006,

- TSA screened 708,400,522. The average wait time was 3.79 minutes and the average peak wait time was 11.76 minutes.
- TSA screened 535,020,271 individual pieces of checked luggage. Opened 16 percent of these checked bags (85,571,710 bags) searching for prohibited items.
- TSA intercepted 13,709,211 prohibited items at our security checkpoints. Of this, 11,616,249 were lighters and 1,607,100 were knives.[14]

A Transportation Security Administration report revealed that screeners at Los Angeles and Chicago O'Hare airports failed to find fake bombs in more than 60 percent of tests run in 2007. Rich Roth, an aviation security expert with CTI Consulting in Bethesda, Md., stated that screeners failed to detect fake dynamite hidden in bathroom kits and bomb residue on shoelaces. He notes, though, that the problems the tests revealed have since been addressed. Besides, the undercover agents had an advantage over would-be terrorists. They did not fear arrest while sneaking the fake bombs through security. A "bad guy" would likely be much more nervous, which might tip off screeners, Roth says. The report also tested private screeners, and unlike their federal counterparts, only 20 percent of the fake bombs made it through security. Roth says this might be because the private screeners are accustomed to being tested.

Therefore, regular testing for TSA and private screeners, plus the changes that have been made in the last year, could improve the screening process at the nation's airports.[15]

Passenger Profiling

Most civil liberty groups have denounced the practice of "profiling" airline passengers. The concept behind profiling is to utilize skilled practitioners to identify passengers who warrant more in-depth security screening before they board an aircraft. The screeners are trained in security-related issues and human behavior. El Al, the Israeli national airline, uses profiling and, of course, its safety and security record is second to none.

In November 2004, the U.S. Transportation Security Agency (TSA) began testing a new form of passenger prescreening called "Secure Flight." The program, which was intended to replace the now-defunct Computer-Assisted Passenger Prescreening System (CAPPS II). CAPPS II was a very controversial and expensive U.S. government experiment that has been slow to get off the ground.

Under Secure Flight, TSA will receive information for each passenger (from the airline). TSA will then determine any matches of information with government watch lists and transmit matching results back to aircraft operators. To this end, the TSA has issued the *Secure Flight Notice of Proposed Rule Making* (NPRM), which lays out the Department of Homeland Security's plans to assume watch list matching.

Secure Flight will match limited passenger information against government watch lists to identify known and suspected terrorists, prevent known and suspected terrorists from boarding an aircraft, facilitate legitimate passenger air travel, and protect individuals' privacy. Secure Flight will:

- Identify known and suspected terrorists.
- Prevent individuals on the No Fly List from boarding an aircraft.
- Identify individuals on the Selectee List for enhanced screening.

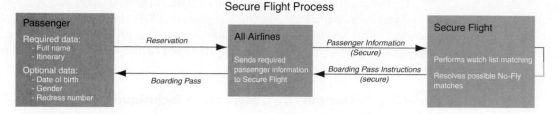

FIGURE 14-2   Secure Flight Process—DHS. (U.S. Department of Homeland Security).

- Facilitate passenger air travel by providing fair, equitable, and consistent matching process across all aircraft operators.
- Protect individuals' privacy.

The NPRM initiated a public comment period that enabled the traveling public and industry to voice comments and concerns. Initial implementation of Secure Flight is expected to occur in 2008.

Secure Flight compares passenger records to expanded "selectee" and "no-fly" lists already in use. Passengers whose records match names on the lists will be subject to commercial background checks to verify their identities.[16]

The TSA began Secure Flight by compiling a "Terrorist No-Fly Watch List."

It compares names on passenger manifests to this list. One problem with the program is the number of people who have been falsely identified as "terrorists" because their name matches, or closely resembles, names on the No-Fly list. Once a name is on the list, it is impossible to remove it and then some "innocent" travelers are detained every time they fly and they can't do anything to get their name off the list. The effectiveness of the Secure Flight program is yet to be determined. Certainly, the U.S. Government Accountability Office (GAO) has some serious reservations about the safety and security of the information being gathered and compared. GAO reviewed the program in January 2005 and listed ten specific points that must be addressed before the full activation of this program. This review, mandated by Congress, effectively stops the launch of Secure Flight. Of the ten areas that Congress asked the GAO to evaluate, the TSA had only addressed one. Because so little progress has been made, the GAO cannot certify the program and TSA cannot launch Secure Flight.[17]

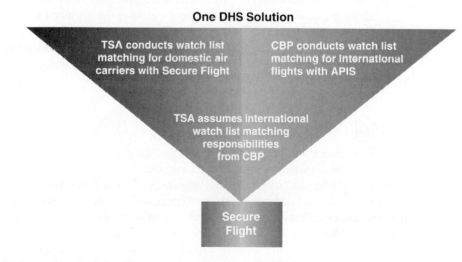

FIGURE 14-3   Secure Flight—DHS (U.S. Department of Homeland Security).

TSA was expected to launch Secure Flight in August 2005 and again the program was delayed and its implementation is ongoing through 2008 with full compliance in 2010. The GAO also noted that TSA has not addressed the identity theft problem, which, as the American Civil Liberties Union has repeatedly pointed out, would render the whole program meaningless and provide a false sense of security.[18]

Screening Passengers by Observation Technique (SPOT)

The Israeli national airline El Al has been profiling passengers attempting to board its flights for the past thirty plus years with considerable success. Passengers and the public are monitored for behavior traits as they enter the airport and the observations extend to the airport perimeters and parking areas. In Canada in February 2008, the Chair of the International Pilots Association called for the Canadian authorities to adopt SPOT, claiming that it was already in use by the TSA in the United States. Under the U.S. SPOT program, TSA stopped 70,000 passengers between January and December 2006 for questioning and although no terrorists were arrested, they did arrest more than 700 individuals. But that 1in100 hit rate involved alleged money laundering, drugs, and weapons possession to immigration violations to outstanding warrants. Following the Glasgow airport attack in 2007, the British have installed the technology version of the same process by funneling images from CCTV cameras to a computer system that will detect 10,000 separate facial "microexpressions," including signs of fear and deception and, reportedly, even an individual's skin temperature.

European Civil Aviation Conference (ECAC)

Nations are responsible for implementing effective aviation security systems for flights leaving their country. Terrorism is an international issue as modern air travel allows terrorists to strike anywhere within hours. Therefore, it is necessary to have an international body to work with governments to develop measures, standards, and recommended practices . . . that body is the **European Civil Aviation Conference (ECAC)**. The ECAC operates with the active support of the International Civil Aviation Organization (ICAO). ECAC, formed more than twenty years ago, has the following three principles in the area of aviation security:

1. That the threat of unlawful interference with civil aviation in its many forms of violence is likely to persist.
2. That ICAO Standards and Recommended Practices in aviation security have to take into account the widely varying provisions available for their implementation in more than 180 Contracting States of ICAO.
3. Mutual understanding and close and constant co-operation between all State authorities concerned are necessary to achieve and maintain a high standard of aviation security.[19]

COMBATING TERRORISTS

One of the first considerations any would-be hijacker would have looked for during the last two decades of the twentieth century was the amount of mass media publicity he or she could hope to achieve for the "cause." Certainly, hijacking an aircraft and demanding it be then flown to JFK Airport in New York, or to London's Heathrow Airport, would gain worldwide media attention. Because of the size and complexity of these airports, the ensuing chaos and disruption to the traveling public would be horrendous. In combating a hijacking, it is imperative that authorities have the option to "direct" the hijacked aircraft to an airport of their choice. Authorities must be able to handle the incident without disrupting the major airports and airline systems of the world.

U.S. Sky Marshals (Federal Air Marshal Service—FAM)

In response to the hijacking of TWA Flight 847 in 1985, President Ronald Reagan directed the Secretary of Transportation, in cooperation with the Secretary of State, to explore expansion of the armed Sky Marshal program aboard international flights for U.S. air carriers. Congress responded by passing the International Security and Development Cooperation Act (Public Law 99–83), which provided the statutes that supported the Federal Air Marshal Service.

The "Sky Marshal" program has in fact been around since the late 1960s, when armed U.S. Customs agents operated in plain clothes on U.S. flagged international flights. At the time of the 9-11 attacks, there were around fifty operational U.S. Sky Marshals. That was to rapidly change and the U.S. government announced an immediate increase in the numbers required to protect U.S. civil aviation from future terrorist attack. Currently, air marshals staff several positions at different organizations such as the National Counterterrorism Center, the National Targeting Center, and on the FBI's Joint Terrorism Task Forces. They are also distributed among other law enforcement and homeland security liaison assignments during times of heightened alert or special national events.

Aircraft Hijack Response Location—Stansted Airport, UK

London's third airport is little known to the international traveler, who will normally arrive at the gateway airports of Heathrow, on the outskirts of London, or Gatwick, about one hour south of London. Stansted, located to the east of London, has become the venue of choice for authorities in dealing with a hijacked aircraft. This supposes, of course, that they are able to hoodwink the terrorist into believing the plane is actually landing at Heathrow. The airport was first used to receive a hijacked aircraft in 1975, when a BAC1–11 was hijacked on a domestic flight between Manchester in the north of England and London. The hijacking took place as the aircraft was approaching Heathrow. The pilot managed to divert, without the hijackers' knowledge, to Stansted. The hijacker then demanded money and to be flown to France. By the time the pilot had flown around and landed at Stansted, the hijacker was convinced he was in France. Few police were available in those days to cover Stansted airport and, as a result of inadequate police power, some valuable lessons were learned. These lessons were incorporated into the training of the **Special Air Service (SAS) Regiment** for dealing with terrorist hijackings in the future. Security operations were lacking in:

- Numbers of police on hand to deal with an emergency of this magnitude.
- Designated emergency rendezvous points for emergency services.
- Communications between pilot and ground.
- A designated command post for the operation.

The requirement to train and maintain a level of response became of great importance. A second hijacking, originating in central Africa in 1982, ended up with an Air Tanzania Boeing 727 landing, after a circuitous route around Europe, at Stansted. On this occasion, the response was a combined police and military operation with the elite SAS in attendance to mount a hostage rescue if police negotiations failed. While police negotiated, a team of SAS members embarked on similarly configured British Airways 737 and flew directly from Heathrow to Stansted. As a result of protracted negotiations involving the Tanzanian High Commissioner, the siege was brought to a peaceful conclusion some twenty-four hours later. What was also apparent in this incident was the role of the media and their release of sensational and news-breaking pictures to an eager public. However, images of armed police lying in wait near the aircraft could have been a considerable problem for the negotiators had the pictures reached the hijackers. In any democratic society, the value of the press and its principal focus of newsgathering must be weighed against the impact on the situation at hand. Close cooperation between the media and authorities is an issue that must be addressed in terror and hijacking incidents.

In August 1996, a Sudan Airways A310 Airbus, which originated in Khartoum, was hijacked by an Iraqi group demanding that the plane be flown to Italy. Because of insufficient fuel, the aircraft landed in Cyprus, refuelled, and then took off for London. Stansted, as a result of the valuable lessons of the last twenty years, was ready and waiting to receive the aircraft. This particular hijacking was to end peacefully. Stansted remains the airport of choice for receiving terrorist-controlled flights into the United Kingdom.[20] On February 7, 2000, an Afghan Airlines Boeing 727 was hijacked during a flight to the Afghan city of Mazar-i-Sharif and was then flown to the Uzbeki capital of Tashkent. It eventually landed at London's third airport . . . Stansted. Stansted has been the scene of international hijacking dramas three times in the past thirty years . . . all of which ended in the surrender of the hijackers without any loss of life.

The Media Angle

Interfering with the media's "right to know" is, of course, frowned upon by reporters on TV media. However, there must be limits placed on the release of pictures and information while an incident is ongoing. As preservers of order in the fabric of democracy, the police and military are bound to come into conflict with the media about the control and dissemination of information. One example of such a conflict occurred during the Falklands War, when the media were given briefings by the government and the content of news was tightly censored so as not to give critical information to the enemy. During the Gulf War, the commander himself, General Norman Schwarzkopf, conducted press briefings. These briefings contained the diluted information that the military chiefs allowed for media release. The press was not allowed on the field of battle during the invasion's operations. In a terror incident taking place in a city, it is impossible to control media coverage in the first phase of the action. The bombing of the Federal Building in Oklahoma City brought the television crews to the scene at almost the same time rescue and police services were arriving, some even quicker. The graphic television coverage of the heroic deeds of firefighters and police officers goes a long way toward winning the public's acceptance of the methods they may subsequently use to catch terrorists. Police are seen as the front line against terrorism; they are part of the community and are, therefore, better appreciated.

Media coverage can also have negative effects in combating terror, even when government censors have neutralized the information. A disastrous media mistake involved a hijacked American airliner at Beirut International Airport in 1985. A rescue unit of Delta Force commandos was dispatched to the region, only to be thwarted by news coverage of their imminent arrival. This allowed the hijackers' time to hide and move their captives throughout Beirut. Many analysts have discussed and reviewed the effects of media coverage on terrorist actions and many conclusions both for and against media coverage can surely be reached. The media, however, must understand that they should remain at "arms' length" so as not to become a tool of the terrorist.

Much media coverage is aimed at showing the horrors of the unfolding situation. The motivational drives of the terrorists are seldom considered, and the dramatic effects of the horror become the main coverage. Without intention, the media begins presenting the terrorists' side of the issues. When that happens, the media inadvertently serve the purposes of the terrorists, giving them precisely the attention they seek.

After all, terrorist actions are all about sending a message. Their preferred method of sending the message is via the broadest media coverage possible. No doubt, studies might conclude that sensational pictures of terrorist events do nothing to get "the message" out to the public but may in fact, fuel public anger. Consider the insurgent/terrorist actions in Iraq in 2004 and 2005. Insurgents kidnapped Westerners, recorded their subsequent execution by grisly beheadings, and then broadcast the atrocity on the Internet. Although the broadcasts severely aggravated the sensitivities of those who viewed them, in the long run, they have had no effect on the resolve of the majority of governments to acquiesce to any demands for troop withdrawal. However, the terrorist attacks on trains in Madrid certainly had serious political implications for Spain and resulted in the pullout of Spanish troops from Iraq and a change in the democratically elected government of the day.

In a free society, the media and the government will invariably clash on what gets coverage and what should not. However, much of what is reported will generally be acquired through government sources, which may appear to be manipulating the media. No one has suggested that the media were manipulated on 9-11, unless of course, you listen to the meanderings of the Iranian leadership who openly espoused that it was all a conspiracy theory! So back to reality; we believe that the media coverage awoke a nation to the true and cowardly nature of terrorists and their despicable acts, so often perpetrated against civilians. In this instance, live news footage of the World Trade Center attack as the second plane crashed into the second of the twin towers was more vivid than any Hollywood portrayal. The cataclysmic events of 9-11 were also viewed and broadcast in Middle Eastern countries. The following day, newsprint articles and television news coverage showed joyful Palestinians dancing in the streets. To most people, that was abhorrent, but it needed to be shown. Censorship of the press and restrictions placed on it is undoubtedly a common practice in many countries, especially where military dictatorships and totalitarian governments are in power. A good example is the tactics and laws imposed by the Robert Mugabe government in Zimbabwe, which makes it a criminal offense to criticize the government and its ministers.

Arabic news media, **Al Jazeera**, is the largest and most controversial Arabic news channel in the Middle East. It offers news coverage twenty-four hours a day from around the world, focusing on the hottest regions of conflict. Al Jazeera could be termed the Arabic version of Atlanta's CNN. Programming also includes a wide selection of high-pitch political talk shows, documentaries, emotional debates, and sensational arguments covering events of the moment. Founded in 1996, and based in Qatar, the Al Jazeera news network is the fastest-growing and most controversial network among Arab communities and Arabic-speaking people around the world. The station has earned the loyalty of a large audience and the enmity of various critics who argue that Al Jazeera is overly sensational. Critics claim the network tends to show bloody footage from various war zones and gives disproportionate coverage to various fundamentalist and extremist groups. Criticism from various governments has helped the channel increase its credibility with an audience that is familiar with censorship and biased coverage from official government outlets. Al Jazeera is not likely to criticize its own benefactor, the Emir of Qatar and the government of Qatar.

Al Jazeera's programs are available worldwide through various satellite and cable systems. In the United States, it is available through satellite.[21] During 2004, U.S. commanders in Iraq were openly critical of the coverage they received from Al Jazeera, particularly during the battle for Fallujah. The news network claimed that U.S. forces were killing hundreds of innocent women and children . . . a claim the military hotly denied.

Policy

Western governments reacted to terrorist activity by responding to them swiftly and effectively. The use of military and spy satellites to track down terrorists has enhanced this effort. Is the problem of defining and dealing with terrorism a police or a military problem? Certainly, the bombing of U.S. embassies in Nairobi and Dar es Salaam in the summer of 1998 was very difficult for the local police to deal with. In trying to come to terms with an enemy not residing within its own borders, the United States responded with a preemptive military strike at the bases of suspected terrorists in both Sudan and Pakistan. Was the United States violating sovereign territory of these two countries? The primary target was Osama bin Laden and his al Qaeda network, who were suspected of being behind the two bombings, as well as the subsequent attacks against the U.S.S. *Cole* in Yemen. As a result of the two bombings, and the U.S. retaliatory strikes, we wondered who would fire the next shot in anger. We now know the next shot was from the Islamic extremists of bin Laden's al Qaeda terror organization deep into the heart of the American public in New York, Washington, and Pennsylvania.

International cooperation in dealing with global terrorism was previously addressed at the Lyon Summit Conference in 1996. Ministers responsible for state security agreed on a framework of some twenty-five measures. The agreement focused on the following main points:

1. Adopt internal measures to prevent terrorism by improving counterterrorism cooperation and capabilities. By adopting this strategy, governments could focus on training of counterterrorism personnel to prevent all kinds of terrorism actions including the use of chemical, biological, and toxic substance attacks.
2. Accelerate the research and development of methods to detect explosives and other harmful substances that cause death or injury, and also to develop standards for marking explosives in order to identify their origin in post-blast investigations.
3. In respect to prosecution and deterrence, the agreement noted that where sufficient justification existed according to national laws, that states must investigate organizations, groups, and associations, including those with charitable social or cultural goals, used by terrorists as a cover for their operations. (An example of such a group would be the Irish Northern Aid Committee or NORAID, which supports and collects funds for the IRA in the United States.)
4. Adopt laws for the restriction and control of weapons and explosives including export controls, to prevent their use by terrorist organizations.
5. Review and amend all current anti-terror legislation.
6. In dealing with political asylum issues, states must ensure that the rights and freedoms of a country are not taken advantage of by terrorists who seek to fund, plan, and then commit terrorist acts.
7. Facilitate the exchange of information through central authorities to provide speedy coordination of requests. Direct exchange of information between competent agencies should be encouraged.
8. The exchange of information should specifically identify:
   • The actions and movement of persons or groups suspected of belonging to or being connected with terrorist networks.
   • Travel documents suspected of being forgeries.
   • Trafficking in arms, explosives, or sensitive materials.
   • The use of communications technologies by terrorist groups.
   • The threat of new types of terrorist activities including those using chemical, biological, or nuclear materials and toxic substances.[22]

UN SECURITY COUNCIL RESOLUTION 1373

After the terror attacks of 9-11, the General Assembly of the United Nations, by consensus of the 189 member states, called for international cooperation to prevent and eradicate acts of terrorism on a worldwide basis. The United Nations also held accountable the perpetrators and those states that harbor and support them. UN Security Council Resolution 1373 was unanimously adopted on September 28, 2001, under Chapter VII of the UN Charter. Resolution 1373 is a legally binding resolution on all member states. It defined the new international campaign to deal with terrorism. It required, among other things, that all member states prevent the financing of terrorism and deny safe haven for terrorists. Resolution 1373 makes it imperative for all states to review and strengthen their border security operations, banking practices, customs and immigration procedures, law enforcement and intelligence cooperation, and share pertinent information with respect to these efforts. The full implementation of 1373 will require each member state to take specific measures to combat terrorism; most will have to make changes to laws, regulations, and practices.

The United States took the following steps:

- September 23, 2001—Executive Order 13224 froze all the assets of twenty-seven foreign individuals, groups, and entities linked to terrorist acts or supporting terrorism and authorized the freezing of assets of those who commit or pose a significant threat of committing acts of terrorism.
- September 28, 2001—The United States sponsored the UN Security Council Resolution 1373, calling on all UN members to criminalize the provision of funds to all terrorists, effectively denying terrorists' safe financial haven anywhere.
- October 5, 2001—The U.S. Attorney General re-designated twenty-five terrorist organizations, to include al Qaeda, as foreign terrorist organizations pursuant to the Antiterrorism and Effective Death Penalty Act 1996. Giving material support or resources to any of these foreign organizations is a felony under U.S. law.
- October 12, 2001—Under Executive Order 13224, thirty-nine names were added to the list of individuals and organizations linked to terrorism or terrorist financing.
- October 26, 2001—The United States enacted the USA Patriot Act, which significantly expanded the capability of U.S. law enforcement to investigate and prosecute persons who engage in terrorist acts.
- October 29, 2001—The Foreign Terrorist Tracking Task Force was created and aimed at denying entry into the United States of persons suspected of being terrorists and locating, detaining, prosecuting, and deporting terrorists already in the United States.
- November 2, 2001—The United States designated twenty-two terrorist organizations located throughout the world under Executive Order 13224, thus highlighting the need to focus on terrorist organizations worldwide.
- November 7, 2001—The United States added sixty-two new organizations and individuals, all of whom were either linked to the Al Barakaat conglomerate or to the Al Taqwa Bank, which have been identified as supplying funds to terrorists.
- December 4, 2001—The United States froze the assets of the Holy Land Foundation in Richardson, Texas, whose funds are used to support the Hamas terrorist organization, and two other entities, bringing the total to 153.
- December 5, 2001—The Secretary of State designated thirty-nine groups as terrorist organizations under the Immigration and Nationality Act, as amended by the USA Patriot Act.[23]

THE PATRIOT ACT

This hastily formed Act was the Congressional response to the events of 9-11, however, like other timed legislation, the Bush administration sought to have this Act reinvigorated and the provisions in it made permanent. The Act has allowed for expanded surveillance of terrorist suspects and increased the use of material witness warrants, which allow suspects to be held incommunicado. The Act also authorized secret proceedings in immigration cases. Many of the provisions are due to expire. While Congress attempts to rework the Act, it has been criticized from both Republicans and Democrats as a law that severely limits the rights and freedoms of individuals and infringes on the rights of law-abiding American citizens.[24]

U.S. NAVAL STATION—GUANTANAMO BAY—CUBA

U.S. Naval Station Guantanamo Bay is the oldest U.S. base overseas and the only one in a Communist country. Located in the Oriente province on the southeast corner of Cuba, the base is about 400 miles from Miami. The United States leased the 45-square-mile parcel of land in 1903 to use as a coaling station. The U.S. Department of Defense has been holding "detainees" at GITMO since the invasion of Afghanistan in 2002. The base is under a strict military rule and the majority of "detainees" are suspected Islamist militants who have been handed over to the DOD by both military and CIA.

The Joint Task Force is tasked with observing, interviewing, and interrogating the detainees. No doubt a certain amount of intelligence has been gathered in regard to bomb making activities and many have been identified as having studied at U.S. universities before embarking on their jihad with Osama bin Laden's al Qaeda movement. Unclassified reports from the DOT in 2005 indicate that one detainee identified eleven fellow detainees as Osama bin Laden bodyguards, who all received their terrorist training at al Farouq, a known terrorist training camp. Another detainee, the probable twentieth 9-11 hijacker, confirmed more than twenty detainees as bin Laden bodyguards. The detainees in many cases when captured were wearing a type of watch that has been linked to al Qaeda and radical Islamist IED's. The particular watch is favored by al Qaeda bomb makers because it allows alarm settings and therefore detonations more than twenty-four hours in advance.

Methods of interrogation have been surfacing and one of the more popular claims from released detainees and detainee lawyers is that some have been subjected to a form of torture termed water boarding . . . an interrogation technique in which the detainee is put in fear of drowning. The use of this practice has been denied at GITMO; however, the CIA admitted to using the technique on al Qaeda detainee Khalid Sheik Mohammed.

Military Commissions (Tribunals)

Military Tribunals are not a new concept and have historically been used to prosecute enemy combatants who violate the laws of war. The last time they were used by the U.S. Military was during WWII. The concept and goal of the commission is to provide the accused with a full and fair trial and at the same time provide protection for classified and sensitive information and the protection and safety of all personnel participating in the process and that would include the accused.

In accordance with his Military Order of November 13, 2001, the President must determine if an individual is subject to his Military Order. This decision is the jurisdictional basis for prosecution; until the President determines that an individual is subject to his Military Order, no prosecution is possible. However, this determination does not require that criminal charges be brought against the individual; that decision is made by the Appointing Authority after the Chief Prosecutor recommends that charges

FIGURE 14-4   Guantanamo Bay—military observation station to monitor detainees (U.S. Department of Homeland Security).

be approved. In the current text of the Military Commissions at GITMO, in order for a suspect to be subject of the President's Military Order, the President must determine that the said individual:

- Is or was an al Qaeda member.
- Has engaged in, aided or abetted, or conspired to commit acts of international terrorism against the United States; or
- Knowingly harboured one or more of the individuals described above; and
- It is in the interest of the United States that such individual be subject to this order.

Once charges have been determined and laid by the Chief Prosecutor, a Military Commission Panel is appointed and this panel will consist of a Presiding Officer who must be a judge advocate and at least three other military officers as members. Questions of law are ruled on by the Presiding Officer. Unlike a civil court, the Panel members vote and if necessary on a sentence; however, the Presiding Officer does not have a vote in this process. From the perspective of the accused he is entitled to hire a civilian defense counsel at no cost to the government as long as that counsel is a U.S. citizen and is admitted to practice in a U.S. jurisdiction, has not been sanction to disciplinary action, is eligible for and can obtain SECRET clearance and will agree to follow the rules of the Commission. In the modern era these commissions have come in for a considerable amount of press and civil liberty scrutiny. So much has changed since WWII it is not surprising that is now the case. The lack of transparency to the overall process does not sit well with civil libertarians in particular.

INTERNATIONAL POLICING

International police cooperation has existed for several decades through the efforts of the **International Criminal Police Organization (Interpol)**. Interpol considers terrorism to be: "a crime, characterized by violence or intimidation, usually against innocent victims in order to obtain a political or social objective." Interpol distinguishes between terrorism and organized crime: organized crime has a profit motive, whereas terrorism's goals are not primarily for financial, but rather for ideological gains. Interpol considers terrorism to be its number-one focus. The international organization supports the 182 member countries with a multi-pronged approach in providing intelligence on terrorist groups and identifying terrorist suspects. Due to its European location, Interpol has lent support to the member states for training assistance in building counterterrorism capability. Interpol also fashions itself as the authority that is ready, able, and willing to facilitate liaisons among the agencies of law enforcement, immigration, and customs as well as military intelligence organizations.

INTELLIGENCE GATHERING

Intelligence gathering for terrorist offenses is the domain of police forces throughout the world, many of which grudgingly share information. When spectacular IRA attacks occurred in London in the early 1990s, the intelligence-gathering operations were transferred from the police to the arm of British intelligence known as MI5. MI5's analysis encompassed not only IRA terrorists, but all groups that could pose a threat. In March 1996, the British government published a report by the Parliamentary Committee on Security and Intelligence which detailed that about 39 percent of the government's resources went toward compiling data on terror group membership, infrastructure, and methods. When cases of terrorism are brought to trial on evidence painstakingly gathered by both police and MI5, it would be counterproductive for a spy to appear on the witness stand to give testimony. Cooperation between these agencies is essential, and there has been successful coopera-tion between the British police and the intelligence community.

In the United States following 9-11, much was made of intelligence failings on the part of the U.S. intelligence community. It is, of course, easy to be critical after the event has taken place. However, there were indicators that were missed and relevant reports that were not followed up on. In order to determine the problems, we should first make an analysis of the current and historic state of the U.S. intelligence services. It could be said, and has been said, that the United States has the greatest intelligence in the world. However, if the right people do not listen and react to the information, it just becomes another secret file to be uncovered in future decades. Many U.S. intelligence agencies have been focused on preventing large-scale conflicts. And there is a serious need for such intelligence; however, the risk from modern terrorism and unconventional attacks appears to warrant the same level of resources. The Cold War era of intelligence, by comparison, is viewed as a simpler mode. It was easier to train covert operators to operate in the former Soviet Union than it is to train operatives to go native and assimilate into Arabic cultures and communities, mainly due to the constraints of culture, religion, and self-identification.

Budget constraints on **human intelligence (HUMINT)** can be traced as far back as the 1970s, when the United States began spending huge sums on improving the eyes and ears of the intelligence community with modern technology and satellite programs. On the other hand, the field operative has the capability to make judgments that are specific to a designated target country or culture that an analyst located thousands of miles distant would be unable to achieve. A very good example of such a failing in a military context was the inability of the U.S. administration to have adequate intelligence about what Iraq's intentions were prior to its invasion of Kuwait. Similarly, it may also have been important to have intelligence targeting the activities of the Pakistan Inter Service Intelligence (ISI) agency and its support of the Taliban and Osama bin Laden's mujahideen.

In addition to the lack of HUMINT resources, there is a balance in signals intelligence (SIGINT), in developing new systems and technologies to penetrate more sophisticated communications without forgetting how to decode the old systems of encryption. Since 9-11, the fear of "sleeper cells" has become a threat to the nation's security and this becomes a challenge for the forces charged with protecting domestic security. Quite obviously, any Islamic extremist elements would likely conceal themselves in regions where other members of the same religious ethnicity reside. The ability of the sleeper to elude possible detection relates to the likely communications gap among the U.S. State Department, which controls and issues visas; the Immigration and Naturalization Service (INS), which has responsibility for investigating and deporting illegal immigrants; and the Federal Bureau of Investigation (FBI), the organization tasked with domestic counterintelligence. The massive bureaucracies that have developed have also been the impeding factor in creating an effective means of performing counterterrorism operations and investigations within the United States. Harry S. Truman, for this very reason, combined the country's intelligence efforts under the Central Intelligence Group, the forerunner to the CIA more than fifty years ago. However, with the speed in the development of technology and the vying for political influence and budgetary constraints, the notion of a synergistic approach to the development of intelligence has been overlooked.[25] The Department of Homeland Security, which was designed to be the all-encompassing body that would meld the intelligence communities together, runs the serious risk of being a bureaucratic behemoth that will fail. With control and oversight in so many areas of enforcement, it is natural to think that with its huge budget and vast array of departments; it is set up to fail. Although it is easy to be critical, your authors believe that protecting the homeland is the priority, but whether the amalgamation of so many diverse operations will be a long-term success story is yet to be established.

As the planning for terrorist attacks often spans countries and regions, fighting terrorism requires the same level of effort and cooperation among nations. Spearheading the International Police agency's (INTERPOL) anti-terrorism efforts is the Fusion Task Force (FTF), created in September 2002 in the wake of the alarming rise in the scale and sophistication of international terrorist attacks.

FTF's primary objectives are to:

- Identify active terrorist groups and their membership.
- Solicit, collect, and share information and intelligence.
- Provide analytical support.
- Enhance the capacity of member countries to address the threats from terrorism
- And organized crime.

As terrorist organizations' far-reaching activities are inextricably linked, the task force investigates not only attacks, but also organizational hierarchies, training, financing, methods, and motives. INTERPOL has identified public safety and terrorism as a priority crime area, and countries can benefit from INTERPOL's unique position in the international law enforcement community in the fight against terrorism. The INTERPOL officials involved with the FTF are all terrorism specialists seconded from their home countries.

Regional and Global Efforts

Six regional task forces have been created in regions considered to be particularly susceptible to terrorist activity: Project Pacific (Southeast Asia), Project Kalkan (Central Asia), Project Amazon (South America), Project Baobab (Africa), Project Europe, and Project Middle East. An immediate goal is to increase the number of officers from the above regions to develop region-specific initiatives and enhance the effectiveness of the task force in these areas. In January 2008, 119 member states were contributing to terrorism related matters.

Fusion Task Force in Action

INTERPOL works closely with organizations such as the United Nations al Qaeda and Taliban monitoring teams and the International Criminal Tribunal for the former Yugoslavia to maintain its lists of suspected terrorists. FTF also maintains a secure Web site for member countries which includes all information on the Fusion Task Working Group Meetings, including presentations and analytical reports; photo boards of suspected terrorists; notices and diffusion lists. In January 2008, 545 users were accessing the FTF restricted Web site.[26]

INTELLIGENCE SERVICES

MI5 (Secret Intelligence Service)

The origins of the British Secret Intelligence Service (SIS) are to be found in the Foreign Section of the Secret Service Bureau, established by the Committee of Imperial Defence in October 1909. The Secret Service Bureau was soon abbreviated to "Secret Service," "SS Bureau" or even "SS." The first head of the Foreign Section, Captain Sir Mansfield Cumming RN, signed himself "MC" or "C" in green ink. Thus began the long tradition of the head of the Service adopting the initial "C" as his symbol.

Cumming sought to ensure that the Foreign Section of the Secret Service Bureau maintained a degree of autonomy, but the War Office, in particular, managed to exercise extensive control over his actions. The outbreak of the First World War in 1914 brought a need for even closer cooperation with military intelligence organizations within the War Office. The most significant manifestation of this was the virtual integration of the Foreign Section within the Military Intelligence Directorate. Thus, for much of the war, Cumming's organization was known as MI1(c). The debate over the future structure of British Intelligence continued at length after the end of hostilities but Cumming managed to engineer the return of the Service to Foreign Office control. At this time the organization was known in Whitehall by a variety of titles, including the "Foreign Intelligence Service," the "Secret Service," "MI1(c)," the "Special Intelligence Service" and even "C's organization." Around 1920, it began increasingly to be referred to as the Secret Intelligence Service (SIS), a title that it has continued to use to the present day and which was enshrined in statute in the Intelligence Services Act 1994.

"MI6" has become an almost interchangeable title for SIS, at least in the minds of those outside the Service. The origins of the use of this other title are to be found in the late 1930s when it was adopted as a flag of convenience for SIS. It was used extensively during the Second World War, especially if an organizational link needed to be made with MI5 (the Security Service). Although "MI6" fell into official disuse years ago, many writers and journalists continue to use it to describe SIS.[27]

Joint Terrorism Analysis Centre (JTAC)—UK

The Joint Terrorism Analysis Centre, or JTAC, was created as the United Kingdom's center for the analysis and assessment of international terrorism. It has been in existence since June 2003 and is based in Thames House. Although the head of JTAC is responsible to the Director General of the Security Service, JTAC operates as a self-standing organization comprised of representatives from eleven government departments and agencies. JTAC analyzes and assesses all intelligence relating to international terrorism, at home in the United Kingdom and overseas, and produces assessments of threats and other terrorist-related subjects for customers from a wide range of government departments and agencies. Within the Security Service, JTAC works especially closely with the International Counter Terrorism branch, which manages investigations into terrorist activity in the United Kingdom, in order to assess the nature and extent of the threat there. JTAC is also the agency that sets threat levels pertaining to threats from international terrorism.

America's National Strategy for Combating Terrorism—UPDATE September 2006

America is at war with a transnational terrorist movement fueled by a radical ideology of hatred, oppression, and murder. Our National Strategy for Combating Terrorism, first published in February 2003, recognizes that we are at war and that protecting and defending the Homeland, the American people, and their livelihoods remains our first and most solemn obligation. Our strategy also recognizes that the War on Terror is a different kind of war. From the beginning, it has been both a battle of arms and a battle of ideas. Not only do we fight our terrorist enemies on the battlefield, we promote freedom and human dignity as alternatives to the terrorists' perverse vision of oppression and totalitarian rule. The paradigm for combating terrorism now involves the application of all elements of our national power and influence. Not only do we employ military power, we use diplomatic, financial, intelligence, and law enforcement activities to protect the Homeland and extend our defenses, disrupt terrorist operations, and deprive our enemies of what they need to operate and survive. We have broken old orthodoxies that once confined our counterterrorism efforts primarily to the criminal justice domain.

Successes

- We have deprived al Qaeda of safe haven in Afghanistan and helped a democratic government to rise in its place. Once a terrorist sanctuary ruled by the repressive Taliban regime, Afghanistan is now a full partner in the War on Terror.
- A multinational coalition joined by the Iraqis is aggressively prosecuting the war against the terrorists in Iraq. Together, we are working to secure a united, stable, and democratic Iraq, now a new War on Terror ally in the heart of the Middle East.
- We have significantly degraded the al Qaeda network. Most of those in the al Qaeda network responsible for the September 11 attacks, including the plot's mastermind Khalid Sheikh Muhammad, have been captured or killed. We also have killed other key al Qaeda members, such as Abu Musab al-Zarqawi, the group's operational commander in Iraq who led a campaign of terror that took the lives of countless American forces and innocent Iraqis.
- We have led an unprecedented international campaign to combat terrorist financing that has made it harder, costlier, and riskier for al Qaeda and related terrorist groups to raise and move money.
- There is a broad and growing global consensus that the deliberate targeting of innocents is never justified by any calling or cause.
- Many nations have rallied to fight terrorism, with unprecedented cooperation on law enforcement, intelligence, military, and diplomatic activity.
- We have strengthened our ability to disrupt and help prevent future attacks in the Homeland by enhancing our counterterrorism architecture through the creation of the Department of Homeland Security, the Office of Director of National Intelligence, and the National

Counterterrorism Center. Overall, the United States and our partners have disrupted several serious plots since September 11, including al Qaeda plots to attack inside the United States.

- Numerous countries that were part of the problem before September 11 are now increasingly becoming part of the solution . . . and this transformation has occurred without destabilizing friendly regimes in key regions.
- The Administration has worked with Congress to adopt, implement, and renew key reforms like the USA Patriot Act that promote our security while also protecting our fundamental liberties.

Yet while America is safer, we are not yet safe. The enemy remains determined, and we face serious challenges at home and abroad.

Challenges

- Terrorist networks today are more dispersed and less centralized. They are more reliant on smaller cells inspired by a common ideology and less directed by a central command structure.
- While the United States Government and its partners have thwarted many attacks, we have not been able to prevent them all. Terrorists have struck in many places throughout the world, from Bali to Beslan to Baghdad.
- While we have substantially improved our air, land, sea, and border security, our Homeland is not immune from attack.
- Terrorists have declared their intention to acquire and use weapons of mass destruction (WMD) to inflict even more catastrophic attacks against the United States, our allies, partners, and other interests around the world.
- Some states, such as Syria and Iran, continue to harbor terrorists at home and sponsor terrorist activity abroad.
- The ongoing fight for freedom in Iraq has been twisted by terrorist propaganda as a rallying cry.
- Increasingly sophisticated use of the Internet and media has enabled our terrorist enemies to communicate, recruit, train, rally support, proselytize, and spread their propaganda without risking personal contact.[28]

CIA and FBI

Following the 9-11 attacks, two major pieces of U.S. legislation, the U.S. Patriot Act and the Intelligence Reform and Prevention of Terrorism Act, were designed, in part, to provide a more cohesive level of coordination for intelligence and information sharing between the CIA and FBI. Prior to 9-11, each agency jealously guarded the information it gathered. Post 9-11, the FBI has subtly changed direction and does not only investigate terrorist events after they occur, but it has now been brought into line with the rest of the U.S. intelligence community to investigate events before they occur. The FBI intelligence program was built on the following core principles:

- Independent Requirements and Collection Management: While intelligence collection, operations, analysis, and reporting are integrated at headquarters divisions and in the field, the Office of Intelligence manages the requirements and collection management process. This ensures that the FBI focuses intelligence collection and production on priority intelligence requirements and on filling key gaps in its knowledge.
- Centralized Management and Distributed Execution: The power of the FBI intelligence capability is in its 56 field offices, 400 resident agencies, and 56 legal attaché offices around the world. The Office of Intelligence must provide those entities with sufficient guidance to drive intelligence production effectively and efficiently, but not micromanage field intelligence operations.
- Focused Strategic Analysis: The Office of Intelligence sets strategic analysis priorities and ensures they are carried out both at headquarters and in the field.
- Integration of Analysis with Operations: Intelligence analysis is best when collectors and analysts work side by side in integrated operations.

Concepts of operations (CONOPs) guide FBI intelligence processes and detailed implementation plans drive specific actions to implement them. CONOPs describe the Intelligence Requirements and Collection Management system and are supported by lower-level collection and collection support processes and procedures defined in the FBI's *Intelligence Requirements and Collection Management Handbook*. These concepts and processes complement FBI operations and are enhanced by the Commission's recommendations.[29]

COUNTER-TERRORISM UNITS

Great Britain

In the world of counter-terrorism operations, few are as effective as the British SAS. Terrorism in the twentieth century has taken place primarily in the fifty-year period after World War II; therefore, counter-terror and counterinsurgency units have also developed since the war. An eccentric Scot, David Stirling, formed the SAS during World War II. A commando officer, Captain Robert Laycock, ably assisted him. During the war, conventional army theoreticians frowned upon the activities being proposed by the unconventional Stirling. At 6'5", he was an impressive figure of a man, and he believed passionately that there was an important role for "special operations" behind enemy lines. In Egypt, Stirling teamed up with a Welsh Guardsman and an Australian named Jock Lewes, and these three men created the Special Air Service. Protocol was the order of the day, and for Second Lieutenant Stirling to communicate his ideas to the General commanding Middle East operations, would require going through a long chain of command. Stirling thought the war would be over before his ideas reached the General. By fortuitous accident, he met with the Deputy Commander, General Ritchie, who was so impressed with the Lieutenant's ideas that they were soon put into practice for operations behind German lines in North Africa. This first unit was named "L' Detachment, Special Air Service Brigade," and the SAS was born.

Special Air Service (SAS) motto . . . "Who dares wins." The SAS of the 1990s is a far cry from that of the war years, and it has developed into what is arguably one of the best counter-terror units in the world. Many counter-terrorism organizations around the world have been modeled after the SAS. The SAS regiment is headquartered in Hereford in the west of England, but with government spending cuts, it was destined for a new home at Royal Air Force base at Creedenhill. The Special Air Service is made up of a Special Projects Team, and it is from this team that the Counter Revolutionary Warfare Squadron was formed to handle both foreign and domestic terrorism issues. Training for the SAS is constant, with one squadron always on standby to leave at a moment's notice to deal with a terrorist situation. An Operations Research Unit supports all SAS projects and has developed weaponry specific to the needs of the Regiment. This unit developed the stun grenade, which is widely used by counter-terrorism units around the world. The unit also developed night-vision goggles and special ladders for aircraft and train assaults.

As a peacetime unit, the SAS has been primarily involved in dealing with the IRA. The Provisional IRA referred to the British application of the SAS in Northern Ireland as death squads sent to terminate Irishmen. Unfortunately, for the Provisional IRA, the SAS was extremely effective in the urban warfare of Northern Ireland. The speed and efficiency with which the unit carried out operations stunned the Irish terrorist community.

SAS activity is not restricted to the United Kingdom, however, and it is believed that the regiment has been involved in operations against Libya. Adding to the mystique surrounding this elite regiment is the anonymity of its members. A plethora of news cameras from around the world covered the hostage drama at the Iranian Embassy in London (April 30, 1980) and captured live the sudden and dramatic rescue by armed men dressed in black fatigues. The success of that raid, which led to the death of all but one of the terrorists, placed Britain firmly in the spotlight as a country that did not deal lightly with terrorists and was prepared to use whatever force was necessary to end a crisis. It is important to note that this operation had been under the control of the civil police authorities until the conservative Home Secretary William Whitelaw gave the authority for the military (SAS) to advance an assault on the Embassy. This was the first time the public saw the SAS in action, and although there was an outpouring of indignation from extremists, the vast majority of Britons strongly supported the actions of the elite SAS team.

The success of the SAS has to be coupled with a highly competent intelligence network and through a variety of ways the security services in Northern Ireland became adept at infiltrating as well as coercing information from informants. In 1987 the SAS carried out one of its most successful operations in Northern Ireland when it ambushed a team of PIRA terrorists about to attack a police station in Loughall. Their intelligence was so precise that they knew all the details of the attack right down to the equipment to be used and the exact time date and location for the attack.

Several RUC & SAS men stayed in the Police Station to act as decoys. Outside, the SAS set up ambush positions, alongside the road past Loughgall Police Station. Apart from the main ambush force, several cut-off groups were put in place to cover for possible escape routes.

The attack on the police station began at 7 P.M., a stolen blue Toyota van was seen driving past the Police Station, presumably scouting the area ahead of the main attack group. A few minutes later, it returned, followed by a stolen JCB (digger), with three hooded men in its cab, and a large oil drum in its front bucket. The JCB crashed through the wire fence around the Police Station. The SAS watched as the three hooded men jumped from the cab, one of them lighting the fuse on the oil drum. As the three IRA men ran from the JCB, five armed men leaped out of the Toyota van and started firing at the station. The SAS immediately opened fire and within seconds all eight PIRA men were dead—cut down in a hail of automatic fire.

It had been the largest and most ferocious firefight between the SAS and the IRA and had a decidedly one-sided result. The incident seemed, at least temporarily, to rattle the IRA, who were troubled by the breach of security that led to the ambush.[30]

The SAS has also been used effectively against the IRA in Europe. In 1988, the SAS followed an IRA unit to Gibraltar, where intelligence sources indicated the terrorists would detonate a bomb during a military parade. The SAS carried out an attack on the three IRA members and, according to witness reports, gunned them down in cold blood. The subsequent outcry over claims of the government's "shoot-to-kill" policy seemed too much for a democracy to handle. The IRA now had its "martyrs" to bury at home in Northern Ireland and the opportunity to haul the British government before the European Court of Justice, which condemned the assault. The resulting court decision showed that caution was required, lest the counter-terrorist forces go too far. Of course, for the IRA, it meant the group had the right to not only shoot first, but to kill as well!

The SAS is on good terms with numerous countries and it has actively assisted in training many counter terror units around the globe. It is believed that the SAS is present, either officially or unofficially, at every terror incident to view how it was handled and to determine what went well and what went wrong. Thorough debriefs are held, and every minute detail of the operation is analyzed. The SAS was present and provided assistance to the Peruvian government when terrorists took control of the Japanese Ambassador's residence in Lima in 1996.

The British Royal Navy has its own counter-terrorism unit to rival the SAS . . . the **Special Boat Squadron (SBS)**. This unit is highly trained to respond to maritime acts of terrorism, though it has not been widely used. Most notably, the unit responded with the SAS to the bomb threat on the ocean liner, Queen Elizabeth II in the North Atlantic. Specifically designed for naval operations, the unit was deployed prior to the arrival of the Naval Task Force off the Falkland Islands at the outbreak of the war between Great Britain and Argentina.

SAS Associates . . . because of the proven effectiveness of the SAS regiment and its legendary exploits since World War II, other Commonwealth countries have modeled their counter-terrorism units on the SAS. The Australian SAS and the New Zealand SAS have even adopted the same name.

On the international stage Special Forces units have teamed up in Iraq 2006 was one of the bloodiest years for suicide and car bombings in Iraq and particularly in Baghdad. The environment in Baghdad would be uniquely suited to the expertise of the British SAS and the U.S. Delta Force. It is not by coincidence that the number of daily bomb attacks had all but dried up in Baghdad in 2007 and 2008 and this was not from a lack of will on the part of groups like al Qaeda in Iraq who have been responsible for a vast majority of the suicide and car bombings. British military sources indicated in late 2008 that over 3,000 terrorists had been either killed or captured by Special Operations units and this had reduced the number of attacks down from over 150 a month to around three or four.

Australia

The Tactical Assault Group (TAG) and the Special Air Service Regiment (SASR) were originally formed in 1957 and comprise Australia's response to any outbreak of domestic terror. The Australian SAS was originally a single company. By 1964, two additional companies had been added and the unit was renamed the Special Air Service Regiment (SASR). The regiment saw military action in Borneo, and with the outbreak of the Vietnam War, was instrumental in training the Australian army for its role in Southeast Asia. By the time the Vietnam War ended, the SASR had achieved some impressive results in the area of "special operations." Since the Vietnam War, Australia has not seen terrorist activity at home and the unit has been scaled down. Like its British counterpart, SASR engages in training and assists other units in the West. SASR has staff based at Fort Bragg and Little Creek in the United States. A specialist unit, the Offshore Installations Assault Group (OAG), is also available for seaborne counter-terror response. Since its creation, the SASR has lost a total of seventeen men: six were killed on active duty in Vietnam, three in operations in Borneo, and eight were killed during a training exercise near Townsville in 1996.

Rhodesia

The Rhodesian SAS is part of the original regiment that was disbanded at the end of World War II. That regiment was so effective that German radio stations referred to David Stirling with respect and fear. Rhodesians have a long and proud history of engagements on foreign soil. One World War II Rhodesian, Mike Sadler, served with the SAS in North Africa and was considered to be the best navigator in the vast Western Desert.[31] When the war was over, members of the SAS were returned to their respective countries. The regiment was almost disbanded, but survived as a territorial unit.

After defeating Germany and Japan in World War II, the next problem facing the allied powers was the rise of Communism in the Far East. It was the Malayan crisis of 1951 that established the reasons for retaining a Rhodesian SAS regiment for actions at home and abroad. The Commonwealth countries were asked to supply volunteers for a force to be dispatched to Malaya to handle the entrenched Communist terrorists in the region. It was commanded by Major "Mad Mike" Calvert, who had been given the go-ahead to form a self-sustaining warfare unit, trained in jungle conditions to operate for long periods of time. Its mission would be to deploy for continual harassment and disruption of Communist terrorist activity. Major Calvert flew to Rhodesia to meet with the contingent of 100 men and briefed them on the Malayan operation. The unit from Rhodesia would become C Squadron 22 SAS (Malayan Scouts).[32]

The Malayan emergency was to last until the end of that decade, and the Rhodesian SAS remained on station for two years. On returning to Africa, the unit was disbanded and the men returned to their civilian lives. However, the lessons learned in that Far East operation were of value in the country's development as it struggled for its identity and independence in the 1960s. Rhodesia's army was in need of specialized expansion and development. Following an assessment, it was decided that the Special Air Service Squadron would be established as a branch of the Rhodesian army. Training would be conducted under the auspices of the British SAS at Sterling Lines in Hereford, England. The Rhodesian military had a long and successful history of graduates at the Sandhurst Military Academy in Berkshire, England, and several cadets have been awarded the coveted Sword of Honor. Among those selected to join the newly formed Rhodesian SAS were remnants of the old Malayan task force of C Squadron.[33]

The Rhodesian SAS was exceptionally well-trained and schooled in jungle warfare techniques and its members were also accomplished paratroopers. The squadron assisted the 22 SAS Regiment in operations with the British army in the Crater District of Aden (now Yemen) during that crisis. The 1960s were a time of rationalization and decolonization. Great Britain was divesting itself of major parts of its empire and Africa was in constant turmoil, as other European empires were doing the same. The breakup of parts of Rhodesia began: the northern part becoming Zambia, and Nyasaland became independent Malawi. In 1964, Ian Smith, a Rhodesian-born former World War II fighter pilot, became prime minister of the country, determined to take Rhodesia to full independence from Britain. Politics would play a major role in the gradual demise of the SAS in Rhodesia. When Ian Smith was unable to convince the British government to grant independence to Rhodesia, he declared a Unilateral Declaration of Independence (UDI). This resulted in sanctions by Britain and a full trade embargo by the United Nations. The following fourteen years of turmoil in the region would end with a Black Nationalist government in power and the dissolution of the SAS. On December 31, 1980, the Rhodesian SAS disbanded and its members fled south to South Africa, taking with them the memorial to their war dead.

Republic of Ireland

The Army Ranger Wing (ARW) is classified as an elite counter-terror force and Ireland's front line against terrorism. Not as well known as its British counterparts, the SAS, the ARW has an impeccable reputation. The unit is made up of approximately 100 members and is subordinate to the chief of staff of the army. Like its SAS neighbors, it has some of the same kind of the basic responsibilities, including:

- Hostage rescue in extreme situations such as hijackings, both maritime and aircraft.
- Search and rescue operations.
- Close protection security details to VIPs and selected government officials.
- Ongoing maintenance of contingency planning processes for terrorist attacks.

Although there are no current details of actions undertaken by the group, the unit has maintained close ties with many European counter-terrorism units, including the French GIGN and the German GSG-9. ARW has been involved in peacekeeping operations through the United Nations in Somalia, Bosnia, and Lebanon.

Spain

Grupo Especial De Operaciones (GEO) Spain, which has had problems with the ETA terrorist group, and also GRAPO, was late in establishing an effective counterterrorism unit. In 1978, following the successes of the German GSG-9, Spain sought help from Germany in setting up GEO. One of Spain's difficulties was finding fiscal and political resources with which to staff the unit. Spain has both left-wing and right-wing terrorist problems, so there was a desperate need for apolitical members of any elite unit for this type of activity. Spain's GEO is not well-known outside that country, but is a highly trained and effective force. Although Spain has a thriving munitions industry of its own, the GEO uses the same assault weapons as their counterparts in GSG-9, favoring the Heckler and Koch MP5. As secretive as their comrades in both the SAS and GSG-9, GEO has had some unsung successes in dealing with terrorists. In May 1981, twenty-four right-wing terrorists occupied the Central Bank of Barcelona and took over 200 hostages. GEO stormed the bank using its standard assault weapon, the MP5. Only one of the hostages was injured and ten of the terrorists were captured. One terrorist was killed. The remainder fled the bank with the hostages in the ensuing confusion.[34]

Guarda Civil . . . Spain's second unit, the Unidad Especial de Intervencion (UEI), handles hostage-taking and terrorist activity and operates within the structure of the Guarda Civil (National Police). UEI is responsible to the ministries of the interior and defense and forms part of Spain's national police force. Like the GEO, it is deployed across the country and has had notable successes in rescuing kidnapping and hostage victims from both ETA and GRAPO.

The Persian Gulf

Cobras (Sultan of Oman Special Forces, SSF) . . . The SAS continued its tradition of providing training and logistical support for friendly Middle East countries with close ties to the Royal Military Academy at Sandhurst. The tiny sultanate of Oman has seen very little terrorist activity but, when the region started to destabilize with pro-Communist guerrillas under the Popular Front for the Liberation of Oman (PFLO), the sultan requested assistance from Britain. The rebellion in Oman lasted almost thirteen years between 1962 and 1975. During that time, the British SAS was actively involved in counter-terrorism operations with the sultan's army. However, the sultan was not prepared for the kind of terror and insurgent tactics the guerrillas would use. The SAS was more than happy to oblige and was instrumental in bringing down the opposition forces opposing the sultan. When the fighting was over, Sultan Qaboos made the decision that his country would never again be without a response unit for insurgency and terrorism.

The British SAS gave support and training in setting up the SSF for the sultan. The Cobras, based in Dhofar, are now considered the most elite force in the Persian Gulf region. Cobra teams are set up along the same military lines as the SAS, and are on constant, fifteen-minute standby. From their bases in Dhofar and Muscat, they have provided assistance to neighboring Kuwait. In a peculiar setup, the Cobras are seconded to the Omani police, who are less well-equipped and trained. The police retain jurisdictional control of incidents. Jealousy and inter-service rivalry have not helped efforts to maintain this effective force in the Gulf.

France

Groupment d'intervention de la Gendarmerie Nationale (GIGN) . . . Unlike the British SAS, this elite counterterrorism response force in France was formed following the terrorist attacks at the Munich Olympic Games and the takeover of the Saudi Embassy in Paris. The Groupment d'intervention de la Gendarmerie Nationale (GIGN) is a police unit, not military. The recruits to this unit come from the ranks of the paramilitary police service, the Gendarmerie Nationale (National Police). All members undergo eight months of rigorous training similar to that of the SAS, to include parachute qualification. On successful completion, they are based at the Maison Alfort near Paris. As a police unit, the GIGN is called on to deal with criminal incidents as well as terrorist attacks. The unit is heavily armed with Heckler and Koch MP5 submachine guns, as well as an assortment of sophisticated handguns. The GIGN is also trained in negotiating skills and recognizing psychological weaknesses and changes in the state of mind of the terrorist. Like the SAS, GIGN shuns publicity. It has had remarkable success in rescuing kidnapping victims. GIGN's most widely known and spectacular action was the storming of an Air France airbus at Marseilles, which resulted in the death of all thirteen hijackers. The Research, Assistance, Intervention, and Dissuasion (RAID) unit is currently the lead counter-terror unit in France and has been leading the fight against radical Islamists in France. This special tactical unit was the result of the rapid rise in terror attacks in France during the 1970s and 1980s at a time when the French National Police were unable to handle rising numbers of terror attacks. Headquartered outside Paris in Bievres and consisting of around 100 members, this elite organization reports to the Director General of French Police. It gathers and selects its members from the French National Police and like other western style elite units, its organizational structure include sections for intervention, negotiation, and tactical support units that flex to the threat being dealt with. RAID was first seen in action during a hostage standoff in Nantes in 1985 . . . the same year it was officially launched. RAID was developed by Robert Broussard a police/special operations expert who had been given the task of tackling rising criminal networks and terrorism.

Netherlands

Bijondere Bijstands Eenheid (BBE) . . . "Qua Patet Orbis" (The Whole World Over) is the motto of the Netherlands Marine Corps. "Send in the marines" has always been an option for Western governments and is an often-used phrase. In the case of the Netherlands, that is exactly what takes place in response to hostage-taking and terrorist actions. The Netherlands has one of the oldest military organizations in the world (the Dutch Marine Corps), which was founded on December 10, 1665. Today's modern Royal Netherlands Marine Corps numbers about 2,800. The corps is split into two separate areas for operational purposes: one group in the Netherlands for NATO duties and the other stationed in Aruba in the Dutch Antillies. The Marines represent a strike force that can respond to any terrorist situation. A section of the Marine Corps is devoted to counter-terrorism functions and is called the BBE. Translated, this has the literal meaning "different circumstances unit." The Dutch government, like other Western European countries, does not negotiate with terrorists, although the country is not beset with severe terrorist problems. One incident that happened which resulted in conflict, relates to Dutch colonialism in Indonesia. In 1975 a group from South Molucca hijacked a train hoping to bring pressure to the Dutch government. The hijackers were members of the Free South Moluccan Youth Organization (VZJ) demanding an independent homeland.

The Netherlands' response was to send in the Marines (BBE). On this occasion, as with others involving the South Moluccans, the siege was ended by extreme force resulting in the death of the terrorists and minor injuries to the rescuers and the rescued. Each attack unit of the BBE consists of two, thirty-three-man platoons, each comprised of four assault teams. They are further broken down into five-man units. The unit's functions are similar to those of the British SAS and are assisted with maritime operations from the 7th Special Boat Squadron, another elite unit made up of four, six-man intervention teams.

Norway

Forsvarets Spesialkommando (FSK, Special Defense Commando) . . . Norway's elite military response unit was formed in 1982, primarily as a defensive unit to deal with terrorist attacks against its many North Sea oil rigs. It is also responsible for the close protection of the Norwegian Royal Family, the national assembly, and other government officials. The FSK is a branch unit of the Norwegian Army Jegercommand. This is another unit that has used the example of the SAS, and the start-up of the unit involved five years of close involvement between the two. FSK and SAS have maintained close ties and often train together on exercises. The close nature of the two units brought the FSK some unwanted publicity when it was reported in the Norwegian press that it had been involved in SAS operations against the IRA in Northern Ireland in 1994, a report that both governments strenuously denied. FSK has also seen service overseas when it was dispatched to Kashmir to help locate a Norwegian being held captive by Al-Faran guerrillas.

Germany

Grenzschutzgruppe 9 (GSG-9) stands alongside the major elite terrorist responders in the world today as one of the most successful units. The unit was formed following the disaster at the Munich Olympic Games. After the horrendous events of the Olympics, the Germans were not prepared to allow such atrocities to happen again. In the case of the Olympics, it was the soft target with worldwide media coverage that the Black September movement was after. In the two decades after the end of World War II, Germany had taken pains not to produce any elitist forces for any purpose. This unit was formed and fully operational by April 1973, six months after the Munich massacre. Unlike the SAS, this unit would become part of the Federal Border Police service and not part of the German military. Each member must be a volunteer and a member of the Border Police. The iconic leader and founding leader of GSG-9 was Colonel Ulrich Wegener who joined Germany's Federal Border Police in 1958. His training with both the FBI and the Israeli Secret Service gave him expert knowledge on terrorism and was the logical choice to lead the group. He is believed to have been involved with the Israeli raid at Entebbe in 1976. Wegener's orders had been to create a small and highly flexible anti-terrorist unit that could be used and deployed at a moment's notice. Following his success at Mogadishu, he was promoted to Brigadier and given ultimate control over the whole of the Federal Border Police.[35]

The group is split into three definable units, each with fifty members: GSG-9/1 is responsible for counterterrorism; GSG-9/2 handles maritime counterterrorism; and GSG-9/3 deals with airborne issues. The federal government supplies GSG-9 with the best and most advanced equipment available. The group operates in five-man units and is outfitted with two sets of combat gear . . . one for day and the other for nighttime operations.

Israel

SAYERET MAT'KAL Sayeret Mat'kal is also known as the **General Staff Reconnaissance Unit #69,** and was founded in 1957. This unit has been in the forefront of every Israeli anti- and counter-terrorism strategy since its inception. It is the unit that is also dedicated to handling hostage-taking incidents. In wartime, this unit takes on the role of intelligence gathering. The Sayeret Mat'kal actively does the bidding of the Israeli government and has hunted down and executed known terrorists. After the Munich massacre, it was mandated to track down and kill those involved. Operation Spring Youth was an offensive strike carried out by the Sayeret Mat'kal in 1973. It has carried out actions that for nearly every other Western power would be unacceptable; however, to the embattled Israelis, the group's actions are accepted as a requirement in the protection of the state. On April 9 and 10, 1973, Sayeret infiltrated Beirut, which had to be considered extremely hostile territory, and assassinated the leaders of the Black September organization. This action was carried out successfully at three separate locations in West Beirut.

Czech Republic

Utvar Rychleho Nasazeni (URNA) is the Czech Republic's rapid response counter-terrorist police and crime-busting force. URNA is modeled to be similar to its elite counterparts in the German GSG-9 and the French GIGN. It has specific responsibilities and as such is tasked directly from the Ministry of the Interior to protect foreign heads of state, secure major sporting events against sabotage, and assist the police in drugs and serious crime interdiction. By far, its most important role is its intervention in extreme terrorist situations, including hostage-taking and hijackings. Although not as well known as other Western European counter-terror units, URNA is considered one of the elite reaction units and is held in very high regard.

HOSTAGE RESCUE UNITS (HRU'S)

Hostage rescue units (HRUs) are in operation throughout the world. Most countries designate, train, and equip teams to deal with hostage-taking crises and the protection of VIPs and government officials. These units in the Philippines are called the Aviation Security Commando (AVESCOM) Unit. In Thailand, HRU functions are the responsibility of the Royal Thai Air Force. In India, the extremely efficient and well-trained Special Counterterrorist Unit (SCU) is considered to be the best in Asia. Malaysia uses the Special Strike Unit of the Royal Malay Police, and Sri Lanka has the Army Commando Squadron. In the Middle East, Bahrain and Saudi Arabia have units trained by the British SAS and the French GIGN, respectively. The Hashemite Kingdom of Jordan maintains the 101st Special Forces Battalion, which also provides sky marshals for Alia, the national airline of Jordan. Egypt has had a colorful history of failures in hostage rescue in recent decades. Both of the incidents occurred in the Mediterranean. Egypt uses the Saiqa unit for counter-terrorism operations, as well as Force 777, created in 1978. The countries of Latin and South America use sections of the military and federal police services for HRU functions in most cases.

The United States of America

The United States has, only in the last decade, begun to experience at home what most European and Middle Eastern countries have been experiencing for nearly four decades. Hostage rescue, kidnapping, and their negotiations have long been the province of the Federal Bureau of Investigations (FBI), assisted by special police squads that are formed in almost every jurisdiction in the United States. These units are termed Special Weapons and Tactical (SWAT) units. The FBI is the U.S. federal agency responsible for information and intelligence gathering at home, which is not, as many believe, the domain of the Central Intelligence Agency. The CIA is mandated for intelligence and field operations outside the United States and for protecting U.S. interests. With varying gun laws throughout the United States, weapons offenses are a daily diet for the state police, with SWAT teams regularly called upon to deal with many criminal activities, particularly bank holdups. With the hostage crisis in Tehran in the 1970s, the need arose to have dedicated and well-trained tactical teams to deal with subversive activities both at home and abroad.

Hostage rescue is a risky business and usually when rescues go wrong they get wrong very quickly and usually with disastrous results. In 1985 Egypt Air 648 was hijacked to the island of Malta in the Mediterranean. The Egyptian government dispatched its counter terrorism strike force, Force 777, to the island to assist with the hostage-rescue operations. The Maltese government gave the go-ahead for Force 777 to take action against the terrorists. The assault began at about 8:00 P.M., lasting for more than a minute and a half, which is nearly four times longer than most anti-terror groups will take to storm an aircraft and release hostages. The series of mistakes, miscalculations, lack of intelligence, and planning resulted in the death of the passengers . . . some of whom were shot by snipers, who mistook escaping passengers for terrorists and gunned some of them down.[36]

"Delta Force" was the brainchild of Charles Beckwith in the 1970s. Beckwith realized that the United States did not have the same capability for hostage rescue and counter-terrorism response as the Europeans and proposed establishing an elite unit from the ranks of the U.S. Special Forces. Selection began, using the same harsh and disciplined methods as used by the SAS, which Beckwith himself had experienced with the SAS in the 1960s. After the seizure of the U.S. Embassy in Tehran, in November 1979, the Delta Force was placed on standby to handle the rescue and evacuation of the hostages. Considerable intelligence gathering and logistical planning went into the plans to rescue the hostages, and the Delta team was front and center. The mission was to fail due to dust storms. One of the mission's helicopters crashed into a C-130 that was carrying munitions, resulting in the deaths of eight members of the U.S. Marine Corps.

The members of Delta Force managed to escape injury and returned to the United States without completing their mission. After the abortive mission to Iran, a Special Operations Group was initiated, and from that came the creation of SEAL Team Six in 1980. SEAL Team Six is the Navy's equivalent to the Delta Force and is responsible for handling counter-terrorism in any maritime environment. Its beginnings relate directly to the failure of the Tehran operation, which had been designated by the code words, "Eagle Claw." The name SEAL Team Six was chosen as a ploy to confuse the Soviets as to exactly how many SEAL units the United States then had available at that time. All of the SEAL platoons were trained in counter-terrorism. SEAL Team Six went through an extensive training regimen that involved training overseas with members of the SAS, GSG-9, GIGN, and other counterterrorism organizations. SEAL Team Six would undergo further changes to its structure, including a name change due to its poor reputation within the Navy. SEAL Team Six was embarrassed by its founding member, Commander Richard Marcinko, who was charged with an assortment of offenses, ranging from fraud to bribery, and was sentenced to a brief term of imprisonment. Following this fiasco, the unit designation was changed to the Naval Special Warfare Development Group (NSWDG). Structured on the same lines as the SAS and numbering approximately 200 men, the NSWDG covers a wide spectrum of abilities, much the same as the SAS and the SBS. Unlike their European counterparts, they have not had the opportunity to prove themselves, as the SAS had at Prince's Gate or the GSG-9 had at Mogadishu, although they have been in both covert and overt operations since the 1980s.

In 1985, NSWDG was on standby in the Mediterranean during the *Achille Lauro* hijacking, which claimed the life of Leon Klinghoffer, but it was not called into action. In the same year, the unit was used during the U.S. invasion of Grenada to rescue the governor of the island, Sir Paul Scoon. During that operation, four SEALs drowned during the helicopter insertion offshore. In a more criminal response operation for the U.S. government, NSWDG was involved, alongside the Delta

Force, in locating and capturing Manuel Noriega from Panama in 1990. Following a coup in Haiti in 1991, it is believed the unit was involved in rescuing deposed President Aristide. The SEALs were used for the initial landings in Somalia in 1992, when they came ashore in scuba gear to a throng of media people with video cameras and floodlights who broadcast their invasion, live, around the world. This was a prime example of poor understanding between operational forces and the media.

In domestic situations, the United States has also used the Alcohol Tobacco and Firearms (ATF) unit for dealing with criminals who are stockpiling illegal weapons. For weeks, the news media covered a major ATF operation in Waco, Texas. The ATF went to execute a warrant against the Branch Davidians, led by David Koresh. An ensuing gun battle and a long standoff later resulted in an ATF assault. A fire erupted and all inside the compound were incinerated. It was discovered after the event, however, that many had been killed or committed suicide before flames overtook the buildings.

CANADA

Joint Task Force Two (JTF-2)

From 1993 onward, responsibility for counter-terror operations in Canada changed from a Royal Canadian Mounted Police (RCMP) role to a military function. A rather secretive military force known as **Joint Task Force 2 (JTF-2)** functions much in the same way as its SAS British counterparts. The unit is known to have operated in Eastern Europe, particularly in Bosnia and in regions of Afghanistan in pursuit of al Qaeda leader Osama bin Laden. JTF-2 arrived in Afghanistan in December 2001 and joined other Special Ops forces from the United States, Britain, and Australia, based at the former Taliban stronghold of Kandahar. The Canadians were assigned to Task Force K-Bar, a multinational special operations group led by U.S. Navy SEAL Captain Robert Harward.

K-Bar consisted of some 2,800 personnel, including support and air staff, and under Harward's command were Special Forces units from the U.S. Navy, Army, and Air Force, as well as forces from Denmark, Germany, Norway, Australia, Canada, New Zealand, and Turkey. U.S. Marine helicopters provided air transport.[37]

PIRACY

The Oxford English Dictionary defines "piracy" as "Robbery, kidnapping, or violence committed at sea or from the sea without lawful authority, especially by one vessel against another." The International Maritime Bureau Piracy Center provides a more recent definition of piracy: "The act of boarding any vessel with the intent to commit theft or other crime and with the capability to use force in the furtherance of the act." Article 101 of the United Nations Convention of the Law of the Sea defines piracy as:

Piracy consists of any of the following acts:

a. Any illegal acts of violence or detention, or any act of depredation, committed for private ends by the crew or the passengers of a private ship or a private aircraft and directed
   i. On the high seas, against another ship or aircraft, or against persons or property on board such ship or aircraft;
   ii. Against a ship, aircraft, persons or property in a place outside the jurisdiction of any State.
b. Any act of voluntary participation in the operation of a ship or of an aircraft with knowledge of facts making it a pirate ship or aircraft;
c. Any act of inciting or of intentionally facilitating an act described in subparagraph a or b.

A less well-known, but very serious, threat continues to exist throughout the shipping world . . . sea piracy. Although sea piracy has been in existence for centuries and, to many, it will conjure up an almost romantic or exotic event, the truth is far from that. Sea piracy is a major economic and security threat. The areas of the globe most affected by sea piracy are located in the waters of the Far East . . . the South China Sea and the waters surrounding Indonesia and the Philippines. Frequent attacks on shipping go virtually unnoticed in the news media; however, crew deaths are not an uncommon result of sea piracy. In earlier days, almost all trade around the globe went via ships, and the lucrative routes between the Middle East and the Far East were the hunting grounds for myriads of pirates. The well-known, sixteenth-century English sea Captain Sir Francis Drake could also be likened to a pirate. His ships' targets were invariably those belonging to Spain. Britain had been on and off at war with Spain and the seizing of Spain's ships was not considered to be piracy, at least not by the British. Drake was deemed to be a "privateer," and his many countrymen operated under the same royal protection. However, the Spanish government considered Drake and Walter Raleigh to be dyed-in-the-wool pirates. Piracy on the high seas has developed and become more sophisticated with the passage of time and with obviously higher risks and greater rewards for the pirates. The International Maritime Organization has defined three types and levels of piracy:

1. An attack on a ship operating close to shore, often an opportunist attack, by pirates in small, high-speed, seagoing craft, with the intent to steal cash and personal valuables from the crew and the ship's safe. This is defined as a Low-Level Armed Robbery (LLAR).
2. Medium-Level Armed Robbery and Assault (MLAAR). This level of attack is invariably a deadly assault on the ship's crew and/or passengers, often by well-armed and equipped pirates. This type of attack has often been coordinated with the aid of a mother ship, enabling the attack to take place in international waters.
3. The most serious level defined by the organization, **Major Criminal Hijack (MCHJ)** . . . invariably involves international criminals who are well-equipped and trained. These groups will either take total control of the vessel, stealing the vessel's entire cargo and off loading it to another ship, or casting the crew adrift and re-naming the ship.

What makes sea piracy so lucrative and accomplishable in the twenty-first century? A large number of states have depleted their navies, thus leaving them unable to have a presence to deter pirate attacks on ships, both in international and territorial waters. Add to this a dimension of high technology in which many vessels are now dependant on much smaller operating crews, creating an opportunity for pirates to operate unhindered. Shipping in international waters is protected by the "flag" of the country in which it is registered. Many countries adopt a "flag of convenience" for their vessel which means that a vessel owned in one country (such as the United States or Great Britain), can be registered in another country (Panama, Liberia, or Cyprus, for example), thus avoiding international safety and taxation regulations. Nearly 90 percent of ocean-going cargo ships entering U.S. ports are operating under foreign flags. Many of these ships, such as Greek flagged and flag-of-convenience ships (officially called "open-registry ships"), operating out of Piraeus employ low-wage seamen from the developing countries of Pakistan and the Philippines. Flag-of-convenience countries are often unwilling to take any significant diplomatic action against countries from which pirates are operating. The International Maritime Bureau has a piracy center located in Kuala Lumpur, Indonesia, that has responsibility to provide information around the clock on piracy activities in all the regions of the globe.

The legal aspects of piracy and maritime hijacking are somewhat convoluted, if not complex. The international community recognizes that an act of piracy can only be committed in international waters and must therefore be dealt with under international law. Should the commission of a seaborne attack on a maritime vessel occur inside territorial waters, the responsibility for pursuing and prosecuting the incident as robbery falls to the state that claims the territorial right over that region of the ocean. International law requires any warship or government vessel to "repress piracy on the high seas" and to come to the aid of any vessel under attack. The rules of engagement for sea piracy, as it affects government vessels, are that force should only be used as a means of self-defense against piracy. There are, in fact, no listed rules of engagement for sea piracy. The action of individual member state's navies is governed, therefore, by each state.

Historical data on piracy does not date back much more than the last two decades of the twentieth century. However, some areas of the globe have suffered from acts of piracy to such an extent that action had to be taken. In the early 1980s, private groups targeted ships at anchor and waiting to berth in the Nigerian ports of Lagos and Bonny. They would attack after dark and break into containers on board. The eventual outcome was a concerted crackdown by Nigerian police and customs to root out the pirates and their bases of operation. Piracy has also been highly prevalent in the Far East in the Straits of Malacca, one of the busiest shipping lanes in the world. In efforts to contain and minimize the attacks against commercial and other shipping, the International Maritime Organization established a working group to study the problem and come up with a methodology and recommendations. The results of the study were that the under-reporting of acts of piracy should be discouraged and that masters should immediately report acts and attempted acts of piracy. Probably the most significant effort was the assistance of technology through the International Telecommunications Union and the International Mobile Satellite Organization (Inmarsat). This technology enabled the inclusion of "piracy/armed robbery attack" as a category of distress message that ships are now able to transmit through Digital Selective Calling (DSC) or by using Inmarsat.[38] The message will be received automatically by ships and shore stations in the area. Maritime piracy continues in many regions of the world and particularly in areas where it is easy for pirates to escape without detection. The vastness of the South China Sea is testament to that, and there are attacks on fishing vessels around the many islands of the Philippines. In these attacks, pirates take the fish and any other valuables on board or take the entire vessel.

The Piracy Reporting Center in Kuala Lumpur, Indonesia, works around the clock and provides daily commentary and bulletins on pirate activity throughout the globe. The center is actually supported on an annual basis by voluntary contributions from shipping lines and insurance companies. The worldwide use of such modern technological breakthroughs as global positioning and tracking systems has enabled shipping companies to adopt such innovations as the SHIPLOC system, which is an inexpensive method of using satellite technology and the internet to track an individual ship. Irrespective of technology and the will to combat the scourge of piracy, it is likely to continue and the pirates themselves will likely become more sophisticated in their modus operandi. Whether a ship will be used in a wider terrorist attack, such as the destruction of a passenger cruise liner, with massive loss of life, is no doubt on the list of scenarios being looked at by the security and intelligence communities at large. By international agreement, as of July 2004, ships above 500 tons had to be equipped with alarm systems that silently transmit security alerts containing tracking information in case of emergency. Vessels are also required to emboss their International Maritime Organization (IMO) number on their hulls. And since 2003, ship owners have been able to install high-voltage electric fencing to discourage intruders, although ships carrying highly volatile cargo (including oil) cannot use such fencing.[39]

Certain areas have seen increased pirate activity and in recent years Nigeria has become the global hotspot. Pirate attacks rose worldwide in the first quarter of 2008, with Nigeria overtaking Indonesia as the country worst plagued by sea bandits. Seafarers suffered forty-nine attacks between January and March around the world, up 20 percent from the forty-one recorded in the same period last year. Nigeria ranked as the No.1 hotspot amid a lack of effective law enforcement, with its ten reported attacks—mostly off its main city of Lagos—accounting for one-fifth of the global total.[40]

The UN Convention of the Law of the Sea, Article 105

The seizure of a pirate ship or aircraft: On the high seas, or in any other place outside the jurisdiction of any State, every State may seize a pirate ship or aircraft, or a ship or aircraft taken by piracy and under the control of pirates, and arrest the persons and seize the property on board. The courts of the State which carried out the seizure may decide on the penalties to be imposed, and may also determine the action to be taken with regard to the ships, aircraft, or property, subject to the rights of the third parties acting in good faith.[41]

FIGURE 14-5 Cruise ships make for a ready target for terrorists (Jeremy R. Spindlove).

Countering the Threats from the Sea

Terrorist groups such as Hezbollah, Jemaah Islamiyaah, the Popular Front for the Liberation of Palestine-General Command, and Sri Lanka's Tamil Tigers, have long sought to develop a maritime capability. Intelligence agencies estimate that al Qaeda and its affiliates now own dozens of phantom ships . . . hijacked vessels that have been repainted, renamed and then operate under false documentation, manned by crews with fake passports and forged competency certificates. Security experts have long warned that terrorists might try to ram a ship loaded with explosive cargo, perhaps even a weapon of mass destruction, into a major port or terminal. Such an attack could bring international trade to a halt, inflicting multi-billion-dollar damage on the world economy.[42] In 2004, Panama and Liberia agreed to allow countries that formed part of the Proliferation Security Initiative (PSI) to board ships sailing under both Liberian and Panamanian flags. The obvious value of this agreement was that any ships owned and operated by al Qaeda would likely be registered and flagged as either Panamanian or Liberian. More than half the ships that traverse the globe are covered by the so-called "flags of convenience." Intelligence gathered on al Qaeda suggests that the group has had the opportunity to operate more than 300 vessels of varying sizes, posing a serious threat to ports, particularly in the United States and Europe. To complement the ability of the major navies of the world to board "suspect" ships on the high seas, additional measures have been established to protect the integrity of cargo—not just at the port of final destination, but also at the port of export. Stringent global strategies came into force on June 1, 2004, including the International Code for the Security of Ships and Port Facilities (ISPS) and amendments to the International Convention for the Safety of Life at Sea (SOLAS). The new ISPS code and the amendments to SOLAS adopted by the 162-member International Maritime Organization (IMO) require all companies operating ships of more than 500 tons on international voyages to designate security officers, prepare contingency plans, and be fitted with new security alert systems.

There is one act of piracy/hijacking in the last quarter of a century that stands out not just for its boldness but for the cruelty and callous actions of the terrorists involved. In 1985 an Italian cruise ship, the Achille Lauro was taken over by members of the Palestine Liberation Front, at the exact same time as Palestinian/Jordanian talks were being conducted in London. The Palestinians demanded the

FIGURE 14-6 Shipping container area, Port of San Pedro, California (Jeremy R. Spindlove).

release of fifty Palestinians being held in Israeli prisons in exchange for the safe return of the cruise ship. Among the cruise ships passengers were American Jews, one an elderly U.S. citizen Leon Klinghoffer, who was confined to a wheelchair, was tossed overboard and drowned.

The hijackers eventually agreed to surrender to Egyptian authorities including the leader of the PLF Abu Abbas. As they began their flight from Tunis to Egypt the aircraft was intercepted by U.S. Navy fighters and forced to fly to a NATO base in Sicily. Italian police arrested the hijackers, but not before diplomatic wrangling between the United States and Italy was eventually resolved with the intervention of President Reagan. It is believed the intended target was not the cruise liner and in fact, the terrorists were planning a raid in Egypt when they were discovered on the *Achille Lauro* with weapons and explosives. Klinghoffer's family and the travel agents who booked the cruise liner sued Arafat and the PLO for damages. In August 1997, they reached a legal settlement with the PLO. Although it is not known what that settlement was, it appears that restitution has been paid for the family's suffering as a result of Klinghoffer's murder.[43]

While piracy is an ongoing problem for shipping in areas such as the South China Sea and off the east coast of Africa, particularly Somalia, the concern is also generated by the vast numbers of containers and container ships that circumnavigate the world's oceans. The potential that just one of these containers could contain a nuclear, chemical, or biological weapon for detonation at a U.S. port is of grave concern. Prior to 9-11, the numbers of containers being screened as they enter the United States amounted to less than half of 1 percent of all container traffic. Since then, significant effort has gone into U.S. port strategy. Reporting requirements are now placed on shipping lines prior to a ship's arrival; security officers, are now required on board ships; and tight security controls are now in place at originating ports. The threat to the food chain and controls on imports of foods is the domain of the U.S. Food and Drug Administration (FDA), an agency not under the umbrella of Homeland Security. The FDA has oversight in areas of bio-defense when it comes to contamination of foods. The FDA is responsible for about 80 percent of the U.S. food supply and its oversight includes safe production, processing, storage, and holding of domestic imported food. Past concerns related to food safety have revolved around individual attempts to contaminate a specific food or food service location. In 2002, a restaurant owner in China added chemicals to a competitor's food, killing dozens and sending several hundred to hospitals. A more serious threat emanated from the United Kingdom in January 2003, when British police arrested a group attempting to place the deadly "Ricin" into the food supply of a British military base. The FDA has formulated four major regulations under the authority of the Public Health Security and Bioterrorism Preparedness and Response Act of 2002. Owners and operators of foreign or domestic food facilities that manufacture, process, pack, or hold food products for human or animal consumption in the United States must submit information to the agency about their facility and emergency contact information.

Container Security Initiative

In January 2002, the U.S. Customs and Border Patrol (CBP) announced the introduction of the Container Security Initiative. This measure is intended to ensure that maritime containers posing a risk for terrorism are identified and examined at foreign ports before they are shipped to the United States. The Initiative is founded on four core principles:

1. Using intelligence and automated information to identify and target containers that pose a risk for terrorism.
2. Pre-screening those containers that pose a risk at the port of departure before they arrive at U.S. ports.
3. Using detection technology to quickly pre-screen containers that pose a risk.
4. Using smarter, tamper-evident containers.

The CSI focused on the twenty foreign ports that ship approximately two-thirds of the volume of containers to the United States. Governments from these twenty foreign ports have agreed to implement the CSI. Since 2002, the program has expanded to include more ports based on volume, location, and strategic concerns. CSI is a reciprocal program that offers participant countries the opportunity to send their customs officers to major U.S. ports to target ocean-going, containerized cargo destined for their countries.

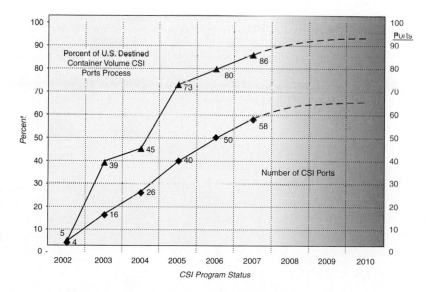

FIGURE 14-7   CSI Program Status (U.S. Department of Homeland Security).

FIGURE 14-8 Shipping container area, Port of San Pedro, California (Jeremy R. Spindlove).

The following is an up-to-date list of those ports currently operating under this initiative:

Europe:

- Rotterdam, The Netherlands
- Bremerhaven and Hamburg, Germany
- Antwerp and Zeebrugge, Belgium
- Le Havre and Marseilles, France

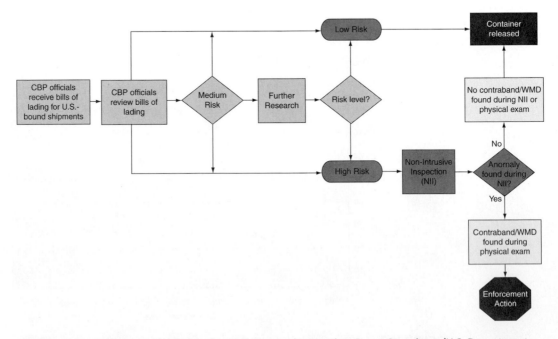

FIGURE 14-9 CBP's Domestic Process for Targeting and Inspecting Cargo Containers (U.S. Department of Homeland Security).

FIGURE 14-10 U.S. Customs inspects a container (U.S. Department of Homeland Security).

- Gothenburg, Sweden
- La Spezia, Genoa, Naples, Gioia Tauro, and Livorno, Italy
- Felixstowe, Liverpool, Thamesport, Tilbury, and Southampton, United Kingdom
- Pireaus, Greece
- Algeciras, Spain

North America:

- Montreal, Halifax, and Vancouver, Canada

East Asia and the Pacific:

- Singapore, China
- Yokohama, Tokyo, Nagoya, and Kobe, Japan
- Hong Kong, China
- Pusan, South Korea
- Port Klang and Tanjung Pelepas, Malaysia
- Laem Chabang, Thailand

Understanding Chemical, Biological, and Nuclear U.S. Food and Drug Administration Strategies

Prior Notification of Food Shipments: This regulation became effective in December 2003 and requires the FDA to receive prior notice of imported food shipments before the food arrives at a U.S. port. This would amount to more than 25,000 notifications about incoming shipments every day.

Establishment and Maintenance of Records: Manufacturers, processors and packers, importers, and others are required to keep records that identify the source from which they receive food and where they send it.

Administrative Detention: The FDA has authority to detain any food for up to thirty hours for which there is credible evidence that the food poses a threat to humans or animals.

Combating the Proliferation of Weapons of Mass Destruction

The threat from chemical, biological, and nuclear weapons may well be overstated and, then, depending on your individual viewpoint, the threat may be understated. What is clear is that since the end of the Cold War, the world is awash with nuclear products and material. Whether terrorists have the desire to obtain and use such material is a matter that has to be addressed in a national security strategy. There has been considerable debate about nuclear stockpiles and their accessibility in the former Soviet republics. Accounting for those stockpiles has not been an exact science. At a Global Threat Reduction Initiative conference in Vienna in 2004, the head of the UN Atomic Energy Agency (AEA) stated that there are about 350 sites in 58 countries that possess highly enriched uranium (HEU) and approximately two dozen of them have enough material to build a nuclear weapon. The Director General believed it was just a matter of time before terrorists deployed a nuclear device. There are tens of thousands of unprotected, suitable radioactive sources available to terrorists, even in wealthy and well-ordered societies. There were fifty cases of illicit traffic in radioactive materials in 2003, and the smugglers often target materials used in the medical and science industries.[44] The last four years have seen a furious debate in the United Kingdom and, to a lesser degree, in the United States, as to whether the Iraqi regime of Saddam Hussein had acquired chemical, as well as other weapons of mass destruction. Although none have been found, it does not necessarily mean they are not still there. An official report by the UN Special Commission to Iraq (UNSCOM) in 1991, stated that inspectors had found 46,000 chemical munitions in Iraq. From that, 20,000 were 120-mm CS-filled bombs; 14,000 contained

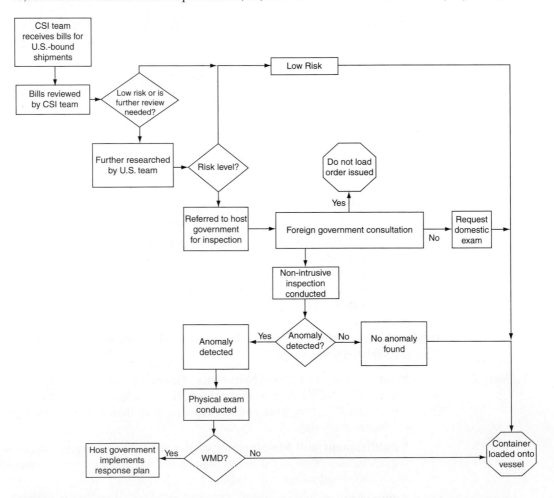

FIGURE 14-11   CSI Process for Targeting and Inspecting Cargo Containers Overseas (U.S. Department of Homeland Security).

mustard gas; and a further 11,000 were filled with the nerve agent sarin. UNSCOM later discovered hidden stockpiles of 200 anthrax bombs and 80 Scud rockets at Salah Ad Din near Tikrit.

Chemical Weapons

The current history of chemical agents used in warfare, dates back to the Great War . . . World War I, when the first known use of a chemical agent occurred. The German army began dispersing chlorine gas against British and allied troops in the battlefields of Europe. And the Germans further developed chemical weapons and the means to deliver such chemicals during World War I; mustard gas was first used during the trench wars of that time. The majority of the chemical casualties were from the effects of mustard gas. Records show that the Italians also used mustard gas against the Ethiopians when they invaded Ethiopia in 1935, and the Japanese used mustard gas and also chlorine gas during their invasion of China in 1930. The Germans made further developments in the production of nerve agents in the late 1930s. Both the Germans and the allied armies had significant stockpiles of chemical weapons but neither side used them during World War II (1939–1945). Mustard gas was further utilized by the Soviets and the Egyptians in Yemen between 1963 and 1967. The United States used chemical defoliant agents such as Agent Orange, Agent Blue, and Agents Purple and White in the Vietnam War. Agent Orange, an herbicide made of two common weed killers, was used frequently—over 50 million pounds were dropped over Vietnam during the war. The Soviet army used nerve agents and mustard gas against the mujahideen in Afghanistan between 1977 and 1989. Both Iran and Iraq used mustard gas in their war from 1979 to 1989.

History of Chemical Terrorism

There has been a long history of terrorists and criminals using poisons and toxins for political assassination and other crimes with political motivation:

- In 1976, the Arab Revolutionary Army injected mercury into citrus food products.
- In 1979, the West German police raided a safehouse of the Red Army Brigade and seized 400 kilograms of chemical precursors used to make nerve agents.
- In 1985, an Israeli military base discovered that its supply of coffee had been contaminated with a nerve agent.
- In 1984, several people died from arsenic poisoning after the drug Tylenol was contaminated with arsenic poison.
- In Tokyo in 1994, the Aum Shinrikyo sect released sarin gas into the subway system, killing twelve people and injuring more than 5,000.
- In the Ukraine in September 2004, Viktor Yushchenko, President of Ukraine, was poisoned by dioxin . . . probably orally administered and some suggest it may have been "Yellow Rain" a chemical agent used by the Soviets in the Afghan War.

There are a large number of chemical agents in existence today that could cause serious disruption if released into a general population:

- **Nerve agents:**
    GA—tabun
    GB—sarin
    GD—soman
    VX—V agents

- **Vesicants or blistering agents:**
    H—mustard
    HD—distilled mustard
    HN—nitrogen mustard
    CX—phosgene oxime
    L—lewisite

- **Blood agents:**
    AC—hydrogen cyanide
    CK—cyanogen chloride

- **Choking agents:**
    chlorine
    phosgene
    chloropicrin

- **Irritating agents:**
    CN—standard tear gas
    CS—stronger tear gas; induces vomiting
    DM—adamsite vomiting agent

Nerve Agents

These chemicals are designed to attack the body's nervous system in such a way as to cause convulsions or death. Nerve agents are liquid at ambient temperatures and are some of the most dangerous of all the chemical agents. Looking at Aum's attack on the Tokyo subway, all the symptoms of a nerve gas attack were prevalent: pinpoint pupils, blurred vision, eyes aggravated by light, excessive sweating, runny nose and nasal congestion, coughing and difficulty with breathing, nausea and vomiting, anxiety, and giddiness.

Some of the outward warning signs that could indicate a nerve agent attack include:

- Explosions that dispense gas, mists, or liquids
- Unscheduled or unusual spraying activities
- Localized explosion that destroys only a package or parcel
- Abandoned spray equipment
- Presence of large numbers of dead fish or animals and bird life
- Mass casualties without obvious trauma
- Definite pattern of casualties and symptom commonality
- Casualties located in possible obvious target locations, such as government and military establishment buildings, mass-transport systems, etc.

Vesicants

These chemicals are blistering agents. They were first produced for use in World War I. The vesicant used in the war was called mustard gas because it smells like mustard. These agents cause severe skin burns and damage to the eyes and respiratory system, if inhaled. If a large area of skin is exposed to the gas, absorption into the blood stream is usually inevitable. Vesicants are heavy, oily liquids and, in pure state, are almost colorless and odorless. They have a high propensity for penetration into layers of clothing and quickly absorb into the skin. They are extremely powerful but are far less lethal than nerve agents. A few drops of mustard gas on the skin can cause severe injury and three grams absorbed through the skin will likely be fatal.

Symptoms of vesicant poisoning include reddening of the eyes; congestion, tearing, a burning, gritty feeling in the eyes, followed by pain and spasm of the eyelids. The skin will blister depending on the level of exposure and initial itching and redness, followed by pain and tenderness. Blisters will appear and likely be fluid-filled and are most common in warm, moist areas of the body, such as in the groin area and under the armpits. There will also be a burning sensation in the nose and throat, coughing, and shortness of breath.

Blood Agents

Most blood agents are derivatives of cyanide compounds and, therefore, packages of cyanide salt and acid precursors may be present in any attack scenario. Blood agents produce casualties by interfering with the blood's ability to transfer oxygen to the cells, which can lead to death by asphyxiation. These agents are common industrial chemicals and information is publicly available on them. The outward warning signs include large numbers of casualties displaying common symptoms; the strong smell of peaches or bitter almonds is also a good indicator of blood agents.

Choking Agents

These chemical agents attack the respiratory system and cause acute distress. They also produce copious amounts of fluid, which can result in death by asphyxiation which resembles drowning. The most common symptoms are choking and coughing. Outward signs are the obvious chemical odor, such as the strong smell of chlorine, while phosgene has the odor of freshly cut hay.

Irritating Agents

These are likely the most commonly seen agents and are found in tear gas used in riot-control situations. They are designed to cause respiratory distress and copious tearing. They have the irritating smell of pepper (pepper spray) and are generally nonlethal. Chemical agents are relatively easy to manufacture and just as easy to disperse. They are easier to control than a biological agent and, although not contagious, may contaminate by persitence. Chemical agents can be mass-produced and are easier to hide and disguise, rather than a conventional weapon. The mere mention of the words "chemical weapons" will spread terror.

BIOLOGICAL WEAPONS

Biological weapons are, by their very nature, indiscriminate and difficult to contain and control. The delivery system for such a "weapon" continues to pose significant problems for a terrorist group. While a chemical attack would be the simpler attack to mount, the bio-attack weapon remains an ultimate weapon for the twenty-first-century terrorist.

History of Biological Weapons

- In 1346, the Tartar Army, led by Khan Janiberg, attacked the city of Kaffa and catapulted plague-infested bodies of their own men over the city walls.
- In the fifteenth century, the Spanish conquistador Pizarro gave clothing contaminated with smallpox to natives in South America.
- In 1940, the Japanese dropped "plague" on China.
- In 1972, 103 countries signed the Biological Weapons Convention, which prohibited the development of both biological and chemical weapons, as well as their use.
- In 1980, the German Red Army Faction was found in a Paris safe house making Botulin toxin.
- In 1984, Cuba reportedly was stockpiling toxins.
- In 1991, the Iraqi government admitted research in the use of anthrax, Botulinum, and Clostridium toxins.
- In 1994, the Aum Shinryko sect in Japan attempted an aerial drop of anthrax over Tokyo.
- In 1995, an Aryan nation's member was arrested in Ohio with a container of plague.
- In October 2001, envelopes containing spores of anthrax were sent to U.S. news media and government offices, causing nationwide panic.[45]

Our most recent attack in North America involved the anthrax bacterium, which produces shell-like spores that allow the bacterium to live in a dormant state in the soil. However, when anthrax is used as a weapon, the spores can become airborne and enter the lungs, where they become active. If enough of the spores are inhaled, the results can often be fatal. Anthrax is a serious infectious disease caused by the bacterium *Bacillus anthracis.* Anthrax is a disease that is common in cows, sheep, horses, and goats. The occasions of human contamination have been as a result of infection by persons coming into close contact with an infected animal. Until 2001, there had only been one case of anthrax in the United States in the previous ten years.

Inhalational Anthrax

This is the most serious form of anthrax. It results when a person inhales anthrax spores into the lungs. The symptoms do not appear immediately, but usually within two to six days after being infected. It is possible that symptoms will occur as late as sixty days after initial infection. Symptoms included headache, fever, coughing, and difficulty in breathing, chills, weakness, and chest pain. This disease can be controlled by antibiotics if diagnosed promptly. Inhalation anthrax is not contagious and does not spread from person to person.

Cutaneous Anthrax

This form of anthrax occurs when the anthrax spores come into direct contact with a cut or break in the skin. Evidence of infection will become apparent within one to seven days of contamination with an itchy bump reminiscent of a small insect bite. The bump will develop blisters and then turn to a painless sore with a black center. Lymph glands in the area or near the affected area may begin to swell. This form is not as dangerous as the inhaled anthrax, but if not treated, this anthrax has a 20 percent mortality rate. This form is also not contagious and responds well to antibiotics.

Intestinal Anthrax

This form of anthrax occurs when a person eats meat from an infected animal that has died from anthrax, or drinks water or other liquids contaminated with anthrax spores. This form will cause vomiting, fever, pain in the abdomen, and diarrhea. Symptoms appear within seven days of infection. If left untreated, the form has a 60 percent mortality rate and, like the two previous forms, is also non-contagious.

Smallpox

This is a highly infectious, viral disease. The last recorded naturally occurring cases of smallpox were prior to 1977, when it was eradicated following a worldwide vaccination campaign. Smallpox comes with influenza-type symptoms and a rash spreading over the body. Pus-filled blisters develop and serious complications can result in blindness, pneumonia, and kidney damage. Infected persons who have not been vaccinated have a 30 percent mortality rate.

Toxins

The poisonous by-products of microorganisms, plants, and animals are called toxins. They tend to be stable because they are not living; however, toxins such as ricin and botulinus have the advantage of being relatively simple to manufacture and are extremely lethal. Toxins can cause almost immediate paralysis of the cardio respiratory system in humans. Ricin is probably the deadliest known plant toxin and is a protein extracted from the castor bean seed. Ricin poisoning will result in nausea, muscle spasms, convulsions, and vomiting. There is no anti-toxin or vaccine currently available. Death from ricin poisoning can occur in three days.

Botulism

This neurotoxin is released by the bacterium Clostridium botulinum and is associated with rotting food. It is a very poisonous substance. If a person ingests or breathes in the toxin, symptoms of nerve disruption will occur. Cold and flu-like symptoms, with a trace of numbness in the lips and fingertips, double vision, and chest paralysis are its many symptoms. Death occurs from respiratory failure. With the quick administration of an anti-toxin, the mortality rate for botulism is 25 percent, however, if left untreated the mortality rate is 100 percent.

Pneumonic Plague

This condition is a rare result of *bubonic* plague and is caused by bites from an infected flea. It turns into pneumonic plague and then becomes a highly contagious and virulent from of pneumonia. Symptoms include fever, chills, coughing, difficulty breathing, and rapid shock. There is a 50 percent to 90 percent mortality rate if left untreated and 15 percent when diagnosed and treated with antibiotics.

Tularemia

Tularemia is also known as "rabbit fever" or "deer fly fever." Tularemia is extremely infectious. Relatively few bacteria are required to cause the disease, which is why it is an attractive weapon for use in bioterrorism.[46]

Severe Acute Respiratory Syndrome (SARS)

In general, SARS begins with a high fever (temperature greater than 100.4°F [38.0°C]). Other symptoms may include headache, an overall feeling of discomfort, and body aches. Some people also have mild respiratory symptoms at the outset. About 10 percent to 20 percent of patients have diarrhea. After two to seven days, SARS patients may develop a dry cough. Most patients develop pneumonia. According to the World Health Organization (WHO), a total of 8,098 people worldwide became sick with SARS during the 2003 outbreak. Of these, 774 died.

SARS seems to spread by close person-to-person contact. The virus that causes SARS is thought to be transmitted most readily by respiratory droplets or droplet spread, which are produced when an infected person coughs or sneezes. Droplet spread can happen when droplets from the cough or sneeze of an infected person are propelled a short distance (generally up to 3 feet) through the air and deposited on the mucous membranes of the mouth, nose, or eyes of persons who are nearby. The virus also can spread when a person touches a surface or object contaminated with infectious droplets and then touches his or her mouth, nose, or eye(s). In addition, it is possible that the SARS virus might spread more broadly through the air (airborne spread) or by other ways that are not now known.[47]

Avian Flu

Avian flu, or the "bird flu," is a highly contagious disease of animals caused by viruses that normally infect only birds, and less commonly, pigs. There have been recent incidents starting in Southeast Asia in 2003 and throughout 2004 and 2005, where the virus has crossed the species barrier and infected humans. The highly pathogenic bird flu is extremely virulent. It spreads very rapidly through poultry flocks, causing disease and affecting multiple internal organs, and has a mortality that can approach 100 percent, often within forty-eight hours. The causative agent, the H5N1 virus, has proved to be especially tenacious. Despite the death or destruction of an estimated 150 million birds, the virus is now considered endemic in many parts of Indonesia and Vietnam and in some parts of Cambodia, China, Thailand, and possibly also the Lao People's Democratic Republic. Control of the disease in poultry is expected to take several years. The widespread persistence of H5N1 in poultry populations poses risks for human health. Of the few avian influenza viruses that have crossed the species barrier to infect humans, H5N1 has caused the largest number of cases of severe disease and death in humans. Unlike normal seasonal influenza, where infection causes only mild respiratory symptoms in most people, the disease caused by H5N1 follows an unusually aggressive clinical course, with rapid deterioration and high fatality.

Of even greater concern, is that the virus, if given enough opportunities, will change into a form that is highly infectious for humans and spreads easily from person to person. Such a change could mark the start of a global outbreak (a pandemic). A pandemic can start when three conditions have been met: a new influenza virus subtype emerges; it infects humans, causing serious illness; and it spreads easily and sustainably among humans. The H5N1 virus amply meets the first two conditions: it is a new virus for humans and it has infected more than 100 humans, killing over half of them. No one will have immunity should an H5N1-like pandemic virus emerge. All prerequisites for the start of a pandemic have therefore been met save one: the establishment of efficient and sustained human-to-human transmission of the virus. The risk that the H5N1 virus will acquire this ability will persist as long as opportunities for human infections occur. These opportunities, in turn, will persist as long as the virus continues to circulate in birds, and this situation could endure for some years to come.[48]

Contingency planning to meet and counter the threat of WMD since 9-11 has taken on monumental proportions. The U.S. government is spending in excess of $2 billion per annum to counter these threats.

Developing an effective response plan is critical to not only community and governments but also in the private business sector. While the likelihood of a terrorist attack having a sudden and direct impact on a particular business is relatively low, there is always the need to act prudently and prepare Business Resumption and Interruption Plans, as well as Disaster Planning and Critical Incident Command procedures. Although these plans are more likely to have been part of the planning process for national and state governments, there is every reason for individual companies to consider plans for disaster events, which should include flood, tornado, earthquake, major fire, chemical accident, and terror attack. Although the terror attack is the one significant incident that comes to most people's attention, the likelihood of the preceding five events occurring is much higher. It has been suggested that up to 70 percent of small- to medium-size businesses fail to recover from a disaster. For a national- or state-level plan to be implemented, it should include the following components:

- Information-gathering system
- Threat awareness . . . be able to determine what threats the organization must be aware of
- An effective communications plan and early-warning system coupled with evacuation procedures
- Particularly in the United States, interagency agreements on command and control in disaster situations
- Detailed procedures on how to identify the release of chemical or bio agents and equipment needed to respond to such a threat or incident
- An appropriate disposal capability
- Procedures for setting up and deploying decontamination stations and personnel to man them

Practical training either in a real-life setting, or a "table top" setting, should be conducted on a regular basis to determine the capability of responders to a specific incident involving mass casualties. This will involve having all the significant players represented at a "table-top" exercise to ensure that each group or organization is fully conversant with the role it has to play. 9-11 was an example of the flaws in the emergency communications coordination, which seriously contributed to the high number of emergency responder losses on that fateful day.

DIRTY BOMBS

To better inform the public on what a dirty bomb is, and what terrorists might intend to try to accomplish in setting off such a weapon, the following information from the U.S. Regulatory Commission is provided.

Given the scores of exercises . . . federal, state, and local . . . being staged to assure that all emergency response organizations are properly equipped, trained, and exercised to respond to a terrorist chemical, biological, or radiological attack, we believe members of the public, as well as news organizations, will benefit from receiving concise, straightforward information.

Basically, the principal type of dirty bomb, or radiological dispersal device (RDD), combines a conventional explosive, such as dynamite, with radioactive material. In most instances, the conventional explosive itself would have more immediate lethality than the radioactive material. At the levels created by most probable sources, not enough radiation would be present in a dirty bomb to kill people or cause severe illness. For example, most radioactive material employed in hospitals for diagnosis or treatment of cancer is sufficiently benign that about 100,000 patients a day are released with this material in their bodies.

However, certain other radioactive materials, dispersed in the air, could contaminate up to several city blocks, creating fear and possibly panic and requiring potentially costly cleanup. Prompt, accurate, non-emotional public information might prevent the panic sought by terrorists.

A second type of RDD might involve a powerful radioactive source hidden in a public place, such as a trash receptacle in a busy train or subway station, where people passing close to the source might get a significant dose of radiation. A dirty bomb is in no way similar to a nuclear weapon. The presumed purpose of its use would be, therefore, not as a weapon of mass destruction, but rather as a weapon of mass disruption.

Impact of a Dirty Bomb

The extent of local contamination would depend on a number of factors, including the size of the explosive, the amount and type of radioactive material used, and weather conditions. Prompt detectability of the kind of radioactive material employed would greatly assist local authorities in advising the community on protective measures, such as quickly leaving the immediate area, or going inside until being further advised. Subsequent decontamination of the affected area could involve considerable time and expense.

Sources of Radioactive Material

Radioactive materials are widely used at hospitals, research facilities, and industrial and construction sites. These radioactive materials are used for such purposes as in diagnosing and treating illnesses, sterilizing equipment, and inspecting welding seams. For example, the Nuclear Regulatory Commission, together with thirty-two states, which regulate radioactive material, has over 21,000 organizations licensed to use such materials. The vast majority of these sources are not useful for constructing an RDD.

Control of Radioactive Material

NRC and state regulations require licensees to secure radioactive material from theft and unauthorized access. These measures have been stiffened since the attacks of September 11, 2001. Licensees must promptly report lost or stolen material. Local authorities make a determined effort to find and retrieve such sources. Most reports of lost or stolen material involve small or short-lived radioactive sources not useful for an RDD. Past experience suggests there has not been a pattern of collecting such sources for the purpose of assembling a dirty bomb. Only one high-risk radioactive source has not been recovered in the last five years in the United States. However, this source (Iridium-192) would no longer be considered a high-risk source because much of the radioactivity has decayed away since it was reported stolen in 1999. In fact, the combined total of all unrecovered sources over a five-year time span would barely reach the threshold for one high-risk radioactive source. Unfortunately, the same cannot be said worldwide. The U.S. government is working to strengthen controls on high-risk radioactive sources both at home and abroad.

What People Should Do Following an Explosion?

Move away from the immediate area—at least several blocks from the explosion—and go inside. This will reduce exposure to any radioactive airborne dust.

- Turn on local radio or TV channels for advisories from emergency response and health authorities.
- If facilities are available, remove clothes and place them in a sealed, plastic bag. Saving contaminated clothing will allow testing for radiation exposure.
- Take a shower to wash off dust and dirt. This will reduce total radiation exposure, if the explosive device contained radioactive material.
- If radioactive material was released, local news broadcasts will advise people where to report for radiation monitoring, blood and other tests to determine whether they were, in fact, exposed and what steps need taken to protect their health.

Risk of Cancer

Just because a person is near a radioactive source for a short time, or gets a small amount of radioactive dust on himself or herself, does not mean he or she will get cancer. The additional risk will likely be very small. Doctors will be able to assess the risks and suggest mitigating measures, once the radioactive source and exposure level have been determined. It should be noted that potassium iodide (KI) would not be protective except in the very unlikely event that the dirty bomb contained radioactive iodine isotopes in large quantities. Radioactive iodine isotopes are not particularly attractive for use in an RDD for a variety of technical reasons. KI only protects the thyroid from radioactive iodine, but offers no protection to other parts of the body or against other radioactive isotopes. A number of federal agencies have responsibilities for dealing with possible detonations of dirty bombs.[49]

Summary

The terrorist attacks on September 11, 2001, the Madrid train station bombings, the London subway bombings, and the Bali night club bombings, are a reminder that terrorism is a global issue. Not a day goes by without some form of atrocity in the name of terrorism perpetrated on an unsuspecting public. Protecting the public at large has been the main consideration of the United States and many Western governments U.S. efforts have been centered on protecting the homeland and the rapid rejuvenation of its intelligence services and apparatus. While the tragic events of 9-11 recede somewhat from our memories, new terror events are taking shape daily such as the ongoing insurgency in Iraq and the threat to Western interests in Indonesia and the Persian Gulf. We continue to wonder what will happen next. Will we see an attack using chemical, biological, or radiological weapons against cities in the West? While governments attempt to make national security a front-line topic, how far do we go in this respect? How vulnerable are we to attack against our infrastructure? The internet is a tool we have all come to rely on, so will the hacking of systems and the insertion of worms and viruses become serious enough as to affect our daily lives? The world does not appear to be any safer since the advent of the War on Terror. We are at war against an unknown and unseen enemy who wants nothing less than the seeming destruction of democratic societies. Where is the middle ground? How do we get to the point where negotiation can take place? Wars have a beginning and an end, although we see no end to the War on Terror. With whom can we negotiate a lasting peace?

Specialized counter-terrorism units have been used as a response mechanism and may be viewed as a well-advertised deterrent by governments unwilling to deal with terrorists. As can be seen with Northern Ireland, both police and specialized units have been deployed in the common cause of fighting terrorism. Special military powers to restrict, control, search, and intern suspected members of illegal or proscribed organizations have also been instituted. In democracy, specialist units like the SAS, GIGN, and GSG-9 can operate effectively and have the support of the government and the public they serve. It is also necessary and prudent to have strict guidelines and controls for the use of such counter-terrorism units. In orthern Ireland, the accusations of a "shoot-to-kill" policy and "death squads" were hurled by the IRA in a desperate attempt by that subversive group to halt the activities of a response mechanism that was too effective for their purposes. Piracy on the seas shows that there are regions of the globe susceptible to this type of rabid activity and the dangers it poses to the international community. Many ships containing extremely hazardous cargoes circumnavigate the globe, and the risks to nation-states and the opportunity for terrorists to take advantage must not be discounted.

Web Sites

1. **Comptroller of the Currency Administrator of National Banks**—*http://www.occ.treas.gov/bsa/BSARegs.htm*
2. **Central Intelligence Agency**—*www.odci.gov*
3. **UK Security Services**—*www.mi5.gov.uk*
4. **Center for Disease Control**—*www.bt.cdc.gov*
5. **International Air Transport Association** — *www.iata.org*
6. **Transportation Security Administration**—*www.tsa.org*

Endnotes

1. Paul Wilkinson. *Terrorism and the Liberal State* (New York: New York University Press, 1979, p. 121).
2. http://www.racerealtions.about.com, "Is racial profiling a non issue in the age of terrorism?"
3. Paul Wilkinson. *Terrorism and the Liberal State*, p. 155.
4. United Nations Conventions Against Terrorism.
5. *Terrorism*, vol. 13, nos. 4, 5 (July–October 1990); Aviation Terrorism Air Carrier Security Programs: Statement before the U.S. House of Representatives, vol. 13, pp. 353–357; Homer Boynton. Government Activities and Transportation Subcommittee (Taylor Francis, 1990).
6. Report to the President's Commission on Aviation Security and Terrorism (1990), www.frac.com.
7. Ibid.
8. Cathal Flynn. "Aviation Security Is Tight," *USA Today* (March 19, 1999), 14A.
9. Billie Vincent. "Aviation Security and Terrorism." *Terrorism: An International Journal*, vol. 13 (December 1990, p. 404).
10. Commander David Tucker—London Metropolitan Police—Avsec World 94 Proceedings Chicago, October 23–26, 1994.
11. "Protect Airliners from Missiles," *The Post and Courier*, Charleston, SC (December 31, 2002, p. 10A).
12. Political Science Monitor (1999).
13. Ed Stephen Ulph. *Jane's Terrorism and Security Monitor* (London: Jane's Information Group, 2002).
14. Transportation Security Agency—http://www.tsa.gov/research/screening_statistics.shtm.
15. NPR. www.npr.org/templates/story/story.php?storyId=15445779.
16. Electronic Privacy Information Center. www.epic.org/privacy/airtravel/profiling.html.
17. ACLU Press Release. "GAO Fails to Green Light Controversial Secure Flight Program; ACLU Points to Recent Privacy Failure of Agency" (March 28, 2005).
18. Ibid.
19. Alan Pangborn. "How Far Has Europe Come Since Pan Am 103?" *Intersec* vol. 6 (Three Bridges Publishing, May 5, 1996, p. 195).
20. Gerry Edwards. "Hijackers' Gateway." *Intersec*, vol. 8, no. 14 (Three Bridges Publishing, April 1998, p. 168).
21. Allied Media Corporation. http://www.allied-media.com/aljazeera.com.
22. Summary of the Ministerial Conference on Terrorism, Paris (July 30, 1996), ww.efc.ca/pages/doc/g7.html.
23. Report to the United Nations Security Council Counterterrorism Committee (December 19, 2001), www.fas.org/irp/threat/unsc.html.
24. Deb Reichmann. "Bush Campaigns for Patriot Act Renewal," Associated Press, *Writer*, Yahoo News (Friday June 10, 2005).
25. Sean Hill. "The Complexity of Intelligence Gathering." *Sam Houston University Crime and Justice International*, vol. 17, no. 56 (October/November 2001, p. 5).
26. Interpol—Fusion Task Force, Operational support www.interpol.int/Public.
27. Mi5. https://www.mi5.gov.uk/output/Page57.html.
28. The White House. http://www.whitehouse.gov/nsct/2006/.
29. "Creating a National Intelligence Director." Statement of John S. Pistole, Executive Assistant Director, Counterterrorism/Counterintelligence, Federal Bureau of Investigation, before the House Judiciary Committee Subcommittee on Crime, Terrorism and Homeland Security (August 23, 2004).
30. Elite Forces. http://www.eliteukforces.info/special-air-service/sas-operations/loughgall/
31. Barbara Cole. *The Elite: The Story of the Rhodesian Special Air Service* (Transkei: Three Knights Publishing, 1984, p. 6).
32. Ibid.
33. Ibid., p. 15.
34. Leroy Thompson. *The Rescue* (Bolder, CO: Paladin Press, 1986, p. 84).
35. Ibid, p. 64.
36. Ibid, p. 20.
37. David Pugliese is author of Shadow Wars: Special Forces in the New Battle Against Terrorism as well as Canada's Secret Commandos: The Unauthorized Story of Joint Task Force Two.
38. The Maritime Safety Division, International Maritime Organization, www.imo.org/home.asp.
39. Terrorism Goes to Sea—Gal Luft and Anne Korin *Foreign Affairs*, November/December 2004, http://www.iags.org/fa2004.html.
40. www.msnbc.com/id/245153680/.
41. United Nations. http://www.un.org/Depts/Cos/Conventies.agreements.htm.

42. Terrorism Goes to Sea—Gal Luft and Anne Korin *Foreign Affairs*, November/December.

43. "Jane's Special Report—Hunt for Scattered Nuclear Material." *Janes Terrorism and Security Monitor* (October 2004).

44. Anthony A. Lukin, Ph.D. "Understanding Nuclear, Biological and Chemical Weapons," a presentation at the Justice Institute of British Columbia Provincial Emergency Program Academy (April 7–8, 1997).

45. Centers for Disease Control (CDC) and OSHA.

46. Basic Information about Sars—Centers for Disease Control and Prevention. http://www.cdc.gov/ncidod/sars/factsheet.htm.

47. World Health Organization. http://www.int/csr/disease/avian_influenza/avian_ fags/en/print.html.

48. UN Nuclear Regulatory Commission—Fact sheet on Dirty Bombs.

49. Ibid.

CHAPTER 15

The Future and the "War Against Terrorism"

Predicting stuff is difficult, especially when it's about the future.

Pogo Possum

Learning Objective

The study and review of this chapter will enable you to

1. Debate terrorism trends over the next decade based on current events;
2. Discuss how increased use of technology will assist in detecting terrorist threats;
3. Detail the timeline for the attack on Iraq;
4. Discuss how the Internet is used as a tool to inspire jihad and radical terror attacks.

OVERVIEW

The above quote, written by the great cartoonist Walt Kelly in the 1950s for his "Pogo" comic strip, is so perfect in our turbulent and changing world that we had to share it with students who may have never heard of the great satirist. Sadly, in the world of counterterrorism and intelligence, predictions often turn out to be wrong. After the first attack on the World Trade Center in 1993, authorities were concerned about the fact that the terrorists had not succeeded in destroying the entire building, as had been their intention. There was also serious concern that they had intended it to be a biological attack. So much for predicting the future! When we began writing the first edition of this book, the hopes for future peace between Northern Ireland and Britain were high, and a Peace Accord was written and signed. Peace has come at last to Northern Ireland but mainland Britain is suffering threats and attacks from Islamic extremists. The Israelis and the PLO, who at one time may have seemed near to a viable peace plan, seem at opposite ends of the spectrum again. The best we can hope for is to provide the student with a valid review of what has happened in past involvements of serious terrorism and violence, hoping that such a broad background will provide some clues about the future from social, economic, religious, psychological, political, and economic standpoints. While the past may often be prologue, trying to plan for the future by using only the past as a guide is about as logical as driving a truck by looking only in the rearview mirror, and talking on a cell phone—you are probably going to be in for a serious and devastating event!

How do we conclude this edition of a book that has engrossed our minds and time for so long? It seems that all we can do now is make some modest comments as to the warning signs for the future. Many of these statements are extensions of what we have covered somewhere in the fourteen previous chapters. What remains remarkably clear to us in regard to the future is that more than 50,000 terrorists were trained in the camps in Afghanistan, and many are now hidden "sleepers" who are blending into the civilian populations of more than sixty nations. This chilling information indicates there could be many thousands of sleeper cells lying dormant in European countries, Canada, Mexico, and the United States. Another disturbing phenomenon is the appearance of suicide bombers in Western cities. How have radical Islamists been able to recruit and corrupt intelligent young men to wage jihad against their adopted countries? Answers to these questions will be a major factor for the future of terrorism in the West. The July 2005 bombings in London saw young men of Pakistani and Jamaican descent—some who had been born, raised, and educated in England—turn into suicide bombers. They apparently achieved this without raising any fears or concerns among their closest friends and family—a worrying trend, indeed. We must remember that these fanatical Islamists seek to overturn and destroy Western values and to supplant it with an Islamic Caliphate, by causing mayhem, fear, and panic on public transit. Transit attacks, and in particular bus bombings by suicide bombers, have been a hallmark of Palestinian terrorists inside Israel, a country with hitherto much more invested in its security apparatus than Western states. Defeating terrorism will have to be about treating the underlying, deeply rooted causes that tempt and pull in young and intelligent minds. Do the recruits lack belief in themselves or in their adoptive country? Is it despair at how they view the world? Or, perhaps, is it possibly how their religion is viewed by the West that turns them against their friends and families? Many have speculated that perhaps the London events could have been averted had the British government withdrawn its troops in Iraq. The failure of that argument is that this breed of Islamic terrorism was around long before the United States and its coalition, including the British, invaded Iraq. Iraq was invaded in 2003; New York and Washington DC were attacked in September 2001, and, prior to that, the U.S. embassies in Kenya and Tanzania, and before them, the suicide attack on the U.S.S. *Cole* in Yemen. Intelligence analysts, counterterrorism agencies, and police have long stated that it was not a question of *if* an attack will come in Britain but *when*.

TERRORISM GETS A LARGER STAGE

Osama bin Laden is alleged to control a personal fortune estimated at over $250 million and spends it freely on his personal war against the United States and the Western democracies that he despises. He has combined financial muscle with religious extremism—a deadly cocktail! He is likely to continue his attacks against soft targets such as transportation systems, but is also likely to turn his attention to "soft countries" that have supported the United States. One example is Canada, a country known for its liberal views and with a large and ethnically diverse population, including many Muslims residing in the large urban centers of Toronto, in central Canada, and in other parts of that vast nation. Bin Laden and a coalition of Islamic extremist groups issued a fatwa (similar to that issued against Salman Rushdie in Iran) and named Canada specifically as being a "legitimate target." Its wording is chilling: "To kill the Americans and their allies, civilian and military, is an individual duty for every Muslim who can do it, in any country in which it is possible to be done." We carried these words in our first edition of *Terrorism Today*, and we now know that he meant what he said. He will continue his jihad (Holy War) with the West, whether it is in the Middle East, Spain, the United Kingdom, or the United States. One fear is that the next attack could involve weapons of mass destruction. The use of chemical or biological weapons is an obvious concern for intelligence analysts and national security organizations alike.

Prior to 9-11, our angers and fears were focused on terrorism committed in far-off lands like Tanzania and Kenya—of course we are referring to the bin Laden-sponsored attacks on the two

U.S. embassies in Africa. The U.S. response to such terror attacks was defined and targeted, limited to bombing attacks on bases in the Sudan and Afghanistan. As we noted before, however, predicting the future is difficult and analyzing the past is always a lot easier. The al Qaeda as we now know is probably more predictable than we might have imagined. Over the last decade it has responded to every U.S. operation mounted against it. The passage of time between attacks by extreme Islamic groups purporting to represent al Qaeda seems to be due, in part, to the planning that goes into each mission/assault. They plan their attacks carefully and leave nothing to chance. If the attack plan is put at risk, the perpetrators retreat until the timing is correct. Intelligence sources indicate that on 9-11, there were other terrorists in the air who could not or did not follow through with their missions. More recently, the attacks on the London subway system were very well-planned, coordinated, devastatingly effective, and timed similar to previous attacks to get the most media attention. In Spain, the Madrid train station bombings went off during the morning rush hour; 9-11 also took place in the morning; and both the Madrid and London attacks occurred on a Thursday. As time and events unfold, it is this kind of information that will be used to further identify trends and bring the full weight of the intelligence and counterterrorism apparatus to bear. London's attack on July 7, 2005, came on the opening day of the G8's Economic Summit in Scotland. The world media and British security were focused primarily on this event in Scotland. A distracting bonus for the terrorists, in this case, was that on the previous evening, Londoners were celebrating the city's selection as host of the 2012 Olympic Games and were in a euphoric and celebratory mood.

As we become further removed from the horrific events of 9-11, the other spectacular events taking place in such centers as Madrid and London are bringing home the ever-present threat of terrorist attack. The world is just as dangerous today, perhaps more so, than in the last decade of the twentieth century. The threat is real—as real as it was in 2001. In fact, it is a permanent condition to which all of us must ultimately adapt. What's important is to remember that we can adapt; we can do something about it.

We already know what the terrorists want to do to us. We have it from their illusive leader, Osama bin Laden, in his own words, from a December 2001, videotape, broadcast by the Arabic television news station Al Jazeera:

- "Our terrorism is against America. Our terrorism is a blessed terrorism . . ."
- "It is very important to hit the U.S. economy with every available means . . . [It] is the base of its military power."
- "If their economy ends, they will busy themselves away from the enslavement of oppressed people . . . it is important to concentrate on the destruction of the American economy."

So with some clarification of mind we can see what is in store for us. In 2008, we saw the economy of the U.S. slide deeper into recession and no doubt if bin Laden was into money lending for mortgages we could probably suggest that it was all down to his vision that the U.S. economy would collapse through the sub prime lending scandals!

Clearly, bin Laden and his followers want to take innocent lives and destroy the American way of life. The very first "mission" in the President's Executive Order that created the Office of Homeland Security reads: "To develop and coordinate the implementation of a comprehensive national strategy to secure the United States from terrorist threats or attacks." The Director of Homeland Security was Governor Tom Ridge, and he took every word of that Executive Order seriously. The Office of Homeland Security helped to build the consensus, but the action will always happen on the front lines, carried out by people who have the experience and expertise to get the job done, and who prove it every single day. The leaders of the Department of Homeland Security must now wrap their arms around every aspect of homeland security. Its strategy must not be just to raise questions, but to provide reasonable, quick, and achievable answers and solutions. National strategy is not just a federal task—the states and localities, the private sector and academia, and the American people must work together to make it happen. Therefore securing the United States means preserving a physical, financial, and electronic infrastructure, its people, its freedoms, and its way of life from the immediate threats and long term threats of terrorism. Securing them is the core responsibility of government. Anticipating all threats or attacks is critical and means the United States must not only improve its preparedness, but it must preempt and deter attacks at their source, whether in Afghanistan, Europe, or in America's own backyard.

WEAPONS OF MASS DESTRUCTION (WMD)

An even greater threat to U.S. and Western security is the potential for biological, chemical, and nuclear attacks. The United States is making alliances around the world, not just to track down the pockets of al Qaeda, but also to identify those countries that are trying to acquire the materials to develop and construct such weapons of mass destruction.

A GAO report to the Senate Intelligence Committee in February 2002 reports then CIA Director George Tenet's comments in a detailed briefing on national security threats. Tenet outlined the key dangers:

1. The al Qaeda is working on "multiple-attack plans" and putting cells in place to carry them out.
2. Iran continues to support terrorist groups and has sent arms to Palestinian terrorists and the group Hezbollah. Tenet said: "Tehran also has failed to move decisively against al Qaeda members who have relocated to Iran from Afghanistan."
3. Terrorists could attack U.S. nuclear plants or chemical industry sites using conventional means "to cause panic and widespread toxic or radiological damage."
4. Al Qaeda cells in major European and Middle Eastern cities could launch attacks, and al Qaeda is connected with groups in Somalia, Yemen, Indonesia, and the Philippines.
5. There are fears that al Qaeda and other terrorists will attack using nuclear, chemical, or biological weapons. Director Tenet said: "Terrorist groups worldwide have ready access to information on chemical, biological, and even nuclear weapons via the Internet, and we know that al Qaeda was working to acquire some of the most dangerous chemical agents and toxins."
6. Tensions between India and Pakistan continue to remain high over a December 13, 2001, terrorist attack on the Indian parliament, and the two nations could resort to nuclear weapons. Tenet said: "We are deeply concerned that a conventional war, once begun, could escalate into a nuclear confrontation."
7. Terrorists could attempt to attack the United States by conducting cyber-strikes designed to cripple U.S. electronic-based infrastructures. Countering the terrorist threat and determining the response will present the biggest challenge challenges for the coming months, and for years to come.

This 2002 report may seem somewhat dated however in order to assess the future it's valuable to look back and comment on the past as we predict the future. In review of the first two items above al Qaeda has spread into a global movement and multiple attack plans have been launched and fortunately not many with success, and certainly we have seen the presence of trained fighters engaged in the Iraq insurgency and supported by Iran. Item #3 has not taken place, #4 we have observed the presence of more al Qaeda affiliated factions across Europe and North Africa as al Qaeda reorganizes, reinvents and rejuvenates itself. Item #5—we have seen in the United Kingdom incidents of potential attacks using ricin being disrupted by police as well as planned attacks of similar nature in Italy and Germany. Item #6—India is currently the fastest growing economy but there are incredible tensions between Muslims and Hindus that could erupt in violence at any time.

GOING TO WAR

In the ten years since the first Gulf War ended, former Iraqi president/dictator, Saddam Hussein stated that he had always considered himself at war with America, and during that time, the United States had always considered him a threat. While America's military had unleashed its might against the Taliban and al Qaeda, President G. W. Bush and powerful forces in Washington considered attacking a much bigger target. The events of 9-11 re-energized Saddam's strongest opponents in Washington. The weekend following the suicide attacks on the World Trade Center and the Pentagon, President Bush met at Camp David with his top advisers to formulate an attack strategy for Iraq.

Then U.S. Secretary of State, Colin Powell, stated that the Bush administration was examining a full range of options on Iraq in dealing with Iraqi President Saddam Hussein's refusal to permit UN international weapons inspections to resume. President Bush was "leaving no stone unturned as to what we might do," Powell stated. Secretary of Defense Donald Rumsfeld asserted that "previous weapons inspections inside Iraq were often ineffective and relied upon defectors." "Any new inspections program," he added, "must be much stronger and more intrusive to end Saddam Hussein's efforts to build weapons of mass destruction." Speaking on the CBS-TV program "Face the Nation" on February 24, 2002, Rumsfeld said, "The Iraqis have had more time to go underground. They've had lots of dual-use technologies that have come in. They've had lots of illicit things that have come in. They have advanced their weapons of mass destruction programs." As a result, Rumsfeld pointed out, "If you try to use the old regime, it wouldn't work. You would have to have a much more intrusive regime and many more inspectors and the Iraqis with no control as to when they could come in, where they could go, what they could do." President George Bush declared a "War on Terror" after 9-11, and singled out Iraq as part of an "axis of evil." Any evidence of Iraqi involvement in the 9-11 attacks is somewhat tenuous and relates to information that an Iraqi intelligence agent had met one of the 9-11 hijackers in Czechoslovakia. This was followed by a series of actions to begin the offensive in Iraq.

IRAQ ATTACK TIMELINE

- September 20, 2001—U.S. and British jets attack Iraqi missile defense batteries.
- September 21, 2001—Iraqi defectors claim that the 9-11 hijackers were trained at Salman Pak air base in Iraq.
- January 29, 2002—In his State of the Union address to the U.S. Congress, George Bush includes Iraq in a list of countries forming the "axis of evil."
- May 2002—Kofi Annan, UN Secretary General, is unsuccessful in trying to get Iraq to allow weapons inspection teams back into Iraq.
- July 2002—UN-brokered talks in Vienna with the Iraqi foreign minister collapse.
- July 25, 2002—Iraq insists any agreement on inspections must include the lifting of sanctions and an end to the no-fly zones.
- September 12, 2002—One year after 9-11, George Bush calls on the United Nations for multilateral action against Iraq. Iraq responds favorably, stating it will allow inspections, but quickly retracts the offer making it conditional on there being no new resolutions.
- September 22, 2002—British Prime Minister Tony Blair produces an intelligence report confirming Iraq possesses significant quantities of WMD.
- November 8, 2002—UN Security Council Resolution 1441 calls for Iraq to declare all WMD and not to delay or obstruct UN inspection teams. Declaration of WMD in Iraq must be completed by December 8, 2002.
- December 7, 2002—In compliance with UN SC 1441, Iraq submits documentation that U.S. experts claim to be false and incomplete.
- March 1, 2003—Arab summit calls on Iraq to disarm.
- March 7, 2003—Following the submission of the report by chief weapons inspector Hans Blix, both the U.S. and Great Britain call for a further resolution to authorize war against Iraq. France, Russia, Germany, and Arab nations oppose the resolution.
- March 19, 2003—The U.S.-led invasion of Iraq commences with support from Britain.
- April 9, 2003—Baghdad falls and George Bush subsequently claims an end to hostilities.

- June 2003—The insurgency begins in Iraq.
- 2004—The al Zarqawi group and affiliated factions continue kidnappings and beheadings of foreign captives.
- Throughout 2003, 2004, and 2005—Widespread insurgent attacks continue, not only on U.S. and British forces, but also against UN and Iraq's interim-government targets.
- Through 2005—Suicide missions aimed at U.S. forces continue unabated. Suicide bomb attacks are a part of daily life in and around Baghdad. They are aimed at both Shia and Sunni areas in attempts to destabilize and create an atmosphere ripe for civil war in the region.

June 2006—Abu Musab al Zarqawi, an Al Qaeda leader, is killed by U.S. forces in Iraq.

- December 2006—Former Iraqi President Saddam Hussein executed.
- January 2007—President Bush authorizes a surge of 20,00 extra troops for Iraq.
- September 2007—Sunni leader and ally Abdul Sattar Abu Risha is killed in Iraq just ten days after meeting with President Bush.
- February 2008—Turkey launches ground operations in northern Iraq to battle against Kurdish separatists.

History will look back and determine the long-term merits and failings of prosecuting a war in Iraq and the subsequent destabilization of the region. As for the future, both U.S. and British troops have been mired in conflict with a deadly insurgency—with no end or political solution in sight. Many have commented that the British and the United States were unprepared for a long campaign such as this in Iraq. The intelligence on the Iraqi threat of WMD was not only incorrect, but no threat existed! Linking Saddam Hussein to the War on Terror has also come in for much discussion as to what links, if any, the Iraqi leader had with Osama bin Laden. Strong evidence has linked Iraq to a network supporting the Abu Nidal group and also providing $25,000 rewards to the families of Palestinian suicide bombers. Other terrorists also received sanctuary from the Ba'ath Party regime in Baghdad after escaping Italian police in October 1985 following the *Achille Lauro* hijacking. Thanks to Abu Abbas's Iraqi diplomatic passport, he finally ended up in Baghdad in 1994, where he lived comfortably as one of Saddam Hussein's guests. U.S. soldiers caught Abbas in Iraq in April 2003. He died on March 9, 2004, in American custody, reportedly of natural causes.

AL QAEDA—THE FUTURE

Al Qaeda, little known before the September 11, 2001, attacks, is now linked to almost every terrorist atrocity around the globe—rightly or wrongly—this is the most notorious movement of the late twentieth and early twenty-first century that will shape the lives of westerners over the coming decade. While al Qaeda has managed to successfully keep its omnipotent leader in hidden seclusion likely somewhere near the Afghan/Pakistan border it continues as the movement that rallies and influences jihad throughout the world. There is no indication from the al Qaeda leadership that there will be any let up in its plans to intensify attacks against the West. The goal posts appear to be in the same spot but the name of the game will change. While we see no calls for moderation from al Qaeda what we do see is the continued decentralization of the pan Islamic jihadist movement, which makes it much more resilient. We believe as do many observers that the glorification in mass casualty attacks is part and parcel of its grass roots movement and is typified in the low cost suicide attacks taking place in Iraq, North Africa, Afghanistan and Pakistan. The more determined attacks which require a higher level of planning and sophistication to target more hardened targets such as airports, oil production and military bases will continue to be a focus of the core of al Qaeda and its professional jihadists. We have seen the spread of al Qaeda into the Islamic regions of North Africa and in particular the movement has been noticeably backing Algerian jihadists who have rebranded as the al Qaeda in the Islamic Maghreb (AQIM). If we then consider the proximity of Pakistan to Afghanistan the natural spread across the borders through the inhospitable North West Frontier region al Qaeda's ascendency in Pakistan is assured and there is little that the security forces in the West can do about its spread.

In 2006, the prospects for all out civil war in Iraq were an almost certainty but with the military surge in early 2007 that has changed. Al Qaeda inspired extremists, having announced the establishment of the Islamic State of Iraq and incited massive sectarian violence, are hell-bent on tearing the country apart. Faced with the prospect of living in a destitute, rump state dominated by hard-line Islamists, Sunni Arab leaders began to see the U.S. as a useful ally and not as their worst enemy.[1] That al Qaeda continues to grow and inspire globally is a major problem. Muslims in many western countries are being drawn into jihad movements inspired by al Qaeda affiliates and while getting into countries such as the U.S. is not as simple as it used to be one must consider that those inspired to jihad may already be residing in the United States and have been living the "American dream" for several decades as sleepers.

The renowned terrorism expert Bruce Hoffman offered the following points in relation to the future and al Qaeda. The success of the 9-11 attacks was based on three capabilities that al Qaeda likely still retains:

1. The ability to identify vulnerabilities of the enemy (i.e., the West) that could mercilessly be exploited.
2. The effective use of deception (e.g., the passengers on board the hijacked airliners were lulled into believing that if they cooperated they would not be harmed).
3. The use of a suicide mission to ensure success.

As counter terrorism continues to improve the al Qaeda and its affiliates will be challenged to adapt to new and probably untried strategies or to work on established strategies used in other theaters such as Israel. Target selection and the need to show that they can inflict heavy casualties on their enemy with attacks on airports and aircraft will continue to be targets of choice to jihadists. The use of portable weapon systems such as SAM-7 missiles and suicide attacks on lightly protected mass transit systems and other events such as the Olympic Games will be areas where jihadists will concentrate their intelligence efforts for the future.

The future threats from WMD

Nations of the world and, more particularly, Western nations, have had to come to the realization that future threats from terrorists will undoubtedly come from the "unthinkable"—the use of chemical and biological agents as a means of mass destruction. But, let's not forget that bin Laden and his cohorts want nothing except our destruction! There is wide discussion about the countries that have the desire and capacity to build components for WMD. In fact, there are more than twenty-eight countries around the globe with the ability to build chemical agents, and some of them are not deemed "friendly states." The United Nations Special Commission to Iraq found over 46,000 munitions filled with chemical agents; of these, 20,000 were 120-mm CS-filled bombs, 14,000 contained mustard gas, and 11,000 contained Sarin. Later discoveries were made near Saddam Hussein's Tikrit base, including 200 anthrax bombs. The fears for the future are real. UN inspectors were kept out of Iraq for years and there is little doubt that development and production of chemical agents continued in secret, unabated. The key question is whether the Iraqi regime passed on any of its deadly technology or hardware to Islamic extremists with desires to continue attacks against the West—the United States in particular.

North Korea, according to a 1996 U.S. DOD report, "has the ability to produce limited quantities of traditional infectious biological-weapon agents or toxins." A 1988 comment by Iran's parliamentary speaker Hashemi Rafsanjani stated, "Chemical and biological weapons are a poor mans' atomic bombs and can easily be produced. We should at least consider them for our national defense." Syria is also considered to have one of the largest chemical warfare capabilities in the Middle East. So, is the threat of an attack by chemical or biological agents a credible threat? In the context of the 9-11 attacks, the future scenario seems just right for such an attack. If the aim of terror groups like al Qaeda, and individuals like bin Laden, is mass destruction, it behooves all of us to be cognizant of the risk of such an attack in the future.

Nuclear Threats

The threat of a terrorist attack with nuclear weapons may be the least likely, although there has been much international concern about security of facilities in the former Soviet states and the rumors of accessibility of materials for arming nuclear weapons. Preparing and constructing a nuclear device is no small feat—it is hard to achieve and it requires a massive investment and considerable technical expertise. Osama bin Laden certainly has the wealth to achieve the goal of acquiring some kind of a nuclear weapon, but his next problem would have to be the preferred method of delivery. Bin Laden appears to be a terrorist in hiding and with no fixed base from which to work at creating a nuclear device. The main constituent of a nuclear weapon is highly enriched uranium (HEU) or plutonium. The quantities of HEU estimated around the globe amount to around 2,000 tons, plus an additional 300 tons of plutonium. Building a nuclear warhead can be achieved with as little as 25 pounds of HEU. Without the sophisticated machine tools, electronic circuitry, and triggering devices needed to make a proper nuclear weapon, merely blowing up a lump of plutonium or HEU with conventional high explosives could still cause widespread and deadly radioactive pollution.[2]

Chemical and Biological Threats

In 1972, 103 countries signed the "Biological Weapons Convention," which prohibited the development of biological and chemical weapons and their use. We now know that the risks of biological and chemical attacks are very real. The anthrax attacks against U.S. public officials and their offices after 9-11 showed how easy it was for a relatively insignificant amount of "white powder" to stampede a public into mass panic and hysteria—presumably one of the aims of that specific act. The anthrax attacks of 2001 made whole governments sit up and take notice of the threat and also made governments realize how unprepared they were to respond.

Our research has provided some understanding of how chemical and biological weapons work. Biological weapons are created in naturally occurring organisms that cause diseases. Two of the most common examples are the bacterium *Bacillus anthracis*, which produces a toxin, and smallpox, a viral disease that is highly infectious. Chemical weapons are poisons, such as the nerve gas Sarin used in Japan's subways, and mustard gas, which was used in trench warfare in World War I. Smallpox, on the other hand, was virtually eradicated worldwide by the end of the 1970s after an aggressive two-decade-long, worldwide vaccination campaign. This highly infectious viral disease could now be used against a generation that has not been so vaccinated, and the unvaccinated death rate would likely be about 30 percent. The only known remaining smallpox cultures being kept under tight security are in Kosovo, Russia, and Atlanta. Starting up a biological weapons laboratory merely requires a person with full knowledge of microbiology and a few thousand dollars' worth of equipment. Development may be one issue, but maintaining control over the culture could pose a very significant problem for the would-be terrorist. Probably one of the most significant reasons why we have not witnessed broad attempts at biological terror is the issue of containing the culture. Bacteria and viruses do not discriminate between terrorist and target and the person who releases the bioweapon can easily suffer its effects.

On the chemical front, Sarin gas, which was used by the Japanese Aum Shinrikyo terror group to attack a Tokyo subway, has a devastating effect. The gas is odorless, colorless, and attacks the central nervous system. Death can occur within two to fifteen minutes. Cyanide, a more commonly known chemical agent, is a gas that can be produced in massive quantities with apparent ease. Cyanide acts almost instantly and the target that ingests it usually die within seconds. Tabun is a nerve agent that has been around since the 1930s and has been used as a pesticide in many regions of the world. Like many other nerve agents, it is absorbed via the skin. Tabun is resistant to heat and can be delivered in aerosol format, which would make it capable of delivery by artillery shell.[3]

A 1991 audit by the U.S. General Accounting Office indicated that nine chemical sites in the United States were potentially vulnerable to aerial attack, and that four of these sites may be susceptible and vulnerable to ground attack. Since 9-11, Homeland Security has focused resources on many of such sites in the United States. The use of chemical and biological agents may be restricted to those organizations bent purely on destroying democracy, rather than those that are using terrorism as a "bargaining chip" for their own styles of democracy.

HOLY TERROR

Terrorism motivated by religious imperatives is growing rapidly. So great is this change, according to Bruce Hoffman, an advocate for woman's choice that we may have to consider revising our notions of the stereotypical terrorist organization. Hoffman explained that traditional terrorist groups could be characterized as those that engage in conspiracy as a full-time avocation, living underground and constantly planning and plotting terrorist attacks, perhaps even under the direct control or at the behest of a foreign government. What we viewed as an amateurish attack on the World Trade Center in 1993 now reveals to us the kind of individual/terrorist groups that we must contend with in the future. From that investigation, it seems evident that the Islamic extremists had not fully completed the attack. It was, however, completed eight years later by their brothers-in-arms in the suicide attacks of 9-11.

"Holy terror" and the purely so-called "secular terror" have radically different value systems, mechanisms for justifying their acts, and concepts of morality. For the religious terrorist, violence is a divine duty and divine writ. Secular terrorists generally regard indiscriminate violence as immoral and counterproductive; on the other hand, religious terrorists view such violence as both morally justified and necessary. Also, whereas secular terrorists will attempt to appeal to a constituency composed of sympathizers and the aggrieved people they claim to speak for, religious terrorists act for no audience but themselves and their faith. This absence of a constituency, combined with an extreme sense of alienation, means that such "holy" terrorists can justify almost limitless violence against virtually any target or group of people that are not considered adherents to their religious beliefs.

Religious or ethnic extremism could more easily allow terrorists to overcome the psychological barriers to committing mass murder than a radical political agenda has provided in the past. Many White supremacists actually welcome the prospect of a nuclear war or all kinds of terrorism. They see it as an opportunity to eliminate their avowed "enemies" and permit the fulfillment of their objectives—to create a "new world order" peopled exclusively by the White race. Any doubts about the seriousness of such hate groups were dispelled when police and federal agents raided a White supremacist compound in rural Arkansas in April 1984, and discovered a stockpile of some thirty gallons of cyanide to be used to poison municipal water supplies. The targets and tactics of "holy terror" operations that have occurred or been attempted during the past decade clearly lead to a conclusion that a possibility exists for far more destructive acts. Ominous examples already abound:

- Poisoning of water supplies of major urban centers—not only American White supremacists, but also terrorists in India are alleged to have made such plans.
- Dispersal of toxic chemicals through internal building ventilation systems, which has been attempted by White supremacist "skinheads" in Arizona.
- Indiscriminate, wanton attacks on busy urban centers' transportation systems, as in Madrid, Spain, and London.
- Attacks on power grids to disrupt electrical service to large population areas, conducted by a Black Muslim sect in Colorado.
- Poisoning of food, undertaken in Oregon by followers of the Bhagwan Rajneesh to influence a local election.

As the new millennium approached, the somewhat superstitious fears of a nation became real, when Ahmed Ressam was intercepted entering the United States from Canada with a bomb planned for use on the Los Angeles International airport. Ressam was convicted in July 2005 and sentenced to twenty-two years in prison. While our attention is now fully averted toward terrorist cells at large in the cities and the countryside, we should not discount other threats that could still pose a significant danger. If we simply ignore the right-wing militias and the network they have stitched together across the nation, we will do so at our own peril. It is clear that militia movements are continuing to grow rapidly. We need only type in the word "militia" on any Internet browser and we will find dozens of examples like those discussed in earlier chapters.

SUICIDE AND RELIGIOUS TERRORISM

Suicide as a means to attack an enemy is not a new tactic; it dates back in the modern era to 1881, when a group of Nihilists wielding homemade bombs assassinated Tsar Alexander II in St. Petersburg, Russia, as he rode in his armored carriage near the Winter Palace. During World War II the Japanese used Kamikaze pilots to dive bomb into U.S. and allied shipping with devastating results. First used intentionally during the October 1944 Battle of Leyte Gulf, the kamikaze attackers succeeded in damaging allied warships, most notably the U.S.S. *St. Lo*, U.S.S. *Intrepid*, U.S.S. *Franklin*, U.S.S. *Bunker Hill*, and the Australian HMAS *Australia*. In addition, the Japanese developed weapons designed to carry out suicide attacks, including the Kaiten manned torpedo, the Ki-115 purpose-built kamikaze plane, and the Ohka rocket-powered kamikaze plane.

U.S. Air Force intelligence has reported that the use of suicide bombers has spread worldwide since 1990. Between 1980 and 1990, suicide bombings occurred in three countries: Lebanon, Sri Lanka, and Kuwait. From 1991 to 2002, however, the tactic had spread to fifteen countries, from Algeria and Chechnya to Argentina and Croatia, and to the United States.[4]

Terrorism associated with suicide attacks had for the most part been the signature style of the Palestinian bombers in Israel and the occupied territories and of the Tamil Tigers in Sri Lanka. In the Iraq insurgency and in Afghanistan suicide attacks have been regular occurrences. Suicide had been an alien form of attack in the West until the terrorist suicides and hijackings on 9-11 and the suicide bombing attacks in London. Britain was prepared and had consistently warned of an attack by Islamic militants. The British alert level had been high during the run-up to the spring 2005 general election, which returned Tony Blair to his post as Prime Minister. The security posture was somewhat heightened when the world leaders attended the G8 Economic Summit in Edinburgh, Scotland, with opening ceremonies slated for July 7, 2005. The attack on the London Underground transport system for all its planning and audaciousness shook British politicians and the public to the core—this was not the work of external groups but second generation immigrants born, raised, and educated in England to mainly middle class families!

In 2004–2005, there were over 400 suicide attacks, mostly in Iraq and 2007 saw a total of 658 globally with 543 being in the Iraq/Afghanistan theater. The bombings have spread to dozens of countries on five continents, killed more than 21,350 people and injured some 50,000 since 1983, when a suicide attack blew up the U.S. Embassy in Beirut. In addressing the root causes of terrorism, we believe that comments presented by the former British Prime Minister Tony Blair in the days after the London attack were overstated and not germane. He stated to a BBC interviewer that the underlying causes of these attacks were lack of democracy, the Middle East conflict, and poverty. Blair's belief that these are the root causes of terrorism is fundamentally flawed; if he believes that by creating democracy or removing poverty, terrorism will be eliminated, he is incorrect. The poorest nations of the world are not the ones producing the terrorist phenomenon. In discussing democracy, it is certainly not clear-cut that this is an important goal for the terrorists' agenda. With respect to the Middle East conflict, there is no evidence to support whether or not that conflict is a lightning rod for terrorism anywhere other than in that geopolitical region. The terrorists who perpetrated the 9-11 attacks, the Madrid train bombings, the London Underground attacks and the attack on Glasgow airport in 2007 have been described as foot soldiers who had little front-line involvement in terrorist activities prior to the attacks. In all of these attacks, none of the perpetrators lived in abject poverty—in fact, the British attackers could be described as middle class and reasonably well educated and in the Glasgow attacks the perpetrators were medical doctors. We need to focus on the root cause of international terrorism. The terrorist ideology supports a system of beliefs that allows for the devaluation of the lives of innocent victims, in most cases civilian victims of so-called targeted enemy societies; and encourages and promotes extreme violence, including suicide, as a method of responding to grievances. Why do extreme promoters of the Islamic faith use such an ideology to make use of poverty, repression, and conflict to aid in recruitment? Terrorist organizations are fundamentally organizations or businesses. While they may have been founded as a response to some grievance either real or perceived, they soon become focused on their own continuity and perpetuation; otherwise they sooner or later would just disappear. A successful terror organization does what is necessary for its own survival. To that end, it requires resources and recruits, so it produces ideology, propaganda, and terror attacks to compete for these inputs. We clearly need to understand that terrorism is an industry, and terrorist organizations are not about to go out of business because of any social or political improvements we can bring about. We need to attack these organizations directly, reducing their ability to motivate, raise funds, recruit, and organize attacks.[5]

Because suicide attacks are dramatic and often effective for a relatively small economic cost, suicide bombings will continue to increase. There are approximately 1.6 million Muslims in Britain, according to the British Home Office. A 2004 report by the Home Office detailed that 13 percent of British Muslims believed that suicide attacks against Western targets were justified. Respondents linked this attitude to anger over foreign policies and the presence of British and U.S. troops in the Middle East. It is, therefore, easy to link that attitude with the ability of bin Laden's network to recruit Western suicide bombers from second-generation immigrants!

Children as Suicide Bombers

As ghastly as the heading may appear this will be a reality in certain areas of the globe. That suicide bombers were traditionally young males has also changed as now we see more female and elderly suicide attackers and in Iraq we have witnessed the use of the mentally challenged to deliver suicide bombs. As for child bombers we have already seen photographs of Palestinian children in combat fatigues and mock suicide belts in training for missions. In 2005, we saw a mixed gender suicide attack on the Jordanian capital—although the target of the 2005 attack was not unusual, the make up of the suicide bombers was. Both were from al Qaeda in Iraq and were a married couple. In 2004 an Israeli soldier manning a checkpoint near the city of Nablus discovered a 13 pound explosive device in the back pack of a twelve-year-old Palestinian boy. The schoolboy had been tricked into carrying the bag by members of a Palestinian terrorist group. The soldier was alerted by the cell phone ring tone in the back pack. In 2006, a Palestinian mother of nine and grandmother of twenty-six were killed by Israeli security as she attempted to detonate a suicide vest. Currently this lady is the oldest recorded suicide bomber to have successfully carried out a mission.

PRIVATE SECURITY

The war in both Iraq and Afghanistan has led to a proliferation in the use of private security contractors to act in both theaters. They have come from across the globe to participate in the war and have been subject to indiscriminate attacks in much the same fashion as military personnel.

A large percentage of these security operatives have come from military backgrounds both in North America and Europe. A calling that is made slightly more bearable by the excellent remuneration they receive. With the heavy load being carried by NATO, U.S., and British troops there will be a continued need for "security contractors" to provide a security presence in such "hot zones" as Iraq and Afghanistan. Training standards will be a key issue for survival and for those without the military background being proficient in weapons handling is but a small part of the overall training.

FIGURE 15-1   Private security contractors undergoing live fire training at a secure facility in Tennessee in late 2007 (Mike McGuire).

FIGURE 15-2   Private security contractors undergoing live fire training at a secure facility in Tennessee in late 2007 (Mike McGuire).

TECHNO TERRORISM

While the Internet offers great opportunity for good and is the fastest-growing business sector the world has ever seen, it must be aligned with commercial market forces and operate on an international basis. Some observers believe that encryption software must be developed to prevent industrial and other espionage. The proliferation of strong encryption will have the opposite effect of that envisioned by the Bush administration—that it will help fight crime by keeping information secure in the new borderless world. Testifying before a Senate committee, Jerry Berman, executive director of the Center for Democracy and Technology, stated that data security demands strong encryption to foil threats wherever they are in the world. And good data security and privacy policies must recognize that the Bill of Rights in the U.S. Constitution is nothing more than a local law. As the Internet user reaches the unnerving conclusion that terrorism, like the Internet, recognizes no national boundaries, law enforcement officials will seek more ways to ferret it out and take preventive actions. In the past, investigators have wielded telephone wiretaps against terrorists, but the Clinton administration pointed to the use of encrypted files by child pornographers, militia members, and spies to avoid discovery. Grave crimes, such as a plot to shoot down several airliners over Chicago, have been foiled by the use of wiretaps. Had the FBI been unable to read those transmissions, a major tragedy might have occurred. Strong language calls for regulation of the Internet's content, such as the Clinton administration's ill-fated attempt to curb child pornography via the Communications Decency Act.

Senator Dianne Feinstein (D-California) introduced a bill that would make it illegal to distribute explosives-making information "by any means," including online, if the distributor intends or knows the information would be used in committing a crime. Encryption that is difficult to decipher should not be distributed to anyone. It's almost the same argument as that for gun control. The good citizen doesn't need a background check, but how can you tell that person from a bank robber without one? The use of the Internet has been dramatic for legitimate businesses, as well as for the business of terrorism and organized crime. The Internet has been used as a tool to frighten and export fear in "real-time," with almost instantaneous video footage of terrorist attacks. This has been a powerful tool and has likely been used not only for the value it gains from fear, but also for recruiting and training. It seems that no self-respecting terrorist will venture out without his camcorder and laptop computer!

TERRORISTS FOR SALE OR EXCHANGE

In an ideal world, governments would deal with any terrorists they apprehended. Alternately, if requested to do so and with good reason, they would hand them over to the government of the country where the crimes were committed, for the purpose of trial, with the barest of formalities or delays. And, countries should fully expect reciprocal and similar treatment. Unfortunately, this seldom happens because one man's "terrorist" is another man's "freedom fighter" and suspicious governments seldom give away something for nothing. All want to retain a few bargaining terrorist chips, just in case—a terrorist in hand often has value. Years ago, the expression "he has a price on his head" was clearly understood: It meant that a person was "wanted" by justice authorities, for either escaping from legal custody or being on the run for having allegedly committed a crime. A cash reward was invariably offered for the criminal's apprehension and conviction, especially in the days before modern police forces, to induce the public to bring him or her to justice. Cash rewards for these purposes brought about bounty hunting, a practice which lingers on in some countries. Nowadays, the expression that "every government has its price" might be more appropriate, particularly when dealing with the extradition of terrorists.

Extradition has always been a delicate subject, touching as it does on national sovereignty, seeming at times to be regarded more as a personal favor to the government asking for it than a routine, international transaction. Many suspect that there must be secret exchange channels, as all such transactions are carried out with the utmost discretion and are publicly denied.

Terrorists for Sale: Cash Will Do Nicely

In August 1994, the French government "purchased" the notorious terrorist "Carlos the Jackal" from the Sudanese government for a reputed U.S. $2 million. The French admitted only that he had been arrested "outside the usual legal framework." Carlos (Ilyich Ramirez Sanchez) was a star terrorist captive, wanted for killing eighty-three people in a series of terrorist attacks, several in France. In December 1975, he had led the terrorist team that kidnapped eleven OPEC oil ministers in Vienna.

Carlos had long been sheltered in Middle Eastern states, courtesy of the KGB, but with the end of the Cold War, he had become an embarrassment. He was subsequently ejected from Syria, refused entry by Yemen and Libya, and forced to accept asylum in Sudan. Carlos still resides in a French prison, having been convicted in the killing of two gendarmes. The French government thought it made a good bargain; perhaps, so too did the Sudanese government.

The Carlos incident established the fact that terrorists have a monetary value. We may be able to look forward to "transactions" involving other international terrorists—bin Laden would, obviously, be the biggest prize. If a government happens to be sheltering a high-value terrorist, and it needs a cash infusion, it would certainly be tempting to bring him to trial for a price. Such show trials provide a major boost to the morale of national security services. Lower-profile terrorists could be obtained for lower prices—a process that might have been in operation for some time for all we know, as secrecy surrounds the process. Either the media were well ahead of the diplomats in the Carlos case, or the French government deliberately sought publicity.

The Western hostage crisis in Lebanon (1984–1992), saw most of them being ransomed eventually. Often, wealthy international concerns pay huge sums of money for the release of employees since it is against most governments' policy to deal directly with terrorists. In 1992 the last two German hostages, Kemptner and Strubig who were kidnapped in Beirut were released after three years in captivity when the two Hamadi brothers who were convicted of hijacking a TWA airliner in 1985, were released in a hostage for prisoner exchange. In June 1995, the German government paid a reputed $1 million to the poverty-stricken Yemeni government for the extradition of Johannes Weinrich, a colleague of Carlos in his heyday. He was wanted for murder and explosions in Berlin and, after twenty years on the run, is now in prison in Germany. When the United States began its assault on Baghdad and the regime of Saddam Hussein in 2003, it created a pack of playing cards, with each card displaying the face and name of a wanted person—the higher the card in the deck, the higher the monetary reward.

Bounty Hunting

While the much-publicized Carlos incident may have alerted the world to the cash value of a terrorist, some countries, especially the United States, have long been offering cash rewards for the apprehension of criminals in order to tempt bounty hunters, many of whom have been highly successful. No film about the Old West would ever be complete without a poster reading "**WANTED—REWARD**" in the background.

In October 1985, the Italian cruise ship *Achille Lauro* was hijacked in the Mediterranean, and one U.S. citizen was killed. The situation was resolved with the help of the Egyptian government, which provided an aircraft to the terrorists. Under President Reagan's "you can run, but you can't hide" policy U.S. aircraft forced the plane down in Italy. There, the leader, Abu Abbas, a Palestinian terrorist mastermind, was allowed to escape to Yugoslavia. The other terrorists involved stood trial and were convicted in Italy. One, Magied al-Mulkil, was sentenced to thirty years' imprisonment and later jumped his parole, whereupon the U.S. government immediately offered a $2 million reward for his recapture. After the terrorist massacre at Luxor (Egypt) in November 1996, the Egyptian government condemned the British government for harboring the Islamic fundamentalist terrorist leaders thought to be responsible. Britain through the 1980s and 1990s had long been a refuge for those wanting to escape harsh regimes in Africa and the Middle East giving its capital city the unenviable nick name of "Londonistan." The United States offered a reward of $2 million (which seems to be the going rate at that time for a top terrorist) for the apprehension of Ramzi Ahmad Yousef. He was the mastermind and "evil genius" behind the conspiracy to blow up the World Trade Center in New York and other buildings and bridges. The CIA believed that Yousef was in Pakistan. Pakistani men smoke a lot, so the CIA issued thousands of small, green (a favorite Islamic color) matchboxes with Yousef's likeness on one side and details of how to obtain the reward on the other. This did the trick. Yousef was subsequently captured and is currently in a U.S. prison.

One hopes that the CIA will issue its green matchboxes by the hundreds of thousands in Afghanistan, where many Islamic fundamentalist terrorists, including bin Laden, are reputed to have sought refuge. The hope is that money—lots of it—may overcome religious scruples. In Afghanistan the challenge was to cut off funding to the Taliban which has gained much of its income from heroin trade. While you would think that with so many troops and UN agencies in Afghanistan would have had the effect of stifling the drug trade—unfortunately that is not the case and in 2008 the country was listed by the UN as one of the biggest exporters of opium! As of this writing, there have been no takers for the U.S. $25 million reward offered for the capture, of Osama bin Laden.

The Exchange Market

Through fact and fiction during the Cold War, we came to accept that spies were sometimes exchanged, so why not "wanted terrorists" too? In the turbulent Middle East, terrorists have sometimes been selectively exchanged under cover of Red Cross prisoner-of-war transfers. Exchanging hostages is an ancient military custom, revived during the Lebanese civil war (1975–1992), when warring factions had their own private prisons where hostages were held as security insurance for vengeance and for selective exchange actions.

Israel has, on occasion, indulged in kidnapping raids to seize terrorist leaders, including Sheikh Abdul Rahman Obeid and Mustafa Dirani. This practice is known locally as "cross-border terrorism." According to the Israeli press, the Israeli government offered to release forty-seven Palestinians, including certain political prisoners loosely referred to as terrorists, for the freeing of one captured Israeli soldier. There have been other instances when "Arab guerrillas," meaning terrorists, have been released in exchange for Israeli prisoners.

Jordanian authorities captured two Mossad agents after their failed attempt to assassinate Khaled Mishal, a Hamas leader, in Amman (Jordan), four others, all with forged Canadian passports, took refuge in the Israeli Embassy in Amman. In exchange for the safe return of the Mossad agents, Israel agreed to exchange Sheikh Ahmad Yassin, imprisoned spiritual leader of Hamas. Israelis have made a few selective key terrorist exchanges over the years, with censorship invariably concealing precise details.

Hostages: A Sliding Scale

High prices have been demanded and obtained for the release of certain terrorist-held hostages, but the success of these extortion plans depended on someone's (usually not a government) ability to pay large sums of money. Wealthy commercial concerns might be prepared to meet a terrorist's demands for the release of one of their employees, but would hesitate to embark upon such an illegal and secretive process. However, a few have done so, as indirectly as possible. Not all were wealthy, but many were able to raise lesser sums of money, so it is probable that there was a terrorists' sliding scale of ransom demands—a sort of actuary's table, understood only by terrorist masterminds and their intermediaries.

Comparatively few hostages are killed, as lucrative prospects seem to out-weigh political scruples and vengeance. This does happen sometimes, particularly when terrorists quarrel among themselves over possession of the hostage and what to do with him or her. On occasion, one terrorist group will snatch a kidnapped hostage from another. Generally, however, terrorist groups more often quarrel with each other over spoils and territory than over political dogma.

Occasionally, hostages have been sold or bartered between groups. One example is that of Ron Arad, an Israeli airman shot down over Lebanon in 1986 and taken hostage by Islamic fundamentalist Amal militia and subsequently sold into the custody of the Iranian Revolutionary Guards, and has not been seen since. Led by Mustafa Dirani, the group, according to some intelligence sources, held Arad for two years before selling him for $300,000. Hopes are that Arad may still be alive somewhere in Iran.

Terrorists with Shelf-Life Expired

In 1999, when the Lebanese army was reasserting its control over parts of the lawless Beka'a Valley, it cleaned out a nest of miscellaneous international terrorists, including five members of the Japanese Red Army. They were all former prisoners of the Israelis who had been freed in a mass Red Cross-organized Arab/Israeli exchange. One was Kozo Okamoto, the surviving terrorist of the May 1972 massacre at Lod Airport, in which over twenty people had been killed and more than eighty injured. Another was Kazuo Tohira, the group's master passport forger. The JRA members had disappeared from public view and notice. Japan showed no interest in them at all, as their shelf-life had expired and Japanese authorities were reluctant to resurrect the emotions of past terrorist dramas. In July 1999, the Lebanese government was reduced to charging the five JRA terrorists with illegal entry into Lebanon, and they were sentenced to three years' imprisonment, after which they were deported.

Open Negotiations for Hostages

Communications between terrorist hostage-takers and those who ultimately pay the ransoms are invariably shrouded in secrecy. An exception seems to be the case in Chechnya, where a twenty-one-month separatist war (1994–1996) between Russia and Chechnya left an open expanse of "no-man's land" between the two hostile military forces, across which illicit contacts and trade flourished. Russian mothers seeking missing soldier sons placed notices on general information boards in the area, giving details and asking for information. Terrorist go-betweens were also using these well-read notice boards for communication (not always in code), quoting demands for ransom and how negotiations may begin.

Terrorist leaders in Chechnya have already kidnapped several international aid and humanitarian workers, demanding food, medical supplies, and money in return for their release. An unofficial exchange of military prisoners seems to be conducted through the medium of the general information notice boards, while military authorities look the other way, as the end result is often to their own benefit. Russian authorities admit that a prosperous market in kidnapping for ransom exists in Chechnya. What of the future? Sadly, one must forecast more of the same, with governments forever seeking to extradite wanted terrorists, and terrorists forever seeking valuable hostages. Market forces influence the prices and we can predict a lot more terrorists being turned in for thirty pieces of silver.[6]

As we look to the future, we continue to look back over our shoulders at what has taken place. If 9-11 was a watershed for the West, what effect is it having on the aspirations of the Islamic extremist movements? We continue to believe that the Islamic terror threat emanates from Osama bin Laden and al Qaeda-affiliated groups. Al Qaeda has not made inroads into any political organizations around the world. In countries like Sudan, Egypt, Kashmir, and Indonesia, we have witnessed attempts by Islamic groups to organize and destabilize the political roadmap. In each, we have witnessed failure and in each there have been somewhat spectacular acts of violence. If bin Laden and his terror-minded sympathizers expected a popular uprising from the millions of Muslims around the world, it has not happened. Nor does it seem likely. After the coalition invasion of Afghanistan, there were no calls from Muslim clerics to declare a holy war against an infidel West. Not only has there been silence, but there have even been calls from other extreme agents of Islam against the actions of al Qaeda. Following the London attacks in July 2005, the British Muslim community roundly condemned the actions of the minority that sought this destruction and brought shame on their religion. In Egypt, the imprisoned leader of al-Gama'a al-Islamiya issued a public declaration distancing his organization from the extreme activities of bin Laden and al Qaeda—hardly a recommendation for a worldwide holy war!

THE FUTURE THREATS AND PROBABLE TRENDS

If we accept the theory that al Qaeda and its like-minded affiliates and followers are fanatically bent on the destruction of non-Islamic governments, then strategies and long-term plans aimed at prevention have to be defined and determined.

The growing appeal and worldwide spread of al Qaeda to Muslims in both Western European countries and the United States cannot be understated. As we continue to watch trends in methods of attack being employed by terrorists believed to be affiliates of the al Qaeda network, it becomes more apparent how their modus operandi changes with the amount of pressure brought to bear from opposing security forces. Temporarily gone, but not forgotten, are the large-scale car and truck bombs of the type that destroyed the Alfred P. Murrah Federal Building in Oklahoma City and attempted to destroy the World Trade Center in 1993. What we are now seeing are terrorists groups, and particularly those al Qaeda affiliates, attempting to stay ahead of the "security curve" by adapting to the changes in security posture. Smaller, but nonetheless equally deadly are the individual suicide bombings that characterized 2005–2008. Suicide attacks from the terrorist perspective are relatively low cost to carry out, and similarly the planning and execution of such attacks like the London Underground attacks were relatively simple to carry out on a subway system, however in the planning phase for this attack the location of detonation and the method of delivery was all important to the terrorists. Relatively small in size, easily transported in an unobtrusive rucksack, the terrorist suicide bombers were able to complete dummy runs on the intended target as part of the build-up in the planning phase of their operation. Al Qaeda operatives are well trained, sophisticated, and dedicated to their attack plans giving us some insight into the amount of planning, training, physical fitness, intelligence gathering, surveillance, and counter surveillance that they conduct in the weeks or months prior to an attack. In 2000, police in Manchester, England, discovered a military training manual, which has come to be known as the "Manchester document," while searching computer files found in the home of a known al Qaeda member. The contents were introduced as evidence into the 2001 trial of terrorists who bombed the U.S. embassies in Tanzania and Kenya in 1998.

Many theorize that this is an al Qaeda-produced document but there is not a single mention of al Qaeda within the translated pages. It is probable that this manual may have been produced by the Muslim Brotherhood and either shared with or adapted to al Qaeda operations. The contents of this manual certainly support what we know about al Qaeda and the manner in which its operatives have been trained to behave. The manual was translated into English and released to the public. The manual covers in great depth the myriad levels of security and surveillance necessary to carry out an operation and gives instruction on how to carry out counter-surveillance and gather target information as unobtrusively as possible.

Staying one step ahead of the security forces at a planned target is something we see with deadly clarity. As the security postures are intensified worldwide, so too changes are made in the methods of attack. Many smaller improvised explosive devices (IEDs) and vehicle borne explosive devices (VBIEDs) are being used to target locations where security may be considered light by the terrorists.

Such incidents as the attacks on the three U.S.-owned hotels in Amman, Jordan, on November 9, 2005, that claimed more than fifty lives indicates that smaller deadly devices with shrapnel components are being used against civilian targets. In the Amman Hotel attack almost all of those killed and injured were Muslims of Jordanian Palestinian descent. Selecting a high visibility location seems to become of primary importance and therefore the size of the bomb less important. The London Underground bombings occurred in packed carriages during rush hour, in narrow tunnels over 100 feet below ground. The impact of even these small bombs in those confined spaces was catastrophic. The same results occurred in the location of the suicide bombings in Amman, Jordan.

TECHNOLOGY AND SURVEILLANCE

It is a fact that there has been no successful jihadist attacks on the West since 2005 and that can be down a number of reasons, stepped up global intelligence and intelligence sharing, emphasis on homeland security both in Europe and the U.S., a centering of jihadist attacks in the Middle East (Iraq and Afghanistan) where there are numerous western military as well as non military western targets. Be that as it may technology will continue to play a role in effectively preempting a terror strike. While some will advocate that advancements in technological protection and detection of terrorists has resulted in a far greater intrusion into peoples privacy many seem not to mind such intrusion. Technological advances in protecting the public in areas such as public transport, airports, and railroads where smart cameras are deployed to identify people by their mannerism, gait, and facial expressions are now deployed. Human intelligence coupled with technology will help detect and prevent an attack. Sensors have been developed to identify the minutest trace of explosives or deadly microbes in a water system.

Shipping and shipping containers are the lifeblood of the U.S. economy and vast numbers of ships loaded with containers cross and criss-cross the world's Oceans. With the technology and globally agreed practices to screen products and identify shipments will go a significant distance to deter and delay the terrorists. However, the further we get away from the target date of September 11, 2001, the more likely we are to forget those events and let down our guard; the terrorists only need to get lucky once—security forces need far more than luck on their side. As we have said previously the terrorists of the twenty-first century still regard aviation as a target of choice and protecting against attacks both at airports and elsewhere continues to occupy the minds of security officials. Systems to prevent a successful MANPAD attack have centered on such companies as BAE Systems, Northrop Grumman, and Saab Avitronics in a bid to design and install systems for commercial aircraft rather than military craft. In January 2008, some four years after the DHS sought to have BAE develop its military counter measures technology to commercial aircraft it awarded a contract to BAE Systems.

As part of the Department of Homeland Security's (DHS) counter-man-portable air defense system (MANPADS) program, BAE Systems will install its JETEYE aircraft missile defense system on up to three American Airlines aircraft. The company will evaluate the system's compatibility with daily passenger airline operations and maintenance.

DHS selected BAE Systems in 2004 to adapt the company's military countermeasures technology to protect commercial aircraft against shoulder-fired missiles. Since then, BAE Systems has received $105 million in funding, and has delivered more than 14,000 infrared countermeasure systems worldwide—more than all other participating companies combined.

The counter-MANPADS program, created by DHS and Congress, is designed to commercialize proven military technology and gauge its suitability for protecting U.S. commercial aircraft by evaluating its performance, impact on aerodynamic drag, weight, reliability, maintainability, and system cost.[7]

Looking into the future we worry about the nature of the next major attack and where it is likely to be carried out. We try to determine if it will be chemical, biological, nuclear or more conventional means. Can the current trends in suicide attacks in the Middle East, the United Kingdom, United States, and Indonesia be a window to future attacks against the United States and its interests both at home and abroad?

As the United States and its close allies continue with the War on Terror it is time to take stock of where we are. Certainly the world has changed since 9-11 but have our attitudes changed as well? Are we becoming too complacent? Do we honestly believe that with all the legislation in place to fight terrorism and the increases in budget spending will prevent the next catastrophic event from taking place? How do we address this problem of global terrorism that seemingly will not go away? Perhaps it is time to take a long hard look at how we handle the scourge of terrorism. This is, and has never been solely an American problem. There is a need to educate schoolchildren, college students, blue collar and white collar workers on the causes, sources, and history of terrorism. From the way police and intelligence agencies recruit, to the skills they demand, to the relationships they build with one another, the whole approach must change. Extensive role playing of the way terrorists might operate in both an urban or rural setting, using a government wide cross-section of expertise is essential. Partnerships and exchange of ideas must become a critical element in the future fight against terrorism. It is apparent the United States cannot go this way on its own and must foster more solid global relations and use ideas and innovations from elsewhere. The ultimate goal in such a process must be to outwit and outthink the terrorists and expose to the whole world an unflinching resolve and determination supported by a strong coalition of governments by conveying a message of what the United States stands for and the exposing of terrorist hypocrisy.

INTERNET JIHAD

The Ubiquitous Power of the Internet and Cyber Jihad

The use of the Internet by terrorist groups will continue to become more sophisticated. As a tool used daily in the world of business and pleasure it is also widely used in the murky world of terrorism and not just for the practice of recruiting but all forms of terrorist logistics, fundraising, money laundering, and of course propaganda activities. The Internet has become the modern day communication tool for Osama bin Laden and others to reach impressionable minds around the globe. Connecting with like minded individuals particularly those in the West is an important tool to help radicalize and inspire jihad. Many of the young Western jihadists are likely self-radicalized and self recruited without ever having contact with al Qaeda or its affiliates. Thus the Internet plays a key role in the recruiting and radicalization process. The Internet has become the virtual world for training jihadists and although it is no substitute for hands-on training at a training camp in Pakistan or Afghanistan, the risks of being detected on the Internet are considerably lower. The publishing of material on the Internet has influenced operational terrorist activity and will continue to do so. The Global Islamic Media Front published an article in the year prior to the Madrid Train station attacks in 2004, which according to the Spanish investigating judge was what had inspired the perpetrators of the attack. Certainly the Internet is helping geographically dispersed groups and individuals who are enthusiastically wanting to join the jihad. It also encourages individual actions by small groups or individuals, which maybe why events such as the airport attack in Glasgow Scotland in 2007 was relatively unsophisticated and crude in its execution.

Summary

Prior to 9-11, the United States never anticipated it would be at war with terrorism and, most certainly, not in the dimensions to which we are now witnessing. The risks, the dangers, and the threats from groups or individual cells—all hell-bent on the destruction of Western democracies—are now at hand. Could they produce another 9-11? Are the London bombings a wake-up call? As should be abundantly clear, your authors have only been able to present the "tip of the iceberg" and we have not used nearly as much material as we would have liked. Events often move faster than we can get them down on paper! In this chapter, we have touched on just a few of the issues facing our terror struck world as it stumbles forward deeper into the twenty-first century among all the probable threats for the future. It appears that it will be up to the next generation to try to find effective ways to eliminate bigotry and the conditions that separate people financially, ethnically, religiously, racially, tribally, politically, and traditionally. We know that, worldwide, we have failed to gather all the available intelligence and accurately analyze and spot the signs to interpret it. This will change, and the wheel will turn. We hope that this book has opened a window through which the reader will forever view the evening news from a far different perspective and with serious skepticism. If we have whetted the reader's appetite for knowledge about how violence and terrorism came about, we are pleased and will feel that all this effort in writing it for you has been worth it.

In conclusion, the words of General Barry R. McCaffrey U.S. Army, Retired, seem to us to be most pertinent:

> Osama bin Laden suggests that nineteen young men, in four domestic airliners, had brought the powerful America to her knees. The terrorists reasoned that America had been unable to tolerate the blood of 350,000 American casualties in Vietnam, had withdrawn its fleet when U.S. Marines were slaughtered in Beirut, and had been humbled and forced to leave Somalia by the large number of U.S. Ranger casualties. The al Qaeda calculation was clear. . ."these American people are powerful in material but weak in spirit; they are politically divided; they have no real allies."[8]

As we attempt to look toward the future and what may lie ahead in the world of terrorist acts, we anticipate that terror networks and affiliates that attack in the guise of Islam will concentrate on spectacular events, but likely not on the dramatic scale of 9-11, which required a considerable amount of planning and training. The suicide bomber is able to strike at will and without warning and cause a large number of casualties. There is currently an almost unending supply of young fanatics willing to become suicide operatives in what might best be described as the poor man's smart bomb or mini WMD! In terms of modern-day terrorism, military occupation of Muslim lands by foreign armies is a contributing factor in the creation of a suicide bomber. From a broad perspective, suicide bombers are usually from outside the country they are attacking. The U.S. military notes that a significant number of attacks by suicide bombers in Afghanistan are carried out by foreign Arabs, while the suicide attacks in London were carried out by young British men of Pakistani and Jamaican descent. The ideology of al Qaeda has not become extinct through the War on Terror—rather; it has become entrenched at the grassroots level. There is no doubt that suicide attacks will continue in the foreseeable future. We will continue to see enhancements in technology as governments attempt to prevent the next "Big One."

Web Sites

1. **Homeland Security/Defense Education Consortium—** *http://homelandsecurity.osu.edu/NACHS/index.html*
2. **World Future Society—***www.wfs.org*
3. **American Society for Industrial Security—** *www.asisonline.org*
4. **International Center for Political Violence and Terrorism Research—***http://www.pvtr.org/*

Endnotes

1. James Binnie. *War on Terror Shifts Focus* (January 2008), Jane's Terrorism & Security Monitor, Jane's Information Group.
2. Paul Cornish. "Sabotage by Sarin." *Intersec: The Journal of International Security*, vol. 7, issue 9 (Surrey, UK: Three Bridges Publishing, September 1997).
3. www.milnet.com.
4. Strategic Forecasting Inc., analysis@stratfor.com.
5. Dan Radlauer. "The London Bombings and the Root Causes of Terrorism." Paper to the International Policy Institute for Counterterrorism (July 10, 2005).
6. Edgar O'balance. "Terrorists for sale or exchange," *Intersec, The Journal of International Security* vol. 8, no. 1 (Surrey, UK: Three Bridges Publishing: January 1998, pp. 9–10, 12).
7. BAE Systems News Release—BAE Systems Awarded Homeland Security Contract to evaluate Missile Defense System on U.S. passenger aircraft—www.baesystems.com, extracted May 3, 2008.
8. General Barry R. McCaffey, USA-Retired. "Challenges to U.S. National Security," *Armed Forces Journal International* (February 2002).

GLOSSARY

Abu Sayyaf Group (ASG)—A small but effective Islamic terror group that seeks an independent Islamic state along the Sulu archipelago.

Accion Nacional Espanila (ANE)—Spanish National Action, a right-wing terror movement that specifically targets Basque separatists.

Active service unit (ASU)—A term used by the Provisional IRA to describe one of its active terror units.

Aden Protectorate—An area of southern Arabia that, by treaty, was under British Protectorate rule during the early to mid-twentieth century; today, the area is part of the Republic of Yemen.

African National Congress (ANC)—A center left political party that traces its roots back to the early twentieth century. In 1944, the ANC youth wing was formed by Oliver Tembo and Nelson Mandela. The ANC was established to defend the rights of the Black majority in South Africa and has been in power in South Africa since 1994.

Afrikaner Weerstandsbeweging (AWB)—The Afrikaner Resistance Movement; an extreme left-wing group that was forced out of the National Party by 1971.

Agca, Mehmet Ali—Turkish nationalist who attempted the assassination of Pope John Paul II in St. Peter's Square, Rome, on May 13, 1981.

Al Jazeera—Arabic TV station located in Qatar in the United Arab Emirates; since the 9-11 attacks it has aired many video messages from Osama bin Laden. Literal translation from Arabic means "an island."

al-Majid, Al Hassan—"Chemical Ali," first cousin to Saddam Hussein; the developer and executor of the Iraqi chemical weapons program through the 1980s and 1990s.

Al Qaeda—An international terrorist movement first heard of in the late 1980s. Founded by Mohammad Atef and Osama bin Laden. The movement was based in Afghanistan and supported by the Taliban government throughout the 1990s. Its aims are the destruction of non-Islamic governments. It is now spread throughout the world with many fighters in the mountains of Pakistan.

Al-Sabah Dynasty—Succession of rulers in Kuwait; Sabah al-Ahmad al-Jabir al-Sabah is the current prime minister of Kuwait and was appointed to this position by his brother, the emir of Kuwait, Jabir al-Sabah in 2003.

Algerian Salafist Group for Preaching and Combat (GSPC)—An Islamic terrorist organization that has gained much support from disenfranchised Muslim youth in Europe and has emerged in recent years as a major source of recruiting and support for al Qaeda operations. A splinter faction of the Algerian Armed Islamic Group (GIA), the GSPC, is engaged in efforts to overthrow the secular government of Algeria and to organize high-profile attacks against Western interests.

Anti-Fascist Resistance Group of October First (GRAPO)—Formed in 1975 as the armed wing of the illegal Communist Party of Spain during the Franco era. GRAPO advocates the overthrow of the Spanish government and its replacement with a Marxist-Leninist regime. The group is anti-United States and seeks the removal of all U.S. military forces from Spanish territory. The group issued a communiqué following the attacks of September 11 in the United States, expressing its satisfaction that "symbols of imperialist power" were decimated and affirming that "the war" has only just begun. Designated under EO 13224 in December 2001.

Antiterrorism and Effective Death Penalty Act of 1996—A set of laws enacted by the United States to deter terrorism and provide justice for victims of terrorism.

Anti-Terrorism Crime and Security Act 2001 (ATCSA)—A counterterrorism bill introduced into law by the government of the United Kingdom.

Apartheid—The policy of segregation along racial lines; prominently practiced in South Africa.

Arafat, Yasser—(August 24, 1929–November 11, 2004) Awarded the Nobel Peace Prize in 1994. He was symbolically portrayed as the leader of the Palestinian struggle for an independent Palestinian state. A stubborn leader often viewed by outsiders as a corrupt politician and a stumbling block to any peace in the Middle East. Israel considered him a terrorist who promoted violence against Israel and they deeply mistrusted him.

Armed Islamic Group (GIA)—Islamic terrorist group operating in Algeria.

Armed Proletarian Nuclei (NAP)—Left-wing movement originating in the Italian prison system.

Armee Republicaine Bretonne (ARB)—Breton Liberation Army is a small nationalist anti-globalization movement with its roots in the Breton region of France. It consists of a small cadre of around thirty members.

Armenian Secret Army for the Liberation of Armenia (ASALA)—Marxist-Leninist Armenian terrorist group formed in 1975 with stated intention to compel the Turkish government to acknowledge publicly its alleged responsibility for the deaths of 1.5 million Armenians in 1915, pay reparations, and cede territory for an Armenian homeland. Led by Hagop Hagopian until he was assassinated in Athens in April 1988.

Army of God—U.S. domestic terror group that engages in violence; targets abortion clinics and medical practitioners.

Army Ranger Wing (ARW)—Republic of Ireland's elite counter terror unit.

Assassination—The targeted killing of an important person for political or ideological reasons.

Aum Shinrikyo—Japanese terror group known for the sarin gas attack on the Tokyo subway in 1995.

Autodeterminaziorako Bilgunea (AuB)—Formed in February 13, 2003. Comprised of prominent representatives from the Basque left-wing pro-independence movement, as well as those from other political backgrounds. Political agenda to demand the right of the Basque people to make decisions regarding their future and supporting a democratic solution to the Basque political conflict.

Aviation Security Commando (AVESCOM)—Philippines hostage rescue unit.

Ba'athist regime—Pan-Arabic socialist party that was prominent in Iraq and continues in Syria; party of Saddam Hussein.

Baader Meinhof Wagon (BMW)—Nickname for the BMW vehicle used by the Baader Meinhof gang in its terrorist attacks.

Bab el Mandeb—A strategic stretch of water linking the Red Sea to the Gulf of Aden.

Bahraini Hezbollah—Organization believed to be supported by Iran; seeks to overthrow the Bahrain government and replace it with a fundamentalist Islamic regime.

Balfour Declaration—Lord Balfour's 1917 declaration pledging British support to a Jewish homeland in Palestine.

Basque Region—An area in northern Spain and southwest France (Pyrenees); the Basque people (approximately 2 million) inhabit the region.

Basque Socialist Coalition—Known as the Herri Batasuna (People's Unity) Party; led by Arnoldo Ortiz.

Batasuna, Herri—The People's Unity Party; Spanish organization led by Arnoldo Ortiz; officially denies any links or involvement with the ETA terrorist organization; a.k.a. The Basque Socialist Coalition.

Black and Tans—British paramilitary force recruited to assist the Royal Irish Constabulary; members wore black and tan uniforms.

Black September—Group of Palestinian fighters who attempted to seize power in Jordan; subsequently, the Jordanian military expelled thousands of Palestinians from Jordan in September 1970. Black September gained notoriety for the killing of eleven Israeli athletes at the Munich Olympic Games in 1972.

Boevaya Oranisatsia (BO)—Terror suborganization within the Social Revolutionary Party; given autonomy under the party (means "the fighting organization").

Bolshevik—Extreme left-wing radicals, who favored revolution; led by Lenin.

Bureau of State Security (BOSS)—The South African state security service.

Cali cartel—A powerful drug cartel operating in Colombia.

Canadian Security Intelligence Service (CSIS)—A relatively young organization that tracks threats to national security within Canada.

Carlos the Jackal—Illich Ramirez Sanchez, an infamous terrorist in Western Europe in the 1960s; currently in a French prison.

CBP—U.S. Customs and Border Patrol.

Cheka—Communist secret police organization established during the Russian Revolution in 1917.

Chiapas—A state in southeast Mexico where a peasant uprising led by the Zapatista National Liberation Army continues to press for greater autonomy.

COBRAS—Sultanate of Oman elite special forces unit.

Communist Combatant Cells (CCC)—A Belgian terror group.

Condera, Monsignor Juan Gerardi—The bishop of Guatemala who was beaten to death two days after releasing a human rights report on April 26, 1998.

Contras—Terrorist organization and armed opponents of Nicaragua's Sandinista Junta of National Reconstruction following the July 1979 overthrow of Anastasio Somoza Debayle and the ending of the Somoza family's forty-three year rule.

CSI—U.S. Container Security Initiative—global security initiative established by U.S. Customs and Border Protection in 2002 to target and screen container traffic.

Customs and Border Patrol (CBP)—The United States Border Patrol was the mobile uniformed law enforcement arm of the Department of Homeland Security (DHS). It was officially established on May 28, 1924, by an act of Congress passed in response to increasing illegal immigration.

Dada, Idi Amin—Self-declared president for Life of Uganda who came to power following a coup in 1971; he purged the military and the country of most of his opponents and exiled 70,000 Ugandan Asians with British passports. He died in exile in Saudi Arabia in 2003.

Dal Khalsa—Sikh terrorist organization supported by ex-patriot Sikhs; their aim to establish the independent Sikh state of Khalistan.

Decommissioning—Provision in the Northern Ireland Peace Agreement that puts weapons beyond the use of Irish terror organizations.

Democratic Front for the Liberation of Palestine (DFLP)—Marxist-Leninist organization founded in 1969 when it split from the Popular Front for the Liberation of Palestine (PFLP). The DFLP believes Palestinian national goals can be achieved only through revolution. Joined with other rejectionist groups to oppose the Declaration of Principals signed in 1993. In the 1970s, the DFLP conducted numerous small bombings and minor assaults and some more spectacular operations in Israel and the occupied territories, concentrating on Israeli targets. They have only been involved in border raids since 1988, but they continue to oppose the Israel-PLO peace agreement.

Democratic People's Republic of Korea (DPRK)—A communist state dominated by a one-man dictatorship. North Korea's long-range missile development and research into nuclear, chemical, and biological weapons and massive conventional armed forces are of major concern to the international community. The current ruler of North Korea is Kim Jong II.

Democratic Progressive Party (DPP)—Taiwanese opposition party.

Department of Homeland Security (DHS)—U.S. government agency created after the attacks of 9-11.

Dev Sol—A left-wing Marxist group that has its origins in the Turkish People's Liberation Army.

Diplock Commission—Commission set up in 1972 to consider legal measures against terrorism in Northern Ireland, which led to the establishment of courts without jury; named after Kenneth Diplock.

Directorate of Inter-Services Intelligence (ISI)—Pakistani intelligence organization; founded in 1948 and has more than 10,000 members; it collects foreign and domestic intelligence and co-ordinates intelligence functions of the three military services.

Doc, Papa—The long-time dictator of Haiti, aided by the Ton-Ton Marquette terrorists.

domestic terrorist acts—Terrorist actions conducted by Americans.

Drive-by shootings—The shooting of a victim, sometimes random in nature, from a moving vehicle; popular method of attack by urban gangs.

Emergency Provisions—Powers given to the military by the Northern Ireland Emergency Provisions to combat urban terror in Northern Ireland.

ETA-Military—Military branch of the Basque terrorist organization.

Ethnic cleansing—A term originally used to describe the Serbs attack on Muslims in Bosnia during the breakup of Yugoslavia; a softer term than "genocide."

European Civil Aviation Conference (ECAC)—European organization responsible for developing policies and standards for civil aviation.

Euzkadi Ta Azkatasuna (ETA)—The Basques formed ETA (Basque Fatherland and Freedom) in 1959 and it has dedicated itself to promoting Basque independence and has become one of Europe's oldest terrorist organizations.

Extraordinary rendition—Secretive U.S. practice of seizing foreign terror suspects and transporting them to foreign countries, such as Egypt and Syria, where torture of suspects is a matter of course.

Falun Gong—Spiritual movement that came to prominence in the People's Republic of China and is widely repressed in that country.

Fedayeen—Arab commando unit.

Federal Air Marshal Service (FAMS)—Federal Sky Marshall program designed to place armed guards on U.S. aircraft in flight.

Ferdinand, Archduke Franz—His assassination in Sarajevo in 1914 triggered the start of World War I.

Fertile Crescent—Region of the Middle East stretching from the deserts of Syria through Iraq.

Fatwa—A legal ruling or Islamic decree issued by a Muslim religious lawyer.

Fiahs—Indonesian term for terrorist cellular structures; for fundraising, religious work, security, and operations.

Frankincense—Aromatic resin widely used in religious rites.

Freedom of Access to Clinic Entrances Act (FACE)—Activities by pro-life activists in the United States attempted to block free access to abortion clinics by surrounding clinics with picketers attempting to shut them down. This activity was prohibited by the FACE Act.

Frente Revolucionario Anti-Fascista Y Patriotico (FRAP)—Left-wing Maoist group.

Front de la Liberation Nationale de la Corse (FLNC)—A group of Corsican separatists.

Front de Liberation du Quebec (FLQ)—Canadian extreme separatist movement active in the 1960s and 1970s.

Front for the Liberation of Angola (FNLA)—The FNLA was founded in 1954 as the Union of Peoples of Northern Angola to advance the interests of the Bakongo rather than to promote independence.

Front for the Liberation of Mozambique (FRELIMO)—Movement against Portuguese rule; originated in early 1960s.

G-8—A group of eight countries: the United States, Canada, Great Britain, Russia, France, Germany, Italy, and Japan—that meet as a world economic forum.

GAO—United Sates Government Accountability Office.

Gastarbeiter Program—Program that brought Turkish workers to Germany to help rebuild the country after World War II.

Genocide—The systematic and planned extermination of an ethnic, religious, political, or national group.

Good Friday Agreement—Plan for devolved government in Northern Ireland signed on April 10, 1998; includes terms of early release of prisoners and decommissioning of weapons.

Great Trek—1835–1843 journey by Afrikaner farmers from Cape colony of South Africa to escape British domination.

Grenzschutzgruppe 9 (GSG-9)—German counterterrorist group founded after the Munich Olympic Games attack by Palestinian terrorists.

Groupment d'intervention de la Gendarmerie Nationale (GIGN)—A French counterterror unit with a ninety-men-strong unit designed to anti-terrorism and police operations similar to U.S. police SWATs. It is organized in four 15-men groups. The GIGN have conducted counter terror actions outside France in Djibouti, Lebanon, and the Comoros Islands.

Grupo Especial De Operaciones (GEO)—Belgium's Para-commando Regiment contains two small units that are special operations capable. The first, ESR (Equips Speciales de Reconnaisance Compagnie) dates back to 1960, when it was formed to give the I Belgium Corps a long-range reconnaissance capacity. This unit is company sized, and uses the standard weapons of the Belgium Army. Two similar units exist within the reserve structure. The second unit is a small frogman section. It is a highly secretive unit, but is known to be about platoon sized and is similar to the British Special Boat Squadron (SBS).

Guantanamo Bay—U.S. military base in Cuba where "detainees" and suspected Islamic militants from Iraq and Afghanistan are being held.

Guevara, Che—Dr. Ernesto Rafael Guevara de la Serna, Argentine-born Marxist revolutionary and Cuban guerrilla leader.

Gulags—Forced labor camps set up by the Soviet internal police for dissidents and politicians.

Gulf Cooperation Council (GCC)—Council comprised of Qatar, Oman, the UAE, Saudi Arabia, Kuwait, and Bahrain; set up in 1981 to address common economic and social issues within the region.

Hajj—Muslim pilgrimage to the Holy City of Mecca.

Hamas—Offshoot of the Islamic Brotherhood and an acronym for the Islamic Resistance Movement.

Hamza al Masri, Abu—Former imam of London's Finsbury Park Mosque.

Harakat-ul-Ansar (HUA)—Pakistani Islamic militant group that operates primarily in Kashmir.

Hashemite Kingdom—The official name for the Middle East kingdom of Jordan.

Hashish-eater—Origin of the word "assassin" in ancient times.

HEU—Highly enriched uranium.

Hezbollah—Radical Arabic organization that established itself following the Israeli invasion of Lebanon; the group is often linked with terror attacks in the Middle East.

Home Rule—The principle of self-government.

Human Intelligence (HUMINT)—An intelligence gathering by tracking suspects, interviews, and interrogations; primarily under the domain CIA in the United States.

IED—An improvised explosive device.

Immigration and Customs Enforcement (ICE)—Is the largest investigative arm of the Department of Homeland Security. As part of its homeland security mission, ICE seeks to maintain the integrity of the immigration system through effective enforcement of U.S. immigration laws.

Indian National Congress—Created in 1885, the Indian party that led the drive for an independent India from British rule; its iconic leader after World War I was Mahatma Gandhi.

Information Analysis and Infrastructure Protection (IAFP)—The Department of Homeland Security would merge under one roof the capability to identify and assess current and future threats to the homeland, map those threats against current vulnerabilities, inform the president, issue timely warnings, and immediately take or effect appropriate preventive and protective action.

International Atomic Energy Agency (IAEA)—Formed in 1957 to promote the peaceful use of nuclear energy and to inhibit its use for military purposes.

Internment—Confinement, often used in wartime; in this case, used in Northern Ireland during the 1980s.

INTERPOL—International Criminal Police Organization created in 1923 to assist with international police cooperation; headquartered in Lyons, France; has 184 member countries making it second in size to the United Nations.

Iranian Revolutionary Guard Crops (IRGC)—The Persian name for the Guards is Sepah and translated

means Pasdaran. Formed in 1979 as a loyal force for the Ayatollah Khomeini, it is a military organization that functions to protect the revolution. The Guards fought alongside the military during the Iran–Iraq war.

Irgun—Hebrew term for the National Military Organization, a Zionist group that operated between 1931 and 1948 in British-mandated Palestine.

Irish Free State—Established by treaty with Great Britain as a dominion within the Commonwealth of Nations in 1922, and become a sovereign state in 1937 (Eire).

Irish National Liberation Army (INLA)—Irish Republican paramilitary organization was founded in 1974. Its terrorist activities have spread to mainland Britain and were responsible for the assassination of Airey Neave, a close political friend of British Prime Minister Margaret Thatcher.

Irish Republican Army (IRA)—A Catholic paramilitary organization.

Islamic Jihad—An umbrella organization of Palestinian terrorist groups operating from the Middle East; many terrorist groups add the word "jihad" to their title.

Islamism—Islamic ideology demanding total adherence to Islamic laws.

Jaish-e-Mohammed (JEM)—The Army of Mohammed; an Islamic extremist group based in Pakistan formed by Masood Azhar upon his release from prison in India.

Jamaat al-Fuqra—Islamic sect that seeks to purify Islam through violence. Its leader is Pakistani cleric Sheikh Mubarik Ali Gilani, who established the organization in the early 1980s. Gilani now resides in Pakistan, but most Fuqra cells are located in North America and the Caribbean.

Janjaweed—Armed militia group operating in Darfur, western Sudan.

Japanese Red Army (JRA)—Marxist revolutionary terror group active in Europe during the 1970s.

Jemaah Islamiyaah (JI)—Shadowy Islamic terror group that has spread throughout southern Asia.

Jihad—Islamic term used to describe a holy war against religious or political oppression.

Joint Task Force-2 (JTF-2)—Canadian Special Forces unit established in 1993 when the Canadian armed forces took responsibility for counterterrorism operations within Canada; very secretive unit about which little is known.

Joint Terrorism Analysis Center (JTAC)—Organization that analyzes and assesses international terrorism in the United Kingdom; established in 2003.

Justice and Equality Movement (JEM)—Organization in Darfur challenging the administration in Khartoum.

Keiretsu—Japanese term used to describe a close-knit group of manufacturers, suppliers, and distributors.

KGB—The Committee for State Security; Soviet secret police, founded by Felix Edmundovich Dzerzhinsky in 1954; lasted until the collapse of the Soviet Union and was dissolved in 1991.

Khalistan—Country formed on October 7, 1987, where the Sikh nation declared its independence from India.

Khmer Rouge—The Communist Party of Cambodia; during its reign of power from 1975 to 1979, it was responsible for the execution of several million Cambodians.

Khmer Royal Armed Forces (KRAF)—The 1993 merger of the Cambodian People's Armed Forces and the two non-Communist resistance armies; also known as the Royal Cambodian Armed Forces, or RCAF.

Killer College—A major training facility for terrorists in Russia.

Killer instinct—Predilection to kill, not in anger, not in the heat of the moment, but in cold blood.

KINTEX—Bulgarian weapons-producing company.

Kirov, Sergei—Bolshevik who took part in the 1905 Russian Revolution and the Russian Civil War of 1920. He was a popular and loyal supporter of Josef Stalin, and was assassinated in December 1934.

Kurdistan—Region of the Middle East inhabited by Kurds and covering areas of Turkey, Iraq, Syria, and Armenia. The region is not recognized demographically; however, it accounts for approximately 25 million Kurds.

Kurdistan Freedom and Democracy Congress (KADEK)—a.k.a. Kurdistan Workers' Party; was established in 1974; is a Marxist-Leninist insurgent group, which aims to create a democratic Kurdish state.

Kurdistan Workers' Party (PKK)—Marxist-Leninist insurgent group made up of Turkish Kurds; founded in 1978. The group's goal has been to establish an independent, democratic Kurdish state in the Middle East.

Lashkar i Jhangvi (LJ)—Extreme Sunni Muslim group that has its roots in a sectarian movement calling itself Sipah-i-Sahaba Pakistan; its main targets for attack are from the Shia religious sect. The group had ties to the Taliban in Afghanistan.

Laws—Rules established for the orderly operation of a society.

Letter bomb—Small, improvised explosive device hidden inside an envelope or a package mailed to a targeted person or organization.

Liberation Tigers of Tamil Eelam (LTTE)—Sri Lankan terrorist movement seeking an autonomous homeland.

Lockerbie—Small village in southern Scotland where Pan Am 103 crashed, destroying many homes and taking the lives of all on board as well as many on the ground.

MI5—British intelligence organization.

Macheteros—Armed Forces of Puerto Rican National Liberation, a.k.a. the Popular Boricua Army (Ejercito Popular Boricua), commonly known as the Macheteros, claimed responsibility for numerous bombings and robberies, causing a reign of terror in Puerto Rico. The goals of the Macheteros were complete autonomy and sovereignty for Puerto Rico.

Man-Portable Air Defense System (MANPADS)—Systems as the Russian (SA-7 and SA-14, Igla SA-16 and SA-18) and the U.S.-manufactured FIM-92 Stinger; easy to use and readily available on the black market; pose an acute threat to military aircraft and civilian airliners.

Mancino Law—Italian law aimed at hate crimes.

Mandela United Football Club—Name given to the bodyguards of Winnie Madikizela-Mandela, wife of former president of South Africa, Nelson Mandela.

Mandela, Nelson Rolihlahla—The first Black president of South Africa.

Mau Mau—Insurgent movement in Kenya that attacked Europeans in the 1950s; comprised mainly of Kikuyu tribesmen.

McVeigh, Timothy James—American who was convicted for the bombing of the Federal Building in Oklahoma City on April 19, 1995, killing 167 people; he was executed on June 11, 2001.

Middle East—A region of the world comprised of Israel, Lebanon, Syria, Jordan, the Gulf states, and Saudi Arabia.

Militia—A militia is a group of citizens organized to provide paramilitary service.

Milli Görüs—Largest Muslim organization in Germany with over 27,000 members; its influence is felt within the tight-knit Muslim communities particularly in the Turkish Muslim areas; a.k.a. National Vision.

Montoneros (Movimiento Peronista Montonero)—Argentinean leftist guerrilla group active during the 1970s. *Montonero* was a local name for nineteenth-century guerrillas. The group formed around 1970 from the socialist supporters of Juan Domingo Perón.

Morazanist Patriotic Front (FPM)—A radical, leftist Honduran terrorist group that first appeared in the late 1980s; its attacks were in protest of U.S. intervention in Honduran economic and political affairs.

Mores—Accepted behaviors and customs within a social group.

Moro Islamic Liberation Front (MILF)—An Islamic terrorist group fighting for an independent Islamic state in the southern Philippines.

Moro National Liberation Front (MNLF)—Terror group that signed a peace deal with the Philippines and was integrated into the Philippine army.

Mossad—Institute for Intelligence and Special Assignments; Israeli intelligence organization, founded in 1949 by David Ben Gurion.

Movimiento Revolucionario Tupac Amaru (MRTA)—Peruvian guerrilla organization during the late 1980s and early 1990s; smaller than The Shining Path but equally as dangerous and ruthless.

Movimento Politico Occidentale (MPO)—(Political Movement of the West)—Italian Skinhead organization.

Mujahedin-e Khalq (MEK)—Formed in the 1960s, the organization was expelled from Iran after the Islamic Revolution in 1979, its primary support came from the former Iraqi regime of Saddam Hussein starting in the late 1980s. They conducted anti-Western attacks prior to the Islamic Revolution. Since then, it has conducted terrorist attacks against the interests of the clerical regime in Iran and abroad. The MEK advocates the overthrow of the Iranian regime and its replacement with the group's own leadership.

Mujahideen—Muslim fighters engaged in jihad.

Muslim Council of Britain—Established in 1997 with membership from more than 250 Muslim organizations in Great Britain—its first Secretary General was Iqbal

Sacranie who received Knighthood from Queen Elizabeth II in 2006.

Myanmar—Originally Burma; the country was renamed in 1989.

Narodnaya Volya (NV)—A nineteenth-century Russian terrorist organization, translation means "The People's Will."

National Liberation Army—A terminology often adapted by a terrorist group in a fight against legitimate authority.

National Organization of Cypriot Combatants (EOKA)—Was a Greek Cypriot military resistance organization that fought for self-determination and for union with Greece in the mid- to late 1950s.

National Targeting Center (NTC)—Part of the U.S. Department of Homeland Security; provides tactical targeting and analytical research in support of customs anti-terrorism efforts.

National Union for the Total Independence of Angola (UNITA)—Formed in 1966 by Jonas Savimbi, its charismatic leader. The group was formed from the politicized split in the Angolan independence movement. Unit 2002, the group was largely a military force and had been fighting a civil war since 1975. Jonas Savimbi headed the group from its formation until his death in 2002.

Nerve agents—Chemical agents used to attack and disable the human central nervous system.

New World Order—Term used to describe what some extreme believers think the U.S. government is determined to create; often referenced by U.S. militia organizations.

Nidal, Abu—Born in 1937 Sabri al Banna; prior to Osama bin Laden, Nidal was considered one of the most dangerous terrorists. He spent many years in Syria, Libya, and Iraq, where he died under mysterious circumstances in 2002.

NORAID—Irish republican organization that (Irish Northern Aid Committee) actively collected funds in the United States to support republican activities in Northern Ireland.

North American Free Trade Agreement (NAFTA)—Trade agreement among the United States, Canada, and Mexico.

North Atlantic Treaty Organization (NATO)—Alliance of twenty-six countries from North America and Europe committed to fulfilling the goals of the North Atlantic Treaty signed in April 4, 1949.

November 17—Greek terrorist revolutionary organization; is Marxist-Leninist, anti-imperialist, anti-United States, anti-Europe, and anti-NATO.

NPA—Maoist group formed in December 1969 with the aim of overthrowing the Philippine government through protracted guerrilla warfare; the military wing of the Communist Party of the Philippines (CPP).

Ocalan, Abdullah—Imprisoned leader of the Kurdish Workers' Party in Turkey.

Oklahoma City Federal Building—Building destroyed by a truck bomb placed by Timothy McVeigh.

Operation Desert Storm—The first Gulf War of 1991; led by the United States and a coalition of countries to remove Iraqi forces from Kuwait.

Organization of Petroleum Exporting Countries (OPEC)—Headquartered in Vienna, Austria, the principal aim of the organization is the determination of petroleum policies of its member countries and the determination of the best means for safeguarding their interests, individually and collectively. The member states are Algeria, Iran, Indonesia, Kuwait, Iraq, Libya, Nigeria, Qatar, Saudi Arabia, Venezuela, and the United Arab Emirates.

Palestine—Region of the eastern Mediterranean coast from the Red Sea to the Jordan valley and from the southern Negev desert to the Galilee Lake region in the north. The word itself derives from "Plesheth," a name that appears frequently in the Bible and, translated to English is "Philistine."

Palestine Liberation Front (PLF)—Small breakaway group from the PFLP based in the West Bank and Lebanon.

Palestine Liberation Organization (PLO)—Established in 1964 as a political body representing the Palestinian people. It is also a paramilitary organization that has dedicated itself to the establishment of a Palestinian state in former Palestine. Yasser Arafat became chairman of the PLO in 1969 until his death in 2004.

Palestinian Islamic Jihad (PIJ)—Formed by militant Palestinians in the Gaza Strip during the 1970s; committed to the creation of an Islamic Palestinian state and the destruction of Israel.

Palestinian National Liberation Movement (Fatah)—Founded in 1959 by Yasser Arafat—Fatah joined the PLO in 1967 and Arafat took over as leader.

Pan Am Flight 103—Pan Am Boeing 747 destroyed by a terrorist bomb over Lockerbie, Scotland.

Partisans—An irregular army evading and attacking an invading or occupying force.

People's Consultative Assembly—Indonesian legislative body largely appointed by the president himself; re-elected Suharto to a seventh term.

People's Republic of China (PRC)—Often referred to as Red China, a Communist country in Asia with a population of 1.3 billion.

Police Service of Northern Ireland (PSNI)—Predominantly Protestant police force formally known as the Royal Ulster Constabulary; name changed under the terms of the Northern Ireland Peace Agreement.

Popular Front for the Liberation of Palestine (PFLP)—Terrorist group under the umbrella of the PLO.

Popular Revolutionary Army (EPR)—Left-wing Mexican group; ranks second in strength to the Zapatista movement based in the southern states of Oaxaca and Guerrero; considered by Mexicans to actually be several different movements operating under one banner.

Pot, Pol—Leader of Communist regime in Cambodia, which he renamed Kampuchea; in 1976, he unveiled a "4-Year Plan" that detailed the collectivization of agriculture, the nationalization of industry, and the financing of the economy through increased agricultural exports. Thousands starved to death as a result.

Prescribe—To establish rules, laws, and direction.

Proscribe—To outlaw and ban terror organizations.

Provisional Irish Republican Army (PIRA)—A splinter from the original IRA movement that has waged a terror campaign in the United Kingdom and Northern Ireland.

Pushkin Square—Locality in the center of Moscow; renamed after Alexander Pushkin in 1937.

Racial Profiling—The inclusion of race as a specific indicator as to whether that person is likely to commit a crime—used widely in the United States and challenged by human rights organizations as racism at worst.

Rebel Armed Forces (FAR)—Leftist Guatemalan terror group. Formed in 1962 by junior officers of the Guatemalan military who had previously led an unsuccessful coup attempt against the conservative Guatemalan government; the officers created the FAR to continue their anti-government attacks. The FAR allied with several leftist terrorist organizations in 1982 to form the Guatemalan National Revolutionary Unity (URNG).

Red Army Faction (RAF)—Western Germany's most active left-wing terrorist organization post-World War II. Also known as Baader-Meinhof Group (in German: Rote Armee Fraktion); operated during 1970–1998.

Reign of Terror—The period between 1793 and 1794 during the French Revolution when thousands were executed.

Revolutionary Armed Forces of Colombia (FARC)—Established in 1964 as the military wing of the Colombian Communist Party, FARC is Latin America's oldest and best-equipped insurgency of Marxist origin.

Revolutionary People's Struggle (ELA)—A Greek, violent Marxist-Leninist organization.

Robben (Island) University—Prison situated off the coast of South Africa prison for members of the previously banned ANC; where many prisoners learned the art of political debate.

Roe v. Wade—1973 U.S. Supreme Court case that established that most laws against abortion violate the U.S. Constitution and the right to privacy.

Rogue states—Countries that support terrorism actions and groups.

Royal Ulster Constabulary (RUC)—Paramilitary police force of Northern Ireland; the removal of the word "Royal" came about during the Northern Ireland Peace Agreement. The force is now the Police Service of Northern Ireland.

Russian Federation—The current government structure of the former USSR.

Sandinistas—Nicaraguan group whose primary goal was to overthrow the Somoza regime and replace it with a Communist government. Taking advantage of public unrest and massive demonstrations against the dictatorial Somoza regime, the Sandinistas successfully ousted the Somoza regime in 1978–1979. The Sandinistas ruled Nicaragua until democratic elections forced them out in 1990.

Sarin toxin—Deadly airborne poison used in the subways in Tokyo.

Satanic Verses—Novel written by British author Salman Rushdie in 1989, contained some unflattering references to Islamic history, which resulted in Iran's Ayotollah Khomeini calling for Rushdie's death.

SAVAK—Ministry of State Security during the reign of the Shah of Iran.

Sayeret Mat'Kal—Also known as General Staff Reconnaissance Unit #69—is the Israeli elite counter terrorist organization.

Sectarian—Strict or rigid adherence to a particular religion; where two or more religions come into conflict, extreme actions and violence often occur, as seen in Northern Ireland.

Selassie, Emperor Haile—Born in July 23, 1892; was emperor of Ethiopia from 1930–1936 and 1941–1974. He was an Ethiopian Orthodox Christian his entire life. He was removed from power in 1974 and died in suspicious circumstances under house arrest in 1975.

Shari'a—Arabic term for Islamic law, most often stemming from the Quran.

Sharon, Ariel—Israeli prime minister; elected in 2001.

Shining Path (Sendero Luminoso)—Peruvian radical, Marxist group that grew out of the Communist movement in the 1960s. Its radical Marxist ideology was shaped by its founder, Abimael Guzmán Reynoso. Guzmán, a former university professor, was able to use his position within academia to gain credibility and entice students to his fledgling Communist movement. He was captured in 1991 and remains in prison.

Shiromani Gurudwara Prabandhak Committee (SGPC)—Is the major Sikh terrorist organization in India.

Signals Intelligence (SIGINT)—The discipline of intelligence gathering through electronic intercepts of messages by varied means.

Sithole, Ndabaningi—Leader of the Ndonga faction of Zimbabwe African Union (ZANU).

Special Air Service Regiment (SAS)—The elite British military unit used for counter terrorist operations - established in North Africa in WWII and based in the west of England.

Special Boat Squadron (SBS)—British special forces unit; waterborne counterpart of the Special Air Service Regiment; employed in waterborne special ops for the British Royal Navy.

Special Immigration Appeal Commission (SIAC)—UK Act established in 1997 providing a method of appeal for immigrants ordered to deport from the United Kingdom.

SPOT—A method employed to Screen Passengers by Observation Techniques.

Stalin, Joseph—Russian leader from 1928 to 1953; summarily executed millions of his opponents. "Stalin" means "Man of Steel."

Stansted Airport—An UK airport situated to the east of the capital and used as a hijack response location for aircraft hijackings.

Stammheim Prison—Prison where members of Germany's Baader-Meinhof Gang were imprisoned.

State Law and Order Restoration Council (SLORC)—Burmese military junta that controlled the region in 1988.

State Peace and Development Council (SPDC)—Burmese military renaming itself from SLORC in 1997.

Sudan Liberation Movement (SLA)—Group originating in the region of Darfur to challenge the administration in Khartoum.

Sunni—The largest division of Islam; Sunni Muslims range from Indonesia through the Middle East and Africa.

SWAT—U.S. Special Weapons and Tactical units—established as hostage rescue units by most U.S. police forces.

Symbionese Liberation Army (SLA)—U.S. group made prominent by the kidnapping of Patty Hearst in 1974.

Sympathizers—Someone or a group that share and understand the same common goals.

Task Force on Violence against Abortion Providers (TFVAAP)—An investigative arm of the Department of Justice, the Civil Rights Division of the Department of Justice. The TFVAAP investigates any instance in which customers or providers of reproductive health services are criminally threatened, obstructed, or injured while seeking or providing services.

Terrorist incident—An attack or threat of an attack carried out by terrorists.

Terrorist No-Fly Watch List—A compilation of suspicious names gathered from airline passenger manifests.

Transportation Security Agency (TSA)—U.S. agency created after 9-11 to replace low-paid, poorly trained airport screeners.

Turkish Revenge Brigade—A little-known, ultranationalist, extreme right-wing group operating in Turkey.

UN Security Council Resolution 1373—Resolution that called for international cooperation to prevent and eradicate acts of terrorism worldwide; unanimously adopted on September 28, 2001, under Chapter VII of the UN General Assembly by consensus of the 189 member states.

Unilateral Declaration of Independence (UDI)—Declared on November 11, 1965, by Ian Smith of Rhodesia.

Union of Islamic Communities and Organizations in Italy (UCOII)—The largest Muslim group in Italy. UCOII has a network of more than fifty mosques throughout the country. It has a network throughout Europe and supports an International Muslim Brotherhood.

UNRA—Utvar Rychleho Nasazeni (URNA) is the Czech Republic's rapid response counter-terrorist police and crime-busting force.

United Self-Defense Forces of Colombia (AUC)—Group formed to combat the leftist terrorist organizations operating in Colombia, primarily the FARC and ELN. The AUC grew out of the paramilitary and self-defense groups formed in the 1980s.

U.S. Patriot Act—Law passed in 2001 following the 9-11 attacks in the United States; Uniting and Strengthening America by Providing Appropriate Tools Required to Intercept and Obstruct Terrorism Act came into force.

Uighur—Separatist movement in Turkistan with possible ties to al Qaeda.

VBIED—Term used to identify a Vehicle Borne Improvised Explosive Device.

Vesicants—A blistering agent developed for use in chemical warfare. A well-known chemical weapon used in World War I and by Saddam Hussein of Iraq against the Kurds.

Waco Massacre—Armed raid by members of the FBI and ATF on the Branch Davidian base in Waco, Texas.

Wahhabism—Islamic religious movement within Islam founded by Muhammad ibn Abd al-Wahhab (1703–1992).

War on Terror—Phrase established after the attacks on the World Trade Center and the Pentagon in September 2001 to detail the coming "war" against terrorism on worldwide scale led primarily by the United States.

World Trade Center—Group of buildings in New York City destroyed on September 11, 2001, by two hijacked aircraft that were flown into two of the towers.

Zapatista National Liberation Army (ELZN)—Violent Mexican organization that opposes NAPTA.

Zimbabwe African National Union (ZANU)—Robert Mugabe's ruling political party.

Zimbabwe African People's Union (ZANPU)—Opposition group opposed to ZANU.

Zimbabwe People's Revolutionary Army (ZIPRA)—Opposition group opposed to ZANU.

INDEX

Note: the letter 'n' after the locators refers to note numbers.